FROM JAMES TO ELIOT

Boris Ford was the General Editor of *The New Pelican Guide to English Literature* (in 11 vols.), which in its original form was launched in 1954. At the time it was being planned he was Chief Editor and later Director of the Bureau of Current Affairs. After a spell on the Secretariat of the United Nations in New York and Geneva, he became Editor of the *Journal of Education* and also first Head of Schools Broadcasting with Independent Television.

Following a period as Education Secretary at the Cambridge University Press, Boris Ford, until he retired in 1982, was Professor of Education at the universities of Sheffield, Sussex and Bristol, where he was also Dean of the School of Cultural and Community Studies. He edited *Universities Quarterly* from 1955 until 1986. He was General Editor of *The Cambridge Guide to the Arts in Britain* (in 9 vols. 1988-91) retitled *The Cambridge Cultural History of Britain* (1992); and edited *Benjamin Britten's Poets* (1994).

HAVANT &
SOUTH DOWNS
COLLEGE

New Road
Havant
Hants PO9 1QL

**Study Central
Havant Campus**

Tel : 023 9387 9999 extension 5005.

Email : library@hsdc.ac.uk

*Please return by the last
date stamped below or
contact the us to renew.*

PENGUIN BOOKS

Published by the Penguin Group
Penguin Books Ltd, 27 Wrights Lane, London W8 5TZ, England
Penguin Putnam Inc., 375 Hudson Street, New York, New York 10014, USA
Penguin Books Australia Ltd, Ringwood, Victoria, Australia
Penguin Books Canada Ltd, 10 Alcorn Avenue, Toronto, Ontario, Canada M4V 3B2
Penguin Books (NZ) Ltd, Private Bag 102902, NSMC, Auckland, New Zealand

Penguin Books Ltd, Registered Offices: Harmondsworth, Middlesex, England

First published in *The Pelican Guide to English Literature* 1961
This revised and expanded edition published 1983
Reprinted in Penguin Books 1990
Reprinted with a revised and updated Bibliography 1996

3 5 7 9 10 8 6 4 2

Copyright © Boris Ford, 1983
All rights reserved

The acknowledgements on p.577 constitute an extension
to this copyright page.

Filmset in Bembo 'Monophoto'
Printed in England by Clays Ltd, St Ives plc

CONTENTS

PART I

PART II

PART III

CONTENTS

PART IV

GENERAL INTRODUCTION

The publication of this *New Pelican Guide to English Literature* in many volumes might seem an odd phenomenon at a time when, in the words of the novelist L. H. Myers, a 'deep-seated spiritual vulgarity ... lies at the heart of our civilization', a time more typically characterized by the Headline and the Digest, by the Magazine and the Tabloid, by Pulp Literature and the Month's Masterpiece. Yet the continuing success of the *Guide* seems to confirm that literature – both yesterday's and today's – has a real and not merely a nominal existence among a large number of people; and its main aim has been to help validate as firmly as possible this feeling for a living literature and for the values it embodies.

The *Guide* is partly designed for the committed student of literature. But it has also been written for those many readers who accept with genuine respect what is known as 'our literary heritage', but for whom this often amounts, in memory, to an unattractive amalgam of set texts and school prizes; as a result they may have come to read only today's books – fiction and biography and travel. Though they are probably familiar with such names as Pope, George Eliot, Langland, Marvell, Yeats, Dr Johnson, Hopkins, and the Brontës, they might hesitate to describe their work intimately or to fit them into any larger pattern of growth and achievement. If this account is a fair one, it seems probable that very many people would be glad of guidance that would help them respond to what is living and contemporary in literature, for, like the other arts, it has the power to enrich the imagination and to clarify thought and feeling.

The *Guide* does not set out to compete with the standard Histories of Literature, which inevitably tend to have a lofty, take-it-or-leave-it attitude about them. This is not a Bradshaw or a Whitaker's Almanack of English literature. Nor is it a digest or potted version, nor again a portrait gallery of the Great. Works such as these already

7

abound, and there is no need to add to their number. What it sets out to offer, by contrast, is a guide to the history and traditions of English literature, a contour map of the literary scene. It attempts, that is, to draw up an ordered account of literature as a direct encouragement to people to read widely in an informed way and with enjoyment. In this respect the *Guide* acknowledges a considerable debt to those twentieth-century writers and critics who have made a determined effort to elicit from literature what is of living value to us today: to establish a sense of literary tradition, and to define the standards that this tradition embodies.

The New Pelican Guide to English Literature consists of eleven volumes:

1. Part One. *Medieval Literature: Chaucer and the Alliterative Tradition* (with an anthology)
1. Part Two. *Medieval Literature: The European Inheritance* (with an anthology)
2. *The Age of Shakespeare*
3. *From Donne to Marvell*
4. *From Dryden to Johnson*
5. *From Blake to Byron*
6. *From Dickens to Hardy*
7. *From James to Eliot*
8. *The Present*
9. *American Literature*
   A Guide for Readers

Most of the volumes have been named after those writers who dominate or stand conveniently at either end of the period, and who also indicate between them the strength of the age in literature.

This particular volume, *From James to Eliot*, deals with the literature of the first half of the twentieth century. The major writers of this period – and by any standards they *are* major – are still very much part of our time. Yet they and particularly the lesser writers are subject to changing fashions and tastes, which makes it harder to write about them with the critical assurance that was possible when discussing writers of earlier ages. None the less, it has been imperative to make the effort, for the writers of today and of the immediate past need to be read and enjoyed and evaluated with the same kind and quality of attention as their well-established forebears. It is an enormous testimony to the richness of the period covered by the volume that its writers stand up so well to the comparison.

Though the *Guide* has been designed as a single work, in the sense that it attempts to provide a coherent and developing account of the tradition of English literature, each volume exists in its own right and sets out to provide the reader with four kinds of related material:

(i) *A survey of the social context of literature* in each period, providing an account of contemporary society at its points of contact with literature.

(ii) *A literary survey* of the period, describing the general characteristics of the period's literature in such a way as to enable the reader to trace its growth and to keep his or her bearings. The aim of this section is to answer such questions as 'What *kind* of literature was written in this period?', 'Which authors matter most?', 'Where does the strength of the period lie?'.

(iii) *Detailed studies* of some of the chief writers and works in the period. Coming after the two general surveys, the aim of this section is to convey a sense of what it means to read closely and with perception; and also to suggest how the literature of a given period is most profitably read, i.e. with what assumptions and with what kind of attention. A number of writers like Eliot, Auden, Waugh, Greene and others, continued writing well after the notional end of the period covered by this volume. So the boundary between this and the next volume is not at all rigid, and though this volume ends around 1940, a number of chapters extend forward well into the post-war years. This section also includes an account of Wyndham Lewis as artist, as perhaps throwing a helpful if indirect light on the literature of the twenties.

(iv) *An appendix of essential facts for reference purposes*, such as authors' and general bibliographies, books for further study, and so on.

BORIS FORD

PART I

THE SOCIAL AND INTELLECTUAL
BACKGROUND

G. H. BANTOCK

Introduction: The Writer's Predicament

When Logan Pearsall Smith confessed to Henry James that he
wished to do the best he could with his pen, James replied that, if such
was the case, 'There is one word – let me impress upon you – which
you must inscribe upon your banner, and that word is Loneliness'.
James caught at the eremitic implications of Pearsall Smith's pursuit
of 'the best' at a time inimical to a display of the finest awareness. And,
indeed, the advice implied both an individual dilemma – for obviously it reflected back on the experience of its author – and the
formulation of a representative perplexity. It arose, biographically,
out of the experience of a man caught between two cultures, American and European, who had found that his subtlety of social analysis
and moral insight had isolated him from the publics of both. It
constituted, therefore, an acceptance of isolation in a world where
the masses newly arrived to prominence yet remained totally ignorant of certain fundamental cultural and moral conflicts and where
even the intelligentsia – the 'clerks' of Benda or the 'clerisy' of
Coleridge – no longer fostered a coherent and accepted set of values.
By implication, therefore, it recommended a defiance of all accepted
organs of social intercommunication – for instance, what James himself called 'newspaperism' or, at the higher levels, the 'associational
process' which constituted the medium of opinion formation; it also
bore witness to a developed ideology of secular individualism and
psychological privacy and linked with an essentially romantic self-
image of isolation. Ultimately, it indicated, one was thrown back on
one's own integrity and sense of moral responsibility as a defiant
assertion (a 'banner') in an increasingly hostile world; it represented
the artist's refusal to compromise with the unifying and homogenizing tendencies of the age.

Two basic themes of modern literature have been those of isolation

13

and relationship within a decaying moral order. The fact that, in the earlier years of the century, really serious literature (as opposed to the ephemera fostered by increasing literacy) had become a peripheral occupation may induce a feeling that the writer's diagnosis of moral confusion or perplexity was suspect, springing from a wounded ego or dramatizing a self-pity. Though many eminent Victorians had regarded their age as one of transition, for the great unthinking the Edwardian weekend was little disturbed by intimations of 'chaos' and 'multiplicity', such as afflicted Henry Adams; and Henry James's comment to A. C. Benson in 1896, 'I have the imagination of disaster – and see life as ferocious and sinister', would have fallen strangely on many ears at that time. Yet it was clear that by the inter-war years every newspaperman and popular pundit had become aware of a 'crisis', a translation into journalese of Adams's intimation of moral confusion. A world war and a consequent accelerated degree of social change had produced profound alterations from even the nineteenth-century ethos, which we now know to have been less stable and free from doubt than was once imagined.[1]

Nor has the serious artist in the end been able to remain aloof from social movements. Gradually, the extreme concern for the individual consciousness characteristic of writers like James has succumbed to subtle collectivist pressures. For all the comparative indifference they received, writers less and less felt able to retreat into private worlds; instead, they became increasingly committed to social, political, and therefore public comment. Indeed, E. M. Forster, one of the most significant of twentieth-century novelists, explained in a television interview his lack of fecundity as being due to precisely such altered pressures:

... I think one of the reasons why I stopped writing novels is that the social aspect of the world changed so much. I had been accustomed to write about the old-fashioned world with its homes and its family life and its comparative peace. All that went, and though I can think about the new world I cannot put it into fiction.

In James's play, *The High Bid*, Mrs Gracedew pleads for the values of the 'old human home' of Coverings End, the country house loca-tion of the play: 'What ... is more precious than what the Ages have slowly wrought?'. Captain Yule, the 'rabid Reformer', proclaims 'something else ... than the vanity of old show-houses'. Thousands in England had no houses at all. The values of intimate relationships and aesthetic beauty are challenged by a cry for impersonal justice arising out of a developing awareness of 'under privilege'. Symptomatically, the fashionable audience applauded the sentiments of Yule, and greeted those of Mrs Gracedew with silence.

Economic and Social Change

For James, the country house, the 'happy rural seat', continued to embody certain important minority values even if he also glimpsed its less attractive side. But in any case, the values of rural community embodied at its best in the great house were doomed. The later years of the nineteenth century saw the almost final breakdown, in the limited areas in which it still survived, of a pre-industrial way of life and economy. The agricultural depression of those times (1870–1902) hit particularly hard the landed aristocracy and the agricultural labourer; and it was then that the 'change in the village' denoted the end of rural England on any significant scale; as Lawrence noted, even the countryman became a 'town bird' at heart. Of the forty-five million inhabitants of the United Kingdom in 1911 (an increase of fourteen million in forty years), nearly 80 per cent lived in England and Wales; and, of these, again roughly 80 per cent came to live in urban districts. The development of the American wheat prairies and the importation of refrigerated meat from the Argentine meant that four million arable acres, £17 millions of landed rents, and 150,000 agricultural labourers disappeared during a period of forty years – some place the numbers a good deal higher. Free Trade, and the increasing urbanization it provoked, 'gorged the banks but left our rickyards bare' (Rider Haggard).

'Agriculture,' as G. M. Trevelyan has said, 'is not one industry among many, but is a way of life, unique and irreplaceable in its human and spiritual values.' The decline of the rural way of life has certainly been reflected in the tenuousness of this century's nature poetry and in the veering of interest, noted by John Holloway in his literary survey in Part II of this volume, towards urban and cosmopolitan themes. True, the country house continued to provide something of a nostalgia for a number of writers – Yeats, Forster,

Galsworthy, Waugh among others; and even Wells, from the below-stairs vantage point of Up Park, where his mother was housekeeper, the Bladesover of *Tono-Bungay*, urged that

modern civilization was begotten and nursed in the households of the prosperous, relatively independent people, the minor nobility, [where] men could talk, think and write at their leisure.

(*Autobiography*)

The profound human implications of the change in the village have been mourned by Hardy, George 'Bourne', Richard Jefferies, Edward Thomas and others, though, as a way of life, it had a shadier side to it than they always confessed. For the evidence of Commissions on the state of the rural poor ought not to be forgotten in assessing the implications of rural depopulation. The Rev. J. Fraser, reporting on the Eastern counties for the Royal Commission on Women and Children in Agriculture (1867–70), said that 'The majority of the cottages that exist in rural parishes are deficient in almost every requisite that should constitute a home for a Christian family in a civilized community'. Certainly, then, the 'organic community' of rural England may not have existed quite as its more naïve exponents believe; in re-animating the past it is easy to omit the stresses that are inseparable from the human condition. Nevertheless, this idealization of rural values is important because many writers have accepted its essential truth and have involved it, if only as a regret, in their work. One response to a complex, urbanized, 'much-divided' civilization has been the evocation of simpler, more organic communities – the ship's company in Conrad's works, the primitivism of certain artists, forms of pastoralism. The pervasive feeling was that material gain must be balanced against a perceptible spiritual loss, and it was the spiritual loss which received the literary attention, even though one realizes in saying so that the division itself over-simplifies the situation.

The altered social emphases following on urbanization extended the encroachment of a changed pattern in social relations which was already to be found over an ever greater part of the country throughout the nineteenth century. Considering the enlarged role of money in the new village economy, George 'Bourne' points to the alterations necessitated by the slow but remorseless enclosure of the commons after 1861, a phase which in his area lasted until 1900:

... the common [was], as it were, a supplement to the cottage gardens, and [furnished] means of extending the scope of the little home industries. It encouraged the poorest labourer to practise, for instance, all those time-honoured crafts which Cobbett, in his little book on Cottage Economy, had advocated as the one hope for labourers.

(*Change in the Village*, 1912)

With the enclosure of the common, 'the once self-supporting cottager turned into a spender of money'. The implication of this struck at the very heart of his human relationships; what emerged was a new ethic, familiar enough by then in the towns but less known in the country, the ethic of competition. The effect of this was to reduce man to the level of economic man, one whose community relationships were at the mercy of the cash nexus, and whose psychological motivations were thought of largely in terms of self-interest. (There were protests, of course, but not on a socially significant scale.) In such circumstances, '"the Poor" was regarded not as a term descriptive of a condition of society but of the character of a group of people' (Beatrice Webb, *My Apprenticeship*). Darwinian notions, interpreted by Herbert Spencer and others, helped to afford a set of fortuitous economic arrangements with the force of an apparent natural law. The chance interaction of economic atomic particles pursuing their rational self-interest was regarded as the inevitable and exclusive model of social behaviour. Notions of a public morality in terms of a diffused public good hardly existed among ordinary people – as the work of C. F. G. Masterman makes clear.

Private morality, at least on the face which it turned towards the world, was initially authoritarian and taboo-ridden. Serious personal oddity was dismissed as a sign of degeneracy, not diagnosed as neurosis. The bringing-up of children, as Samuel Butler bore witness, was strict; and the overt decencies of family life and relationships were maintained, whatever went on under the surface. The 'great ladies of the day' sent for Lord Templecombe when the question of divorce arose, in Miss Sackville-West's *The Edwardians*:

'Noblesse oblige, my dear Eadred', they had said; 'people like us do not exhibit their feelings; they do not divorce. Only the vulgar divorce.'

The twentieth century has seen the breakdown of the old familiar authoritarian pattern in private and social, as opposed to political, life. A similar type of moral questioning to that which, in the later

eighteenth and nineteenth centuries, undermined the old hierarchic
political order, affected many of the assumptions of family and social
life. By way of compensation, private dilemma provoked, or at least
went along with, a growth of public concern, particularly a developing guilt over wealth. Divorce in the 1930s carried no moral stigma
comparable to that of exploiting the poor, or of ill-treating a child.
To some extent, indeed, the realm of the public expanded at the
expense of the private, almost as if the pressure of uncertainty had
been resolved by a transfer of responsibility. The individual and the
social ('the social' understood to imply the primary sub-group as well
as society at large) came to seem inter-dependent to a degree which
would have appeared strange to a Victorian, to the detriment of that
individual atomization inherent in Victorian economic arrangements, and of that sense of individual self-responsibility which characterized the morally earnest Victorian ethos. As Lord Annan has
pointed out:

Nothing marks the break with Victorian thought more decisively than
modern sociology – that revolution at the beginning of this century which
we associate with the names of Weber, Durkheim, and Pareto. They no longer
started with the individual as the central concept in terms of which society
must be explained. They saw society as a nexus of groups; and the pattern
of behaviour which these groups unwittingly established primarily determined men's actions.
  ('The Curious Strength of Positivism in English Political Thought', 1959)

The notion, inherited from the Enlightenment, that man was the
product of his circumstances rather than an autonomous moral agent,
gained ground; it was used to justify collectivist intervention which
was increasingly advocated – by the Fabians, for instance. They
pointed to a profound moral perplexity concerning – among other
things – the boundaries of the public and private worlds.

Moral Perplexities

A theory basically economic had deeply affected social and political
thinking about relationships in society for nearly a century, then. In
its replacement, the empirical, sceptical spirit of science played a large
part and helped in the dissolution of old social acceptances based on
a priori assumptions. Beatrice Webb refers to the 'belief of the most

original and vigorous minds of the seventies and eighties that it was by science, and by science alone, that all human misery would be ultimately swept away'.

Social investigations were mounted on 'scientific' principles; economic theory was likewise affected. From trying 'to solve the largest possible problems from the least possible knowledge' (Postan), Cambridge economists from Marshall to Keynes have infused their theoretical constructions with particular observations of reality. No Gradgrind could have pursued the facts more relentlessly than the investigators into social conditions at the end of the nineteenth century. The wife of Charles Booth, whose *Life and Labour of the People of London* (1891–1903) was one of the first great social surveys, stated clearly in a *Memoir* of her husband's life:

The *a priori* reasoning of political economy, orthodox and unorthodox alike, fails from want of reality. At its base are a series of assumptions very imperfectly connected with the observed facts of life. We need to begin with a true picture of the modern industrial organism.

'The primary task [is] to observe and dissect facts', urged the Webbs. Yet at the very moment when social investigators were about to enter upon an empirical, positivist phase, a number of blows were struck at nineteenth-century rationalist self-confidence. There had always been a few to swim 'against the current' of the Enlightenment's conviction in the homogeneity of human nature behind the façade of local custom and its susceptibility to the same sort of scientific scrutiny that had been so resoundingly successful in the physical world: men like Vico, Herder and Herzen. Now disenchantment grew apace. There was the mighty but equivocal figure of Freud. True, Freud worked within the conventional framework of nineteenth-century assumptions – deterministic, materialistic, and rationalistic. At the same time, there were also features of his work which to the careless reader seemed to point to a considerable scepticism about the findings of reason. Rooted in a theory of biological instincts, Freud's view of the developing psyche placed a great emphasis on the power of the unconscious to affect conduct; intellectual convictions seemed to be rationalizations of emotional needs – 'rationalization' being a word introduced by Freud's disciple, Ernest Jones. Freud's teleology was firmly rooted in nineteenth-century hedonism; but the discovery that man's actions could be 'motivated' by forces of which he might know nothing introduced a probable irrationality into human behaviour which was profoundly disturbing. This 'entirely unsuspected peculiarity in the constitution of human nature', as William James not quite accurately called it, meant that a new dimension in the assessment of human behaviour had to be taken into account. The 'normal' scale of events demanded a new measuring rod, for analysis might reveal a profound significance in the apparently trivial. The firm line which nineteenth-century psychiatrists had drawn between the normal and the abnormal, the latter being explained largely in terms of degeneracy, disappeared; dreams and slips of the tongue, if nothing else, showed that we all displayed neurotic symptoms. Above all, the implied criticism of the traditional model in terms of which reason ruled the will in the interests of moral behaviour, and the discovery that the super-ego could profoundly distort the ego, so that 'in our therapy we often find ourselves obliged to do battle with the super-ego, and work to moderate its demands', had a profound effect on twentieth-century moral attitudes. Rationalist though Freud was, therapeutically speaking, his 'ego' is a feeble thing, fighting for its life against the encroachments of the super-ego and the id. And then, of course, there was the enormous importance, in the theories of instincts, placed on the demands of libido (those, that is, of sexuality), particularly on those manifested in the Oedipus phase.

Thus a considerable blow was struck at man's sense of self-responsibility and at the ordered emphases of behaviour on which he had come to depend: the consequences for fiction can be sensed in the comments of Virginia Woolf, who knew of psychoanalytic doctrine early because of her affiliations with the Strachey family:

... the accent falls differently from of old; the moment of importance came not here but there ... Let us not take it for granted that life exists more fully in what is commonly thought big than in what is commonly thought small.

('Modern Fiction' in *The Common Reader*, 1919)

The results in the spheres of private and family relationships were profound, especially during the twenties and thirties. Jealousies were recognized where no such imputations would previously have been made. Mothers, particularly, were suspect as seeking to devour their sons; *Hamlet* was interpreted in terms of an Oedipus situation. The theme of sexual renunciation practically disappeared as subject for a novel; the dilemma of Isabel Archer *vis-à-vis* Gilbert Osmond in James's *The Portrait of a Lady* (1881) no longer appeared real. Interest in perversion grew. The relation between the generations profoundly altered; and the Freudian phenomenon of infantile sexuality, though initially received with horror, focused attention on the importance of early developments and gave childhood a status it had only previously had in the pages of Rousseau and the writings of other 'progressives'. Before the First World War, male hegemony had suffered a reverse in the rise of the 'new woman' and the suffragette movement. Shaw's analysis of femininity in *Man and Superman* (1903) and *Candida* (1898) implied an error in the conventional nineteenth-century assessment of the relative role of the sexes. Little wonder that D. H. Lawrence, writing in 1913, found in the relations between man and woman '*the* problem of today, the establishment of a new relation, or the readjustment of the old one . . .'; and that, where parents and children were concerned, there was a break-up of the old authoritarian pattern. For Ronald Knox's sister, Lady Peck, parents had been 'a race apart'. To Robert Graves, during the twenties, his children were 'close friends with the claims of friendship and liable to the accidents of friendship'.

The growing crisis of confidence was further exacerbated when a generation of scientists at the turn of the century called into question the fundamental postulates of classical physics, notably that of causality. The increased emphasis on the hypothetical nature of science, so that 'models' of behaviour became, in the words of Poincaré, 'neither true, nor false, but useful', the realization of a subjective element in scientific findings introduced the note of 'relativity' which, among the cognoscenti, if not so much in the public at large, increased uncertainty and 'indeterminacy'. The 'world out there' lost its putative solidity; and art – painting and sculpture – began to lose that basic structural certainty which arose out of the fixed viewpoint of Renaissance perspective. Hence the dissolution of forms of the cubists and the increased subjectivity of the surrealists; the way had been prepared by the momentary and essentially fluid evocations of the impressionists – whose musical counterpart was Debussy. Thus

scientists and creative artists were, often quite independently, threatening hitherto received ideas about space and time – more generally still, about all such principles of order in the world. They showed increasing awareness . . .

that the previously accepted structures of reality were simply reflections of men's own frequently arbitrary assumptions. From this important stand-point the scientific revolution was being complemented by the verbal experimentation of Mallarmé, the probing into memory of Proust, the rebellion against perspective in Picasso and against phenomenal representation in Kandinsky, or the revolution of tone, rhythm and harmony in Schoenberg and Stravinsky.

(M. D. Biddiss, *The Age of the Masses*, 1977)

The traumatic event which hastened, though it did not initiate, the dissolution of familiar social and intellectual boundaries was the First World War of 1914–18. The conflicts between the generation too old to fight and the generation of the trenches did a great deal to re-shape the old authoritarian pattern. Those in authority – the politicians and generals – had, many of them, been wasteful and incompetent. Nor did their mutual recriminations help to preserve the façade of authority. The peace of Versailles seemed, to a generation which distrusted the politicians as much as it had learnt to despise the generals, simply to play the old imperialist game: 'oil was trumps', as dos Passos put it in *Nineteen Nineteen*. The war has been the subject of a hundred memoirs, defining in their varied terms its impact on the shocked nerves of a generation. What in essence died, Lawrence tried to reveal:

It was in 1915 the old world ended. In the winter 1915–16 the spirit of old London collapsed; the city, in some way, perished, perished from being the heart of the world, and became a vortex of broken passions, lusts, hopes, fears and horrors. The integrity of London collapsed and the genuine debasement began, the unspeakable baseness of the press and the public voice, the reign of that bloated ignominy, *John Bull* ... The well-bred, really cultured classes were on the whole passive resisters. They shirked their duty. It is the business of people who really know better to fight tooth and nail to keep up a standard, to hold control of authority. *Laisser-aller* is as guilty as the actual stinking mongrelism it gives place to.

(*Kangaroo*, 1923)

As Charles Madge has indicated recently in his reminiscences concerning the 'minority' principle: 'We all knew that this was true ... But we all wished it was not'.

The reaction of the post-war world, then, was to suspect too easily all manifestations of authority. The 1920s became an era of 'revolt' against signs of the assertive will – the diffusion at an increasingly popular level of that intellectual and artistic resistance to the conventions already noted in artistic and scientific circles. Acton's dictum about power corrupting became so popular that it came to symbolize the unease of a generation. The temper of the age was anti-heroic; Oxford in the 1930s, for example, refused to fight for King and Country. E. M. Forster pointed to an early reaction against the moral imperatives of the war period when he commented in 1917:

Huysmans's *À Rebours* is the book of that blessed period that I remember best. Oh, the relief of a world which lived for its sensations and ignored the will – the world of des Esseintes. Was it decadent? Yes, and thank God. Yes: here again was a human being who had time to feel and experiment with his feelings, to taste and smell and arrange books and fabricate flowers, and be selfish and himself. The waves of edifying bilge rolled off me, the newspapers ebbed.

The 'will' (the instrument of the moral 'super-ego') had, then, in some degree exhausted itself in the war effort; it was, in any case, suspect through its association with Victorian strenuousness and the subtle dominations of family relationships. D. H. Lawrence was insistent on its power to cramp and thwart in the field of personal relationships between 'men and women' – the 'insensate love will' marred the intimate growth of psychic uniqueness. He saw in it, too, the motive force behind developments in machine technology, dehumanizing in the industrial field.[2] Strength became a questionable value and 'success' in a worldly sense was only for the insensitive – Babbitt on Main Street. The theme was not by any means entirely new, of course, as witness Gissing's *New Grub Street* (1891). And, further back, there was Blake's 'Damn braces; bless relaxes', not to mention Wordsworth's 'wise passiveness'. But there was an increasing tendency, in the inter-war years, for the hero in novels to be a person to whom things happen, rather than someone who to any extent imposes his will on life – Eustace rather than Hilda – a whimper replaces a bang. In the 1930s, the life of action itself (except, of course, in defence of the Workers' Republic) was often suspect; Auden's *Ascent of F6* (1937) posed the dilemma of action and contemplation.

In the social sphere increasing knowledge tended only to confirm and strengthen intimations of moral unease and to destroy faith in the essential and unquestioned rightness of Western ways of behaviour. Advances in anthropology, for instance, helped to undermine the absoluteness of religious and ethical systems in favour of the more relativistic standpoint. Westermarck's *Ethical Relativity*, denying objectivity of moral judgements, was followed by Frazer's *Golden Bough* (1890–1915), beneath which, as Lord Annan put it, 'runs the theme that all Christian ceremonies are merely sophistications of savage rituals and that as magic was superseded by religion, so religion will vanish before reason'. Further developments conceived primitive societies as integrated structures, 'patterns of culture', and, in this way, a large variety of different ways of organizing a society was demonstrated. The Enlightenment myth of a universal human nature was finally exploded; modes of behaviour obviously varied immensely in different environments. To grow up in Samoa was obviously not the same thing as to grow up in, say, Chicago. Ruth Benedict herself pointed out, whilst she deprecated, a typical Western reaction to these findings:

> The sophisticated modern temper has made of social relativity . . . a doctrine of despair. It has pointed out its incongruity with the orthodox dreams of permanence and ideality and with the individual's illusions of autonomy.
>
> (*Patterns of Culture*, 1934)

Behind all these manifestations of confusion and uncertainty there lay a deeper and more profound problem – the inability to arrive at a commonly accepted metaphysical picture of Man. To Freud man was a biological phenomenon, a prey to instinctual desires and their re-direction in the face of 'harsh' reality; he was, therefore, in the Darwinian tradition, simply a part of nature. To Marx he was the outcome of economic and social forces, the alienated product of an evolutionary necessity as rigid as any the nineteenth century found in the natural world. The declining but still manifest rationalistic picture of man derived from the liberal, laissez-faire tradition rested upon an assumed harmony among men's varying rational desires, which, when not interfered with, reflected the pre-established harmonies to be found in nature; this view reflected the shrinking but still pervasive optimism of the Enlightenment. A pessimistic scientific humanism saw man's aspirations and hopes as 'but the outcome of chance collocations of atoms' (Bertrand Russell). The Christian notion of man as inherently the child of sin, as belonging at once to the natural and to the transcendent world, and owing his possibilities of salvation to the grace of God, a man whose essence was free self-determination and whose sin was the wrong use of his freedom, retained only an echo of its former vitality. Though Christianity, especially in its Catholic forms, underwent spasmodic revivals of influence – witness Chesterbelloc, T. S. Eliot, Graham Greene –

or was sometimes condescended to by sociologists as fulfilling a social 'function', religious controversy no longer vitally affected public issues. Many of the greatest writers, however, like D. H. Lawrence and L. H. Myers, found empirical accounts of experience totally insufficient to the ultimate mystery of human existence; certain theologians like Kierkegaard enjoyed spells of popularity because they depicted an angst which echoed the emotional despair of the times. Nineteenth-century reactions to the 'death of God' persisted into the twentieth century for a few at least.

For the majority, however, these uncertainties were not removed or lessened by current theorizing in philosophy or ethics. The ontological and metaphysical concerns of continental philosophers – such as the Thomists and later the existentialists – made, in general, little impact in this country. English philosophy, indeed, ceased to involve system-building and became linguistic and analytical. Philosophers within the tradition of British empiricism concentrated on 'second order' activities concerned with the analysis of terms and the logical rigours of argument. They sought to emulate, within their own field, the austerities of the scientists.

In the early years of the century, Bradley's absolute idealism began to give way to the realism of Russell and Moore. Russell urged in 1914 that philosophers 'should give an account of the world of science and daily life'; Moore put forward the claims of common sense. From this and from Moore's practice of clarification and analysis in the *Principia Ethica* (1903) and *Ethics* (1911), through the aridities of logical atomism and logical positivism, developed a concern with the analysis of ordinary language. On the way, metaphysics was repudiated, as could be seen in A. J. Ayer's *Language, Truth and Logic* (1935). The later Wittgenstein, posthumously published in the *Philosophical Investigations* (1936–49), dismissed any desire to reveal *the essential* function of language and sought to investigate *how* language was used in daily existence. A revived interest in metaphysics belongs to the period after the Second World War. In general, the tendency of the dominant school of English philosophy during the period under review was '... not to increase what we know ... but to rectify the logical geography of the knowledge we already possess' (Gilbert Ryle, *The Concept of Mind*, 1949).

This changed focus of philosophical discussion was accompanied

by the belief that moral statements did not constitute genuine propositions. With the decline of intuitionism, the view of the American,
C. L. Stevenson, that ethical judgements had 'no objective validity
whatsoever ... [but] are pure expressions of feeling and as such do
not come under the category of truth or falsehood', was widely accepted among ethical theorists in the late 1930s and 40s and reflected
a widespread scepticism about the objectivity of moral judgements.
Ethics, for many moral philosophers, became 'the logical study of
the language of morals' (R. M. Hare, 1952). In the late 1940s ethical
statements were reinstated as being supportable on rational, and not
merely emotive, grounds; though ethical judgements were, strictly
speaking, neither true nor false, they could be better or worse. Nevertheless, the ethical philosopher still largely denied that his job was
to tell us what we ought to do:

Generalization [about moral advice] is possible only in so far as men are
psychologically and biologically similar ... it is vain, presumptuous, and
dangerous to try to answer these questions without a knowledge both of
psychology and of the individual case.

(P. H. Nowell-Smith, *Ethics*, 1954)

Philosophers had become technicians; they had abandoned the role
of sage.

Something of the same spirit infected the field of political
philosophy. Political and party propagandists and left-wing theorists
like the British Marxist, Harold Laski, continued to discuss or imply
the function of the state. But, after the generation of Hobhouse, Lindsay, and Ernest Barker, academic political theorists either, like
Michael Oakeshott, reacted against ideological system-builders, finding in the pursuit of 'intimations' a sufficient guide to political action,
or, like T. D. Weldon, urged the uselessness of attempting to discover
the ideal purpose of the state and assigned to the philosopher a subordi-
nate role as 'consultant'. Though writers such as Collingwood were
not totally neglected nor the work of foreign existentialists unknown,
the empiricists increasingly dominated the native philosophical scene,
bringing with them an element of scepticism: '... in science there
is no *"knowledge"* in the sense in which Plato and Aristotle understood
the word, in the sense which implies finality' (Karl Popper, *The Open
Society*, 1945). As noted earlier, twentieth-century physical scientists
abandoned their claim to depict 'reality' as something independent

of the observer's position and of the conceptual system adopted for the purpose of interpretation. Science, traditionally, had seemed open and 'democratic', on the grounds that the behaviour on which it was based was – at least theoretically – open to public inspection and hence revision in a way in which *a priori* moral postulates derived from authoritative texts were not. Hence moral philosophers in the central English 'liberal' tradition have avoided the deduction of abstract schemês of human betterment from axioms within a postulational system, and the bolstering up of existing structures by similar means. This also contributed to the gradual dissolution of authority and certainty and left the door ajar for the entry of alien authoritarian systems like Marxism.

At the practical political level the development of Imperial relations strikes the note of moral dilemma and uncertainty full in the hearing of autocracy and power. The period from 1883, when Seeley's *Expansion of England* proclaimed the Imperial Mission, to the period after the Second World War, when Empire dissolved into Commonwealth, represented a time of remarkable political transformation concerning notions of Imperial hegemony and white superiority. By 1900 the Empire had reached nearly 13,000,000 square miles and 370,000,000 people; the colonies were being used as sources of raw materials, markets and incomes, and outlets for emigration. But the Boer War went a long way to puncture British complacency. The developing conception of Imperial relations was exemplified most clearly in the history of India where the high promises of Empire, in Kiplingesque terms, took on an increasingly hollow emphasis amidst the twentieth-century hatreds and discordances. As Lord Chelmsford wrote to George V on 4 October 1918:

We have an educated class here, 95 per cent of whom are inimical to us, and I venture to assert that every student in every university is growing up with a hatred of us.

After the Amritsar shootings in 1919, Gandhi transformed 'an intellectual agitation into a mass revolutionary movement'. Political struggle and negotiations lasted off and on for nearly thirty years, until on 15 August 1947, India and Pakistan became independent republics within the Commonwealth. This constituted the beginning of the end of England's imperial mission.

The trend of events in India and elsewhere was assisted by the pervasive scepticism about political power among writers and intellectuals. Political subjection was repugnant to those, like George Orwell, in whom it aroused strong feelings of guilt, and like E. M. Forster, who thought in terms of personal relationships based on equality and the feeling heart. About Ronnie, his complacent young Anglo-Indian in *A Passage to India* (1934), Forster says:

> One touch of regret – not the canny substitute but the true regret from the heart – would have made him a different man, and the British Empire a different institution.

This criticism involved a comment on a whole ethos, one far transcending the comparatively local manifestations of imperial relations. It was a protest of the 'heart', solicitous for a fellow feeling where social and political subjection have no place, against the divisive implications of the will-to-power and of that 'intellectual hatred' which, as Yeats has reminded us, 'is the worst'. Forster proclaimed, scandalously, a willingness to betray country before friend. For the world, he believed, 'is a globe of men who are trying to reach one another ... by the help of goodwill plus culture and intelligence' – a remark which betrays a true English insularity in the era of Freud (*homo homini lupus*) and Hitler. Tragically, it became a period of decadent romanticism when the dynamics and inescapable demands of power were little understood by the British people at large. Classical humanism had addressed itself to the essential conditions of rulership; the romantics lacked a sense of public order and retreated into private worlds or exploded into violence against the current conformity in the interest of some Utopian outcome. Bewitched by abstractions implicit in the romantic search for new forms of community, intellectuals ignored the simple, concrete actualities implicit in the plain unadorned directness of a statement by Ortega y Gasset: 'The function of commanding and obeying is the decisive one in every society' (*Revolt of the Masses*, 1932).

A New Social Ethic

In their most extreme form, these Utopian longings, as indicated, focused on the continental creed of Marxism. Marxism combined in a curious way a moral relativism – after all, it was ultimately intended as a doctrine of liberation – a relativism which fitted the sceptical mood of the times, with a historical necessitarianism which evoked a comforting political absolutism. The nature of such an absolutism was not understood, in the main; it simply provided a refuge from the all too pressing horror of nearer, more visible absolutisms which threatened the safety of Europe. (Russia, in any case, appeared the natural enemy of German expansionist ambitions.) For a writer like L. H. Myers – and there were a number like him in this – a sentimental Marxism provided at once a tool for sceptical analysis of the prevailing class structure and a vision of a New Society. Such writers found themselves agreeing that

... all former moral theories are the product, in the last analysis, of the economic stage which society had reached at that particular epoch. And as society has hitherto moved in class antagonisms, morality was always a class morality.

(Engels, *Anti-Duhring*)

Positively, Marxism filled an uncomfortable vacuum which liberalism – 'a movement not so much defined by its end, as by its starting point', as Eliot observed – had left. Lacking the continental *feel* of absolutism, many hastened to abet the new manifestation of necessity, the victory of the proletariat.

The attractions of Marxism served to highlight in dramatic form the emergence of a new communal ethic. The Protestant, individualistic, liberal outlook seemed to be giving way to a social group ethic, in no way universally accepted, even though it had been developing spasmodically during the nineteenth century, but providing considerable evidence of a trend. The old atomization met the challenge of new key concepts: 'organic', 'integration', 'relation', 'adaptation'. The new hell was to be that of other people. The empirical philosopher often spoke as if disagreement sprang from inadequate factual data; the 'organization man' suspected a breakdown in communication. The solution involved 'imprisonment in brotherhood'.

Indeed, there would be reasons for thinking that some of the earlier questionings in the private sphere arose out of a changing social awareness. The nineteenth century, of course, had a long minority tradition of comment and criticism unfavourable to the cultural and social consequences of industrialization and commercialism. Cobbett, Robert Owen, Dickens, Matthew Arnold, Ruskin, William Morris had all, with a variety of stresses, pointed to the human unsatisfactoriness of the dominant trends. At the end of the century, a number of circumstances combined to bring this minority criticism into greater prominence. Signs of a relative decline *vis-à-vis* certain foreign nations, the exclusion from certain primary markets by the imposition of heavy duties, a decline in the birthrate and an increase in emigration, induced unaccustomed uncertainties into the economic situation. The third Reform Act of 1884 and the County Councils Act of 1888, together with the development of universal education after 1870 and the rise of the grammar schools after 1902, implied a change in political balance; the lower middle classes were arriving. Though the predominant class structure was still strongly authoritarian, it came to be realized that the boasted 'freedom' extended only to the employer of labour; the implications of 'water plentiful and labour docile' were examined and found wanting.

There were signs that the upper classes were no longer quite what they had been. Henry James bluntly referred to the 'clumsy conventional materialized vulgarized brutalized life of London', and found the state of the upper class in England 'in many ways very much the same rotten and *collapsible* one of the French aristocracy before the revolution'. The old aristocracy of birth and inheritance was being replaced by one of wealth and economic power during all the Victorian period. By its end, even the degree of 'respectability' exacted, in moral and sexual terms, was, as Beatrice Webb saw, graded to the degree of social, political, or industrial power exercised. Ramsay MacDonald proclaimed that 'the Age of the Financier' had come and expressed the belief that 'such people' (they included 'the scum of the earth which possessed itself of gold in the gutters of the Johannesburg market place') 'did not command the moral respect which tones down class hatred'.

What was distasteful in this society to the sensibilities of the writer was the total lack of concern for personal relationships, the judging of people by exclusively 'social' standards; though, perhaps, what was new was the sensitivity of the artist rather than the behaviour of exclusive social sets:

What was demoralizing ... because it bred a poisonous cynicism about human relations, was the making and breaking of personal friendships according to temporary and accidental circumstances in no way connected with personal merit: gracious appreciation and insistent intimacy being succeeded, when failure according to worldly standards occurred, by harsh criticism and cold avoidance.

(Beatrice Webb, *My Apprenticeship*)

This diagnosis was confirmed from the early years of the century by L. H. Myers who, with his aristocratic affiliations, was able to observe the ethics of the 'cult of first-rateness', as he calls it in *The Pool of Vishnu* (1940), at close quarters. His letters betray his profound hatred of upper-class life in precisely Beatrice Webb's terms. Vita Sackville-West's *The Edwardians* (1935) afforded further evidence; the people of whom she wrote knew only, she suggested, that they '[needed] plenty of money and that they must be seen in the right places, associated with the right people ... Whatever happens, the world must be served first'. Forster, with his theory of the un-developed heart, linked this insensitivity to 'persons', in contrast to extreme awareness of social atmospheres, with the public-school out-look. Such analyses should perhaps warn us against accepting sureness of values as in itself a virtue. The value of the values, so to speak, is also in question.

Politically, the aristocracy, with the passing of the Parliament Act of 1911, suffered a great loss of direct influence. And when George V, after much anxious thought and consultation, accepted the advice of Lord Balfour and, in 1923, sent for Stanley Baldwin in preference to Lord Curzon to form the new Conservative ministry, the highest political office in the land was forever closed to a member of the House of Lords. At the same time, the persistence of what has been termed an 'Establishment' – a network of social–political–commer-cial–economic relations involving the decision-makers of our gener-ation – was amply demonstrated in an article by T. Lupton and C. Wilson published in *The Manchester School*. The network of family, school, club, and personal relationships there revealed would suggest that personal influence had not given way before the insistent claims of the new social meritocracy as much as might have been thought. Even in the Labour Party, after the first generation of members had passed, a public-school education at Haileybury or Winchester proved no bar to advancement; and though Lloyd George had pro-claimed 'the day of the cottage-bred man', the personnel of the House of Commons remained obstinately middle class. Nevertheless, there was an immense increase in social mobility; and the struggle for status, based on education not birth, became a characteristic mid-century phenomenon. This both accompanied and sustained a predominance of the economic motive.

Beatrice Webb's father, she recalled, had no conception of 'general principles ... no clear vision of the public good'. The new ethic of which she herself was symptomatic was to be much concerned with 'public good'; state action was to replace the 'freedom of the market' but without fundamentally altering the anti-traditional, rationalistic basis of political behaviour. For the spirit of Bentham rather than that of Burke still triumphed; indeed, both laissez-faire liberalism and socialism stem from the ideas of the Enlightenment. The new sense of 'community' was dependent very much on the functioning of the 'upper centres', as Lawrence would have put it. Old custom was to be replaced, after the nineteenth-century vacuum, by positive law as the guiding force of the new communal spirit; at this level relationship was willed rather than the result of a genuine 'organic' growth, though to say that is not to deny it the possibility of a positive value.

Several groups at the end of the century demanded change: the Marxist Social Democratic Federation under A. M. Hyndman provided the revolutionary element, though its influence was not great. The Socialist League produced Morris, even if otherwise its effect was slight. Above all, the Fabian society became the 'symbol of social democracy, of gradualism, of peaceful permeation, of avoidance of revolution'. Wedded to fact-finding, its empirical approach forbade any enveloping philosophical theory and substituted a detailed programme of action based on the careful collection of factual data. As Helen Lynd puts it, the Fabians 'applied the method of social engineering to questions hitherto left to the realm of sentiment'. Their only common principle was the 'condemnation of the profit motive [which condemnation] was the G.C.M., the greatest common measure, of socialists'.

The Gladstone Parliament of 1880–85 was 'the "no-man's land" between the old Radicalism and the new Socialism'. The new spirit not only manifested itself in a spate of social legislation and royal commissions, but received theoretical justification at the hands of T. H. Green and the neo-Hegelian philosophers in the universities. The stage was set for the predominant twentieth-century developments, both in social philosophy and legislation. 'Every period has its dominant religion and hope,' as Arthur Koestler says, 'and "Socialism" in a vague and undefined sense was the hope of the early twentieth century.' The changing attitude was reinforced by developments in social psychology – notably in the American's, Charles Cooley's, *Human Nature and the Social Order* (1902), which, in Dewey's phrase, conceived 'individual mind as a function of social life'. Even Freud, who started from a firmly rooted theory of biological instinct, came latterly to see the importance of the social environment.

Not everyone, however, was satisfied with the Fabian purview or the Fabian rate of progress. H. G. Wells, who so interestingly represents a facet of modern rationalistic political thinking, was struck by the wastefulness of contemporary conditions, the Victorian formlessness, and welcomed the forces tending to 'rationalize' and systematize, those which tend

to promote industrial co-ordination, increase productivity, necessitate new and better-informed classes, evoke a new type of education and make it universal, break down political boundaries everywhere and bring all men into one planetary community.

(Experiment in Autobiography, 1934)

The effects of this, in terms of immediate personal relations, Wells approvingly defines as a 'progressive emancipation of the attention from everyday urgencies ... conceptions of living divorced more and more from immediacy'. Though he deprecated any repudiation of the 'primaries of life' – personal affection and the like – he admitted the desire to control them in order to 'concentrate the largest possible proportion of my energy upon the particular system of effort that has established itself for me as my distinctive business in the world'. Modern conditions admitted the revolutionary question: ' "Yes, you earn a living, you support a family, you love and hate, but – *what do you do?*" ' What *he* did he summed up: 'We originative intellectual workers are reconditioning human life.'

The mechanical, abstract basis of community relationship could hardly be more clearly illustrated. We can see why D. H. Lawrence had to ask:

Why do modern people almost invariably ignore the things that are actually present to them ... They certainly never live on the spot where they are.

33

They inhabit abstract space, the desert void of politics, principles, right and wrong, and so forth ... Talking to them is like trying to have a human relationship with the letter X in algebra.

('Insouciance', 1928)

The reconditioning process involved an appreciation of the planned world state as the answer to Victorian untidiness. Fabian interpenetration was rejected as a 'protest rather than a plan'. Wells thought in terms of large administrative units rather than of the adaptation of existing governmental machinery. 'I listened to *Arms and the Man* with admiration and hatred. It seemed to me inorganic, logical straightness and not the crooked road of life': Yeats's comment is equally applicable to Wells's Utopian schemes.

Many others took up the notion of the planned, particularly as the moral climate concerning personal responsibility for misfortune and poverty changed so that, as Richard Titmuss puts it: 'Inquiry [moved] from the question "who are the poor" to the question "why are they poor".' The progress of events – war, unemployment, economic depression – favoured the concentration on social and economic problems. Alfred Marshall, in his *Principles of Economics* (1890), had already urged that there was 'no moral justification for extreme poverty side by side with great wealth'. Maynard Keynes, in the 1920s, resisted the hereditary 'lethargy' of the orthodox view of laissez-faire:

It is *not* true that individuals possess a prescriptive 'natural liberty' in their economic activities. There is *no* 'compact' conferring perpetual rights on those who Have or on those who Acquire. The world is *not* so governed from above that private and social interest always coincide ...

(*End of Laissez-faire*, 1926)

and so on. The need was to distinguish, more comprehensively but in Bentham's terms, the *Agenda*, and the *Non-Agenda*, of government.

Keynes, of course, was not a socialist planner; he aimed rather at 'improvements in the technique of modern Capitalism by the agency of collective action'. Others, during the economic crisis of the 1930s, were much more forthright in demanding full planning. The example of Russian planned economy was frequently evoked, sometimes with cautious warning against the violent means employed, as in Barbara Wootton's *Plan or No Plan* (1934), sometimes with an

34

acceptance of the inevitable possibility of violence, as in John Strachey's *The Theory and Practice of Socialism* (1938). The Webbs visited Russia and proclaimed its virtues: A New Civilization.

For, indeed, as Kingsley Martin pointed out in his biography of Harold Laski, the effect of the 1931 crisis, when MacDonald, Snowden, and Thomas defected from the Labour party and the National Government was set up, was to change the philosophy of a large part of the Labour party. Previously, among the intellectual strands which had gone to form British Socialism,

including Chartist Radicalism, Owenite optimism, Christian socialism, William Morris romanticism, Fabianism and Marxist materialism, the last had been the least important. After 1931 it became dominant, not yet in action, but as a matter of increasingly accepted theory.

Arthur Koestler evoked, in his autobiography, the emotional impact and the intellectual attraction of Marxism:

... born out of the despair of world war and civil war, of social unrest and economic chaos, the desire for a complete break with the past, for starting human history from scratch, was deep and genuine. In this apocalyptic climate dadaism, futurism, surrealism and the Five-year-plan-mystique came together in a curious amalgam. Moved by a perhaps similar mood of despair, John Donne had begged: 'Moist with a drop of Thy blood my dry soule.' The mystic of the nineteen-thirties yearned, as a sign of Grace, for a look at the Dnieper Dam and a three per cent increase in the Soviet pig-iron production.

The age of anxiety evoked, in some hearts, a desire for the comforts of a simplifying formula or of a closed system, like Marxism, providing all the answers. R. H. S. Crossman refers, in his introduction to *The God that Failed* (1930), to the attractions of an 'unquestioned purpose', the peace of intellectual doubt and uncertainty in subjecting one's soul to the 'canon law of the Kremlin'. Symptomatically, some disillusioned communists turned to the Catholic church. In the period following the Second World War Marxism as an influence in the sphere of practical politics suffered an eclipse because of the expansionist behaviour of the Russians. It continued, however, to play a significant role as an analytical tool in the hands of certain intellectuals – especially, of course, social scientists and historians; political disillusionment, indeed, had already been expressed before the war by writers like Orwell and Gide, though wartime exigencies temporarily silenced doubts. Nevertheless, in the immediate post-war period concern for social improvement which was one of the motive forces of the 'pink decade' continued, in psychological as well as economic terms. 'Security', as defined by Sir William Beveridge, rather than simply 'wealth' – the cash-nexus – becomes politically important. 'Want, Disease, Ignorance, Squalor, and Idleness' were the giants against which Beveridge tilted: the terms in which Ignorance was tackled represent, even if rather tritely, the extent to which we had moved beyond the cynicism of educating our masters:

In the development of education lies the most important, if not the most urgent, of all the tasks of reconstruction. The needs of civilized man are illimitable, because they include the wise, happy enjoyment of leisure!

Thus the two mighty forces unleashed by the reconstructive aspirations of the Enlightenment to replace outmoded privilege and 'superstition' continued to coexist in uneasy association – the desires towards individuality and collectivism, freedom as self-expression and freedom as obedience. The former was manifest in a growth of permissiveness in sexual and cultural expression: resultant gains in personal freedom, however, have been matched by new manifestations of group tyranny. Modern psychology stressed group dynamics rather than individual behaviour, the total configuration rather than the isolate. Group therapy appeared alongside individual treatment; group methods involving 'projects' were recommended in schools to replace the old individualistic competitive pattern. Apologists for a comprehensive experiment in education urged the benefits of social intermingling in the same breath with which they played up the needs of the meritocracy. Business men with advanced views proclaimed industry as fulfilling a social as well as an economic function. The notion of 'adjustment' to society came to play an important part as a value concept. Diseased aspects of society or a variety of other external causes, rather than individual wickedness, have for long been blamed for increased delinquency and crime; as Barbara Wootton summed it up in her *Social Science and Social Pathology* (1959), 'the logical drive, in modern social science, away from notions of individual responsibility is very powerful'. A social psychologist, like J. A. C. Brown, could write that 'the primary group' is the basic unit of society, not the individual. Equality was sought even at the sacrifice of liberty.

Though the movement in England was as yet fitful, tentative, and spasmodic, and had not yet warranted the riposte it had earned in William H. Whyte's *Organization Man* (1956) in America, the book could be appreciated here in terms of current trends. The problem of the old ethic was man's indifference to man; that of the new, man's too confident and complete assumption of concern. With typical insight and brilliance de Tocqueville foresaw the dilemma which had been evolving since the late nineteenth century.

> In the principle of equality I very clearly discern two tendencies; the one leading the mind of every man to untried thoughts, the other inclined to prohibit him from thinking at all. And I perceive how, under the dominion of certain laws, democracy would extinguish that liberty of the mind to which a democratic social condition is favourable; so that, after having broken all the bondage once imposed on it by ranks or by men, the human mind would be closely fettered to the general will of the greatest number.
>
> (*Democracy in America*, 1840)

At the same time, warnings against the totalitarian implications of state interference grew apace in the immediate post-war period. There had been Orwell's *Nineteen Eighty-Four* (1949) and Koestler's *The Yogi and the Commissar* (1945). Karl Popper's *The Open Society and its Enemies* (1945) reasserted liberal values, and his *Poverty of Historicism* (1957) protested against notions of historical inevitability. F. A. Hayek's *Road to Serfdom* (1944) was anti-left in attitude; and when, in 1951, Michael Oakeshott replaced Harold Laski in the chair of Political Science at the London School of Economics, so long associated with socialist views, a philosopher in the Burke tradition replaced an English Marxist. English liberalism was to prove toughly resistant to the extremes of continental absolutist systems, whether of the right or the left. Nevertheless, the decline of the liberal intelligentsia, its abdication of responsibility in the face of growing classlessness, its elite anti-elitism, boded ill for the future.

Problems of Popular Culture

In his book *The Age of the Masses* (1977) M. D. Biddiss indicates that:

In the context of European history, it is the emergence of mass society, and the associated development of mass politics and culture, which most essentially and dramatically distinguishes this period [post 1870] from what has gone before.

Nearly fifty years previously, Ortega y Gasset in *The Revolt of the Masses* (1932) had proclaimed that

the characteristic of the hour is that the commonplace mind, knowing itself to be commonplace, has the assurance to proclaim the rights of the commonplace and to impose them wherever it will ... The sovereignty of the unqualified individual, of the human being as such, generically, has now passed from being a juridical idea or ideal to be a psychological state inherent in the average man.

The decline of classical humanism, already under attack in the eighteenth century, had removed one of the two central energizing forces of European civility (the other was Christianity). The growing prestige of science introduced two new elements into the situation: a cultural force of increasing potency entirely lacking in moral content apart from the initial pre-supposition that increased understanding of and control over nature constituted an unqualified good; and the attribution of prestige to minds which, apart from the innovative few (and Thomas Kuhn in his book *The Structure of Scientific Revolutions*, 1962, has shown how comparatively rare they were and are), were essentially mediocre – 'shut up in the narrow cell of their laboratory', ignorant of much even in their own fields, outside the narrow confines of their research. We encounter the modern phenomenon, the prototype of the specialist, and thus savour the brutality of minds who know a great deal about a little and not necessarily much about anything else.

The increasingly precarious position of the man of wide cultivation has become apparent since the early years of the nineteenth century: it lay behind Coleridge's advocacy of a 'clerisy', Arnold's analysis of culture and anarchy, Henry James's cry of 'loneliness'. De Tocqueville, indeed, in the passage quoted above, foresaw that gradual cultural homogenization (outside the areas of specialization) which has become so marked a feature of the twentieth century. Expectation that the spread of literacy to all, following the Acts of 1870–80, would revivify a perceptibly declining cultural vitality has been sadly disappointed. The commercial development of various media of mass communication has fostered further that trading spirit which de Tocqueville diagnosed as having already affected literature by 1840. Since the aim, cynically overt or sententiously wrapped up, was so often quick profits, the tendency was to appeal at a low level of public taste on the assumption that this would bring about the largest quantitative return.

The case for the new age of industrial democracy was stated by John Dewey: he pointed out how learning was no longer a 'class matter':

> ... as a direct result of the industrial revolution ... this has been changed. Printing was invented; it was made commercial. Books, magazines, papers were multiplied and cheapened. As a result of the locomotive and telegraph, frequent, rapid and cheap intercommunication by mails and electricity was called into being ... the result has been an intellectual revolution. Learning has been put in circulation ... Stimuli of an intellectual sort pour in upon us in all kinds of ways.
>
> (*School and Society*, 1900)

James's analysis of the phenomenon of the 'newspaperized world' would seem to imply the more perceptive comment:

> One sketches one's age but imperfectly if one doesn't touch on that particular matter: the invasion, the impudence and shamelessness, of the newspaper and the interviewer, the devouring *publicity* of life, the extinction of all sense between public and private. It is the highest expression of the note of 'familiarity', the sinking of *manners*, in so many ways, which the democratization of the world brings with it.
>
> (*Notebooks*)

As F. R. Leavis remarked, 'It is as if society, in so complicating and extending the machinery of organization, had lost intelligence, memory and moral purpose.'

The coming of universal literacy produced no such anticipated advances in rationality as the utilitarian theorists had prophesied. Indeed, developing educational dilemmas merely served to highlight the inability to find an adequate substitute for the old culture of the people – expressed in folksong and dance, rustic craft and natural lore – which industrialism had destroyed. Where the secondary-modern school curriculum was concerned, for instance, neither the encouragement of that 'practical' bent said to characterize those of inferior intellectual capacities nor the more 'democratic' suggestion of the common core curriculum met the case satisfactorily.[3]

Where popular reading was concerned – and here the effect of the new literacy can be assessed – there would seem to be some evidence of a decline in quality.[4] Certainly, popular reading matter of the twentieth century has demonstrated a distressing poverty in the imaginative life of the people. The sort of cultural and moral desiccation represented by the attitudes of a Northcliffe and those of his heirs revealed itself in a variety of ways. What was almost worse than the vulgarity, triviality and sensationalism implicit in the sort of emphasis the news received and in the methods of exploitation and presentation, was the standard of human relationship tacitly accepted in the journalists' search for news. Harold Laski described his humiliation during the libel case he brought in 1946 in a bitterly felt account of what modern publicity entails:

... the photographers – a merciless and determined race – await you as you enter the big doors of the Courts, begging you to pose ... They run in front of you as you approach the bus ... The notion that you have some right to privacy either does not enter their minds, or is mercilessly thrust on one side in the knowledge that your temporary publicity is the basis upon which they may earn an extra half-guinea ...

James's analysis received a striking confirmation.

If the ethics of business enterprise, with its consequent emphasis on material consumption, were accepted, then advertising had a necessary place in the economy. But its effect in creating stereotypes, in stimulating the baser aspects of human nature – fear of social non-conformity, snobbery, resentment at the demands of work – must rank high in any assessment of deleterious influences on the twentieth-century consciousness. In the same way, the various forms of popular literature – crime or love stories – were to be condemned, not because they incited to violence and rape (violence was a major characteristic of the popular culture of the 1960s, not of the 1920s and 30s) but because the attitudes they involved in important matters of human relationship and moral choice were obstructive to finer or more subtle responses. The expectations about human behaviour aroused by the ordinary work of popular fiction or the popular magazine story involved grossly over-simplified stereotypes which, to addicts, must to some extent have interfered with their ability to understand those with whom they had to live in close personal contact, as in family life. At the very least, they debased the medium of social intercourse, language, and when that happens, 'the whole machinery of social and individual thought and order goes to pot', as Ezra Pound put it.

Again, twentieth-century technical developments produced a variety of mass media of communication – the cinema, the radio and, after the Second World War, the television – of a potency not susceptible to precise measurement, though it is already clear that the radio and television are of considerable political effectiveness. Think of Hitler over the radio:

> Through technical devices like the radio and the loud-speaker, eighty million people were deprived of independent thought. It was thereby possible to subject them to the will of one man. (Albert Speer)

As important is the fact that night after night a selection of pro-grammes of inane triviality seemed to be acceptable to millions of people. And these, it is necessary to remind ourselves, were the 'educated' and literate descendants of the people who produced the folksong and the folktale, who built the parish churches and nourished Bunyan.

The whole problem of the effects of bad art became one of in-calculable importance. I. A. Richards wrote in *Principles of Literary Criticism* (1924):

> At present bad literature, bad art, the cinema, etc. are an influence of the first importance in fixing immature and actually inapplicable attitudes to most things. Even the decision as to what constitutes a pretty girl or a handsome young man, an affair apparently natural and personal enough is largely de-termined by magazine covers and movie stars.

In the years following the Second World War a good deal of work has been done in America, and latterly in this country, in an attempt to measure these influences in more precise terms than those provided by the 'moralizing literati' of the last two hundred years. Effects, it has been realized, are matters of some complexity; a simple extrapola-tion from content analysis is insufficient. The manifestations of popular culture need to be seen as influences working amid other factors in a total configuration. In the words of a social scientist:

> ... the effects of communications can be many and diverse, they may operate at different levels and in different strengths, they may manifest themselves in different ways or they may be latent, and they may derive from different

aspects of the content and different parts of the communication process. However, in spite of these difficulties and with due allowance for the incomplete nature of the evidence, it will be seen that what evidence there is suggests that the media have effects and that it would be wrong to assume that these effects are wholly good.

(J. D. Halloran, *The Effects of Mass Communication*, 1964)

Indeed, evidence of the deleterious effects of the cheaper manifestations of the media continue to grow even though it is realized that these effects differ in relation to the predispositions of the receiving agent. At best there is often the negative result of wasted opportunities and emotional energies dissipated in unselective television viewing – as Halloran again points out:

The defenders of television are ever ready to claim that the medium can improve and widen tastes and stimulate interests in creative activities. The evidence available does not support these claims.

Positive effects on cinema goers, as in matters of personal dress, hair style, make-up and house furnishing, as well as in some of the intimacies of human behaviour, such as love-making, have been recorded since the creation of the Hollywood 'dream factory' – witness the Valentino phenomenon of 1924. The implication was that, at times at least, many people lived fantasy existences derived from the shadow lives of the screen: they acquired, if only temporarily, models of behaviour. It may be that 'conclusive evidence about communication effects is still inadequate'; but there is enough to show that the 'moralizing literati' had a case. In any event, Marshall McLuhan caused us to suspect that even the medium itself may have unsuspected implications: the medium, as well as the content, 'is the message'. This at a time, too, when the nature of the work performed by the masses stimulated less and less to a sense of reality, to a grappling with the intractable nature of materials and substances in the individual and personal creative effort of the craftsman to induce form on the formless. The impersonal machine functioned instead. Hannah Arendt's indictment had behind it a complex and powerful analysis of the development of modern attitudes. It is, she wrote,

... as though individual life had actually been submerged in the over-all life process of the species and the only active decision still required of the individual were to let go, so to speak, to abandon his individuality, the still individually sensed pain and trouble of living, and acquiesce in a dazed, 'tranquillized', functional type of behaviour ... It is quite conceivable that the modern age – which began with such an unprecedented and promising outburst of human activity – may end in the deadliest, most sterile passivity history has ever known.

(The Human Condition, 1958)

In the very early days of the cinema, D. H. Lawrence realized the danger it offered of 'fixing' psychic expectation and 'idea':

The girl who is going to fall in love knows all about it beforehand from books and the movies ... she knows exactly how she feels when her lover or husband betrays her or when she betrays him: she knows precisely what it is to be a forsaken wife, an adoring mother, an erratic grandmother. All at the age of eighteen.

Growth, then, was fixated. Richard Hoggart diagnosed something similar when he noted that so much popular music consisted of

strictly conventional songs; their aim is to present to the hearer a known pattern of emotions; they are not so much creations in their own right as structures of conventional signs for the emotional fields they open.

(The Uses of Literacy, 1957)

Constant Lambert in his *Music Ho!* (1934) made the same point. To use Lawrence's terminology, such 'idealization' implied the death of the dynamic personality. It has seemed to many critics of the twentieth century that it is precisely the function of great literature to foster growth, to break down such stereotypes: in Leavis's view to speak out for 'life'.

Part of the trouble, of course, has been the increasing 'rootlessness' of the modern world:

'Was that', my friend smiled, 'where you "have your roots"?'
No, only where my childhood was unspent,
I wanted to retort, just where I started.

(Philip Larkin)

Greatly increased mobility implied a lack of continuity of environment and a consequent superficializing of relationships. The antagonism between the generations, a theme as old as the gods, had become more overt and uncontrolled owing to the moral uncertainties of the older generation, the acceptance of adolescence as a time of 'revolt' and the insidious exploitation of young people for commercial and political reasons by affording them a spurious 'importance'; hence the development of the teenage market. Symptomatic of the moral rootlessness was the kaleidoscopic progression of fashions, intellectual and otherwise, already marked in the earlier years of the century.

> The generations are extraordinarily short-lived. I can count up the intellectual fashions that have taken and held my students for a brief space. When I began in 1907 there was a wave of social idealism. Then ... suffrage, then syndicalism, then the war ... then Freud ... It's lost labour to refute these things – they just die out in time.
>
> (L. T. Hobhouse)

That this diagnosis of cultural malaise has been attacked from a number of quarters is itself revealing. It has been argued that such an indictment sprang from a sentimentalization and overestimation of a past which only *seemed* to offer more coherent and preferable standards – things have never really been different – and that it underestimated the very real advantages of the present and ignored 'growing-points' of our civilization. Moral uncertainty has been a positive gain: 'It is precisely our uncertainty which brings us a good deal closer to reality than was possible in former periods which had faith in the absolute' (K. Mannheim). There have been immense strides in material well-being and in the banishing of poverty. In a world increasingly aware of the dangers of over-specialization, the relative popularity of the agencies for cultural dissemination – the work of the Arts Council, the Third Programme, the encouraging sales of good-quality paperback books and classical gramophone records, and so on – has seemed to indicate a more widely diffused seriousness of interest. Vigorous experiment in the fields of music, painting, architecture and industrial design was cited as evidence of vitality, change being thought a mark of cultural vigour rather than a symptom of breakdown of cultural continuity. Science certainly flourished (affecting literature itself) and has been identified as an essential element in vital culture since Thomas Huxley proclaimed in 1880 that 'for the purpose of attaining real culture, an exclusively scientific education is at least as effective as an exclusively literary education'. New versions of pastoralism have detected signs of altered vitality in the working classes or the young as groups hitherto not generally accepted for their contribution to the quality of the age. The identification of both carried on traditions established in the nineteenth century, explicit in the writings of people like Herzen and Tolstoy or in the student movements of middle and eastern Europe following the great festival on the Wartburg in October 1817 – 'the first major conclave of students in modern history', as Lewis S. Feuer calls it. (It is well to be reminded that what are sometimes regarded as essentially manifestations of the period following the Second World War have their roots deep in the past.)

The complexities of assessing the relative movements of a whole civilization are so immense that it is only right that such counter-charges should be carefully noted. Certainly, that my indictment has been repeated from Wordsworth and Coleridge to Lawrence and Leavis seems to indicate a continuity of awareness which is encouraging and does something to nullify the charges made – this one can grant. Yet, some writers and critics might reply, the new complacency side-stepped the assumption on which their work was based, that great literature is not peripheral, but remains, after the decay of organized religion, one of the few means through which we can appraise the nature and quality of our lives, and is therefore vital to any strenuous attempt to define the nature of the good life. (There is, indeed, nothing new in this claim, as the humanists of the Renaissance bear witness.) Indeed, it cannot be a matter of in-difference that earlier in our period practically no writer of major stature failed to lament an isolation enforced on him by public apathy or even hostility. Nor, if literature is accepted as a presentation of 'felt' life, is it possible to brush aside as mistaken the testimony of its most powerful practitioners on a matter so fundamental as their relationship with their audience. For the nature of their analysis was of a very different sort from that of Johnson's easy and unself-conscious appeal to the 'common voice of the multitude, uninstructed by precept and unprejudiced by authority', or Dryden's complacent comment on his Elizabethan predecessors: 'Greatness was not then so easy to assess, nor conversation so free, as it now is'. It may be that this is the price of democratization; it is no use, however, burking the fact that there is a price and that it is a serious one. In the inter-war years there was none of that interpenetration of artistic, social, and political life that characterized the Augustan age.

The Disintegration of the Elite

The pleading to which I have referred is symptomatic of one of the supreme manifestations of the modern age, the disintegration of the elite. The notion of 'Mass Civilization and Minority Culture' (to quote the title of one of F. R. Leavis's first books) has been attacked on the grounds of its inadequate formulation of the complexities inherent in 'mass' civilization. It would be as relevant to note that the 'minority', in the literary field alone, subdivided, proliferated, and disagreed. Bloomsbury's all too self-contained aestheticism, *Scrutiny*'s reassertion of the puritan, ethical virtues, and 'Eng. Lit.'s' academic cohorts intent on the claims of scholarship, indicated a serious cleavage in what was still exiguous opinion. *Scrutiny* (1932–53) contained major revaluations over a wide range of literature in addition to challenging repudiations of 'aesthetic' and 'academic' values manifest, one in the belle-lettrist tradition and the other in scholarship uninformed by critical sensibility, and of the 'associational process' which accompanied both. This brought it into conflict with Bloomsbury, which countered with charges of a 'scientific' intrusion into the proper work of aesthetic criticism, and with certain academics, who flung charges of inadequate learning against a few of *Scrutiny*'s historical reassessments.

It will be argued, however, that these were simply the internal disagreements likely to be found among any group of the highly conscious. Even if this is accepted (and it is pertinent to note that these disagreements strike at the very foundations of the significance of a literary culture and its rationale), it takes no note of the highly significant manipulation of the avant-garde. This, essentially an offshoot of romantic stress on originality, was characterized by 'the myth of the new'. Its sociological implications have been admirably analysed by Renato Poggioli in *The Theory of the Avant-garde* (1962):

A cultural sociology for our time can only be constructed from the now certain hypothesis that a plurality of diverse and contradicting intellectual strata exists ... Our cultural-social situation is in a continual state of flux. From the political point of view, this situation produces an antithesis of what Pareto called 'the circulation of the elites', which really means a circulation within the elites. What happens is a continual up and down from one to another elite, from elite to non-elite ... What we then have is a continual process of disintegration ...

A major phenomenon of our period illustrating this process was that of Dada and its later associations with surrealism. Dada was largely if not quite nihilistic, sceptical of all programmes and ideologies: surrealism at least recognized a tradition of protest. As Robert Short has pointed out in his recent *Dada and Surrealism* (1980), their differences could be symbolized by their respective attitudes to automatism, Dada seeing it as the intimation of the ultimate chaos of man and nature, the surrealists as firmly within automatic 'creativity' patterns revelatory of the human unconscious. What then appeared to stem from common roots in European scepticism and romanticism exacerbated by the cataclysm of war gradually brought about shifting allegiances and realignments in the manner described by Poggioli. There was also the phenomenon of homogenization between the elite and the non-elite to which Poggioli refers. What I am getting at has been admirably diagnosed by Saul Bellow:

> In the 17th and 18th centuries the public was small, but highly educated and cultivated ... In the 19th century there appeared a mass public, the readers of Dickens, Thackeray and Trollope. By the end of that century, there had appeared a second and very small public interested in Baudelaire, Mallarmé, and, a little later, Proust and Joyce. There were two publics. Now again we have a single public. The methods of the small-public masters have been generally assimilated. Even the mass media employ the techniques of Joyce ... In fact, all the traditions of art have been absorbed into the movies, television, fashion and smart journalism. Our new public is by now university-educated, but it would be incorrect to compare it to the aristocratic public of the 18th century. University education has not instilled good taste, has not refined the judgement of readers. The literary conversation of educated people can frighten a writer to death.
>
> (*Observer*, 8 December 1968)

What Mr Bellow perhaps failed to bring out with sufficient explicitness was that this absorption had been a two-way process. If the techniques of the *former* 'advanced' writers and painters (Joyce, Picasso) were absorbed and utilized by the mass media and the world of fashion (thus undoubtedly helping to make the mass public more alert and quicker witted), it is equally true to say that the avant-garde increasingly looked for its source material and its emotional circumambience within the world of popular artefacts and culture. The minority and the majority, in fact, drew together: Dada's cult of the ready-made revealed a sophisticated reductionism. Advertising by the 1930s had absorbed the avant-garde techniques of collage. The necessary outcome of this process was in the sphere of the arts, a homogenizing of emotional range; this became increasingly apparent. The themes chosen by 'serious' writers more and more exploited violence and an interest in the cruder forms of sex. The net result was to display a restricted and inadequate account of human possibility and potentiality; and human beings were correspondingly diminished. We saw the heroic deprecated, pride and honour under a cloud, decorum ignored. What Lytton Strachey began was implemented even by writers with pretensions – Greene, Isherwood, and, at the end of our period, Kingsley Amis. In becoming assimilated to the largely corrupt world of popular art, the writer forgot the first rule of artistic integrity, the need for fidelity to the range of man's potential. Otherwise he becomes sentimental, reductionist or eccentric; and this, in fact, is just what he did become.

A hundred years ago Matthew Arnold expressed certain doubts about Swiss democracy: it had become, he said, 'socialistic, in the sense in which that word expresses a principle hostile to the interests of true society – *the eliminating of superiorities*'. What, indeed, is needed in even a democratic society, if it is to survive, is 'superiority' in two senses; superiority of insight on the part of writers, so that the worst *and the best* can be faced without distorting emphasis on the one or the other; and superiority of manners as a part of general social behaviour so that literature has a context in which it can perform its traditional function of refining understanding and assisting moral discrimination. The two processes, of course, are interdependent; literature both feeds and is fed by the social process. When, however, literature focuses its attention, for reasons of profit or fashion, on a restricted aspect of the social situation it both offends against its own nature and furthers the disintegration of civility which rests, at even the best of times, on slender and brittle foundations. The net effect of the cultural débâcle of Nazi Germany and of Soviet Russia – Soviet 'realism' constituted simply the totalitarian counterpart of the avant-garde movement in persistently 'liberal' countries in that both are equally reductive and false to the complexities of living – was to demonstrate the vital need for the preservation of a sense of cultural continuity (so that the eccentricities of the present can be more fully realized) and of loyalty to the circumstances of artistic integrity as opposed to those of fashion and over-anxious though selective social commitment.

Fashion, it will be realized, constituted a key concept in the understanding of the modern period. As Quentin Bell put it:

> The art of painting has today something in common with *haute couture*: the artist need shrink from no audacity so long as he is audacious in a socially acceptable way and so long as his inventions have the charm of novelty.
>
> (*Crisis in the Humanities*, ed. J. H. Plumb)

In what has been called the 'radical empiricism of the avant-garde', with its rejection of tradition, causality, its dissolution of form, its acceptance of the chaos of chance, we can detect the obliteration of the ideals of the Renaissance. Certainly, the penetration of high culture by popular (initially *petit bourgeois*, but latterly proletarian) models pointed to the decay of elitism, a decay symbolized by the attacks on the private education system, the call, after the American model, for the common school and the 'massification' of higher education which was chronicled by Flexner in America as early as 1930. In education, the first great revolution of the Renaissance enthroned the ideal – essentially elitist – of the literate man of affairs nurtured on the 'commonplaces' (*topoi*) of classical wisdom; the second – that of our own country – rejected such 'amateurism' in favour of a narrow expertise. Thus the lack of a generally informed public invited any eccentricity that could make itself heard. The crisis of the mid-century was not only a crisis at popular level – it permeated our whole society. D. H. Lawrence's sense of decay (noted in the passage from *Kangaroo* previously quoted) had been confirmed.

The Great Writer's Response to his Age

It is now apparent, to an extent which can only be realized in the light of the preceding diagnosis, that the 'isolation' referred to in the opening paragraph of this essay was a source of strength as well as of weakness. This isolation explains, too, what has often been a matter of reproach levelled against some of the greatest figures of the earlier twentieth century, especially Eliot – their conservatism. While at one level they protested against much that was mechanical and materialistic in our society, they countered not by an irresponsible flight to chance, momentary sensation, sexual titillation and anti-rational mindlessness but by a reassertion of the need for roots, the traditions of their craft. While they sought to change the nature of continuity they confirmed its necessity: as D. H. Lawrence put it, 'Thank God I'm not free, any more than a rooted tree is free', a remark which balances Eliot's 'Tradition cannot mean standing still'.

So, in examining the greatest writers' responses to this age of disintegration and confusion it is important to remember that not all protests are the same protest; the informed, carefully detailed criticisms of great artists, balanced by acceptable positive affirmations of substance and quality, constitute very different indictments from those of a reductionist avant-garde or of youthful agitators. The latter afford evidence of a widespread and growing repudiation of the disciplines necessary for civilization – even for civility; the former constitute an awareness of dislocation in a context of analysis and reaffirmation which 'placed' current discontents in the permanent context of the human predicament.

A high degree of social and experiential awareness on the part of the modern writer enables us, without much difficulty, to relate social and intellectual background to the preoccupations of the greatest writers of the twentieth century. Rarely, indeed, can there have been a time when 'background' more readily obtruded as an essential part of foreground. Sensing the disintegration around them, these writers took it upon themselves both to explore the state of the social order and to propound ways of dealing with it. They inherited the preoccupation of nineteenth-century writers with how to live.

Their contribution manifested itself in a very different guise from that of the social scientist, whose increased importance has been commented on earlier. The writer ideally committed himself to a process of defining the implications of experience as a prerequisite to the right ordering of personal and social life. Particularly in the modern period he has been the enemy of those abstractions which have clogged our consciousness as a result of the rationalist, positivist tradition. He pursued his sense of the 'real' beneath the level attainable (as yet, at least) by the scientific sociologist; where the latter conceptualized the former, at his best, attempted to employ a more unified interplay of feeling and intellect, one which defined itself through the emotive complexities of language. He felt *into* situations rather than subjected them to rational and therefore extroverted analysis. He was essentially the practitioner of '*Verstehen*'.

Lawrence, in the name of that ultimate spark of spontaneity, the essential uniqueness and untouchable naïvety at the centre of all true human beings, rejected both the false 'individuality' of the liberal tradition and the increasing socialization of his times. His triumph was to see them as joint manifestations of the same basic outlook, involving the elevation of the '*ego* or spurious self, the conscious entity with which every individual is saddled' – the conceptualizing self, not the unified sensibility. In essence, too, this was his case against the positivist assault. In reaction against the abstractions of the intellect, the failure of 'reason' to capture adequately the sheer flux and flow of experience, there has been a counter-assertion of the need to convey emotional immediacy, a grasping after the moment, a subjective insistence on the force of inner feeling, what John Holloway, in his survey, describes as the Romantic preoccupation.

T. S. Eliot's notion of the 'dissociation of sensibility', whatever it may indicate about certain movements of consciousness in the seventeenth century, revealed a diagnostic impulse of the twentieth-century poet in recognizing an unhealthy split between 'thought' and 'feeling'. His summing-up of Donne's sensibility – 'An idea was an experience; it modified his sensibility' – implied a contemporary criticism of the conceptualizing ego. Part of its tyranny was over the tool of the artist, language: Yeats repudiated the Ibsenite tradition, the drama of ideas, as that of those who

write in the impersonal language that has come, not out of individual life, nor out of life at all, but out of the necessities of commerce, of parliament, of Board Schools, of hurried journeys by rail, [and this] death of language, this substitution of phrases as nearly impersonal as algebra for words and rhythms varying from man to man, is but a part of the tyranny of impersonal things.

In praising Synge for being 'by nature unfitted to think a political thought', Yeats had in mind the same sort of criterion as had Eliot in appraising Henry James for having too fine a mind for it ever to be violated by an idea.

Yet, in accepting Eliot's diagnosis of 'dissociation', we were still in a world where the 'idea' is acknowledged – even if as something to 'touch and stroke', to '*feel*' rather than to inter in conceptualization. What he (and Lawrence, for that matter) advocated was the *unified* sensibility; the aim was to catch 'the whole man alive' in terms of the feeling intellect, not to surrender to pure emotion or intellectual abstraction. Thus D. H. Lawrence protested against 'idealization':

> The ideal – what is the ideal? A figment. An abstraction ... It is a fragment of the before and after. It is a crystallized aspiration, or a crystallized remembrance: crystallized, set, finished. It is a thing, set 'apart', in the great storehouse of eternity, the storehouse of finished things.
>
> (Preface to *Poems*)

What was being insisted on was an updated version of that view of the imagination formulated by Coleridge as involving 'a *coalescence* of subject and object', a matter of the mutual modification of person and environment in the very act of apprehension. The relationship between mind and world became one of 'transaction' in John Dewey's sense of the word rather than of 'interaction' with its implications of discreteness. William James as well as anyone formulated the theory of consciousness which lay behind these attempts to define psychic life:

> ... consciousness, then, does not appear to itself chopped up in bits ... It is nothing jointed; it flows. A 'river' or 'stream' are the metaphors by which it is most naturally described. In talking of it hereafter, let us call it the stream of thought, of consciousness, or of subjective life.
>
> (*Principles of Psychology*, 1901)

Psychological atomism, inherent in associationist ideas, was being challenged by 'gestalt' theories. To William James, as we see, experience, reality constituted a continuum. (It is relevant to remember that Henry James, after receiving his brother's book, confessed to having been a pragmatist all his life.)

> I found myself compelled to *give up* logic, fairly, squarely, irrevocably ... It has an imperishable use in human life, but that use is not to make us theoretically acquainted with the essential nature of reality ... I find myself no good warrant for even suspecting the existence of any reality of a higher denomination than that distributed and strung along and flowing sort of reality we finite beings swim in. That is the sort of reality given us, and that is the sort with which logic is so incommensurable.
>
> (*Principles of Psychology*)

Hence the 'stream of consciousness' writing of responsible authors like Virginia Woolf, Dorothy Richardson and James Joyce. Their intention was to reassert a psychic balance against the influence of the mechanical, the atomized self, to cope with an ever changing being and world rather than remain stuck in the repetitions and recurrences of a fixated past. The attempt was to heal the rift between intellectual abstraction and the ever present flow of feeling. In a 'much-divided civilization', when the claims of technology were becoming more and more insistent, the greatest writers, in whose work intellect was suffused with emotion and emotion controlled by intelligence, pointed a way to 'unity of being', psychic wholeness and health. In such a fusion, intuitive insight and moral control could coalesce.

It is important to realize, however, that what marked the great writers off from less effective practitioners who wished to exploit 'the tradition of the new', involving a surrender to flux rather than to its control (as in surrealism and other avant-garde manifestations), was their appreciation that an essential part of the present was derived from the past and that the attempt to repudiate the past, the attack on history and memory explicit in Dadaism, for instance, involved a fundamental falsification of that very present the avant-garde was concerned to capture: as Eliot put it,

> Time present and time past
> Are both perhaps present in time future
> And time future contained in time past.

And Lawrence combined his concern for 'the instant, the immediate self, the very plasma of the self' with the realization that that very self drew its real substance from sources deep in the history of the race:

> The soul must take the hint from the relics our scientists have so marvellously gathered out of the forgotten past, and from the hint develop a new living utterance. The spark is from dead wisdom, but the fire is life.

So the insistent present draws its substance from the living past; hence the 'conservatism' of these writers – Yeats with his invocation of Ancestral Houses, Eliot and Christianity, Conrad with the sense of 'simple fellowship and honourable reciprocity of services' derived from his Polish past and the British Merchant Service. It explains the coexistence of past and present in their work, the individual renewal completed in the sense of the social and historical; it makes inescapable the defining characteristics, in F. R. Leavis's words, of a genuine literary commitment as involving an 'interest in man, society and civilization'. If, on occasions, these writers should appear 'anti-democratic' then their comments should be treated seriously as attempts to correct fashionable doctrines by an appeal to the more permanent manifestations of the human condition, a condition which in the end will exact its penalties from democracy itself if their warnings go unheeded. It is perhaps easier to see this from the vantage point of the 1980s than it was when these writers were actually producing their works. As the great political abstractions – Fascism, Communism, Socialism, Internationalism – have been tried and found wanting, their assertion of unique and irreplaceable individuality is a valuable corrective; as the assertion of individual 'rights' takes precedence over obligation, their evocations of an historical need for order and responsibility act as an antidote to the libertinism of permissiveness. A reinvocation of the Renaissance dependence on an historical literature still seems the only feasible counter-measure to the disassociations of specialization, as Leavis, who can be termed the last of the Renaissance humanists, so strongly advocated.

'The Essence of Modern Man'

The period under review can be considered from a variety of perspectives. In the political sphere, nineteenth-century liberalism is giving way to a growing collectivism with its implications of standardization and uniformity – 'equality' rather than 'liberty'. The corrective response is to stress individuality, the uniqueness of poetic utterance, the purely personal in expression. In psychic terms there is the growing power, clearly manifest from the time of the Enlightenment, of thought, the abstractions of intellect to guide and direct life; hence an important strand of literary practice saw life, by contrast, as a series of emotional intensities involving a logic different from that of the rational world and capturable only in dissociated images or stream of consciousness musings ('These fragments I have shored against my ruins'). The disappearance of philosophical speculation and system-building led the creative writer and the literary critic to reassert the centrality of literature as a guide to the moral perplexities of the age in a manner reminiscent of (though not identical with) the Renaissance humanist; hence the private agonies of writers and artists acquire a public bearing which constitutes the counterpart to their intimations of isolation and 'loneliness'. The difficulty which marks so much 'modern' writing constituted a response to the ubiquity of print and the consequent staling of language, so that certain types of utterance can only recover their freshness in an ironic context – they represent the revivification of the cliché through an implication of equivocation.

But perhaps the most fundamental characteristic of the 'modern' period was itself an irony – its equivocation over the very concept of the 'modern'. Ever since the seventeenth century there has been wave after wave of protest against what have been regarded as the stultifications of the historical consciousness, manifest as a series of scepticisms. Descartes' method of doubt, Locke's dismissal of the *a priori* implicit in his denial of innateness, the reconstructive zeal of the Enlightenment on a basis of universal reason (the 'transcendental pretense' as a recent commentator has called it) all reflect in a variety of ways the battle of the 'moderns' against the 'ancients'. The reconstructive zeal of science has penetrated deeply into the European psyche.

All this has culminated in our own 'modern' period in the growing reductionism which has marked so many features of our cultural life: the cult of primitivism and mindlessness, the desire to see afresh 'with the mind of a child'; the indignation against convention and forms of all kinds, the destruction of boundaries; the constant change in fashion; the restless experimentalism of painters like Picasso. Against this have been quite conscious reassertions of tradition and attempts to define it which have characterized the greatest writers and critics. In them, indeed, 'ancient' and 'modern' constitutes perhaps the fundamental tension that runs through all their work – the acceptance of the romantic notion of 'originality', the new, the fresh perception, the penetration – in Lawrence – below 'the old stable ego' of the character, and the need to suffuse these new perceptions with values derived from former insights, the inescapable historical element of the *a priori* as an essential datum in 'experience', the fact of being born and reared into an historical circumstance before consciousness could intervene. This basic human tension has been exacerbated by the change in audience – the accession to prominence of the historically anonymous masses, those who lack a defined history if not a history. These offspring of the folk, made rootless by industrialization, are the basic new factor in the modern period which has altered the balance (itself traditional) between ancient and contemporary. It is this fact, blatantly visible after the Second World War, but emerging well before the twentieth century, which, culturally, raises the profoundest doubts and uncertainties for the future; for what the masses contribute is surface agitation, what they lack is depth of being. M. Alain Robbe-Grillet's diagnosis – 'The essence of modern man ... is no longer to be found within a hidden soul, but plastered on hoardings ... Therefore study the surface, the object, for it contains the only answer' – has a retrospective force in its relevance to the period under review. At least it helps to account for the unmistakable decline in literary quality once the great 'moderns', who are the subject of this volume, have passed away: 'life' has increasingly manifested itself either in the esotericism of specialized and arcane knowledge or a socially homogenized 'experience'.

NOTES

1. cp. W. E. Houghton, *The Victorian Frame of Mind, 1830–1870* (New Haven, 1957).

2. cp. the rationalization of the coal mines by Gerald Crich in *Women in Love*. It may be that what Lawrence was getting at was 'Taylorism' or 'scientific management', which was a near-contemporary industrial manifestation. On the whole question of modern industrialism and its implications for work satisfaction and human relationships, the reader is strongly recommended to read Georges Friedmann's *Industrial Society* (Illinois, 1964). One of the best attempts to characterize the nature of the mental climate induced by the machine is to be found in Chapter IX of Thorstein Veblen's *The Theory of Business Enterprise*, reprinted in *The Portable Veblen* ed. Max Lerner (New York, 1948), where it is recognized that 'The discipline exercised by the mechanical occupations ... is a discipline of the habits of thought'. These habits of thought are defined at some length by Veblen. M. J. Wiener, in his recent *English Culture and the Decline of the Industrial Spirit, 1850–1980* (Cambridge, 1981), has indicated the extent to which 'the social and intellectual revolution implicit in industrialization was muted, perhaps even aborted' in Britain as a result of the persistence of a nostalgic anti-industrial spirit among certain sections of the elite. He blames this persistence for the relative decline of British industry in recent years.

3. I have examined this situation more fully in my *Dilemmas of the Curriculum* (Oxford, 1980).

4. R. K. Webb's article in the sixth volume of the *Guide, From Dickens to Hardy*, warns against over-emphasis on the homogeneity or seriousness of the Victorian reading public. Yet Miss Dalziel, in her *Popular Fiction 100 years Ago* (London, 1957), considers that there are grounds to support Q. D. Leavis's contention, made in *Fiction and the Reading Public* (London, 1932), that there has been a deterioration in the quality of popular literature over the last hundred years, though those grounds are not quite the ones Mrs Leavis herself expressed.

PART II

PART II

THE LITERARY SCENE

JOHN HOLLOWAY

Introductory

There are certain things which the reader should bear in mind throughout this survey, as fundamentals in the literary scene of the earlier decades of the twentieth century. The first is that this was a period in which, as a result of developments in the religious, political, economic, military, and other fields, men more and more lost faith in certain traditional ways of seeing the world. This was not a change which began in 1900. Something like it was a great feature of the cultural life of the whole nineteenth century. It went conspicuously further, however, in the period which concerns this chapter: a period which saw some writers reach an ultimate point along the line of bewilderment and disillusion, and others (or indeed, the same ones at another stage or in another phase) making a new start, and hammering out the terms of life afresh.

This is a fact about the period which spread so wide, that it would be important for a survey of any aspect of its life; and it has been discussed at length in the preceding chapter. The second fundamental fact also spreads far beyond literature, but it concerns the literary scene quite as much as the first. It is that the age under review was conspicuously one of popularization and commercialization. As a fundamental of modern life, this has also received attention by G. H. Bantock in Part I of this volume. It has meant that literature and serious literary standards had to survive in, and in one sense adapt themselves to, a world which was largely alien to the attitudes, values, and assumptions that they most naturally require. Again, this development has a history throughout the nineteenth century. Wordsworth, Ruskin, and Matthew Arnold – to name only three of many – all noticed it as a deep-rooted feature of English life in their time. But the changes that they noticed proceeded further; and serious writers, with those who most seriously cared for literature and the continuance of literature, were confronted with a society which in part relied, half-indifferently, upon the stock literary judgement, the best-seller, and the polite verse anthology, but which had forgotten that literature could touch life at both its deepest, and its most exhilarating.

These are familiar ideas. They have already been put forward by some of the more notable critical or social studies of the time.[1] Less often commented upon (if commented upon at all) is something which arose strictly within the field of serious literature and serious thinking about it, and which gave these wider facts about the mass nature and the commercialized nature of modern society a quite special importance. This is, that the period under review was one in which most important new work in literature lent itself especially little to general consumption, or to a relaxed taste, or a taste influenced by non-literary interests. The main body of outstanding work written in this period was written under a special kind of influence which necessarily made that work unfamiliar and difficult. This was the influence of contemporary literature abroad; and, in the case of poetry especially, of a foreign school of poetry, that of certain late-nineteenth-century French writers, whose work was uniquely condensed and obscure.

Comparison with the mid-nineteenth century may make this point clearer. Poets like Tennyson and Rossetti, prose writers like Arnold, novelists like George Eliot were not of course devoid of acquaintance with foreign writing: such a suggestion would be absurd. But their interests were not concentrated on, or even much directed to, truly contemporary and avant-garde authors abroad. Moreover, knowledge or interest is one thing, and seeking to learn massively about fundamental questions of writing, to naturalize new basic techniques and insights, is another. Relatively speaking, the mid-Victorian period was one in which English literature pursued a self-contained course. Certainly, this contrast may be over-simplified; it is not a black and white contrast. On the other hand, in seeing the period of this survey as one of major influence from abroad, we see in it something which has been recurrent in the development of our literature over centuries. More than once in the past, a period of comparative native independence has been succeeded by a period of major influence from continental Europe; this has been assimilated, and once again our literature has temporarily become more self-contained in its development. As, in fact, one takes one's studies further on into the century, beyond the close of the present volume of the *Guide*, it is just such a self-containment and indeed insularity which proves to be important.

The Opening Scene

With these guiding ideas in mind, it is time to come to some details which may throw the major changes of the period into relief; and to begin with, to reconstruct as a starting point something of the world, so different from our own, of the turn of the century.

Yeats, retrospecting in 1936, recalled the change at this very time. His tone does not invalidate what he says:

> Then in 1900 everybody got down off his stilts; henceforth nobody drank absinthe with his black coffee; nobody went mad; nobody committed suicide; nobody joined the Catholic Church; or if they did I have forgotten.
> (Introduction to *The Oxford Book of Modern Verse*, xi)

But the literary scene of the 1890s spread far wider than the Rhymers' Club (their intentions, if not their achievement, being more down-to-earth than is usually realized)[2] and the 'Nineties Poets'. It spreads out to the whole opulent plutocratic social world of the time. This means the great country houses (James was an *habitué*) with their fashionable weekends; the great town houses (Lancaster Gate in *The Wings of the Dove*, Princes' Gate in real life, where Leyland the Liverpool shipping merchant collected his Japanese blue-and-white china, and Whistler created the famous 'Peacock Room'); and artistic Chelsea where Whistler, Wilde, Henry James, and Sargent were all near neighbours. It means also the reign of the 'actor-managers' in the London theatre (Irving at the Lyceum, Beerbohm Tree at His Majesty's giving Easter Shakespeare seasons – *A Midsummer Night's Dream* with real woods, bluebells, rabbits, *Macbeth* with witches that flew on wires and real guardsmen from Chelsea Barracks for the battle scenes); of the Leicester Square Alhambra, with its Moorish dreamland architecture and lavish shows, and the adjoining Empire with its notorious promenade, and the 'Gaiety Girls' who married into the peerage (model wives, usually). Again, it means the great divorce scandals – Dilke, Parnell, Lady Colin

Campbell. The third of these gave Frank Harris's scandal-journalism its first great opportunity and doubled his paper's circulation, all of them perhaps did something to strengthen the new preoccupations of Hardy's *Jude the Obscure* (1896) – though Hardy's concern with these matters is visible in *The Woodlanders* (1887) – and certainly supplied the scene for Pinero's *The Second Mrs Tanqueray* (1893) and Wilde's ironically named *An Ideal Husband* (1895). It is against this richly varied background, and as in a real sense not only the critic but also the chronicler of this world, its chronicler with unrivalled fullness, insight, and humanity, that Henry James must be seen.

The Spoils of Poynton (1897) is James's dramatization of the conflict between what Arnold would have called the 'Barbarian' aspect of this plutocracy, and the 'Aesthetic' one: first the vulgarizing, Edwardianizing Mona Brigstock, with her aspirations to transform the house of priceless art treasures by installing a winter garden and a billiard room; second Mrs Gereth, the 'treasure hunter' as James called her, yet herself a vulgarian in conduct (albeit an elegant one) and conscious of the fineness only of fine 'Things'. James makes it clear enough that Poynton in no way stands for the traditions of a true and enduring aristocracy. It has no special claim to its 'Spoils'. They are spoils in the full, satiric sense; the work of another Lord Duveen. The fire which destroys the house at the end (it is one of James's few triumphs purely as a descriptive writer) is no mere re-using of the closing move of Meredith's *Harry Richmond* (1871) or Hardy's *A Laodicean* (1881). James is making clear, finally, the worth as he sees it of 'Spoils' in life.

By the same token, *The Awkward Age* (1899) is not a title which refers merely to the dawning womanhood of its heroine. It is the age as a whole which is awkward: the reign of a plutocracy (shoe magnates, aristo-bureaucrats, an upper class whose chief media of living are elegant talk and the *liaison*) in which an older, plainer kind of integrity is neither possible nor, save to the peculiarly astute, even recognizable. In several of James's more important short stories, the plutocracy of his time is studied from the point of view of the writer: over and over again James reveals his conviction, sometimes with bitterness, that the social world of his time at bottom had little to offer the artist save a velvet-gloved exploitation and the kind of hollow applause which destroyed his real life and real work. *The*

Lesson of the Master (1888) and *The Author of 'Beltraffio'* (1884) show writers spoilt through eagerness for pretty wives and the social veneer in which they mainly shone; yet, certainly in the first of these tales, James's inexhaustible ambiguity of treatment, ultimately leaving all the final interpretations open, for the reader not so much to choose between as simply to contemplate and wonder at, remains as our deepest impression, and accords, indeed, with the lavish opulence, the super-abundance, enjoyed at least by many in the period. *Broken Wings* (1900), shows a man and a woman writer who, for the illusory opulence of a life of country-house visits and the rest, have bartered away not only their best work but also their real lives as lovers. In *The Death of the Lion* (1894) the demands of the literary hostess upon her 'lion' are ultimately those of a homicide. *The Coxon Fund* (1894) shows the other side of the coin: literary patronage issues from a world without grasp or standards ('fancy constituting an endowment without establishing a tribunal – a bench of competent people – of judges') and can therefore do nothing but first select a largely bogus talent and then corrupt it. These two stories were both first published in *The Yellow Book* (1894–7): a fact which serves as reminder that James was nearer to the 'Aesthetic Movement' than one might now assume from the massive moral seriousness of his work; and that, for him, aesthetic perfection and moral significance were not opposed but – as in truth they are – complementary aspects of a single reality.

The interest of James, in this context, does not quite stop there. That one after another of his stories is about story-writing itself is an index, perhaps, that the world in which he moved did not give him as rich a field of real life as he craved for on behalf of the novelist.[3] Deeply and strongly as he saw into that world and grasped its limitations, those limitations elusively grasped him as well. This survey is not the place to enter into a full evaluation of the varied body of James's work. The problem here is of how that work belongs to and reflects its period: its place in a general scheme. In regard to this it seems as if what is best in James's work points mainly back to his American origin; and that the British (or in part European) scene of the turn of the century, as he used it in his later works, gave him something which in part he could turn to good effect, but not wholly so. James's distinction lies in the quick yet strong intelligence which unremittingly controls his work; in the clarity and nobility of his moral vision; and in his great sense of the richness and beauty of what at least is potential in human life. These qualities of intelligence, integrity, and idealism, this sense of what life can offer, are forcibly reminiscent of what was best in the culture of New England, Boston, Harvard, and New York in which James grew up. James's earlier work is largely set in America; and in it these qualities are intact (*The Europeans*, 1878; *Washington Square*, 1880). His genuineness is completely and splendidly reassuring in the larger and more ambitious *Portrait of a Lady* (1881). The work of his closing years, however, cannot be seen in quite the same light. He saw deficiencies in the kind of complexity and refinement which characterized this later period; yet these very things seem to colour his later work. As his world becomes more multitudinously self-reflecting and variegated, a doubt more and more preoccupies the reader. The doubt is, whether James's many-dimensional kaleidoscope of surfaces is after all a true revelation of deeper life in the characters, or only a wonderful simulacrum of deeper life. Nor can that doubt but be strengthened by James's growing tendency to invest his interplaying surfaces with all the grandiosity of Edwardian opulence; his growing dependence on words for his characters and their doings like 'fine', 'lovely', 'beautiful', 'tremendous', 'large', 'grand' ('they insisted enough that "stupendous" was the word': *The Wings of the Dove*, 1902, ch. 34); and this not as part of a total view, admire-but-judge, but rather of characters whom he endorses out and out. In the end, one is inclined to conclude that James and Sargent were not near neighbours quite for nothing. Nor is to perceive this to deny James's exhilaration and indeed his greatness; but to recognize that he was of his time.

Conrad had, as his strongest link with James in literary terms, his sense of life as a sustained struggle in moral terms: an issue between good and evil, in the fullest sense of these words, which individual men find they cannot evade. But James and Conrad should be seen together in the period in which they wrote, because the latter, with the former, is registering, and searchingly criticizing, basic realities of his time. Moreover, Conrad's realities relate to those which pre-occupied James. *Nostromo* (1904), unquestionably Conrad's master-piece, provides the definitive picture of how Western financial imperialism (that its roots are American makes no difference), prof-

fering to bring to an equatorial American society material advancement and an end to the picturesque banditry of the past, in fact
brings only spiritual emptiness and an unnoticed compromise with
principle, or progressive blindness to it.

It may seem wilful to link, to Conrad's richness of substance, deep
humanity of insight, and comprehensive, almost faultless control, the
name of Kipling. Yet to see in Kipling only a vulgar Imperialist is
crude. His values are largely the mid-Victorian ones of earnest effort
and personal genuineness (*The Mary Gloster* or *MacAndrew's Hymn*,
1894). His chief aversion was to the smooth representatives of plutocracy who both censure and exploit the pioneering generation
(*Gentleman Rankers*, 1892; *The Explorer*, 1898; *The Pro-consuls*, 1905).
His chief fear, the point of *Recessional* (1897), was that the exploiters,
the parasites, were winning. What limits his achievement is that he
submits to the trend of his time. Even as a poet, he writes for the
audience to which his journalistic years directed him, and the
result is an embarrassingly buoyant heavy-handedness under which
the finer distinctions disappear and the plainest issues of good and
evil seem without weight. This applies also to his prose, though it
must be remembered that in *Kim* (1901), at least, there is an immediacy, richness, and exactitude which put Kipling high among the
chroniclers of British expansion.

Kim's Russian agents were in the Himalayas. Other writers were
to sense, nearer home, some of the threats to the world of opulent
liberalism. Conrad's *Under Western Eyes* (1911) depicts the nineteenth-
century Russian police state with the brilliance of one who knew it
at first hand; and is little less outstanding in dealing with the extremist
exiles from it in Western Europe. In *The Secret Agent* (1907) it is
not the terrorists themselves, but the (thinly disguised) Russian
embassy and its *agent provocateur* which preoccupy the author, and the
quite unexpected but in the end quite decisive presence of Irish
Fenians in a minor, picturesque, largely comical novel like Quiller-
Couch's *The Astonishing History of Troy Town* (1888) adds a curious
confirmation to the general point. James's *The Princess Casamassima*
(1886) cannot be seen as dealing successfully either with Bakuninism
or with the life and mind of the London poor. But that James of
all writers should have taken up the subject is itself illuminating; it
is a forcible reminder of how widely the writers of the closing years

of the nineteenth century were aware of all that existed in their society outside its circle of opulence. One can see, in this work, an awareness in James of those forces which were soon to bring sweeping social changes, and in the end, contribute decisively to the transformed social scene of two generations later. If the *fin-de-siècle* or Edwardian periods were opulent, it was an opulence which arose out of a sea of poverty. General Booth's *In Darkest England* (1890) began with an account of the opening up of Central Africa, only to point out that there was a social jungle, with its three million slaves to destitution, at home. Hardy, in both his prose and verse, reflected the rural side of poverty and deprivation. Gissing (*The Unclassed*, 1884) revealed a London which seemed to have lost the variegatedness it had for Dickens, and to have become a sea of undifferentiated anonymity which destroyed all the individual's vital energies.

New Influences in Fiction

One section of Gissing's most forceful work, *New Grub Street* (1891), is particularly helpful in throwing light on what was happening in English fiction towards the close of the century. In chapter 10 of this book, several of the characters discuss the kinds of novel they would like to write. Among them, they stress the importance for fiction of new ideas in natural history (above all, Darwin) and religious thinking. This fact is helpful in that it is a brief reminder of how English fiction had for several decades been coming to deal with new and more 'intellectual' subjects; had been gaining, as with Hardy and indeed Meredith, a dimension which might almost be called philosophical. George Eliot, in real contrast to Thackeray or Trollope, and superficially (though not fundamentally) in contrast also to Dickens, based her fiction on a comprehensive, systematic sense of society and the inter-relations within it; a sense which must owe something to her early study of the social sciences and contact with the circle of the *Westminster Review*. The trend had been going on for some time, and it remains important for a twentieth-century writer like Bennett. The debate in *New Grub Street*, however, also throws something else into relief; and this new factor is one which rapidly became more important towards the end of the century. As they discuss the fiction they would like to write, Gissing's characters not only decide that Dickens's treatment of common life is lacking in seriousness because of his leanings towards humour and melo-drama; they also consider Zola's treatment of common, everyday life – dry, patient, comprehensive, seemingly non-committal – as a contrast and a superior alternative to Dickens.

Here, in this interest in, this impact of, the continental model, is a basic and enduring new influence. Zola's *L'Assommoir* (1877) was the detailed model not only of the Victorian melodrama *Drink* (1879: arranged by Charles Reade) but also for George Moore's *A Mummer's Wife* (1888), the first serious attempt in English at fiction like Zola's; and to some extent (though the influence of Dickens is also asserting itself) for Maugham's first novel, *Liza of Lambeth* (1897). Arnold Bennett's work displays not only the influence of the new, systematic, intellectual approach to fiction ('Herbert Spencer's *First Principles*, by filling me up with the sense of causation everywhere, has altered my whole view of life ... you can see *First Principles* in nearly every line I write,' Bennett says in his *Journals* for September 1910) but the French influence as well. 'I ought during the last month to have read nothing but de Goncourt,' he wrote when *Anna of the Five Towns* (1902) was begun; or again, 'The achievements of the finest French writers, with Turgenev and Tolstoy, have set a standard for all coming masters of fiction' (*Journals*, September 1896, January 1899). James and Conrad, as will transpire later, in part belong to this story also.

The newer influences were not only French. It is not a long step from the realism of Flaubert or Zola to that of Ibsen; and when Ibsen decisively 'arrived' in the 1891 season of G. T. Grein's Independent Theatre Group,[4] Shaw not only decided that Ibsen's topical concern with current abuses was his most conspicuous achievement (*The Quintessence of Ibsenism*, 1891), but himself followed at once in the same direction as a writer. Admittedly, we do not now see this kind of topicality as Ibsen's chief merit: but the point at issue for the present is the importance of continental influences, and Shaw's response to Ibsen is another aspect of this. *Widowers' Houses* (1892) was staged the year after the Ibsen season (by the same director and company in the same theatre) and it was the first in a series of plays which were Ibsenite in dealing with questions and abuses of the day, though by no means in the Irish rodomontade with which they did so. These included *Mrs Warren's Profession* (written 1893), *Man and Superman* (1903), and *Major Barbara* (1907); the two latter works reflecting Ibsen's own particular interest in problems connected with the 'New Woman'.

Ibsen was also the recurrent point of reference (reference largely, though by no means wholly, by opposition)[5] for Yeats as he developed his ideas of poetic drama in the 1890s and early 1900s. Long before, James in a number of critical essays had struggled repeatedly with what he saw as the radical defect of the whole French school, its preoccupation with the drab intricacies of mere material or sensuous or narrowly sexual realities at the expense of genuinely humane and spiritual insight. Moreover, James studied foreign literature deeply, but he was clear that learning from abroad had to go with continuing to learn from what had been done at home. He pointed to George Eliot as a writer who had achieved the massive and integrated richness of external or material facts of writers like Flaubert or Zola, without forfeiting realism in a richer sense, the realism which sees into psychology, character, and moral values.

On the other hand, he had stressed how Turgenev had also achieved this richer, more human realism in some respects more successfully than George Eliot. It is important to see how the native strand and the foreign were working together. George Eliot was also singled out for just such praise in the first decisive Western European recognition of the greatness of Russian fiction, de Vogüé's *Le Roman russe* (1886, translated 1913); and this work began to exercise an immediate effect on English thinking about fiction. George Moore wrote the Introduction for a reissue of Dostoyevsky's *Poor Folk* (1894), and Edward and Constance Garnett's translations from Turgenev began to appear during the nineties. In Galsworthy's *Villa Rubein* (1900) and Conrad's *Under Western Eyes*, the influence of Turgenev is clear; though Conrad's novel may in part satirize what it draws on. Tolstoy's influence dates also from this period, which is that of Arnold's essay on him (1887); his *Kreutzer Sonata* (1889) helped to intensify the questioning of the marriage institution in the 1890s, and its radical thinking on art and society were influential too. The vogue of Dostoyevsky came later, among the sufferings and disorientation of the First World War. All in all, the Russian impact was a profound one. It related to matters of technique, at one extreme, and of the spirit in which both art and life were conducted at the other.[6]

It is difficult to sum up in specific detail what was acquired from abroad by each individual writer. In James, French influence shows in such things as his reproving Trollope for lack of detachment in portraying character (Trollope was too much the Thackerayan 'puppet-master'); in his intense interest in self-conscious construction, controlled tone, and calculated effect ('Ah, this divine conception of one's little masses and periods in the scenic light – as rounded Acts'); or in his repeated imitation of how Flaubert in *Madame Bovary* (1857), say, shows the whole course of the novel from the standpoint of the central character. If James's immense admiration for Turgenev can be localized in his work, it lies in the poetry, tenderness, and tact with which he handles some of his scenes – the heroine's tea-party in *The Awkward Age*, for example. Bennett, despite his admiration for the Russians, seldom has this deep feeling, restraint, and dignity; the humanity of his characters (*Riceymann Steps*, 1923, illustrates this well) tends to be submerged in analysis of how they are the creatures of their environment. But Bennett's sense of half-impersonal historical continuity (notably in *The Old Wives' Tale*, 1908), and his accumulation of factual detail to produce a dense and rich, if limited, context for the action, are achievements of no mean order; and the point, in the present context, is that such an achievement as they represent must certainly be related to the influence of Zola.

Conrad's rigid economy of style, his taut and sequacious construction, his effects that seem so carefully timed, have their counterparts in Flaubert or Stendhal rather than in any Victorian novelist. Lawrence in a letter of 1 February 1913 likens his own work to that of Chekhov in contrast to 'the rule and measure mathematical folk' – Shaw, Galsworthy, Barker. He is in fact speaking of plays; but the parallel and the contrast are plain enough in his short stories also. Moreover, there is a poetry and symbolism, a poignant strangeness, and often a seemingly disjointed surface creating in the end a deep inner unity, which are plain in his work as they are also, in different terms, in that of Virginia Woolf or Ford Madox Ford. Such qualities have no clear counterpart in mid-nineteenth-century English fiction; though they have, undoubtedly, in Dostoyevsky.

Tradition and Experiment in Poetry

Late-nineteenth-century French literature had not been Realist only. If it had included Zola and the brothers Goncourt, it had also included Rimbaud and Mallarmé and Laforgue; and the early-twentieth-century movement in English poetry which came to terms with these writers should be seen as part of a whole continental impact. But there is a prior question: what sort of poetry occupied, as it were, the field? Upon what in English poetry did the influence of continental models impinge?

Just as in discussing developments in fiction it was important not to oversimplify the picture of the mid-nineteenth century in England, and necessary to remember that that period included George Eliot just as much as it did Dickens, so it is important to remember the complexity and variety of the situation in poetry. F. R. Leavis has said: 'Nineteenth-century poetry was characteristically preoccupied with the creation of a dream-world.'[7] This points forcefully to much of the poetry of the later years of the nineteenth century.

> Sunlight from the sun's own heart
> Flax unfolded to receive
> Out of sky and flax and art
> Lovely raiment I achieve
> Summer is time for beauty's flowering
> For the exuberance of day,
> And the cool of the evening,
> Summer is time for play,
> And for joy, and the touch of tweed.

That, without a word altered, is part of a poem from the closing pages of the *Oxford Book of Victorian Verse*, and part tailor's advertisement (*c.* 1950) from a Sunday newspaper. It brings out not merely what was worst in the verse of the later nineteenth century, but also how that tradition of bad poetry was something which created an established taste for itself: a taste, a taking-for-granted, which could later be exploited by the world of commerce because it was in no way essentially different from that world. One can glimpse in the very possibility of amalgamating those two passages, some of the underlying causes why the poetry of Pound and Eliot should have seemed, to the man in the street and also to much organized literary taste, an affront to what was truly poetic.

Yet to think of the later nineteenth century as typically represented by 'Sunlight from the sun's own heart' and rubbish like it would be to oversimplify. ('Not all of the poetry, or all of the poets,' Dr Leavis added to his remark just quoted.) 'Dream-world' is a term which does not bring out the strength – though one must add at once that it was a modest strength – of much later nineteenth-century verse; and once that relatively sound and strong kind has been identified, it can be seen as a tradition of English verse which is firmly in being before the time of Pound and Eliot, and which runs steadily through, and after, the years in which they were making their impact.

This other tradition of verse displays a use of language which is unquestionably vernacular, but rather too deliberate (one might put it) to be termed colloquial; an intimate, personal; yet unassertive tone: a modest lyric artistry; and a thoughtful receptivity before the poet's environment, especially nature seen in a somewhat domestic way, by the cottage, not on the mountain. Later developments in English poetry will prove baffling to those who do not recognize the quality and provenance of this kind of verse, and its strength as a tradition in being at the close of the nineteenth and in the early twentieth century. Here it is in Hardy's *An August Midnight* (1899):

> A shaded lamp and a waving blind,
> And the beat of a clock from a distant floor:
> On this scene enter – winged, horned, and spined –
> A longlegs, a moth, and a dumbledore;
> While 'mid my page there idly stands
> A sleepy fly that rubs its hands ...

Hardy, it must be remembered, was writing verse steadily from the 1860s; and, with its plain vernacular language, and its strong (if nostalgic) awareness of everyday life, his large body of verse forcibly invites us to see nineteenth-century poetry itself in other than 'dream-world' terms.

Hardy's long period of activity as a poet – from the 1860s to the 1920s – significantly bridges the nineteenth and twentieth centuries, and does so not only in the matter of dates, but of outlook, technique and diction as well. For Hardy the uncertainties of the nineteenth century, the displacement of man from any assured place at the centre of things, had become a deep habit of mind. Hence his sense of a kind of uneventful tragedy everywhere in life, his disillusion, and the aura of nostalgia that issued from it. Surprisingly, though, these newer viewpoints cannot easily be separated from Hardy's unornate, often seemingly clumsy language, with its dialect and bluntly unpoetic coinages. Also, in many of Hardy's best poems the dominance of folksong as a model, or of the street-ballad, is clear; this is another respect in which he parted company with the traditions of 'polite letters'. These qualities of language and of technique are not surface qualities, but point to how Hardy wrote out of a full, detailed and realistic knowledge of rural and natural life, and was profoundly at home with the everyday existence, and the work, of ordinary country-people. A range of experience and sympathy that, backwards in time, has no parallel until we reach Clare or Crabbe, called out a new kind of work. These facts make Hardy a key figure in the whole development of later poetry; and one may note that the poetry of the middle and later twentieth century has probably followed him, consciously or unconsciously, more than anyone else.

Hardy is not the only poet to represent, at the turn of the century and just after, the tradition of writing described above. Edward Thomas does so as well:

> And yet I still am half in love with pain,
> With what is imperfect, with both tears and mirth,
> With things that have an end, with life and earth,
> And this moon that leaves me dark within the door.
> (Liberty, c. 1915)

So does Lawrence, for example, in *End of Another Home Holiday* (c. 1913):

> When shall I see the half-moon sink again
> Behind the black sycamore at the end of the garden?
> When will the scent of the dim white phlox
> Creep up the wall to me, and in at my open window?

and finally, with a slight yet salient difference in the closing lines, to which the discussion must revert, so does Robert Graves's *Full Moon*, written (before 1923) at a time when Pound and Eliot were beginning to dominate the scene:

> As I walked out that sultry night,
>   I heard the stroke of one.
> The moon, attained to her full height,

74

> Stood beaming like the sun:
> She exorcized the ghostly wheat
> To mute assent in love's defeat,
> Whose tryst had now begun.

Those who see how the first of these passages is reminiscent of Wordsworth's *Green Linnet*, say, or the second of the opening lines of Keats's *Endymion* and the simple, more introspective passages of his *Epistles*, or the fourth of *The Ancient Mariner* (though the links are not all equally strong), will recognize that this kind of verse was no isolated or merely local freak of poetic development, but had a good deal of English poetry behind it. But what is also clear is that the range of experience which lies behind this verse was mainly a traditional and rural one. It did not easily come nearer to the city than the suburban garden.

Because of this, the verse of Hardy, Edward Thomas, and also D. H. Lawrence in his first years as a poet, for all its soundness and modest strength, was not abreast of the time; and could barely develop to meet its challenges. The centre of life had moved away from what was rural. This shows earlier, and later too, in the declining quality of the rural inspiration. There is a note of retreat, of weariness, even in Richard Jefferies; but the indications elsewhere are clearer. They are clear, for example, in some of the townified versions of rurality which were poeticized for the Georgian Anthologies (1912–20); in Wells's picture in *The History of Mr Polly* (1910) of the countryside as a place for afternoon bicycle excursions or escapist idylls; and in the fragile, fey quality which colours the achievement of a fine talent like that of Walter de la Mare. Most revealing of all, perhaps, is the work of T. F. Powys. Here a deep sense of the total round, rich fertility and sour brutality of rural life, and a command over both fable and symbol as fictional vehicles, seem recurrently to be marred by relapses into a kind of jasmine frailty or coy whimsy, or a response to sex and to cruelty which not infrequently seems disquietingly ambivalent. So devious, so various, are the signs that a way of life can no longer abundantly sustain a body of literature.

The new poetry which came into being from about 1910 did not modify the English tradition which has just been discussed, but departed sharply from it. Pound called for poetry at 'such a degree of development ... that it will vitally concern people who are accustomed, in prose, to Henry James, ... and in music to Debussy' (*Pavanes and Divagations*, 1918). This new poetry looked not to the countryside, but to the great city.[8] Already, in this fact alone, the complex story of its affiliations begins to emerge. From one point of view, Eliot's 1917 poems (*Preludes, Rhapsody on a Windy Night*) stand in a loose continuity with Laforgue, with Rimbaud's *Illuminations*,[9] and above all with the *Tableaux Parisiens* of Baudelaire, probably the first poet in Europe to take his stand as the poet of the '*Fourmillante cité, cité pleine de rêves*' of which the poet can say '*tout pour moi devient allégorie*'. As Eliot said, '(Baudelaire) gave new possibilities to poetry in a new stock of images from contemporary life.'[10] The new poetry was also a city poetry, however, in a rather special sense. Hardy's *A Wife in London*, Symons's *City Nights: In the Train*, Dowson's sonnet *Spleen* and a number of works by other poets, all bear testimony to how London as a vast and at that time unique capital city was intriguing and preoccupying the writers. Impressionist painting, and the new powers of vision that it made current, caused London, and especially 'London River', to be seen with its own haunting beauty. This whole trend in writing also in part illustrates the force of Pound's reference, quoted above, to the new poetry and its links with other arts. Henley's *London Voluntaries* are arranged in movements like a symphony, recalling music such as Elgar's 'Cockaigne' (ie, 'Cockney'-Land) Overture; they are full of Impressionist pictures of London, and in what corresponds to the sombre slow movement, at a number of points prefigure Eliot's morose vignettes of life in the capital.

In Pound and Eliot, however, the range of intellectual, cosmopolitan and culturally polyglot interests is far wider than in earlier poets like Henley, Dowson and the rest. Pound's interest in Far Eastern literatures,[11] and Eliot's Sanskrit studies, bear witness to that; and one might link to it T. E. Hulme's interest (see his *Speculations*) in the German art critic Worringer and his (admittedly amateurish) admiration for the intensity and stylization of Byzantine and Egyptian art. In fact, the links which the new verse had with Impressionism in painting are less substantial than its contrast and hostility to that: and its stronger links with Post-Impressionist and indeed Expressionist trends are firmly underlined by Pound's insistence, in the 1913 Imagist Manifesto, on the integrated image, stark and clear, and on a maximum economy of words in the poem (see the chapter on Wyndham Lewis, p. 213).

The ambitiously cultural-elite aspect of the new poetry, and its repudiation of the prosperous middle class of city life and its values, has also its links with later nineteenth-century poetry. That prosperous middle class, after all, was what in Dublin, for several reasons but in particular for its failure to respond to the work of the Abbey Theatre, notably Synge, in Dublin during the 1900s, had disgusted Yeats. That modern poetry started with this repudiation of the broad city middle class affords a link between the new poets of the 1910s and those of the Aesthetic Movement of the 1890s, and helps one to see how it was natural enough that Pound's earliest verse should have *fin-de siècle* qualities, or that like the nineties poets Pound should have had a special interest in Old French or Provençal. The point also emerges in early essays of Yeats like *What is Popular Poetry?* (1901) or *The Symbolism of Poetry* (1900) written under the immediate influence of Arthur Symons's *The Symbolist Movement in Literature* (1899); itself the first book significantly to introduce English readers to French Symbolists, even if it a little tinged these with Celtic twilight in the process. For Yeats, poet and peasant could come together (and Yeats reflected the distinctive quality of Irish life and of the Irish peasantry in the ease with which he envisaged that); but grocer and politician were in another world. This amounted in practice to a firm repudiation of what was seen by Yeats as the whole Tennysonian stance, the poet as public figure writing for the broad middle class and diluting his poetry until that class could take it in.

Repudiating this particular social status for poetry seems actually to underlie the more technical features of the new verse. It issued, in the first place, in the demand that social respectability should not be allowed to impose restrictions of subject-matter upon the poet, nor literary convention impose restrictions of diction or emotion. This is why Jules Laforgue particularly interested both Pound and Eliot. Again, this change in social orientation led to an insistence on the supreme virtue of economy and concentration: poetry was not to be made easy for the relaxed general reader. Yeats in his early essays made it clear that, for him, refusing to do this underlay dropping what binds normal discourse tidily together: a sequacious logic, a self-explaining easy-to-follow train of thought.[12] This repudiation of tidy logical exposition in poetry brought with it perhaps the most characteristic quality of all, a constant laconic *juxtaposition* of ideas, rather than an ordering of them in a banally lucid exposition.

Again, the immediate roots of this principle of style are foreign; but though they are partly from France, they are not wholly so. Pound himself did not speak of juxtaposition, but of 'the mode of super-position', which he recognized above all in the Japanese seventeen-syllable poems, the *hokku*.[13] Ernest Fenollosa's brilliant *The Chinese Written Character* (finished before his death in 1908, published by Pound in 1920) finds a paradigm for this, the true poetic texture, in the very nature of Chinese as a language. But T. E. Hulme, an influential member of the circle of Pound's intimates, goes clearly back for his conception of the truly poetic use of language to the contrast which Bergson drew between the order of logic and the continuity of life; and when Eliot, in 1920, writes that certain lines of Massinger

exhibit that perpetual slight alteration of language, words perpetually juxtaposed in new and sudden combinations, meanings perpetually *eingeschachtelt* into meanings

he is writing in the tradition of Mallarmé's *Crise de vers* (1895):

l'oeuvre pure implique la disparition élocutoire du poète, qui cède l'initiative aux mots, par le heurt de leur inégalité mobilisés; ils s'allument de reflets réciproques comme une virtuelle trainée de feu sur des pierreries.[14]

Indeed, this also has an affinity of thought with the best known of Rimbaud's letters, the 'Lettre du Voyant', written to Démeny on 15 May 1871.

When, further, Eliot distinguishes in *Tradition and the Individual Talent* (1917) the radically non-logical nature of the poetic process, he draws heavily on Rémy de Gourmont's *Le Problème du style* (1902). 'Sensibility' and 'fusion' were the key terms for both in their account of the working of the poet's mind; and it is in de Gourmont that we find a classic account of what probably lies at the centre of later British thinking about poetry, the power, depth, and suggestiveness of metaphors.[15] If this whole sense of the intricate surface and deeper evocativeness of poetry could be related to music (as it was), that goes back ultimately to the especial reverence of Mallarmé and those who followed him for the music of Wagner, and their recognition of

Wagner's peculiarly intricate and comprehensive inter-relatedness of texture. But it goes back further to Wagner's own idea of what this enabled the artist to achieve: nothing less than a half-mystic glimpse of true Reality behind Appearance.[16] The idea chimed in well with the Neo-Platonist and occultist strains which were plain enough in the work of the French poets; and indeed, it is this idea that the ostensible subject of the poem may be the key to an ulterior Reality which is really the justification for calling them 'Symbolists'.[17] The term is less helpful in discussing English literature, because (save with Yeats) this train of thought was usually dropped when their ideas were imported. This dropping-out of the idea of deeper truth behind the sharply focused surface fact is especially clear in the *Imagist Manifesto* (1913), where the stress is laid upon economical presentation of a brilliant visual reality. But the Imagists, apart from Pound, and also Lawrence who had a slight and brief connection with them, have no importance.

From these considerations, and from the fact that Eliot had completed *Prufrock* and *Portrait of a Lady* by 1914, it is clear enough that so far as the central creative work of this circle went, the articles of their creed had been established well before 1920, and Eliot's work at that time on Jacobean literature constituted the development of them in one particular field, rather than homage to the decisive source of inspiration. Some distinctions, in fact, need to be drawn at this point. The new qualities of Eliot's earlier verse have often been seen as standing in very close connection with his special interest in early-seventeenth-century dramatic and lyrical verse, especially Donne. In reality, this interest now seems to show more prominently in Eliot's critical work (it should be remembered that he by no means began the revival of Donne)[18] than in his verse. Close study reveals that there is surprisingly little sign of a direct and detailed influence of Donne on Eliot as a poet; less so, indeed, than on Yeats.[19] Again, the fact that Eliot broke sharply with nineteenth-century verse does not mean that Pound did so to the same extent. The continuity in his case has already been touched on (p. 77), and in an important letter of May 1928 he relates it also to one of the greatest of Donne's nineteenth-century admirers: '*überhaupt ich stamm aus Browning. Pourquoi nier son père?*' though he adds that his father in poetry was a Browning '*dénué des paroles superflues*'.

Poetry and the War Crisis

These were the trends: to what sort of poetic achievement did they lead? On the surface, to writing which was brilliant and exhilarating for its intelligence and complexity; in essence, to what was much more powerful and moving than the conventional verse of the time, because its many-sidedness could touch and move the whole depth and capacity of the mind. As an example, here are the closing stanzas of the first part of Pound's *Hugh Selwyn Mauberley*:

> His true Penelope was Flaubert,
> He fished by obstinate isles;
> Observed the elegance of Circe's hair
> Rather than the mottoes on sundials.
>
> Unaffected by 'the march of events',
> He passed from men's memory in *l'an trentiesme*
> *De son eage*; the case presents
> No adjunct to the Muse's diadem.

The sub-title is *E. P. Ode pour l'Election de son Sepulchre*: that is to say, a dryly ironical imitation of Ronsard becomes the vehicle by which the minority poet will express his sense of failure in a society which is radically hostile to serious art ('a half-savage country'). But the astringent compression, the powerful suggestiveness of these widely ranging but tightly juxtaposed references to literature, mythology, and public life, pass beyond intellectual excitingness to achieve true and deep feeling. The 'elegance of Circe's hair' image, picked up again in the 'Muse's diadem', conveys Pound's service to a destructive enchantress; but this is, at one and the same time, true devotion to Penelope, his faithful mate and equal. Again, the poet is seen at once as the wily Odysseus and a crafty fisherman ('obstinate isles'), and also, through the terse reference implied in '*l'an trentiesme de son eage*', as the hapless, hopeless Villon. The mottoes on sundials which he misses are not only those about transience, but those about happiness too. His acute predicament emerges movingly from these seeming-fragments, dry and sophisticated.

But something has been omitted from this account of development. What has been said so far can largely explain *Hugh Selwyn Mauberley* ('an attempt to condense the Jamesian novel', Pound called it),[20] and still more so the new astringency, bluntness, irony, many-sidedness, vernacular quality – and emotional charge – of such poems as Yeats's *The Fascination of What's Difficult*, or Eliot's *Mr Apollinax*. But Yeats's *The Second Coming* (1921) or Eliot's *The Waste Land* (1922) strike a new note, and one that contradicts Yeats's early ideas, or those of the French poets discussed above.

> 'On Margate Sands.
> I can connect
> Nothing with nothing.
> The broken fingernails of dirty hands.
> My people humble people who expect
> Nothing.'
>
> la la
>
> To Carthage then I came
>
> Burning burning burning burning
> O Lord thou pluckest me out
> O Lord thou pluckest
>
> burning

Using much the same method of terse and esoteric reference as Pound's, these closing lines of the third part of *The Waste Land* provide the very title of the poem. 'To Carthage then I came' are the opening words of Book III of St Augustine's *Confessions*: and he closed the preceding book with the words 'I wandered, O my God, too much astray from Thee my stay, in these days of my youth, and I became to myself a *waste land*'.[21] But this, and the echo of Amos 4:11 which follows it in the poem, and leads into the title of the section ('The Fire Sermon'), do not merely create a satirist's vision of society or an artist's private sense of personal predicament. They go with the terse indications of humble Thames-side scenes ('la la' is the strumming of a mandoline) to evoke a genuinely prophetic vision (none the less real because it comes, as in poetry such things almost must come, with an intensely personal and subjective vibration) of a breakdown in life itself: a waste land, general to humanity, in which nothing connects with nothing. Here is no notion of keeping art free from middle-brow preoccupations like social reality; but an anguished concern to register a sick world and to make contact with something which might restore the springs of human goodness and vitality.[22]

This radical shift becomes easier to understand if one remembers that Yeats and Pound were studying the Japanese plays, and the latter exercising his commanding influence on *The Egoist* and *The Little Review*, during the years of the Great War. This traumatic experience marked a decisive phase in British civilization, and was registered in the emergence, over the years following, of several outstanding war autobiographies: Blunden's *Undertones of War* (1928), Graves's *Goodbye to All That* (1929), Wyndham Lewis's *Blasting and Bombardiering* (1937).

Also published in 1937, and strongly autobiographical in content if not in presentation, is the painter David Jones's *In Parenthesis*, the most remarkable of all books in English to come out of the First World War. This long prose-poem of life in the trenches belongs with *The Waste Land* and with the Hell-sequence in Pound's *Cantos*, not only in its 'mode of superposition' technique and gamut of dictions, but also because of its starkly Expressionist stylization ('The candle-end by the coffee-tin, flickered and went out'). It not only draws together the New Poetry and the War Prose, but also links writing and painting in the period, and looks forward to Jones's later verse, which carried on the techniques of Pound and Eliot into the very different post-war age (see Volume 8 of the *Guide*). Besides this, though, the length and intensity of the 1914–18 experience brought it about that English poetry of the more traditional and indigenous kind itself underwent a remarkable change, and one which ran parallel to those now more conspicuous changes initiated by Pound and Eliot.

The early poets are among the weaker representatives of a poetic line which has already been discussed (pp. 72–5 above). At bottom, lyricism and rurality were there to guide them:

> The fighting man shall from the sun
> Take warmth, and life from the glowing earth.

Julian Grenfell wrote *Into Battle*. England gave Rupert Brooke's *Soldier* 'her flowers to love, her ways to roam'; and Edward Thomas's *A Private* (who had been a ploughman) suggests that, decisive as are the differences in other respects, Thomas is part of this picture. But after the holocausts of the middle war years these poets gave place to others, such as Siegfried Sassoon; and now a style prominent from

his time to our own (1980) may be seen in the very act of breaking
out of the shell of the old:

> I see them in foul dug-outs, gnawed by rats,
> And in the ruined trenches, lashed with rain,
> Dreaming of *things they did with balls and bats*
> And mocked with hopeless longing *to regain*
> *Bank holidays and picture shows and spats*
> *And going to the office in the train.*   (*Dreamers*)

But the laconic diction (tautened everywhere by paradox) and the
restless, evocative rhythm of Wilfred Owen's *Exposure* represent a
much more distinguished achievement; they also show an un-
expectedly interesting flowering, it might be claimed, of *Imagisme*,
and an expression of tense yet aimless awareness coming near to some
purely civilian scenes in *The Waste Land*:

> Our brains ache, in the merciless iced east winds that knive us ...
> Wearied we keep awake because the night is silent ...
> Low, drooping flares confuse our memory of the salient ...
> Worried by silence, sentries whisper, curious, nervous,
>   But nothing happens.

War and Crisis in Fiction

The most remarkable record in fiction of change and disruption
from the Great War is surely Ford Madox Ford's 'Tietjens' tetralogy
(*Some Do Not, No More Parades, A Man Could Stand Up, Last Post*;
1924–8). The sheer bulk of Ford's minor output, and his early prominence in the literary scene as an editor (see below, p. 102), have concealed his achievement as a novelist. *The Good Soldier* (1915) resumes
the trend of French influence touched upon earlier (see the reference
to Conrad, p. 66 above), but in this novel Ford went further than
those from whom he learnt. Not only is the persona of the amateurish, extempore teller of the tale really a mask for intricate premedi-
tatedness on the author's part, as to how the fiction shall eventually
assemble itself together. Another aspect of Ford's subtle artlessness
is to make this seemingly artless 'saddest story' the damning indictment of a lavish but at bottom empty 'social' world. In this, Ford
is with James (see above, p. 64).

If this novel has an underlying defect, it is one to which one might also point in works by Arnold Bennett. Both novelists, inclined to seek a representation of life which is more complete, sensitive, and humane than what they found in de Maupassant or Zola, were a little inclined to do so on too easy terms. The result is a certain relaxing of detachment and control, a manipulatory holding up of the characters and their situation for comprehension, sympathy, a feeling of pathos even, which betrays the general influence of Dickens or Thackeray in the background. The Tietjens books probably lack the delicacy of perception and movement of indisputably great fiction. But in their large, loose organization, their outstanding resilience and vitality, and their comprehensive, unflinching grasp of a complex pattern of cultural change, they are very notable works; and they suggest that Russian fiction (with its assured achievement in displaying how near the order of art can come to the disorder of life, and how novels may have poignant compassion, sympathy, and insight without manipulation or straining for emotion) was once again exerting its influence upon English.

Virginia Woolf put this better. Speaking of the novels of Turgenev she said: 'They are so short and yet they hold so much. The emotion is so intense and yet so calm. The form is in one sense so perfect, in another so broken.'[23] In her own complex of affiliations, the Russian one is clear enough; but a complex it certainly is, and other links are clearer. Behind her emphatic repudiation of the pedestrian, in a sense the peripheral realism of Bennett or Wells,[24] lies not only a more sharply differentiated concern for art as such, but also a sense of the inexhaustible interest and significance and *goodness* of experience, even at its most immediate and transient, which connects her with G. E. Moore (in a work like *Principia Ethica*, 1903), and with Walter Pater. This side of Virginia Woolf, at its slightest, can be disconcerting. It leads occasionally to a kind of perky incompleteness in her criticism, and an almost dithery brightness in her fiction, in which there is even a streak of vulgarity ('somehow or other, loveliness is infernally sad': *Jacob's Room*, 1922).

Yet to say no more than that is to caricature. Her preoccupation with the immediate and always-changing surface of life is based upon substantial grounds. These are much the grounds which Bergson would have offered for the same preference: and it is noteworthy that her well-known remark in the essay on *Modern Fiction* (1919), 'life is not a series of gig-lamps symmetrically arranged; life is a luminous halo, a semi-transparent envelope', seems to be following a passage in Bergson's *Introduction to Metaphysics* (1904).[25] But if the lamps are Bergson's, the luminous halo and the envelope may come from Henry James's *Art of Fiction* (1884).

Another link with painting must also be noticed. Virginia Woolf's concern for surface impression and immediacy brings Monet to mind, and the infiltration of the Impressionist painter's vision at least into poetry is something which may be often traced in English poetry from the 1880s on: but she was also in the circle of Roger Fry, whose main achievement was to introduce English taste to the first gener-ation of Post-Impressionist painters (Cézanne, Van Gogh, and the rest) in the famous London exhibitions of 1910 and 1912. Virginia Woolf is no Cézanne, but if Cézanne used the discoveries of earlier Impressionist painters in order to capture not the surface but the essence of his subjects, it is not altogether pointless to liken her to him. Her best work embodies a vision of how richly the immediacy of experience engages also what is substantial in experience; a sense reminiscent of James (though flimsy by comparison) that life's deli-cate surfaces reveal what T. S. Eliot has called 'the boredom and the horror and the glory' which can be just below them. Virginia Woolf brings to the more aesthetic or Impressionist side of her work an interest in human values which plainly shows the influence of her father, Leslie Stephen. The 'stream of consciousness' which her writ-ing endeavours to capture (and for this purpose she was no inconsider-able technical innovator) reflects a genuine humanity, a real and compassionate concern for what makes life rich and what dries it up.

Finally, her position in these matters fits properly into its historical context. It is the position of the liberal intellectual surviving in the post-war world. Fullness of individual life stands over against brutal dominance. *Mrs Dalloway* (1925) is polarized between the abundant if uninsistent life of the heroine, and the sheer not having of ex-perience of Sir William Bradshaw, the doctor who drives his shell-shocked patient to suicide. In *To the Lighthouse* (1927), life and the self-assertive negation of life interact within the experiences of Mr Ramsay, of his children, even of Mrs Ramsay herself.

In view of certain deeply contrasting attitudes which became prominent later in the century (see Volume 8 of the *Guide*), it is to the point to notice a certain wider aspect of liberal humanism in some of the writing of the 1910s and 1920s. Often enough what the writer seems to care about most of all is the striving of the individual to achieve a fullness of psychic independence and self-realization. *Sons and Lovers* (1910), *The Rainbow* (1915) and *Women in Love* (1921) are not irrelevant here, but will be discussed later (see below, pp. 95–8). The boat-journey in *To the Lighthouse* is the self-realization of the young Ramsays, and Lily Briscoe, who stays at home and paints, achieves the consummation of her picture as the boat reaches its goal. Wolf Solent, in John Cowper Powys's novel of that name (1929), gives up his job and position in a definitive attempt to be himself to the full. Other novels by Virginia Woolf and Powys, and short stories by Lawrence, show the same trend. Crucial interest attaches to the individual's supreme attempt to achieve selfhood. It is significant that this is the key motif in a talented novel of the time, Richard Garnett's *Go She Must!* (1927): the title neatly expresses the theme. Dorothy Richardson's *Pilgrimage* series (from 1915) focuses upon the same idea from the standpoint of Woman; though perhaps the relaxed but subtle, sensuous awareness and immediacy that she often depicts is characteristic of people in general at their best, not of women only; and a man, anyhow, may find that her reiterated sweeping condemnations of men are self-defeating.

If there is a lack in Virginia Woolf's work, it is that she has also the weakness of the liberal intellectual. It is a lack not of values but of confidence, ultimately of vitality. What she cares for is always made tentative and exploratory, and – she is typical of the period after 1918 in this – it survives within a perimeter of threatening violence, deeply feared and half-understood. The meaningless death of the hero of *Jacob's Room* in battle, the thread of tragedy and brutality running so close to life's most exquisite striations in *Mrs Dalloway*, the suppressed vindictiveness of *To the Lighthouse*, the spiritual deprivation, squalor, physical violence, that everywhere surround the village pageant in *Between the Acts* (1941), all at bottom reflect the plight of the liberal in the modern world. It is surely significant that the same two attitudes – a care for the immediacy of private living, a sense of its being surrounded and threatened by meaningless violence – combine prominently in the work of E. M. Forster. It shows that the plight of the liberal was one which could be diagnosed before 1914; and in Forster's works also, the pervasive sense is of how the good of life, ordinary kindly private living, is everywhere surrounded by unpredictable violence, the product of random change or of uncomprehending self-assertiveness. If Forster, in the end, is a less exciting but more reassuring novelist than Virginia Woolf, it is because, though he lacks her exuberant subtlety of sensuous perception, he never radiantly obscures what is central to his purpose by technical virtuosity. His integrity is always, sometimes even a little nudely, in view. Moreover, he ranges further than Virginia Woolf, and is more aware than she of how the goodness of private experience is something which the individual shares with others. *A Passage to India* (1924) has a humanity and modesty, a plain and strong sense of values, and at the same time a half-poetic imaginativeness, which put it far above his other works, and above anything of Virginia Woolf's also.

The works of Forster and Virginia Woolf represent an early phase in a probing and challenging of that polite liberal culture which, more and more, came to seem radically incommensurate with the challenges confronting it in the twentieth century. That it did so has been a fundamental reality of the period, and a recurrent feature of its fiction. In the novels of Huxley, too, there is a sense of a world for cultivated people closely surrounded by a bigger world of horror and brutality:

> At this very moment ... the most frightful horrors are taking place in every corner of the world ... screams of pain and fear go pulsing through the air ... after travelling for three seconds they are perfectly inaudible ... The Black and Tans harry Ireland, the Poles maltreat the Silesians, the bold Fascisti slaughter their poorer countrymen: we take it all for granted. Since the war we wonder at nothing.
>
> (*Crome Yellow*, 1921)

But in Huxley the doubts have entered deeper than in Forster or Virginia Woolf. They impugn the centre itself; and leave in his works a paradoxical central emptiness, in that the writer seems still to believe in the elements of the culture he knows (music, art, rational conversation) but sees only a restless sterilized fatuity in those who transmit that culture. It is, indeed, the world of one part of the 1920s: that of the first jazz, the Charleston, the first sports car. In Huxley's later novels (as in *Eyeless in Gaza*, 1936, where a dog falls from an aeroplane to bespatter the liveliest intimacies of two roof-top lovers) the sense of circumambient violence has become obsessive; and in the novels of Evelyn Waugh (e.g. *Decline and Fall*, 1928) a further stage still may perhaps be traced. Here, the social group is an élite of money rather than ostensible culture, but even so it is not far remote from Huxley's; yet now the elements of culture are themselves valueless. There is nothing for a world of absurd violence either to surround or threaten; the result is to make violence both ubiquitous and insignificant.

Something with affinity to this is to be seen in the long-forgotten 1930s novels of Jean Rhys (*After Leaving Mr Mackenzie*, 1930; *Good Morning, Midnight*, 1939; see also Volume 8 of the *Guide*). These books show a strong yet delicate mastery of stream-of-consciousness techniques, but deploy them in the new field of the isolated woman on the verge of social collapse and destitution: their terse, vivid tragedy is an outstanding achievement. With them should be mentioned *Olivia* (1949) by 'Olivia', the pseudonym of Dorothy Bussy, sister of Lytton Strachey. Here another vivid, economical, tragic book presents the pleasures and stresses of the life of women together. The dexterous lightness of Stevie Smith's early books (e.g., *Novel on Yellow Paper*, 1936) might also be mentioned along with William Gerhardie's exquisitely poised and amusing, if slightly inane novels. All these works, in their various ways, fit into a pattern of immense fictional skill and sophistication: the high point, or, rather, somewhat beyond that, of a great period of development.

Wyndham Lewis's later work throws his earlier work into a new focus, and shows him not only as one of the major destructive critics of our time, but as seeing in fundamental terms what the writers just discussed saw in isolation or did not see so much as merely use.[26] In *The Apes of God* (1930) Lewis does little more than toy disgustedly with the social levels that also half repulsed Huxley. But in *The Revenge for Love* (1937) and still more in *Self Condemned* (1951), what threatens life is seen not as among the preoccupations of a class, but as having its roots deep in the modernity of the modern world, committed as this is to the rhythms of the great city and the machine. The machine, moreover, can take control of men's lives because in the end there is something of the mechanical even about men themselves; the idea is already clear enough in *Tarr* (1918) and in the outstanding short stories published in *The Wild Body* (1927). The same insights are prominent in Lewis's remarkable paintings. There are things to be said against his sprawling works and his largely (not wholly) negative vision, but it must also be said that Lewis is the only English writer who establishes his full comprehension of the basic realities of life in a mid-twentieth-century society, that of a mass civilization, wholly mechanized and essentially megalopolitan. His last important work, *The Human Age* (1955), is perhaps the most memorable picture, in the form of fable rather than realistic fiction, that we have of our own time.

Lewis was no isolated phenomenon: he was one of the great seminal creative group of whom the main figures were Eliot, Epstein, and Pound. His work, straddling literature and the visual arts, reproduced the range of interest of the group as a whole; and Pound's immediate recognition of his power (*Letters*, 9 March 1916) should be known:

> Lewis has just sent in the first dozen drawings . . . the thing is stupendous. The vitality, the fullness of the man! Nobody has any conception of the volume and energy and the variety . . . It is not merely knowledge of technique, or skill, it is intelligence and knowledge of life, of the whole of it, beauty, heaven, hell, sarcasm, every kind of whirlwind of force and emotion.

Probably the most enigmatic associate of this group, however, remains to be mentioned. It was Joyce. Like Pound, Joyce has a link with the Aesthetic Movement of the nineties, and it shows in his early poems and in some of the most evocative passages of his early short stories (*Dubliners*, 1914). The independent reality of art is endorsed in *A Portrait of the Artist as a Young Man*, which Pound published in *The Egoist* in 1916; but that work is also a searchingly realistic picture of intense emotion and decisive spiritual development. Moreover, although Joyce took his stand as a rebel against Irish life and the Roman Catholic religion which dominated it, this novel shows how deeply his own mind had been influenced by both. The combined variety and shabbiness of the social milieu, and the rich facility and inventiveness of language, point to Joyce's emergence from a distinctively Irish society; the pervasive sense of incessant sinfulness and incessant redemption point to his roots in Catholicism. All these things retain their importance (indeed, they extend further) in his later fiction.

Joyce's admiration had also gone out to the realism that gave ample place to the sordid: he found it in Ibsen, and it led him to his own play *Exiles* (1918). Again, his frequent residences in France and consequent contact with French experimental writing, as also his connections with Pound and Eliot, brought him to a turning away from logic, to a reliance upon laconic juxtaposition as the staple ordering principle of contemporary literature, and to a densening verbal texture, until the kaleidoscopic inter-relatedness and inter-suggestiveness of his work make it, in some respects, a clearer example of the linguistic idea of Symbolist writers than anything else in English.

Thus, many lines of origin and development help to create the difficulty of Joyce's case. Taken even at its simplest, there is a problem about the consciousness of reality revealed by his chief novel: *Ulysses* (1922). This work, first published in part in *The Little Review*, with which Pound was connected, carries realism to the length of an encyclopaedic portrayal of one single day, pursued by the author with dogged yet inexhaustible vitality. The result is a unique picture of life, seen (paradoxically) with disillusion and delight at one and the same time. Joyce stands as the last and in some ways unquestionably the most gifted of a line of novelists, running back through the previous century, who sought to depict the inner radiance of what is most ordinary and commonplace in how men live. His compassion and insight enter life at its littlest, its most trivially prurient. This prurience can even seem to infect the writer (Lawrence spoke of his 'dirty-mindedness'): but his vitality and many-sided awareness sustain a true sense of human sympathy and genuine care for life at the very same time.

Yet to leave the account there would be to omit what Joyce himself would have seen as of major significance. There is a core of truth in the aesthetic ideal that Joyce early encountered. 'Art for great art's sake,' one might perhaps put it. The idea is relevant to *Ulysses*. Like all great art, this novel is no mere picture of reality, but a re-making of reality into the unique reality of the work; a re-making where substance and medium cannot be divorced, where almost a new world of language, a progressive energizing and then debilitating of style sustained in an extraordinary way over the whole book, and an unhesitating medley of pastiche, quotation, extravaganza, dramatization, complex literary allusion, all interfuse with story and character and grotesque realistic immediacy so as to create the richness and heterogeneity of a new cosmos. *Ulysses* itself is an undoubted masterpiece. In *Finnegans Wake* (1939), the incessant polyglot punning, far denser and richer, one may note, than is listed even in such encyclopaedic works as Roland McHugh's *Annotations to Finnegans Wake* (1980), ranges over thirty or more languages including Swahili, Roumansch and Irish tinkers' lingo; and is sustained with such continuity and density that character and event both disappear save for those who (as Joyce in fact required of his readers) give their lives over to the book. These unparalleled linguistic pyrotechnics are enriched also from a large repertoire of traditional and popular songs, and with occultism, proverbs, Irish, English and Continental history, and a great range of other miscellaneous knowledge, all made available to inexhaustible paronomasia through the gap between standard English spelling and a Dublin Irish accent. Whether the central purposes of literature (if such be admitted) are served by such a use of a unique gift is another question.

The Search for Values in Poetry

There is a diagnosis, a representation of life, in both Huxley and Joyce; though it is much more impressive in the latter than in the former. But literature can be something which is distinguishable from a representation of life. It can offer to re-invigorate the very forces which lend life validity. T. S. Eliot made clear his own concern for this function of literature in his essay on *The Pensées of Pascal* (1931). Here he implicitly contrasts his own position with that of 'the unbeliever' who

... is, as a rule, not so greatly troubled to explain the world to himself, nor so greatly distressed by its disorder; nor is he generally concerned (in modern terms) to 'preserve values' ...

The Waste Land (1922) is, from the point of view of its substance, an attempt, articulated with peculiar clarity, to diagnose the 'disorder'; to render its challenge inescapably insistent; and in its final section to deliver a 'message' emphasizing certain human values, on the strength of which the poet can add, 'Shall I at least *set my lands in order*?' Admittedly, there is something a little arbitrary or bookish about Eliot's solution, which suddenly makes its appearance from the

Upanishads; but this is representative of a certain negativeness or distaste in the face of experience which runs widely through Eliot's earlier work.

Yeats goes far beyond the present train of thought. He does not have his roots in the Aesthetic Movement for nothing, nor for harm only; and if he had never written a line of 'prophetic' verse, he would still be a major poet for his great body of lyric and dramatic poems (*The Cold Heaven*, 1914; *An Irish Airman Foresees his Death*, 1919; *Leda and the Swan*, 1928; *Long-legged Fly*, 1939, are merely a few among many). Moreover, as perhaps the last of these poems makes clear, Yeats's outlook and philosophy (and his philosophy of history) are sometimes present in his verse when they do not dominate it. Those who rightly see Yeats's knowledge of the Neo-Platonist tradition widely in both his later verse and later drama should bear in mind that Yeats chiefly valued the philosophy for the poetry, not conversely:

... ours is the main road, the road of naturalness and swiftness, and we have thirty centuries on our side. We alone can 'think like a wise man, yet express ourselves like the common people'. These new men are goldsmiths, working with a glass screwed into one eye, whereas we stride ahead of the crowd, its swordsmen, its jugglers, looking to right and left. 'To right and left' – by which I mean that we need, like Milton, Shakespeare, Shelley, vast sentiments, generalizations supported by tradition.[27]

Here may be seen Yeats's enduring sense of the poet as taking up a stance and sustaining a role. That in its turn should probably be seen as one aspect of Yeats's distinctive position: not an English but an Irish poet. Sometimes, as with Joyce, language could also for him be a rich and splendid and even intoxicating thing. Yeats's adaptation of the minority views of the French poets to the special conditions of Ireland, with its archaic Western peasantry that still had something of the Homeric about them, has already been noticed (p. 77 above). Essentially Irish too were his points of reference in history, from his early attachment to the Irish Heroic Age, to his later admiration of the eighteenth-century Ascendancy. Nor did his attachment to the Irish Heroic Age give place to a merely 'Anglo-Irish' awareness of the eighteenth century. Much as Yeats admired the Ascendancy of that time, and checked as he inevitably was by his family background and his virtual ignorance of the Irish language, he nevertheless acquired (largely through Douglas Hyde) some vivid glimpses, any-how, of Irish culture in the Penal Age; and these entered intimately into some of his later poems.[28] *An Irish Airman Foresees his Death* brings out in how un-English a way Yeats naturally saw the events of the 1914–18 war which had so affected English poets; and if it is true that he, as much as any writer, saw the quality of nightmare in his own time, it is true also that he did so through distinctively Irish realities:

> Things fall apart; the centre cannot hold;
> Mere anarchy is loosed upon the world,
> The blood-dimmed tide is loosed, and everywhere
> The ceremony of innocence is drowned ...
> *(The Second Coming*, 1921)

To his awareness Yeats was brought not by the 1914–18 war but (as *Nineteen-Nineteen* or *Meditations in Time of Civil War* set beyond doubt) by the period of 'Troubles' in Ireland which were a direct consequence of that war, coinciding with it and prolonged after it. Yet if Yeats's more or less esoteric philosophy of history explains and dramatizes both good and evil in the world, it is not this philosophy which his work advances as a source of re-invigoration, so much as an intense energy which goes into creating the poem as an elaborate artefact at the same time as, with fierce intimacy, it takes hold of the validity of life itself: a validity of which the living moment is the sole and decisive warrant. This is the conviction which blazes out in *A Dialogue of Self and Soul* (1933):

> What matter if the ditches are impure?
> What matter if I live it all once more?
> I am content to live it all again
> And yet again, if it be life to pitch
> Into the frogspawn of a blind man's ditch –

and in *The Gyres* (1939):

> What matter though dumb nightmare ride on top,
> And blood and mire the sensitive body stain?
> What matter? Heave no sigh, let no tear drop,
> A greater, a more gracious time has gone;
> For painted forms or boxes of make-up
> In ancient tombs I sighed, but not again;
> What matter? Out of cavern comes a voice,
> And all it knows is that one word 'Rejoice!'

The 'cavern' may be the Neo-Platonic Cave of the Nymphs, but its message is not of return to the Heavenly world: it is of a universal, joyous transformation and energy within which both evil and good belong to a greater good. Moreover, this vital conviction, imposed for Yeats by the act of life itself, underlay all his findings when he looked to his own Irish scene for abiding points of reference and sources of vitality. Two more quotations will make this point. The immediate all-deciding vigour of life is as clear to the beggar-woman in *Crazy Jane Grown Old looks at the Dancers* (1933):

> God be with the times when I
> Cared not a thraneen for what chanced
> So that I had the limbs to try
> Such a dance as there was danced –
> *Love is like the lion's tooth.*

– as it is in *Ancestral Houses* (1928):

> Surely among a rich man's flowering lawns,
> Amid the rustle of his planted hills,
> Life overflows without ambitious pains;
> And rains down life until the basin spills,
> And mounts more dizzy high the more it rains ...

Yeats's stature is not self-evident. He wrote enough for a number of his poems to be unimportant or unsuccessful, and an element of grandiose silliness appears in some of his ideas, parts of his life, and a little of his verse. His work exposes itself to cavil more openly than that of a more circumspect writer like Eliot. But the range and variety of what he has done in prose and verse, and, at the best, its splendid vitality, its humanity and positiveness, and its irresistible artistry, set beyond question his greatness as a writer, and his supremacy in this century as a poet.

Values in Fiction

Of all the writers of this century, D. H. Lawrence was the most impassioned and persistent in seeking to diagnose some of the psychic dangers besetting his society, and the potential sources of strength from which they might be combated. His position on the literary scene may, in external terms, be plotted easily enough:

I hate Bennett's resignation. Tragedy ought really to be a great kick at misery. But *Anna of the Five Towns* seems like an acceptance – so does all the modern stuff since Flaubert.

(Letter to A. W. McLeod, 6 October 1912)

Here is Lawrence's revulsion from the French Realist tradition. His indebtedness to the more spiritual realism of the Russian novelists shows in a letter to Catherine Carswell of 2 December 1916:

... don't think I would belittle the Russians. They have meant an enormous amount to me; Turgenev, Tolstoi, Dostoievski – mattered almost more than anything, and I thought them the greatest writers of all time.

(That by the date of this letter he could go straight on to condemn Russian fiction does not affect the issue.) He may, in loose terms, be connected with the same nonconformist Midlands as George Eliot; though he was not intimate with anything comparable to the radical intellectual circles of her early years (see p. 62 above). But Lawrence has a clearer literary continuity with Hardy's less systematized and more poetic conception of the novel, and with the deep sense pervading Hardy's work of man's life as one with its environment in nature. Richard Jefferies's link with Lawrence is also strong: it involves not merely the Hardyesque qualities of Jefferies, but the fact that the terse yet offhand rhythms, and the flexible, sarcastic, slightly truculent tone of much of Lawrence's polemical prose seem also to go back directly to Jefferies.[29]

While Hardy was preoccupied with a rural world in decline, however, Lawrence saw one in the more characteristically modern condition of transformation to industry and urbanism. This runs steadily through *The Rainbow* (1915). Little by little, the Brangwen circle move out from a life bounded by the rhythms of the traditional farmer's year, into more modern worlds: to the local high school, to London 'into a big shop' or to study art, to a working-class town school, to a Teachers' Training College where folk-song and morris-dancing appear, their own ghosts, in the curriculum, to 'a fairly large house in the new, red-brick part of Beldover ... a villa built by the widow of the late colliery manager'. 'Out into the world meant out into the world.'

Thus *The Rainbow* registers how a wider, looser, more complex, more ambitious pattern of life came in; and recognizes also that the archaic springs of strength could no longer meet its needs. Most of what Lawrence was to write after *The Rainbow* conducts the search, in fictional terms, for a new source of vitality. What Lawrence, in fact, saw himself as discovering was that in any individual there is a unique and inexpungeable source of vitality lying deep in the psyche; and his concern with the intimacies of sex is best seen as a derivative from this belief, a conviction simply that in sex the central psychic forces can most abundantly flow and most easily and naturally assume their uninsistent yet powerful kind of control. Much of his outstanding later work may be seen as an exploring of the essential difference between the sham strength of those who lack this kind of integration, and the essential reality of those who have it. Particularly is this true of the short stories: for example, *St Mawr*, *The Captain's Doll*, *The Fox*, *Sun*, *The Virgin and the Gipsy*.

Moreover, the psychic ideal – an inner, intangible, relaxed but sinew-strong integrity and unity – becomes a literary one; and the topicality of this fact will by now be plain. The 'old stable ego' of character disappears,[30] and so does that of plot. 'Tell Arnold Bennett that all rules of construction hold good only for novels which are copies of other novels.'[31] In *Women in Love* (1920), his most clearly unique achievement,[32] the characters are caught in all their disjointed wholeness; and the wavering episodic movement, the abrupt transitions of the story, leave the book itself with the same kind of unity – massively and cumulatively present in spite of much that would seem at first to preclude it. Lawrence's personal quality is insistent throughout, to be sure. But there is more to say. The abrupt transitions, the calculated disjointedness, the organic kind of unity, belong to the period, and (leaving the differences for the moment aside) have affinity with the modes of organization of Eliot's *Love Song of J. Alfred Prufrock* or of *Ulysses* (see p. 90 above).

Lawrence's verse follows a similar course. The more traditional inspiration of the passage quoted above (p. 74) gives place, even before 1941, to a progressively freer verse style, to the new, looser kinds of transition and unity which have just been discussed in his prose, and to a related overriding concern for the essential, individual reality of living things. Finally, the *Preface* which Lawrence wrote for the 1927 edition of his poems shows him clearly as one who, from the point of view of the period, should be seen in relation to Bergson, to

Imagism (although it is an Imagism taken to new and transforming depths), and in general to the new sense, both of life and of technique, which had entered English poetry.

It is the quality of Lawrence's interest in life which justifies his claim: 'Primarily I am a passionately religious man'. But with the clarity of the great artist he went straight on, in the same sentence, to make clear how a struggle against difficulties, a struggle indeed to overcome weakness, is integral to his work:

> ... and my novels must be written from the depth of my religious experience. That I must keep to because I can only work like that. And my Cockneyism and commonness are only when the deep feeling doesn't find its way out, and a sort of jeer comes instead, and sentimentality, and purplism.
>
> (Letter to Edward Garnett, 22 April 1914)

Lawrence becomes a master in fiction through the struggle to become master of himself. If self-absorption is an evil, he was not wholly free of it. A few months before the battle of the Somme he could write:

> ... I will not live any more in this time ... as far as I possibly can, I will stand outside this time, I will live my life, and if possible, be happy, though the whole world slides in horror down into the bottomless pit ... What does it matter about that seething scrimmage of mankind in Europe?
>
> (Letter to Lady Ottoline Morrell, 7 February 1916)

And if *Women in Love* exposes the self-assertive determination of one human being to dominate another, one should have in mind that Lawrence can also write:

> Frieda says I am antediluvian in my positive attitude. I do think a woman must yield some sort of precedence to a man ... I do think men must go ahead absolutely in front of their women, without turning round to ask for permission or approval from their women. Consequently the women must follow as it were unquestioningly.
>
> (Letter to Katherine Mansfield, December 1918)

Above all, it is necessary to recognize that Lawrence's deep sense of how modern man may become rootlessly cut off from the proper springs of his vitality is not a calm and magisterial diagnosis of weakness in others, but a brave and persevering response to the challenge of his own predicament:

> We're rather like Jonahs running away from the place we belong ... So I am making up my mind to return to England during the course of the summer. I really think that the most living clue to life is in us Englishmen

in England, and the great mistake we make is not uniting together in the strength of this real living clue – religious in the most vital sense.

(Letter to R. P. Barlow, 30 March 1922)

Five years later Lawrence is still writing in much the same way:

It is our being cut off that is our ailment, and out of this ailment everything bad arises. I wish I saw a little clearer how you get over this cut-offness ... Myself, I suffer badly from being so cut off. But what is one to do? ... One has no real human relations – that is so devastating.

(Letter to T. Burrow, 3 August 1927)

It may be that this alienation from his own country ('the thought of England is entirely repugnant,' he wrote in 1921; he never really abandoned this position and never returned save as a fleeting and dissatisfied visitor) lies behind another achievement in Lawrence which is close to his own weakness. If we value him as the writer who, more than any other in this age, has striven to affirm and renew life, we should remember that this was in response to his own tendency to indiscriminate exasperation and disgust, to something not unlike the 'doing dirt on life' that also disgusted him in his other phase. 'This filthy contemptible world of actuality' in a letter of 1 April 1917 is both echoed, and controlled, in the words of the Lawrentian hero of the last novel:

When I feel the human world is doomed, has doomed itself by its own mingy beastliness, then I feel the colonies aren't afar enough. The moon wouldn't be far enough, because even there you could look back and see the earth, dirty, beastly, unsavoury among all the stars: made foul by men. Then I feel I've swallowed gall, and it's eating my inside out, and nowhere's far enough away. But when I get a turn, I forget it all again.

(*Lady Chatterley's Lover*, ch. 16)

If Lawrence is the greatest English writer of the century (Yeats, in this respect, stands nearest to him) it is largely because art feeds upon the tensions in the artist as well as on their resolution; and the tensions hinted at by the above quotations are what help to give Lawrence's people their rich and flexible complexity and their astonishing vitality. Thus it is exactly as an artist that Lawrence is so greatly superior to, say, a writer with serious and sensitive interests in human personality like L. H. Myers (*The Clio*, 1925; *The Root and The Flower*, completed 1935; *Strange Glory*, 1936). Myers's preoccupation with what is real and what is hollow in life is akin to

Lawrence's, but the best part of his work specifically as fiction is his rendering of the equatorial forest as expressing rich relaxed spontaneity. Aside from this, there is a recurrent tendency for the action of the books to become progressively divorced from what is most seriously at issue in them, and to degenerate into a kind of slow-moving and wooden intrigue.

Largely, it is also Lawrence's talent as a writer, in a comparatively conventional sense, that makes him more satisfying than an important though still much neglected novelist of his period, John Cowper Powys (*Wolf Solent*, 1929; *A Glastonbury Romance*, 1933; *Weymouth Sands*, 1934). Powys, like Lawrence, responded as a moralist to the needs of the modern world (see his long prose essay, *In Defence of Sensuality*, 1930). His highly idiosyncratic kind of sensualist Manichaeism is sometimes a trifle ridiculous; but so, one must surely admit, is Lawrence at his most speculative and dogmatic. Powys's sense of life, though crabbed and contorted, can be powerfully vivid; and his awareness of natural beauty is deeply moving, and reminiscent of both Lawrence and Hardy. It must also be said in his favour that he was not an alienated writer as both these were in part. His work never displays either melancholy, or waspish despair; and is confident and zestful, with a kind of tempestuous geniality. But it is also usually awkward and (despite its almost Dickensian elaboration) curiously same, with characters and incidents that can be both wooden and forced. Surprisingly, the immediately striking contrast with Lawrence is in respect of literary competence. Viewed generally, Powys's work leaves the impression of a lifelong amateur of gigantic ambition and real if ill-directed genius. All in all, however, he requires fuller treatment than he can receive here.*

Many will remain dubious of Powys's ragged immensities; and in the context of the present discussion will find a more congenial figure in Joyce Cary. Cary, though, has something important in common with Powys. Also a moralist, he is also no 'Modernist'. In his work too, a loose episodic structure and a boisterous sense of character are akin to Dickens rather than Lawrence. His predilection for the chronicle novel, straddling several generations, hints at Galsworthy, and there is little that is cosmopolitan and sophisticated about it – it is

* For a discussion of J. C. Powys's work, see pp. 187–90.

the resumption of a homely and traditional form. But as this discussion proceeds, it will transpire that this does not make Cary an isolated throw-back. On the contrary. It is what makes him belong to the middle and later years of the century; for that period will prove to be one in which the continental influence spent itself, and, for a time at least, English writers resumed certain links with the native past. (See Volume 8 of the *Guide*.)

Cary's political novels (*Prisoner of Grace*, 1952; *Except the Lord*, 1953) have something in common with a work like Wells's *The New Machiavelli* (1911) in their sense of the contrast between the corruptions of public life and the restoring strength of private affection; but Cary's sense of this is easily the fuller, and his rendering of it correspondingly more substantial. At its richest his work is almost poetic in its imaginative apprehension of life and its lyrical expression of this in metaphor. A novel like *A Fearful Joy* (1949) is deeply impressive for its sense of the continuing collapse of traditions in the social revolutions of the two wars; and yet at the same time of this as urgent transformation rather than mere decline, of life continually reasserting itself through its own deepest, strongest, yet crudest drives. Finally (to revert to Lawrence) at one point Cary is strong where Lawrence is weak. Throughout his work runs a confident sense, made real in the fiction itself, of how each man or woman lives and thrives by virtue of bonds with many others; of how everyone is a unit in the whole social fabric of the family and of society. Lawrence is very different. Birkin says to Ursula, 'I don't want a definite place ... it is a horrible tyranny of a fixed milieu'.[33] Mellors and Connie (*Lady Chatterley's Lover*, 1928) find their fulfilment in isolation in an unsympathetic world. Great as are the differences, the reader of Lawrence will sometimes find himself recalling Arnold's *Dover Beach*:

> Ah, love, let us be true
> To one another! for the world ...
> Hath really neither joy, nor love, nor light,
> Nor certitude, nor peace, nor help for pain;
> And we are here as on a darkling plain ...

Developments in Literary Criticism

The development of literary criticism in this period is a topic which receives detailed discussion later, and what is said here is by way of preliminary to that. Perhaps it is as well to indicate at the start, in broad terms, the two interests which have lain behind what has been new and forward-looking in criticism since Eliot began his career. Of these one has started from the fact that a literary work is nothing other than certain words in a certain order; and it has taken the form of a close and detailed concern with how the verbal texture of the work, through the exact quality and interplay of its details, creates the richness and depth of meaning of the whole work. This, as is suggested by the comparison between Eliot and Mallarmé (made on p. 78 above), largely derives from the ideas and theories about poetry of the late-nineteenth-century French poets and critics who have already been discussed.

The other guiding idea – the best critics have necessarily seen both in the closest inter-connection – has spread much wider, and run parallel in fact to the writers' concern with how society has been disrupted and endangered. Reacting from the idea (as sometimes expressed by Wilde, say) that literature, being art, stood apart from life, critics have insisted that literary values were ultimately one with those of living itself. From this point of view, critical issues are inseparable in the end from general cultural ones. Serious writing has been seen as one of the major forces sustaining general cultural health; and the weakening of society, the decline of its standards of discrimination through the spread of either commercial or scientific values beyond their proper spheres, stood out as matters directly concerning the critic. Moreover, much that is distinctive of criticism in the modern period developed along with the development of English literature as a major part of higher education (at school or university) in the humane, non-vocational 'cultural' sense (see pp. 37–40).

It is Matthew Arnold who stands at the point of origin of this way of studying literature; and his reasons for stressing its value help to explain how criticism (with literature itself) was reaching forward to a new social role. 'More and more mankind will discover,' Arnold wrote in 1880, specifically with the decline of religion in mind, 'that we have to turn to poetry to interpret life for us, to console us, to sustain us.' Some of the implications of this for the function of the critic emerge from what the most important of modern teacher-critics, F. R. Leavis, said in the context of Arnold:

Many who deplore Arnold's way with religion will agree that, as the other traditions relax and social forms disintegrate, it becomes correspondingly more important to preserve the literary tradition.[34]

In part, literary criticism and the educational institutions associated with it were moving towards some of the social functions – such as sustaining an awareness of cultural tradition and moral values – once chiefly exercised, and in part still exercised, by organized religion. Criticism was gaining a place which spread wider in society, and went deeper, than might at first appear.

Turning from these general matters to brief detailed illustration of them, the main point is that there was no sudden break in development. Throughout the nineteenth century, there was a strong tradition (Ruskin, Coventry Patmore, and Leslie Stephen have their places in it, besides Arnold) that the values of life and art were ultimately one. The critical writings of A. R. Orage (editor of *The New Age*, 1908–21) constantly take up problems of moral wholeness ('moral decadence may be discovered in style itself . . . its sign-manual in style is the diffuse sentence, the partial treatment, the inchoate vocabulary, the mixed principles'[35]) and also of cultural decay, commercialization, shortage of serious criticism, and debasement of standards. Moreover, they insist steadily on the critic's duty to distinguish decisively between the first-rate and the second-rate, and they employ both crushing irony and also close poetic analysis. They point clearly backwards to Arnold (whom Orage constantly praises, and whose method of 'touchstones' in poetic criticism he regularly employs) and forwards to more recent criticism. Not only in singling out a writer like George Bourne for commendation, but also in its *bêtes noires* (the military critic of *The Times*, 'the frivolous Professor Murray', the Poetry Society, Masefield, Landor, polite essayists like 'Alpha of the Plough', popular reviewing, literary weeklies, and the 'kept Press') Orage's work seems to radiate out almost equally towards Arnold, Eliot, and Leavis. As his work becomes better known, Orage is now proving to be one of the decisive figures in the continuity of criticism over the last century.

A number of others, however, must also be taken into account. Ford Madox Ford (or Hueffer) was a more relaxed and less incisive critic, but he deserves mention in the same context as Orage, and the columns of his *English Review* (he edited this from 1908) often dealt seriously with central issues of criticism and culture, even if Orage's *New Age* was ill-satisfied with how they did so. Before 1912, T. E. Hulme had repudiated 'romantic' poetry and the primacy of emotion, and had stressed how writing which is not trivial uses words precisely and concretely.[36] J. Middleton Murry's *The Problem of Style* (1922) was also something of a landmark, for it brought clearly together the ideas that literature is the expression of the writer's whole response to life seen in its deepest terms, and that it is so through its exploratory and creative use of language and especially of metaphor. Moreover, Murry anticipated much later work in insisting that the greatness of Shakespeare himself lay precisely here.[37] Eliot's importance and influence must be gauged not only by his early critical essays, but also his editorship (1922–39) of the *Criterion*, which published important critical work by Pound, Hulme, and Eliot himself, and stressed such ideas as that literature is an integral part of life, that it should show a response in particular to the facts of contemporary life, that humane culture is threatened by the spread of a crudified scientific outlook and that a loss of standards has occurred through the invasion of literature by commerce. 'The almost impregnable position . . . that one should write in some way that will not depreciate the value of the electro-plates now possessed by the elder British publishing firms', Pound put it in the opening issue. As the *Criterion* went on, however, its editorial commentaries proved more stilted in tone, and less concerned with critical than with ecclesiastical, architectural, theatrical, or publishing issues.

Much superior to it as a critical journal was *The Calendar of Modern Letters* (1925–7), edited by Edgell Rickword and Douglas Garman. This not only published essays of central importance like Lawrence's *Art and Morality* and *Why the Novel Matters*, but spoke out, with consistency and often with pungent asperity, against the 'annihilating of standards' ('the subservience of criticism to publishers' advertisements') as reflected by certain literary weeklies, the literary 'Establishment', or the modern section of the *Oxford Book of English Verse*; and also against the harmful influence, in the sphere of spiritual values, of science. On the positive side, much that is best in later criticism was already clear, for example, on the claim of satire to a high place in literature, the ultimate identity of 'poetic and real values', and the fact that in all literature (fiction as much as verse) it is the organization of language, 'the verbal and differentiated qualities of writing', which should determine the critic's judgement. To turn from A. R. Orage or the *Calendar* to *Scrutiny* (1932–53), which with the writings of its editor F. R. Leavis is the outstanding critical achievement of the century in English, is to see that *Scrutiny*'s merits lay less in bringing original and powerful new ideas into criticism than in the comprehensive and detailed working out of ideas which had already been formulated; and in a recognition, sustained over several decades, of what makes a significant argument in critical matters, and what a trivial one.

The technique of detailed 'analysis' was developed in several important books of the 1920s. I. A. Richards's *Principles of Literary Criticism* (1924) supplied an elaborate (if in the end inadequate) theory on which analysis could be based, and that theory also gave poetry a central place as contributing not merely to amusement, but also to fundamental cultural health. *A Survey of Modernist Poetry* (1927), by Robert Graves and Laura Riding, was a pioneer work anticipating much later writing, now better known, in the field of poetic ambiguity; and G. Wilson Knight began his detailed if often erratic analyses of poetry and symbolism in Shakespeare just before 1930.[38]

One must distinguish two trends in the criticism of this period: trends by no means mutually antagonistic, but in essence quite distinct. On the one hand there are Eliot's more analytic and detailed pieces, Richards's *Practical Criticism* (1929), the detail of Leavis's analyses in *Revaluation* (1936), Empson's *Seven Types of Ambiguity* (1930), and much else of the kind. Yeats's remarks, long before, in his early essays on Symbolism and the infinite subtle suggestiveness of 'symbolic writing' should be mentioned in the same context, and so should the work, later on, of the American 'New Critics'. In all that line of thinking, the prominent ideas were of complexity and ambiguity in the local poetic texture, of subtle 'equipoise' (Eliot's word) between contrasting attitudes, of ironical play.

Eliot's exact words, in a phrase much quoted to articulate that line of criticism, ought, however, to be recalled. True enough, he spoke of 'a network of tentacular roots': a phrase that lies behind Richards's extraordinary mythology-diagram (*Principles*, p. 126) of the neurological intricacies of the poetry-reading process. But Eliot went on to write: '... tentacular roots *reaching down to the deepest terrors and desires*'. That is the other dimension of the critical effort of the period: a conviction that the major literary work, in prose or verse, speaks with some kind of finality to the fundamental and ultimate realities of human experience; beside that, the other and 'politer' things that writing may do are insignificant. Such convictions may be seen most plainly in some of Lawrence's critical pieces (the general essays on the novel in *Phoenix*, the *Study of Thomas Hardy*, and 'A Propos of Lady Chatterley') and in some of Leavis's later criticism, where an almost conspicuous absence of analysis, and an oracular though sometimes very convincing, or at least deeply disturbing, presentation make the point, and the contrast between the two critical procedures, particularly noticeable.

The Closing Years of an Age

It is at this point that the reader should recall what was said above about Cary (p. 100); and that the general picture of literary development over the period starts to become clear. From 1930 onward the avant-garde writers of the two preceding decades begin to retire from the scene. Pound had left England and wrote in comparative isolation abroad; Lawrence, Joyce, and Virginia Woolf were removed by death, and Eliot produced no verse (other than his plays) after *Four Quartets*, completed by the early 1940s.

On the question of relative value, the 1910–30 period was one of the great epochs of English literature. It stands with 1590–1612, or 1710–35, or 1798–1822. What has been written since then does not bear comparison with it for a moment. The trends which have been referred to, however, throw light not on the quality of recent development, but on its direction. They suggest, in fact, that Eliot and Pound must surely leave a permanent mark on English verse, but did not re-orientate it once and for all.

To turn, for example, to Auden, Spender, and the other 'political' poets of the 1930s (though they were not writers of political verse only) is at once to encounter work which is very far from continuing the traditions of Pound and Eliot. Certainly, their concern about social and cultural disorder is reminiscent of *The Waste Land*:

> In unlighted streets you hide away the appalling;
> Factories where lives are made for a temporary use

Like collars or chairs, rooms where the lonely are battered
Slowly like pebbles into fortuitous shapes.
                                        (*The Capitol*, 1940)

But the resemblance is a strictly limited one. Eliot's gaze was upon
the culture and society of his own time, but he saw it in the abiding
terms of one whose ultimate solutions were spiritual and universal.
Topicality in the work of these new poets was at once sharper, less
portentous, and more limited: the counterpart of a less serious or at
least less solemn conception of verse, as also of an interest in left-wing
politics, combined with the mounting political tension created by the
Slump, the rise of Hitler, the war in Spain, and the unemployment
and industrial policies of the government (see pp. 34–5). These
differences of attitude and approach show clearly in the texture of
their verse. Auden does not employ Pound's 'mode of superposition',
but an organization which, in both logic and syntax, is like that of
ordinary discourse. Moreover, his work draws on a narrower range
of cultural reference, and offers a narrower range of emotion, at least
within the single poem. He reflects a new admiration for dryness,
irony, easy vernacular diction, and self-deflation in verse; but because
his mode of organization was, in several respects, different from that
of Pound or Eliot, his verse lacks the poignant intensity of those poets,
though it offers something instead.

Indeed, Auden to some extent drew upon the very cast of thought
– external, scientific, classifying – which lay behind the social organizations he condemned: perhaps the most distinctive feature of his
verse is the almost uninterrupted succession of class-words (plural
nouns, or singular nouns employed with plural force) which run
through it. 'Streets', 'Factories', 'rooms', 'the appalling', 'the lonely',
make this decisively clear in the passage quoted above. All this is to
say that the continuity with Pound and Eliot was superficial rather
than profound. Certainly, from 'Lay your sleeping head, my love' to
The Shield of Achilles, there is a more lyrical side to Auden's work;
one which grew more prominent in quantity, if not quality, as his
later verse ceased to be political, and became personal, historical and
religious.[39] But this spare lyrical poignancy, musical though vernacular, can in no way be referred back to Eliot. Influenced perhaps by
Yeats, it points mainly to Hardy, and is a partial resumption of the
tradition of verse discussed above on pp. 73–5.

The work of Dylan Thomas often conspicuously conforms to Eliot's guiding ideas. These lines are from *A Refusal to Mourn the Death, by Fire, of a Child in London*:

Never ...
Shall I let pray the shadow of a sound
Or sow my salt seed
In the least valley of sackcloth to mourn
The majesty and burning of the child's death.

I shall not murder the mankind of her going with a grave truth
Nor blaspheme down the stations of the breath
With any further
Elegy of innocence and youth.

'Valley of sackcloth', 'stations of the breath', 'mankind of her going', and several other turns of phrase in this passage bring to mind Eliot's 'words perpetually juxtaposed in new and sudden combinations, meanings perpetually *eingeschachtelt* into meanings' (see above, p. 78). But when he wrote this, Eliot was discussing a passage from Tourneur, and pointing to the firm-set muscularity of its language. Thomas's conformity to Eliot's principle is superficial. In these lines it appears as a harmless idiosyncrasy of diction; often elsewhere as distracting cleverness. His strength (and it must be remembered that he was a most obviously gifted poet – the words imply clear reservations) lay elsewhere: in a half-naïve, half-mystical, delighted sense of the livingness of man's environment and his oneness with it, which emerges in a few only of his poems, such as *A Refusal ...*, *Poem in October*, and 'Especially when the October Wind'. But again, though in a different way, the case is one of a poet who conforms on the surface to Eliot's dicta, but is independent in substance; for this deeper and more genuine side to Thomas does not point at all towards Eliot, Pound, Donne, or the Symbolists, but to Hopkins and still more to Blake, poets whom Eliot ignored or disparaged.

The important poet of this period who seems to have been decisively influenced by Eliot was William Empson. His case is a very different one, but in the end, surprisingly, it seems to bring out the same general direction of change. In his slender though distinguished production of verse there is a dry but impassioned or half-tortured intellectuality which indeed looks back to Donne; and with that, often, a coolness and casualness of tone which seem to stem from the criticism of Eliot or Richards:

> It is the pain, it is the pain endures.
> Your chemic beauty burned my muscles through.
> Poise of my hands reminded me of yours.
>
> What later purge from this deep toxin cures?
> What kindness now could the old slave renew?
> It is the pain, it is the pain, endures.   (*Villanelle*)

Moreover Empson, as these lines show ('Poise of my hands', 'this deep toxin'), has a particularity of apprehension and of language which Auden lacks. Yet although Empson has been an important influence on later writers of verse, his influence has not been contrary to that of Auden so much as parallel to it. This is because Empson's recondite, contorted, and powerful poems (*Arachne*, say, or *High Dive*) have not been imitated. Later writers have taken their direction rather from those of his poems, like *Villanelle* and *Aubade*, where an adroit and suave easiness prevails – where, indeed, Empson is nearest to a kind of verse which Auden both practised, and identified as 'the fencing wit of an informal style'. The result has been that Empson at his most distinctive has been least influential: and most influential at his most Audenesque. John Wain, for example, has claimed to have followed Empson's lead; but this must be seen in the light of a characteristic poem of Wain's like *Who Speaks my Language?*:

> Ah, no. It seems the simplest words take fright
> And shape themselves anew for every ear,
> Protected by a crazy copyright
>
> From ever making their intention clear.
> And yet one cannot blame the words alone ...

The nearest parallel is not in Empson at all, but Auden, and it is decisively close:

> Verse was a special illness of the ear;
> Integrity was not enough; that seemed
> The hell of childhood: he must try again.
>   (*Rimbaud*, 1940)

Empson's work, that is to say, has a very distinctive place for its intrinsic qualities, but as an influence it contributed to the general direction of movement rather than made against it.

The perspective will become clearer if the reader refers again to the poetic continuity noticed (pp. 73–5) in Hardy, Edward Thomas, Lawrence, and Graves. The full point of the dry, witty tone in the closing lines of Graves's stanza may now be seen: it shows, at an early stage, what has emerged as a very definite change in that continuity, but not a lasting repudiation of it. The impact of Eliot and Pound and all that they stood for has been profound; but it remains true that Eliot and Pound now seem to have constituted a highly distinctive *phase* of poetic history, one which was at bottom a continental impact rather than the decisive restoration of a central English tradition.

Pound, writing after 1920 on his own in Italy, seems to have continued in the *Cantos*,[40] with extraordinary consistency, to work in the vein of 1920. There is the same principle of structure through juxtaposition, the same dislocating medley of references, the same density and compression, the same constant extension into new meanings (reaching in the end to the Chinese character and the Egyptian hieroglyph), the same emphatic shifts of voice, often the same casual yet sarcastic tone. That the *Cantos* seem as a whole to be a profound quest, blocked out through example after example taken in all its fullness, for the qualities which can validate public life and thus make true art possible, does not affect the question of continuity. Pound has gone on in a direct line from how he began.[41]

By contrast, Eliot spent his later years in England, more and more as an established landmark in its literary scene. His later work shows it. Already by the 1930s he was praising, in his prose:

> poetry so transparent that we should not see the poetry but that which we are meant to see through the poetry, poetry so transparent that in reading it we are intent on what the poem points at, and not on the poetry; this seems to me to be the thing to try for.

With these points in mind, certain features of *Four Quartets* (1935–42) take on a special interest. Among these are the clear-cut yet buoyant quality of several of the lyrics; the sombre lucidity of expression going with an elusiveness less of subtle evocation than of argument and idea; the acceptance of something like philosophical generalization; the notable absence of abrupt and cryptic juxtapositions such as are so frequent in *The Waste Land*; and the tone, seldom satirical or throw-away, but often quiet, sincere, intimate, unhappy –

sometimes reminiscent of the meditative verse of Arnold. These things make it clear that from several points of view the *Four Quartets* are traditional poems in a sense of that word which Eliot's 1917 essay, *Tradition and the Individual Talent*, implicitly condemned. They have a continuity with areas of English literature from which that essay turned away. This is neither to praise nor to condemn them, but to point towards the kind of work which they comprise.

There is no reason to suppose that the span of writers' lives will correspond to the period over which they bring in such innovations as transform the literary scene; nor that they will conform to their avant-garde positions right through into old age. Eliot's last works – his final plays – seem rather to take their colour from new and quite other forces, forces which became influential in Britain in the years after the Second World War. That matter belongs to the next Volume of the *Guide*, and will be resumed in it.

NOTES

1. See Q. D. Leavis, *Fiction and the Reading Public* (1932); F. R. Leavis and D. Thompson, *Culture and Environment* (1933); George Orwell, 'Boys' Weeklies' (1939) and 'Raffles and Miss Blandish' (included in *Critical Essays*, 1946); M. Dalziel, *Popular Fiction 100 Years Ago* (1957); Richard Hoggart, *The Uses of Literacy* (1957).

2. W. B. Yeats, 'The Rhymers' Club' (1892) in *Letters to the New Island* (1934): see especially 144–6.

3. See his essay 'The Art of Fiction' (1884; in *Partial Portraits*, 1888, and *Henry James and Robert Louis Stevenson*, ed. Janet Adam Smith, 1948).

4. For sporadic earlier productions see Una Ellis-Fermor, *The Irish Dramatic Movement* (1939), Appendix B; and the *Guardian*, 28 November 1959, 6.

5. *Plays and Controversies* (1923), 157–8; but compare 12 and 155.

6. See Gilbert Phelps, *The Russian Novel in English Fiction* (1956); a short but illuminating book.

7. *New Bearings in English Poetry* (1932), 10.

8. Some confirmation of this is given by references in Pound's *Letters*, ed. D. D. Paige (New York, 1950) 90, 239.

9. See, e.g., Wallace Fowlie, *Rimbaud's 'Illuminations'* (1953), 109n; also, among the *Illuminations* themselves, 'Villes I and II', and 'Métropolitain' (which may be a source for Eliot's description of the fog in *Prufrock*).

10. *Selected Essays* (1932), 373.

11. See also, however, Pound's series of essays and notes on recent French poets (*Little Review*, 1918; reprinted in *Make it New*, 1934).

12. See the essay, 'What is Popular Poetry?' (1901), reprinted in *Ideas of Good and Evil* (especially 7, 1914 edn).

13. Earl Miner, *The Japanese Tradition in British and American Poetry* (Princeton, 1958); an informative book, despite its improbable title.

14. Eliot, *Selected Essays*, 209; Mallarmé, *Œuvres* (Pléiade, 1945), 366.

15. F. W. Bateson, 'Dissociation of Sensibility', *Essays in Criticism*, July 1951; *Le Problème du style* (13th edn, 1924), especially 91–101.

16. Wagner, *The Music of the Future* (1861); *Prose Works*, trans. W. A. Ellis (1894), Vol. III, 317–18; and Vol. V, 65, on Schopenhauer's 'Platonic' theory of music.

17. See Gwendoline Bays, *The Orphic Vision* (1964).

18. See, e.g., K. Tillotson, 'Donne in the Nineteenth Century' (in *Essays Presented to F. P. Wilson*, 1960).

19. J. E. Duncan, *The Revival of Metaphysical Poetry* (Minnesota, 1959), especially chs VI–VIII.

20. Letter of 9 July 1933.

21. Augustine, *Confessions* (trans. E. B. Pusey, 1930), 53–4.

22. John Holloway, 'The Waste Land Revisited', *Encounter*, August 1968.

23. 'The Novels of Turgenev' (1933), in *The Captain's Deathbed* (1950), 54.

24. See her essays, 'Modern Fiction', in *The Common Reader* (1925), and 'Mr Bennett and Mrs Brown', in *The Captain's Deathbed*.

25. But compare J. W. Graham, 'A Negative Note on Bergson and Virginia Woolf', *Essays in Criticism*, January 1956.

26. I have discussed these points more fully in 'Wyndham Lewis: the Massacre and the Innocents', *Hudson Review*, summer 1957; reprinted in *The Charted Mirror*, 1960.

27. Letter to Dorothy Wellesley, April 1936; in Yeats's *Letters*, ed. A. Wade (1954), 853.

28. John Holloway, 'Yeats and the Penal Age', *Critical Quarterly*, 1966.

29. See for example *Amaryllis at the Fair* (1887), ch. 27, or the closing pages of ch. 32.

30. Letter to Edward Garnett, 5 June 1914; in the context, it is relevant to note, of several foreign writers, Russian or Italian, as possible guides or models.

31. 16 December 1915; *Letters*, ed. Aldous Huxley (1932), 295.

32. It was described as 'Mr Lawrence's most significant and most characteristic novel' by E. D. McDonald as early as 1925 (*Centaur Bibliography*, 49).

33. *Women in Love*, ch. 26 (Phoenix edn., 1954, 348).

34. 'Arnold as Critic' in *Scrutiny*, 1939, Vol. VII, 323.

35. A. R. Orage, *Selected Essays and Critical Writings*, ed. H. Read and D. Saurat (1935), 13–14.

36. See *Speculations*, ed. H. Read (1924), 113–40; and also *Further Speculations*, ed. S. Hynes (Minnesota, 1953), especially 79–80.

37. *The Problem of Style* (1922; lectures, 1921), 26–31; 83, 97–9; and 13 and elsewhere.

38. See also, however, Graves's earlier pamphlet, *Contemporary Techniques in Poetry* (1925).

39. John Holloway, 'Auden: The Master as Joker', *Art International*, January 1969.

40. *A Draft of XXX Cantos*, 1933; *Cantos XXXI–XLI*, 1934; *The Fifth Decade of Cantos*, 1937; *Cantos LII–LXXI*, 1940; *The Pisan Cantos* (LXXIV–LXXXIV), 1949; *Section: Rock Drill* (*Cantos LXXXV–XCV*), 1957; *Thrones* (*96–109 de los cantares*), 1960.

41. Pound's splendid but in a certain sense traditional translations from the Chinese *Classical Anthology* (1956) should however be noted.

PART III

HENRY JAMES:
THE DRAMA OF DISCRIMINATION

HENRY GIFFORD

'I have made my choice, and God knows that I have now no time to waste.' This memorandum of 1881, written for his own eye, reveals the essential Henry James in his power of lonely decision and his uncommon ardour. The particular choice was to live in England: a step often deplored but, given the peculiar genius of James, strictly logical. In taking it he overcame the last of his disabilities. Almost from infancy he had known his talent – that of 'the visiting mind', to gather impressions and to read aspects – but for making use of it he needed faith in his own lights. The elder Henry James, his father, thought little of 'mere' literary men, since any kind of 'doing' was a restriction on 'being'. William James teased and harassed his younger brother with cordial insensibility until at length – in 1905 – Henry rejected his point of view as too 'remotely alien' for the beginnings of appreciation. He waged a further struggle with his American environment. An essay in *French Poets and Novelists* (1878) speaks of Turgenev as 'having what one may call a poet's quarrel' with his native land. 'He loves the old, and he is unable to see where the new is drifting.' James recognized this 'poet's quarrel' as necessarily his own, though for him the conditions were even less favourable. Turgenev at least could rejoice in the wealth of type under his eye, whereas the American novelist had still like Hawthorne to content himself with coldness, thinness, and blankness. 'It is on manners, customs, usages, habits, forms, upon all these things matured and established, that a novelist lives ...' In the second chapter of his *Hawthorne* (1879), James drew up a list of 'the items of high civilization' missing from American life: a court, an aristocracy, an established church; country houses, cathedrals, old universities and schools; the arts, a political society, a sporting class. Another kind of novelist – Melville, for instance, of whom James apparently knew nothing – may live immensely without these things, or on their sparest counterparts. But for James, with his indefeasible sense of Europe, America gave too little suggestion. He coveted the 'deep, rich English tone' of George Eliot, and the density of Balzac's France. Instead, America offered too often scenes like this in *The Bostonians* (1886):

... the desolate suburban horizons, peeled and made bald by the rigour of the season; the general hard, cold void of the prospect; the extrusion, at Charleston, at Cambridge, of a few chimneys and steeples, straight, sordid tubes of factories and engine-shops, or spare, heavenward finger of the New England meeting-house. There was something inexorable in the poverty of the scene, shameful in the meanness of its details ... loose fences, vacant lots, mounds of refuse, yards bestrewn with iron pipes, telegraph poles, and bare wooden backs of places.

The activity these things betoken meant very little to James. He pleaded ignorance of the business world – which formed, on his own reckoning, nineteen-twentieths of American life. His family and friends were all among the 'casually disqualified', so that eventually, like White-Mason in *Crapy Cornelia* (1909), he would find himself shut out from 'the music of the future', together with

the few scattered surviving representatives of a society once 'good' – *rari nantes in gurgite vasto*.

But that predicament – seen in terms of 'social impossibilities' – was reserved for Edith Wharton to render. James's concern, growing over the years, is more profound. Like Hawthorne, he came to know the pains of the separated artist: the American writer who lived for discrimination and his own approval was forced to contend against the current of national life.

If his experience was narrow – and the James children had scarcely seen a clergyman, a military man, or a politician – he had the advantage of a 'formed critical habit'. There are times when 'critic' and 'creator' are for James interchangeable terms. The critical impulse, as T. S. Eliot long ago pointed out, was remarkably strong in him. We may accept from Eliot that James stands nearer to Hawthorne than to any foreign novelist;[1] but what enlarges his scope beyond Hawthorne's, enabling him to read similar problems with more subtlety, was perhaps the study of Sainte-Beuve and Arnold. These latter displayed (what he might find also in George Eliot and Turgenev) the values of intelligence and irony and of the finely disinterested mind. The young Henry James, according to a letter he wrote in 1867, even had visions of himself as a Sainte-Beuve in English letters.[2] Doubtless it was Sainte-Beuve's marked novelistic sense – his desire to present the whole man in his proper setting – that appealed to James. *Partial Portraits* (1888) owe more than their title to Sainte-Beuve, two collections of whose 'portraits' James had reviewed earlier in the *Nation*. It may even be that there is a hint of derivation, however remote, in *The Portrait of a Lady*.

The American privilege, as James saw it then, was to 'pick and choose and assimilate and in short (aesthetically etc.) claim our property wherever we find it'. Deprivation at home caused a hunger to appropriate and claim possession. Fullness of life was something promised in books, as the small boy discovered from reading *Punch* on the hearth-rug in 'medieval New York'. There he saw the varieties of English life; subsequent visits to Europe beset him thickly with recognitions. Henry James had, like T. S. Eliot and Ezra Pound, the *instructed* imagination, proceeding from books to life and holding the two in mutual enrichment.

The 'necessity of his case' brought James to the international theme: a restless childhood divided between Europe and America fitted him perfectly for this kind of counterpoint. 'It was as if I had, vulgarly speaking, received quite at first the "straight tip" – to back the right horse or buy the right shares.' The 'mixture of manners', their contrast, the possibilities of a higher civilization than either hemisphere could show by itself – these interests held his attention from the beginning, and never wholly passed out of sight. The sense of Europe involved him, as it had involved Cooper, Hawthorne, and Melville, in a continuing dialectic between present and past, present and future, between innocence and experience, good and evil.[3] Usually he preferred to try 'the bewilderment of the good American, of either sex and of almost any age, in presence of the "European" order'. European bewilderment in presence of America he found less treatable: such attempts as *An International Episode* (1879), *Pandora* (1884), and *Lady Barbarina* (1884) could not be renewed indefinitely. There was in fact a risk of monotony: they had too little to confront. Far more numerous, and generally more rewarding, are the studies of American innocence in a fascinating but more or less corrupt Europe. A brief comparison of *The Europeans* (1878) with *The Portrait of a*

Lady (1881) will show what each end of the relation had to offer him.

In presenting the American scene to European eyes he needed to avoid 'the poor concussion of positives on one side with negatives on the other'. Just this difficulty arose in the working of *Washington Square* (1880), which is a provincial story, *mœurs de province*, revealing a corner of the past, 'medieval New York', with a light, caressing irony. Though James's subject is a bad case of parental despotism, it receives something of an idyllic frame. *The Europeans* gains by bringing the European values – merely implied in *Washington Square* – into an active relation with those of Boston. Felix Young and the Baroness not only provide two differing registers of the scene, two projections of European intelligence: they must in their turn face criticism from the Wentworths, they too are weighed in James's fine balance. The author himself, as F. R. Leavis demonstrated in his alert commentary,[4] does not directly intervene. His sympathies may well lean to the American order – homely, pious, frugal, earnest, candid – but nothing is made simple or schematic. We are called upon to appraise various notes. There is the note of Mr Wentworth and Mr Brand: New England sense of duty; the note of Gertrude Wentworth: a shy originality not altogether at ease in Zion; the note of the Baroness: European worldliness and lack of scruple; the note of Felix: a free intelligence at play, too ingenuous to be wholly European, too light for New England. The comedy of manners, then, defines tacitly an ideal of civilization, where wit shall be tempered with morality, and morality enlivened with wit.

James's own loyalties, it should be stressed, were to patrician New York.[5] As a young man at Newport he had felt a 'particular shade of satisfaction' in 'being in New England without being of it'. He is therefore the impartial onlooker at his comedy in this novel. Boston had struck him as still a rural centre: in the Harvard Law School he used to study his professors for 'type', and, Sainte-Beuve assisting, divined 'those depths of rusticity which more and more unmistakably underlay the social order at large'. That is the style of the Wentworths ('It's primitive,' Felix informs the Baroness, 'it's patriarchal; it's the *ton* of the golden age'). The first encounter with Gertrude staying at home from church on a fine Sunday morning in springtime conveys this exactly. It is done by exhibiting 'the

simple details of the picture' to form 'the items of a "sum" in addition'. 'A large square house in the country'; 'neatly-disposed plants'
over against a muddy road; doors and windows thrown open 'to
admit the purifying sunshine' – here is order, confidence, a quiet
joy in 'the abundant light and warmth'.

> It was an ancient house – ancient in the sense of being eighty years old;
> it was built of wood, painted a clean, clear, faded grey, and adorned along
> the front, at intervals, with flat wooden pilasters, painted white.

The specification of eighty years is not wholly ironic. Almost the
same span in *The Jolly Corner* (1908) provides the sense of continuity
over three generations. Here it serves as a passport into the eighteenth
century – General Washington had slept there. It belongs to the past
in which James felt at ease; the more remote past was 'dusky' for
him, the past of Hawthorne's House of the Seven Gables and of
iniquitous feudal Europe. But the 'big, unguarded home' in its
cleanliness and sobriety has no guilty secrets: it reflects faithfully its
master, also 'a clean, clear, faded grey'.

James may have been helped to this vision by certain passages in
Turgenev (behind which one discerns the second chapter of Pushkin's
Onegin). Mr Wentworth is perhaps seen with the aid of George
Eliot: a more sympathetic, an unselfish if still pedantic kinsman of
Mr Casaubon. Certainly the notation is similar:

> It seemed to him that he ought to find [the materials for a judgement] in
> his own experience, as a man of the world and an almost public character; but
> they were not there, and he was ashamed to confess to himself ... the
> unfurnished condition of his repository.   (*The Europeans*)

> Hence he determined to abandon himself to the stream of feeling and
> perhaps was surprised to find what an exceedingly shallow rill it was.
>
> (*Middlemarch*)

When a page or two later Felix offers to paint Mr Wentworth 'as
an old prelate, an old cardinal, or the prior of an order', we may
recall Ladislaw's idea of Mr Casaubon as a model for Aquinas. Felix
indeed is a Ladislaw properly conceived – a convincing and not
wearisome Bohemian (something George Eliot could never do). Such
derivations often suggest themselves in James's work – there is a
hint of another when he says that Turgenev's heroines 'have to
our sense a touch of the faintly acrid perfume of the New England

temperament'. The art of working the American scene depended on a faculty for relations: hence the critical vision turning to literature for perspective. What he required was the appropriate tone. One might say that his delicacy is Hawthorne's, his mild asperity – the light brush of satire – George Eliot's. But the 'very atmosphere of the mind' that 'takes to itself the faintest hints of life' was entirely his own. Henry James brought an abundant gift of consciousness, controlled in part by what he read, but never submitting to mere imitation.

In *The Europeans* his scrutiny of manners is serious but gentle. The novel was called by him a sketch: it has the brightness of the American air, and its values are put in with a light dexterity. Mr Wentworth's 'doctrine ... of the oppressive gravity of mistakes'; Gertrude's puzzling out of the unfamiliar concept, to 'enjoy'; the Baroness's attitude towards 'fibbing': these revelations of character and social ethos are in their essence playful. The Baroness quits the scene, a superior woman disabled by American rural worth. Like Lord Lambeth in *An International Episode*, and the Prussian Count in *Pandora*, she had expected to conquer. But American simplicity holds the field.

The Portrait of a Lady carries on the debate in much graver terms. The tone has utterly changed:

> She could live it over again, the incredulous terror with which she had taken the measure of her dwelling. Between those four walls she had lived ever since; they were to surround her for the rest of her life. It was the house of darkness, the house of dumbness, the house of suffocation.

Isabel Archer's situation might be compared with Catherine Sloper's in *Washington Square*. Each is the victim of a domestic tyrant, each has been deceived in her generous affections. Isabel, of course, is the more finely aware, and that makes for a higher intensity. But she also matters more for James: her plight deeply engages. There is Ralph Touchett to focus our anxiety for her; and sinister apparitions lurk along her path – Madame Merle at the piano that rainy afternoon, Osmond waiting in the villa which 'had heavy lids, but no eyes'. The symbolism obtrudes: the 'silent, motionless portal' in the Albany house leading in her imagination to 'a region of delight or of terror'; the reminder that there were other gardens in the world than those of her remarkable soul, and that there were moreover a great many places which were not gardens at all – only dusky pestiferous tracts, planted thick with ugliness and misery.

The sense of Isabel's predicament seems to be Hawthorne's: her native innocence cannot brook the uncleanness of Osmond. 'She was not a daughter of the Puritans, but for all that she believed in such a thing as chastity and even as decency.' It was Hilda of *The Marble Faun* – a trusting and exalted American girl in guilt-laden Rome – who told the priest in St Peter's after confession: 'I am a daughter of the Puritans'; and James regarded that scene as one of the great moments in Hawthorne's novel.

Isabel, of course, stems from a proved social reality. She is the unique American girl, 'heiress of all the ages', and for her as for Milly Theale in *The Wings of the Dove* (1902), a novel that returns upon this theme, there must be 'a strong and special implication of liberty', to bring out the poignancy of her case. The American girl in Europe – 'a huge success of curiosity' who had 'infinitely amused the nations' – confronted the old order with an entire freedom: she was not 'placed' socially, and wealth made its own privileges. Ralph Touchett sees to it that Isabel receives wealth. Thereby he fosters her illusion of being superior to conditions.

Isabel's self-regard, her habit of 'treating herself to occasions of homage', her 'confidence at once innocent and dogmatic', are grievously punished, and thus James may be seen to explore the American theme of spirit and refractory circumstance. At the same time he offers Isabel a choice between representative men: Lord Warburton the English magnate, Caspar Goodwood the New England entrepreneur, Osmond the American divorced from the native values by long residence in Europe, Ralph Touchett the American who has become in Mr Eliot's sense 'a European – something which no born European, no person of any European nationality, can become'. *The Portrait of a Lady* is indeed brilliant on its social surface. Keen observation; the surest of touches in placing Osmond, Madame Merle, Henrietta Stackpole, the Countess Gemini, Lord Warburton; so much of control, intelligence, the large critical view and sense of relations: having all these, it is indeed a highly accomplished novel. In our gratitude for such mastery, we may not recognize the presence of an undertow, pulling James into a region where the intelligence can be blinded. Two jottings from his notebook scenario point this weakness:

Isabel awakes from her sweet delusion – oh, the art required for making this delusion natural! – and finds herself face to face with a husband who has ended by conceiving a hatred for her own larger qualities.

Ralph's helpless observation of Isabel's deep misery . . . This to be a strong feature in the situation.

These notes give too much away. As a matter of fact, Isabel's 'sweet delusion' never is made quite convincing. Both her martyrdom and Ralph's 'helpless observation' seem things contrived, things James needed to bring about for the expression of some deep personal theme. His mind was fixed on suffering and renunciation.

Popularity – never very certainly in his grasp – deserted James altogether in 1886, the year of *The Bostonians* and *The Princess Casamassima*. If *Daisy Miller* (1878) – an exhibition of the American girl made, as he admits, in poetical rather than critical terms – won him a fairly wide success, *The Bostonians* blighted his fortunes with the public at home. It happens that James's intentionally 'very *American* tale' started to run in the *Century Magazine* for February 1885 which was then publishing two other fictions deeply American: *The Rise of Silas Lapham* by W. D. Howells, and Mark Twain's *Huckleberry Finn*. Howells, the old friend and editor of James, had set his novel also in Boston, and what he produced – a clean square of local colour, rendered with acuteness and sympathy – couldn't fail to please the American reader looking out for the depiction of national type. Lapham, the simple and stubborn Yankee who found his fortune in a paint-mine on the old farm, was well understood by Howells, and the novel has survived much of his other work. *The Bostonians* – a daylight raid on an unsuspecting city, merciless and complete – is brilliant in a manner quite beyond Howells (who has marked affinities with the author of, say, *Washington Square* or *A New England Winter*(1884)). Understandably, its brilliance did not appeal to Mark Twain. Although *Huckleberry Finn* shares at least one of James's preoccupations – the incorruptible young mind, and Huck is, like Maisie Farange, wiser than the adults – Mark Twain and Henry James differ in their knowledge, their irony, their divinations, and their beliefs. The spell of *Huckleberry Finn* arises from two things, Huck's intimacy with the river, and the native resource of his language. The world of the frontier was closed to James; and Huck's range of expression (so suggestive to later American novelists) could not be his: it wasn't his birthright. 'The lightning kept whimpering'; 'it was a steamboat that had killed herself on a rock' – the truly American force of such phrases is bound up with attitudes even hostile to James. (Mark Twain 'would rather be damned to John Bunyan's heaven than read' *The Bostonians*.) A very large side of American life James had to take on trust. All the camp-meeting background of Selah Tarrant is supplied, perhaps, from a book he once reviewed, Nord-hoff's *Communistic Societies*; and there is, of course, as F. R. Leavis has noted, a real debt in *The Bostonians* to *Martin Chuzzlewit*. Yet James's novel, even beside a nonpareil like *Huckleberry Finn*, at once folktale and poignant record of the American prime, doesn't appear what one might expect, artificial and 'genteel'. It is extremely animated, and it strikes hard.

James knew very well the intellectual tone of Boston (he made one year later a compensatory gesture in his portrait of Emerson); the absurdities of the lecture hall and the passions of female insurgence did not escape his eye searching for the 'salient and peculiar'. He noted 'the situation of women, the decline of the sentiment of sex' as an index to the whole society, and chose therefore to organize his drama of conflicting values around 'a study of one of those friendships between women which are so common in New England'. The battle for Verena Tarrant's soul between the implacable female zealot, Olive Chancellor, and the rude Southern knight-errant, Basil Ransom, enacts in passionate and personal form a conflict of ideas – between North and South, reform and reaction, the feminine and the masculine principles. The periphery is richly comic – a world of queer female missionaries under the gas lamps, of fraud and exaltation and selfless service and crude publicity. But the centre is other-wise conceived:

> There was a splendid sky, all blue-black and silver – a sparkling wintry vault, where the stars were like a myriad points of ice. The air was silent and sharp, and the vague snow looked cruel. Olive now knew very definitely what the promise was that she wanted Verena to make ...

This might almost be the desolate world of ice and snow in which

Gerald Crich dies. Lionel Trilling has read a Laurentian meaning into James's novel, and 'fear of the loss of manhood' may be among the promptings to James's imagination.[6] But more essentially – and here too he is akin to Lawrence – James is concerned with the will to dominate. Olive Chancellor is a more awful Hermione Roddice, white-hot and armed with a gospel.

The Princess Casamassima, a novel in which divination frankly replaces the inward knowledge of *The Bostonians*, is in certain ways a companion piece. Its thesis, however, remains somewhat abstract, and James's rendering lacks the complete assurance of *The Bostonians* (Miss Birdseye is given far more circumstantially than Lady Aurora). Again, a group with a fixed design (here they are anarchists) wish to make use of a gifted but immature being. Ransom's words to Verena – 'you are unique, extraordinary ... outside and above all vulgarizing influences' – are even more true of Hyacinth Robinson. But this latter is the conscious artist; and when he too betrays the cause, he does so not as a hustled captive to superior force like Verena, but of his own deliberate choice. Hyacinth's dilemma somewhat resembles that of Nezhdanov in *Virgin Soil*, whom James in a review of Turgenev's novel had characterized as 'drifting ... into the stream of occult radicalism' and then finding himself 'fastidious and sceptical and "aesthetic"'. Nezhdanov kills himself through a sense of his own ineptitude and unworthiness: Hyacinth, because the ideal no longer convinces him. Lionel Trilling in a most persuasive essay[7] sought to show that James hit off the revolutionary movement of his time with a 'striking literary accuracy', and that every detail of his picture could be 'confirmed by multitudinous records'. Even so, Hyacinth himself – who 'sprang up ... out of the London pavement' – isn't appropriate for the kind of novel – 'grainy and knotted with practicality and detail' – that Trilling made out *The Princess Casamassima* to be. He springs (as Trilling also argued) from a necessity of James's own spirit. One has the sense that the author imposes a scheme upon his story, perhaps in part unrecognized by himself. 'The dispute between art and moral action', from which Hyacinth at last escapes into death, had its unhappy familial side for James. And the theme of the exquisite nature cut off in its first flowering was to return with Milly Theale.

James's possession of 'the great grey Babylon' (with some help from Dickens) proves how little time he had lost in assimilating the English scene. He was also alive to the drawbacks of his situation. Powerful and privileged Englishmen cared little for ideas: Lord Canterville's 'den' in *Lady Barbarina* was part office and part harness-room – 'it couldn't have been called in any degree a library'. James admired the massive confidence and unconcern of these people, but he became increasingly aware that they missed their opportunities. The young American sister-in-law in *A London Life* (1888)

marvelled at the waste involved in some human institutions – the English landed gentry for instance – when she noted how much it had taken to produce so little ... all that was exquisite in the home of his forefathers – what visible reference was there to these fine things in poor Lionel's stable-stamped composition?

James clung to the forms of English life, but his sense of alienation grew, in a society where art received every kind of empty homage: 'the line is drawn ... only at the importance of heeding what it may mean'.

In the last decade of the century he wrote numerous stories about the ordeal of the modern artist. These proclaim the duty of sacrifice, of abiding by the 'inspired and impenitent' choice. Two of his most deeply felt tales on this theme, *The Death of the Lion* and *The Middle Years*, came out in the volume called *Terminations* (1895). Only a few months before, James's desperate fling at the theatre had been ended by the miscarriage of *Guy Domville*. These five years of deluded endeavour betray something like a failure of nerve. He had dropped the writing of long novels after *The Tragic Muse* (1890) to win wealth and glory as a dramatist. He found neither: and it is difficult to see what he gained from the whole misadventure except perhaps 'the divine principle of the scenario', which enabled him to project an entire novel in its articulation before rendering it. A novelist whose public begins to desert him is bound to meet the temptation of confronting them more directly, either through the theatre or, as Dickens did, through public readings. James wanted to receive acclamation in person. He swallowed his pride; he made too many concessions; he even put himself in the hands of George Alexander, who on relinquishing James took up Oscar Wilde. *Guy Domville* had some merits, as A. B. Walkley recognized. But 'fastidious, frugal quietism' does not make good theatre. Henry James returned to attempt the work of his life, with no illusions about his solitude.

R. P. Blackmur has well said that 'James made the theme of the artist a focus for the ultimate theme of human integrity'. This engaged him very often during his English years: Laura Wing in *A London Life*, Rose Tramore in *The Chaperon* (1891), Fleda Vetch in *The Spoils of Poynton* (1897) all face temptations of the wilderness, in which 'the free spirit' is put to proof. Nanda Brookenham in *The Awkward Age* (1899) is left at the end to muster her courage and 'let Van down easily'; Maisie Farange endures in *What Maisie Knew* (1897) a culminating ordeal of moral responsibility to which only an angelic child would be equal. James cannot remit these fierce probations. The sins of greed, the rages of a ruling passion, prey on his mind. Mrs Gereth suffers 'the torment of taste'; the researchers in *The Aspern Papers* (1888) and *The Figure in the Carpet* (1896) that of an obsessed curiosity: the eyewitness in *The Sacred Fount* (1901), for whom 'the condition of light' is 'the sacrifice of feeling', exposes the common case. All these figures are living in what might be Dante's hell. Eliot was surely wide of the mark in referring once to James's 'idealization' of English society. *What Maisie Knew* fixes with unfaltering verve and scorn the barbarities of a world at once feral and ridiculous.

The three major explorations of moral responsibility which James now undertook – *The Ambassadors* (1903), *The Wings of the Dove* (1902), *The Golden Bowl* (1904) – are notorious for their difficulty – a difficulty which first declared itself in *The Sacred Fount*. The notation is almost excessively fine, the issues often appear tenuous, the atmosphere has been pumped 'gaspingly dry'. Readers who delighted in the pictorial brilliancy of his earlier work and its neatness of style, must now grope in a world where for all the animation of James's figurative speech both meaning and action often hang in suspense; they must give unremitting attention to a new kind of discourse – the passional language of disembodied intelligences. And yet – is the later style really so cumbersome? F. O. Mathiessen examined the revisions made in *The Portrait of a Lady* for the New York edition:[8] almost every one is a gain in dramatic power and lucidity. A few random samples from *The Pension Beaurepas* illustrate this: I give the earlier versions in brackets:

'Poor Mr Ruck [who is extremely good-natured and soft] who's a mush of personal and private concession ...'

Mrs Church [looked at me a moment, in quickened meditation] with her cold competence, picked my story over.

But if he ate very little, he [talked a great deal; he talked about business, going into a hundred details in which I was quite unable to follow him] still moved his lean jaws – he mumbled over his spoilt repast of apprehended facts; strange tough financial fare into which I was unable to bite.

The abounding images – in *The Golden Bowl* there is the Palladian church in the Piazza (ch. vii), the Pagoda in the garden (ch. xxv), the 'tortuous stone staircase' of Prince Amerigo's moral sense in contrast to the high-speed elevator of Mr Verver's (ch. ii), and the overworked device of the bowl itself – are all planted as 'aids to lucidity'. Often they give a patterning to the whole work. Their effect is that of the classical simile as Johnson saw it, which 'must both illustrate and ennoble the subject'. They yield always an explicit meaning: 'the breakage [of the golden bowl] stood not for any wrought discomposure among the triumphant three – it stood merely for the dire deformity of her attitude toward them'. Such images must necessarily be inferior to those which, like the moon in a difficult chapter of *Women in Love*, compose meanings in no other way to be apprehended. They are expository, for the most part brilliantly contrived, but seldom, one feels, forcing their way up from the deepest levels of imagination.

The Golden Bowl in particular makes heavy demands on the reader's willingness to suspend disbelief. Princes and innocent millionaires and sublime little American girls, acting out between them a drama of wonderful intensity, stand a poor chance with the contemporary reader. Meticulously charting the course, James leads Maggie Verver to a kind of Gethsemane: seeing her father, her father's wife, and that wife's lover – her own husband – at cards from the darkness outside, she divines their appeal to save them; to contrive a relation; to lighten them of their sins, like the scapegoat. James's theme of redemption has its moments when high drama breaks out – Maggie, for instance, confronting Charlotte, the uncaged beast, in her splendid and dangerous pride. Yet the conclusion of the novel, with Charlotte safe in the silken halter, worries our sense of fitness. Adam Verver, the saint of acquisition; Maggie herself, in that fug of filial piety (the two Ververs, like the James family, being most of the time 'genially interested in almost nothing but each other'); and the Prince as final trophy and reward – are they quite credible? Such apparent allegories, which confront evil and yet seek to resolve it through the fearless innocence of youth, are essentially romantic: they proceed by 'the beautiful circuit and subterfuge of our thought and our desire'. One might see a distant parallel to Shakespeare's final plays, his 'romances'. It should not be pushed too far, because James demands from his reader the kind of acceptance that every novel tied to actualities must be given. The only magic he can use is that of operative virtue, in his heroines. And this must inevitably meet with scepticism. *The Golden Bowl*, like its two companion novels, didn't quite enact the intended truth.[9]

Those who are dissatisfied with these novels should not forget that James was still to write excellent smaller pieces (as in that collection of 1910, *The Finer Grain*, to which Ezra Pound gave especial praise). Much could be said in a discussion of James's pre-eminent skill in the slighter thing – the short story and *nouvelle*. After his visit to America in 1904 he began a moving 'interrogation of the past', originally in the pages of *The American Scene* (1907), where the daunting present drove him to 'felicities of the backward reach'; next in the Prefaces written for his New York Edition, where he narrated the story of each story; and finally in the volumes of autobiography prompted by his brother's death. If these last describe the 'growth of a poet's mind', and the Prefaces trace the processes of that mind in particular acts of creation, *The American Scene* itself is the most beautiful long poem yet to have come out of America. From his first appalled view of the villas on the New Jersey shore – loneliness and inanity written all over them – to the tragic plea on his last page, James displays a gift of divination which seldom fails him. Wells's book of the same time, *The Future in America*, for all its acuteness and verve, looks flimsy indeed beside James's deeply felt record of a signal experience.

The First World War found him no better prepared than most of his contemporaries. At one moment he cried out in panic that 'the subject-matter of one's effort has become *itself* utterly treacherous and false — its relation to reality utterly given away and smashed'. He abandoned *The Ivory Tower*, which nevertheless showed the keenest sense of realities — the black dishonoured roots of colossal fortunes flaunted in contemporary Newport. James in this last phase of social understanding (attained through the experience of *The American Scene*) stands not very far from Conrad. Though the outward forms of the civilization he knew have largely decayed, his meaning is still actual; very little in the vast body of his work can be disregarded. He has become widely recognized as a pattern of the dedicated artist, who exists to create values, to extend life, 'to be finely aware and richly responsible'. In the last of his Prefaces he claimed for himself the title of poet. There is nothing extravagant in this claim, since poets, no less than novelists, have much to learn from him. Henry James is a master for all who prize (in Marianne Moore's words) 'certainty of touch and unhurried incision'.

NOTES

1. Eliot's essay on 'The Hawthorne Aspect' and the detailed exploration by Marius Bewley in *The Complex Fate* set James firmly in his native tradition: Balzac, Turgenev, George Eliot, Dickens seem to have been *consciously* assimilated, Hawthorne's hold on his imagination was not perhaps perfectly clear to him.

2. Both James and T. S. Eliot in early manhood wrote review articles greatly outnumbering their attempts at original work. This allowed each to think over the bases of his art. James's fullest statement on this subject before the Prefaces was 'The Art of Fiction' (1884), reprinted in *Partial Portraits*.

3. On the significance of these themes for the American novelist of the the nineteenth century see *The Complex Fate* and its sequel *The Eccentric Design*.

4. In 'The Novel as Dramatic Poem (III): *The Europeans*', *Scrutiny*, XV (1948).

5. W. D. Howells defined 'New Yorkishness' as 'a sort of a Bostonian quality, with the element of *conscious* worth eliminated, and purified as essentially of pedantry as of commerciality'.

6. See his preface to *The Bostonians* in the Chiltern Library edition (London, 1952); reprinted in *The Opposing Self*.

7. In *The Liberal Imagination*.

8. See his appendix to *Henry James: The Major Phase*, entitled 'The Painter's Sponge and Varnish Bottle'.

9. Quentin Anderson in *The American Henry James* takes them rather as a

'divine novel', in which James sought to dramatize the religious views of his father. One may readily acknowledge Mr Anderson's insight into the delicacies of James's moral sense. It goes without saying that James like his father abhorred greed and domination; and we must treat with caution the view that his moral sense in these later novels surrendered to ambiguities. One can only enter here the plea that it is preposterous to conceive of father and son as standing perpetually in the same Swedenborgian pew. Mr Anderson has suffered the novelist's mind to be violated by an idea.

FROM *HEART OF DARKNESS* TO
NOSTROMO: AN APPROACH TO CONRAD

DOUGLAS BROWN

Conrad's art has its limitations. It does not explore human relation-
ship; it offers few triumphs of feminine portraiture; it lent itself to
a good deal of plainly inferior work, and two or three even among
the masterpieces are flawed – *Lord Jim*, for instance, and *Chance* and
Victory. But there is no point in making much of the limitations, for
Conrad's astonishing *range* of achievement is part and parcel of them.
To testify to that variety, there are successively *The Nigger* (1897),
Lord Jim (1900), *Heart of Darkness* (1902), *Typhoon* (1903), *Nostromo*
(1904), *The Secret Agent* (1907), *Under Western Eyes* (1911), *The Secret
Sharer* (1912), *Chance* (1913), *Victory* (1915), and *The Shadow-Line*
(1917).[1] Consider what distinction of styles separates the affirmative
eloquence of much of *The Nigger* from the discomposing astringency
of *The Secret Agent*; what distinction of scale separates the epitomizing
The Secret Sharer, and *Nostromo*. The Congo terrain of *Heart of Darkness*, the London streets of *The Secret Agent*, the South American
province of *Nostromo*, and the Gulf of Siam and the shipboard life
of *The Shadow-Line* call to mind the Polish expatriate, his adventurous
and disordered youth and early manhood, seemingly at the beck of
some compulsion to make terms with the sheer multiplicity of the
world. In his own experience he knew both far-ranging styles of life
and nature, and a strict commitment to one tested tradition – that of
the mercantile marine. It was a unique equipment for a novelist;
moreover, behind his subtle judgement of appropriate style and scale
and method, lay his equally strict service of his artistic vocation, once
the decision for that new *métier* was taken. It meant 'the intimacy
and strain of a creative effort in which mind, and will, and conscience
are engaged to the full'.

So the organization of his novels and tales is not to be taken
lightly: it expresses a scrupulous, sceptical intelligence. Several of the
finest use a present moment, still not oversure of its perspectives, to

look back into past experience and recreate it, its immediacy still vivid but its meaning enlarged and clarified by distance. The recurring figure of the raconteur, his experience separated from the novelist's own, or the aligning of a series of distinct attitudes, deny the reader simple certitudes. *Nostromo*, supremely, exhibits this structural scepticism. Now it reflects back from a forward point in time, when consequences have become evident; now contemporary events reach us through a variety of distinct consciousnesses established at various points along the chronological route; now one style of appraisal – Decoud's, now another – Mitchell's; now meditation and now drama. Add the oppressive presence of darkness or shadow through so much of the novel, and we are kept steadily in mind of the insufficiency of anyone's comprehension. Reading, we lack orientation. Nobody is thoroughly understood, no situation is perfectly clear. And the scepticism tapers off – is it the sardonic manner? or the elliptical method? – into the enigmatic. It is to the point that the novel's pivotal figure, Nostromo, is an enigmatic figure.

It may be right to associate this facet of Conrad with the expatriate wanderer. Other elements in his art express the commitment of the sailor. His artistic manifesto, the Preface to *The Nigger*, speaks of imaginative creation that shall address the senses irresistibly and so reach down to 'the secret springs of responsive emotions'. The process does not stop there; it calls into being our sense of our involvement in mankind. Conrad shares with George Eliot a concern for 'the latent feeling of fellowship', 'the subtle but invincible conviction of solidarity'. They share also the concern to give imaginative authority to the sense of obligation and rectitude, to the word 'ought' which surmounts the noise of the gale on Macwhirr's lips. So Conrad's best work gives full play to disquieting scepticism, yet celebrates fidelity and heroic discipline. It probes anxiously at traditional moral sanctions; it preserves something nearer to respect than to confidence; we move along a tightrope. Each vantage point in *Nostromo* questions or invalidates some other, no focus for authority emerges. Yet the sense of quest for some such focus prevails: the novel's structure insists upon it. It seems, on one hand, that no traditional or social code withstands the catalyst of the silver, or that other catalyst of solitude and darkness towards which repeatedly the narratives tend. But even the unillusioned cynic Decoud, who trusts nothing but the truth of his sensations, finds he desires at the crisis to leave behind him a true record of his acts. It's a sort of desolate gesture to human solidarity. And there is always some note of compassion, or regard, for those in Sulaco who do live by 'some distinct ideal'. Conrad's preoccupation with betrayal is itself suggestive: betrayal in his world has social roots, it presumes a collaborative morality – people to fail, dues to forfeit. It is affirmative. Jukes's experience in *Typhoon* presents the sway between anarchy and discipline in plainer terms. On one side of him is Macwhirr's unshakeable commitment to the demands of his tradition: on the other, the typhoon's immeasurable and destructive potency. It saps resolve, and the sense of obligation, and self-respect. As the novels and tales lead out of the nineteenth century and into our own, we are made to feel more of the limited, contingent validity of moral claims and of collaborative endeavour. We are confined in a gleaming engine-room while natural forces beyond imagination wreak havoc on the deck above and threaten to overwhelm the ship. Or, with Jukes, we suffer 'the thick blackness which made the appalling boundary of his vision', or discover in the Placid Gulf of *Nostromo* 'the limitations put upon the human faculties by the darkness of the night'.

Conrad's art addresses our senses, then, and goes on from there.

The yarns of seamen have a direct simplicity, the whole meaning of which lies within the shell of a cracked nut. But . . . to him the meaning of an episode was not inside it like the kernel but outside, enveloping the tale which brought it out only as a glow brings out a haze.

These words are Marlow's, the protagonist of *Heart of Darkness*, whose memory pieces together and re-lives the journey into the Belgian Congo. The image is important. A kernel can be extracted and the shell discarded: and recently there has been a good deal of such extraction from Conrad's work – symbols, and Jungian motifs, and so forth. The effect is to falsify and simplify the truth and depth of his art, and not surprisingly the plain force of his tales often gets obscured too.[2] We are to attend, rather, to the luminous quality of the tale itself, its 'glow'; we are to depend on the evidence of our senses, and our power to respond delicately enough to the story-teller's arrangement of his scenes, and to his tone of voice. (Though he was Polish by birth, Conrad became a master of our speech. He learnt it from the talk of seamen first, as he learnt our language generally from manuals of navigation, entries in ships' logs, as well as studies in our literature. He felt 'a subtle and unforeseen accord of my emotional nature with its genius'.) His artistic austerity led him to present no more than was necessary. Even through the vast span of *Nostromo*, one comes to feel that a thorough sifting has already taken place. There is point in every paragraph, and though there is lightness and humour, there is no give in the prose. At every moment it matters whose voice we are listening to or whose tone is prevalent. And if the montage, the shifting viewpoints, impose a condition of incertitude upon the reader, they also elicit an activity of clarification. Evidence confronts us and we are drawn to judge, and implicate ourselves in the consequences of judgement – or of incapacity to judge. Frequently the way of the narrative itself suggests this: as the *Patna* inquiry does, or the circle of auditors to whom Marlow relates his Congo ordeal as if testifying; as the manner of the young captains in *The Secret Sharer* and *The Shadow-Line* does, in no way solemn, yet seeming to bear witness before some ultimate tribunal. (*The Shadow-Line* is sub-titled 'A Confession'.) *Nostromo*'s key figure – if such it has – Dr Monygham, lives under the same constraint.

Beyond question, *Nostromo* is Conrad's greatest achievement. Yet its very magnitude and cogency sometimes obstruct readers; and it does not yield the measure of its worth at one reading, though it offers rewards enough to be going on with. It has certainly not lacked critical advocacy and no detailed fresh appraisal would earn its place here.[3] An appraisal of *Heart of Darkness* perhaps may. It is a novel that can be read, considered, and re-read in a short time; and once engaged with, it is not likely to leave a reader alone until *Nostromo* and *The Shadow-Line* have had their say. It has now received much recognition if rather less understanding although it is characteristic Conrad and includes passages that are by common consent among his very finest. Most important, and when due regard has been given to its dramatic fibre, it exhibits – like *The Shadow-Line* – a profoundly personal art: both tales handle distressing personal experience such as extends a man's knowledge of himself and of what the world is like. It is safe to say that Conrad's own Congo journey and its attendant breakdown were decisive in confirming him in his vocation as an imaginative artist. His own laconic remark prepares us for what the novel is about: 'before the Congo I was only a simple animal'.

Marlow's journey is an initiation into a fuller scale of human being. Jukes's ordeal, in *Typhoon*, relates to it, as do those of the later captains of ships. In *Nostromo* such ordeal is absorbed into and changed by a more extensive pattern, but it counts. In Sulaco, where yet more various political and economic forces are at work than make their presence felt in the Congo, Nostromo at first commits his whole identity to his public role. He is the common folk's mysterious chieftain, the creator and devotee of a cult of public fidelity. The ordeal of the pitch-dark night on the Gulf marks the point of his awakening to the nature of his city, and its silver, and his part in both. Like the adolescent in ritual, he goes out into the night and sleeps alone. In solitude he must forge an adult identity for himself. Then he puts on a man's strength and resolve and returns to his city. But Sulaco has the complex and entangling character of modern civilization, and in Sulaco Nostromo cannot escape what he has been, nor the pressures of the silver. They bear even more strongly and corruptingly upon the adult. Soon he is romanticizing his new manhood, his resentful duplicity, his subtlety, and his power. He plays alternately the hero and the villain of some adventure story of his own contriving. The enigmatic knight-errant of the silver-grey mare becomes a sort of corrupt Robin Hood: fittingly, he ends half highwayman, half cavalier.

Adult manhood is not simple or unconfined in Conrad; confusions, tensions, disappointments, and corruption strengthen their hold. Growth brings to the Marlow of *Heart of Darkness* a radical discomposure of the self. But the feeling of growth and fuller participation in the human condition carries its own worth. Conrad appears to have altered little the biographical data from his own past. His creative energy goes into acts of selection and juxtaposition, into sensuous prose, and into the provision and use of Marlow: so securing a holdfast upon the discomposure, a detached view of the changing self.

   'I don't want to bother you much with what happened to me personally,' he began ... 'Yet to understand the effect of it on me you ought to know how I got out there, what I saw, how I went up that river to the place where I first met the poor chap. It was the farthest point of navigation and the culminating point of my experience. It seemed somehow to throw a kind of light on everything about me – and into my thoughts. It was sombre enough, too – and pitiful – not extraordinary in any way – not very clear either. No, not very clear. And yet it seemed to throw a kind of light.'

There is a subtle command of the tone of voice. A slightly mannered colloquial unpretentiousness, nervous hesitations and reticences, alert the reader, and give authority to that 'farthest point of navigation'. Navigation, and the duty of the helm, and the experience of dangerous or uncharted waters, 'glow' continually in Conrad with issues of direction, of responsibility, of purpose. A memorable line runs through Singleton in *The Nigger*'s storm and Hackett ('fixed to look one way') in *Typhoon*'s, through the nearly blind Whalley of *The End of the Tether*, and the African steersman here, through Nostromo at the helm for Decoud on the Placid Gulf; towards those later vindications of responsible purpose, the terrified but obedient helmsman of *The Secret Sharer*, and the sharing of the helm at the end of *The Shadow-Line* between the captain himself and the frail, indomitable Ransome. As for Marlow's 'farthest point of navigation', the hint finally takes us to the presiding figure of Captain Giles, imagined with such serene humour in *The Shadow-Line*, who

had his own peculiar position. He was an expert. An expert in – how shall I say it? – in intricate navigation. He was supposed to know more about remote and imperfectly charted parts of the Archipelago than any man living.

The novelist himself is among the group of listeners to Marlow's voice, aboard the yawl that night on the Thames. His eyes see Marlow as an object, 'sunken cheeks, a yellow complexion, a straight back, an ascetic aspect', and his mind prepares to contemplate one of 'Marlow's inconclusive experiences'. The laconic note indicates a considered distance from the raconteur, and Marlow's own variety of tone and nuance secures a further perspective. A grim or playful sardonic understating manner remains Marlow's staple; but it becomes liable to a jarring flippancy here, a callowness there, that register the disturbing power of the memories; and later still, to a vacant rhetoric symptomatic of evasive fears and embarrassments, of memory working upon a nervous disorder. Conrad's art is that of a consummate stylist, and to read his novels well is to cultivate the utmost sensitivity to style, style as moral imprint, and to the implications of tone and arrangement. Arrangement, here, includes the company director – 'our captain and our host' – the lawyer, and the accountant, alongside the novelist, comprising Marlow's audience. For the codes and vocations of all these are implicated in the tale to come, and the novel sharpens in many ways our perception of such involvements.

Using style and arrangement like this, and by abundant sensuous life, the opening pages begin to connect many modes of exploration. We experience a movement towards the dead of night, and towards an indistinct region in which London – its lights brilliant on the water – and the Thames of now and of earliest history, and the Congo river, become one; and the various darknesses merge. Conrad purposes not only to penetrate the tenebrous moral and physical world of the Congo, and to trace the web that joins it to London's Thames, and joins its present with our past; his art is also to vibrate with the potentialities of the self that the exploration releases, to suggest the tremors suffered by the stable and complacent levels of judgement. Not that the tale is to become a mere image for the soul's 'night-journey' (after Jung): any more than the Leggatt encountered in the night of *The Secret Sharer* emanates from the psyche of the young captain. These are real meetings with people and the natural world, that so disturb the sensitive regions of the self as to require some new orientation. So far as *Heart of Darkness* records a journey into the darks of the self, those darks awaken at the touch of the actual Congo experience, and what it brings of confusion, fascination, guilt, the sense of nightmare. 'It seemed to throw a kind of light upon everything about me – and into my thoughts.'

Then there is a grandiose note, too, in these opening pages, to be discountenanced by the progress of the tale, like the initial complacencies of *Nostromo*, or the overweening confidence in the securities of the naval tradition in *The Secret Sharer* and *The Shadow-Line*. A boyish review of the piratical, the expeditionary, and the colonizing glamour in the British past follows the path of the Thames: and Conrad traces another filament of the all-connecting web. And there is one more note, perhaps the most significant. The prose suggests many forms of stillness and inertia blent with the darkness: a brooding immobility accompanies and lures on the unfolding tale. The Conrad of *The Nigger* and *Typhoon* is still recognizably a nineteenth-century novelist; what threatens the human order with tragedy appears as storm, and invites heroic resistance. The twentieth-century Conrad of *Nostromo* and *The Shadow-Line* expresses a profounder and more disturbing intuition of menace, under the image of becalmed or stagnant conditions, with the collapse of the power or the will to act. This is more insidious, it turns the mind in on itself to probe at the rationale of living and question its own identity. Decoud at the time of his suicide is the extreme term, pointing to nihilism. More positively there are the diary entries in *The Shadow-Line* and the hours just before the rain comes. *Nostromo* tends to reflect one focal image from episode to episode, as though the human condition in Sulaco is perpetually this: a lighter loaded with the silver that all factions and individuals adjust themselves to, suspended motionless in pitch darkness on a motionless Gulf. There are three figures abroad, Hirsch, impotent with fear, Decoud, impotent with nihilism, and Nostromo at the helm: a steersman whose identity has been bound up with public endorsement, and who can accomplish nothing in that Gulf. They are there to serve the instincts of acquisition or of power. And this 'Night of the Gulf' pervades the whole novel. It continues all the while, whatever men or factions may believe. This is what Charles Gould's activity amounts to in the end; and his wife's impotent grief – as the poignant chapter at the end of the book discloses. One reason why the narrative line has often to fall below the surface is to prevent the apparent form of men's doings from concealing the lighter on the Placid Gulf from us. Nostromo's hands seem still to be on that tiller when he lies dead.[4]

Heart of Darkness is heavy with brooding at the outset, and still and sombre gloom seems to be the agent, as much as the setting, of the unfolding experience. But just before the first uttered words draw everything together, 'the stir of lights going up and down' catches the eye. Energy and movement continue through the novel to stand over against inertia and stillness. Here, the ordered navigation of ships about their business momentarily sets off the dark places of the earth, and of history, and of human being – undeveloped or deranged. (Just so, the last light to go out in *Typhoon* before anarchy is unloosed is 'the green gleam of the starboard light', the navigation light for ocean traffic.) ' "And this also", said Marlow suddenly, "has been one of the dark places of the earth".' The weight falls memorably on the first three words. Marlow's mind is already active in the Congo and in the past: the brooding stillness promotes that activity. So the grim speculations upon the bygone Roman invasion of *our* interior, added to that 'also', seem to be both a pertinent tableau of the invasion of Africa, and a disconcerting shift in the point of view. At the same time Marlow's uneasy tone suggests memories so disruptive that he has now to re-live them deviously, and diminish the tremor by reference to common historical experience. What the experience has done to Marlow, how it has wounded him – this, as much as the journey itself, is Conrad's subject. The sardonic, the mordant, or the facetious note in the raconteur's manner preserves detachment: but there is something else. The caustic flippancy with which he recounts his predecessor's death, for instance, conveys some insecurity. For the fatal eruption of rage in that quiet Danish skipper hints at a transformation of the ego under the pressures set up 'out there' by the jungle and the trading milieu. It is another filament of the web; Marlow discerns himself in his predecessor; their roles are the same. The episode makes an embryo of things to come. Both the naval community and the African community disintegrate:

The steamer Fresleven commanded left also in a bad panic, in charge of the engineer, I believe ... The village was deserted, the huts gaped black, rotting, all askew within the fallen enclosures ... The people had vanished.

It presages the eventual arrival at Kurtz's trading station; it offers the first sight of crazy physical destruction; and 'black' goes on to attach itself to one thing after another – another filament of the web. Marlow, replacing the Danish skipper, finds his way to the shadowed and deserted Company Offices, to the two women knitting black wool and 'guarding the door of darkness'. And so the web has him. His interview with the doctor, if it adds an ingredient of observant humour, quickens our apprehension of quiescent unbalance. 'The changes take place inside, you know.'

With the voyage towards the Congo, forms of immobility and of activity group themselves on either side. We observe in a more extended passage such as this, how the Trading Company's new representative encounters the Africans: he idle, isolated, deluded, they zestful and purposeful. The 'lugubrious drollery' of the French warship aimlessly firing into the continent – the power behind the trade – seems like energy warped, slowing to a standstill. 'The merry dance of death and trade goes on in a still and earthy atmosphere like that of an overheated catacomb.'

   The idleness of a passenger, my isolation amongst all these men with whom I had no point of contact, the oily and languid sea, the uniform sombreness of the coast, seemed to keep me away from the truth of things, within the toil of a mournful and senseless delusion. The voice of the surf heard now and then was a positive pleasure, like the speech of a brother. It was something natural, that had its reason, that had a meaning. Now and then a boat from the shore gave one a momentary contact with reality. It was paddled by black fellows. You could see from afar the white of their eyeballs glistening. They shouted, sang; their bodies streamed with perspiration; they had faces like grotesque masks – these chaps; but they had bone, muscle, a wild vitality, an intense energy of movement, that was as natural and true as the surf along the coast. They wanted no excuse for being there. They were a great comfort to look at. For a time I would feel I belonged still to a world of straightforward facts; but the feeling would not last long. Something would turn up to scare it away. Once, I remember, we came upon a man-of-war anchored off the coast. There wasn't even a shed there, and she was shelling the bush. It appears the French had one of their wars going on thereabouts. Her ensign dropped limp like a rag; the muzzles of the long, six-inch guns stuck out all over the low hull; the greasy, slimy swell swung her up lazily and let her down, swaying her thin masts. In the empty immensity of earth, sky, and water, there she was, incomprehensible, firing into a continent. Pop, would go one of the six-inch guns; a small flame would dart and vanish, a little white smoke would disappear, a tiny projectile would give a feeble screech – and nothing happened. Nothing could happen. There was a touch of insanity in the proceeding, a sense of lugubrious drollery in the sight . . .

This has poetic force; and so has Conrad's command of montage and juxtaposition. A mordant commentary rises from within, needing no further expression, as episode and attitude draw power from contiguity. Consider as a sequence the scenes and impressions that follow immediately upon Marlow's arrival at the trading station. If there is a connecting thread, it is his instant reflection as the chain-gang moves by: 'I foresaw that in the blinding sunshine of that land I would become acquainted with a flabby pretending weak-eyed devil of a rapacious and pitiless folly.' First, a scene of desultory mess: the half-buried boiler, the railway truck with its wheels in the air, the dilapidated machinery. Then the sound of blasting (quite purposeless, it soon appears) recalls the warship pouring out its shells. The chained gang of forced labourers comes very close, in one of the most incisive and pitiful paragraphs anywhere in our fiction. The eye fastens again on material disorder: a heap of broken drain-pipes, 'a wanton smash-up' in a quarry dug for no purpose and abandoned. Then, to draw these sights and sounds into the larger web of the novel, comes an extraordinary impression simultaneously of violent motion and infernal stillness in the African scene. Next, the pity owing to the human victims of this wanton smash-up is summoned by a painful closeness of vision to sick African labourers cast aside to die. Sounds of the objectless blasting go on. As the eye accustoms itself to the gloom of the grove, the 'black shadows' define themselves poignantly as individual human beings. To complete the sequence, there comes into sight the absurd, immaculate figure of the company's chief accountant.

I saw a high starched collar, white cuffs, a light alpaca jacket, snowy trousers, a clean necktie and varnished boots. No hat. Hair parted, brushed, oiled, under a green-lined parasol held in a big white hand. He was amazing, and had a penholder behind his ear.

The horror out in the grove gives place to an equal horror indoors, where the impeccably kept trading accounts deflect in turn every human claim. The scenes have the same quality of significant series. The emergence of that accountant, and all that transpires in his office, point up Conrad's creative relationship with Dickens, at the same time as they exhibit a sensuous animation, a rendering of the external, that seem uncanny. Appropriately, it is on this accountant's lips that Marlow first hears Kurtz's name. Kurtz seems to emanate from trade distorted into crass lust of gain; from 'the work of the world' distorted into a perfect accountancy of predatory spoliation; and from the presence there, in that room, of a dying agent. The later and more shameful horrors that gather about him adhere to his function, agent for the Company, who 'sends in as much ivory as all the others put together'. The manager's account of him comes next, and adjoins Marlow's finding the steamer he should command, wrecked and half-submerged. The effect is to locate Kurtz in this crassness that smashes pipes and overturns trucks and abandons steamers and dissolves human solidarities. He is both the instrument and the consequence of power at the service of greed. He personifies the exploiter's dis-avowal of moral obligation towards the African community, whether in trade, law, or financial probity. (We may recall that circle of auditors to Marlow's tale.)

Hence the peculiarly suggestive force of ivory. It serves as a point of focus like the silver in *Nostromo*. That is mercantile wealth and a focus for acquisitiveness. As the silver of the mine involved in the operations of finance houses and eventually breeding industrial strife, it is a focus for human labour. As the silver of the mountain Higuerota it focuses power; and as the contemporary equivalent for the 'legendary treasure' it fastens upon the mind, possessing those who seek to possess it. As the 'incorruptible metal that can be trusted to keep its value for ever' it is the emblem all rally to, it holds the question of final ends continually before us. This is not to expand symbolic levels but to respond to the pressures of Conrad's art: the silver manifests itself in all these ways. The ivory of *Heart of Darkness* is the raw material of wealth: raw, for its resonance affects one more intimately than mineral silver. This is bone that was once part of the living animal, it is more and other than natural resource for human plunder. And then particularly ivory is the material of luxury, the ornament of civilization. Raw or refined, it evokes pallor, personality gone bloodless and impenetrable. By its use for fetish and idol it insinuates the religious quest, devotion or possession or idolatry – and these may distort or corrupt the mind and appetite. The very first pages of the novel propose this issue. What, they ask, is the 'ideal' that sustains colonial enterprise? What may the apparent ideal conceal? – The lust of power? Greed of gain? Or may it really be 'a humane idealism, a civilizing mission'? What do these men (the phrase is Marlow's) 'bow down to'? The raconteur himself sits there motionless, like an idol, presenting the question to his listeners. All the suggestions latent in the ivory, and this last especially, come together in the sardonic designation of the waiting traders and agents at that station: the pilgrims. From now on Marlow never sees them as anything else. 'The word "ivory" rang in the air, was whispered, was sighed. You would think they were praying to it. A taint of imbecile rapacity blew through it all, like a whiff from some corpse.' While he waits, dejected and inactive, the suggestions implicit in the ivory increase and become more distinct. At the same time through rumour and surreptitious gossip and the story-teller's hints of what is to come, Kurtz also becomes more distinct: what he does and what he has become.

The wilderness had patted him on the head, and, behold, it was like a ball – an ivory ball; it had caressed him, and – lo! – he had withered . . . Ivory? I should think so. Heaps of it, stacks of it . . . It was no more fossil than I am; but they call it fossil when it is dug up . . . We filled the steamboat with it, and had to pile a lot on deck. Thus he could see and enjoy as long as he could see . . . You should have heard him say, 'My ivory.'

Marlow first remembers him as 'an animated image of death carved out of old ivory'. 'I saw him open his mouth wide – it gave him a weirdly voracious aspect, as though he had wanted to swallow all the air, all the earth, all the men before him.'

As the actual appearance of Kurtz to Marlow's memory comes nearer, his style of narrative loosens its hold. The sardonic manner still maintains some foothold in these shifting nightmare-like places. But more and more he lapses into mordant quirks, spasmodic advances and withdrawals, and a hollow rhetoric like that of Kurtz's report for the International Society for the Suppression of Savage Customs, 'vibrating with eloquence, but too high-strung, I think'. The yells of a beaten African get into his mind, words like 'jabber' and 'fantastic' recur, there are tremors of hysteria. The novelist chooses this place, therefore, to return to the actual present, the night on the Thames, the equable circle of listeners; and significantly he does so twice more before the tale is done. For the unstable and hectoring quality of the narrative as we approach Kurtz are Marlow's, they register its renewed impact upon his memory: they are not Conrad's. And Marlow's tone, too, can suddenly adjust itself to our normality:

'Do you see the story? Do you see anything? It seems to me I am trying to tell you a dream – making a vain attempt, because no relation of a dream can convey the dream-sensation . . .'
He was silent for a while.
'No, it is impossible, it is impossible to convey the life-sensation of any given epoch of one's existence – that which makes its truth, its meaning – its subtle and penetrating essence. It is impossible. We live, as we dream – alone.'
He paused again as if reflecting, then added –
'Of course in this you fellows see more than I could then. You see me whom you know.'
It had become so pitch dark that we listeners could hardly see one another.

There are limits to what can be communicated of the farther reaches of Marlow's memories, except obliquely. And part of the obliquity is this way the prose has of giving the resurgence of Kurtz and his fascination in a style of absurd vehemence. 'The man presented himself as a voice.' 'What carried the sense of his real presence was his ability to talk, his words.' The horror of Kurtz is in part an evil done upon style; upon the decorum and usefulness of language – that lucidity of speech that makes for relationship and clear perception. During the journey downriver we find that at any moment the ordinary detail of work to be done, or the sensory facts of wilderness and river, may re-establish their equilibrium. And other vital parts of the horror of Kurtz, too, may be defined with sardonic vigilance. The extravagant rhetoric is no artistic accident: it gives part of the memory's response to the experience itself, and it indicates the quality of the fascination which so subtly disturbs Marlow's own moral categories at that time with the menacing 'and yet'. In him, too, during the ordeal, and drawing him towards the corrupted trader, it is a rhetoric to bolster egotism, even at the hideous price of proposing something 'moral' about Kurtz's final state.[5] The final scenes concerning him suggest something insupportable in the direction and purpose given to life by the hallowing or authorizing of economic forces at work beneath the ostentation of a civilizing mission, and by the 'wanton smash-up' of primitive communities. It is Conrad's achievement to communicate a powerful sense of sacrilege, independently of any traditional religious sanctions. Sacrilege, essentially, against human dignity. The black shadows of diseased and cast-off African workers first call it into play, and that grotesque parody of what collaborative work ought to be, the chain-gang. And in Kurtz himself we get the maniacal assertion of the self against traditional morality, integrity in human dealing, and law. The diversity of race and nation drawn into the novel's web, and the interlocking responsibilities of warships, soldiers, traders, and seamen, provide authority for the claim thrown out as if accidentally – 'All Europe contributed to the making of Kurtz.' The predatory lust that possesses him takes support from the objects of the Company he serves, and that Company is felt in a ghastly way to be active on behalf of all acquisitive Europe, requiring its civilized ivory luxury, and disengaging the human ties in pursuit of wealth for power, power for more wealth, without end.

This is not all that needs to be said of the darkness, the horror, that Marlow encounters; but this is its plain force, and to minimize it is to read glibly, in Kurtz's own fashion. Other darknesses, too, inhabit the jungle interior, and something especially sinister seems to emanate from the collision between what the traders are, and bring with them, and what they find already there. And again, inhabiting those voids of rhetoric and anxiety on Marlow's later pages is the sense of delusion, of nightmare. There is an abyss at hand, the human tenure of any moral categories feels insecure. We are nearing the darknesses and solitudes of *Nostromo*, the shadow of Koh-ring and the uncharted seas of *The Secret Sharer* and *The Shadow-Line*. In *Heart of Darkness*, this particular insecurity seems partly to lurk in the wanton disregard of the smaller, traditional morality, operative in the charted places. These suggestions, then, are present, but the plain meaning stands. The novel's first movement opened with the grim tableau of the Roman expeditionary force penetrating our own interior. The movement ends with the return from the African interior of the Eldorado expedition. Conrad never wrote a page more laconically savage.

But the rivets are quite another matter. By contrast with the ivory and the darkness there is the salvage of the steamer, the order of work and purpose. The need of ships to be under way, in other Conrad tales, is to enable seafaring activities and skills to be exercised in purposeful collaboration. So here, the work of repair. 'Waiting for rivets' Marlow 'stuck to his salvage night and day'. Those rivets are a characteristic triumph: the symbolism proposes itself perfectly naturally. The salvage briefly restores the social bonds that rapacious folly disrupts, and it resists the paralysis all round it. Marlow doesn't relinquish the sardonic manner altogether, but respect prevails. A man can 'find himself' in such work, it is life-enhancing; and the self he finds in work for and with others is both a social reality, and yet a profound private reassurance. As soon as Marlow's work begins, here, relationships grow between mechanics, foreman, boiler-maker, and Marlow himself. The only real human relationships the novel records come of the work of repair and the work of navigation – and the finding of a manual of seamanship. As they go downriver, the skill demanded, and the collaboration, repeatedly offset the hints of nightmare, the darknesses, or the Kurtz rhetoric. And there is work to be done, with the same effect, before and after the actual death of Kurtz: leaky cylinders to mend, connecting rods to straighten, the helm to look to.

Taking this aspect of *Heart of Darkness* with such things as Singleton's unrelieved thirty hours at the helm through the storm of *The Nigger*, Macwhirr's all-sufficient 'He isn't on duty' after his second mate's insubordination, or the marvellous pages that follow the coming of rain at the climax of *The Shadow-Line*, we are left in no doubt of the place of 'the work of the world' in Conrad's art. It is honoured; but by a sceptical intelligence. If Macwhirr's ship goes down, the gleaming engine-room with its harmonious power and 'builders – good men' behind it, and disciplined engineers within it, go down too, and the man at the helm: and this at the behest of a captain's obstinate folly in misjudging nature's potencies by simple reference to his own experience and code. The selfless work Charles Gould gives to the mine in *Nostromo* has to subserve forces beyond his control; and Marlow's spiritual bravado in making the steamer seaworthy is offset at once by the appearance of the dreadful Eldorado expedition. What, the juxtaposition asks, is the work *for*? And later, where is the helmsman steering to, and why? In a sense the purposeful work only obscures a grim reality of the kind insinuated by stillness and inertia. The slow voyage up the Congo 'crawled towards Kurtz, exclusively' towards 'this Kurtz grubbing for ivory in the wretched bush'. When Marlow comes upon Towson's manual of seamanship and feels 'its singleness of intention, an honest concern for the right way of going to work which made these pages luminous with another than a professional light', the 'delicious sensation of having come upon something unmistakably real' can only be enjoyed in a moment's oblivion of 'the jungle and the pilgrims'. At once he catches sight of the manager and traders, puts the book in his pocket, and 'started the lame engines ahead', now and again picking out a tree 'to measure our progress towards Kurtz by'.

So energy takes more grotesque and irrational forms, activity becomes more sluggish, as the ulterior purposes they serve loom clearer. The superb movements of Africans paddling their boats from the shore: the merry dance of death and trade: the chain-gang: the jig Marlow dances with the foreman in the hope of rivets: jungle dwellers capering wildly, fighting crazily: and at last the orgy round

Kurtz at dead of night. Even navigation becomes (in Marlow's grim phrases) 'monkey-tricks' and 'performing on a tightrope'. As we approach the shrine, the last trading station, we experience many penetrations at once: into a distinct and fearful African territory; into the darks of time; into mingled social forms, neither barbaric nor civilized but profoundly disordered and spoiled; into the darks of moral anarchy; and into the darks of the self that the sense at once of repulsion and fascination disturbs. We could take for close reading in this light the pages immediately following the finding of the manual, and leading to that wild cry of despair with which the jungle dwellers greet the approaching traders, and which they take to be the war cry of attacking savages.[6] Such subtly organized sequences, with their questioning ironies, their variety of vocal nuance, their tentative hints at the protagonist's instability and suffering and his disintegrating confidence – above all, with their discomposing particularity – have no superior in Conrad's work, and may stand as the essence of his contribution to our fiction. Inevitably, this experience of penetration, of absorption, this loss of moral clarity and of certitude, feels sluggish: the very voyage a kind of paralysis:

The current ran smooth and swift, but a dumb immobility sat on the banks. The living trees, lashed together by the creepers and every living bush of the undergrowth, might have been changed into stone, even to the slenderest twig, to the lightest leaf. It was not sleep – it seemed unnatural, like a state of trance. Not the faintest sound of any kind could be heard. You looked on amazed, and began to suspect yourself of being deaf – then the night came suddenly, and struck you blind as well. About three in the morning some large fish leaped, and the loud splash made me jump as though a gun had been fired. When the sun rose there was a white fog, very warm and clammy, and more blinding than the night. It did not shift or drive; it was just there, standing all round you like something solid.

It is the kind of experience we have at the scene of Decoud's suicide, and again as Mrs Gould suffers her own death-in-life desolation at the end of *Nostromo*. Its last form is the embodied intuition of 'a sense of finality' just before the rain falls in *The Shadow-Line*. But even upon the horror of that paralysis there supervenes 'the seaman's instinct alone survived whole in my moral dissolution'. The contrary forces stand over against each other: that of the gulf, the typhoon, the wilderness, beyond the scope of moral certitudes and obligations, isolating and dissolving personal consciousness; and that of traditional human codes, reciprocal service, vocation, the sense of the human bond. On either side they stand at the culmination of Marlow's journey, and the needle still swings between them in Conrad's next major achievement, *Typhoon*: 'Both the typhoon and Captain Macwhirr presented themselves to me as the necessities ...'

There is a fine ease about the later parts of Conrad's best work, which is the earned ease of genius. One thinks of the last stages in the relationship of Leggatt and the young captain in *The Secret Sharer*; of the pages just before the final onslaught of the typhoon; of the handling of Ransome towards the end of *The Shadow-Line*. Having worked so hard for his imagined world, having so profoundly gauged and charted its significances, Conrad has finally only to log accurately and in order the physical and the spiritual facts. So it is with the coming upon Kurtz himself at last, the nocturnal orgy, the return journey, and the superb scene of Kurtz's death. That outing at dead of night, and the orgy, draw all the filaments of the web visibly together. This is the dance of death and trade: like the lighter on the Placid Gulf in the greater novel, this is what has happened throughout, manifestly or covertly. Everyone seems to be part of it: the manager, the pilgrims ('squirting lead in the air out of Winchesters held to the hip' so that we remember the crass violence of those warships), the Africans, Marlow, Kurtz himself, even the Company's head offices – 'the knitting old woman with the cat ... a most improper person to be sitting at the other end of such an affair'.

The achievement of the closing pages is more equivocal. The collision between the Congo wilderness, and the elegances and proprieties of the Europe at the other end; the sepulchral city replacing the ivory pallor – this is well managed. But it seems that Conrad tries to accomplish too much, after enough has already been done for the scale of his invention, when the deceptions and speculations and moral somersaults perceptible through the haze of memory as it works over the experience of nervous breakdown, occasion the scene of Marlow's visit to Kurtz's fiancée, and of his romantic lies to her. The absurd vein of sentimental heroics fits the unhinged adventurer with the diseased imagination all right; but the reader is hard put to find and keep his bearings. Not until we reach the equable tones of the last paragraphs does the grotesque ardour of Marlow's account fall into perspective. The final words are often quoted, but

those that precede it have as distinct a place in the total economy
of the novel:

> Marlow ceased, and sat apart, indistinct and silent, in the pose of a medi-
> tating Buddha. Nobody moved for a time. 'We have lost the first of the ebb,'
> said the Director, suddenly. I raised my head. The offing was barred by
> a black bank of clouds, and the tranquil waterway leading to the uttermost
> ends of the earth flowed sombre under an overcast sky – seemed to lead into
> the heart of an immense darkness.

NOTES

1. See, for critical guidance on most of these, F. R. Leavis, *The Great Tradition*.

2. For example in parts of the writing on Conrad of A. J. Guerard, R.
W. Stallman, Robert B. Haugh, and a number of other American critics; and
such essays by English critics as those on *The Secret Sharer* by D. Hewitt
(*Conrad: a reassessment*) and J. Wain (*London Magazine: Conrad Symposium*).

3. Notably by F. R. Leavis, A. Kettle (*Introduction to the Novel*, Vol. II),
and D. Hewitt.

4. *Nostromo*, 465–8 – Nostromo's return to Viola's Inn – gives very poignantly this omnipresence of the Gulf.

5. It seems perverse and sentimental to attribute to anyone except Marlow
the notion that Kurtz represents a character to be admired, or his end some
sort of 'moral victory': a Marlow, moreover, recording the disorder and
fascination remembered from a state of nervous collapse. Yet a good deal of
criticism appears to suppose simply this to be Conrad's own view of the
matter.

6. *Heart of Darkness*, 100–114.

DE LA MARE, HARDY AND
EDWARD THOMAS

H. COOMBES

Georgian poetry derives unduly, that is to say with a minimum of significant modification, from early and later nineteenth-century romantic poetry. From that poetry it mostly took over the weaker characteristics such as vague emotion, inexpressive sing-song rhythms, emphasis on surface verbal music for its own sake, and the tendency to fantasy or dream without any very strong human interest. We can usefully make discriminations, but it remains generally true that the Georgians allowed themselves only a limited range of feelings and mostly stereotyped techniques. Hardy, de la Mare, and Edward Thomas (who is often associated with the Georgians though he never appeared in Edward Marsh's Georgian Books) stand out by their refusal to wear the label of a category.

Of the three poets of permanent value to be here considered, Walter de la Mare is the most readily assimilable to nineteenth-century techniques and habits of thought and feeling, but to say this is not to question the individuality of his poetic gift. And if, as is likely, the factor of 'escape' must come into our final estimate of de la Mare, we shall nevertheless be wise not to insist on 'reality' as in all conditions a fixed and all-redeeming criterion. It is indisputable that most of his poetry evades reality in various important ways. Yet precisely because of his evasion, his gifts being what they were, he created a body of exquisite minor poetry.

He was, of course, perfectly aware of the dream-like quality of his poetry: he cultivated fantasy, he aimed consciously at entrancement. But he was not wholly aware of the hazards for a poet in postulating, as he repeatedly does, a dichotomy between 'the day's travail' and 'the garden of the Lord's' in which he is enchanted by the dream that brings poetry:

> Ev'n in the shallow, busy hours of day
> Dreams their intangible enchantments weave.

Happy childhood, harsh adult world, happy recollections of child-hood, pleasure and profit in dreaming, beauty and transcendental worth of nature, the duty to love: this seems a reasonably fair account. An innate tenderness saved de la Mare from the danger Yeats saw in such a creed:

> We had fed the heart on fantasies,
> The heart's grown brutal from the fare.

But the habit did involve for him a certain narrowness of sympathetic response as well as repetition and monotony. And though his general delight in flowers, trees, insects, birds, streams is unquestionable, his apprehension of the natural world is nothing like so full or delicate as Hardy's or Edward Thomas's.

There is validity in the common view of de la Mare's poetry as 'making the actual magical and the magic actual': the issue here is one of the magic of dream and of the child's world. This does not mean that it is a poetry of the nursery, though much of it does in fact delight children. Many readers feel 'that beneath the murmur of childish voices we hear a more ancient and wiser tongue, the lan-guage of myth and fairytale, dream and symbol'.[1]

There is little need here to point to de la Mare's skill in creating atmosphere idyllic or foreboding (*Nod*, *The Tailor*, *At the Keyhole*, *Never-to-be*), or the aptness of his rhythms in various kinds of narrative and situation (*The Dwelling-Place*, *Off the Ground*, *Nicholas Nye*), or the wistful or humorous fancies (*Sam*, *The Quartette*, *Where*), or the small pathetic pieces (*The Silver Penny*, *All But Blind*, *Fare Well*); these are plain for all to see. But this habit of mind, impelling him to handle his themes in a particular way, does involve him too often in a dependence on a 'verbal magic' which is overmuch a matter of dex-terity with vowels and consonants. And in moving about his world — green shadows, cool clear water, slim hands, unfolding buds, starry tapers, steps on stairs, dark hair and shining eyes, moths at evening, dew, faint shrill cries of birds, sailors' bones, tranquil dreams, dying fires, woods, musicians — we do need to discriminate between the genuine poetry and a routine use of the properties.

Our concern as adult readers is finally with adult poetry, with those poems in which an interesting play of mind accompanies the en-chanted atmosphere and the word-music. *Old Shellover* is one of many poems, slight but real, which do not wholly rely on power to charm with mystery. The snails and the scene have their own small reality, and a touch of feeling implicit in the dialogue makes the poem just that little more than a 'pretty fancy':

> 'Come!' said Old Shellover.
> 'What?' says Creep.
> 'The horny old Gardener's fast asleep;
> The fat cock Thrush
> To his nest has gone,
> And the dew shines bright
> In the rising moon;
> Old Sallie Worm from her hole doth peep;
> Come!' said Old Shellover.
> 'Ay!' said Creep.

The Witch tells how her pack of spells and sorceries, as she slept under the churchyard wall, was plundered by the dead who thereupon assumed the shapes of wild creatures. The poem is lively with crisp action and has genuinely created atmosphere; everyday 'unromantic' terms — 'jerked it off her back', 'squats asleep' — play their part in a final effect of 'romantic' economy:

> Names may be writ; and mounds rise;
> Purporting, Here be bones:
> But empty is that churchyard
> Of all save stones.
>
> Owl and Newt and Nightjar,
> Leveret, Bat and Mole
> Haunt and call in the twilight,
> Where she slept, poor soul.

Sometimes, as in *John Mouldy*, atmosphere is subtly achieved with a minimum of supernatural story. Mould in a cellar has moved the poet to a creation lightly but convincingly sinister:

> I spied John Mouldy in his cellar,
> Deep down twenty steps of stone;
> In the dark he sat a-smiling,
>   Smiling there alone.
>
> He read no book, he snuffed no candle,
> The rats ran in, the rats ran out;
> And far and near, the drip of water
>   Went whispering about.

> The dusk was still, with dew a-falling,
> I saw the Dog Star bleak and grim,
> I saw a slim brown rat of Norway
>   Creep over him.
>
> I spied John Mouldy in his cellar,
> Deep down twenty steps of stone;
> In the dark he sat a-smiling,
>   Smiling there alone.

Here a variety of elements, of facts and things with widely dissimilar associations have been brought into unity. The subject has engaged the poet; the word-music serves imagination.

The Ghost and *The Song of the Mad Prince* are two of those poems in which the poet aims at expressing more profoundly personal emotion. Both deal with love and loss. In the first of them a dialogue between the man and the ghost, movingly within the 'wistful' range, is followed by the characteristic de la Mare 'magic':

> Silence. Still faint on the porch
> Brake the flame of the stars.

In context the self-conscious poeticality is effective enough, but then the gloom is laid on heavily, and the poem ends with 'vast Sorrow', and the ghost of the loved one has become almost an occasion for indulgence in the 'sweet cheat' of illusion. The reality of sharp personal feeling has in the end been evaded. In *The Song of the Mad Prince* the idealization is purposive and seems a quite natural movement of feeling in the totality of the poem:

> Who said, 'Peacock Pie'?
>   The old King to the sparrow:
> Who said, 'Crops are ripe'?
>   Rust to the harrow:
> Who said, 'Where sleeps she now?
>   Where rests she now her head,
> Bathed in eve's loveliness'?
>   That's what I said.
>
> Who said, 'Ay, mum's the word'?
>   Sexton to willow:
> Who said, 'Green dusk for dreams,
>   Moss for a pillow'?
> Who said, 'All Time's delight
>   Hath she for narrow bed,

153

Life's troubled bubble broken'?
That's what I said.

The mad prince is of course the poet as well as Hamlet, and in the seemingly inconsequential images he makes a comment on life which contains his feeling. The echoes of *Hamlet*, and the suggestions of colour and feasting, harvest and the passage of the seasons, death, both intensify the poignancy of lost love (stressing its universality too) and serve with their width of reference as a check to disproportionate indulgence in grief. If we feel some uneasiness at the underlining that occurs in the last but one line of the poem, it will be at least lessened if we think of the incantation of the Weird Sisters in *Macbeth*. *The Song of the Mad Prince* is perhaps the strongest poem that de la Mare wrote.

A reading of the whole of de la Mare's poetry would reveal many shortcomings: a tendency to repetition which shows that enchantments can become stale; flat emotional commonplaces in explicit terms like 'heart's vacancy' and 'anguished sigh'; portentousness and melodrama in his treatment of such actualities as (say) a prisoner in the dock; simple horror-reactions to evil; excess of self-pity and of yearning for rest and peace; clichés and poeticalities when women and beauty are the set themes; over-elaboration of the idyllic and the eerie; ponderous moralizing about time and eternity; a lack of experience to guarantee the solidity of his affirmations of the value of love and beauty; a sensuousness which is too often the effect of accumulating items from other poets. This is an alarming list. It is a measure of de la Mare's gifts that when all has been said in question of his total achievement, there remain poems of his fine enough and numerous enough to ensure him a permanent place among twentieth-century poets.

Thomas Hardy, also a prolific poet, needed in a high degree the quality we commonly designate as 'courage to live'. His writing has almost nothing of the dream about it, and in his rare evocations of childhood it is never the magic that he emphasizes. His sense of change and of bereavement was exceptionally acute; furthermore he was dogged by a view of life which could afford him no illusory comforts. And the power of these agencies in his life was the stronger because his interest in humanity and in phenomena was great and lasting. He was a humane, sensitive man who could not entertain any suggestion of a Deity other than an indifferent or a malevolent one, and who did not believe in any form of personal survival as it is usually understood; who yet had deep loves in his life and who keenly observed and seriously pondered. Out of his beliefs and the tensions generated between his beliefs and his intimate feelings sprang his poetry, first-rate and third-rate alike.

Perhaps his one escape is to be found in the pertinacity with which he held to his conception of a Vast Imbecility or a neutral Spinner of the Years or a sightless Mother presiding over a mankind endowed (or cursed) with sentience; this pertinacity led him often into heavy protests, portentous and uttered with a prosy clumsiness which, while unquestionably sincere, is too simply explicit to impress deeply:

AN ENQUIRY

A Phantasy

Circumdederunt me dolores mortis. – Psalm XVIII

> I said to It: 'We grasp not what you meant,
> (Dwelling down here, so narrowly pinched and pent)
> By crowning Death the King of the Firmament:
>   The query I admit to be
>   One of the unwonted size,
> But it is put to you sorrowingly,
>   And not in idle-wise.'

Or he was betrayed – if the phrase is appropriate to writing that was so completely deliberate – into anecdotes and episodes which reveal a perverse preoccupation with 'life's little ironies' and a prepossession with gloom: the young Parson in *The Curate's Kindness* has succeeded in persuading the Guardians of the Workhouse to annul the regulation separating man and wife, but the narrator is dismayed when he hears about it:

> 'I thought they'd be strangers aroun' me,
>   But she's to be there!
> Let me jump out o'wagon and go back and drown me
>   At Pummery or Ten-Hatches Weir.'

And it is a fixed, unalive cynicism that calls in despair for a return of human impercipience:

> Ere nescience shall be reaffirmed
>   How long, how long?

Sometimes the language corresponds in luridness or inflation to the melodrama of the subject; at other times it is merely metrical and low-pitched rhymed prose. A failure in self-criticism leads him sometimes into humourless solemnities and bathos.

Yet the bent of Hardy's mind is ultimately conditioned by a sympathy for human and animal suffering and usually even the banalities, in their context, have saving sincerities. There are, moreover, many poems (*The Sleep-Worker*, for instance) which, though we may consider their prompting idea to be unduly partial, show a steady progression of thought which is impressive.

The case that Hardy makes out for 'pessimism' in the Apology to *Late Lyrics and Earlier* (1922) cannot at any rate be dismissed on the ground of insincerity: 'What is today,' he writes, 'in allusion to the present author's pages, alleged to be "pessimism", is, in truth, only "questionings" in the exploration of reality, and is the first step towards the soul's betterment, and the body's also.' He claimed that his poems were 'a series of fugitive impressions', and not the expression of anything like a systematized view of life. This is certainly true of a limited number of the poems, but if they are taken altogether most readers will feel that there was a certain amount of self-deception in the claim.

But despite being based too often on a view of life which seems to inhibit a free responsiveness, Hardy's poems provide an abundance of people and incident and perceptions; they are the work of a man who is also a novelist. Eye and ear are delicate and vigilant: he notes 'the smooth sea-line with a metal shine', and May's 'glad green leaves . . . Delicate-filmed as new-spun silk.' In *Old Furniture*, where he thinks with characteristic affection of the hands that have owned and handled the 'relics of householdry', he imagines a finger setting the hands of the clock right,

> With tentative touches that lift and linger
> In the wont of a moth on a summer night.

Moments of everyday life are seen and presented with a quite individual intimacy:

> Icicles tag the church-aisle leads,
> The flag-rope gibbers hoarse,
> The home-bound foot-folk wrap their snow-flaked heads.

This intimate knowledge of village and small town life, rendered as it is with a deep regard for its value simply as life, is one of the 'positives' in Hardy's poetry. He does not of course attempt, as he does in some of the novels, any big or sustained account of the rural civilization which he saw changing and decaying. But there is enough of church and churchyard and music gallery, ballroom and pub, lovers' walks, sea-port, watering-place, tea under the trees, fields and woods and barns, and it is given in such a way as to impress itself on us as a profound element in Hardy's personal history. He appreciates the deftness of the turnip-hoer as he does the 'junketings, maypoles, and flings'; cider-makers and field-women and fiddlers catch his interest. He can be humorous on the 'ruined maid' (see the poem of that name) from the country. When William Dewy, in *Friends Beyond*, is recalled from the past and made to say 'Ye mid burn the old bass-viol that I set such value by', an ancient way of life is woven into the poet's feeling and habit of thought. When Beeny Cliff, Yell'ham Wood, Mellstock Churchyard, and so on come into Hardy's poetry it is normally with a strong personal note: places are important to him, his feeling for them is one of his buttresses against the gloom of his general view of life and the universe.

The middle range of Hardy's poetry – lying between, on the one hand, patriotic jingles and banal-darksome tales and simplified love-idylls and heavy explicit statements of his 'philosophy', and on the other the small number of his wonderful best poems – displays in general the Hardy stoicism and truthfulness in the face of uncomforting experience. *Afterwards*, speculating on what people will say about him after his death, makes the quietest of claims for the gifts of loving observation and kindness to living things, at the same time envisaging with detachment his 'bell of quittance'; the poem is full of particular perceptions played off beautifully against the idea of death. In *An Ancient to Ancients*, tone and movement are more formal, but there remains a distinctive pathos in his account of the changes of fashion in dancing, opera, painting, poetry. *His Visitor* pictures the ghost who has 'come across from Mellstock while the moon wastes weaker' to revisit her home; disappointed by the changes she sees, she leaves 'to make again for Mellstock to return here never And rejoin the roomy silence . . .': the tone is low-pitched and the rhythms (though regular) unemphatic, and the feeling comes from the quiet manner of conveying the sense of the importance to the ghost of the domesticities whose changes now trouble her. The feeling, it should be said, is comparatively unsubtle, as it is in *Beeny Cliff, March 1870–March 1913* and in *Five Students*, two other moving 'middle-range' poems with a poignant significance for the writer.

What justifies the use of 'wonderful' near the beginning of the previous paragraph is the extraordinary power and originality with which Hardy records in his best poems a tragic sense derived from intense personal experience. In these poems (most of which were written late in life and are the subject of Henry Gifford's chapter on p. 166) we have the stoicism which has not involved any evasion of the felt multiplicity and force of life. There is none of the simplifying division into ideal and actual which Hardy was prone to fall into, no over-spiritualization of women. The actual in these poems is imbued by the fineness of Hardy's spirit with a profound significance. Most, though not all, concern a man–woman relationship. All are an outcome of intensely pondered experience. There is simultaneously a vivid evocation of the past and a vivid rendering of the feeling of the present moment.

The grey bleakness of loss is conveyed as strongly in *Neutral Tones*, written in his twenties, as in *The Voice*, written in his seventies, though the earlier poem has a note of bitterness not present in the later one. Both poems make wonderful use of the natural scene: in the first, 'the pond edged with greyish leaves', and in the second

> the breeze, in its listlessness,
> Travelling across the wet mead to me here

are powerful agents of feeling.

The Self-Unseeing, in the space of twelve short lines, gives the scene now before the poet, with recollection of the fiddler and the dance and the woman, and realization of their failure to live that past moment to the full. The bareness of

> Here was the former door
> Where the dead feet walked in

combines with the momentary strong glowing excitement of

> Blessings emblazoned that day

to produce a rich economy. In contrast, though equally poignant, is *A Broken Appointment*: nothing of the scene is given except a suggestion of the clock striking the hour which should have brought her, and the poem rests upon the steady painful recognition of the significance of her non-appearance and the quiet rebuke which the poet offers with such delicacy:

> ... But, unto the store
> Of human deeds divine in all but name,
> Was it not worth a little hour or more
> To add yet this: Once you, a woman, came
> To soothe a time-worn man; even though it be
> You love not me?

In *After a Journey* the poet is at the edge of the sea, at night, communing with the 'ghost' of the woman he had been there with forty years before. The long deliberate lines suggest exact contemplation in memory, and the loved memory of the dead woman is simultaneously present with the sense of irretrievable loss. The remembered mist-bow above the waterfall and the present voice of the cave below are elements of the natural scene which are at the same time images charged with particular emotions. Unbeglamoured truthfulness conveys the profound loyalty of the poet, and as dawn comes the 'ghost' is as nothing to the creatures, who carry on life as if she had never been: 'The waked birds preen and the seals flop lazily.' In a superb analysis of the poem F. R. Leavis has shown how the apparently awkward phrases are actually felicities aiding in the revelation of a rare integrity: 'The real focus for me,' he shows Hardy as saying, 'the focus of my affirmation, is the remembered realest thing, though to remember vividly is at the same time, inescapably, to embrace the utterness of loss.'[2]

During Wind and Rain is hardly less fine and moving, though less intensely personal, than *After a Journey*. Here again the past is vivid in consciousness. In each of four stanzas a warmly recalled moment or scene is brought sharply up against a refrain-like line whose burden is 'the years', and this is followed by a last line which gives with great force and immediacy a detail of the wild autumn day now before the poet. The deliberation of the stressing in the final line of the poem,

Down their carved names the rain-drop ploughs,

clinches, with precisely that implication of mortality, the poet's confrontation of reality in the beauty and vividness of art.

The epic-drama, *The Dynasts* (1903–8), has been claimed by some admirers to be Hardy's greatest work. But while it is impressive by its manifestation of the peculiar strength and quality of its author's character, it seems in its magnitude to be more a matter of determined accumulation for preconceived ends than of impulsion from Hardy's deepest emotional being.

It is one of the triumphs of Edward Thomas that with the character and temperament he possessed he could move quite away from the kind of shadowiness that marks de la Mare's poetry, and also out of the landscape that Hardy too often colours with his own greyness of spirit, into an open and fresh air. When we call him a poet of minute particularity and fidelity we have in mind both phenomena and mood. His poetic output, compared with that of Hardy and de la Mare, is small, but a high proportion of it bears his characteristic excellences. The fact that he did not start writing poetry until he was thirty-five accounts in part for a degree of self-awareness and self-criticism that served him well. He knew from the start that there were certain things he wished to avoid in his poetry, and it was because he was an original poet with the original poet's disturbing power that editors to whom he submitted poems were almost unanimously discouraging.

Reviewing Robert Frost's *North of Boston* in 1914 Thomas wrote: 'These poems are revolutionary because they lack the exaggeration of rhetoric.' This is a way of saying that he welcomed a departure from at least some of the aspects of nineteenth-century poetry. His own poems were alleged, by friends during his lifetime and by many critics after his death, to lack 'form'. He was felt to be disturbingly different from the typical Georgian poets (several of whom he was friendly with). His refusal to take the influential Edward Garnett's advice to 'chisel' *Lob* is characteristic of his steady perseverance in the way he wanted to go. We can now see Edward Thomas as a poet of great distinction, English in a profound sense, a voice that is contemporary in the middle of the twentieth century.

It is only on the superficial ground of broad similarity of subject-matter that Edward Thomas can be assimilated to the Georgians. Nature and the countryside, though intensely and exquisitely appreciated for their own sake, are mainly in his poetry an occasion for exploring and presenting his mood and character and a whole mode of experiencing; while his best love poems are quite personal. The presentment is quiet, delicate, and strong, and the quality of the man profoundly interesting.

He had the gift of putting character, mood, attitude to life, into a seemingly small situation, into a moment's perceiving. And the records he unassumingly offers will enhance the more our own power of experiencing because he is in close and vitalizing touch with the natural world. He can give us enlightenment on sincerity and beauty.

This poem is entitled *A Tale*:

> There once the walls
> Of the ruined cottage stood.
> The periwinkle crawls
> With flowers in its hair into the wood.
>
> In flowerless hours
> Never will the bank fail
> With everlasting flowers
> On fragments of blue plates, to tell the tale.

A small poem, as serious though not as powerful as Wordsworth's *A Slumber Did My Spirit Seal*. The cottage and scene are actual and now; but what they tell is not simply the tale of themselves but *the* tale of man's life, of nature and change, of disappearance and also of relics that are emblems of endeavour. Thomas perceives a depth in the seen. In another small poem, *The Hollow Wood*, a goldfinch flits and feeds on thistle-tops at the edge of a wood, while other birds pass to and fro inside the wood: we can abstract an idea-feeling if we wish from the juxtaposition in the poem of the known and bright with the strange and dark. But what is essentially communicated is a way of seeing and feeling that has depth and innerness while still remaining fresh and physical.

'Forest' or 'wood' is a recurring symbol in Edward Thomas, and its introduction is invariably a spontaneous and unforced item of the experience he is describing. With its various significances – obscure regions of human experience not wholly susceptible to rational explanation, or the gulf 'where nothing is But what is not', or thoughts of death – it is connected in Thomas's poetry with his well-known melancholy. But he does not simplify and narrow them down; his poetic analysis of his feeling is finer than (say) the typical Victorian or Georgian piece in being immeasurably more than an expression of regret or sorrow or apprehensiveness. There are no inert or merely weary poems in Thomas. He never fails in sharp sensuous perceiving and rarely in a precision of phrasing which retains a hauntingly natural manner.

In *The Gypsy* he goes home at night after the Christmas fair and market, carrying with him the image of what he has seen and heard:

> ... Not even the kneeling ox had eyes like the Romany.
> That night he peopled for me the hollow wooded land,
> More dark and wild than stormiest heavens, that I searched and
>   scanned
> Like a ghost new-arrived. The gradations of the dark
> Were like an underworld of death, but for the spark
> In the Gypsy boy's black eyes as he played and stamped his tune,
> 'Over the hills and far away', and a crescent moon.

The feeling of a dark unknown immensity is very powerful, but it is not all-conquering: against the blackness and the words of the tune (suggesting an even farther recession) there are the spark, the strength of stamping, the new moon. Even in the most stark among the poems, *Rain* for instance –

> Rain, midnight rain, nothing but the wild rain
> On this bleak hut, and solitude, and me
> Remembering again that I shall die ...

– and in the poems, such as *Lights Out*, where he seems near to surrender, there is no defeat and no flaccidity. A sensitiveness of movement and an exactness of statement show the poet to be in full and alert control.

In many of the poems it is a subtle intermingling of diverse sense-impressions and delicate observations that is largely effective in conveying a feeling of elusive experience which the poet has nevertheless firmly caught. *Ambition* has an extraordinary interplay of images of energetic life with a sense of silence and emptiness. *The Brook* has child paddling and man seated, butterfly on stone, silent bird and silent man, a horse galloping and a horse at rest. The dualities in Thomas's poetry – clear and misty, near and far, sound and silence, present and past, movement and stillness, thought and sensation, and so on – are never posited by the poet. We may or may not note them consciously as we read, but they have their effect in a seemingly inevitable whole.

What is in fact subtly organized poetry sounds often like the poet speaking easily but with beautiful precision, revealing an inner life by a remarkably sensitive account of the outer world. The second half of *March* follows on a vivid rendering of a bitterly cold day of hail and wind, with the sun now near the end of the day filling earth and heaven with a great light, but no warmth:

> ... What did the thrushes know? Rain, snow, sleet, hail,
> Had kept them quiet as the primroses.
> They had but an hour to sing. On boughs they sang,
> On gates, on ground; they sang while they changed perches
> And while they fought, if they remembered to fight;
> So earnest were they to pack into that hour
> Their unwilling hoard of song before the moon
> Grew brighter than the clouds. Then 'twas no time
> For singing merely. So they could keep off silence
> And night, they cared not what they sang or screamed;
> Whether 'twas hoarse or sweet or fierce or soft;
> And to me all was sweet: they could do no wrong.
> Something they knew – I also, while they sang
> And after. Not till night had half its stars
> And never a cloud, was I aware of silence
> Stained with all that hour's songs, a silence
> Saying that Spring returns, perhaps to-morrow.

To appreciate this in all its rich significance, it would of course be necessary to see it with the first half of the poem. But the extract may show how the feelings and perceptions, the thankfulness that overcomes the distress of the cold, the exquisite way the silence comes into his consciousness, the sense that the Spring of the poem is happiness (without ceasing to be Spring), are given – to use Thomas's words about Frost – 'through fidelity to the postures which the voice assumes in the most expressive intimate speech'.

His language is quite free from stale poeticalities. It frequently has, it is true, words common in 'romantic' poetry of nature and love and disillusion – sweet, solitary, once, strange, hidden, vainly, happy – but they are never simply exploited for their stock emotional content; they are *used* as an essential item, modifying and modified by other items. He makes good use also, with a sort of homely vividness, of phrases which were deemed unpoetical by many of his contemporary readers: his thrushes *pack* into an hour their 'unwilling *hoard* of song'. It is ultimately his complete lack of condescension, his openness to impressions, which give his language (like his rhythms) a certain easy breadth; the breadth contributes to a total complexity born of a rare union of fastidiousness and democratic sympathy, including humour:

> Women he liked, did shovel-bearded Bob,
> Old Farmer Hayward of the Heath, but he
> Loved horses. He himself was like a cob,
> And leather-coloured. Also he loved a tree.

A certain robustness-with-shrewdness, like that which he portrays with such a light touch in Old Jack (to use one of Lob's several folknames), is an ingredient of his own character:

> He is English as this gate, these flowers, this mire.
> And when at eight years old Lob-lie-by-the-fire
> Came in my books, this was the man I saw.
> He has been in England as long as dove and daw . . .

Old Man, The Glory, The Other, are among the finest of many poems that present a self-questioning which does not preclude a wealth of outgoing feeling, and a reaching for fulfilment which we feel cannot for him be dependent upon any possible creed or any group-support. The nature of the statement and the self-searching that we get in the following superb lines from *The Glory* are quite different from Hardy's expressions of solid views and attitudes:

> The glory of the beauty of the morning –
> The cuckoo crying over the untouched dew;
> The blackbird that has found it, and the dove
> That tempts me on to something sweeter than love . . .
>
> Or must I be content with discontent
> As larks and swallows are perhaps with wings?
> And shall I ask at the day's end once more
> What beauty is, and what I can have meant
> By happiness? And shall I let all go,
> Glad, weary, or both? Or shall I perhaps know
> That I was happy oft and oft before,
> Awhile forgetting how I am fast pent,
> How dreary-swift, with naught to travel to,
> Is Time? I cannot bite the day to the core.

Thomas was sharply aware not only of the difficulty of fulfilment in human relationship but also of the impact of new knowledge and of the destructive effects of certain new attitudes on many of the things he cared for.

Prufrock appeared in the year Edward Thomas died. But though the externals of Mr Eliot's urban world are probably the more relevant now to the majority of readers (and poets), those of Edward Thomas's are in some important aspects still with us and must continue to be so. Furthermore the partial supersession of the rural civilization which he himself saw declining, does not affect his status as a poet, for fundamentally he deals with permanent things in human nature. Although he does not offer either a fullness like that of Keats's *Autumn* or the kind of dramatic force and concentration that Hopkins won from his self-division, he has his own delicate richness and his own explored stresses. If he had lived longer he might have widened his range, perhaps making discoveries that would have enabled him to present more of himself and of life. As it is he remains a remarkable original poet.

NOTES

1. William Walsh, in *The Use of Imagination* (London, 1959).
2. In *Scrutiny*, XIX, No. 2.

HARDY IN HIS LATER POEMS

HENRY GIFFORD

There is no parallel that springs to mind for Hardy's late flowering. He had entered his seventies when he wrote the poems for which he is most admired. Hardy was an assiduous reviser; his reading of life remained constant, and it is not easy to tell whether most of the undated poems are early or late. He went his own way from the beginning, safe, because so long unpublished, from the ill effects of purblind criticism or from a disabling sense of responsibility to the public.

Hardy's major undertaking after he gave up novel-writing was *The Dynasts* (1903–10), his 'epic-drama' on the Napoleonic Wars. This subject had always stirred his imagination. *The Trumpet-Major* (1880), though situated on the margin of these events, is the more convincing for its local immediacy. It tells how the rumour of history reached Wessex. The *Victory*, a 'great silent ship, with her population of blue-jackets, marines, officers, captain, and the admiral who was not to return alive', passes by Portland Bill 'like a phantom'. In its final words the novel evokes – far away – 'one of the bloody battle-fields of Spain'. *The Dynasts* opens with 'a ridge in Wessex', where passengers on a stage-coach are talking about the war, and it visits many battle-fields. In a 'Fore scene' Hardy presents 'the Overworld', populated with a cast of 'impersonated abstractions, or Intelligences, called Spirits', time-saddened refugees from *Prometheus Unbound*. Hardy's perspective is vast: 'the peoples, distressed by events which they did not cause, are seen writhing, crawling, heaving and vibrating in their various cities and nationalities'. He retains his eye for the vivid particular; but this is a laborious work, though quickened by the prose passages that set the scenes, in contrast to much of its lumbering blank verse. Hardy had read *War and Peace*, but in a poor translation; and when writing *The Dynasts* he never enjoyed the creative freedom that Tolstoy had in a form wholly responsive to the artist's hand.

In his lyric poetry, however, such freedom was generally the rule. Although the critics were slow to acknowledge it, Hardy's technical resource is unflagging. *Time's Laughingstocks* (1909), though not as impressive as the two books that followed, *Satires of Circumstance* (1914) and *Moments of Vision* (1917), is the work of a considerable craftsman. It contains an entirely successful modern ballad, *A Trampwoman's Tragedy*; *Reminiscences of a Dancing Man*, a spirited ballad in the other sense of a song for music; *Julie-Jane*, a Wessex country song –

> Sing; how 'a would sing!
> How 'a would raise the tune
> When we rode in the waggon from harvesting
> By the light o' the moon!
>
> Dance; how 'a would dance!
> If a fiddlestring did but sound
> She would hold out her coats, give a slanting glance,
> And go round and round ...

– *The Dead Quire*, a deftly moving verse-tale in which

> the Quick pursue the Dead
> By crystal Froom that crinkles there;

and such varied notations as *The Pine Planters* (*Marty South's Reverie*), *Misconception*, which reads almost like a secular adaptation of George Herbert, or the finely cadenced *Shut Out That Moon*:

> Step not forth on the dew-dashed lawn
> To view the Lady's Chair,
> Immense Orion's glittering form,
> The Less and Greater Bear ...

In these poems the movement is sure, the situation firmly seized, and Hardy's verbal inventiveness never uncouth ('crystal Froom that *crinkles* there'). Most of his lyrics at this time are short of greatness, apart (perhaps) from *A Trampwoman's Tragedy*. But who among English-speaking poets then displayed such versatility, or tempered it so well? Kipling's ear, as Eliot has shown, is accomplished, yet he lacks the subtle responsiveness of Hardy; Yeats had still to arrive at his mature work foreshadowed in *Responsibilities* (1914).

The assurance of this poetry is grounded upon the tradition of rural song alive in Hardy's youth. His provincialism was a great strength when he used it confidently. He faltered only when describing scenes from middle-class life with an eye on literary London. This becomes evident in *A Conversation at Dawn* from *Satires of Circumstance*. Its scene of genuine misery is enacted in a hotel bedroom at a seaside resort, and the dialogue shows uncertainty of touch from the beginning:

> 'Then what has kept, O reticent one,
>   Those lids unlatched –
> Anything promised I've not yet done?'

It can be crassly eccentric:

> ' – So you've lost a sprucer spouse than I?'

or

> 'I own this last is enough to freeze
>   The warmest wight'.

These artificialities drop away at the bleak climax:

> 'And you became as his wife?' – 'I did.' –
> He stood as stiff as a caryatid,
>   And said, 'Indeed! . . .
> No matter. You're mine, whatever you've hid!'

It is beside the point that a caryatid should be feminine: Hardy achieves with it the effect he needs, of a living person turned to stone. The desolation in such tales is absolute:

> She answered not, lying listlessly
> With her dark dry eyes on the coppery sea,
>   That now and then
> Flung its lazy flounce at the neighbouring quay.

Hardy's dramatic awareness always seizes on 'the body's life' – 'her dark dry eyes'. In another poem from this book, *The Woman in the Rye*, he matches the traditional ballad for intensity:

> 'Why do you stand in the dripping rye,
> Cold-lipped, unconscious, wet to the knee,
> When there are firesides near?' said I.
> 'I told him I wished him dead,' said she.

The sensibility that rendered so well the misery of Tess at Flintcomb-Ash is here marvellously alive to the destitution in grief. And the numbness of her feeling is confirmed by the last line, with its weary repetition 'I told him I wished him' and the dull thud of ' "dead", said she.'

In April 1912 Hardy wrote one of his most eloquent public poems, *The Convergence of the Twain*, on the loss of the *Titanic*. With grave and elaborate irony it records how the liner met a predestined 'sinister mate', the iceberg. Hardy cannot resist using his machinery of 'The Immanent Will that stirs and urges everything', familiar from *The Dynasts* and certain speculative poems. It is made acceptable in this lyric by the relentless movement of the verse:

I

In a solitude of the sea
Deep from human vanity,
And the Pride of Life that planned her, stilly couches she.

II

Steel chambers, late the pyres
Of her salamandrine fires,
Cold currents thrid, and turn to rhythmic tidal lyres.

III

Over the mirrors meant
To glass the opulent
The sea-worm crawls – grotesque, slimed, dumb, indifferent.

IV

Jewels in joy designed
To ravish the sensuous mind
Lie lightless, all their sparkles bleared and black and blind.

V

Dim moon-eyed fishes near
Gaze at the gilded gear
And query: 'What does this vaingloriousness down here?' ...

The next five stanzas describe the growth, parallel to the ship's, of the iceberg 'in shadowy silent distance': the phrase seems to hint that this 'Shape of Ice' is her shadow. The 'twin halves' of the 'one august event' are brought closer 'by paths coincident',

XI

Till the Spinner of the Years
Said 'Now!' And each one hears,
And consummation comes, and jars two hemispheres.

The visionary strangeness of the poem is announced by its opening phrases, slightly unexpected: not in '*the* solitude of the sea,' but '*a* solitude', not '*far* from human vanity', but '*deep*' from it, 'stilly couches she', like some marine creature. One aspect of the scene might have been foretold: Hardy delighted in bizarre contrast, and here it flourishes even to rankness:

> Over the mirrors meant
> To glass the opulent
> The sea-worm crawls – grotesque, slimed, dumb, indifferent.

The adjectives mass inertly. Those for the jewels that 'Lie lightless, all their sparkles bleared and black and blind', cluster like barnacles. But the baroque rendering recalls Milton's description of the flood which 'overwhelm'd' and 'with all their pomp/Deep under water roll'd' the dwellings of thoughtless mankind:

> and in their Palaces
> Where luxury late reign'd, Sea-monsters whelp'd
> And stabl'd ...

There is a Miltonic grandeur in the conception of the poem which deplores 'the Pride of Life' and 'this vaingloriousness', the fate of which had been invisible to 'mortal eye'. Hardy invoked Aeschylus extravagantly at the finish of *Tess*. This poem is more truly imbued with the spirit of Greek tragedy. It stands in contrast to the one that precedes, *Channel Firing*. There the dead in their tombs are shaken by the guns into supposing that Judgement-day has arrived:

> Till God called 'No;
> It's gunnery practice out at sea.' ...

He tells them about the perversity of the nations:

> 'Mad as hatters
> They do no more for Christés sake
> Than you who are helpless in such matters.'

A precedent for this casual, even slangy talk exists in medieval morality plays ('for Christés sake' may point to affiliation). But the calculated changes of tone are disconcerting, as when Parson Thirdly's expression of regret that he had not 'stuck to pipes and beer' is followed by the solemnly prophetic lines:

> Again the guns disturbed the hour,
> Roaring their readiness to avenge,
> As far inland as Stourton Tower,
> And Camelot, and starlit Stonehenge.

Hardy's verse, until the overwhelming shock of his wife's death in November 1912, had nearly always maintained the stance of the onlooker, ironic, pitying or both. There are rare occasions when he speaks out for himself, as in *I Look Into My Glass* at the end of *Wessex Poems*. In the novels he had lived through imaginary situations that were deeply painful – the miseries, for example, of Tess and Jude. Now sudden bereavement compelled him to face some bitter truths in his own life. Latterly there had been no communication between Emma and himself, but after her death he chanced on two things she had written. These were her resentful diaries of twenty years, which he destroyed, and a little volume entitled *Some Recollections*, completed in January 1911. It described her happy childhood and their first rapturous meeting on the coast of North Cornwall. The innocent joy of these memoirs made real to him the young woman of that time and their romance which had been reflected in *A Pair of Blue Eyes* (1873). Its setting, even after twenty years, could still move him to write in a new Preface to the novel:

The place is pre-eminently (for one person at least) the region of dream and mystery. The ghostly birds, the pall-like sea, the frothy wind, the eternal soliloquy of the waters, the bloom of dark purple cast, that seems to exhale from the shoreward precipices, in themselves lend to the scene an atmosphere like the twilight of a night vision.

It returned to him from his wife's impressions noted so recently:

... the wild Atlantic ocean rolling in with its magnificent waves and spray, its white gulls and black choughs and grey puffins, its cliffs and rocks and gorgeous sunsettings sparkling redness in a track widening from the horizon to the shore.

With childish vanity Emma had visualized herself in their lost youth (they were already thirty then) and he was willing to be led by her.

A more attentive husband might not have been so unprepared for her death as Hardy was. Now, after the initial numbness and forlorn sense of guilt, Emma appeared to be calling to him from the re-opened past. His *Poems of 1912–13* were published with Dido's words as their epigraph, *Veteris vestigia flammae*, 'the signs of an old flame'.

This flame burns again, more vividly even than it may have done in the 1870s; but Hardy must have remembered that the injured shade of Dido turned away from Aeneas in the underworld. His affirmation in these poems triumphs over such a dread possibility.

The Going, which opens the sequence, is one of three poems dated December 1912. The unexpectedness of it all staggers him: he

> Saw morning harden upon the wall,
>   Unmoved, unknowing
>   That your great going
> Had place that moment, and altered all.

Why did Emma 'give no hint'? Robert Gittings has protested that her condition should have been plain enough without any hints, and maintains that unbearable remorse drove Hardy into self-deception. The final stanza communicates a 'depth of guilt' which his 'catalogue of relatively small omissions of sympathy and understanding hardly seems to justify':[1]

> Well, well! All's past amend,
>   Unchangeable. It must go.
> I seem but a dead man held on end
> To sink down soon . . . O you could not know
>   That such swift fleeing
>   No soul foreseeing –
> Not even I – would undo me so!

The question arises: are these poems flawed by Hardy's evasion (if that it was) of the truth? His biographer will be concerned with the event itself and the total evidence – provided not only by the poems – of its effect upon Hardy. Our attention must be limited to the poetry, as the sufficient record of an exploration which sought to harmonize his discordant and lacerated feelings in the impersonality of art. The *Poems of 1912–13* were called by him an 'expiation'. They tell of a recovered intimacy which restores the 'dead man' to his youth and the 'voiceless ghost' to hers, 'all aglow' as she was in the days before his present frailty and her dissolution. Hardy had never before written a cycle of poems like these, forming a 'book' in the manner of Yeats's collection *The Tower*. Such ramifying sequences are for modern poets the equivalent of a major form – if not the only feasible one, at any rate the most successful. Not all the poems he wrote about Emma at that time, but the best of them, were given a place in it.

Hardy's appeal to his wife as she lay dying had been 'Em, Em, don't you know me?' The first seven poems are centred on the fact of her not knowing or caring (these words often recur together). In *Your Last Drive* he confesses that he would never have read what her face had to tell him:

> 'I go hence soon to my resting-place;
>
> You may miss me then. But I shall not know
> How many times you may visit me there,
> Or what your thoughts are, or if you go
> There never at all. And I shall not care.'

The silence that began when 'latterly, we did not speak', as he admits in *The Going*, is now irremediable. 'Dear ghost,' he addresses her – but the term as yet allows no possibility of a ghostly response: he concludes drearily, 'You are past love, praise, indifference, blame.' Hardy was unusually sensitive to touch, and in the fourth poem, *Rain on a Grave*, it is by this tactile awareness that he re-animates her image:

> Clouds spout upon her
>   Their waters amain
>   In ruthless disdain, –
> Her who but lately
>   Had shivered with pain
> As at touch of dishonour
> If there had lit on her
> So coldly, so straightly
>   Such arrows of rain:
>
> One who to shelter
>   Her delicate head
> Would quicken and quicken
>   Each tentative tread
> If drops chanced to pelt her
>   That summertime spills
>   In dust-paven rills
> When thunder-clouds thicken
>   And birds close their bills.

The momentum of 'quicken and quicken' is also that of his memory surprised, the 'old flame' renewing itself from the ashes, so that in the next poem he may surmise for her an escape from insentience:

> Yet her shade, maybe,
> Will creep underground
> Till it catch the sound
> Of that western sea
> As it swells and sobs
> Where she once domiciled,
> And joy in its throbs
> With the heart of a child.

This too is a 'tentative tread', for throughout the sequence Hardy does not lose his sense of the literal and the tangible. The poem in question, *I Found Her Out There*, has a markedly romantic setting which, as Robert Gittings and Evelyn Hardy have pointed out, is coloured by the passage quoted above from *Some Recollections*:

> I found her out there
> On a slope few see,
> That falls westwardly
> To the salt-edged air,
> Where the ocean breaks
> On the purple strand,
> And the hurricane shakes
> The solid land.

'Salt-edged air' is tingling to the senses; the 'solid land' as sobering as the waggonette and the 'sturdy pony' in *At Castle Boterel*. When he suggests that Emma's 'shade . . . will creep underground' to the scenes of her youth, it is no sentimental fancy. In her posthumous memoirs she had done this, 'with the heart of a child'.

Already, in the third December poem, *The Voice*, he had brought her near to him, and then doubted:

> Woman much missed, how you call to me, call to me,
> Saying that now you are not as you were
> When you had changed from the one who was all to me,
> But as at first, when our day was fair.

'Can it be you that I hear?' he asks, and for a moment he can visualize her 'in the original air-blue gown'. But 'air-blue' (replacing what he had first written, '*hat and* gown') could prefigure a melting into the elements, and the certainty of the start now wavers:

> Or is it only the breeze, in its listlessness
> Travelling across the wet mead to me here,
> You being ever dissolved to wan wistlessness,
> Heard no more again far or near?

> Thus I; faltering forward,
>   Leaves around me falling,
> Wind oozing thin through the thorn from norward,
>   And the woman calling.

Leavis preferred the earlier coinage, 'existlessness', for 'wan wistless-ness'; but it is her *unknowingness* that has pained Hardy, and 'wan' gives the keynote for the final tottering stanza. The wind is 'oozing thin through the thorn', like his own difficult belief – suddenly re-affirmed in the decisive phrase:

> And the woman calling.

By March 1913 Hardy had arrived in Cornwall, and could say in *After a Journey*, which triumphs over the hesitancies of *A Voice*:

> Yes: I have re-entered your olden haunts at last ...

It begins with his former sense of desolation:

> Hereto I come to view a voiceless ghost;
>   Whither, O whither will its whim now draw me?
> Up the cliff, down, till I'm lonely, lost,
>   And the unseen waters' ejaculations awe me ...

She, 'the thin ghost that I now fraily follow', has become 'voiceless', and is momentarily reduced to an object – '*its* whim'. Encountering the actual scene of *Some Recollections* was bound to challenge their veracity. But then her presence becomes overpoweringly real, and he calls out:

> Where you will next be, there's no knowing,
>   Facing round about me everywhere,
>   With your nut-coloured hair,
> And gray eyes, and rose-flush coming and going.

And he is able to ask:

> What have you now found to say of our past –
>   Scanned across the dark space wherein I have lacked you?

Regret that 'Things were not lastly as firstly well' can now be over-arched by joy – the certainty of

> I see what you are doing: you are leading me on
>   To the spots we knew when we haunted here together ...

An earlier poem, *The Haunter*, represents Emma as the unseen companion whose love can still 'give no hint':

> How shall I let him know
> That whither his fancy sets him wandering
> I, too, alertly go?

Its concern is to comfort Hardy:

> Tell him a faithful one is doing
> All that love can do
> Still that his path may be worth pursuing,
> And to bring peace thereto.

After a Journey assumes, as *The Haunter* had, her listening; but since she leads him to their familiar haunts, and can hear his plea –

> Trust me, I mind not, though Life lours,
> The bringing me here; nay, bring me here again!

– mutuality has been restored: he can claim

> I am just the same as when
> Our days were a joy, and our paths through flowers.

The paths had been shared. Hardy refers to 'the spots we knew when we haunted here together', and the double sense of haunting, which can refer to an ordinary visitor or a supernatural visitant, is crucial. Emma haunts him as a 'thin ghost', which, because of the *Recollections*, takes on a vivid embodiment; and Hardy, haunting the familiar scene, – 'a dead man held on end/To sink down soon' – has almost become ghostly himself.

At Castle Boterel is the central poem of five in the next group, exploring the validity of transient happiness in a world which, as Hardy had so often stated, does not reckon with human sentiments. *A Death-Day Recalled* mourns the disregard by the places dear to Emma of their 'former friend'; and *Beeny Cliff* declares, with a Swinburnian coloratura ('O the opal and the sapphire of that wandering western sea'), that while the glory of the elements is unchanged the love between the two has no part in the scene: joy that had once been is removed for ever:

> What if still in chasmal beauty looms that wild weird western shore,
> The woman now is – elsewhere – whom the ambling pony bore,
> And nor knows nor cares for Beeny, and will laugh there nevermore.

But this reversal is not the end. *At Castle Boterel* marks the culmination of Hardy's thought in the series. He holds no colloquy with
his dead wife (nor had he in the two previous poems). Yet here he
manages to encompass the whole experience of these months and to
resolve his difficulty. He achieves it by scrutinizing one particular
moment, which he relates not only to his own past and that of the
race, but also to geological time. (The immensity of this had been
revealed in *A Pair of Blue Eyes* to Knight, hanging on the cliff face,
by the stony stare of a fossil.) Hardy presents with a delicate exactitude
his moment of vision, and then, as the poem continues, the sequence
of his perceptions:

> As I drive to the junction of lane and highway,
>   And the drizzle bedrenches the waggonette,
> I look behind at the fading byway,
>   And see on its slope, now glistening wet,
>   Distinctly yet
>
> Myself and a girlish form benighted
>   In dry March weather. We climb the road
> Beside a chaise. We had just alighted
>   To ease the sturdy pony's load
>   When he sighed and slowed.

The break between these stanzas prepares for the displacement of
normal time. This is helped by the aural link between 'I drive', with
the alliteration to follow of 'drizzle bedrenches', and 'dry March
weather'. The actual scene has yielded to one so irresistibly there that
he says in the present tense: 'We climb the road'. But his sense of
fact restores the distance: 'We had just alighted ...' The elaborate
play of tenses throughout the poem helps to establish the certitude
at which it arrives. So precise is Hardy's notation of temporal modes –
with the contrast between 'transitory' (though not less real) and
'Earth's long order', between his own helplessness to stay with the
moment, and his sense of its imperishability – that the affirmation
must be respected:

> It filled but a minute. But was there ever
>   A time of such quality, since or before,
> In that hill's story? To one mind never ...

And he feels emboldened to claim of the 'primaeval rocks' that

> What they record in colour and cast
>   Is – that we two passed.
>
> And to me, though Time's unflinching rigour,
>   In mindless rote, has ruled from sight
> The substance now, one phantom figure
>   Remains on the slope ...

The waggonette bears him away from that vision: 'I look and see it there, shrinking, shrinking.' The honesty which returns Hardy to his sole self, which admits too that he alone can vouch for the conviction that possessed him, makes this a truth by which he can live.

In the last poem of his original eighteen, *The Phantom Horsewoman*, Hardy pictures himself, 'a man I know', as 'he comes and stands/In a careworn craze', to contemplate the 'phantom of his own figuring', the vision he carries everywhere:

> A ghost-girl-rider. And though, toil-tried,
>   He withers daily,
>   Time touches her not,
> But she still rides gaily
>   In his rapt thought
>   On that shagged and shaly
>   Atlantic spot,
> And as when first eyed
> Draws rein and sings to the swing of the tide.

Thus he returns to the image of his first poem, *The Going*, when Emma,

>   reining nigh me,
>   Would muse and eye me,
> While Life unrolled us its very best.

The distinction of these poems – unequalled in the five hundred that were to follow – is twofold: it lies in their close relationship and cumulative force, and in the aptness of metre and diction. As the later volumes continue to show, he was almost invariably the skilled practitioner (consider only *He Never Expected Much*, written for his eighty-sixth birthday). He liked – perhaps because of his critics' obtuseness – to parade this a little. Thus, the very first of his *Wessex Poems*, is designated *The Temporary the All* (Sapphics); *On Sturminster Footbridge*, in *Moments of Vision*, similarly has *Onomatopoeic* in brackets. *The Later Life* boasted that many schemes of classical metres would be found among his papers. Wordsworth complained that the diction of Gray was 'curiously elaborate'; and Hardy wanted the language of 'passion and sentiment' to have the simplicity of prose, whereas ' "poetic diction" (of the real kind) is proper, and even necessary', in poems of a fanciful nature. *The Pedigree* (again from *Moments of Vision*) illustrates what might sometimes pass with him for 'poetic diction (of the real kind)':

> The first of them, the primest fuglemen of my line,
> Being fogged in far antiqueness past surmise and reason's reach.

This is too heavily brocaded. In *Beeny Cliff* the language is ornamental, but it matches his observations:

> A little cloud then cloaked us, and there flew an
>   irised rain,
> And the Atlantic dyed its levels with a dull
>   misfeatured stain,
> And then the sun burst out again, and purples
>   prinked the main.

Hardy does sometimes fall into banality, or an over-complicated form will contort his language to become downright wayward. Yet he is (Yeats having not then reached maturity) the most rewarding poet to read in English between Hopkins and Eliot. He surprises by his capacity to breathe new life into much that might have seemed repetitive. There is a kind of innocence in his highly personal idiom; his eye and ear are continually alert. The emotional range of his work is fairly narrow, but for their depth and variety of response and disciplined ease the *Poems of 1912–13* can be compared with the finest verse of this century.

NOTE

1. Gittings, *The Older Hardy* (London, 1978), 153.

THE RURAL TRADITION

DENYS THOMPSON

By the turn of the century agriculture had ceased to be of importance in the life of the nation. Yet there remained a deep belief in the supreme value of country life; rural communities were supposed to preserve the virtues of historic England; and in an age of industry the general outlook was backward, towards a farming society. The results of this have been numerous, widespread, and persistent; in literature, for example, there has been a steady and continuing flow of books with a rural interest or background, and many of these followed in the wake of Thomas Hardy.

Hardy's idea of nature was formed by his own experience and his wide reading. He believed, for instance, that all organic creatures were members of one natural family:

I sit under a tree, and feel alone: I think of certain insects around me as magnified by the microscope: creatures like elephants, flying dragons, etc. And I feel I am by no means alone.[1]

He saw human beings influenced by natural forces beyond their control, and he shaped the characters in his novels accordingly. If they were wise, men co-operated with these forces – the climate, the seasons, their environment – by winning food and clothing and shelter for themselves through agriculture. In the seasonal round of tilling the soil were rooted the ancient rituals, observances and festivals that gave pattern and meaning to human life, and sealed the right relationship between men and their world. The mill in *Tess*, the flour in *The Trumpet-Major* ('the blessed staff of life') and the barn in *Far From the Madding Crowd* ('So the barn was natural to the shearers, and the shearers were in harmony with the barn') were all symbols of man's success in getting his livelihood from his habitat. In *The Woodlanders* Hardy expressed unstinted admiration for human beings who fit in perfectly with the natural scheme of things through their dedicated work – Giles with his 'marvellous power of making trees grow' and the 'heroic girl', Marty South, who had an equally 'intelligent intercourse with nature'. On the other hand a wrong relationship with nature was exemplified by the men who tried to till and fertilize Egdon, and were killed or ruined by it; the five Wessex novels contain characters who do not accept the natural order of things, and meet with disaster.

The peasant economy had been an example of successful adaptation, but it had come to an end with the enclosures before Hardy was born. Though his aim was 'to preserve for my own satisfaction a fairly true record of a vanishing life', he could not observe much at first hand. What he could still recognize and describe were the peasant qualities, the loss of which he lamented in the decline of agriculture in his lifetime. Writing on 'The Dorsetshire Labourer' in *Longmans Magazine* in 1883, he deplored the replacement of stationary cottagers by migrant labourers, with the consequent

breach in continuity of local history, fatal to the preservation of legend and folk-lore, close inter-social relations and eccentric individualities. For these the indispensable conditions of existence are attachment to the soil of one particular spot by generation after generation.

One such 'replacement' is movingly described in *Tess* (chs 51 and 52). Even when the peasant had become a landless labourer,

the fields were those he had ploughed and sown from boyhood, and it was impossible for him, in such circumstances, to sink altogether the character of natural guardian in that of hireling.

There is an aching sense of loss in Hardy's observations, but it is not nostalgic; he did not wish for the impossible – for any kind of return. The farm labourers' lot in the middle of the nineteenth century was often intolerably miserable: bad wages resulted in cases of actual starvation, while well-to-do farmers treated their employees – men, women and children – with a cruelty (Hardy remarked) and contempt that could not have been exceeded in the days of real serfdom. Hardy noted too that the villages used to contain an interesting and well-informed class, the backbone of village life – the blacksmith, the carpenter, the shoemaker – who, as a result of not being wanted as tenants by landowners, had to seek refuge in the boroughs. In his words, 'This process, which is designated by statisticians as "the tendency of rural population towards the large towns", is really the tendency of water to flow uphill when forced.'

Hardy's feeling for the past and his dismay at the plight of agriculture supply a common pattern to the five Wessex novels (*Far From the Madding Crowd, The Return of the Native, The Mayor of Casterbridge, The Woodlanders, Tess of the d'Urbervilles* and to a less extent their prelude, *Under the Greenwood Tree*).* This and a good deal else about the novels was first noticed by Lionel Johnson in 1892. They are set in the same tract of country, peopled by a few men and women of powerful character, surrounded by the rank and file of country labour. These people are then brought into contact with outsiders, superior in education and perhaps social position, but inferior in strength and fineness. Love affairs make the contrast sharper, and rural values come into conflict with those of the town. Throughout, the ordinary villagers provide a stable background against which the main characters are seen in relief. Hardy said that the Mellstock rustics were 'the characters that I like best in my own novels', and he stood up for them again and again, in opposition to the views of Fielding and the Victorians. He praised their oral culture: 'how vast and striking is the body of unwritten human experience in this so-called literary age'; and when it came to illustrating *Far From the Madding Crowd* he wanted the rustics to appear intelligent, and not boorish at all. Their feet, like Hardy's, were always firmly on the ground, and they found guidance in their ancient peasant culture with all its limitations. Through it they embodied a morality, a fund of immemorial wisdom and experience; and from this strength they pronounced their choric comments on the action, as inheritors rather than individuals. The typical heir of peasant virtues was kindly, humorous and cheerful, accepted things as they were, stoically endured pain and misfortune, kept to the middle way, and lacked ambition. A reading of the novels leaves the impression that Hardy's own values tend to approximate to those of his country people; as Lawrence commented in his *Study of Thomas Hardy*, 'all but the average people die'.

However much Hardy protested that in writing novels he sought merely to boil the pot, his shaping purpose was always a moral one.

---

* Hardy's novels are the subject of a chapter by G. D. Klingopulos in Volume 6 of the *Guide, From Dickens to Hardy*.

In contrast, the aim of the next two writers to be discussed here, Hudson and Barrett, was to set down what they themselves had enjoyed so much. W. H. Hudson, an American who came to England as a young man, wrote mainly as a naturalist, but produced his best work in old age: *Far Away and Long Ago* (1918), an account of his childhood, and *A Shepherd's Life* (1910). In the latter Hudson recorded the life and times of Caleb Bawcombe, who had worked on the Wiltshire downs seven days a week for fifty years, and died a man fulfilled. It is an absorbing story of one whose vocation called for knowledge and skill and judgement of men as well as of animals. Hudson draws freely on a memory richly stored by experience, and also includes vivid sketches of individuals, descriptions of the countryside, and much observation of 'the humble cottagers, the true people of the vale who were rooted in the soil':

> The labourer on the land goes on from boyhood to the end of his life in the same everlasting round, the changes from task to task, according to the seasons, being no greater than in the case of the animals that alter their actions and habits to suit the varying conditions of the year. (p. 39)

The gipsies especially achieved a 'perfect correspondence between organism and environment'. But it was not an animal existence that all these people led, for their power of endurance, their independence, zest in work and pleasure in their flower gardens were tokens of their true humanity. Like so many social historians of the nineteenth century, Hudson learned how brutally the farm labourers were treated, and how savagely punished when unemployment and actual starvation drove them to protest and to smash machinery. There are some graphic passages on a drama in which the farmers and gamekeepers were consistently the villains. In all his writing, both on the land and its inhabitants, Hudson's tone and feeling are infallibly appropriate at a time when a lush style and a patronizing note were too common; his brief account of a shepherd's death (p. 222) is a beautiful example.

Hudson wrote of an agricultural order that was not without its graces, of folksong and folk art. W. H. Barrett (*Tales from the Fens*, 1963) lived in a different milieu. As a child at the turn of the century he used to ease the loneliness of crow-scaring or sheep-tending by memorizing the tales he had learned from the local story-tellers, whose art would earn them drink and tobacco at the pub. In later years he was encouraged, just in time, to write them down. The stories come from a small area near Ely, where dwell the descendants of the original wild fenmen who lived by trapping and fishing until the drainage of the seventeenth century turned them into wage-earners. As labourers they were worse off than their fellows in other parts of England, for in the nineteenth century at least the misery and poverty of the East Anglian working class were unparalleled elsewhere. This emerges from such tales as 'The Littleport Riots' (of 1816) in which men driven desperate by starvation, while wealthy farmers prospered, assembled and broke some windows. No one was hurt, but the Bishop of Ely appointed hanging judges and five men were executed. Such a background did not encourage the growth of popular art; yet these tales show how people preserved their courage, manhood and humour (sometimes crude and cruel) in the midst of oppression and hardship. When they could, they took savage revenges, yet 'agitators' who came from outside to preach politics were tarred and feathered. Some of the stories are about tough and resourceful individuals; others are legends, of which one about Tennyson includes a jingle attributed to him that is not in the collected poems; and yet others speak of traditions that go back to the Roman occupation, some of them now being verified by archaeology. They range from the very funny to the macabre and grimly realistic; all have the run of living speech and the narrative skill of oral literature. They were and still are excellent entertainment, with the addition for the modern reader of their considerable contribution to social history. Products of a real popular culture, they offer splendid material for teaching English and history, and ought to be available in paperback.

Hardy's consciousness of change has been shared by most of this century's writers on the country. Feeling his sense of irreparable loss, they have developed, filled in, and brought up to date what he only hinted at. George Sturt, for example, has affinities with the older writer, though he did not much like what he read of him. Both had an acute sensitivity to what was happening, and an awareness of its significance. Both had the novelist's ability to enter into the lives of others; both admired the qualities of the 'peasant' and felt that he had been much ill-used. Sturt looked ahead more often than Hardy – he was a more 'political' author – and in his awareness of the modern lack of roots he was close to Lawrence's insight into what happens 'when the peasant suddenly leaves his home and becomes a workman'. Sturt had inherited the family wheelwright's business, but his real interest lay in writing, to which eventually he was able to devote himself. He finished two novels and a work on aesthetics, but his claims rest on a handful of books about life and work in the country, most of them published under the name 'George Bourne', since he feared that his local reputation might suffer if he were known to be an author.

His first substantial publication, *The Bettesworth Book* (1901), was noted down from the garrulous talk of an old gardener, whom Sturt found interesting and quaint; the uncertainty of tone is reminiscent of the early Hardy's patronizing attitude towards his fictional rustics. *Memoirs of a Surrey Labourer* (1907), from the same source, is more assured and more perceptive. Though dragged up as an orphan, Bettesworth had a receptive mind, a sense of order and a gift of expression. In a life that was far from easy, he was never dull; he responded sensitively to the changes of the year, and endured suffering with unselfpitying cheerfulness:

Alone, of his own inborn instinct for being a decent man, he strove, through all his life, not to be rich, but to live upright and unashamed. Fumbling, tiresome, garrulous, unprofitable, lean and grim and dirty in outward appearance, the grey old life was full of fight for its idea of being a man; full of fight and patience and stubborn resolve not to give in to anything which it had learnt to regard as weakness ... think of the patient, resolute spirit, which had almost never indulged its weaknesses, but had its self-respect, its half-savage instincts towards righteousness, its smothered tastes, its untold affections and its tenderness.

From the old man's chatter Sturt was able to piece together a picture of a peasant economy that had effectively come to an end two generations earlier; and thus alerted he went on to collect evidence for the nature of this home-made civilization and the opportunities it afforded. The result was *Change in the Village* (1912), a remarkable feat of reconstruction, for all that Sturt sensed about a much earlier period has been confirmed, both by historians such as W. G. Hoskins and Joan Thirsk, and by other observers, notably George Ewart Evans and Flora Thompson. Evans has carried out valuable research, especially on the fresh ground covered by *Where Beards Wag All* (1970) on the relevance of the oral tradition. Flora

Thompson's *Lark Rise to Candleford* (1939) records the traces, in a rather poor area of Oxfordshire, of a self-sufficient society, living off open fields and common land. Its tough loyalties and values survived even the Industrial Revolution and the enclosures, till they were over-run by suburbia. With a powerful grasp of her subject she noted precisely what Sturt observed, with the difference that she was much more in and of the village than Sturt as an employer ever could be.

In *Change in the Village* Sturt followed up the clues he had gathered from Bettesworth, and the truth came home to him: the peasant economy afforded more prosperity, more independence and more rewarding work than the life of a wage-earner. It had subsisted on what the industry of the people could produce, and its well-being depended on their intimate knowledge of the resources at hand. Moreover, 'this life of manifold industry was interesting to live. It is impossible to doubt it.' Most important of all:

> To the exigent problems of life it furnished solutions of its own – different solutions, certainly, from those which modern civilization gives, but yet serviceable enough. People could find in it not only a method of getting a living, but also an encouragement and a help to live well ... best of all, those customs provided a rough guidance as to conduct.

All this has gone beyond recall:

> There is no going back to the land, for English people, on the old terms of social life there. A taste for the wider outlook ... only possible in towns has almost certainly awakened in us. We can cultivate the land for a living, as a business; we shall hardly be able again to endure the restricted folk life which was the solace of our rural ancestors two hundred years ago.
>
> (*Journals*, p. 551)

The Wheelwright's Shop (1923) dealt with another aspect of pre-industrial England, a craft that required in those who practised it a close knowledge of their environment and its inhabitants. Sturt wrote of his employees:

> In them was stored all the local lore of what good wheelwright's work should be like ... They knew each customer and his needs; understood his carters and his horses and the nature of his land; and finally took a pride in providing exactly what was wanted in every case. So, unawares, they lived as integral parts in the rural community of the English. Overworked and underpaid, they none the less enjoyed life, I am sure. (p. 54)

They exercised traditional skills that brought out the best in them and allowed them to be fully alive at work. The major loss that Sturt recorded was the close relation between cultural values and the economic basis of life; as he learned the job from his men he found that 'truly, it was a liberal education to work under Cook's guidance . . . his tiresome fastidiousness over tools and handiwork sprang from a knowledge as valid as any artist's'. But in his time he saw the men become machine hands, 'under the power of molecular forces', and the satisfaction in their tasks diminish as the skill required lessened. As Sturt reflected,

> The products of work are, to be sure, as important as ever – what is to become of us all if the dockers will not sweat for us or the miners risk their lives? That civilization may flourish a less-civilized working-class must work.

Sturt stands out above most writers of his day because he insisted, with a wealth of illustration, that we must not allow ourselves to be blinded by material progress to the insights of cultural tradition.

Such insights are numerous in the *Journals*, which (as Sturt himself felt) represent his best work. They are a quarry of material for the books he wrote, as well as for those he hoped to write but was prevented by ill-health from starting. His knowledge of the living past enabled him to see the present – the era of applied science and technological autarchy – with the utmost clarity. He was one of the earlier critics of 'efficiency' and 'labour-saving' and of powerful syndicates with big capital and dead consciences. He repeatedly raised the question of leisure in a system wherein men begin to live only after their working hours. Sturt hoped, not entirely in vain, for success in the literary world, but he remained somewhat isolated. This meant that, when he found subjects that really interested him, his ability to write was engaged without external pressures. He was adept at describing rural scenes and people, and for this alone his admirable prose, unforced but lively, would be represented in any anthology. His distinction lies in his capacity to detect the trends of a civilization that had lost its way – a capacity not present in some of his better-known contemporaries.

John Cowper Powys and his brother Theodore Francis were among the eleven children of the incumbent of Montacute in Somerset. John greatly admired Hardy, and set some of his best fiction in Hardy's Wessex; but the resemblance does not go much further, for their chief common quality is a liability to stylistic lapses which are unimportant in the totality of their work. Hardy had naïve ideas of how to improve his own style, and chose quite unsuitable models for the purpose. Powys on the other hand tended to disapprove of 'art', for the cultivated person, he thought, 'will meddle little with contemporary fashions'. So he went his own way, though he might have been a better writer had he been able to learn from his contemporaries. Joyce and Lawrence, for instance, were ten years younger, but they were in print first: *Sons and Lovers* appeared in 1913 and *Portrait of the Artist as a Young Man* in 1915, but Powys's first success, *Wolf Solent*, was not published till 1929. He spent most of his working life as an itinerant lecturer in America, and was sustained throughout by his childhood memories of the Somerset and Dorset countryside. Its beauty had impressed him deeply; he was unhappy at school, and wrote of this period: 'Deep has that West Dorset countryside sunk into my soul! Nature has conquered in the end and overcome all the miseries I suffered in that place'.[2] These years powerfully influenced his novels; he was able to adapt his childhood feelings to mature experience, and as a result brought out very sensitively the childlike aspects of his characters.

What nature meant to Powys throughout his life and in his writing emerges clearly from his *The Meaning of Culture* (1930). Here he stressed the need for men to form a philosophy of their own, based on an habitual way of response to nature: a sensitivity to the life of the earth is the beginning and end of true education. This is not a matter of being inspired by beauty spots, for in Powys's view the genuine nature-lover thinks not about her beauty, but about her life and the sense of human continuity given by a well-tilled landscape, deriving thence 'a healing calm'. A further stage in the cult of nature is reached when the individual comes to feel an identity between his own inner being and that of other things, inanimate as well as conscious. Powys reiterated this time and time again: 'I could flow through every material object ... in a rapture of identification'.[3] Again, 'I could become any one of all the animals, birds, snakes, insects and even the tree roots that exist'.[4] As a result he felt that 'every swamp-pool, every rushy brook, every weedy estuary, every turnip-field, every grey milestone, every desolate haystack [in

Cambridgeshire] became part of my spirit'.[5] Another side of his rapport with animal, vegetable and even dead matter ('the organic body of some living being') was his Jungian belief in inherited memory, the experience in our own lives of emotions and gestures that have recurred through the ages. To Powys this meant the 're-birth of the ... feelings of the human race itself; not merely of certain Welsh ancestors, not merely of my ancestors, but of *all* our ancestors'.[6]

The descriptions of landscape in Powys's fiction help to shape the reader's response to the characters. This is especially remarkable in *Wolf Solent*, for the novel is organized around the protagonist's inter-course with his natural surroundings, which are also material in presenting to us the two girls, Gerda and Christie, with whom he is in love. When Wolf has a vision of a coal forest he becomes 'a leaf among leaves'; and

Each calamitous event that occurred during those deciduous months seemed to be brewed in the oozy vat of vegetation, as if the muddy lanes and the wet hazel-copses ... were conspiring with human circumstances. (pp. 389, 390)

Wolf is very much on his own in receiving these impressions of nature; they make for him the private world, which to Powys is

the grand secret of cosmic happiness ... It is only by this feeling of loneliness that we can escape ... and return to the calm reservoirs of earth, air, water and fire, the constant enjoyment of which constitutes the only indestructible ecstasy of life. (*In Defence of Sensuality*, 1930, p. 287)

Powys's word 'escape' is not appropriate to the recourse to powers that increase awareness and strengthen the capacity for living in the world. Far from being escapist, his outlook was that of his time and often ahead of it. He saw technological progress depriving people of the simple and natural, and he showed his Wolf Solent, for example, as very much enmeshed in the problems of the twentieth century. The sight of a lorry raising clouds of dust prompts Wolf to reflect:

He felt as though with aeroplanes spying down upon every retreat like ubiquitous vultures, with the lanes invaded by ironclad motors like colossal beetles, with no sea, no lake, no river free from throbbing, thudding engines, the one thing most precious of all in the world was being destroyed ...

and later he sees human nature being undone by 'the cold clutch of scientific discovery'. Powys wished to look at the stars, 'eliminating from my consciousness all those bewildering astronomical and mathematical calculations with regard to their size and distance'.[7] His beliefs that there is 'no such thing as scientific truth' and that 'Faster and faster every year is the purely mechanistic conception of life receding and being discarded' have been much echoed since his day. A particular application of science that evoked his persistent protests (especially in *Weymouth Sands*) was vivisection, which (like Dr Johnson) he condemned because, as well as being cruel, it was bad for those who practised it. Altogether his response to such a feature of civilization as this is likely to develop the consciousness needed for being fully alive today.

Theodore Francis Powys farmed for a short time in Suffolk, and then retired to Dorset. In 1915 he wrote *Soliloquies of a Hermit*, in which he expressed an attitude that lies behind most of his novels and short stories. The background of the book was the horror of the First World War: 'I see torn bodies, broken, buried in blood, that were a year ago very thoughtless young men; and I see the evil eye of our greed blinking and cruel' (p. 149). 'Hermit' suggests that the writer has opted out of social responsibilities; he does not want to be bothered with the 'mob', his 'conforming' fellow-men, who would try to 'pump petrol' into his soul. He hates work 'with a foreman biting behind; not the work of a ploughboy who has plenty of time to think of his dinner and to sing a song, but the work that has no song in it at all ...' (p. 36). He loves the light of the fire and the sun, walks with friends, silence and nature in some of its aspects. He writes much of 'the moods of God' into which he is thrown as one of the 'priest class'. God himself, the Judaic tyrant of the Old Testament, seems mainly an object to be dreaded; made in the image of man, he contains the evil which forms a large part of every human being. Evil alone is immortal, so the greatest gift of God to man is death, the only escape from divine cruelty and the loathsomeness of human life. (Christ, however, who first planted the seed of love, does not in any way resemble his terrible father.) The manner of the book is gnomic and authoritative, but this is belied by whimsicality, patches like the prose of a Georgian poet, and contradictions. For example, after hearing much of an evil God, we read: 'It is much better, I have found, to love a chair than to love a person; there is often more of God in a chair' – a notion different from that of the vindictive Old Testament despot.

Mr Tasker's Gods (written 1916, published 1925) is the most notable of the early novels, in which the main character worships the pigs that make money for him. His father is a tramp, and a nuisance, who in return for a bottle of spirits kicks to death one of the book's two saintly and courageous characters. In a drunken stupor he is killed by a dog belonging to his son, and devoured by the pigs; Mr Tasker then shovels the remains of his father under a dung-heap. The figures in the novel, most of them vicious, are two-dimensional; by the end Mr Tasker is purely a symbol of evil. There is a sharp division between black and white: the bad are embodiments of vice, and the good are martyrs who come to grief automatically. Powys indulges in a savage irony that reminds one of Swift, and prompts the same comment: this man is unbalanced. The writer's bitterness leads to the crude and melodramatic presentation of violence.

Mark Only (1924) is a more mature work. The opening scene is forebodingly dramatic; the misnaming at his christening foreshadows disaster for Mark. He is one of Powys's more human figures, and this makes him large enough to carry the weight of the tragedy; he has about him an air of the sacred fool. The other persons have something to contribute; they are presented with an effective ironic humour. As the novel advances, the feeling of impending doom is developed; by contrast, in *Mr Tasker's Gods* chapters could be re-arranged or omitted without loss, while the general feeling induced is of revulsion. The more disciplined *Mark Only* looks forward to the achievement of *Mr Weston's Good Wine* (1927).

This is the most carefully wrought of the novels, and the most satisfying; it is the finest allegory to have appeared in English since *Gulliver's Travels*. Mr Weston, a wine merchant, and his assistant Michael come to the village of Folly Down one afternoon to call on customers with samples of his light and dark wines. The clocks all stop at seven and Mr Weston goes round taking orders, while a number of well-integrated sub-plots are resolved. For once the scales are not weighted against the good and innocent, and the black villains receive their dues. When all is arranged Mr Weston tells Michael to drop a lighted match in the petrol tank of their car, and they vanish in a pillar of smoke that ascends to heaven. The revelation that Mr Weston is God, a more tolerable deity than the earlier versions, is gently managed in the first fifty pages or so, and his light and dark wines are seen to be love and death. He shows 'the power of kindness' in his face; he is powerful, perhaps omnipotent, and in some respects is the God of the New (with a hint from the apocryphal one) rather than the Old Testament. He stands for the better hopes and aspirations of humanity instead of the worst, as in some of the other books, so that the novel offers encouragement to go on living.

The other mature fruit of Powys's meditations on man and God, usually concluding that true happiness is found in death, is the collection of short stories called *Fables* (1929). Here he pursues the idea, quoted above, from *Soliloquies* that it is better to love a chair than a person; and endows inanimate objects with the consciousness of human beings. Remembering the title, we are to look for lessons; and we learn that the aim, which is brilliantly achieved, is to make the reader think again about accepted attitudes. These inanimates feel and talk like men and women, but they are so much more agreeable than most of Powys's human figures that to enter their world is a relief from the scene as he so often describes it.

Powys is not a country writer in the sense that Hardy and Adrian Bell are. He wrote about types of human beings found in all countries and periods, depicted in two dimensions as in a morality; and to this end he chose country people in the small and simplified world of a village. Dialect, not a very real one, provided stylization and contributed to the detachment required. Allusions to literature helped to form Powys's style, especially the Bible with its small vocabulary, uncomplicated expression, and narrow range of ideas and attitudes. He could never have written as he did if he had moved on from Job to Greek tragedy. He was a superb storyteller, and within his chosen limitations he evolved a manner perfect for his purpose, the writing of allegories.

This discussion of a group of writers from the large number who form the rural tradition is rounded off by looking at a journalist and a novelist. H. J. Massingham's journalism, impelled by conviction, active interests and zest in writing, marks him out as an exceptionally valuable middleman of ideas. He links the first and last authors discussed here, because he had met Hardy and was a friend of Adrian Bell. His substantial *Downland Man* (1926), deeply influenced by the diffusionist theory of culture, gave him a base for exploration in several directions. He came to query the claims of western civilization and to regard it as morally bankrupt. He believed that the theory of evolution had been misapplied to human life when its canons of survival were used to sanction both actual war and the rapacious conflict of commercialism; and that primitive man had been non-aggressive. Wars were caused by greed for wealth and power, working through civilized institutions.

The ugliness and sterility of civilization were to Massingham signs that it had gone astray, especially in its neglect of agriculture. Thus industrial man's adjustment to his environment had been dislocated, and looking back he argued: 'Our future lies in our past, our pre-industrial past ... one can but examine the past and seek to detect therein the more permanent elements of man's life upon earth'.[8] The lost balance had been attained by farming, the foundation of national well-being; and he wanted to see that equipoise restored, with the emphasis on small farms – though without waging war on industry or large farms. There would, however, be an attack on chemical farming, whereby after the abstract study of problems in the laboratory artificial fertilizers and weedkillers are unloaded on to the land. A short account such as this necessarily distorts, but Massingham himself avoided simplification in his range of still-rewarding books on farming, tools, craftsmanship and regional culture.

Massingham described his autobiography, *Remembrance*, as 'a story of conversion' to a 'unified perception of life'. Adrian Bell was also a convert, from being a member of an urban professional family to life as a farmer, married and permanently settled in Suffolk. All this, from apprenticeship to ownership, is described in his trilogy, *Corduroy* (1930), *Silver Ley* (1931) and *The Cherry Tree* (1932). As he gained experience as one of the dying class of small farmers, he realized that even in his time unindustrialized agriculture offered opportunities for skill, judgement and knowledge in work that was interesting and rewarding. The men still spoke a dialect: 'Its physical expressiveness was its attraction for me, its merry-hearted similes, and the fact that it always seemed to be on the verge of breaking into song.' Without wanting to do away with the modern roller mill, he saw bread as the symbol of farming as the proper and normal activity of man. He observed the changes as they happened around him: young people foreign to their own land in 'lethargic disrelation to their surroundings', factory farms, and concentration camps in which birds and animals served life sentences. On the other hand he liked the big fields of modern East Anglia, because there the country looked as it must have done before the enclosures.

He felt that he was a steward in charge of an inheritance:

I now have care of this soil which former men cherished. I feel such a compulsion towards it: it is the most important thing in life to me, far beyond the level of a paying proposition; because ... it is the greatest parable of ultimate truth.[9]

He sensitively related the activities of the past with the present and the future; he urged that the ideas of literature must be tested by 'the winds and waters and man's handiwork'; in short he was, as he said, a man 'in love with unity'. His novels are consistently enjoyable, and as we read them their author emerges as a deeply religious figure, with a faith born not of books (though he was widely read), but of work, observation and finding in Christianity a source of unity and sanctity. He wrote, of Norwich Cathedral:

I must tell myself again and again that this place of praise houses man's true nature, and the great issue to which his ordinary daily life is addressed. It should not be just a quarter of an hour stolen from the traffic of life, but the very business of life itself – to work as if to pray, to build a granary expressive of grain, or a house as true to the cherishing of life as a bird's nest is.[10]

Though his work, which includes an excellent anthology of country life, and compiling *The Times* crossword puzzle for many years, must have cushioned the agricultural depression between the wars, farming alone supplies the basic material of his fiction. 'The garden roses are coming out, but they are not as heartening a sight to me as spring cabbages are in March.' Most of his books are novels in name, but they mainly consist of accounts of his life, descriptions of the Suffolk countryside in its various phases, and a good deal of reflection and casual comment. Characteristically, mention of a warbler leads to a discussion of folk song – how could a people harassed to misery produce 'The Seeds of Love'? – and so on to the labourer's lot, Easter and the meaning of resurrection. The prose is lucid and unemphatic, as it follows the writer's thoughts and impressions; pages on winter, a false spring, the sounds of farm and field, for example, are beautifully written, not as set pieces but integral with their contexts. (*My Own Master*, 1961, has a wonderful description of a cow blind from birth.) And the criticism of our civilization, though never at all radical, becomes more incisive.

A full survey of writers on the country would consider E. M. Forster and D. H. Lawrence, as well as a number who were closer to the scene, such as J. S. Collis (*The Worm Forgives the Plough*, 1973), Raymond O'Malley (*One-Horse Farm*, 1948) and R. S. Thomas in his poetry. Those discussed here would accept a number of propositions: the country is a source of health and energy; primary production is man's most important activity; the changes that have taken place are irreversible; the past is a reminder, too readily neglected, of human potential. What they have to offer is not outdated but of increasing concern, for implicit in their work are questions that demand attention. Is it possible to restore the values that work used to stand for before it was devalued? Are 'growth' and 'the gross national product' adequate measures of prosperity, if the products represent moral and spiritual retrogression? Is our technological civilization conditioning us to accept the pattern of life it dictates? Our authors do not supply answers, but the quality of their writing insists that they be taken seriously. They write well because they see clearly.

NOTES

1. Florence Emily Hardy, *Life of Thomas Hardy* (1962), 107.
2. *Autobiography* (1934), 134.
3. *Autobiography*, 61.
4. *Letters* (1958), 296.
5. *Autobiography*, 183
6. *Autobiography*, 291
7. *Autobiography*, 171
8. *Remembrance* (1942), 127.
9. *The Flower and the Wheel* (1949), 94.
10. *The Flower and the Wheel*, 27.

THE LITERATURE OF THE FIRST
WORLD WAR

D. J. ENRIGHT

While Wilfred Owen, Siegfried Sassoon and Isaac Rosenberg may not have contributed to the establishment of what we call 'modernism', the poetry of the First World War has a clear right to be considered part and parcel of modern poetry. It would be strange were this not so; for the experience of the war was emphatically one which could not be conveyed in debilitated nineteenth-century poetic conventions. Owen's poetic antecedents and personal tastes were of the nineteenth century; he was in no sense a conscious innovator of the kind of T. S. Eliot or Ezra Pound or even the Imagists; he was a 'bookish boy' rather than a literary intellectual, he was probably unaware of any crisis in poetry, quite possibly he had read neither the Jacobeans nor the metaphysicals. Simply, the war, a devastating non-literary event, forced him, as a poet and an honest man, to find another way of speaking.

The compulsion behind this war poetry, that is to say, arose out of its subject-matter. This is particularly true of Sassoon, whose style, when one becomes aware of it, is unashamedly old-fashioned. In the more successful war poetry, the style capitulated to the subject-matter; in the best of it, and predominantly in Owen's work, the style was *in* the subject-matter.

Since the reputations of the war writers are by now variously established, this essay will largely take the form of an anthology accompanied by a minimum of commentary. We begin with a brief comparison between Rupert Brooke as old-style war poet and Wilfred Owen as new-style war poet, which, though hackneyed, is still useful. For one thing, the comparison serves as a simple illustration of a basic difference between early-twentieth-century 'traditional' poetry and modern poetry: the abandonment by the latter of high- or at least nice-mindedness, of prescribed 'romantic' paraphernalia, of the conception of poetry as 'dream'. But the war only accelerated the development of modern poetry: it did not instigate it. What the difference between

> Safe shall be my going,
> Secretly armed against all death's endeavour;
> Safe though all safety's lost; safe where men fall;
> And if these poor limbs die, safest of all
> > (Brooke, *Safety*)

and

> One dawn, our wire patrol
> Carried him. This time, Death had not missed.
> We could do nothing but wipe his bleeding cough.
> Could it be accident? – Rifles go off ...
> Not sniped? No. (Later they found the English ball.)
> > (Owen, *S.I.W.*)

implies is actual experience of war – and its effects on a poet who, whatever his earlier allegiances, was able to perceive and follow the new directives of experience.

There is little compulsion behind Brooke's peace-time poetry: apart from some pleasant light verse, it is only accomplished, self-consciously graceful, and vaguely portentous within the bounds of good manners, except when setting out to be bad-mannered and turning into schoolboyish cynicism. It is his war poems we are concerned with, however: the sequence of sonnets entitled *1914*.

The first, *Peace*, advances the idea that war is clean and cleansing, rather like a good swim: a change from 'all the little emptiness of love' and from 'half-men, and their dirty songs'; the only thing that can suffer in war is the body (not true, as events showed). The second, *Safety*, seeks to testify to the safeness of war: it may even lead to death, the safest shelter of all against the (unspecified) dangers of life. The third, *The Dead*, is a conventional trumpet-piece, with none of the perverse 'logic' of the first two sonnets, though later witnesses were not so sure about its grand generalization, 'Honour has come back, as a king, to earth ...' The fourth, also called *The Dead*, is equally free from that anti-life petulance, indeed reverses it; the sestet describes waves that have frozen over, and is presumably a relatively tactful way of equating the peace of the dead with the animation of the living as two forms of natural beauty.

The fifth sonnet, *The Soldier*, I quote in full since it is not only Brooke's most celebrated poem but also interesting as a document.

> If I should die, think only this of me:
> That there's some corner of a foreign field
> That is for ever England. There shall be
> In that rich earth a richer dust concealed;
> A dust whom England bore, shaped, made aware,
> Gave, once, her flowers to love, her ways to roam,
> A body of England's, breathing English air,
> Washed by the rivers, blest by suns of home.
>
> And think, this heart, all evil shed away,
> A pulse in the eternal mind, no less
> Gives somewhere back the thoughts by England given;
> Her sights and sounds; dreams happy as her day;
> And laughter, learnt of friends, and gentleness,
> In hearts at peace, under an English heaven.

Today this sonnet strikes us as very much a period piece, not lacking in the factitious charm of 'nostalgia', and standing as a pre-eminent expression of sentiments to which many bosoms must have returned an echo and perhaps found solace in – even to the cloudy 'mysticism' of the sestet whereby the 'riches' enumerated in the octave are somehow, somewhere, to be given back to somebody. The poem is 'innocent', in the sense of Philip Larkin's comment in his poem *MCMXIV*: 'Never such innocence again'.

In several senses, Brooke's war poetry is typically pre-war poetry. And what has been said above is no more than was said, with far greater authority, by a number of poets within a short time of Brooke's death. It was as a schoolboy, in 1912, that Charles Sorley declared: 'The voice of our poets and men of letters is finely trained and sweet to hear ... it pleases, it flatters, it charms, it soothes: it is a living lie.'[1] Later he made the radical criticism of Brooke's work: 'He has clothed his attitude in fine words: but he has taken the sentimental attitude.' And in a sonnet Sorley makes an implicit rejoinder to Brooke's *1914* sequence:

> When you see millions of the mouthless dead
> Across your dreams in pale battalions go,
> Say not soft things as other men have said,
> That you'll remember. For you need not so.

> Give them not praise. For, deaf, how should they know
> It is not curses heaped on each gashed head?
> Nor tears. Their blind eyes see not your tears flow.
> Nor honour. It is easy to be dead.

Sorley's attitude to the conflict – an attitude which grew stronger in later writing, where the conflict came to seem one of soldiers against politicians rather than nationality against nationality – was already far more thoughtful, humane and accurate than Brooke's:

> ... in each other's dearest ways we stand
> And hiss and hate. And the blind fight the blind.[2]

Relevant on this point is Herbert Read's remark in *Annals of Innocence and Experience*:

It must be remembered that in 1914 our conception of war was completely unreal. We had vague childish memories of the Boer War, and from these and from a general diffusion of Kiplingesque sentiments, we managed to infuse into war a decided element of adventurous romance. War still appealed to the imagination.

A little later it was to appeal, violently, to the senses, and the imagination underwent a forcible transformation. There are the few poems of Arthur Graeme West to show how that old imagination was exploded:

> Next was a bunch of half a dozen men
> All blown to bits, an archipelago
> Of corrupt fragments ...
> (*Night Patrol*, March 1916)

In a letter written early in 1917 Owen comments, '... everything unnatural, broken, blasted; the distortion of the dead, whose unburiable bodies sit outside the dug-outs all day, all night, the most execrable sights on earth. In poetry we call them the most glorious.' Finally, there is Robert Graves, in *Goodbye to All That*, reporting a conversation with Siegfried Sassoon in November 1915:

... he showed me some of his own poems. One of them began:

> 'Return to greet me, colours that were my joy,
> Not in the woeful crimson of men slain ...'

Siegfried had not yet been in the trenches. I told him, in my old-soldier manner, that he would soon change his style.

In considering the real poetry of the war, or the poetry of the real war, we may most conveniently begin with Siegfried Sassoon, the one major war poet (one would not include Robert Graves or Edmund Blunden, in the category of war poets) to survive the war.

The great compulsion here, as to a lesser extent or less exclusively in Owen's work, was to communicate reality, to convey the truth of modern warfare to those not directly engaged in it. For this was the first modern war, in respect of destructive power; at the same time it was (for the British people at least) the last of the old wars in which the civilian population were at a safe distance from the destruction. As Vivian de Sola Pinto has pointed out, by 1916 a change had taken place in English society whereby a vertical division, cutting across class distinctions, separated the Nation at Home from the Nation Overseas (i.e. the armies on the Continent). Inevitably civilian attitudes were, to use Herbert Read's term, largely Kipling-esque. Information and correction were necessary, and all the more so in view of the romantic lies of the politicians, the nobility-in-absentia of the newspapers, and the vicarious altruism of the profi-teers. The common soldier could not speak for himself, and the casualty lists apparently did not speak plainly enough. Thus the writers in the trenches felt it a duty, not simply to write poems or prose, but to write about the trenches.

The mood in Sassoon's early verse of

> War is our scourge; yet war has made us wise,
> And, fighting for our freedom, we are free
>
> *(Absolution)*

was soon replaced by a sober documentary manner:

> He was a young man with a meagre wife
> And two small children in a Midland town;
> He showed their photographs to all his mates,
> And they considered him a decent chap
> Who did his work and hadn't much to say ...
>
> *(A Working Party)*

And in turn this manner was pushed aside by the angry violence of the collection entitled *Counterattack* (1918):

> 'Good-morning; good-morning!' the General said
> When we met him last week on our way to the line.
> Now the soldiers he smiled at are most of 'em dead,

And we're cursing his staff for incompetent swine.
'He's a cheery old card,' grunted Harry to Jack
As they slogged up to Arras with rifle and pack.

     .   .

But he did for them both by his plan of attack.
                               (*The General*)

Counterattack is first-class propaganda, and rather more: angry polemical verses, technically simple, rough and ready, concerned only with the obvious meanings of the words used, never suggesting more than is actually said, but never suggesting less than is said:

> I knew a simple soldier boy
> Who grinned at life in empty joy,
> Slept soundly through the lonesome dark,
> And whistled early with the lark.
>
> In winter trenches, cowed and glum,
> With crumps and lice and lack of rum,
> He put a bullet through his brain.
> No one spoke of him again.
>
>   .   .
>
> You smug-faced crowds with kindling eye
> Who cheer when soldier lads march by,
> Sneak home and pray you'll never know
> The hell where youth and laughter go.
>   (*Suicide in the Trenches*)

Not poetry, perhaps? But did that matter? The poetry – to adapt a phrase from Owen – is in the anger. While its impact would have been more powerful, or more permanently powerful, had the mode of satire been more controlled, more calculated, and had Sassoon drawn these victims less sketchily, we must yet admit that in the best of his poems it is the spontaneity, the lack of calculation, which impresses us. They were so clearly written out of honest rage and decent indignation.

Perhaps it is significant that since the war Sassoon only wrote as forcefully when remembering it. One of his best pieces was provoked by the erection of the great War Memorial near Ypres, *On Passing the New Menin Gate, 1927*:

> Who will remember, passing through this Gate,
> The unheroic Dead who fed the guns?
> Who shall absolve the foulness of their fate, –

> Those doomed, conscripted, unvictorious ones?
> Crudely renewed, the Salient holds its own.
> Paid are its dim defenders by this pomp;
> Paid, with a pile of peace-complacent stone,
> The armies who endured that sullen swamp ...

There is also the satirical collection, *The Road to Ruin*, written in the early 1930s: a prefigurement of similar ambitions, euphemisms, and lies, leading to another great war, with greater weapons and more radical destruction. The opening poem describes the Prince of Darkness standing with his staff at the Cenotaph, 'unostentatious and respectful', and praying, 'Make them forget, O Lord, what this Memorial means ...' The best is probably *An Unveiling*:

> The President's oration ended thus:
> 'Not vainly London's War-gassed victims perished.
> We are a part of them, and they of us:
> As such they will perpetually be cherished.
> Not many of them did much; but all did what
> They could, who stood like warriors at their post
> (Even when too young to walk). This hallowed spot
> Commemorates a proud, though poisoned host.
> We honour here' (he paused) 'our Million Dead;
> Who, as a living poet has nobly said,
> "Are now forever London" ...'

Its effectiveness is much increased by memories of the poet's earlier piece on the New Menin Gate and of Brooke's *Soldier*, reincarnated in the form of a civilian casualty list.

Yet Sassoon's poems of 1949 revert to Brooke in sentiment, though they are considerably less lush in language and rhythm. *Silent Service* —

> Now, multifold, let Britain's patient power
> Be proven within us for the world to see

— is no more than a dash of Winston Churchill in an ocean of water; and one turns with relief to Herbert Read's poem, *To a Conscript of 1940*:

> But you, my brother and my ghost, if you can go
> Knowing that there is no reward, no certain use
> In all your sacrifice, then honour is reprieved.

If Brooke has played the war poet for those who are fascinated by the 'idea' of poetry (or indeed of war), Wilfred Owen is the war poet for those who desire the reality. For a brief account of his life and thought there is the excellent memoir by Edmund Blunden, affixed to *The Poems of Wilfred Owen*.[3] Owen began to write poetry at an early age and, as Blunden points out, the influence of Keats, to whom he was devoted, is clear in his first poems. Along with imitation of the late-nineteenth-century 'decadents', the Keatsian influence ('Five cushions hath my hands, for reveries;/And one deep pillow for thy brow's fatigues') remained in force up to and some way beyond his enlistment in 1915. In his last two years he showed himself increasingly self-critical, as C. Day Lewis indicates in referring to successive drafts of his poems.[4] In January 1917 he wrote from the Somme,

> I can't tell you any more Facts. I have no Fancies and no Feelings ... [A few days later:] Those 'Somme Pictures' are the laughing-stock of the army – like the trenches on exhibition in Kensington ... The people of England needn't hope. They must agitate. But they are not yet agitated even.

And in August 1917, in hospital near Edinburgh, he refers thus to Tennyson's personal unhappiness:

> as for misery, was he ever frozen alive, with dead men for comforters? Did he hear the moaning at the Bar, not at twilight and the evening bell only, but at dawn, noon, and night, eating and sleeping, walking and working, always the close moaning of the Bar; the thunder, the hissing, and the whining of the Bar? – Tennyson, it seems, was always a great child. So should I have been, but for Beaumont Hamel.

While convalescing from his 'neurasthenia', Owen met Sassoon, and the two became close friends. Sassoon's example confirmed Owen in his resolve to speak out against the war, in harsh, clear and unpleasant words, unsoftened by any poetic or patriotic euphemisms. He entered his brief brilliant maturity.

These two extracts come from a poem called *Disabled*:

> One time he liked a blood-smear down his leg,
> After the matches, carried shoulder-high.
> It was after football, when he'd drunk a peg,
> He thought he'd better join. – He wonders why ...

> Some cheered him home, but not as crowds cheer Goal.
> Only a solemn man who brought him fruits
> *Thanked* him; and then inquired about his soul.

Now, he will spend a few sick years in Institutes,
And do what things the rules consider wise,
And take whatever pity they may dole.
Tonight he noticed how the women's eyes
Passed from him to the strong men that were whole.
How cold and late it is! Why don't they come
And put him into bed? Why don't they come?

It may be that this poem found its originating impulse in anger; but it goes far beyond anger. Just as much as the best poems of Sassoon, this is the expression of a lacerated moral sensibility: even so, it is poetry of a different and higher order. The success of Sassoon's anti-war verse depends to a great extent upon the reader's personal attitude: you will only *agree* with what is said if you are already tending towards the same opinion. The power of Owen's poetry is greater. It can create an attitude, starting from nothing: it can impel agreement by the depth, the 'density', of its expression. The 'he' of *Disabled* has a life, a presence, which is only hinted at in the convenient satirical shorthand of Sassoon's 'Harry' and 'Jack'. Sassoon's most interesting poetry is composed of what have been called the 'negative emotions' – horror, anger, disgust – and outside that field he inclines to become sentimental in a conventional way. (Robert Graves hit the nail on the head in saying, 'Modernism in Mr Sassoon is an intelligent, satiric reaction to contemporary political and social Bluffs; it is not a literary policy.'[5] In Owen's work, the 'positive emotions', of love, compassion, admiration, joy, are present as well, and this coexistence strengthens the poetry.

These comments should not be taken to suggest that Owen ever reverted to the simple-minded romanticism of Brooke or Julian Grenfell. (It is touching to read in the Appendix to Blunden's edition of his *Poems* that Owen was collecting photographs of war wounds, mutilations, and the results of surgical operations.) On the contrary, some of his poems are almost unbearably painful, in that they permit us no escape into cursing or self-righteousness or other defences or satisfactions afforded by the squib or lampoon. The quiet accurate accounts of gas casualties, men who have gone mad, men who are technically alive although their bodies have been destroyed – these are in the end a more powerful indictment of war than Sassoon's fluent indignation. And they do not 'date'.

Anthem for Doomed Youth is one of Owen's best-known poems:

> What passing-bells for these who die as cattle?
>   Only the monstrous anger of the guns,
>   Only the stuttering rifles' rapid rattle
> Can patter out their hasty orisons.
> No mockeries now for them; no prayers nor bells,
>   Nor any voice of mourning save the choirs, –
> The shrill, demented choirs of wailing shells;
>   And bugles calling for them from sad shires.
>
> What candles may be held to speed them all?
>   Not in the hands of boys, but in their eyes
> Shall shine the holy glimmers of good-byes.
>   The pallor of girls' brows shall be their pall;
> Their flowers the tenderness of patient minds,
> And each slow dusk a drawing-down of blinds.

The opening seems obvious in its intention: the poet protests at the discrepancy between the suffering of the Nation Overseas and the smugness of the Nation at Home. The 'cannon-fodder' cliché hovers near. But the third line demonstrates the poet's ear: 'the stuttering rifles' rapid rattle': and sends us back to see (or hear, rather) whether the second line really is a cliché. The word 'patter', similarly, when listened to as well as looked at releases an unexpected complexity of meaning. The following lines appear to be an obvious and easy success in the line of sarcasm: 'no mockeries now for them; no prayers nor bells ...' But Owen was too much of a poet to be content with resting on those laurels. There is, paradoxically, a kind of glory in the next two lines:

> The shrill, demented choirs of wailing shells;
>   And bugles calling for them from sad shires,

though a very different kind of glory from the official one. Then, when we arrive at the sestet of the sonnet, the bitterness of the opening has faded, and what prevails is the quiet restrained sorrow appropriate to a tragic close. (The quietness of tone may prevent us from noticing what a risk Owen took in his last line, how narrowly he brought it off.)

It is instructive to set side by side a poem of Owen's and one of Sassoon's, the originating impulses of which were clearly similar:

The Bishop tells us: 'When the boys come back
They will not be the same; for they'll have fought
In a just cause: they lead the last attack
On Anti-Christ; their comrades' blood has bought
New right to breed an honourable race,
They have challenged Death and dared him face to face.'

'We're none of us the same!' the boys reply.
'For George lost both his legs; and Bill's stone blind;
Poor Jim's shot through the lungs and like to die;
And Bert's gone syphilitic: you'll not find
A chap who's served that hasn't found *some* change.'
And the Bishop said: 'The ways of God are strange!'

(Sassoon, 'They')

I mind as 'ow the night afore that show
Us five got talking, – we was in the know.
'Over the top to-morrer; boys, we're for it.
First wave we are, first ruddy wave; that's tore it.'
'Ah well,' says Jimmy, – an' 'e's seen some scrappin' –
'There ain't no more nor five things as can 'appen:
Ye get knocked out; else wounded – bad or cushy;
Scuppered; or nowt except yer feeling mushy.'

One of us got the knock-out, blown to chops.
T'other was hurt, like, losin' both 'is props.
An' one, to use the word of 'ypocrites,
'Ad the misfortoon to be took be Fritz.
Now me, I wasn't scratched, praise God Amighty,
(Though next time please I'll thank 'im for a blighty).
But poor young Jim, 'e's livin' an' 'e's not;
'E reckoned 'e'd five chances, an' 'e 'ad;
'E's wounded, killed, and pris'ner, all the lot,
The bloody lot all rolled in one. Jim's mad.

(Owen, The Chances)

'*They*' is one of the poet's most effective outbursts, but as a poem
it is weakened by the too-amenable Bishop: Sassoon has shot, right
through the heart, a sitting duck. We feel less indignant than the
poem wants us to feel. *The Chances* – one of the very few successful
English 'proletarian' poems, incidentally – is an altogether richer
piece, a poem which will hold even though every bishop should take
a vow of pacifism or silence. The humour in the speaker's style –
with the implied modesty of one who has no intention of 'preaching'
– lays the reader open to the full onslaught of the last short sentence.
As for anger: that is not in the poem, it is in the reader.

Blunden quotes a friend's description of Owen: '... an intense pity for suffering humanity – a need to alleviate it, wherever possible, and an inability to shirk the sharing of it, even when this seemed useless. This was the keynote of Wilfred's character ...' It is also the keynote of his poetry. An instance is the fine lyric, *Futility*, as bare and cool and natural in its English as the poetry of Edward Thomas:

> Move him into the sun –
> Gently its touch awoke him once,
> At home, whispering of fields unsown.
> Always it woke him, even in France,
> Until this morning and this snow.
> If anything might rouse him now
> The kind old sun will know.
>
> Think how it wakes the seeds, –
> Woke, once, the clays of a cold star.
> Are limbs, so dear-achieved, are sides
> Full-nerved – still warm – too hard to stir?
> Was it for this the clay grew tall?
> – O what made fatuous sunbeams toil
> To break earth's sleep at all?

And the note sounds, more explicit, in the last stanza of *Insensibility*, beginning 'But cursed are dullards whom no cannon stuns':

> By choice they made themselves immune
> To pity and whatever moans in man
> Before the last sea and the hapless stars;
> Whatever mourns when many leave these shores;
> Whatever shares
> The eternal reciprocity of tears

– a passage sufficient in itself to prove that Owen is a poet, not a war poet alone. His use of assonantal rhyme (half-rhyme) should be remarked on here: perhaps deriving from his reading of French poetry, it afforded the measure of formal control he desired without the too melodious and (in view of his subject-matter) inexpedient chime of pure rhyme. Simultaneously, and notably in *Strange Meeting* and *Exposure*, it contributes a telling music of its own, ominous in its intonations:

> Watching, we hear the mad gusts tugging on the wire,
> Like twitching agonies of men among its brambles.
> Northward, incessantly, the flickering gunnery rumbles ...

In August 1918, his convalescence over, he returned to France, feeling that life there could not be harder to bear than 'the stinking Leeds and Bradford war-profiteers now reading *John Bull* on Scarborough Sands'. There was a more positive reason for his readiness to go back to the trenches: 'there', he wrote, 'I shall be better able to cry my outcry'. It was this compulsion to speak so as to be understood which guarded him against his Keatsian taste for rich sensuous language. In a letter to Sassoon, he declared: 'I don't want to write anything to which a soldier would say *No Compris!*'

When Owen was killed on 4 November, among his papers was found a draft preface to a future volume of poems. It is the best commentary on the work he left:

> This book is not about heroes. English poetry is not yet fit to speak of them.
> Nor is it about deeds, or lands, nor anything about glory, honour, might, majesty, dominion, or power, except War.
> Above all I am not concerned with Poetry.
> My subject is War, and the pity of War.
> The Poetry is in the pity.
> Yet these elegies are to this generation in no sense consolatory. They may be to the next. All a poet can do today is warn. That is why the true Poets must be truthful ...

In the Table of Contents, against *Strange Meeting*, possibly the last of his poems, possibly the finest, is written: 'Foolishness of War'. This poem is no doubt 'allegorical', but it succeeds through its sheer concretion: 'it is a dream only a stage further on than the actuality of the tunnelled dug-outs', as Blunden remarks, if indeed we think of it as a dream at all –

> It seemed that out of battle I escaped
> Down some profound dull tunnel ...

He rouses one of the 'encumbered sleepers' there:

> And by his smile, I knew that sullen hall,
> By his dead smile I knew we stood in Hell.

The other speaks of the wastage of life, of the ambition, which now cannot be realized, to help humanity by warning, by telling the truth:

> For by my glee might many men have laughed,
> And of my weeping something had been left,
> Which must die now. I mean the truth untold,
> The pity of war, the pity war distilled ...

The poem has its weaknesses, which the poet would surely have dealt with had he lived. The reference to 'chariot-wheels', even though we take the implication that 'all wars are one war', is out of place in the Hindenburg Line; while the half-rhyme works splendidly, the words 'mystery' and 'mastery' are vaguer in meaning than we might wish; and 'trek from progress' is a rather awkward concession to the exigencies of rhyme. But again and again the poet triumphs: in 'lifting distressful hands as if to bless', 'foreheads of men have bled where no wounds were', and the extracts quoted above and below. The poem ends:

> I am the enemy you killed, my friend.
> I knew you in this dark: for so you frowned
> Yesterday through me as you jabbed and killed.
> I parried; but my hands were loath and cold.
> Let us sleep now . . .

Isaac Rosenberg was the other indubitable poetic loss incurred in the war; he was killed at the age of twenty-seven. 'Scriptural and sculptural' are the adjectives by which Sassoon has described Rosenberg's use of language.[6] Isolated lines blaze with energy and colour (he was also a gifted painter); for example, the image of the 'dead heart' in *Midusmmer Frost*:

> A frozen pool whereon mirth dances;
> Where the shining boys would fish

– or the opening of *Day*:

> The fiery hoofs of day have trampled the night to dust;
> They have broken the censer of darkness and its fumes are lost in light.
> Like a smoke blown away by the rushing of the gust
> When the doors of the sun flung open, morning leaped and smote the
>   night . . .

Rosenberg was tougher-minded than Owen, less obsessed with the pity of things (and hence less exposed to the risk of sentimentality), and demonstrating a greater muscularity in his handling of words: 'elemental' is the term Ian Parsons applies to him.[7] But the relatively recent view which holds Rosenberg superior to Owen is, I would say, fairly clearly mistaken. Although in this case comparisons are more than usually odious, or at the very least otiose, it may be that three or four of his poems equal, or even surpass, anything in Owen. But such total successes are rare. The 'scriptural and sculptural' manner often seems merely overwrought, its effects exuberantly but too easily arrived at: this is the writing of an immensely promising poet who needed more time to develop, as well as to extricate himself (as Owen had to) from nineteenth-century conceptions of 'the poetical', than he was allowed. His finest poems are *Returning, We hear the Larks, August 1914, Break of Day in the Trenches* and *Dead Man's Dump*.

The relaxed manner, uncharacteristic of this poet, in which *Break of Day in the Trenches* opens is perfectly attuned to the soldier's light-hearted gesture, plucking a poppy in the quiet of dawn, and to his humorously ironic musings on the 'cosmopolitan' rat (cf. Lear's out-cry: 'Why should a dog, a horse, a rat, have life,/And thou no breath at all?'). There follows a succinct evocation of daily life and death at the front, unironic and sufficiently grim, but reached by a natural transition. Then we are returned, by way of the resonantly meta-phorical poppy whose root is 'in man's veins', to the literal flower tucked behind the speaker's ear and, for the moment, safe:

> The darkness crumbles away.
> It is the same old druid Time as ever,
> Only a live thing leaps my hand,
> A queer sardonic rat
> As I pull the parapet's poppy
> To stick behind my ear.
> Droll rat, they would shoot you if they knew
> Your cosmopolitan sympathies.
> Now you have touched this English hand
> You will do the same to a German
> Soon, no doubt, if it be your pleasure
> To cross the sleeping green between.
> It seems you inwardly grin as you pass
> Strong eyes, fine limbs, haughty athletes,
> Less chanced than you for life,
> Bonds to the whims of murder,
> Sprawled in the bowels of the earth,
> The torn fields of France.
> What do you see in our eyes
> At the shrieking iron and flame
> Hurled through still heavens?
> What quaver – what heart aghast?
> Poppies whose roots are in man's veins
> Drop, and are ever dropping;

But mine in my ear is safe –
Just a little white with the dust.

Mention must be made of Ivor Gurney, a victim of the war in mind if not in body: the odd phrasing and broken, confused course of his poems (*The Silent One* is among the most powerful) seem to enact with little mediation the jolting incoherence of the experiences behind them.[8] I have not included Edmund Blunden and Robert Graves in the province of war poets, though memories of the war have haunted their poetry ever since. They must feature here, however, as the authors of the two finest prose works to deal with the war. Blunden's *Undertones of War*, an established classic, is a work gentler in tone than those we have been chiefly concerned with (it was published in 1928), with literature and the English countryside never very far away, yet accurate and detailed in observation of the war scene and its human figures. *Goodbye to All That* (1929), Robert Graves's 'autobiography' (written at the age of thirty-three), dealing largely with his war experience, is the lively sort of writing we expect from the author, racy without being careless, crammed with short stories and brilliant character sketches, a little too casual and almost callous at times, but continuously readable. With these first-class accounts we must group Sassoon's *Memoirs of an Infantry Officer* (1930), a more painful work characterized by sensitive and minute documentation; and two shorter pieces by Herbert Read, *In Retreat* ('A journal of the retreat of the Fifth Army from St Quentin, March 1918') (1925) and *The Raid* (1930).[9]

David Jones's *In Parenthesis* (1937) is a consciously 'literary' work: its style is alternately tapestried and 'modernistic', mixing prose with free verse, Celtic myth with actualities of infantry life on the Western Front. Paul Fussell has recently defined the misgivings which the work has aroused in some readers: while 'profoundly decent', it is a curiously ambiguous attempt 'to elevate the new Matter of Flanders and Picardy to the status of the old Matter of Britain', and, for all the horrors recorded therein, the effect is 'to rationalize and even to validate the war by implying that it somehow recovers many of the motifs and values of medieval romance'.[10] It may seem as if, in the day, the author is offering future generations the 'consolation' Owen spoke of in his draft preface.

The prose writers too were under the compulsion to report, to inform and, however indirectly, to warn. All were affected by the new human experience of the war (Brooke's idealistic view of fighting and of fighting men had been borne out in part), the relationship between officers and men, with its 'depth of understanding and sympathy for which I know no parallel in civilian life', as Herbert Read has put it: 'the relationship was . . . like that of a priest to his parish'.[11] These writers were not only (as officers) priests, they were also interpreters.

NOTES

In writing this essay I was particularly indebted to Edmund Blunden's pamphlet, *War Poets 1914–1918* ('Writers and Their Work' Series, London, 1958) and to the short but substantial chapter on 'Trench Poets' in Vivian de Sola Pinto's *Crisis in English Poetry 1880–1940* (London, 1951). Later critical and biographical material is listed either in these notes or in the Bibliography.

1. The first comment occurred in a paper on John Masefield; the second in a letter to his mother, 28 April 1915, shortly after Brooke's death. (See Jean Moorcroft Wilson's biography, *Charles Hamilton Sorley*, London, 1985, and *The Collected Poems of Charles Hamilton Sorley*, edited by Jean Moorcroft Wilson, London 1985.) Compare these and the following comments on the need for a change in poetic style with Ezra Pound's statement: 'the poetry which I expect to see written during the next decade or so . . . will, I think, move against poppycock, it will be harder and saner, it will be . . . "nearer the bone" . . . its force will lie in its truth' (*Poetry Review*, February 1912).

2. See *The Collected Poems of Charles Hamilton Sorley* and *Charles Hamilton Sorley: A Biography*, both referred to above.

3. Edited by Edmund Blunden and first published in 1931. The memoir is reprinted in C. Day Lewis's *The Collected Poems of Wilfred Owen* (London, 1963). For a fuller account see Jon Stallworthy's biography, *Wilfred Owen* (London, 1974).

4. In the introduction to C. Day Lewis's edition referred to above.

5. 'Modernist Poetry and Civilization', *A Survey of Modernist Poetry* (with Laura Riding, 1927), reprinted in *The Common Ashpodel* (London, 1949).

6. In the foreword to Rosenberg's *Collected Poems*, edited by Gordon Bottomley and Denys Harding (London, 1937, 1949); included in Ian Parson's definitive edition, *The Collected Works of Isaac Rosenberg* (London, 1979).

7. In the introduction to his edition mentioned above.

8. See *Collected Poems of Ivor Gurney*, edited by P. J. Kavanagh (Oxford, 1982).

9. Both of these were included in the enlarged edition of *Annals of Innocence and Experience* (London, 1946) and subsequently in *Contrary Experience* (London, 1963).

10. *The Great War and Modern Memory* (New York and London, 1975).

11. 'The Impact of War', in the two volumes mentioned in note 6.

WYNDHAM LEWIS AND THE ICONS
OF ART

JOHN HOLLOWAY

The immediate purpose of this discussion is to suggest how Lewis's paintings and drawings, and his writings on art, may be related to his fiction and cast further light on it. The wider purpose is to explore how attention to the world of painting in the early twentieth century sheds light upon the new writing of the period, and shows that some well-established accounts of that writing are incomplete. Wyndham Lewis is the key figure in this respect because he did important work in both writing and the visual arts; while his pronouncements, in regard to the latter particularly, have been plentiful and forthright.

It would be easy to become immersed in the preliminaries to this large subject; perhaps one may begin by asserting that the general sense of what was achieved by the 'new poetry' of the 1910s and 1920s (Eliot, Pound, in part Yeats) has been thought of too closely in the context of *Symbolisme*, as 'Symbolist' or perhaps 'Post-Symbolist'. Chronologically, the latter term cannot but be right in one sense. But if it is to be right in any fuller sense, some unexpected things have to be allowed for, and 'Post-Symbolist' has to mean almost 'anti-*Symboliste*' in some respects.

Many of those interested in the 'new poetry' of that period think about it through some of Eliot's best-known critical remarks. Well known as they are, they had better be recalled here (my italics stress what is most to the present point):

... a gift for combining, for *fusing* into a single phrase, two or more *impressions* ... the metaphor identifies itself with what suggests it; the resultant is one and unique ... that *perpetual slight alteration of language* ... which evidences a very high development ... ('Massinger', 1920)

... the whole effect, the dominant tone, is due to the fact that a number of *floating feelings*, having an *affinity* to this emotion by no means superficially evident, have combined with it to give us a new emotion ...

... the poet has ... a particular medium ... in which *impressions* and experiences combine in peculiar and unexpected ways ... ('Tradition and the Individual Talent', 1917)

One can easily enough associate these remarks with what Pound had to say in *How to Read* about logopoeia as 'the *dance* of the intellect among words', and as taking count of 'known acceptances, of ironical play'. But Eliot's remarks send one back to Yeats's essay 'The Symbolism of Poetry' twenty years before:

... all sounds, all colours, all forms, either because of their pre-ordained energies or because of long association, evoke indefinable and yet precise emotions, or, as I prefer to think, call down among us *certain disembodied powers*, whose footsteps over our heart we call emotions; and when sound, and colour, and form are in a *musical* relation, a beautiful relation to one another, they become, as it were, one sound, one colour, one form, and *evoke* an emotion that is made out of their distinct emotions, and yet is one emotion.[1]

The Pateresque hegemony for music as art, and the link to nineteenth-century Occultism, are clear.

Such assertions send one back to the *Symboliste* poets, to Mallarmé and beyond:

... j'invente une langue qui doit nécessairement jaillir d'une poétique très nouvelle ... Peindre non la chose, mais l'effet qu'elle produit. (Mallarmé to Cazalis, October 1864)

Nommer un objet, c'est supprimer les trois-quarts de la *jouissance* du poème qui est fait du *bonheur* de *deviner peu à peu* ... le *suggérer*, voilà le rêve. C'est le parfait usage de ce mystère qui constitue la symbole; *évoquer* petit à petit un objet pour montrer un état d'âme, ou, inversement, choisir un objet et en dégager un état d'âme, par une *série de déchiffrements*. (Answer to Huret's *Enquête* ...)[2]

Two points become clear. First, the provenance of Eliot's words back to Yeats and Mallarmé points rather contrary to Pound's emphasis on '... known acceptances ... ironical play' – and so away from how those early remarks were to be taken further by Richards, Empson and the American New Critics. Second, we cannot but see an affinity between *Symbolisme* and Impressionist painting; and Wyndham Lewis's links with Pound (see below), alongside his reiterated rejection of Impressionist art, become food for thought.

This is no place for a full discussion of Impressionism; but its connection with *Symbolisme* is clearly suggested by the passages above. One recalls the words of Courbet, who meant so much to the Impressionists, addressing his pupils: 'Paint what you see, what you want, what you feel', later referred to as 'the key words of Impressionism'. Impressionism's characteristic treatment of shadow accords with 'peindre non la chose ...' Shadow is absence of light, hence darkness, hence blackness, only in abstraction. 'L'effet qu'elle produit' is in fact something else, it is the complementary colour of those pure prismatic hues that glow radiantly from Monet's gardens or cathedral fronts, or from Renoir's nubile, nacreous nudes. Corot said 'beauty consists in truth, bathed in impressions we receive from contemplating nature.'

The substantial connection between *Symboliste* poetry and Impressionist painting is by now clear: it could be made clearer by discussion of, for example, English poems like Wilde's *In the Gold Room* or Henley's *London Voluntaries*. But while Impressionist painting may indeed have emerged, directly and explicitly, from laws of colour and theories of vision, its most substantial feature is to represent a certain *Weltanschauung*. Zola said of Camille Pissarro's landscapes, 'You can hear the earth's deep voices'; Octave Mirbeau said of Monet's work that it 'created Nature anew'. Impressionist painting embodies the last great upsurge of European optimism. Monet's 'Houses of Parliament' (1904) are drenched in a celestial gold and violet haze. Pissarro's Paris street scenes of 1897 assert even crowded humanity as the dignified inhabitants of a warm, spacious, light-filled order. Monet's 1877 'Gare St Lazare' endows modern industrialism with relaxed, spacious, idyllic qualities, Renoir's nudes speak the same language again. If we can count Degas among the Impressionists, works like his 'Women Ironing' of 1884 speak of a similar outgoingness and abundance even in the life of toil. Monet's 'Boating Party' of 1881 tells the same happy, outgoing tale.

One can now see a new significance in Mallarmé's remarks above. For why is it a 'jouissance' to 'deviner, peu à peu' what 'la chose' essentially is? Spinning out the discovery of a sombre truth is no 'jouissance' at all. It can only be such because Nature is an endless joyous argosy of light, plenty, order ... 'calme et volupté'. *Symbolisme* reflects the same fundamental optimism.

One sees something else, though, in Degas, even as early as his 'Absinthe Drinkers' (1876); and with Gauguin that something else is also clearly present. Gauguin's paintings of Tahitian women superficially suggest the opposite ('. . . et l'or de leurs corps'); but the enigmatical facial expressions of his models, the pent-up strains and energies in their often awkward poses, tell another tale in both literary and formal terms. 'Bonjour Monsieur Gauguin' (1889) makes the point decisively clear. This landscape is not opulently benign like the Impressionists', but magical-seeming and mysterious. The central figure in it expresses, both by his posture in physical terms and simply as an alien mass in a design, bafflement, bewilderment, a man at a loss. Nor are all of Van Gogh's works like the blossoming trees, happy harvest fields and the like of some of his early works. In his 'Sunrise at Saint Rémy' (1889) the enormous sun, close down to the horizon, seems monstrous and menacing, and the earth glares with its light like a runaway, out-of-orbit planet heading for catastrophe. Four years before, Munch had produced the first version of 'The Cry' – of a Human, lost in a catastrophic world.

Wyndham Lewis repeatedly and scornfully dismissed Impressionism. When, in a late essay, he wrote, 'the painter should sever his connections with nature and should cease to behave like a copyist',[3] he had something utterly different in mind from what Mallarmé meant by 'peindre non la chose . . .' In fact it is T. E. Hulme who seems to make one part of Lewis's position clear, in his essay 'Modern Art'. Following Worringer (as is well enough known, and as he freely acknowledges), Hulme distinguishes two kinds of art: one that, coming naturally to Man, he calls 'vital art', identifies with 'naturalism or realism', sees represented in the achievements of classical Greece or of Europe since the Renaissance, and says that it offers 'pleasure' (*jouissance?*) through 'a feeling of increased vitality'. But that is possible, in Hulme's view, because we believe in a fundamental relation of goodness and harmony between Man and Nature ('a happy pantheistic relation between man and the outside world'); and therefore, since nothing can have a harmonious relation with chaos, also a harmony within Nature itself.

That is not what Gauguin, Van Gogh or Munch represented. Hulme contrasts it with art that expresses 'a feeling of separation in the face of outside nature', or 'lack of order and seeming arbitrariness' that evoke 'a certain fear'. Many will recall Hulme's application of this train of thought to the contemporary scene: 'I prophesy that a period of dry, hard, classical verse is coming': not much like Eliot's 'perpetual slight alterations of language', 'floating feelings', impressions and fusions. If Hulme did not mention Impressionism as the most recent and luxuriant of naturalistic art-forms, that was perhaps because, even in 1914, 'England was in an unusually somnolent condition' (Lewis's words) *vis-à-vis* recent continental developments in painting. 'England is just as unkind and inimical to Art as the Arctic zone is to Life', Lewis said (*Blast*, 1915).

Lewis appears to have got the word 'Vortex' from Pound, but where the latter used it to mean something like 'creative centre', collective or individual, Lewis gave it his own meaning. 'In Vorticism the direct and hot impressions of life are mated with Abstraction in the Combinations of the Will.' Clearly, such 'hot' impressions are remote from those of Impressionism *tout court*. In 1910–12, when Western European art was undergoing its greatest transformation for centuries, Lewis was uncompromising in his remarks on contemporary painting, and his demands as to what art should do. He spoke of the need for 'unadulterated extremism'. He firmly rejected (not always, perhaps, in quite consistent terms) even 'distortions of Nature' in such work no doubt as that of Van Gogh or the Fauves; but he rejected it because it meant that Nature still played some part in the painting. 'They were Naturalists, after all.' He condemned the vestigial naturalistic motifs in Kandinsky's early abstracts, and said that the Cubists were 'half-hearted' in non-representationalism. Vorticism was to be 'a substitute of architecture for painting': or, the essential idea was 'to build up a visual language as abstract as music'. The overtones of that were utterly different from analogies between music and literature drawn by Pater or Mallarmé.

Such remarks make one wonder what happens if Lewis's painting or drawings are set beside the work of other avant-garde artists of the time, like Kandinsky or the Cubists. Lewis and Kandinsky are poles apart: by the time of the publication of *Blast*, Kandinsky was indeed engaged upon fully abstract painting, but repeatedly, with a colourful *brio* and sometimes almost whimsically delicate (if also energetic) sense of form indeed far from Lewis's. On the other hand, many of Lewis's works from, say, the 'Smiling Woman Ascending a Stair' * to

---

*Reproduced in Walter Michel, *Wyndham Lewis, Paintings and Drawings*, 1971, item 27: future references to works by Lewis will be cited simply by 'M' and the number in Michel.

the 'Workshop' of 1915 (M, P15: rediscovered, one may note, in an antique shop in Baltimore in 1963) at least superficially suggests Cubism through their assertive linearity of design and bold effects of stylization. 'Portrait of an Englishwoman' (1913: M, 146) is another example. The work is executed in long narrow black rectangles, or in more nearly square white ones. Some of the 1912 designs for the *Timon of Athens* portfolio (published by the 'Cube' Press in 1913) also suggest Cubism by their intricate, stylized designs built up of straight lines and multiple intersecting geometric curves.

This impression, however, does not survive closer consideration. In the first place, none of Lewis's works displays the least tendency to portray the object through integration in a single design of multiple perspectives, as is generally attempted in analytic Cubism. Rather, Lewis seems occasionally to be exploiting Cubist techniques to serve a literary purpose: that, simply, of the aggressive, even brutal cartooner. The 1912 'Two Mechanics' (M, 144), where the heavy, bowed, stylized figures look as if they are carved out of teak and with the grain of the wood, is one example; the heavily stylized 'At the Seaside' (M, 123) is another.

Besides these particular instances, Lewis made perfectly clear his general rejection of Cubism:

> The Cubists' paintings have a large tincture of the deadness (as well as the weightiness) of Cézanne; they are static and representative, not swarming, exploding or burgeoning with life, as is the ideal of the Futurists, or *electric with a more mastered, vivid vitality*, which is the conception of their mission held by most of the Vorticists.[4]

In particular Lewis asserted that Cubism (of the early years, we ought perhaps to add) was limited by its links to Cézanne and beyond: 'it is essentially the same as Impressionism', because of its start from the 'studio-table with two apples and a mandoline'. Hence its tendency to 'slip back into facile and sententious formulas, and escape invention'. The practice of starting from the still-life model, Lewis declared, 'Vorticism repudiates as an absurdity and sign of relaxed initiative'.

Much early Cubism, seen simply against a background of Monet or even Cézanne, leaves an impression of the boldly, masterfully innovative. Seen beside Lewis's works, what catches the attention in Cubist works is something different: it is a certain gaiety, *brio* and delicacy. Braque's still-lifes of 'two apples and a mandoline',

Picasso's 'Card Player' (*c.* 1914), or his glitteringly crystalline 'Ambroise Vollard' (*c.* 1910), and Léger's 1912 'Woman in Blue' are remote in execution from the Impressionists; but, extreme as are their stylizations, they all start from a joyous, colourful, light-filled world, the *bonheur* and *jouissance* of Monet and Pissarro, the world of optimism, the world favourable to man. That is even true of aggressively anti-lyrical works like Picasso's 'Demoiselles d'Avignon' (1907), where exuberant femininity is clear in the parted thighs and luxuriantly raised arms of two of the figures; or in Braque's famous 'Blue Nude' of 1907–8, where much of the modelling sustains a clear sense of opulence of the female form. Delaunay's well-known 'Tour Eifel' of 1910 takes one straight back to the spacious gaieties of Pissarro's Paris street-scenes or to Monet's rue Montorgeuil and its happy flag-frippery of twenty years earlier. The appropriate contrast would be with Lewis's grimly severe and potently inhuman 'The Crowd' (M, P17) of 1915; of the 'Surrender of Barcelona' of 1936 (M, P61).

Lewis's Vorticist figures, of only several years later than the Cubist pictures just mentioned, tell a wholly different story. Drawings like 'Two Mechanics' (1912), or 'Courtship' of the same year, manifest a violent chiaroscuro, and an urge towards brutal caricature of the human form, as if its interest lay only in how it could be represented in some alien medium (hardwood, metal). Back to the reassuring optimism of the nineteenth century there is no continuity whatsoever. In 'Combat No. 2' and 'Combat No. 3' (M, 161, 162), drawings of 1914, the wrestlers are in heavy, ominous black, half anthropoid, half demonic or machine, 'electric' certainly with 'vivid vitality', while the environment in which we see them is minatory and Martian. The emotional resonance of these works is a blank hostility to humanity. Certain of Hulme's remarks in 'Modern Art' are again to the point:

In the new art ... There is rather a desire to avoid those lines and surfaces which look pleasing and organic, and to use lines which are clean, clearcut and mechanical. If we take this to be the new sensibility, and regard it as the culmination of the process of breaking-up and transformation in art, that has been proceeding since the impressionists ... the history of the last twenty years becomes more intelligible.[5]

Lewis's own position certainly does so.

Lewis's self-portraits in ink of 1920 (M, 423 *et seq.*) have the same effect: a statuesque wood-cut style suggests great power, brutal and largely inhuman. The 1919 portrait of Ezra Pound (M, P 26) is, as one contemporary critic said, 'large and intimidating', with a 'power of expressive feeling in form' that comes from the aggressive physiognomy and posture of the sitter and the harsh chiaroscuro and heavily rectilinear stylization of the treatment. 'Composition' (1919, M, 125) is a fine example of energy in abstract design, coming from dramatic organization around the diagonal, and brutal simplification of form and colour.

Such qualities link with Lewis's experiences on the Western Front, and the stark, inhuman, anti-nature treatment he gave them ('Drag Ropes'; 'The No. 2'; 'A Battery Shelled': M, 273, 295, P25). Of course, the chronology is wrong: those works are from 1918 and 1919. But for all that, Lewis may have been imagining the horrors of war and of the trenches before he actually experienced them. We have 'Slow Attack' and 'Plan of War' (M, P12, P13), both of 1913–14, and the curious 'Design for Programme Cover' (M, 52) of 1912, where the figures unquestionably look like British 'Tommies' of such later works as 'D. Sub-Section Relief' or 'Walking Wounded' (both 1918, M, 309, 322).

Lewis's visual-art work shortly before 1914 thus manifests a more drastic and self-assertive break with the past than either Abstractionism or Cubism. In *Men Without Art* (1934) Lewis formulated the magnitude of the change:

... an artist who is not a mere entertainer and money-maker ... must today be penetrated by a sense of the great discontinuity of our destiny. At every moment he is compelled to be aware of that different scheme, coming up as if by magic, behind all that has been so familiar for so long. (p. 126)

Like the Futurists, Lewis saw his new world in the image of the machine. But the Futurists saw the image of the machine as joyous and affirmative. Lewis brushed them aside: 'Their *paeans* to machinery were stupid'. For him, the machine image brought an emotional reverberation sometimes of impressive if intimidating power; more often, it was bleak, menacing, and anti-human. Both these responses can be traced in Lewis's novel *Tarr* (written 1912–14, published 1918; the quotations now following are from the 1928, somewhat revised edition). The interweaving in the first quotation below of the mechanical, the animal as mechanical function, and the 'magical' as source of power, is especially interesting. This is Anastasya (her beauty is insisted upon):

She wore a heavy black burnous, very voluminous and severe; a large ornamental bag was on the chair at her side, which one expected to contain herbs and trinkets, paraphernalia of the witch, rather than powder, lip-stick and mere beauty secrets. Her hat was immense and sinuous; generally her appearance implied an egotistic code of advanced order, full of insolent strategies. Beside her other women in the restaurant appeared dragged down and drained of vitality by their clothes ... Her large square-shouldered and powerful body swam in the fluidities of hers like a duck.

When she laughed, this commotion was transmitted to her body as though sharp sonorous blows had been struck upon her mouth. (II. 5)

Imagine Renoir – or Henry James – seeing beauty in such terms. The machine-like in human life as blackly absurdist is also easily illustrated from *Tarr*, either in the rape-scene ('the figure [of Kreisler] resembled a switchback, rising slowly in a steady innocent way, to the top of an incline, and then plunging suddenly down the other side in a catastrophic rush ... he was a mad beast') or in some parts of the duel-scene, where again the machine-like and the animal are united:

Soltyk became white and red by turns: the will was released in a muffled explosion ... His blood, one heavy mass, hurtled about in him, up and down, like a sturgeon in a narrow tank ... His hands were electrified ... his enemy was hurled about to left and right, he was pumped backwards and forwards. Otto's hands ... gripped along the coat sleeves, connecting him with *the engine he had just overcharged with fuel* ... (VI. 5)

What Lewis did, in both his visual art and his writing, was to integrate certain stylistic devices (which may have come to him, partly, from Cubism) with an emotional resonance of the bleak and brutal such as is to be found in certain Expressionist painters. One may mention here Beckmann's intense but impassive representations of human tortures and horrors, Rouault's whores and lawyers that become inhuman puppets, savage or absurd, or Max Ernst's grimly lunar fortress cities or nightmare forests. Such paintings are not near to Lewis in style and technique: but they are, in tone and resonance of feeling. Also, one must add, there is no question of Lewis's having evolved through study of Beckmann, Rouault, Ernst or the like. In fact, the works which have most affinity with Lewis (Beckmann's overwhelming self-portrait of 1934 would be an example) were largely executed later. Doubtless it is a matter of artists responding similarly to similar circumstances. In that regard, one should recall how Franz Marc, founder of the *Blaue Reiter* group and a German artist with some affinity, anyhow, to Beckmann and the others, wrote his *Aphorisms* at the Western Front in 1915, not very far away from Hulme when he was killed; and then was himself killed in action against the Allies. Some of Marc's paintings, like the 'Fighting Forms' or the 'Play of Forms', both of 1914, are indeed somewhat reminiscent of Lewis's work at the time, though with an altogether more colourful palette.

It is clear, then, that Lewis's paintings and writings over the 1910s (and much later also, though that is another matter) went on in close relation to each other, and that the visual art helps one to see what Lewis sought to achieve in his writing. But the interest of the comparison extends more widely than in respect of Lewis alone.

Suppose one sets a remark of Lewis's like 'A man could make just as fine art in discords, and with nothing but *"ugly" trivial and terrible* materials, as any classic artist did with only "beautiful" and pleasant means'[6] beside Eliot's lines at the beginning of *Gerontion*:

> ... I was neither at the hot gates
> Nor fought in the warm rain
> Nor knee deep in the salt marsh, heaving a cutlass,
> Bitten by flies, fought.

Or these lines from Eliot's *Sweeney Erect*:

> Tests the razor on his leg
>   Waiting until the shriek subsides.
> The epileptic on the bed
>   Curves backward, clutching at her sides.

(As it happens, Lewis's 'Figure Composition' (1912, M, 61) has a remarkably apt and convincing representation of Sweeney testing the razor.) Or consider *The Waste Land*:

> Here one can neither stand nor lie nor sit
> There is not even silence among the mountains
> But dry sterile thunder without rain
> There is not even solitude among the mountains
> But red sullen faces sneer and snarl
> From doors of mudcracked houses (ll. 340–46)

Doubtless ingenuity can find something of anything in anything; but can one really say that the dominant quality of such passages is 'perpetual slight alteration of language', or 'floating feelings' or the 'fusing' of 'impressions' ? – the ideas that Eliot was bringing forward almost in the same years as he wrote these passages and others like them? Lewis's concepts fit much better: 'electric ... with vivid vitality'; 'direct and hot impressions of life'; 'the mild lunatic asylum that it is our lot to inhabit'. And Eliot's 'hot gates' would well fit Lewis's oils of 1937, 'Inferno'.

Another Lewis oils, 'Inca Among the Birds' of 1933, with its dark masses, harsh striding movement, and remote, haughty expression on the face of the principal figure, helps one to find what is there to be found in a celebrated passage of Yeats, written twenty years after he had spoken of 'evocations' and 'musical relations', and contemporaneous therefore with Lewis's minatory phantasmagorias:

> Hardly are those words out
> When a vast image out of *Spiritus Mundi*
> Troubles my sight: somewhere in the sands of the desert
> A shape with lion body and the head of a man,
> A gaze blank and pitiless as the sun,
> Is moving its slow thighs, while all about it
> Reel shadows of the indignant desert birds.
>
> *(The Second Coming)*

Yeats also, then, was sometimes an 'Expressionist' artist, with the Expressionist note of laconic menace and non-human energy and power.

Lewis's positions are of help also over certain of Pound's *Cantos* which, if we approach them with the expectations that follow from Pound's statements on 'logopoeia' as amplified by Eliot, can seem only revolting. I think particularly of the Hell Cantos, XIV and XV, though also of the Purgatory Canto XVI:

> The stench of wet coal, politicians
> .... e and .... n, their wrists bound to their ankles,
> Standing bare bum,
> Faces smeared on their rumps,
>   wide eye on flat buttock,
> Bush hanging for beard ...
>
> (XIV, 2–7)

.....r less rowdy, ... Episcopus
       ..... sis,
           head down, screwed into the swill,
his legs waving and pustular,
           a clerical jock strap hanging back over the navel
his condom full of black beetles,
           tattoo marks round the anus,
and a circle of lady golfers about him.

(XV, 7-14)

Those last lines are something of a re-writing of Dante's vindictive
anecdote of meeting Filippo Argenti in Hell (see *Inferno*, VIII, 52-4);
but made more 'electric with vivid vitality', galvanized with brutal
humour, filled with more 'Violent life' (Lewis's phrase from the late
novel *Self-Condemned*, where he applies it generally to experience)
than in the original. Pound's Canto XIV, at one point, picks up
Yeats's 'vast image' phrase quoted above:

the blowing of dry dust and stray paper,
foetor, sweat, the stench of stale oranges ...
sows eating their litters
and here the placard ΕΙΚΩΝ ΓΗΣ

(XIV, 38-41)

Εἰκών γῆς is an 'icon', a vast image, of life on earth. Writing to
Wyndham Lewis in 1924, Pound refers to Canto XIV as 'a portrait
of England (specifically London) as she was when I left her'. Lewis
achieved the indelible, stylized solemnity of the 'icon' in his work of
this period ('Gossips', 1917; 'Enemy of the Stars', 1913: M, 252,
143). The 'icon' also recalls Rouault because of his connection with
the tradition of stained glass, the nearest equivalent in Western
ecclesiastical art to the Orthodox icon. One recalls Pound's 'phanopoeia', rather than 'logopoeia'. 'Phanopoeia' was 'a casting of images
on the visual imagination'; but perhaps it has generally been understood as too much like the 'dance' of the intellect, as too much matter
of 'floating', 'fusing', 'music'. Casting of images may also be, as in
Expressionist painting, grimly univocal and minatory, wholly
different from what is thought of when *Imagism* comes to mind.

  Pound's transformation of Dante's account of meeting Filippo
Argenti introduces an element of brutal caricature which should also
not be overlooked in Lewis's work. The 'Tyro' drawings of 1920-21,
and the 1926-7 covers for *The Enemy*, exemplify it dramatically (M,

P31, P27, 470, 620, 633, 634). So does a suaver cartoon like 'The Duc de Joyeux Sings' (1920s; M, 662). From them it is only a step to the stylized caricature-portraits like that of Mosley (1934; M, 845); and thence to the range of more or less realistic ironical portraits of Establishment figures (Chesterton, C. B. Cochran, Priestley, Rother-mere, Spender). Lewis labelled one, at least, of his many self-portraits 'Self-caricature'. This side of his work shows his dazzling flair as a draughtsman and portraitist, even of a rather 'glossy' kind.

Lewis was clear that his work in visual art, and writing, connected:

Vorticism, in fact, was what I, personally, did, and said, at a certain period. This may be expanded into a certain theory regarding visual art; and (much less theoretically) a view of what was excellent in literary art. *The Enemy of the Stars* [he refers of course to the play] and the first version of the novel *Tarr* exemplified the latter of these two intellectual novelties.[7]

Thinking about Lewis's visual and literary art together, however, serves a more important purpose than to elucidate either of the works he mentions. It throws light on what Yeats, Pound and Eliot were writing in their crucial years, and enables us to recognize those works for what essentially they were: contributions to European Expression-ism.[8] It shows us that the seminal critical ideas of Eliot were both incomplete and misleading, as a guide to his verse, or to that of his contemporaries. That verse was more in alignment with the major art-movements of its time than has been commonly recognized.

A brief comparison, in the matter of visual art, is useful as between Lewis and Lawrence; because, with very different results, both often put a curiously similar stress on the idea of 'life' as a key to success in art; though the point of course is that by the same word they meant utterly different things. Lewis strongly repudiates how some relate the two. 'Life is the important thing!', he repeats scornfully, and scornfully adds: 'Life is the important thing, indeed, if much painting of Life that we see is the alternative'. To think like that, he claims, is a rejection of 'the pure painter as snob', and his ultimately dis-ablingly Impressionist affiliations.

Yet in another sense, Lewis sees Life as something like the ultimate artistic value. 'Rubens *imitated* Life ... traced the sprawling and surging of its animal hulks.' But Leonardo '*made new beings*, delicate and severe'. To do so is 'no *equivalent* for life, but *another* life' (his italics). What Lewis wishes to stress is some principle of energy intrinsically embodied in the work: what he calls elsewhere 'mastered vitality', or the 'vivacity' he praises in the Futurists. When he praises Wadsworth's paintings in the London Group Show of 1915, what he singles out is 'the quality of *Life*'; but he immediately explains it in the terms of 'the condensed . . . vivacity' of the painter's bold styliz-ations.[9]

True, for Lawrence something not altogether remote from this is the essence of painting: a 'deep seizure of the consciousness'; great works are 'made by the whole consciousness . . . in unison and one-ness'.[10] But, when he writes of 'the actual *touch* of Life' as essential to true art, or, in 'Making Pictures' (*c.* 1929), of finding in some of his own early trials 'something that delighted me – a certain glow of Life', he means something quite unlike Lewis: he means the paint-ing has caught something of the 'real substance' of its *subject*; the 'appleyness' of the model ('Introduction to these Paintings').

Bearing in mind Lawrence's dissatisfaction with Impressionism, one may ask how he sought this ultimate reality and solidity of, not the painting, but the subject. It is not easy to say, because Lawrence's paintings are even less available as originals than Lewis's. One has only *The Paintings of D. H. Lawrence*, edited by Mervyn Levy (1964) as guide. Even so, certain stylizations on Lawrence's part, though totally different from the stylizations of Lewis, seem to be genuinely part of the dominant effect of his works.

Lawrence said that, for him, landscape was no more than a setting for the human body, which was a painter's central reality; and his dominant effect, repeatedly, is of a great solidity, ponderousness and ultimate self-subsistence of that human body. He made light of the idea of 'being able to draw', and at the close of the 'Introduction to these Paintings' has a long, hilarious passage about the wondrous things to be learnt at Art Schools. All the same, one ought to give weight to his apparent technical limitations, since it is *prima facie* pos-sible that some of the most uncharacteristic and meaningful things about his work are not unrelated to it. That being said, there is cer-tainly a marked immobility about the figures in many of his paintings ('Contadini', 'The Lizard', 'Under the Haystack', 'Close-up – The Kiss', 'Renascence of Man'). Likewise, in certain paintings where movement is an essential, it becomes movement caught in, as it were, a moment of immobility. The leaping nudes in 'Fire Dance' bear a striking resemblance to the immobile ones of 'Yawning', while 'Fight with an Amazon' looks like a momentary pause in the fight; and in consequence surprisingly resembles the early 'An Idyll'.

This last work shows a shepherd embracing a coy yet yielding nymph or the like, and both the nymph's braced backward instep, and her lover's braced arms, make her buxom, sagging weight, her 'appley' heaviness, the main effect. Which is indeed characteristic: in 'The Rape of the Sabine Women', which in reproduction looks like one of Lawrence's finest oils, the whole picture is given over to representing what it means to lift and carry the nubile but passively un-cooperative Sabines. Hence why the painting chiefly depicts the generous calves, breasts and buttocks, or the powerful haunches, backs and shoulder muscles, that create, or effortfully lift, that heaviness. Hence also why of the three faces in the work, two are featureless, and the third looks right out of the picture. The emotions towards which the work is designed lie in musculature rather than physiognomy.

In fact, a non-interrelation between faces and glances is remarkably recurrent in Lawrence's work. 'Fauns and Nymphs' depicts five figures in close, amorous proximity: none looks at any other. 'Flight back into Paradise', closely examined, is the same. In 'Family on a Veranda', the children's heads are turned away and down, the woman is either asleep or gazing sleepily through the window, the man at her feet seems to gaze at her navel. In 'Throwing Back the Apple', Adam's back is turned, and God's exiguous face is at the very edge of the painting. In 'Dance Sketch' the man seems to look at the woman, but she disregards him. In 'Resurrection', none of the three figures meets the gaze of any other: the design throws the emphasis on how the weight of Christ is being taken – under his armpit, under his elbow, his right hand (invisibly) on the Magdalene's left breast. Herbert Read thought that in 'The Feast of the Radishes' the small red figures in the background were 'dancers'. More likely, they are on the 'gaily decorated stalls, each festooned with huge *radishes* carved into human and animal figures'.[11] If so, the 'toy' figures contrast with the dark, heavily draped, immobile human shapes in the foreground. Here, just one couple looks at each other, or almost does; but the rest, hooded or as if veiled, are nearly faceless, while the figure of Lawrence himself is eyeless.

This preoccupation with the physical solidity of the human shows also in the slow, plodding, leaning woman in the early 'Landscape with Figure'. What we see is her back; and the general strong predominance of the back views of figures (see, for another remarkable example, 'Red Willow Trees') ought not to be attributed to inability on Lawrence's part over drawing faces – witness the superbly striking and convincing Eve in 'Throwing Back the Apple', or the work entitled 'The Lizard', or many others – but to Lawrence's preoccupation with bodily weight or bodily power. He depended on this, to achieve the 'reality of substantial bodies', the appley 'woman of flesh, the first Eve who lived before any of the fig-leaf nonsense'.

Lewis's art was avant-garde in an individual way; but Lawrence's was too. His dexterity as a draughtsman was not like Lewis's, which was remarkable; but his recognition of the limitations of Impressionism, though quite different from Lewis's, was every bit as articulate; and his fundamental ambitions as a painter, 'literary' as in a sense they were, went deeper, along their own particular line, than that of any contemporary. 'I can never look on art save as a form of delight', he wrote in 'Making Pictures'. These strong but ordinary faces, these powerful, heavy, sleepy-seeming bodies, indeed have what Lawrence called for in painting – 'real substance', 'the actual *touch* of life', and the 'delight' that he sought and that that can give.

NOTES

1. *Essays and Introductions* (1961), 156–7.
2. See *Modern French Poets on Poetry* (1961), ed. R. Gibson, 143–4. The following are translations of the passages: 'I am inventing a language that cannot but spring from a wholly new poetic ... to depict, not the thing itself, but the effect it produces'; 'To refer to an object by name is to suppress three quarters of the enjoyment of the poem, which is made up of the happiness of intuiting little by little ... to *suggest* something, there is the magical thing. A symbol is a mystery, and doing that is what puts it perfectly to use: evoking an object, little by little, so as to display a condition of the soul, or on the other hand selecting an object and releasing a condition of the soul from it through a series of "decipherings".'
3. See *Wyndham Lewis on Art* (1969), ed. Walter Michel and C. J. Fox, 454.
4. *Wyndham Lewis on Art*, 59.
5. *Speculations*, 97.
6. *Wyndham Lewis on Art*, 50.

7. *Wyndham Lewis on Art*, 451.

8. It should be noted that Lewis himself used 'Expressionist' differently, and identified it principally with Kandinsky. See *Wyndham Lewis on Art*, 63.

9. *Wyndham Lewis on Art*, 32–5, 59, 85.

10. 'Introduction to these Paintings', in *Phoenix*, ed. E. D. McDonald, 1936, 6, 561, 573–4.

11. M. Levy, *The Paintings of D. H. Lawrence*, 67.

THE LATER POETRY OF W. B. YEATS

GRAHAM MARTIN

There seem to be two distinct kinds of difficulty in Yeats's major poems. One, the focus of much discussion, is the relevance of Yeats's beliefs to his verse, and the sometimes cryptic symbolism with which – some claim and some deny – he succeeded in expressing these beliefs. The second has received less attention, and is certainly less easy to identify. Yeats's major work (i.e. from 1918 to his death in 1939) appeared during a period in which the combined influence of Eliot's poetry and criticism was more and more felt to have super-annuated the tradition out of which Yeats grew. Whatever the rights of this view, there is no doubt that to go to Yeats from the Eliot 'quatrain' poems – if I can use them to pinpoint one pervasive in-fluence on a modern reader – entails as thorough a revision of critical expectancy as to go from Pope to Wordsworth. In what follows, I have tried to approach Yeats with this particularly in mind.

The first section of this chapter discusses *Meditations In Time Of Civil War*, the poem in which Yeats most fully expresses his attitude to the common nightmare of his time: in Pound's phrase, to the 'botched civilization'. This allows a useful contrast with Eliot; but more importantly, it details the way in which a specifically Irish event is the stimulus to Yeats's meditation on the common theme in terms which have an honourable nineteenth-century pedigree. Yeats's romantic inheritance is not simple. When in about 1903 he began to re-formulate his poetic idiom in a way that was soon to impress the young Ezra Pound, he seems to be reaching forward into the new century. 'My work has got more masculine. It has more salt in it' ... 'the error of late periods like this is to believe that some things are inherently poetical' ... 'I believe more strongly every day that the element of strength in poetic language is common idiom.'[1] But he is also reaching back into the deeper meanings of the complex relationship between the romantic artist and society which the late

Victorian period of his youth had simplified and narrowed. The Irish
situation was to provide in his life, and by metaphor in many poems,
the arena in which Yeats recapitulated that relationship with unique
intensity.

In the second section, I have concentrated on two issues: the
question of Yeats's 'philosophy', on the way in which ideas enter into
his poems, and the kind of importance – limited in my view – which
they have; and the particular quality of feeling many of his lesser
poems evoke. This seems to me to be sufficiently unlike any other
twentieth-century poet to require some stress. The complex, self-
aware, meditative poems like *Among Schoolchildren* and *Sailing to
Byzantium* are very fine, but it is difficult not to feel that they owe
something of their prominence in Yeats's criticism to the fact that
they are mostly easily discussed in the critical tradition represented
by, for example, Cleanth Brooks's *The Well Wrought Urn*. But
'Those men that in their writings are most wise Own nothing but
their *blind, stupefied* hearts' [2] – that is quite commonly Yeats's centre
and, in the twentieth century, not the least either of his challenges
or of his claims to greatness.

> 'And no one knows, at sight, a masterpiece.
> And give up verse, my boy,
> There's nothing in it.'
> ... Don't kick against the pricks,
> Accept opinion. The 'Nineties' tried your game
> And died, there's nothing in it.
>
> (Ezra Pound, *Hugh Selwyn Mauberley*)

There was certainly not much in it for Yeats – 'never ... more than
two hundred a year ...' he noted of his early career, 'and I am not
by nature economical'[3] – and without Lady Gregory, without the Irish
movement as a whole, it is unlikely that he would have reached even
this precarious independence. Yeats knew what image 'the age demanded'. As much as Eliot, Yeats lived through 'the beating down
of the wise'; even, in a biographical sense, more. Born in 1865, he
was old enough to have had very different hopes about the twentieth
century from those entertained by his younger contemporaries.

New from the influence, mainly the personal influence, of William Morris,
I dreamed of enlarging Irish hate, till we had come to hate with a passion
of patriotism what Morris and Ruskin hated ... We were to forge in Ireland

a new sword on our old traditional anvil for the great battle that must in the end re-establish the old, confident, joyous world.[4]

With memories like these, it is not surprising that the tone of Yeats's dealings with the 'filthy modern tide' has little in common with the mordant commentaries of Eliot and Pound. And in all of Yeats's mature poems, it is *tone* – in an exact sense – that one immediately notices.

> What shall I do with this absurdity –
> O heart, O troubled heart – this caricature,
> Decrepit age that has been tied to me
> As to a dog's tail?
>
> (*The Tower*, 1927)

> A tree there is that from its topmost bough
> Is half all glittering flame and half all green
> Abounding foliage moistened with the dew;
> And half is half and yet is all the scene;
> And half and half consume what they renew,
> And he that Attis' image hangs between
> That staring fury and the blind lush leaf
> May know not what he knows, but knows not grief.
>
> (*Vacillation*, 1932)

> Come, fix upon me that accusing eye.
> I thirst for accusation. All that was sung,
> All that was said in Ireland is a lie
> Bred out of the contagion of the throng,
> Saving the rhyme rats hear before they die.
> Leave nothing but the nothings that belong
> To this bare soul, let all men judge that can
> Whether it be an animal or a man.
>
> (*Parnell's Funeral*, 1934)

> No dark tomb-haunter once; her form all full
> As though with magnanimity of light,
> Yet a most gentle woman; who can tell
> Which of her forms has shown her substance right?
>
> (*A Bronze Head*, 1939)[5]

Self-mockery, visionary exaltation, contemptuous defiance, elegy – Yeats's consistently public tone accommodates an extraordinary range of feeling. It presupposes a listener of even wider experience than that humanistic figure, 'the normal active man', that the poet set himself to express in 1909 when he began to wither into the creative disillusionment of his major work. To write like this out of Pound's 'botched civilization' certainly argues a very surprising command of his own experience, and even when contemporary barbarism is his theme, it is still Yeats's *command* that one principally notices.

> The cloud-pale unicorns, the eyes of aquamarine,
> The quivering half-closed eyelids, the rags of cloud or of lace,
> Or eyes that rage has brightened, arms it has made lean,
> Give place to an indifferent multitude, give place
> To brazen hawks. Nor self-delighting reverie,
> Nor hate of what's to come, nor pity for what's gone,
> Nothing but grip of claw, and the eye's complacency,
> The innumerable clanging wings that have put out the moon.
>
> I turn away and shut the door, and on the stair
> Wonder how many times I could have proved my worth
> In something that all others understand or share;
> But O! ambitious heart, had such a proof drawn forth
> A company of friends, a conscience set at ease,
> It had but made us pine the more. The abstract joy,
> The half-read wisdom of daemonic images,
> Suffice the ageing man as once the growing boy.
>
> (*Meditations In Time Of Civil War*, 1923)

Yeats is writing in the syntax and idiom of ordinary discourse – elaborated only at moments of intensity, and then very slightly – of an experience which on the face of it seems likely to make ordinary discourse impossible. Even though, as he states in the earlier verses, this estranging vision evokes 'monstrous familiar images' which 'bewilder [and] perturb the mind', the mind continues to act, to define, to persuade. 'Brazen hawks' and 'the innumerable clanging wings' point towards nightmare, but the effect – hawks are not made of brass, brazen usually applies to hussies, wings do not clang – of conscious trope is not to draw us into the experience of an alienated mind, but to warn (perhaps to remind) us of the possibility. The tone unites us with the 'I' of the poem, over against his prophetic insight: on the one hand, the hawks, urgent and dreadful; but on the other, the precisely judged '*indifferent* multitude'; and again, 'the eye's *complacency*' balances 'grip of claw', the critical observation is intensified, not obliterated by the monstrous image.[6]

Yeats wrote *Meditations In Time Of Civil War* during the summer of 1922 – the war broke out in June – and, significant enough in his country's history, the event had a particular meaning for the poet. He had already (certainly by 1922, but the following passage was probably drafted in 1916–17) come to accept that fact that

the dream of my early manhood, that a modern nation can return to Unity of Culture, is false; though it may be we can achieve it for some small circle of men and women, and there leave it till the moon bring round its century.[7]

He had, that is, given up hope that Ireland would produce, and that he would contribute to, an art both major and popular. What remained was the limited achievement of writing for a sympathetic coterie, and the verse-plays of *Four Plays for Dancers* (1921) are precisely that. 'In writing these little plays I knew that I was creating something which could only fully succeed in a civilization *very unlike ours*'[8] – Yeats is adjusting his ambitions to the restricted community of 'some fifty people in a drawing room', and the achieved content is correspondingly thin. But in *Meditations*, the old dream reasserts itself in a painful yet fruitful way. The fact that Ireland is no exception to the historical rule has come true in the most tragic terms: the fact of the war resurrects in Yeats's mind the whole structure of youthful hopes, and involves him in a more thorough abandonment of those hopes than he had expected.

Thus, the poem is not only a generous humanitarian response to the war, but stimulus to a far-reaching personal examination, and it was this because the 'Irish' dream was a moving force in the development of Yeats's major poetry. Yeats's sense of his own identity and function as a poet begins to take shape in the context of Irish nationalism, out of his deliberate and many-sided effort to provide the movement with some finer motive than mere hate of the English. He complains in 1909, for example, that

the political class in Ireland – the lower middle-class from whom the patriotic associations have drawn their journalists and their leaders for the past ten years – have suffered through a cultivation of hatred as the one energy of their movement, a deprivation which is the intellectual equivalent to a certain surgical operation. Hence the shrillness of their voices. They contemplate all creative power as the eunuchs contemplate Don Juan as he passes through Hell on the white horse.[9]

The function of the Abbey was to supply 'loftier thought, Sweeter emotion'; to dramatize 'the Ireland of men's affections [as] self-moving, self-creating'.

... in the work of Lady Gregory, of Synge, of O'Grady, of Lionel Johnson, in my own work, a school of journalists with simple moral ideas could find right building material to create a historical and literary nationalism as powerful as the old and nobler. That done, they could bid the people love and not hate.'[10]

The journalists, however, refused to be taught, and it was the recognition of this, forced upon Yeats by the reception of Synge's *Playboy*, and later by the Hugh Lane controversy, that provoked him to the new powers of expression, evident in *The Green Helmet* (1910) and *Responsibilities* (1914). (In the latter volume, the significant group of poems is Nos. II to VIII: see Yeats's note on the 'three public controversies', with which he associated them.)

By 1922, all this deep personal and artistic significance was a matter of accepted history; but to foresee the failure of a dream, and to live through a consequence of that failure are different things. In 1916, for example, Yeats could describe the bloody Easter Rising which destroyed a good part of O'Connell Street, as having given birth to 'a terrible beauty'. But the violence of the Troubles had a different aspect.

> Now days are dragon-ridden, the nightmare
> Rides upon sleep: a drunken soldiery
> Can leave the mother, murdered at her door,
> To crawl in her own blood, and go scot-free;
> The night can sweat with terror as before
> We pieced our thoughts into philosophy,
> And planned to bring the world under a rule,
> Who are but weasels fighting in a hole.
>
> *(Nineteen Hundred and Nineteen*, 1921)

Yeats felt responsible for the Troubles as he had not done for the Rising, and an acute sense of guilt is at the poem's heart:

> We, who seven years ago
> Talked of honour and of truth,
> Shriek with pleasure if we show
> The weasel's twist, the weasel's tooth.

As the over-emphasis indicates, the shock goes deeper than he is able to control, and in the poem's argument – that the particular catastrophe mirrors both a metaphysical condition ('Man is in love and loves what vanishes,/What more is there to say?') and a historical process (see poem VI) – there is a complementary vagueness. The opening stanzas, for example, assert a bond between the 'ingenious lovely things' of art, and 'a law indifferent to blame or praise': 'the nightmare' of violence and terror destroys both, and for Yeats, these are newly significant interconnections. But the poem leaves them unexplored, concentrating instead on the plight of 'He who can read the signs', and upon his emotions of moral outrage and despair.

Meditations is an advance on this. The political catastrophe appears not as an unexplainable revelation of man's state, but as the inevitable period to a whole phase in Irish history. The 'I' of the poem is less a person (confused by double loyalties) than a poet with a clear function, the unambiguous witness not of 'many ingenious lovely things' but of 'life's own self-delight'.

There are seven sections to the poem. In the first, 'Ancestral Houses', Yeats evokes only to discard a familiar image for Unity of Culture, the house-and-garden of the eighteenth-century Anglo-Ireland.

> ... now it seems
> As if some marvellous empty sea-shell flung
> Out of the obscure dark of the rich streams,
> And not a fountain, were the symbol which
> Shadows the inherited glory of the rich.

The very excellence of past creations has exhausted the creative energies, and the present impulses have yet to crystallize. In poems II to IV, he erects symbols appropriate for a poet isolated by destructive social change. In poems V and VI he shows his response – part-envy, part-revulsion – to the actual business of war. Finally, in poem VII he prophesies the threatening future which 'the indifferent multitude' is likely to command. Here, then, is Yeats's 'waste land', his most extended meditation on the contemporary theme, written shortly before the first appearance of Eliot's poem in October 1922. One major difference is clear at once. In both poems the identity of the observer is comparable: both are poets, both witnesses of threatened cultural traditions; but in Eliot's poems, the observer is not distinct from what he observes – we see a state of mind as much as a social condition– whereas in Yeats's what the poet diagnoses exists on its own public and historical terms. This distinction enters each poem's detail, and leads to others:

> DA
> *Dayadhvam*: I have heard the key
> Turn in the door once and turn once only
> We think of the key, each in his prison
> Thinking of the key, each confirms a prison
> Only at nightfall, aethereal rumours
> Revive for a moment a broken Coriolanus.
> (The Waste Land)

> We are closed in, and the key is turned
> On our uncertainty; somewhere
> A man is killed, or a house burned,
> Yet no clear fact to be discerned:
> Come build in the empty house of the stare.

The points of comparison are clear enough: the common metaphor, the common condition of isolation, uncertainty, fear, the common prayer for deliverance (though that is too emphatic a term for the Eliot passage). But it is the differences that matter. Eliot's verse – and in this respect, the lines are typical – is wholly given over to defining the subtle condition, the lost identity and listless self-involvement which are both cause and effect of this condition. Eliot's 'I' is incapable of experience, because incapable of the self-definition which precedes it; and his 'we' is an aggregate of such lost souls. Yeats's lines follow a different direction: the fear and menace are there (who turned the key?), but opposing them is 'uncertainty' – the condition has a name; 'somewhere A man is killed, or a house burned' – it has nameable causes; and though 'no clear fact [is] to be discerned', still, 'facts' exist, and 'discernment' is possible. In the full context, these differences become more exact:

> *The Stare's Nest by My Window*
> The bees build in the crevices
> Of loosening masonry, and there
> The mother birds bring grubs and flies.
> My wall is loosening; honey-bees,
> Come build in the empty house of the stare.

> We are closed in, and the key is turned
> On our uncertainty; somewhere
> A man is killed, or a house burned,

> Yet no clear fact to be discerned:
> Come build in the empty house of the stare.
>
> A barricade of stone or of wood;
> Some fourteen days of civil war;
> Last night they trundled down the road
> That dead young soldier in his blood:
> Come build in the empty house of the stare.
>
> We had fed the heart on fantasies,
> The heart's grown brutal from the fare;
> More substance in our enmities
> Than in our love; O honey-bees,
> Come build in the empty house of the stare.

The prison is both actual and metaphorical, a place as well as a condition of mind, and these two meanings coexist without interfering with each other. Correspondingly, the lines hold two distinct attitudes in a single tension: the fear of inner collapse in 'My wall is loosening'; and the creative purposefulness of 'build', 'mother birds', and 'house'. The subsequent stanzas develop this contrast, and the last one generalizes it. The firm syntax, the detailed report, the ballad refrain work an effect wholly opposite to that of the Eliot lines; they protest against the condition of 'We are closed in', rather than state its fullness, so that the isolation of Yeats's prison becomes not a paralysis, so much as an opportunity for diagnosis and judgement. Moreover, the war – literal cause of the imprisonment – is the appropriate occasion for these thoughts. It involves the poet because the utopian 'fantasies' which brutalize the heart lead through war to 'That dead young soldier in his blood'. The poet's 'We' involves him in that death (contrast the 'we' of the Eliot lines), and this gives conviction to his prayer. Yeats's 'O honey-bees, Come *build* ...' grows from the metaphor which demonstrates his sickness. The invocation is not applied to the situation, it is his intimate response to it. Comparably, Eliot's 'Dayadhvam' is part of the diagnosis, an Olympian comment.

Now the argument which links the various poems in *Meditations* identifies culture, with the poet as witness, with the fountain of 'life's own self-delight'. Just as the 'golden grasshoppers and bees' of *Nineteen Hundred and Nineteen* are, in comparison with the 'honey-bees' of the above verse, merely beautiful objects; so, in the later

poem, 'culture' means no longer 'Many ingenious lovely things ...
That seemed sheer miracle to the multitude', but the self-moving self-
creating energies of life itself.

> Surely among a rich man's flowering lawns,
> Amid the rustle of his planted hills,
> Life overflows without ambitious pains;
> And rains down life until the basin spills ...

> ... Mere dreams, mere dreams! Yet Homer had not sung
> Had he not found it certain beyond dreams
> That out of life's own self-delight had sprung
> The abounding glittering jet ...

The poem shows that two kinds of change threaten the poet's
ability to give proper voice ('Homer') to this meaning. First, there
is the superannuation of the old social forms which throws the poet
upon his own resources of personal symbol – 'My House', 'My
Table', 'My Descendants', and

> An ancient bridge, and a more ancient tower,
> A farmhouse that is sheltered by its wall,
> An acre of stony ground,
> Where the *symbolic* rose can break in flower. [*my italics*]

This change the poet has to accept, because 'if no change appears/No
moon; only an aching heart/Conceives a changeless work of art'. The
real source of life is 'the obscure dark of the rich streams' of history,
and the poet must remain sensitive to this. It is because he does, that
the calamity outlined in the quoted stanzas of *The Stare's Nest* is also
a source of new life.

But there is another change which the poet cannot turn to account:
the portentous vision of poem VII *I see Phantoms of Hatred and of the
Heart's Fulness and of the Coming Emptiness*. Faced with 'Nothing but
grip of claw, and the eye's complacency', with a future 'indifferent'
not simply to the delicacies of art, but callous, insentient, uninvolved
in life itself, the poet can find no possible identity. His towered isolation becomes therefore the refuge of 'life's own self-delight' from
'the coming Emptiness'.

> And I, that count myself most prosperous,
> Seeing that love and friendship are enough,
> For an old neighbour's friendship chose the house

And decked and altered it for a girl's love,
And know whatever flourish and decline
These stones remain their monument and mine.

'Seeing that love and friendship are enough', 'The mother birds bring grubs and flies' – if we think of *The Waste Land* these may seem simple formulas; but they do not emerge from any turning away from the contemplated present; and the strength which makes them convincing is not simple. The central appeal is underwritten by the clear statement of what 'poet' and what 'culture' mean in this situation. Yeats is evoking in terms of his particular experience a traditional protest,[11] less subtly than Eliot, but with a satisfying freedom from hesitation and ambiguity. *The Waste Land*'s use of literature as a means of definition and perspective ('a broken Coriolanus'), and so a shorthand statement of attitude, often gives questionable status to covert 'personal' judgements, to feelings that the poet seems unwilling to declare. Yeats, on the other hand, as the closing lines of poem VII suggest, includes his own failure in the total analysis. Similarly, his '*We* had fed the heart on fantasies' is wholly candid: one sign of his own involvement in the whole historical event.

But the main point is not whether or not Yeats is more 'positive' than Eliot – whose strength in *The Waste Land* is, after all, in being 'negative', in showing what happens when you go beyond the limit of 'brazen hawk' into the experience it points to – but in the different response to the contemporary nightmare. For Yeats, there are established positions, and his response to the threat is to state these. That is not to say that he comes to the event with a ready-made answer: the difference between *Nineteen Hundred and Nineteen* and *Meditations* shows that it took the severe pressure of the whole experience to arrive at the control and understanding of the later poem. There is, in these poems, and in the movement between them, an interplay of individual attitude and public event which it is not easy to parallel; and this participation between Yeats and 'events' – intimate, yet principally on Yeats's own terms, so that the events re-emerge in what people call Yeats's *myth* – is central to his development as a poet. You cannot understand this process simply in terms of a literary tradition, working itself out; simply in terms of maturing 'personal' experience.

> You that would judge me, do not judge alone
> This book or that, come to this hallowed place
> Where my friends' portrait's hang and look thereon;
> Ireland's history in their lineaments trace;
> > (*The Municipal Gallery Revisited*, 1937)

The point needs stressing if only to underline that the ubiquitous assurance of the public 'tone' arises from a genuinely public, a genuinely social poetry – the fact is important whatever final assessment the social ideas and insights require – and if the tone marks Yeats off from Eliot, then his right to it, as the upshot of a continuing relationship with the history of his own country, marks him off from Auden. (Auden often takes over the manner, but he could not inherit the relationship, nor did he create one of his own: compare *Nineteen Hundred and Nineteen* with *Spain 1937*.) Yeats's audience, his capable listener, was neither a fiction nor a coterie ('parish of rich women' as Auden called it). It was, at least in the first instance, a group for whom Ireland was the common theme, the public issue in whose terms Yeats could address himself as a poet and expect to be heard.

> All day I'd looked in the face
> What I had hoped 'twould be
> To write for my own race
> And the reality; ...
> Suddenly I began,
> In scorn of this audience,
> Imagining a man ...
> > (*The Fisherman*, 1916)

But scorn is a relationship, and the tension between the flawed reality and the ideal Unity of Culture was enough for Yeats to work on. In that relation, Yeats could write 'as a man speaking to men' – in, at any rate, a richer, more immediate relation than any other poet of the century.

Yeats's identification of the poet with the affirmation of 'life's own self-delight' offers a useful perspective on his work as a whole, and in particular, on those poems which seem to attempt a different complexity. There is, for example, *The Second Coming* (1920).

> ... Things fall apart; the centre cannot hold;
> Mere anarchy is loosed upon the world,
> The blood-dimmed tide is loosed, and everywhere

The ceremony of innocence is drowned;
The best lack all conviction, while the worst
Are full of passionate intensity.

... The darkness drops again; but now I know
That twenty centuries of stony sleep
Were vexed to nightmare by a rocking cradle,
And what rough beast, its hour come round at last,
Slouches towards Bethlehem to be born?

As often with Yeats's prophetic or visionary poems (where the reciprocal relationship of 'a man speaking to men' is qualified by the
poet's special 'disposition to be affected *more than other men by absent
things as if they were present*; [his] ability of *conjuring up in himself
passions*, which are indeed far from being the same as those produced
by real events'),[12] these lines suggest something unsettled in the poet's
final attitude. Louis MacNeice ascribed this ambiguity to the fact that
'Yeats had a budding fascist inside himself' and therefore heralded
'the rise of this tide ... with a certain relish'.[13] But this is to confuse
Yeats-and-his-reader with Yeats-and-his-subject. The poem's intensity depends primarily upon our familiarity with ideas like 'the
Second Coming ... a rocking cradle ... Bethlehem'.[14] Yeats, that
is, in order to express 'his vision of absent things' lays hold of the
only available public language, and adapts it in a number of bold
paradoxes. The magus foresees, but it is the poet who urges, and here,
at the polemical level,[15] lies the difficulty. The poem's tone is not
coherent. Beside the memorable restraint of 'The best lack all conviction, while the worst/Are full of passionate intensity', the rhetorical attack of the final lines is crude – it exploits the previously established relationship – and with this in mind, it is possible to feel that
the famous 'The ceremony of innocence is drowned' is a discreeter
example of the same exploitation. There is more anxiety than insight
in the line. The poet claims an assurance that he does not feel – this
is one way of putting it; and – crucial in a polemical poem – what
he is not sure about is whether the sanctities invoked in 'sleep ...
vexed ... cradle' can or cannot withstand the future.

It is helpful to relate this uncertainty, if not to the actual details
of *A Vision*, then certainly to the question of its determinism, a point
which Yeats had not settled in 1919, if indeed he ever did settle it.
(The 1925 edition implies a complete determinism, but the 1937

edition develops one of the original suggestions into an explicit allowance of free-will.) By means of the first line 'Turning and turning in the widening gyre', the poem invokes this 'determinism' at one level only to effect a moral protest at its implications at another. Like so many political statements, the poem both hopes and fears at once. This ambiguity recurs in a poem like *The Gyres* (1938), or *The Statues* (1939), and its extreme form is the desperate idealizing of the 'heroic' Irish in the late writing. Yeats seems to have combined a very powerful sense of immediate history with a restricted historical equipment for relating present insight to the determining past. The evidence for the historical patterns of *A Vision* is almost entirely drawn from the arts, and while this may help to organize and project a chosen structure of loyalties and predispositions, it is not much help when it comes to predicting the probable future. In *The Second Coming*, Yeats has tried to generalize his immediate foreboding into a historical statement, but since the historical idea ('gyre') is itself over-simple, it merely ratifies the confusion of fear and hope from which the poet begins. This is then transmitted in the uncertain tone, and unjustified variation of intensity in the rhetoric. Uncertain of his own position, Yeats turns, so to speak, on his listeners. There should not, finally, be any question as to where Yeats stands in relation to the rough beast. The companion poem to his prophecy is, after all, the restrained and assured *A Prayer for My Daughter* (1919).

A more straightforward unevenness in the third section of *The Tower* (1927) shows again that 'ideas' in Yeats are sometimes his way of refusing to think out his position. In this poem, he is stating his final attitude about old age and approaching death.

> Now shall I make my soul,
> Compelling it to study
> In a learned school . . .

and at 'learned', we naturally refer back to the earlier declaration. What is the relation between the two 'learnings'?

> And I declare my faith:
> I mock Plotinus' thought
> And cry in Plato's teeth,
> Death and life were not
> Till man made up the whole,
> Made lock, stock, and barrel

> Out of his bitter soul,
> Aye, sun and moon and star, all,
> And further add to that
> That, being dead, we rise,
> Dream and so create
> Translunar paradise.
> I have prepared my peace
> With learned Italian things
> And the proud stones of Greece,
> Poet's imaginings
> And memories of love ...

When Yeats begins to sound like 'the annual scourge of the Georgian anthology' (T. S. Eliot), it seems fair to protest. What is the basis of this swashing dismissal of Plotinus and Plato? – a quasi-religious idiom ('rise ... create ... paradise'), a clerical boom ('I have prepared my peace'), and a comically unembarrassed display of culture-totems ('proud stones', etc.). Take away these trappings, and there is not much left, certainly not a philosophy, so that it needs to be stressed that the attitude with which the *poem* (as distinct from the poet) faces death is very different.

> In a learned school
> Till the wreck of body,
> Slow decay of blood,
> Testy delirium
> Or dull decrepitude,
> Or what worse evil come –
> The death of friends, or death
> Of every brilliant eye
> That made a catch in the breath –
> Seem but the clouds of the sky
> When the horizon fades;
> Or a bird's sleepy cry
> Among the deepening shades.

A sustained metaphor underlies this conclusion. 'wreck ... decay ... delirium' register the pain of physical ageing; 'dull decrepitude' qualifies the protest with a contemptuous resignation which anticipates the final acceptance. The digression enlarges the perspective to include the death of the poet's friends, and of what he values ('every brilliant eye'), so that his merely personal extinction has disappeared from view by the time you reach the main verb ('seem') and the concluding recognition that death is a natural process, not to be gainsaid. The teaching of the 'learned school' is not new (cf. the last stanza of Keats's *Ode to Autumn*); and if it is profound, then not in the sense in which some of Yeats's critics – certainly encouraged by the poet in some parts of his work – use the term. There is nothing profound about Yeats's 'translunar paradise'. The elaborate paraphernalia of 'ideas' masks nothing more complicated than an instinctual refusal-to-die. When in the final lines, this instinct is confronted with the equally simple fact of death, a genuine 'idea' does emerge: individuals die, but nature, the species, does not. But what matters is not this 'philosophy', but the controlled rehearsal of the approach to death, beside which the earlier protest is a comparatively frivolous display of 'style'. As Yeats's father said to him, 'You would be a philosopher and are really a poet', and the *would be* is often the point for the critic. Yeats's profundity is rarely a matter of complex or intricate thinking about human experience. Ideas enter his poetry in the form of large generalizations which help to organize a particular group of experiences:

> ... Endure that toil of growing up;
> The ignominy of boyhood; the distress
> Of boyhood changing into man;
> The unfinished man and his pain
> Brought face to face with his own clumsiness;
> The finished man among his enemies ...
> (*A Dialogue of Self and Soul*, 1929)

Assume the pain of growth, carry it through the detail of experience, and we get this concentrated statement: 'endure ... toil ... ignominy ... distress ... pain ... clumsiness ... enemies'. In the poetry of 'thinking', idea and detail interact; each alters the other, exists in terms of the other. But in Yeats, the detail of experience does not question, it illustrates the ideas (as the poems on the Troubles show), which have, so to speak, been decided upon outside the poem. Adopt, then, another assumption about 'growing up', and we get these famous lines:

> That is no country for old men. The young
> In one another's arms, birds in the trees
> – Those dying generations – at their song,
> The salmon-falls, the mackerel-crowded seas,

Fish, flesh, or fowl, commend all summer long
Whatever is begotten, born, and dies.
(*Sailing to Byzantium*, 1927)

It is not the greater complexity that is my point, but the different idea – growth as a rich blind trustfulness – the point of view with which in some argument, one might oppose undue insistence on the '*toil* of growing up'. It is by debate, argument, the confrontation of different ideas and so of the different experience each idea engages that Yeats arrives at his most varied insights. And it is the inclusive generalizations of 'thought' ('gyres', 'translunar paradise') which involve him in simplification and ambiguity.

Another group of poems which bears on this occurs in *Michael Robartes and The Dancer* (1921), where the enemy of life is not the historical process, or the 'indifferent' future, but what Yeats calls 'thought' or 'opinion'. He remarks elsewhere that 'A mind that generalizes rapidly, continually prevents the experience that would have made it feel and see deeply',[16] and 'thought' in those poems is the neurotic hypertrophy of this condition. The amusing title poem (1920) announces the theme:

> *He*   ... and it's plain
> The half-dead dragon was her thought,
> That every morning rose again
> And dug its claws and shrieked and fought.
> Could the impossible come to pass
> She would have time to turn her eyes,
> Her lover thought, upon the glass
> And on the instant would grow wise.
> *She* You mean they *argued* ...   [*my italics*]

This maladjustment of 'thought' and experience links the subsequent poems on love, in which some abstracting fantasy interferes with the relationship, with the better-known political poems.

> Maybe the bride-bed brings despair,
> For each an imagined image brings
> And finds a real image there;
> Yet the world ends when these two things,
> Though several, are a single light,
> When oil and wick are burned in one;
> (*Solomon and The Witch*)

> Hearts with one purpose alone
> Through summer and winter seem
> Enchanted to a stone
> To trouble the living stream.
>
> (*Easter 1916*, 1916)

> Did she in touching that lone wing
> Recall the years before her mind
> Became a bitter, an abstract thing,
> Her thought some popular enmity ... ?
>
> (*On A Political Prisoner*, 1920)

> My mind, because the minds that I have loved,
> The sort of beauty that I have approved,
> Prosper but little, has dried up of late,
> Yet knows that to be choked with hate
> May well be of all evil chances chief.
> ... An intellectual hatred is the worst,
> So let her think opinions are accursed.
>
> (*A Prayer for my Daughter*, 1919)

As the various dates show, Yeats has here brought together unpublished and previously published poems which apply a common insight to different situations and relationships. The insight is not explored, nor is it fully realized in any one instance, but provides rather the organizing centre for a number of experiences of introspection or observation. A poem of a decade later shows how such a key-emphasis can resurrect itself, still 'undeveloped', yet just as vital:

> I know not what the younger dreams –
> Some vague Utopia – and she seems,
> When withered old and skeleton-gaunt,
> An image of such politics.
> Many a time I think to seek
> One or the other out and speak
> Of that old Georgian mansion, mix
> Pictures of the mind, recall
> That table and the talk of youth,
> Two girls in silk kimonos, both
> Beautiful, one a gazelle.
>
> (*In Memory of Eva Gore-Booth and Con Markiewicz*, 1929)

Here it is not a metaphor so much as the beautifully managed cadences of the final lines (from 'Pictures') that judges 'such politics'. For dreams of the 'vague Utopia' – and 'vague' is the important word – Yeats offers the precise alternative of his delicately stated feeling for what has gone. This is the stress: the actuality of human interchange, however transient or imperfect, is of 'the living stream', and therefore a test for the questionable truths of 'thought'. Whether the result is heroic, degrading, or even a spiritual certainty, 'thought' distracts from, where it doesn't deform, the difficult intricacy of life. It is at best a superior compensation for failing to live, and with this in mind, the force of saying that Yeats's poetry works from ideas rather than through them should be clear.

A related impulse is important in the unique series of occasional poems which extend from about 1912 till Yeats's death. Yeats's 'modernity' properly begins with *The Green Helmet* (1910) – though its anticipation in one or two poems (subsequently added to) in *In The Seven Woods* (1903) is clear; see for example 'Never Give All The Heart' first published in 1905 – but his first unquestionably great poem is *In Memory of Major Robert Gregory* (1918). One difference between this poem and, say *To A Shade* (1913) has been well underlined by Frank Kermode. It is the first poem fully to incorporate Yeats's romantic inheritance.[17] But it is also the first in a long line of occasional celebrations and laments: *All Souls' Night* (1921), *A Prayer For My Daughter* (1919), *Coole Park and Ballylee, 1931* (1932), and *The Bronze Head* (1939), and this coincidence is important. 'The self-conquest of the writer who is not a man of action is style',[18] and the style of these poems – formal, elaborate, yet easy and humane – can be said to state Yeats's responsibility as a poet to the central human experiences they commemorate.

> He had much industry at setting out,
> Much boisterous courage, before loneliness
> Had driven him crazed;
> For meditations upon unknown thought
> Make human intercourse grow less and less;
> They are neither paid nor praised.
> But he'd object to the host,
> The glass because my glass;
> A ghost-lover he was
> And may have grown more arrogant being a ghost.
>
> (*All Souls' Night*)

The stanza is the poetic expression of what Yeats in *A Prayer For My Daughter* calls 'courtesy': it reconciles the criticism of 'arrogant' with the appreciation of 'boisterous courage'. The sensitive adjustments of feeling depend wholly upon the changes in pace which the elaborate verse and rhyme scheme makes possible. The directness reacts with the formality so that the first is not blunt, and the second not stiff. The poet disappears, so to speak, into the poetry, and the poetry into the permanent experience of what Blake called 'the severe contentions of friendship'.

If one senses the writer's 'self-conquest' in the style of all these occasional poems, it is even more evident in the actual structure of the Gregory elegy.

> I had thought, seeing how bitter is that wind
> That shakes the shutter, to have brought to mind
> All those that manhood tried, or childhood loved
> Or boyish intellect approved,
> With some appropriate commentary on each;
> Until imagination brought
> A fitter welcome; but a thought
> Of that late death took all my heart for speech.

'We are not required to accept as true the statement that Yeats had intended a longer poem,' wrote Peter Ure in his explication of the poem. 'All is device and formality, a mask on the face of grief.'[19] But this, with its suggestion of hidden tears, a suppressed catch in the throat, is a little misleading. The point of the final trope is to dissolve the 'personal' voice with which the poem has been speaking into anonymity, without losing the sense of an actual relationship between the writer and the dead man. The poet's business is to express not his own feelings, but other people's as if they were his own: 'whatever's written in what poets name The book of the people'.[20] The elegy needs an obituary voice, that is still not 'official'. The effect of the last stanza after what has preceded it is to achieve this adjustment of attitude, this difficult generality. The presentation of Robert Gregory who is 'a man of action' and 'all life's epitome' takes place in this context: the projection of the romantic figure who burns his life out is by means of the poem accommodated to the 'damp faggots' of ordinary living – Yeats's term in this poem for himself and for the continuity he is affirming.

The formal elaboration of these poems expresses, then, an important part of their meaning: the terms on which we share in the commemorated experience, but even in much simpler poems, rhetorical device is prominent, and it serves a similar purpose. One can express this roughly by saying that many of Yeats's poems express a familiar general emotion, but in a strange, even an eccentric way. Yet the difficulties are superficial; they do not belong to the experience, so much as guard it from misunderstanding or too-easy acceptance. The experience is very often 'what oft was thought', but the expression shears off the encrustations of habitual response, and protective staleness. Feeling in Yeats is, in general, not complex: i.e. not realized with all the contradictions and qualifications which any particular emotion actually involves; but 'simple': 'disengaged, disembroiled, disencumbered, exempt from the conditions we usually know to attach to it'.[21] The process of disengagement is undertaken in several ways. There is the discreet wit in phrases like: 'that discourtesy of death', 'casual comedy', 'popular rage', 'civil rancour' – where one word discriminates the general emotion suggested by the other. The effect is to invite one's cooperation in the critical refinement (cf. Pope's and Dryden's similar fondness for the construction). More generally, there is the rhetorical syntax which plays off 'artificial' against 'natural' speech rhythms; and the use of dramatis personae or Masks, and of named occasions and situations for the particular experience. To take a familiar example:

Easter 1916

> I have met them at close of day
> Coming with vivid faces
> From counter or desk among grey
> Eighteenth-century houses.
> I have passed with a nod of head
> Or polite meaningless words,
> Or have lingered awhile and said
> Polite meaningless words,
> And thought before I had done
> Of a mocking tale or a gibe
> To please a companion
> Around the fire at the club . . .

The lofty opening rhythms quickly give way to the loose 'casual' movement of the later lines, and this follows the contrast of the 'vivid faces', and the commonplace gossip which the poet retails about them. But before that happens, there is the memorable dissonance of 'faces/houses', forcing its way against the secure 'day/grey', like some flattened seventh in a full statement of the key. The clash has its point. It underlines the heroic opening – by slightly departing from it, that is, it makes an individual statement of this note. The note is essential; the very title demands it; but of course, Yeats's view of the heroism of Macdonagh and Macbride and Connolly and Pearse is very specific and he only adapts the banal emotion of the political tub-thumper because he wants it on his own terms. Admittedly, these are not as clear or satisfactory as they might be: but 'terrible beauty', whatever its failings, sufficiently shows how Yeats *insisted* on his own particular view of 'the heroic emotion'. The title, then, is a first approximation to Yeats's own definition: it is not just a piece of information, but part of the poem's language.

Another example is the first poem of *Supernatural Songs*, *Ribh at the Tomb of Baile and Aillinn* (1934), a title whose strangeness immediately contrasts with the opening familiarity of 'Because you have found me in the pitch-dark night/With open book you ask me what I do'. But Ribh is not a character, and if he is a Mask, that is not because he delivers any special necessary meaning. What he says makes its own point:

> ... when such bodies join
> There is no touching here, nor touching there,
> Nor straining joy, but whole is joined to whole;
> For the intercourse of angels is a light
> Where for its moment both seem lost, consumed.
>
> Here in the pitch-dark atmosphere above
> The trembling of the apple and the yew,
> Here on the anniversary of their death,
> The anniversary of their first embrace,
> These lovers, purified by tragedy,
> Hurry into each other's arms; these eyes,
> By water, herb, and solitary prayer
> Made aquiline, are open to that light.
> Though somewhat broken by the leaves, that light
> Lies in a circle on the grass; therein
> I turn the pages of my holy book.

The natural leaves interfere with the supernatural light; but this light is a metaphor for an ideal love-in-nature. Ribh's eyes see by the light, but *what* he sees is not 'the intercourse of angels', but his 'holy book'. The effect is to interpenetrate the categories of real and ideal fulfilment in an extraordinarily delicate relationship; to convey Ribh's ponderings about the completion beyond death of the full relationship life denies to the lovers without suggesting compensatory nostalgia, or spiritual voyeurism about a love he never experienced. The poem's outworks – Ribh, Baile, Aillinn – make the experience strange, not because it is difficult, complex, and mysterious (as, for example, the rejections and projections of Eliot's *Marina* are) but because it must be very exactly defined. It is the essential heart of the condition which the poem conveys, and in order to insist on this its language (again the title is part of the language) prunes away implication and suggestivity. Yeats's claim that his mind was 'sensuous, concrete, rhythmical' is not more important than the complementary statement '. . . I, whose virtues are the definitions Of the analytic mind' – and the analysis progresses towards general emotions exactly defined. Even where the emotion is 'complex', Yeats arrives at the complexity by accumulating a number of distinct strands. These lines from *The Man and The Echo* (1939) provide a miniature instance:

> O Rocky Voice,
> Shall we in that great night rejoice?
> What do we know but that we face
> One another in this place?
> But hush, for I have lost the theme,
> Its joy or night seem but a dream;
> Up there some hawk or owl has struck,
> Dropping out of sky or rock,
> A stricken rabbit is crying out,
> And its cry distracts my thought.

Each strand – hope for happiness after death, stoical acceptance of human ignorance, sympathy for the suffering of created life – has a separate identity, and they coexist in such a way as to sharpen that identity. Out of context, for example, it is impossible to know how to read lines 3–4: gloomily? toughly? with suppressed self-pity? Only in relation to the other lines can one say: the stoicism is not tough, but a simple statement ('all we can be certain of is . . .'); not gloomy, because the 'great night' – impressive rather than terrifying – offers the possibility of joy; nor self-pitying because the sympathy goes wholly to 'the stricken rabbit'. The effect of the context is to do away with the usual blur of feeling that accompanies the direct commonplace question, to make it more direct without making it any the less commonplace, and so genuinely the question of the generic Man in whose name the poem is written. It need hardly be insisted that this ability, in a culture that has driven the wedge between artist and the 'commonplace' experience of men as deeply as ours has, is uniquely important. Like any great poet, Yeats offers many satisfactions, but there seem to me good grounds for rating the simple direct centrality of much of his work as the most lasting.

NOTES

1. *The Letters of W. B. Yeats* (ed. Allan Wade, 1954), 397, 460, 462.
2. *Collected Poems* (1950), 182. My italics.
3. *Autobiographies* (1955), 409.
4. *Essays* (1924), 307–8.
5. The dates given for these and subsequently mentioned poems are those of the first publication – in some cases earlier by several years than the date of the collection in which the poem finally appears in *Collected Poems*. See Allan Wade, *A Bibliography of the Writings of W. B. Yeats* (2nd edn, 1958). For a list of probable dates of composition, see Richard Ellmann, *The Identity of Yeats* (1954).
6. cf. 'And bats with baby faces in the violet light
   Whistled, and beat their wings
   And crawled head downward down a blackened wall'. (T. S. Eliot, *The Waste Land, Collected Poems 1909–1935*, 1936, 76).
7. *Autobiographies* (1955), 295.
8. *Four Plays For Dancers* (1921), 105–6. My italics.
9. *Autobiographies* (1955), 486. See also 'On Those That Hated "The Playboy Of The Western World", 1907', *Collected Poems* (1950), 124.
10. *Autobiographies*, 494.
11. Discussing the contribution to the total meaning of 'culture' made by the Romantic poets, Raymond Williams notes 'an emphasis on the embodiment in art of certain human values, capacities, energies, which the development of society towards an industrial civilization was felt to be threatening or even destroying' . . . 'The whole tradition can be summed up in one striking phrase used by Wordsworth, where the poet, the artist in general, is seen as "an upholder and preserver, *carrying everywhere with him relationship and love*".' *Culture and Society 1780–1950* (1958), 36, 42. My italics.
12. 'Preface to Lyrical Ballads (1800)', W. Wordsworth. My italics.

13. F. L. MacNeice, *The Poetry of W. B. Yeats* (1941), 132.

14. Allen Tate has pointed out, correctly I think, that this is more generally true of Yeats's esotericism than most critics admit. See *The Permanence of Yeats* (ed. Hall and Steinemann, 1950), 111.

15. That the poem is, in a deep sense, polemical, I take the following letter to indicate '... as my sense of reality deepens ... my horror at the cruelty of governments grows greater ... Communist, Fascist, nationalist, clerical, anti-clerical, are all responsible according to the number of their victims. I have not been silent; I have used the only vehicle I possess – verse. If you have my poems by you, look up a poem called *The Second Coming*. It was written some sixteen or seventeen years ago and foretold what is happening. I have written of the same thing again and again since. This will seem little to you with your strong practical sense, for it takes fifty years for a poet's weapons to influence the issue.' (April 1936) *The Letters of W. B. Yeats* (ed. Allan Wade, 1954), 851.

16. *Essays* (1924), 406–7.

17. Frank Kermode, *The Romantic Image* (1957), 30–42.

18. *Autobiographies*, 516.

19. Peter Ure, *Towards A Mythology* ... (1946), 40.

20. *Coole Park & Ballylee, 1931, Collected Poems* (1950), 276.

21. The phrase is from Henry James's 'Preface to *The American*', *The Art of the Novel* (1953), 33

THE IRISH LITERARY SCENE

GRATTAN FREYER

In the first twenty-five years of the present century, it would have been appropriate to entitle an essay such as this 'The Irish Movement'. Today writers who work or were born in Ireland are not conscious of belonging to any 'movement'. Irish independence, for which the early writers – under the all-pervasive influence of Yeats – struggled to create a cultural consciousness, is a fact. The current existence in many universities in Europe and America of departments specializing in Irish Studies is a handsome indication of the success of Yeats's ambition to forge a literary tradition of Irish writing in English as distinctive as the American literature of Thoreau, Whitman and Bret Harte. It is appropriate, therefore, to consider first the Irish literary movement proper, and to proceed from thence to some account of contemporary Irish writers working within this new tradition. (As Shaw, Yeats and Joyce are treated elsewhere in this volume, and Beckett, Heaney and Montague in Volume 8 of the *Guide*, *The Present*, this chapter will make only passing reference to them. And although this volume extends only to around 1940 in its coverage of English writers, since there is no general discussion of the Irish Literary Scene in Volume 8 this chapter will fill in the background up to the present day.)

Ireland forms part of the British Isles, yet the Irish have never really formed part of the British nation. Race, religion, history, and the ensuing social and economic development have all helped to keep the two peoples distinct. The majority of the Irish have remained Roman Catholics, and though many of her leading writers have come from the Protestant minority, the traditional faith colours the background from which they spring. Class distinctions too are less socially rigid than in Britain. One finds a sense of community and social fluidity in Ireland, which has long since ceased to exist in England. This has proved an asset of particular interest to the dramatist. In Synge's plays, when a stranger enters, he shares naturally in the conversation;

no introduction is necessary. It is sometimes suggested that this community feeling arose from the unity of the Irish people in their historic struggle against British occupation. Yet this is not entirely true, since even the margin between the British 'ascendancy' – the descendants of those who were given land when the native Irish were dispossessed – and the local people was never a sharp one. In Yeats's early novel *John Sherman* (1889), the principal character, who is a member of the lesser gentry, observes: 'In your big towns a man finds his minority and knows nothing outside its border ... but here one chats with the whole world in a day's walk, for every man one meets is a class.' The capacity of the Irish to absorb their invaders and make them 'more Irish than themselves' is proverbial. It is more remarkable in that, unlike the Chinese or even the French, there was never any well-defined or sophisticated civilization into which the invaders were fitted.

This amorphousness of class structure is closely related to another feature of the Irish scene – the easy-going character of the Irish people, at least in those parts that now form the Republic, which, though less marked today than formerly, never fails to strike an outside visitor. This, however, has a negative aspect as far as literature is concerned. There has been an almost complete lack of social purpose or moral earnestness, and writers such as Bertrand Russell or Sartre would be as alien in Ireland as men from Mars. Even Shaw, strangely enough, hardly aroused a flicker of interest in his native country. Moreover, a substantial portion of English writing has depended on exploring the sensibilities and situations to which a well-defined class structure gives rise – one thinks of Waugh or E. M. Forster, but it is equally true of those, like Kingsley Amis or George Orwell, who deprecated the snobbery of a class society. The counterpart of this preoccupation in Ireland is perhaps the relationship of the writer to the dominance of the Catholic church, which will be considered below.

It will be appropriate here to refer briefly to the only native culture Ireland possessed, the ancient Gaelic civilization. Ireland became Christian in the fifth century, and the golden age of Gaelic culture lasted from the seventh to around the twelfth century. The language declined steadily under the British occupation, and by the first half of the nineteenth century Irish had ceased to exist as a tongue for the educated. What survived were a number of peasant dialects, spoken along the western and southern seaboards. A movement to revive the language began at the turn of the present century, and after the Irish Free State came into being in 1921, teaching of the language – and wherever possible in the language – was made compulsory in the schools. It is common knowledge today that this policy has met with scant success and in recent years it has come in for strong criticism. Nevertheless the language has had considerable influence on speaking and writing in English. Synge wrote nothing in Irish, but the English he used drew its peculiar quality from being frequently a direct translation of Gaelic idiom.

With Liam O'Flaherty, who is an Aran islander born and so a native speaker, the influence is even stronger. His first book, *The Black Soul*, appears to have been written in Irish and then translated. Just as in Conrad, there are passages which suggest an extremely vivid but not a native command of English. Most of the later generation of writers had a competence in Irish. Frank O'Connor, Seán O'Faoláin, Donagh MacDonagh, Thomas Kinsella, all published translations from the Gaelic. Brendan Behan's riotously lyrical play, *The Hostage*, which caused a sensation in London in 1958, was originally performed in Irish. Those with a competence in both languages claim that the Irish version, *An Gail*, is a more substantial piece of writing than the English version, which was considerably revised for the stage by Joan Littlewood.

There is one eighteenth-century Gaelic poem of some length which possesses such unique liveliness and interest that it has drawn forth no fewer than four contemporary translations into English, and it deserves mention here. This is Brian Merriman's *The Midnight Court*, and it deals in racy and often ribald language with a peculiarly Irish problem even today: the difficulty of persuading eligible bachelors to marry! The translations of Ussher, O'Connor, Longford, and Marcus all have merit. I quote at random from Marcus's very free rendering to show a rhythm and manner which is directly brought over from the original – the lady is beginning the catalogue of her neglected charms:

> My mouth is sweet and my teeth are flashing,
> My face is never in need of washing,
> My eyes are green and my hair's undyed
> With waves as big as the ocean tide,
> And that's not a half, nor a tenth, of my treasure:
> I'm built with an eye to the maximum pleasure.

Two other translations of unusual interest are Tomas O'Crohan's *The Islandman* and Maurice O'Sullivan's *Twenty Years A-growing*. Both these are autobiographies by peasants from the Blasket Islands off the far south-western tip of Kerry. They portray men whose every-day way of life was not greatly different from that of Homer's fishermen or the Icelanders of the sagas. The value of O'Crohan's book is enhanced by the fact that he was deeply conscious of the new civilization which was soon to engulf them. He states his purpose in writing as 'to set down the character of the people about me so that some record of us might live after us, for the like of us will never be again.'

Before leaving the topic of Gaelic, one may mention the interesting decision of one Irish poet, Michael Hartnett, who, after establishing a not inconsiderable reputation by writing in English, made a firm commitment to write only in Irish in future. His last English col-lection, appearing in 1975, was entitled *A Farewell to English*. His viewpoint, shared by a modest coterie, is that Irish offers a medium unadulterated by the clichés of commercial journalism and that the audience of his peers gains in quality what it must lose in quantity.

The surge of creative writing in Ireland around the opening of this century has often, with mild exaggeration, been spoken of as the Irish Literary Renaissance. Though Ireland's population is less than one-tenth that of Great Britain, she has produced, in Yeats, Joyce and Beckett, three out of the half-dozen or so major writers of this period. She contributed at least her fair share of minor writers, and in the field of the English-speaking theatre was the principal medium for a revolution in dramatic writing and acting technique. What was responsible for this sudden outpouring of talent?

It is neither easy nor necessary to give a precise answer to that question. The troubled history of Ireland and the complete absence of settled, wealthy, middle-class patronage seem to have been re-sponsible for the lack of any tradition in painting or music. Apart from architecture, literature, in fact, was the only art form which did appear under these conditions. But during the greater part of the nineteenth century the enthusiasm and idealism of the country tended to politics rather than literature. In 1890 political nationalism received a sudden and unusual check when the movement was split from top to bottom over Parnell's divorce case. Historical detail would be out of place here, but a glimpse of the anguished disillusion caused among ordinary people is given in Joyce's short story 'Ivy Day in the Committee Room', included in *Dubliners*, and in the family quarrel depicted in the early part of *A Portrait of the Artist as a Young Man*. The point to note here is that in Yeats's and Joyce's formative years nationalist fervour was seeking an outlet outside politics. The Gaelic League, which was the movement to revive the language, and the national theatre movement were the principal beneficiaries. Both date from this time.

Five or six individuals were responsible for launching the new theatre movement, and, quite naturally, their aims were not identical. Yeats was interested from his early days in dramatic verse; he had already had a verse play performed in London. Edward Martyn's enthusiasm was in direct opposition to Yeats's; he admired Ibsen, and though there was a poetic side to Ibsen which appealed to Yeats and Joyce, it was the aspect of his work dealing with problems of local politics – in 'joyless and pallid words', as Synge later put it – which Martyn wanted to apply to Ireland. Martyn's cousin, George Moore, had some practical experience of plays and players in Paris and London, a genuine interest in the Irish countryside and her people, and a natural attraction towards a new medium of self-expression. Moore and Martyn were Catholic landlords from the West, and they met with Yeats in the home of a Protestant neighbour, Lady Gregory, who contributed a little money, several short plays, and much diplomacy to the venture. (A lot was needed.) These were people of letters. From the theatrical side came the Fay brothers, William and Frank, who had for some years been acting in amateur and badly paid productions in Dublin and the provinces. The Fays, in fact, were looking round for more serious plays to perform than the romantic melodramas then current, at the same time as the literary men were seeking an outlet in the theatre. The Fays approached the poet A E (George Russell), and Douglas Hyde, the founder of the Gaelic League. A E put the Fays in touch with Yeats.

The Irish National Theatre Society was founded in 1901 with Yeats as president. Two years later – owing to the financial support of an English drama enthusiast, Miss Horniman – a small theatre seating 500 was acquired. At first, productions were entirely amateur. But the need for professionalism inevitably asserted itself, though it led to the loss of some enthusiasts. The Abbey Theatre Company came into being with Yeats, Lady Gregory, and later Synge as directors. William Fay was its first manager.

From the start the Abbey aroused intense interest and controversy at home. But it was the acclaim and financial success of visits to London, Cambridge, Oxford, Manchester, Glasgow, and other British cities which kept the company solvent. Plays were invariably 'by Irish authors on Irish subjects', but it was the style of acting which took English audiences by storm. The essentials of this style were realism in scenery, dress, and language (except for the verse plays), a refusal to allow any 'star' acting to dominate the group, and a studied absence of unnecessary gesture. (It is said that at one time Yeats tried to get the actors to rehearse in barrels.) This was a style of acting which had just been introduced in France by Antoine with his *théâtre libre*, which the Fays enthusiastically admired. Retrospectively, the scenic realism of the Abbey appears overdone, producing a fresh cramping convention in its turn; but the new purity of diction was to be a lasting innovation which cleared the way for later developments on the English stage.

It is sometimes supposed that the fierce quarrels which broke out in Dublin over the subject-matter of the new plays showed a straightforward cleavage between an enlightened band of artists and patriots and a priest-led mob. This was in fact far from the case. William Fay wrote in his memoirs that every play had to face two questions: Was it 'an insult to the faith'? Was it 'a slander on the people of Ireland'? Most serious plays failed in one test; some, such as *The Playboy*, failed in both. But leading patriots were as concerned over these questions as anyone else and were often opposed to Yeats's vision of artistic integrity within a nationalist mould. Arthur Griffith, the Sinn Fein chief, poured invective on the whole Abbey venture. The pacifist Francis Sheehy-Skeffington signed the protest against Yeats's *Countess Cathleen* – in which a philanthropist sells her soul to the devil to provide for her people in time of famine. And Maud Gonne, who had played the leading role in this play, herself walked out in protest against Synge's *In the Shadow of the Glen*, which she regarded as an attack on the purity of Irish womanhood. Patrick

Pearse, however, who was later executed for his leadership of the 1916 insurrection, was in favour of Synge. Many times it looked as though the theatre would be forced to close either by mob violence or by a newspaper-led boycott. Yet somehow it weathered the storm. A small army of policemen had to be on hand to allow *The Playboy* to finish its first week and only at the end was an audience permitted to hear the play through. Further riots greeted O'Casey's plays after the First World War. The wheel turned, and a few years later two young men forced their way on to the stage to protest against the irreverent way in which one of O'Casey's masterpieces had been acted!

The plays written by the Abbey dramatists reflected the contrasting ideals of the theatre's founders, which have already been mentioned. Yeats wrote one expressly patriotic play: *Kathleen ni Houlihan*, an allegory in which the spirit of Ireland is personified by an old woman who rouses her people to the national struggle. This was a moving play to an Irish audience, but fell flat elsewhere. Yeats's other contributions offered an astonishingly wide range in theme and treatment from the prose farce of country life, *The Pot of Broth*, through the lovely spoken verse of the *Four Plays for Dancers*, utilizing the conventions of Japanese Noh drama, to an extraordinarily dramatic and intellectually satisfying play on Swift, *The Words upon the Window-pane*. All are one-act plays. Lady Gregory, who had never written a line before middle age, translated Molière successfully into West of Ireland dialect, and wrote a number of slight peasant comedies. One short play, *The Rising of the Moon*, with its intermingling of high patriotic seriousness and comedy – the Quixote formula, which was to be so often repeated – has been consistently popular. Her other plays fell into disfavour soon after her death, but still command the interest of the cultural historian.

Many playwrights dealt in the Ibsen manner with the typical problems of contemporary Irish life: the hunger for land (Padraic Colum); the frustrated ambitions of provincial life (Lennox Robinson, Seán O'Faoláin); the asperities of peasant life (T. C. Murray); the role of the priests (Joseph Tomelty, Paul Vincent Carroll); emigration and late marriages (M. J. Molloy). And a new stage-Irish comedy emerged in George Shiels and others. Most of these plays were too topical to last, or to hold interest for non-Irish audiences. But there are two Abbey dramatists whose work forms part of the wider theatre – Synge and O'Casey.

More than any other writer, J. M. Synge may be said to have been the creation of the Abbey Theatre. Yeats describes in one of his auto-biographies how he met Synge in Paris, supplementing a small private income by giving English lessons and making translations from French poets into Anglo-Irish dialect. He advised Synge to return to his own country, learn Irish, and write plays for the new theatre. Synge followed his advice to the letter. It is doubtful if even Yeats anticipated the consequences of this advice.

The plays of Synge rise head and shoulders above the dramatic conventions of his fellow-playwrights. They are not purely poetic plays, nor peasant plays – though they have something of both; still less are they problem plays. The greatest of them, *The Playboy of the Western World*, was soon to be performed in half a dozen European languages. This is the story of a peasant boy who flees home under the impression he has killed his father. He is acclaimed as a hero, and under this acclaim becomes a hero – until his 'murdered da' reappears! Synge's strength, like that of Cervantes, lies in the juxta-position of the most earthy realism with the highest flights of fancy. His characters speak a language which is imaginative and exuberant, just as sixteenth-century English was, because it was not cramped by industrial conformity or newspaper emotions:

> Bravery's a treasure in a lonesome place, and a lad would kill his father, I'm thinking, would face a foxy divil with a pitchpike on the flags of hell.

We forget the wild improbability of the story, because it is both possible and probable at a certain level of the imagination. The patriot hysteria which greeted early productions in Dublin depended on the conviction that no decent Irish country girl would admire a mur-derer. Yet there is a primitive element in all human nature which is eternally ready to rejoice in the heroic, amoral act – until the civilized inhibitions clamp down. Synge's world is not the conven-tional world of modern living, but a small pre-civilized world of the imagination. Within this small world, his characters are com-pletely convincing and enormously alive. It is absurd to try to dis-entangle any 'message' from so unpolitical a writer; what does perhaps emerge is the nostalgia of a lonely and sick man for vital living. Synge died at the age of thirty-eight.

There is a measure of similarity between the work of Synge and Sean O'Casey in that both rejected the 'joyless and pallid words' of the naturalist drama, but that is as far as the parallel goes. Whereas Synge was bred a country gentleman of small means and educated at Trinity College, Dublin, O'Casey was an autodidact from the Dublin slums. Moreover, a radical change had come in the Irish scene in consequence of the First World War, the Irish fight for independence, and the civil war which ensued between those who wished for a compromise within the British empire, and those who, like de Valera, strove for an autonomous republic. Each of O'Casey's three great Irish plays, *The Shadow of a Gunman*, *Juno and the Paycock*, and *The Plough and the Stars*, is set in the poorer parts of the city in which the playwright was born, and in each there is a background of armed fighting and revolutionary catchcries.

A writer using such material started with an initial advantage. His theme is the impact of war and of a national ideal embodying courage and self-sacrifice on lives that would otherwise be merely sordid and without dramatic interest. All these plays verge on melodrama, but the intensity of a real experience, which was shared by the author and his early audiences, saves them from being quite that. The dominant motif is pity, pity for suffering humanity. The national struggle is accepted as a facet of nature, as inevitable as birth or death. But the heroes of these plays are not its soldiers, but their womenfolk who show courage of a different sort – who fight without sentiment and without conscious idealism to aid the suffering and afflicted, and to protect their own. These three plays were followed by what is perhaps the most powerful anti-war play ever written, *The Silver Tassie*. Unfortunately, Yeats made the most consummate blunder of his critical career in rejecting this for the Abbey Theatre.

Largely on account of this, O'Casey made his home henceforward in England, and though some of his later work is set in Ireland it belongs primarily to the English stage. There is a radical difference of opinion among critics as to the value of O'Casey's later work. For some it is overlaid in diffuseness with maudlin sentimentality: the theme is still pity and admiration for the common people, but it is drowned in sardonic and indiscriminate caricature of the upper classes, and this soon becomes monotonous. The failure in organizing intelligence is only occasionally redeemed by the old vitality of language. By this time O'Casey, who had been a syndicalist and follower of Larkin and Connolly in his youth, was a vociferous supporter of the British Communist Party. An American critic, Robert Hogan, has claimed, however, in *After the Irish Renaissance* that these later plays belong to the central tradition of English pastoral comedy and that it is irrelevant to compare them with the early plays – a view apparently authenticated by O'Casey himself during the controversy over the banning of *The Bishop's Bonfire* in Dublin in 1955. The theme, as in Shakespeare's *Winter's Tale*, is the innocence of bucolic love pitted against the hypocrisies of church and state, with modern Ireland as a rather special Aunt Sally. Few of these later plays were performed in Ireland during the author's lifetime, but after a successful performance of *Purple Dust*, treating it as a wild extravaganza, in the 1970s, the Abbey announced an intention of presenting the complete canon.

O'Casey wrote six volumes of autobiography, beginning with *I Knock at the Door* (1939). Often the writer is carried away with the old exuberance of language, but for the Dickensian intensity of the portrayal of Dublin tenement life they are well worth reading.

In several of his writings setting out the ideals of the Abbey Theatre Yeats had mentioned that he hoped its work would be complemented by a move to make the classics of world drama available to Irish audiences. After the First World War this hope materialized. In 1918 a new theatrical grouping was established, the Dublin Drama League, with just this intention. Plays by Pirandello, Eugene O'Neill, D'Annunzio and others were performed. In 1928 this group led to the founding of the Dublin Gate Theatre by Hilton Edwards and Michael MacLiammoir. The work of the Gate was not limited to non-Irish plays. The wider perspectives offered made it also a forum for Irish work which could find no place in the increasingly narrow conventions of the Abbey. The Gate's most notable discovery was Denis Johnston. The title of his play, *The Old Lady says 'No!'*, refers to its rejection by the Abbey directors. This play, together with *A Bride for the Unicorn* and *The Golden Cuckoo*, used an expressionist technique, similar to that of Toller and Brecht. Unfortunately, they depend for their full effect on a close acquaintance with Irish history and tradition and the emotional undertones this involves.

Johnston's most successful play, *The Moon in the Yellow River* (1931), which was welcomed in London and New York as well as in Dublin, is a straight play within the Chekhov–Ibsen tradition. It deals with the impact of material progress on a countryside still dominated by easy-going traditionalism and romantic nationalism. As in O'Casey, there is conflict between an advancing ideal and human nature, and once more comedy and tragedy are juxtaposed. But unlike O'Casey the conflict is presented with full intelligence instead of with despairing pity. It is seen as part of a wider context: the 'message' of the play is to reflect a genuine perplexedness, which is as relevant to Russia or China (from which the title comes) as to Ireland. After the Second World War Johnston concentrated increasingly on work for the BBC and television. In middle life he fell almost completely silent, living in America and teaching drama at a New England university.

The great days of the Abbey run from its foundation to the early 1920s, those of the Gate dominate the 1930s and 1940s. The year 1939 marked both the death of Yeats and a split in the Gate Theatre Company between the artistic directors, Edwards and MacLiammoir, and the sixth Earl of Longford, who had contributed generous financial support and since 1931 had been chairman. Two companies, Gate Theatre and Longford Productions, succeeded the older company with an agreement each to use the theatre for six months of the year and tour the remainder. Both companies produced plays of their own successfully for several more years, but there was a gradual falling-off in experimental work.

The rather humble original Abbey premises burned down in 1951 and were only replaced by a modern government-subsidized building in 1966. Meanwhile a proliferation of miniature theatre groupings had taken place in Dublin and its suburbs. In 1957 the first Dublin Theatre Festival was held. After teething troubles, notably an acrimonious controversy with O'Casey,[1] which led him to refusing permission for any more of his plays to be performed in Ireland, and a decision by Samuel Beckett to withdraw a play in sympathy, the Festival settled down as an annual event which provided the main outlet for new work and experiment. Three playwrights in particular may be said to have emerged with the Theatre Festival, Hugh Leonard, John B. Keane and Brian Friel. Leonard, who was reared by foster parents near Dublin, is a playwright of enormous energy, technical expertise, and success. His early work was mainly adaptations – *The Passion of Peer Ginty*, after Ibsen, *When the Saints Go Cycling In*, from Flann O'Brien's *The Dalkey Archive*, and *Stephen D* from Joyce's *Portrait*. Later, however, he developed his own themes, probing with caustic insight the *mores* of his peers. If the misanthropic note is not to everyone's taste, it is in keeping with a substantial strain in modern Anglo-American drama. *Da* ran successfully in New York in the late 1970s. Keane is a Kerryman by birth and a publican by trade. As might be expected from this background, his varied characters are bursting with vitality and perform with devastating naturalism, though their language sometimes runs to hyperbole. *Sive*, a most popular play for amateur productions, is a poignant re-use of the old theme – the young girl driven by parental greed to marriage with a rich farmer twice her age. *The Highest House on the Mountain*, another tormented play of rural tensions, was the great success of the 1960 Theatre Festival. Keane's plots may fall within a stage-Irish convention, but his dialogue has an earthy vigour it would be hard to match elsewhere.

Brian Friel is a more serious writer than either of these, making no concessions to the groundlings for laughs, as Keane does, nor for sensationalism, as Leonard does. In addition he is a craftsman of dramatic originality. With the international *tour de force* of *Translations* (1980) he has emerged as Ireland's leading dramatist, a successor to the great tradition. In 1964 he spent some months at Tyrone Guthrie's theatre in Minneapolis. His first real breakthrough came with *Philadelphia, Here I Come!* (1964), a play highlighting the pathos and homesickness of emigration, utilizing a 'double' to voice the central character's unspoken thoughts. Fresh plays followed at frequent intervals. *The Freedom of the City* (1973) is based on the fate of three diverse characters caught up in the Derry civil rights riots. *Translations* takes the clash of two opposed but interlocking civilizations back to the early nineteenth century. An unusual subtlety here is that while English only is spoken on the stage, the audience is never in doubt that in reality some of the characters are speaking in Gaelic.

Irish theatre today is alive and well. Thomas Kilroy's *Talbot's Box*

(1977) and Thomas Murphy's *The Sanctuary Lamp* (1975) may be mentioned. In the 1981 Theatre Festival some twenty separate productions were mounted, ranging from *Macbeth* and the *Commedia dell'Arte a l'Avogaria* to first nights by Irish playwrights in English and Gaelic.

The influence of cultural naturalism was strongest in the theatre. It was marked in poetry and least strong in prose fiction. It used to be felt indeed that the novel was the weakest art-form in Irish letters. Joyce, of course, is a case apart: his work transcends the Irish scene. George Moore wrote one or two fine novels portraying, with a tinge of anti-clericalism, life in the Mayo countryside. But although at one moment he aspired to leadership of the Irish Renaissance (his *Hail and Farewell* mischievously tells the tale), his main work lies within the English tradition. After Moore there was a hiatus until a crop of vivid short-story writers appeared soon after independence. In recent years, however, several novelists of distinction have made their presence felt. These writers do not constitute a cohesive group. Nevertheless they stand out from their English or American contemporaries, less perhaps by innovations of style than by their use of characteristic themes.

Five main themes dominated Irish prose writing in the early part of this century and our discussion is best grouped round these: the 'big house' theme, the nature theme, the historical theme ('the Troubles'), the Catholic novel, and the comic novel. The latter leads to a subsidiary theme, that of the experimental novel.

Three (to be precise, four) women novelists made notable contributions within the first theme. The big house of the Irish countryside might superficially seem to resemble the manor-home of England. Politically and socially it lay a world apart. While the English lord of the manor might expect sincere deference from all but a tiny minority of his neighbours, his Irish cousin would look for either fawning subservience or sullen hostility. For the native, he was the descendant of usurpers, and he in his turn was aware of this. This bred a tension not altogether unfruitful for literature. Somerville and Ross was the pen name with which Violet Martin and Edith Somerville elected to sign the long series of novels which included *The Real Charlotte* (1894), *The Experiences of an Irish R.M.* (1899) and *The Big House of Inver* (1925). These used to be dismissed as merely humorous writing, but recent critics have found in them valuable sociological insight, and have realized that the authors were less complacent to the shortcomings of their class than superficial appraisal suggested. Elizabeth Bowen might seem less obviously an Irish writer *The Death of the Heart* (1935) is set in London society. But at the centre of this, as of her other work, is a concern with uncertain allegiance and the threat of social extinction – the basic preoccupations of the Anglo-Irish caste. In *The Last September* (1929) she set this theme in its big house setting during the watershed of the first Irish 'Troubles'. In *Bowen's Court* (1942) she left a history of the family home she once knew, which, like so many of its kind, has since vanished from the Irish countryside.

Kate O'Brien's background was Catholic merchant prince, rather than true ascendancy. Yet the Limerick mansion of her upbringing lay within the shadow of the fox-hunting Anglo-Irish, and when that class fell from power, it carried a portion of the patrician class with it. *The Ante-Room* (1934), recently republished with a penetrating preface by Eavan Boland, carries insight into the ethos of this class.

The finest example of a writer utilizing nature themes is Liam O'Flaherty, who has already been mentioned. A fellow-writer, Seán O'Faoláin, tells in his autobiography how, when O'Flaherty arrived in London fresh from the Aran Islands and determined to be a writer, he attempted a novel of society ladies and their love-affairs. A perspicacious publisher recognized the talent behind it, but advised him to write of things he knew from personal experience. 'But I only know about fields, rocks and cows' was O'Flaherty's unhappy answer. 'Then write about them.' He did, and produced the exquisite tales of country life collected in the volumes *Spring Sowing* (1924), *The Tent* (1926) and *The Mountain Tavern* (1929). It would be hard to think of any European writer with the same power to place himself imaginatively into the anguish of a cow looking at her injured calf or a baby seagull just learning to fly. Rural Ireland of the interwar years found a compassionate chronicle in the stories of Mary Lavin, and a harsher one in Patrick Kavanagh's novel, *Tarry Flynn*.

The bloodshed which took place in Ireland during the years 1916 to 1923 was a shattering experience for all sensitive Irishmen. For English and continental writers who experienced the First World

War, it was the futility and anonymity of mass-slaughter which horrified. In the Irish struggle, particularly in the civil war, personal relationships were tragically close: often a family was divided against itself, and even where this was not so, the existence of a common language between the English soldiery and the Irish insurrectionaries gave it a more private character. The title-story of Frank O'Connor's first book, *Guests of a Nation* (1931), well illustrates this. Seán O'Faoláin produced a first collection on the same theme at the same period, *Midsummer Night Madness* (1932); and Liam O'Flaherty caught the vivid detail of the revolutionary war in such short novels as *The Informer* (1925) and *The Martyr* (1933), some of which were filmed. Peadar O'Donnell was a little older than these three, and was a socialist as well as a revolutionary. His novel *The Knife* (1930) suggests the class alignments that lay behind the national struggle. All these writers were young men who had participated in the fighting they depicted. History had been kind to the poet Yeats in that he reached maturity before the nationalist movement passed from words to acts: he was both involved and detached and so able to produce great reflective poetry, such as the *Meditations In Time Of Civil War*. By contrast, these youngsters were caught and hurt by the raw experience which they could record but not place in any settled perspective. It seemed surprising that Ireland produced no novel of wide canvas to depict the drama of these years. But it should be remembered that *War and Peace* was written nearly sixty years after the events it describes and which Tolstoy knew principally from grandfathers' tales. Michael Farrell's *Thy Tears Might Cease* (1963) was an only partially successful attempt to do the same for Ireland. More recently, James Plunkett's *Strumpet City* (1969) and Eilis Dillon's *Across the Bitter Sea* (1973) have used actual history as the novelist's frame. But the masterpiece of Irish historical novels is that of the Irish-American, Thomas Flanagan, *The Year of the French* (1979), set against the events of the revolutionary year 1798.

It seems relevant here to mention another gifted Irish novelist, who handled non-Irish themes. John Banville has been re-creating in fictional form with extraordinarily vivid detail the lives of the European scientists; *Doctor Copernicus* (1976) and *Kepler* (1981) are the first of a tetralogy. His work has won high praise outside Ireland.

It was not easy for men whose formative years had been spent in guerrilla war to settle to the humdrum business of the middle-class state that emerged from the Irish revolution. The early years of the Irish Free State were still troubled politically, and the absence of any established background to society has been blamed for the tendency of many writers to fall back on the short story rather than the novel in those years. It might be felt that the Catholic church should have been able to offer such a background. But Irish Catholicism had such a narrow and parochial character as to prove rather a millstone round the neck of any creative writer. One of the first actions of the new government was to impose a censorship of books on moral grounds, which soon made Ireland the laughing stock of intellectual Europe. Few writers of world repute failed to figure on the censored list, and Irish writers were under special scrutiny. It was not pleasant for men like O'Faoláin to find themselves branded in their native land as pornographers. O'Faoláin's *Come Back to Erin* and Brinsley Mac-Namara's *Valley of the Squinting Windows* reflect the straitjacketing of the times. In recent years, happily, the censorship has been considerably relaxed and indeed a German literary historian has noted an almost excessive preoccupation with sexual themes.

One novel of maturity and distinction, promptly banned in Ireland, did appear in those early years – Seán O'Faoláin's *Bird Alone* (1936). A subtle and sensitive novel in its own right, it also highlights an important question: What is the Catholic novel? The central character is an old man who in youth, as the story little by little reveals, got a girl with child. The girl dies in childbirth, tormented by her sin. The struggle of carnal desire against Catholic precept is told with immense delicacy and sympathy, and the implied background of transcendental values sets this novel in a world apart from the slice-of-life fiction contemporary in America and England. In the more open Ireland of the 1960s a new group of Irish writers tackled similar themes, notably John McGahern in *The Barracks* and *The Dark*. With *The Leavetaking* (1974) and *The Pornographer* (1979), McGahern has emerged as the most sensitive craftsman of the middle generation. William Trevor, in Irish stories such as 'The Distant Past', combines superb craftsmanship with the jaundiced vision of the expatriate.

The hardest genre to discuss is the comic novel, because too often the effect of analysing humour is to lose it. But if, in spite of that, one dare venture a definition, Irish humour seems characterized by the juxtaposition of seedy, earthy realism with abstruse flights of metaphysical fancy. This is the nature of much of the humour in *Ulysses* and *Finnegans Wake* and in the early writings of Beckett. It is found in unadulterated form in the novels of Brian Nolan, alias Flann O'Brien, alias Myles na gCopaleen, the most outstanding of which are *At Swim-Two-Birds* (1939) and the posthumous *The Third Policeman* (1940). These two are also rare precursors of the anti-novel in English. The protagonist of *At Swim-Two-Birds* announces:

> One ending and one beginning for a book was a thing I did not agree with ... A good book may have three openings entirely dissimilar and inter-related only in the prescience of the author, or for that matter one hundred times as many endings.

It is easy to imagine where this doctrine leads.

Another fine writer, bordering on this category, is Benedict Kiely. A Northerner and an ex-seminarist, he writes with a whimsical compassion. *A Ball of Malt and Madame Butterfly* (1973) is one of his best collections. *Proxopera* (1977) is in a different vein – a sobering *novella* relating to the Northern tragedy.

An odd man out among Irish novelists, as elsewhere, is Francis Stuart. Though Yeats once found in his work 'a cold, exciting strangeness', until recently he was largely ignored but is now highly regarded by a younger generation. Born of Northern Protestant stock, he married Maud Gonne's natural daughter, Iseult, turned Catholic, and took the extreme Republican side in the Irish civil war. Later he spent the Second World War in Germany, and its aftermath in France, only returning to Ireland in the mid-1960s. Though he never propagandized for the Nazis, he lived through the bombing of Berlin and its occupation by the Russians. Probably he is the only novelist of stature writing in English to bring such experiences to bear on his work. His finest novels, *The Angel of Pity* (1935), *Redemption* (1949) and *The Flowering Cross* (1950), reflect the problems of suffering once posed by Dostoyevsky, and a Catholicism that anticipates the Second Vatican Council. A strange, long work, *Blacklist Section H* (1971) is part autobiography, part historical fiction.

The Irish Writers' Co-operative, with the assistance of the Irish Arts Council, is making available the work of a younger generation of sometimes experimental novelists, such as Desmond Hogan, *The Leaves on Grey* (1980), F. D. Sheridan, *Captives* (1980), Leland Bardwell, *That London Winter* (1981) and Maura Treacy, *Scenes from a Country Wedding* (1981).

The titan figure of Yeats inevitably dominated the Irish poetic scene even well into the years following his death. This did not make it easy for younger men to find distinctive voices. F. R. Higgins and Padraic Colum owe something to the early Yeats and more to the older ballads. Colum's fine lyric 'She Moved through the Fair' evokes the anonymity of the bardic tradition and reminds one of Yeats's observation that the country people are fond of verses and stories that 'keep half their meaning to themselves'. Donagh MacDonagh broke new ground by contributing to the Dublin stage two ballad-comedies, *Happy as Larry* (1946) and *God's Gentry*. These are in the manner of Brecht's *Beggar's Opera* and were forerunners of Behan's *The Hostage* and the musical adaptation of *The Playboy* as *The Heart's a Wonder* which achieved passing fame in the 1950s.

Two powerful Catholic poets, Austin Clarke and Denis Devlin, emerged in the 1930s. Clarke owes much to Yeats, to the verbal tricks of Gaelic poetry, and to a Jansenist-tinged vision of the early Irish church. His later collections *Flight to Africa* (1963) and *Old-Fashioned Pilgrimage* (1967) include clipped, sardonic satire on issues Irish and foreign. His long *Mnemosyne Lay in Dust*, perhaps his finest work, agonizingly depicts a nervous breakdown. Denis Devlin was a member of Ireland's diplomatic corps and much of his work was published abroad. His imagery and subject-matter are correspondingly wide. He was better known in Italy and America during his lifetime until the posthumous *Collected Poems* appeared in Dublin in 1963. Neither Clarke nor Devlin can approach their deity with Hopkins's fearful, but positive, apprehension, but if Clarke's approach is Jansenist, Devlin's is Kierkegaardian:

> It being essential to the gall he tasted
> That bitterness only bitterness can share.

But the most original poet to appear since the death of Yeats was Patrick Kavanagh. Born on a poor farm near the Ulster border, the opening lines of his longest poem, *The Great Hunger*, portray this land:

> Clay is the word and clay is the flesh
> Where the potato-gatherers like mechanized scarecrows move
> Along the side-fall of the hill – Maguire and his men.
> If we watch them an hour is there anything we can prove
> Of life as it is broken-backed over the Book
> Of Death?

Any forerunner here is D. H. Lawrence, not Yeats. Kavanagh's unromantic picture of grinding toil in the pocket-handkerchief fields of his homeland is closer to Lawrence's stories of the collieries than to any of the English nature-poets:

> Watch him, watch him, that man on a hill whose spirit
> Is a wet sack flapping about the knees of time.

The poet who wrote that had himself worn an old sack for a cheap apron on muddy work. Here once more we find the problem of Ireland's lonely bachelors, fearful to marry lest they overcrowd the land, this time seen from the inside. The 'hunger' of the title is both the hunger for land and the hunger for life, both finally unappeased:

> ... he is not so sure now if his mother was right
> When she praised the man who made a field his bride.

When this *Guide* first appeared, Thomas Kinsella was cited as the youngest poet of promise. With every collection since, he has handsomely fulfilled this. A rare devotion to craftsmanship, a scholar's knowledge of Gaelic tradition, and an almost unbearably poignant personal vision are his strength. Such early poems as *In the Ringwood* and *A Lady of Quality* have lyric form, tempered by the brooding shadow of Irish history or personal suffering. In his later, often difficult, work, the mood darkens further, leading through self-irony to an exploration of primal existence, sometimes of nightmare intensity: *Notes from the Land of the Dead* (1973) and *One* (1974). No Irish poet has remained untouched by the Northern troubles and in 1972 Kinsella startled his admirers with an overtly political poem, *Butcher's Dozen*. This is a savage tract of the times in the tradition of Swift and Dante: it evokes the accusing shades of the thirteen unarmed Derry citizens who were shot by British paratroopers on 13 January 1972. In 1969, at home on a Guggenheim fellowship from teaching in America, Kinsella produced a complete rendering in prose and verse of the great epic of Ireland's golden age, the *Tain* – with illustrations by Louis le Brocquy. Kinsella now divides his time between Ireland and America.

As mentioned above, John Montague and Seamus Heaney will be discussed in the next volume of the *Guide*. Richard Murphy was slower to mature, but *The Battle of Aughrim* (1968), a long poem in spare classic style, marked his breakthrough to the first rank. Brendan Kennelly has issued a variety of collections combining shrewdness of observation with the vivid phrase in a sometimes surrealist vision. Eavan Boland links the deft, unexpected phrase with a penetrating intellect in her two fine first collections, *New Territory* (1967) and *The War Horse* (1975). She is also a first-class literary critic and political journalist.

An essay such as this must inevitably miss many names other critics consider important. I hope, though, that enough has been said to substantiate the opening claim that Irish writing today forms an autonomous tradition with the English literature of this century.

NOTE

1. See Gabriel Fallon, *Sean O'Casey: The Man I Knew* (London, 1965) for details; also Robert Hogan, *After the Irish Renaissance* (London, 1968).

SHAW AND THE LONDON THEATRE

T. R. BARNES

Dramatic art has long seemed to me a kind of *Biblia Pauperum* – a Bible in pictures for those who cannot read the written or printed word; and the dramatic author a lay preacher, who hawks about the ideas of his time in popular form – popular enough for the middle classes, who form the bulk of theatrical audiences, to grasp the nature of the subject without troubling their brains too much. The theatre, accordingly, has always been a board-school for the young, for the half-educated, and for women, who still retain the inferior faculty of deceiving themselves and allowing themselves to be deceived: that is to say, of being susceptible to illusion and to the suggestions of the author. Consequently, in these days, when the rudimentary and in-completely developed thought-process which operates through the imagin-ation appears to be developing into reflection, investigation and examination, it has seemed to me that the theatre ... may be on the verge of being abandoned as a form which is dying out, and for the enjoyment of which we lack the necessary conditions ... in those civilized countries which have produced the greatest thinkers of the age – that is to say, England and Ger-many – the dramatic art ... is dead.

(Strindberg, Preface to *Miss Julie*, 1888)

The passage is well known, but it has seemed worth quoting at length, not only because it so well typifies the climate of opinion in which Shaw began to write plays, but because it remains so extraordinarily apposite a description of his own work and of much that has been written since. Consider for example, this account, by F. C. Burnand, of the audience at the Royal Court Theatre, during the famous Barker–Vedrenne regime, 1903–6: 'The female element predominates over the inferior sex as something like twelve to one. The audience had not a theatre-going, but rather, a lecture-going, sermon-loving appearance.' And it is easy to compile a list of worthy plays, from *Strife* to *Thunder Rock* or *A Sleeping Clergyman* or *Johnson Over Jordan*, which are, in essence, lessons for Strindberg's 'board-school'.

The attack on the imagination is also relevant. Curiously old-fashioned though it may sound today, it is characteristic of much thinking about the drama at the end of the nineteenth century. There was a naïve belief that the literature of naturalism was, for the first time, revealing the truth. '*Dans l'enfantement continu de l'humanité,*' declared Zola magniloquently in the preface to the dramatized version of *Thérèse Raquin*, '*nous en sommes à l'accouchement du vrai.*' This truth was to be 'scientific'. 'What we wanted as the basis of our plays', wrote Shaw, 'was not romance, but a really scientific natural history'; and this basis was to be arrived at by thinking: 'there is flatly no future for any drama without music, except the drama of thought'. Strindberg would seem to imply that if all we have is 're-flection, investigation, examination', we 'lack the necessary conditions for the enjoyment' and also, presumably, for the creation, of the drama. It seems to be a popular procedure in avant-garde criticism to cut off the branch you are sitting on – Ionesco and Beckett are contemporary examples – and Strindberg's practice belied his theory; but in the attitude to literature expressed in these remarks, above all in the exaltation of the intellect at the expense of the imagination, in the insistence on scientific method and on thought, lies the reason why so much of the well-intentioned, thought-provoking, socially-directed drama of the Shavian period seems so dead today.

Shaw claimed to be in the tradition of Molière. 'My business as a classic writer of comedies', he said, 'is to chasten morals with ridicule'; and part of his technique was to reintroduce to the drama 'long rhetorical speeches in the manner of Molière'. There can be no doubt that his plays amused, stimulated, exasperated, and shocked his contemporaries; that no plays since Congreve's (it is T. S. Eliot's opinion) have more pointed and eloquent dialogue, that he was a man of great intelligence and immense seriousness of purpose, and that only one of his contemporaries, in one play, *The Importance of Being Earnest*, can hold a candle to his best work. But if we compare his work with that, say, of Lawrence, of Forster, or of Eliot, can we say that it still lives for us as much as theirs does, that we can return to it, as we can to theirs, and find new values in it? Does not the reference to Molière, which was seriously meant – it is not a mere piece of Shavian rodomontade – make us feel a bit uneasy?

Consider these fragments of dialogue:

Madelon (one of the Précieuses Ridicules):
  La belle galanterie que la leur! Quoi! Débuter d'abord par le mariage?
Gorgibus (her father):
  Et par où veux-tu donc qu'ils débutent? Par le concubinage?

Don Luis (speaking to his son, Don Juan):
  Apprenez enfin qu'un gentilhomme qui vit mal est un monstre dans la nature ...

Mme Jourdain: ... Il y a longtemps que vos façons de faire donnent à rire à tout le monde.
M. Jourdain: Qui est donc tout ce monde-là, s'il vous plaît?
Mme Jourdain: Tout ce monde-là est un monde qui a raison, et qui est plus sage que vous.

Mendoza: I am a bandit. I live by robbing the rich.
Tanner: I am a gentleman. I live by robbing the poor. Shake hands!

Undershaft: Poverty, my friend, is not a thing to be proud of.
Shirley: Who made your millions for you? Me and my like. Whats kep us poor? Keepin you rich. I wouldn't have your conscience, not for all your income.
Undershaft: I wouldn't have your income, not for all your conscience, Mr Shirley.

All these bits depend for their impact on the weight of certain key words – *galanterie, mariage, nature, monde,* gentleman, poverty, riches, conscience, and so on. If Molière's terms have much greater weight than Shaw's, and I think it could be shown that they have, this is because values were shared between them, because Molière's culture supported him, so that he could assume an understanding on the part of his audience more complete than any contemporary playwright can count on. The fact that this sort of understanding no longer exists makes 'chastening morals with ridicule', as Molière or Ben Jonson understood the matter, most difficult, if not impossible; since before morals can be chastened we must agree on what they are, and by what standards they are to be judged.

This difficulty cripples the dramatist more than any other writer, because he must move a group. The novelist or poet, who addresses the individual, can forge his own language, and hope that his readers will learn it. The dramatist must speak in terms they already understand; he has to use the language of his age, and this language reflects the condition of the society that speaks it. Our society and our language are such that it is far more difficult to produce truly creative and original work in a medium like the drama, which depends for its effect on immediate public consent, than it is to do so in the comparatively private media of poetry and fiction. The dialogue in which Shaw's characters discuss the ideas about society and politics and justice which he wanted his audience to respond to remains brilliantly clear: we have only to turn over the pages of *Strife* or *The Madras House* to see how vastly better he was than his contemporaries. Yet many critics, from A. B. Walkley onwards, have felt that there was something 'wrong' with Shaw's plays. They certainly wear less well than those of his near-contemporaries, Ibsen and Chekhov. The reason lies in his curiously ambivalent attitude to art and literature.

Shaw proclaimed himself uncompromisingly a Puritan: 'My conscience is the genuine pulpit article: it annoys me to see people comfortable when they ought to be uncomfortable; and I insist on making them think in order to bring them to a conviction of sin.' 'For art's sake' he would not 'face the toil of writing a sentence'. Yet literature is part of 'the struggle for life to become divinely conscious of itself', he writes. In *Man and Superman* (1903) he makes Tanner explain to Tavy that 'the artist's work is to show us ourselves as we really are. Our minds are nothing but this knowledge of ourselves; and he who adds a jot to such knowledge creates new mind as surely as any woman creates new men'. A noble definition, expressed with the rhythmic precision and clarity which Shaw's best dialogue always exhibits; but when we remember the whole scene, and the context of this speech, we also remember that it is Tavy who is supposed to be the 'artist', and he is a refined well-to-do version of the usual *vie de Bohème* stereotype that Shaw always represents the artist as being, and of which Marchbanks and Dubedat are the classic examples. It is Tanner whose work is important, and he is no 'mere artist' but an 'artist philosopher' – the phrases were used by Shaw to describe the author of *Everyman*; his literary ancestor is not Shakespeare but Bunyan. Shakespeare, 'who knew human weakness so well, never knew human strength ...', but Bunyan 'achieved virtue and courage by identifying himself with the purpose of the world as he knew it'.

If, then, we are to judge the value of Shaw's work, we must estimate what he has added to our knowledge of ourselves, and how he has explained the purpose of the world. But he has made it very difficult for us to do this on his own terms, because in his view such knowledge is always going out of date, and the purpose of the world (magniloquent but empty phrase) would appear to be always changing. Consider these remarks, from the Preface to *Man and Superman*:

Effectiveness of assertion is the Alpha and Omega of style. He who has nothing to assert has no style and can have none: he who has something to assert will go as far in power of style as its momentousness and his convictions will carry him. Disprove his assertion after it is made, yet its style remains. Darwin has no more destroyed the style of Job nor of Handel than Martin Luther destroyed the style of Giotto. All the assertions get disproved sooner or later, and so we find the world full of a magnificent débris of artistic fossils, with the matter-of-fact credibility gone clean out of them, but the form still splendid. And that is why the old masters play the deuce with our mere susceptibilities.

How did a man whose specific judgements on music and drama were so often so acute, come to write such irrelevant nonsense when he generalized about the arts? Because, I believe, he was uneasily conscious of his talent's limitations. As a wit and a pamphleteer he was impressive: as a creative artist only a minor figure. The epithet he applies to our susceptibilities gives the game away; it gives evidence, like his digs at Shakespeare, of an underlying, perhaps unconscious envy of qualities he knew to be outside his scope. *St Joan* was his attempt at a great play. Its discussions of political motives and class antagonisms are lively; its efforts to move our 'mere susceptibilities' are failures. Shaw commands only the language of assertion and dialectic; when he deals with emotion there is only cliché: 'if only I could hear the wind in the trees, the larks in the sunshine, the young lambs crying through the healthy frost, and the blessed, blessed church bells'. One is reminded of Yeats's remarks about the realistic drama:

Except when it is superficial, or deliberately argumentative, it fills one's soul with a sense of commonness as with dust. It has one mortal ailment. It cannot become impassioned, that is to say vital, without making somebody gushing and sentimental.

Shaw advised us to 'get rid of reputations: they are weeds in the soil of ignorance. Cultivate that soil, and they will flower more beautifully, but only as annuals.' But since, presumably, we cannot agree with this, or with the idea that past works of art are 'fossils', preserved in 'style', we must ask what elements in Shaw's work are still living. His assertions about the Life Force, tolerable in a light-hearted performance like *Man and Superman*, become boring in the over-long and pretentious *Back to Methuselah* (1921); his admiration for the great man, stimulating and even ennobling in *Caesar and Cleopatra* (1901), degenerated into dangerous and sentimental weakness; but his wit, his gaiety, above all his passion for justice, remain undimmed.

Shaw was a pioneer in the matter of publishing plays. 'He realized', says St John Ervine, 'that no one would read a prompt copy of a play unless he had to ... *Plays Pleasant and Unpleasant*, was, therefore, issued in a form which was a mixture of novel and play ... the emotions of the characters at a particular point were described.' The same authority tells us that 'dull people imagined that G.B.S. in writing these accounts was naïvely revealing his inability to write plays at all'. Think, for a moment, of the brilliant paragraph which, at the beginning of *Man and Superman*, describes Roebuck Ramsden in his study:

He wears a black frock coat, a white waistcoat (it is bright summer weather) and trousers, neither black nor perceptibly blue, of one of those indefinitely mixed hues which the modern clothier has produced to harmonize with the religions of respectable men ...

If we remember anything about Roebuck it is likely to be this joke about the colour of his trousers. The specimen is pinned down for our leisurely inspection, its habitat sketched in, and its prejudices, social, political, economic, and aesthetic, neatly indicated:

Against the wall opposite him are two busts on pillars: one, to his left, of John Bright; the other, to his right, of Herbert Spencer ... autotypes of allegories by Mr G. F. Watts (for Roebuck believes in the fine arts with all the earnestness of a man who does not understand them) ...

Our pleasure in this detached and comic portrayal is increased by symbolic and humorous exaggeration. The polish on Roebuck's furniture, made possible by the labour his money can buy ('it is clear that there are at least two housemaids and a parlourmaid downstairs, and a housekeeper upstairs who does not let them spare elbow grease'), is transferred to his bald head: 'On a sunshiny day he could heliograph orders to distant camps by merely nodding.' Shaw's debt to Dickens in passages like this is obvious. But to think of a novelist, is to think that this whole passage might well come from a novel, though it is in fact a stage direction; yet when we consider it from that point of view we see at once that most of it is quite irrelevant, for no audience can be expected to recognize photographs of George Eliot and busts of John Bright and draw from them those conclusions about Roebuck's character which Shaw so neatly deduces.

St John Ervine's dull people were, of course, wrong when they thought Shaw couldn't write plays; but the point they might have made about this description of Ramsden is simply that it is not in the play at all, and that no matter how cunning the scene designer, or how skilled the actor, it can't by any means be got into it. And they might also add that in great drama 'the emotions of the characters at a particular point' are not described, but expressed. Shaw's dialogue, his style, his rhythms, his imagery, though admirably suited to dialectic or pedagogy, won't do for everything he has in mind to put in the plays; and this is largely true of naturalistic drama in general. We need not, in way of comparison, invoke the shades of Shakespeare or Molière: Congreve, Sheridan, Beaumarchais, or even Wilde will do. We don't need elaborate descriptions of Ben the Sailor, or Sir Benjamin Backbite, or Figaro (compared with him how poverty-stricken a character is Henry Straker), or Lady Bracknell, because their creators have expressed them fully and exactly through the speeches and rhythms they have created for them.

In the Preface to *Plays Pleasant and Unpleasant* (1898) Shaw discusses stage directions, complains that there are none in Shakespeare's plays, and goes on to say:

> It is for want of this elaboration that Shakespeare, unsurpassed as poet, story-teller, character draughtsman, humorist, and rhetorician, has left no coherent drama, and could not afford to pursue a genuinely scientific method in his studies of character and society.

If Shaw's drama *is* intellectually coherent, its coherence can only be grasped by a reader. We must agree with Shaw when he says that he has 'never found an acquaintance with a dramatist founded on the theatre alone ... a really intimate and accurate one'; but we may also wonder whether any drama is truly great that depends as much as his does on extra-theatrical considerations.

When we turn from the plays of Shaw to those of his contemporaries and successors who used the naturalistic convention to depict and discuss society and its problems, we find little of permanent interest. Much work, like that of Barrie or Coward, for example, is merely sentimental, frivolous, or trivial. Attempts by such writers as Galsworthy, Maugham, Bridie, or Priestley to deal with serious themes seem already dated. There is a good deal of honest and earnest work, some flashes of humour and fantasy, and useful discussion – for Shaw's success undoubtedly opened the theatre doors to the drama of ideas – but there is nothing truly creative. These writers all handle ideas we have heard before, and manipulate situations and feelings already familiar. They are not trivial, they do not lack a 'worthy purpose', but they are not creative. If effective enough in the theatre, their works do not repay reading; their dialogue is for the most part invincibly dull: words fail them.

Not all voices at the beginning of the century acclaimed naturalism: Yeats, for example, had very different ideas. He had been told, he said, that 'the poetic drama has come to an end, because modern poets have no dramatic power'; but this explanation didn't convince him. He found it

easier to believe that audiences, who have learned . . . from the life of crowded cities to live upon the surface of life, and actors and managers who study to please them, have changed, than that imagination, which is the voice of what is eternal in man, has changed . . . The theatre began in ritual, and it cannot come to its greatness again without recalling words to their ancient sovereignty.

It would, I think, be true to say that most plays of any literary merit produced during the last half-century exhibit the influence of what we might call the Shavian or the Yeatsian points of view. Though naturalism was dominant, there were many besides Yeats who were dissatisfied with what they felt to be the imaginative poverty of realism, and who tried to bring poetry back to the theatre. Mostly they failed, and it is usually thought that they did so because they knew nothing of the stage, or play construction, or how to write dialogue, and this is partly true; but the real reason for their failure is linguistic. Their verse was merely decorative, their idiom devitalized, their rhythms flaccid. They pleased what Lawrence called the 'habituated ear' of the public whose taste approved the Georgian Poetry anthologies, but their plays could only lead a brief obscure theatrical existence in private performances or in occasional appearances in the lists of the more adventurous repertory companies. Believing the naturalistic conventions to be sterile, determined to get away from 'plays with pink lamp-shades', from 'patent leather shoes on Brussels carpets', from a stage dedicated to picturing 'life on thirty pounds a day, not as it is, but as it is conceived by the earners of thirty shillings a week' they escaped for the most part into romantic unrealities. Their works might well have been written by Marchbanks or Tavy.

In the thirties, W. H. Auden, in collaboration with Christopher Isherwood, tried to assimilate elements of the popular theatre into plays which should embody a serious comment on the contemporary situation. The result was an uneasy mixture of satire and nostalgia, of moral indignation and self-pity, seasoned with tags from Freud and Marx, but it had at least a certain energy; it evinced a genuine concern for the human situation, and tried to express that concern in a poetic idiom tough enough to work on the public stage.

That the poet should try to make use of the forms of the commercial theatre, instead of turning his back on them in despair or disgust, was an important departure which has obvious bearings on the dramatic work of T. S. Eliot. Audiences began to welcome verbal exuberance and rhetoric, after a starvation diet of the dullest prose. Terence Rattigan dignified this development of taste by describing it as

a revolution in the contemporary theatre, begun a few years ago by T. S. Eliot and Christopher Fry, [which] has rescued the theatre from the thraldom of middle-class vernacular in which it has been held, with rare intervals, since Tom Robertson, and given it once more a voice.

It is characteristic of the confusion of critical values that Rattigan, and many others with him, should have imagined that the voices of Eliot and Fry had anything in common. Christopher Fry is certainly exuberant. His verse, with its tumbling imagery, almost batters an audience into submission. But if we examine his lines in detail, we find they resemble those of 'poet-dramatists' like Gordon Bottomley, though Fry's idiom is, of course, more fashionable:

> *Thomas:*   Oh no!
> You can't postpone me. Since opening-time I've been
> Propped up at the bar of heaven and earth, between
> The wall-eye of the moon and the brandy-cask of the sun

> Growling thick songs about jolly good fellows
> In a mumping pub where the ceiling drips humanity,
> Until I've drunk myself sick, and now, by Christ,
> I mean to sleep it off in a stupor of dust
> Till the morning after the day of judgement.
> So put me on the waiting-list for your gallows
> With a note recommending preferential treatment.
>   *Tyson:* Go away; you're an unappetizing young man
> With a tongue too big for your brains ...

The Lady's Not For Burning (1949) is not really about anything; it is a sort of conjuring trick – the quickness of the word deceives the ear – and the images, unrelated to any over-all pattern of meaning, remain a series of disconnected bright ideas. A similar criticism may be made of the ingenious phrases:

> Cain ...
>   a huskular strapling
> With all his passions about him ...
> Old Joe Adam all sin and bone ...

which decorate a more serious work like *A Sleep of Prisoners* (1951).

Eliot, we know, long envied the music-hall comedian his direct contact with his audience: and we would, I think, be justified in assuming that one of his reasons for turning to the drama was the desire to break out of the cultural isolation from which the modern poet suffers. 'Our problem should be', he wrote in *The Possibility of a Poetic Drama*, 'to take a form of entertainment of a crude sort and subject it to the process which would leave it a form of art.' The form of entertainment he has chosen is the drawing-room comedy, that 'sets a piece of the world as we know it in a place by itself'. The list of characters in *The Family Reunion* (1939), for example, would suit a play by Maugham or Coward or Rattigan; it is patently 'a play about modern educated people'. The 'process' to which this 'form' is subjected is twofold: first the story or action refers to a Greek original; it has a skeleton of myth, presumably to help represent 'what is eternal in man', though this can be of use only to the author, for he cannot rely today on an audience understanding such an allusion, and Eliot has himself recorded that he had to 'go into detailed explanation' to convince his friends that the source of *The Cocktail Party* (1949) was the *Alcestis* of Euripides. Second, the

284

dialogue is written in verse. ('Surely there is some legitimate craving, not restricted to a few persons, which only the verse play can satisfy.') This verse has a 'rhythm close to contemporary speech'; the lines are 'of varying length and varying number of syllables, with a caesura and three stresses', and the whole is intended as 'a design of human actions and words, such as to present at once the two aspects of dramatic and musical order'.

Few can doubt the value of Eliot's experiments, and of the acute analyses he made of the problems of poetic drama. But in spite of the care, the skill, the intelligence that has gone to their making, these plays lack vitality because they are not informed with human sympathy. In the arbitrary hierarchy of spiritual values that the characters represent there is no charity. We are shown their actions, we are told about their motives, we see their progress to the solution Eliot has arranged for them, but we do not feel any of this. It is impossible to believe in Colby Simpkins's future ordination or to be convinced by the martyrdom of the young lady in *The Cocktail Party*. This lack of warmth and energy is strikingly brought out if we compare a page or two of any of these plays with that remarkable fragment *Sweeney Agonistes* (1932) – surely the finest piece of dramatic verse Eliot ever wrote. We might apply to it his own remarks on Yeats's last play, *Purgatory*, 'in which ... he solved his problems of speech in verse, and laid all his successors under obligation to him'. When we think of *Prufrock* and *Gerontion*, where verse follows with insidious intent and exhilarating vigour the quirk of character, the shift of mood and feeling, we may feel like applying to Eliot the remarks he makes about Browning, in the essay entitled *Three Voices of Poetry* (1953):

What personage, in a play by Browning, remains alive in the mind? On the other hand who can forget Fra Lippo Lippi, or Andrea del Sarto ... It would seem without further examination, from Browning's mastery of the dramatic monologue, and his very modest achievement in the drama, that the two forms must be essentially different. Is there ... another voice ... the voice of the dramatic poet whose dramatic gifts are best exercised outside the theatre?

It may be significant that Eliot's most successful play should be *Murder in the Cathedral* (1935), which was written for the Canterbury Festival, and was therefore intended to fulfil a specific social purpose, a purpose, moreover, with which the drama has still a living and real, if tenuous, connection – the performance in aid of the parish funds. The poet was here playing a traditional role; his gifts served a cause and commended beliefs which he shared with his audience, and this situation seems to have liberated energies which have given the play strength enough to dominate an audience in a public theatre, a greater strength, it seems to me, than is exhibited in any of the plays which use the conventions of drawing-room comedy.

Shaw once said that what was wrong with 'the drama of the day' was that it was 'written for the theatres instead of from its own inner necessity'. The sort of play that Shaw was complaining about is still the staple fare in the West End theatre. But thanks to him that fare now usually includes a few dishes more nourishing than any he had to feed on in the days when he was a dramatic critic. His precepts and his example have had their effect. Shaw cannot be considered a major artist (he ranked himself about number ten among English playwrights); but we can with some justice claim that our best dramatic work is livelier, more serious, more deeply concerned with life than it has been at any time since the days of Fielding. In so far as any one man is responsible for this, that man is Shaw.

THE COMEDY OF IDEAS:
CROSS-CURRENTS IN FICTION
AND DRAMA

R. C. CHURCHILL

There has been a great deal of interest taken in Henry James's abortive flirtation with the drama, it being widely recognized that this experience was one of the chief influences behind the intensely dramatized form of his later novels. What has not been remarked is the curious fact that at the same time as James was trying to get the dramatic virtues into the novel, Bernard Shaw, who had started as a novelist and had the same failure in fiction as James had on the stage, was trying to get the virtues of the novel into the drama. Shaw was to become the leading platform debater, as well as the leading dramatist of ideas, of the twentieth century; and there was nothing that James liked better, whether in writing or in conversation, than to discuss the problems of his art. Yet, though the two men did correspond on this subject, no record of a full-scale debate has survived.

We can, nevertheless, imagine roughly how it would have gone. In the correspondence of James and H. G. Wells[1] we have the classic case of the literary artist versus the journalist, summed up by Wells when he wrote: 'To you literature like painting is an end, to me literature like architecture is a means, it has a use ... I had rather be called a journalist than an artist, that is the essence of it.' He was to satirize the literary artist of the James type in *Boon* (1915), as he had satirized the sociologist of the type of the Webbs in *The New Machiavelli* (1911). Both James and Wells, however, were inclined to exaggerate their position. In reaction against Wells's immense international reputation,[2] James over-emphasized his own unpopularity. He was not in fact so unpopular as he frequently lamented. One of his novels, *The American*, appeared in Nelson's Sevenpenny Library, as 'an example of the best work of one who is regarded with justice as among our greatest living novelists ... as one of the most perfect examples of Mr Henry James's remarkable art'.[3] On his side, in reaction against the beliefs of the James–Conrad–Ford circle, Wells was inclined to over-emphasize the reliance of his fiction on the topics of the moment, saying that most of his work would survive only so long as their ideas remained current. This view is obviously correct in regard to such novels as *Ann Veronica* (1909); but in the best of his social comedies, such as *Kipps* (1905) – which James thought his masterpiece – and in the best of the scientific romances and short stories, like *The Time Machine* (1895) and *The Country of the Blind* (1911), he attains the stature of a literary artist of a minor but decidedly original kind. The 'idea' is still the mainspring, but it involves the moral idea of the novel proper and, though most of such stories had a 'use' in their time, it would be untrue to say that they are now readable only as period pieces.

Shaw in retrospect is connected with Wells: we see them as embattled Socialists and Evolutionists debating endlessly, on platform and in print, with the Distributism and the Christian Liberalism of Hilaire Belloc and G. K. Chesterton, all four very much in the public eye. And he would have echoed many of Wells's remarks in his controversy with James. An inner distinction is there, nevertheless, as well as an outward resemblance. Wells was a teacher of science and a writer of scientific textbooks before he became a novelist; Shaw was a music critic, and one of the best in modern times, before he won fame as a playwright. We are apt to think of him as merely the propagator of Ibsen (or William Archer's Ibsen) and Samuel Butler; we forget his love of music and the fact that his writing was always deeply influenced by the four masters of his youth: Bunyan, Blake, Dickens, and Ruskin. Wells in his novels of ideas may have 'rather been called a journalist than an artist'; in his dramatic criticism and his drama of ideas Shaw would have queried the distinction.

He was convinced that the 'new drama' must compete in elaboration with the contemporary novel. He was thinking of Meredith, Hardy, and Gissing rather than of James,[4] and James of course was writing novels like this:

'She gave me a lot of money.'
Mrs Wix stared. 'And pray what did you do with a lot of money?'

'I gave it to Mrs Beale.'

'And what did Mrs Beale do with it?'

'She sent it back.'

'To the Countess? Gammon!' said Mrs Wix. She disposed of that plea as effectually as Susan Ash.

'Well, I don't care!' Maisie replied. 'What I mean is that you don't know about the rest.'

The rest? What rest?'

(*What Maisie Knew*, 1897, ch. 25)

and was soon to graduate to this:

'... I can bear anything.'

'Oh "bear"!' Mrs Assingham fluted.

'For love,' said the Princess.

Fanny hesitated. 'Of your father.'

'For love,' Maggie repeated.

It kept her friend watching. 'Of your husband?'

'For love,' Maggie said again.

(*The Golden Bowl*, 1904, Book IV, ch. 6)

That is the novel partaking of the dramatic emotion of the stage play. Shaw, at the same time, was writing plays with enormous stage directions, being convinced that the time had gone by when one could just say, like the Elizabethans, 'another part of the field', and leave it at that. Shaw not only set his scene in the utmost detail, but gave his actors an embarrassment of help by describing both the outward appearance and the personality of his characters:

Major Sergius Saranoff, the original of the portrait in Raina's room, is a tall romantically handsome man, with the physical hardihood, the high spirit, and the susceptible imagination of an untamed mountaineer chieftain. But his remarkable personal distinction is of a characteristically civilized type. The ridges of his eyebrows, curving with an interrogative twist round the projections at the outer corners; his jealously observant eye; his nose, thin, keen, and apprehensive in spite of the pugnacious high bridge and large nostril; his assertive chin would not be out of place in a Parisian salon, shewing that the clever imaginative barbarian has an acute critical faculty which has been thrown into intense activity by the arrival of western civilization in the Balkans. The result is precisely what the advent of nineteenth-century thought first produced in England: to wit, Byronism. By his brooding on the perpetual failure, not only of others, but of himself, to live up to his ideals ... [*etc., etc.: continued for twenty more lines in the collected edition*].

(*Arms and the Man*, 1894, Act II)

This massive detail, to say nothing of his lengthy prefaces, makes his plays something of a cross between dramatic literature and the novel; assisted by the accident of his becoming famous in print first, then on the stage afterwards. James's move in the opposite direction was partly due to his irritation at the sprawling habits of the Victorian three-volume novel, particularly those previously serialized in magazines, the novelist padding out his numbers against the clock. It cannot be denied, however, that most of James's later novels, for all their dramatic merits, make heavier reading than he intended; nor that, despite the readability as well as the theatrical qualities of the early Shaw, there was a corresponding limitation in the Shavian conception of the dramatic art.

This is best seen in his view of Shakespeare. Shaw the music critic spoke well of the 'orchestration' of Shakespeare's verse; but his portrait of Shakespeare in *The Dark Lady of the Sonnets* (1910) is one that could only have been produced by a writer who combined a deep appreciation of music with a total misconception of dramatic poetry. His Shakespeare carries a notebook about with him and when anyone utters a 'strain of music' he copies it down for future use. Thus, when the Beefeater exclaims: 'Angels and ministers of grace defend us!', down it goes in Shakespeare's 'tablets' for future use in *Hamlet*! The limited truth behind this misconception is, of course, that the Elizabethan drama, like the Authorized Version of the Bible, was based on the common speech of the time; but what Shaw failed to realize was that poetic drama is not drama with poetry added to it but a separate species in which the drama and the poetry are one and the same.[5] A related point is that Shaw romanticized a poet in *Candida* (1894) and a painter in *The Doctor's Dilemma* (1906), both highly unconvincing figures; he would not have made the same mistake with a composer.

I cannot myself see entire success either in the majority of James's later 'dramatic' fiction or in most of Shaw's early 'novel-plays'. They were written at roughly the same time, *c.* 1890–1910, and they have, I believe, different but related weaknesses. James's intention was so to dramatize the novel that all extraneous matter could be eliminated and the attention of the reader fixed throughout on the main scenes, like a spectator in the theatre; Shaw's intention was to provide plays with so extensive an elaboration that they could bear intellectual comparison with the novels of a Meredith. We cannot doubt the limited success of these endeavours, James's later novels being on as lofty a level compared with the average Victorian three-decker as Shaw's early plays compared with the average Victorian melodrama or farce. But do such novels as *The Awkward Age* and *The Golden Bowl* compare favourably with *Middlemarch* or with the best of James's own earlier work? Is not their comparative unreadability partly due to a misconception of form, similar to Shaw's lack of dramatic art compared with Shakespeare or Synge? It is with the results of this curious juncture in mind that I should like to make some observations on the position of the literature of ideas in the twentieth century.

We can imagine roughly, as I say, the arguments used by James and Shaw in justification of their contrary proceeding. Much of their debate would have been talking at cross-purposes, but not all of it; for James was as profoundly versed in painting as Shaw was in music, so that each had a standard in a different art to which literature could profitably be compared. James's analogies with painting, in the prefaces to the novels, are as frequent as Shaw's orchestral analogies in the prefaces to the plays. Sooner or later, however, they would, as it were, have come to blows: they would have started hurling Dickens at each other, and both would have been justified in their ammunition.

For we cannot proceed very far in any discussion of the relation of the English novel to the English drama without bringing in Dickens. He is the most dramatic of our novelists, though he did not deliberately incur the dramatic responsibilities in the manner of James. In his autobiographies James gives him the title of 'Master' along with George Eliot, and he had the privilege of meeting both Masters personally.[6] There are perhaps two main currents in the English novel, the one flowing from Fielding and Smollett to Scott and Dickens, the other from Richardson and Jane Austen to George Eliot and James. We need not discuss the minor links; it is sufficient for our purpose to note that the novel proper in the twentieth century has mostly stemmed from the latter source, the novel of ideas from the former. There is a tradition of comedy in English fiction which originally sprang from the drama, which reached its highest point in Dickens, and which in our time is principally found in the novel of ideas from Wells to Orwell and in the novel-drama of Shaw. They are the inheritors here, not only of the comic richness and the concern for social justice of Fielding and Dickens, but of that looseness of art in the general run of eighteenth- and nineteenth-century literature against which writers like James and Conrad reacted. They were right so to react; but we must not put all the righteousness on the one side. What a sprawl is *Chuzzlewit* compared with James's *Lady* or Conrad's *Nostromo*! If James had written *Chuzzlewit*, we can be sure that the novel would have been a unified work of art, as Dickens's novel is not; but there would have been no artistic necessity for such characters as Mrs Gamp or Young Bailey, or indeed for the whole Columbian business, and it is precisely there that the comic genius of *Chuzzlewit* mainly resides. Mrs Gamp, like Sam Weller, was an afterthought, a sudden flush of comic inspiration; and when you write a novel on the principles of Flaubert or James you keep to your original plan, with no afterthoughts permitted.[7] It was the practice of James, particularly after his dramatic experience, to draw up what he called 'a really detailed scenario, an intensely structural, intensely hinged and jointed preliminary frame'; it was the practice of the early Dickens to draw up a rough plan and improvise the details as he went along – a practice encouraged by publication in instalments. It is the whole achievement of the work of art which we admire in James (though some of his novels, including *What Maisie Knew*, were serialized in magazines); in Dickens we often forget the over-all plan in our admiration of the details.

I submit the following proposition: that the literature of ideas in the twentieth century is mainly Dickensian, both in its virtues and in its vices, and that to criticize it by the standards of Henry James is beside the point. It is the English tradition of comedy, both in its admirable detail and its casual sprawl, which is inherited by writers like Shaw, Wells, Chesterton, Huxley, and Orwell. In *Unto This Last*

Ruskin praised 'the essential value and truth of Dickens's writings', singling out *Hard Times* ('to my mind, in several respects, the greatest he has written') and advising us not to 'lose the use of Dickens's wit and insight, because he chooses to speak in a circle of stage fire'.[8] This is eminently just and reasonable, but nevertheless it was that disparaged fire which produced Mrs Gamp and most of the other memorable Dickens characters as well as the melodrama and the sentimentality which Ruskin rightly deplored.

Paraphrasing Ruskin, I would say: let us not lose the wit and insight of the best of our literature of ideas because these virtues are embodied in the writings which, as works of art, do not stand comparison with even the lesser productions of our major literary artists. Compared with Synge, Shaw seems as insecure an artist as Wells compared with James, or Huxley compared with Lawrence; but Shaw on the stage, though comparable at his best with Sheridan and Oscar Wilde, is not the whole Shaw: he has a further dimension in non-dramatic literature, as the novels and essays of Wells, Belloc, Chesterton, Huxley, and Orwell are variants of the same species. The literature of ideas in our time is a very untidy business; but no more so than in the novels (or assorted scrapbooks) of Peacock, Disraeli, and Samuel Butler.

Proportion is the essence of the serious literary artist; comic exaggeration, if often for a serious purpose, is the keynote alike of Dickens and the twentieth-century literature of ideas: exaggeration in all its forms, of speech and idea and procedure. Where Dickens in the preface to *Little Dorrit* cannot write simply of 'a small boy carrying a baby' but must needs write 'the smallest boy I ever conversed with, carrying the largest baby I ever saw'; so in *The Truth about Pyecraft* (1903), Wells writes of the '*British Encyclopaedia* (tenth edition)', where the edition is absolutely irrelevant; in *Arms and the Man* (1894) Shaw puts his ideas about Byronism into a stage-direction and writes a preface to the gigantic *Back to Methuselah* sequence (1921) which is itself a hundred pages long and the wittiest summary of the Darwinian controversy ever written; Chesterton pads out to novel length the simplest of short stories, like *Manalive* (1912), as if Hans Andersen had taken three volumes to tell the story of the Ugly Duckling; Huxley in *Brave New World* (1932) cannot resist the temptation to quote the nursery rhymes of the future: 'Streptocock-Gee to Banbury T, to see a fine bathroom and W.C.' etc.; and Orwell in *1984* (1949) inserts some notes about modern idiom he had previously discussed in the essay *Politics and the English Language* ... In all these cases, and any reader will supply a dozen more, there is evidently no premeditation, but ideas springing to the mind of the writers as they go along, too rich to be left out, too absorbing not to be carried to the bitter end. Equally, it is in these details, as it is in Mrs Gamp in *Chuzzlewit*, that the value of their writings mainly resides.

Huxley himself, under the thin disguise of the character Philip Quarles in *Point Counter Point* (1928), discussed the difference between the novelist of ideas and what he termed the 'congenital' novelist. And in that novel he made an attempt to proceed from being the former into being the latter. I believe we should be grateful that the attempt was, on the whole, a failure. Compared with the best of Forster or Lawrence, the novel does not rank very high as a work of art. Huxley later went back to his early style, producing novels of ideas like *Brave New World* and *After Many a Summer* (1939), which, like the early Peacockian Huxley, make up for their artistic weaknesses in the exuberance of their ideas and the fertility of their comic invention. Huxley and Orwell were to the generations of the twenties, thirties, and forties what Shaw, Wells, and Chesterton were to the pre-1914 public; comparison with a James is as irrelevant as comparison with a Joyce. They are writers like Wells's Mr Britling, who have 'ideas about everything ... in the utmost profusion', and proceed to pour them out in an unending series of novels, essays, and pamphlets. It is a matter of comparative unimportance for them whether their views are expressed in fictional or non-fictional form: a state of mind incomprehensible to a literary artist like James or Conrad. Whole chunks of Huxley's novels could be printed as separate essays with only a little alteration; the opening of Chesterton's *Napoleon of Notting Hill* (1904) could have developed into an essay with equal plausibility, and some of the essays in *Tremendous Trifles* (1909) could have developed quite easily into stories.

The literary artist in fiction is interested above all in the personal relations of his characters: 'I have never taken *ideas* but always *charac-*

ters for my starting point,' wrote Turgenev. 'I never attempted to "create a character" if in the first place I had in mind an idea and not a living person.'[9] The writer of the novel or the drama of ideas is apt to conceive of his ideas first, then to invent characters to embody them. We remember *Ann Veronica* as a novel about the condition-of-woman question; it is difficult to recall anything about Ann Veronica Stanley as an individual woman. Wells, like Shaw, however, has something of the Dickensian gift for comic speech; if we do not commonly remember his characters as persons, more often as the mouthpieces of the author, we do sometimes recall their characteristic idiom.

There is a related difference in real life between the literary artist and the novelist or dramatist of ideas. The latter are apt to be 'characters' in themselves, often public figures known to everyone in rough outline, as Shaw the flamboyant Irishman, Wells the Cockney prophet, Chesterton the rolling English rover, Orwell the Old Etonian tramp ... We do not conjure up such a vision, or such a caricature, of writers like Synge, James, or Forster: their personalities are more private, their art more impersonal. It must be difficult for a writer who is 'a character' in his own right to keep himself out of his work, and the plays of Shaw are as full of Shavian figures as the novels (and biographies) of Chesterton of Chestertonian eccentrics. Comstock in *Keep the Aspidistra Flying* (1936) and Bowling in *Coming Up for Air* (1939) are composite figures, composed in equal parts of the ordinary man as seen by Orwell and Orwell himself; this actually makes them very 'uncomstock',[10] liable to speak as often in their creator's character as in their own.

There is subtle, ironic comedy in the work of such writers as James and Forster. But the kind of laughter that Dickens often provokes – 'Laughter holding both his sides' – is more frequently found in our time in the literature of ideas. It is the kind of laughter provoked by the deliberately absurd and exaggerated: qualities – which can so easily become vices – that we do not associate with the literary artists of our age, but rather with those who, like the early Dickens, think of their best strokes as they go along. The most memorable line in Orwell's *Animal Farm* (1945), for instance – the revised revolutionary slogan: 'All animals are equal but some animals are more equal than others' – was evidently, like Mrs Harris, an inspiration of the moment.

'Heavens, how we laughed!' wrote Murry, reflecting on the impact of Wells on his generation. This seems to me the right attitude to adopt, and many readers of a later generation would echo Murry's words in relation to Huxley or Orwell. One would not claim too much for such writers; the distinction between the literary artist and the journalist still holds true. At the same time, we must not forget the significance of James's failure in the theatre and the relative failure of most of his later 'dramatic' novels; Shaw's 'novel-drama' has a similar limitation as literary art. Yet our literature of ideas as a whole has managed to carry on something of the Dickensian tradition of English comedy. In an increasingly cosmopolitan literary world, that is an achievement by no means to be despised.

NOTES

1. *Henry James and H. G. Wells*, ed. L. Edel and G. N. Ray (1958). For the less extensive correspondence between James and Shaw, see *The Complete Plays of Henry James*, ed. L. Edel (1949).

2. '... he had become the chief representative of English literature upon the European continent. In every bookshop in France you would see, in the early years of this century, the impressive rows of his translated works ... I believe it was on the immense sales of his early scientific stories and romances that the success of the great French publishing house, the Mercure de France, was mainly founded.' (J. M. Murry, *Adelphi*, October 1946; reprinted *Little Reviews Anthology*, 1948, 188.)

3. I quote Nelson's advertisement.

4. Meredith is the novelist he actually mentions. See Preface, *Plays Pleasant and Unpleasant* (1898), Vol. I, xxi.

5. To paraphrase Granville-Barker. Eliot has made much the same point. Shaw complained that the Folio 'gives us hardly anything but the bare lines'! If only, he wrote, Shakespeare 'instead of merely writing out his lines' had prepared his plays for publication 'in competition with fiction as elaborate' as that of Meredith, 'what a light they would shed ... on the history of the sixteenth century!' (ref. n. 4 above).

6. See *Autobiography* (1957), reprint in I vol. of *A Small Boy and Others* (1913), *Notes of a Son and Brother* (1914), and the unfinished *The Middle Years* (1917).

7. In *The Maturity of Dickens* (1959) Monroe Engel, whose object is 'to insist that Dickens can and should be read with pleasure and no restriction of intelligence by post-Jamesian adults', treats Mrs Gamp simply as 'an example of the callous brutality bred by poverty'.

8. *Unto This Last*, Essay I, note to para. 10: World's Classics edn, 26.

9. Two separate quotations here juxtaposed: cited in Miriam Allott, *Novelists on the Novel* (1959), 103.

10. The name Comstock is an interesting anticipation of the 'Newspeak' of *1984*. The opposite would be 'uncomstock' – a serious crime in Oceania.

HUGH MACDIARMID: THE EARLY WORK

NANCY K. GISH

Four months before Hugh MacDiarmid's death, the *Sunday Times* carried a feature on his life and work. Entitled 'The Last of the Giants', the article opened with a large photograph of MacDiarmid and Ezra Pound walking down a street in Venice, the slightly bowed old men sharing a grave dignity. It was a belated but appropriate tribute to the man who had dominated Scotland's literary and cultural scene for five decades. For MacDiarmid and Pound shared an era and an enterprise. Like their contemporaries, Eliot and Yeats, they sought a new poetry to render difficult and problematic visions of modern life, but they were distinct in their persistent refusal either to formulate or synthesize. While Eliot moved from the sombre discontinuities of *The Waste Land* to the formal patterns of *Four Quartets*, and Yeats devised a system of 'stylistic arrangements of experience' by which to 'hold in a single thought reality and justice', Pound and MacDiarmid eschewed comprehensive systems or truths. Speaking of Pound's achievement, MacDiarmid emphasized this point: 'The difference between Eliot and Pound, who were very friendly at one time or another, is that Pound kept opening out. That gives the sort of inchoate aspects to his *Cantos*, taking in all kinds of material and so on.'[1] Like the critical comments of most poets, MacDiarmid's are largely a validation of his own method, and his deep admiration for Pound is instructive. Arguing that the important direction in modern poetry is towards the long poem and this its greatest practitioner is Pound, he defines the qualities of great poetry:

It has been said – and I accept the definition – that these qualities are three: (1) robustness of thought; (2) felicity of expression; (3) comprehensiveness of view ... The purely lyric poet, by the very character of his muse, is incapable of excelling in the first quality – robustness of thought.

The aim of longer poetry, on the other hand, is illustrated by Heine, who, after the great success of his early lyrics, found he must cease to write in that way altogether and needed to break up the unity of the lyric, create a new form that would accommodate shifting tonalities and levels so that he could introduce, and grapple with, all manner of diverse subject matter and feelings.[2]

That capacity to take in 'all manner of diverse' feeling and experience distinguishes Pound. 'Ezra Pound shows in the *Cantos* that he has never allowed himself to be (in Sean O'Casey's phrase) drawn away from "the sensitive extension of the world".'[3] Underlying this commitment to comprehensiveness and extension is a fundamental assumption about reality deeply engrained in modern thought. As MacDiarmid puts it, 'It is the complicated which seems to be Nature's climax of rightness.'[4] In his own poetry he sought to reveal this 'climax of rightness'.

Formally, MacDiarmid's poetry falls into distinct groups. His early work consists of brief, intense lyrics in a dense Scots. Throughout the 1920s he followed a consistent line of lyric development, moving from individual lyrics to long poetic sequences of diverse styles and moods. In the 1930s he gradually dropped the lyric, shifting to wide-ranging experiments in technique and theme. The uneven success of these experiments makes any assessment of the canon difficult and subject to disagreement. It is easy to point to frequent weaknesses in conception and style and to an inconsistency that increases as MacDiarmid moves to longer, more open forms. Unusual and problematic, the late work is and will probably remain controversial. It consists of long discursive works, suddenly illuminated by striking images and extended analogies, but including lengthy lists, quotations, names, and obscure technical references. Despite this formal variety and even greater diversity of theme and mood, the central concerns of his poetry remain constant. As we learn to read the massive and unfamiliar late works, the originality and extent of MacDiarmid's achievement will become even clearer. But the unquestionable power of the early work, up to and including *A Drunk Man Looks at the Thistle*, is best understood as deriving from the same impulse that produced the late long poems, the impulse to complexity, inclusiveness, and openness. In focusing on this early great period of lyric development, I am not concerned to place exclusive value on it but to define a vision underlying the whole.

Although he denied that lyric poetry could excel in 'robustness of thought', in fact, MacDiarmid sought for just that in his early poems. In writing a new kind of Scots poetry, his avowed aim was to show that the vernacular could express the whole range of human experience. The journal he published to launch a Scottish renaissance, *The Scottish Chapbook*, announced its purpose in sweeping terms: 'The general aim of the Chapbook is, of course, to conduct experiments into the assimilability into literature of the whole range of Scottish life – including the total content of Scottish minds.'[5] Like Pound's 'taking in all kinds of material', this concept of assimilating assumes a willingness to acknowledge and, in MacDiarmid's words, 'grapple with' all experience. For all their compression and formal control, the lyrics of *Sangshaw* and *Penny Wheep* gain their sense of uncanny insight from the feeling of 'taking in', including, assimilating, far more than from the immediate focus of attention . Yet this vivid sense of *more* being there is not achieved by the symbolist mode of seeing through an object or situation to metaphysical significance. A materialist who yet retains the mystic's capacity for awe in the face of mystery, MacDiarmid creates a world of amplitude and plenitude, any detail of which carries the force of endless interconnections. While Eliot's nightingale or Yeats's swans evoke multiple suggestions and overtones of meaning remote from their existence as birds, an equally suggestive bird in an early MacDiarmid lyric retains a wry individuality and character, its startling thrust into the heavens a literal extension of significance rather than a shift in planes of experience. Or rather, experience is not divided into levels; the move from nest to heavens is not a displacement:

Ex vermibus

> Gape, gape, gorlin',[a]
> For I ha'e a worm
> That'll gi'e ye a slee[b] and sliggy sang
> Wi' mony a whuram.[c]
>
> Syne i' the lift[d]
> Byous[e] spatrils you'll mak',
> For a gorlin' wi' worms like this in its wame[f]
> Nae airels[g] sall lack.

a nestling; *b* sly and cunning, loquacious; *c* crotchet, quaver; *d* heaven; *e* wonderful, musical notes; *f* belly; *g* musical notes of any kind; *h* ablaze.

But owre the tree-taps
Maun flee like a sperk,
Till it hes the haill o' the Heavens alunt[h]
Frae dawin' to derk.

If the title, 'From Worms', prepares us for a comic and familiar tone, it also points outward. The movement is from worms to the heavens, and the tone follows from the opening humorous/conspiratorial line promising the gawky baby bird a special worm, to the awed appreciation of its lighting of heaven: a complex movement from worms to birds to heavens, as the worm becomes first food then music then flames. The bird, too, moves outward, from gaping nestling to musical master filling the skies. Within so brief a poem, the range of possibility is immense, yet it remains pointedly natural. Birds do transform worms into music filling the air. The emphasis is on intricate execution – byous spatrils, whurams, a slee sang. Yet that intricacy also carries us into something greater than the immediate facts account for: the whole of the heavens is ablaze from dawn to dark. But though the tiny bird resonates in every direction, it points to nothing supernatural, ineffable, divine. It insists on a weight of significance within rather than beyond the material world. Such effects, like sound waves on the air rather than the inner ear, create an experience of dense texture and fullness, joined with an openness of possibility.

MacDiarmid's lyrics achieve their characteristic intensity from this union of minute detail with expansiveness. The constant sense one has of experiencing more than can be delineated directs one towards more and more relationships. MacDiarmid achieves this sense of a dense texture of reality in three major ways in the lyrics. He packs images in layers, forcing the reader to move quickly from meaning to meaning and to take in many meanings at once; he extends the tiny and insignificant into cosmic proportions and reduces the vast to human scale; and he joins formal closure with a conceptual openness that leaves room for speculation. His endings seldom seem to end. If the gorlin' is transformed by a worm into a spark to light the heavens from dawn to dark, it is not clear precisely what this means or what power has been set free. What is clear is that MacDiarmid feels a familiarity with the universe which he approaches at times with whimsical affection and at times with uncanny recognition of the strange and unknown. The bird's swift passage from nest to heavens is effected with a surprising ease that is paralleled in lyric after lyric.

MacDiarmid joins an easy movement between vast and tiny with a swift movement from image to image. While it makes great demands on the reader, this packing of associations gives to very brief lyrics a richness and subtlety compounded by extension of significance. In *Scunner* the body of the beloved is almost casually associated with stars, not in a traditional conceit likening her to their brilliance but by an association acknowledging equivalence:

> *Scunner*[a]
> Your body derns[b]
> In its graces again
> As dreich[c] grun' does
> In the gowden grain,
> And oot o' the daith
> O' pride you rise
> Wi' beauty yet
> For a hauf-disguise.
>
> The skinklan'[d] stars
> Are but distant dirt.
> Tho' fer owre near
> You are still-whiles-girt
> Wi' the bonnie licht
> You bood[e] ha'e tint[f]
> – And I lo'e Love
> Wi' a scunner in't.

The poem turns on the notion of disguise viewed with an odd mixture of feeling. Disguises repeat themselves six times in these few lines, each version adding to the complex of feeling. The body hides in graces, the ground in golden grain, 'you' in beauty, the stars in shining light, 'you' in bonnie light, and scunner in Love. And to compound it further, pride seems a 'disguise' that has been given up to be replaced by the 'hauf-disguise' of beauty. The opening comparison sets the tone of ambiguous attraction. The body derns in its graces, and the 'again' makes this hiding a pattern, as if the dull material form had previously revealed itself to disgust, only to be veiled in desire. Like the ground covered with golden grain, it is

---

a disgust, revulsion; *b* hides; *c* dreary, tedious; *d* shining; *e* should; *f* lost.

tedious and dreary in its everyday physicality and yet burgeoning with warm life. Any judgement, therefore, must be suspended; the 'dreich grun' is not more real or significant than the golden grain. Love is a coexistence of conflicting responses. Having given up pride, having presumably, yielded, the beloved yet restores her integrity through the partial protection of beauty. This second contrast slightly shifts the focus of concern from attraction to a kind of uneasy respect and admiration which does not alter knowledge of the hidden. Linking with 'again' as with 'still' in the second stanza, 'yet' points to the perpetual restoration of her power.

The dismissive gesture with which the second stanza opens only enlarges the scope of ambiguity. For if the stars bring to bear a cosmic vastness of scale, unavoidably granting to her a heavenly level of beauty, they are themselves but dirt, also disguised in their own glow. Unlike them she is far too close and surrounded by an equivalent light, one she 'bood ha'e tint'. The easy identification of stars (dirt) with ground and with body is inseparable from the linking of grace and grain and light. Rather than an ironic under-cutting, the reduction of stars is of a piece with the extension of earth; both reflect a world where all is taken in and accepted both in its particularity and in its relations. This acceptance becomes a judgement in itself in the last lines: 'And I lo'e Love/Wi' a scunner in 't'. A curious remark, it is characteristic of MacDiarmid's refusal to categorize and to limit. Love as ideal, as perfected beauty, even as illusory desire, is yet penetrated by the crude and dull and disgusting, perpetually transformed and regenerated. And it is in its very problematic and disturbing nature that it is loved. Like *Ex vermibus*, the poem ends with a formal closure that leaves everything open. For if an assertion of value, defining Love, seems final, the definition opens it up to the uncontrollable and contradictory.

MacDiarmid's opening out is both an acknowledgement of and a participation in process. He delights in reopening final questions and subverting old categories. In *God Takes a Rest* God returns to the sea and lies 'i' the stound o' its whirlpools, free/Frae a' that's happened since.' 'Stounds' extends even this image of whirling birth and creative source. It means throbs, but also resounding noises and moments of time. God is thus back in temporal and sensual flux and the generative surge of life. In *The Innumerable Christ* God's other major finality, the Incarnation, repeats itself on countless stars, and the crucifixion follows over and over. The earth whirling in space is an exciting uproar in *Somersault*. Rushing by at a headlong pace, it carries everything fatalistically down into the night but up again in a perpetual recurrence of morning: 'But the East's aye there/Like a sow at the farrow.' The speaker of *In the Pantry* feels nausea at the finished stagnation of all that is and plans a whole new creation: 'I'll thraw the lot oot/And lippen[a] to get fresh/For the sicht o'ts eneuch/ To turn my soul nesh[b]!' Many poems thus deal thematically with that opening out nearly all suggest by their language and imagery.

In MacDiarmid's hands the lyric becomes an engagement in process; it eschews autonomous unity, that sense of a perfected whole Lawrence attributed to 'the poetry of the beginning and the poetry of the end', and directs the reader into further and further relations. But for such a purpose the lyric does have limitations. The density of texture nevertheless remains part of a single complex of experience, however rich. It points to but cannot follow out lines of development, those 'shifting tonalities and levels' only accommodated in new forms. An interesting characteristic of MacDiarmid's lyrics is the great range of feeling, experience, and mood they cover. Eliot's ironies, Hardy's pessimisms, even Yeats's early dreamy tones seem restricted by comparison. Gentle, sinister, stark, whimsical, fine or crude by turns, they take in, as a group, 'all manner of diverse subject matter and feelings'. But MacDiarmid sought to render the whole as well as the many parts. In *Lucky Poet* he described himself as

a man whose mind has always been on the track of something which required an awareness that was integral and continuous, and, no matter how small the detail of life he was observing, always strove to relate it to something more inclusive, to make it part of a whole – the work of a poet who believes that the poet 'must be able to understand and communicate the complexities of the world that grows daily more complicated'.[6]

MacDiarmid's move to the long poem is an extension of his early method rather than a break from it. What the lyrics do as a group, *A Drunk Man Looks at the Thistle* does as a single whole. Both seek to relate details to something more inclusive, but where the lyrics indicate directions, *Drunk Man* follows them. It moves towards greater and greater integration in a characteristic way, not by making

a trust; *b* nervous, full of awareness.

a pattern of experience which can account in advance for any detail but by 'grappling' directly with conflicting and contradictory experiences, linking all back to one thing, the poet's mind in its struggle to understand and communicate.

Like *The Waste Land*, *A Drunk Man Looks at the Thistle* consists of a mass of disparate lyrics selected and arranged in collaboration with a friend. The composer, F. G. Scott, to whom MacDiarmid regularly gave his poetry for comment, spent a night with the poet over a bottle of whisky, discarding, sorting, and ordering piles of individual pieces. Scott described his involvement as indicating the shape a poem or a musical composition should take, an ordering according to the best sequence and climaxes.[7] If this function resembles Pound's cutting of *The Waste Land*, the differences are instructive; Scott had outlined a plan and supplied a title before MacDiarmid started to write. But whatever was initially intended, the poem's unity derives from a focus of attention and a central symbol that is itself in constant flux. There is no structure of events, no myth to supply formal order, nor did Scott's arrangement supply one. Instead the poem works from a theme and a situation, the meaning of the thistle as seen by a drunk man. Drunkenness supplies a kind of ecstatic vision, freeing the poet from conventional assumptions and ordered patterns. The poem is, in fact, a deliberate plunge into chaos, an extension of the process of taking in and opening out; it shows no linear progression but radiates from a centre. Although each section connects back to the central image and the single voice of the drunk man, the sections do not necessarily lead to one another or to any final resolutions. The movement is accumulative, gathering the many facets of Scotland, poetry, and the poet's struggle into a constantly enlarging vision. Reading it forces one into a double concentration on each movement and on the linking of each part to the centre. The thistle, national symbol of Scotland, offered MacDiarmid a single image capable of expressing the integral and continuous nature of reality. Its roots deep in dark soil and its thistle and roses reaching into heaven, it embodies the opposing and contradictory elements of individual, cultural, and aesthetic life. Oppositions coexist; they do not need to be reconciled into *logical* unity. Integration consists in including what is there. So, the characteristic forms of early lyrics reappear as individual sections, detachable but part of the mass of linked meanings. They join again a formal unity and closure with conceptual openness and inclusiveness that leave way for the next passage. As Pound will end a *Canto* with 'so that . . .' or 'and' or ellipses, MacDiarmid often points to the non-finish with ellipses, as if any finality were an arbitrary choice and any apparent absolute open to reconsideration.

Examining any part of *Drunk Man* reveals a process of discovery both within and between individual sections. An early lyric on a mysterious lady, for example, introduces a long series of intricately related passages exploring the nature of the self, Scotland, and knowledge. Forming one of several broadly related groups of poems, it introduces all the major themes of the poem. A single passage will focus on a particular facet of the thistle's contradictions. The justly famous lyric, *O Wha's the Bride*, for example, presents one form of the question of love and sexuality:

> O wha's the bride that cairries the bunch
> O' thistles blinterin'[a] white?
> Her cuckold bridegroom little dreids
> What he sall ken this nicht.
>
> For closer than gudeman can come
> And closer to'r than hersel',
> Wha didna need her maidenheid
> Has wrocht his purpose fell.
>
> O wha's been here afore me, lass,
> And hoo did he get in?
>   *A man that deed or I was born*
>   *This evil thing has din.*
>
> And left, as it were on a corpse,
> Your maidenheid to me?
>   *– Nae lass, gudeman, sin' Time began*
>   *'S hed ony mair to gi'e.*
>
>   *But I can gi'e ye kindness, lad,*
>   *And a pair o' willin' hands,*
>   *And you sall ha'e my breists like stars,*
>   *My limbs like willow wands.*
>
>   *And on my lips ye'll heed nae mair,*
>   *And in my hair forget,*
>   *The seed o' a' the men that in*
>   *My virgin womb ha'e met . . .*

a glimmering feebly.

Innocence and knowledge are strangely mixed in this virgin carrying the seeds of generation, as are desire and revulsion. But the conventional response of the bridegroom is dismissed by the simplicity of the bride's response: there is no other form of love, no lass inviolate of time and generation. What she offers is an opportunity to acknowledge and accept the ambiguous union of beauty and bestiality, love and loathing. She carries thistles, thorny and rose covered, blinterin' white. Her technical virginity masks a dark meaning, but her young body, containing seeds of death, also promises birth: a maidenhead on a corpse. If the question/response pattern sets up a dialectic between these opposing implications of love and sexuality, it leads to no simple synthesis. The bride encounters her lover's horror with both reality and illusion, yet she leaves the oppositions intact. The oppositions are, in fact, the reality she offers, softened by romance – breists like stars and limbs like willow wands. She offers these as simply and unaffectedly as the kindness and willing hands. In moments of love, they are equally real. But in such moments, lost in lips and hair, he will, she says, forget that violation and death are contained in love. The poem ends on that contradiction, her virgin violated womb, and opens out in an ellipsis. Its ambiguities multiply in a series of lyrics on sexuality that take in the body and soul and enlarge to include the birth of Christ. Sex becomes a metaphor for the soul's intercourse with all reality, the poet's relations with the world:

> A'thing wi' which a man
> Can intromit's[a] a wumman,
> And can, and s'ud, become
> As intimate and human,
>
> He's no a man ava'.
> And lacks a proper pride,
> Gin[b] less than a' the warld
> Can ser' him for a bride! . . .

The interpenetration of man and woman, in fact, points to that central puzzle of human life, the union of body and soul, a mind that ranges the universe with god-like vision tied to deep instinctual urges. Throughout the poem, Dostoyevsky, Christ, and the poet-visionary, MacDiarmid himself, form a trilogy of figures reaching beyond the

a meddle; *b* if.

life of those they know yet caught in the same paradox of birth and death. If the contrast is at times a source of disgust – 'Wull ever a wumman be big again/Wi's muckle's a Christ? Yech, there's nae sayin'' – it can also be a revelation: 'Said my body to my mind,/"I've been startled whiles to find,/When Jean has been in bed wi' me,/A kind o' Christianity!"' Christ, too, grew out of that inherent violation, the virgin seed, and represents not God but the ambiguous human, or the thistle's roses thrown off by thorns.

The series of poems focusing on sex can be taken as a microcosm, gathering into a single facet of life all the complexities and contradiction encompassed by the thistle. It comprehends both life and death: 'Whisky mak's Heaven or Hell and whiles mells baith,/Disease is but the privy torch o' Daith,/ – But sex reveals life, faith.' But the poet can also imagine the act of love as a surreal horror of necrophilia: 'Its a queer thing to tryst wi' a wumman/When the boss^a o' her body's gane,/And her banes in the wund as she comes/Dirl^b like a raff o' rain^c.' Birth and death, desire and loathing, creation and desiccation, triumph and defeat – the multiple divisions of all experience find one expression in sexuality. They are reiterated in society's recurrent progress and decline, in Scotland's aspirations and barrenness, in the poet's vision and despair. All are contained in the thistle, the 'symbol o' the puzzle o' man's soul'. The thistle itself is defined over and over. Protean, endlessly transformational, it exists as a dynamic shape linking Heaven and Hell – Ygdrasil, Christ's cross, skeleton, and link between the heart and the moon. The contrasts embodied in individual elements of inexperience are subsumed in it. It is, then, an image for comprehensiveness, inclusion. Yet unlike Yeats's gyres, it does not stylize in order to include. A living plant, it grows, withers, regenerates. Its roots and branches keep extending in an increasing network of lines. As an image it includes that wholeness with the open-endedness MacDiarmid attributes to Pound's work, expressing integration without arbitrary limits and design. For this reason it is difficult if not impossible to describe the poem as a whole; one can only enter at a specific place, accepting the 'inchoate aspect'. Taken together, two specific passages define the thistle's central nature. Its oppositions and its penetration of the universe appear in a double image that is both thistle and self:

a torso; *b* rattle, move briskly; *c* a few streaks of rain.

> A mony-brainchin' candelabra fills
> The lift[a] and's lowin'[b] wi' the stars;
> The Octopus Creation is wallopin'[c]
> In coontless faddoms o' a nameless sea
>
> I am the candelabra, and burn
> My endless candles to an Unkent[d] God.
> I am the mind and meanin' o' the octopus
> That thraws its empty airms through a' th' Inane.

Here the thistle and poet are defined by penetration, movement out, both up and down. A flame, branching into heaven, is inseparable from the living, writhing, octopus of chaotic creation. No division or distinction of value is implied. In another passage, the thistle is identified also with the infinite particularities massed between the poles of flame and dark tentacle:

> Thou art the facts in ilka airt[e]
> That breenge[f] into infinity,
> Criss-crossed wi' coontless ither facts
> Nae man can follow, and o' which
> he is himsel' a helpless pairt . . .

The thistle, then, is all reality, and also the mind that recognizes and engages with it. Between its extremes of heaven and hell is a texture as dense as any individual lyric but sustained over a book-length poem. This thickness of texture absorbs and fascinates, drawing the reader back over and over to its complexities.

These complexities reach no resolution. MacDiarmid's purpose is not to select and exclude but to understand and communicate what is there. The poem ends with a momentary poise of balanced force that, like the lyric's formal closure, opens out into a renewal of all questions. His vision dissolved in morning-after exhaustion, the drunk man turns to what remains after the total expenditure of thought and language that has been both his night of vision and the poem. In one of his finest lyrics, the poet contemplates a personified Silence, that well of words, the all from which come endless particularities of word and image. Defined by negation, Silence is not those things often associated with it, death, dread, and loneliness, and not anything so impotent as God:

a sky; *b* blazing; *c* thrashing, plunging; *d* unknown; *e* every quarter of the heavens, any direction; *f* move impetuously.

– But Him, whom nocht in man or Deity,
Or Daith or Dreid or Laneliness can touch,
Wha's deed owre often and has seen owre much.

O I ha'e Silence left,

– 'And weel ye micht,'
Sae Jean'll say, 'efter sic a nicht!'

With the sardonic voice of his wife, formal stasis is broken. F. G. Scott said that he thought he remembered adding those words himself to 'bring the thing to some kind of conclusion'. Whoever supplied the words, their effect is only formally conclusive. Jean closes off the drunken night in a wry evaluation, but her voice reintroduces both the nature of the night and herself as emblem of all the world with which 'a man can intromit'. Contemplation gives way to physical immediacy and Silence to the sounds of speech. It is like ending with 'and'.

A language in process, a poem left open, cannot sustain the perfection of closed forms, and MacDiarmid's lapses in taste and style have been well documented, as has his often quoted response to such criticism: 'My job, as I see it, has never been to lay a tit's egg, but to erupt like a volcano, emitting not only flame but a lot of rubbish.' The intermittent and often partial success of MacDiarmid's late work and the inconsistencies throughout the canon do not work against his poetic enterprise. Had he chosen to edit, to select, to exclude, he could have retained a large volume of extraordinary work. But this would be to distort the whole; what mattered for him was a process of discovery which included many attempts, new directions, blind alleys. In the early Scots lyrics and *Drunk Man* that process reached its first major fulfilment. He, too, continued to 'open out', assuming the problems as well as the possibilities that entails. He expressed the ambiguous satisfaction of his own stance in a characteristic remark that he was 'acknowledging chaos with a candour which cannot evade fear, but seeking refuge neither in an irrecoverable way of life nor in oblivion'.[8]

NOTES

1. Nancy Gish, 'An Interview with Hugh MacDiarmid', in *Contemporary Literature*, 20, No. 2 (1979), 151.

2. Hugh MacDiarmid, 'The Return of the Long Poem', in *Ezra Pound: Perspectives*, ed. Noel Stock (Chicago, 1965), 90–91.

3. MacDiarmid, 'Return', 93.

4. 'Return', 93.

5. Hugh MacDiarmid, 'Causerie', in *The Scottish Chapbook*, 1, No. 3 (1922), 62.

6. Hugh MacDiarmid, *Lucky Poet* (London, 1943; Berkeley, 1972), xvii.

7. Scott's account appears in a letter to Maurice Lindsay, 20 May 1947, in the National Library of Scotland.

8. *Lucky Poet*, xxviii.

THE LANGUAGE OF THOUGHT

E. W. F. TOMLIN

It is a commonplace that the behaviour of language in prose is different from its behaviour in verse; what the difference is may not be so apparent. As with many distinctions so fine as to resist precise formulation, an example may illuminate it. The lines are from Yeats's *The Crazed Moon*:

> Crazed through much child-bearing,
> The moon is staggering in the sky.

The image, a brilliant one, is to be seized in itself. The thought behind the image enjoys no independent existence, affords no additional satisfaction. Concept and intuition are one, but only in the sense that the distinction has not yet arisen. The language of prose, though not without this inner quality, enjoys at the same time a kind of external existence; it lives for something beyond itself, namely the communication of a meaning or idea. It is a means to an end. In prose we first become aware of the distinction between what is said and what is meant; and this is evidently a stage which has something to do with man's attainment, if always uncertain grasp, of his 'humanity'. Hence some of the repetitiveness of prose, and the still greater repetitiveness of conversation. The writer or speaker has to struggle to maintain intelligibility – 'I mean . . .', 'What I mean is . . .', etc. Furthermore, within all rational exposition there exist two elements, mutually opposed and therefore generative of tension. These elements may be called the *dialectical* and the *eristical*. Dialectical exposition is that which elucidates its subject after the manner of dialogue. There is statement, counter-statement, and conclusion; the primary appeal is to reason. Eristic has not merely a different but usually a concealed aim; it seeks not to persuade but to impose; and this it does by deliberate appeal to sentiment and prejudice. As the Oxford Dictionary says, the aim of eristic is not truth but victory.

The ideal language – or prose – of thought would be that in which the two elements were in equilibrium.

Given this definition, the prose of thought might be expected to find its most perfect embodiment in works of philosophy. For philosophy, since the time of its systematic development, is committed to the putting forward of arguments; and arguments are valid only in so far as they conform to rational canons of inference. It is true that Hume, and in our century Dewey, tried to demonstrate that inferential thinking arose not from some rational constraint in the mind, but from acquired habit or custom; but in Hume's philosophical works, and in Dewey's logical treatises, the exposition clearly lays claim to be rational; these thinkers are stating a case, not simply reflecting a vagrant 'state of mind'.[1] Nor is conceptual thinking to be regarded as the monopoly of civilized peoples: Lévy-Bruhl came to abandon his idea of a 'pre-logical' stage of thought, and the conceptual ability of primitive peoples has been stressed by Lévi-Strauss. A work such as the 'Memphite Drama', which dates from the fourth millennium, is at least as well argued as many later theological treatises, and remains more intelligible than some; and the myths of the Bushmen and the Ainu, to name two peoples who until recently followed a Neolithic way of life, are not irrational, if by that is meant devoid of sense. Any society in which there is a recognizable legal system, or a set of regulations not arbitrarily to be set aside, must be capable, in its exposition and administration of the law, of the prose of thought.

The analogy with jurisprudence is, as we shall see, strictly relevant; for the task of the courts is not merely to expound the law but to sustain a case. Style is needed. And the same is true of philosophy, or the rational inquiry into the basic principles of any field of speculation. Ideally, the task of philosophy would be, in Brand Blanshard's words, 'to see what is the case' rather than 'to make out a case'.[2] If the case were judiciously and honestly stated to perfection, however, it would at the same time be 'made'. In practice, since almost every word of philosophy has a polemical aspect and arises in a context of argument, the function of style is not merely to present but to persuade; and that is why the language of thought cannot dispense with an element of eristic.

Certainly, British philosophy, to take that alone, can claim its

masters of style. Even those who remain indifferent or allergic to
their thought may find Berkeley, Hume, Mill, and Bradley satisfying
and elegant writers. Latterly, we have witnessed a revolution in the
idea of philosophy, at least in Britain; and this has affected the way
in which philosophy has come to be written. One of the tenets of
this new view is that certain philosophical problems, especially those
termed metaphysical, arise from intractable elements in language. In
other words, our common language is riddled with ambiguity. Artificial languages need to be constructed for the assertion of rational
truth. A purely referential or scientific language would presumably
be one voided of every ambiguity, every emotive element. Moreover, it would be a *fixed* language. What was called the analytical
or linguistic movement in philosophy had a double aim. First, it
sought to achieve the purification of language, even to the point of
trying to escape from common language altogether. Secondly, it
sought to effect the liquidation of systems of thought held to batten
upon linguistic ambiguity. The 'elimination of metaphysics', to use
the common phrase, was the consequence of the supposed elimination of a flaw in language.

The justification for referring thus early to a particular philosophical movement is that the theory behind it has exerted considerable
influence outside the sphere of philosophy proper. Works on theology, history, literary criticism, law, even political theory and
economics, reveal the influence of the linguistic movement. Without
the early writings of Russell, G. E. Moore, and Wittgenstein, such
works as Richards's *Principles of Literary Criticism* and its offspring
Empson's *Seven Types of Ambiguity* might never have been written.
The same applies to more recent studies such as Fraser's *Economic
Thought and Language* (1936), Weldon's *Vocabulary of Politics* (1953),
and the symposium *New Essays in Philosophical Theology* (1955).

By contrast, we find that, in countries in which the analytical
movement has failed to take hold, philosophy and theology are still
written in the traditional manner. To take France as an example, the
Revue de Métaphysique et Morale (January–March 1952, p. 69) referred
to the British analytical school as '*un mouvement imparfaitement connu
en France*'. The philosophical writings of Sartre, Marcel, Merleau-
Ponty, and Bachelard, however revolutionary they may be, belong
to the orthodox classico-literary tradition. There is a stylistic link

between these writers and Bergson, just as there is a link between Bergson and Maine de Biran. The last great English philosophical writer in this tradition, if we exclude McTaggart, is F. H. Bradley. Much of Bradley's writings can be classed as *belles lettres*; they remain a quarry for the anthologist. Bradley is distinguished from Arnold on the one hand and from his fellow-idealists on the other, by his greater analytical powers and his mastery of logic. Yet it would seem that people today read *The Principles of Logic* (1883) less for instruction than for the spectacle of a sustained literary and polemical performance.

The decay of idealism, which set in many years before Bradley's death in 1924, is visible as much in the abstraction-ridden prose of Lord Haldane as in the basic poverty of his thought. (It is only fair to say that Haldane disliked the term idealist; but it is not what one likes to be called, it is what one is.) Similarly, the balance and precision of such an early work as Moore's *Principia Ethica* (1905) marks a new departure in philosophy, the birth of a New Realism. The 'philosophy of common sense', which Moore initiated, needed a medium of expression radically different from that of idealists; it needed plainness, an approximation to common usage. Stripped of its conventional arguments, the idealism of the neo-Hegelian variety consisted for the most part in a prolonged hymn to the Absolute. The flowing periods, the incantatory rhythm, the outbursts of lyricism, were all part of a metaphysical ritual. To embrace Reality-as-a-whole, as Bradley sought to do in *Appearance and Reality* (1893), was necessarily to have recourse to the grand manner. Theology in the nineteenth century was likewise nurtured in the neo-Hegelian tradition; Edward Caird was a theologian as well as a philosopher, and so was T. H. Green. Thus the sermon, once capable of inspiring excellent prose, has suffered degeneration no less from its worn-out phraseology than from the absence of trained congregations. It is surprising to what extent much modern theology has remained linked to a form of philosophy long outmoded.[3] Moral exhortation does not always make for good prose, though it may provide material for rhetoric and for inferior poetry.

By way of illustrating the difference between the old and the new prose of thought, it may be illuminating to compare an extract from Bradley with a passage from Moore. Here is Bradley (*Appearance and Reality*):

Reality is one experience, self-pervading and superior to mere relations. Its character is the opposite of that fabled extreme which is barely mechanical, and it is, in the end, the sole perfect realization of spirit ... Outside of spirit there is not, and there cannot be, any reality, and the more that anything is spiritual, so much the more is it veritably real.

And further:

Spirit is the unity of the manifold, in which the externality of the manifold has utterly ceased.

Here is Moore (*Principia Ethica*):

My point is that good is a simple notion, just as 'yellow' is a simple notion: that, just as you cannot, by any manner of means, explain to anyone who does not already know it, what yellow is, so you cannot explain what good is. Definitions of the kind that I was asking for, definitions which describe the real nature of the object or notion denoted by a word, and which do not merely tell us what the word is used to mean, are only possible when the object or notion in question is something complex. You can give a definition of a horse, because a horse has many different properties and qualities, all of which you can enumerate. But when you have enumerated them all, when you have reduced a horse to its simplest terms, then you can no longer define those terms ... And so it is with all objects, not previously known, which we are able to define. They are all complex, all composed of parts, which may themselves, in the first instance, be capable of definition, but which must in the end be reducible to simplest parts, which can no longer be defined. But yellow and good, we say, are not complex; they are notions of that simple kind, out of which definitions are composed and with which the power of further defining ceases.

I have deliberately chosen Bradley, and not the most rhetorical example of Bradley at that, because the selection of a more impassioned piece, such as one taken from Stirling's rarefied work *The Secret of Hegel* (1865), would scarcely have been fair. Even so, this brief extract, despite its apparent simplicity, is found on examination to be blurred by imprecise terminology and to be informed with an undercurrent of rhetoric. 'Self-pervading', which has meaning in Whitehead's philosophy of organism, acts here rather like a plug of emotive cotton-wool. The use of 'mere' to qualify 'relations', like the use of 'fabled' to qualify 'extreme', is a calculated thrust at less lofty philosophies. 'Veritably' as qualifying 'real' is superfluous. Moreover, in the final sentence, the words 'utterly ceased', besides being curiously inept in the context, form a kind of pseudo-eschatological climax; we are in the world of the *Upanishads*. By comparison, the passage of Moore makes a direct appeal to the reader's intelligence; it is turned outwards, following patiently, perhaps a little pedestrianly, the movement of thought. Its peroration, if such it can be called, is addressed not to the emotions but to the reason. This is demonstrated in the use it makes in conclusion of the same verb, 'ceases', as that which terminates the passage from Bradley.[4]

Moore is a transitional writer; he remains, for all his commonsense, a stylist. He has balance and decorum. As we know, he exerted no small influence on the aestheticism of Bloomsbury;[5] there is even a stylistic link between him and J. M. Keynes. The effort towards plainness, towards the lowering of temperature to that of cold statement, is best observed in certain early associates, though not always disciples, of Moore. Of these, one of the most interesting is Cook Wilson. *Statement and Inference* (1926), a posthumously selected volume of Wilson's lectures and notes, gives the surface-appearance of meticulous, orderly, but essentially 'deflating' expression. A more powerful and complex thinker, likewise reluctant to publish, was Wittgenstein himself. With the exception of the *Tractatus Logico-Philosophicus*, which he wrote when a prisoner of war, and the *Philosophical Investigations*, which he composed to deter the plagiarists, Wittgenstein's philosophy took the form of a conversational game, an exercise in verbal dialect. The *Blue Book* and the *Brown Book* consist of *viva voce* transcripts, but even so the transcription probably dissatisfied him. In the exercise of speaking or thinking aloud, he felt he was less liable to deceive himself, less prone to fall into verbal misrepresentation.

> Consider this example: you tell me to write a few lines, and while I am doing so, you ask, 'Do you feel something in your hand while you are writing?' I say, 'Yes, I have a peculiar feeling' – Can't I say to myself when I write, 'I have *this* feeling'? Of course I can say it.[6]

– and so on. This technique of conversational analysis has been developed, and indeed carried to an extreme, by John Wisdom. Here is a typical example:

> You remember it was said – to stop the worry it was said – 'He has the measle germ' just means 'He will give all the measle-reactions'. Now this is incorrect. But that again is not the point. The point is that this answer

is too soothing. Or rather not too soothing – nothing could be that, every-thing's absolutely all right in metaphysics – but it's too sickly soothing. It's soothing without requiring of us that act of courage, that flinging away of our battery of crutches, which is required in order to realize that everything's all right. This phenomenalist answer soothes without demanding this change of heart only by soothing deceptively and saying that this alarming hippo-potamus is only a horse that lives in rivers. It's true that the hippopotamus is quite O.K. and not at all carnivorous and won't hurt anybody who treats him right – that treats him like a hippopotamus has to be treated; but it's a mistake to soothe people by telling them he's a horse because, though that may soothe them for a moment, they will soon find out that to treat him like a horse is not satisfactory.

(Other Minds, 1952, p. 73)

The point of interest in this passage (which departs so far from philosophical decorum as to betray faint echoes of Gertrude Stein) is that the search for clarity, the unmasking of ambiguity by trying to catch language unawares at its own game, has transported philo-sophy from the heights of fine writing to the ground level of com-mon speech and even lower. With its nervous colloquialism – there is only one technical term, 'phenomenalist', which seems curiously out of place – it makes use of every device of common speech. Yet such writing has significantly failed to pass through the stage of referential language. Despite attempts to write philosophy in logical notation, that stage has remained not so much an ideal as a chimera; for such language, purged of every emotive element, could not remain a means of communication. Its very fixity would render it ineffective. In the work of the philosophical analysts, and even in the most rigorous of logical positivists, we find not the absence of emotion, not an abandonment of the stylistic screen, but the adoption of studied plainness to convey a particular set of emotions. And these emotions are no less powerful in their way than those expressed by metaphysicians. It is hardly an accident that Cook Wilson, like his disciple Pritchard, not to mention Wittgenstein himself, proved ardent and even intemperate in debate. The *Proceedings of the Aris-totelian Society*, together with the issues of the review *Analysis*, pro-vide a wealth of examples of philosophical papers written in the style, at once suave and astringent, customary with linguistic philosophers; but the reader, or better still the listener, comes soon to perceive that this style is meant to convey its own emotional tone. No one is likely to describe the style of Sir Isaiah Berlin, written or spoken, as lacking in emotive power. Indeed it is in such philosophical writers as Berlin that the passion for accuracy, breaking through the fixity imposed upon it by doctrinaire analytical theory, issues once more in a torrent of eloquence.

An example of prose which, avoiding extremes, marshals its ideas with clarity, charm, and the kind of wit without which philosophy may easily fall into pretentiousness, is the following:

Novelists, dramatists and biographers had always been satisfied to exhibit people's motives, thoughts, perturbations and habits by describing their doings, sayings, and imaginings, their grimaces, gestures and tones of voice. In concentrating on what Jane Austen concentrated on, psychologists began to find that these were, after all, the stuff and not the mere trappings of their subjects. They have, of course, continued to suffer unnecessary qualms of anxiety, lest this diversion of psychology from the task of describing the ghostly might not commit it to tasks of describing the merely mechanical. But the influence of the bogy of mechanism has for a century been dwindling because, among other reasons, during this period the biological sciences have established their title of 'sciences'. The Newtonian system is no longer the sole paradigm of natural science. Man need not be degraded to a machine by being denied to be a ghost in a machine. He might, after all, be a sort of animal, namely, a higher mammal. There has yet to be ventured the hazardous leap to the hypothesis that perhaps he is a man.

The Behaviourists' methodological programme has been of revolutionary importance to the programme of psychology. But more, it has been one of the main sources of the philosophical suspicion that the two-worlds story is a myth. It is a matter of relatively slight importance that the champions of this methodological principle have tended to espouse as well a kind of Hobbist theory, and even to imagine that the truth of mechanism is entailed by the truth of their theory of scientific research method in psychology.

It is not for me to say to what extent the concrete research procedures of practising psychologists have been affected by their long adherence to the two-worlds story, or to what extent the Behaviourist revolt has led to modifications of their methods. For all I know, the ill effects of the myth may, on balance, have been outweighed by the good, and the Behaviourist revolt against it may have led to reforms more nominal than real. Myths are not always detrimental to the progress of theories. Indeed, in their youth they are often of inestimable value. Pioneers are, at the start, fortified by the dream that the New World is, behind its alien appearances, a sort of duplicate of the Old World, and the child is not so much baffled by a strange house if, wherever they may actually lead him, its bannisters feel to his hand like those he knew at home.

(Gilbert Ryle, *The Concept of Mind*, ch. x, 'Psychology')

The prose of thought, then, is not prose which lacks emotive ambience; it is prose charged with the emotions most suited to conceptual or dialectical expression. Much hangs on that word 'suited'; it covers not merely 'fitting' but 'sincere'. Bearing in mind our initial distinction between dialectic and eristic argument, philosophy is the subject in which truth must in principle be arrived at; and in order to *arrive* at the truth it is necessary to lay bare every dogma, to unmask subterfuge, to strip away verbiage. Consequently, the movement towards colloquialism in philosophy represents an attempt, if a desperate one, to recapture the true spirit of dialectic, which is realized most effectively in dialogue. For it is only the practice of printing books that obscures the fact that all thought is 'spoken'. By contrast, eristic is an attempt, rarely successful over long periods, to appeal directly to the emotions by by-passing the rational faculty; it is an attempt to manage or manipulate the feelings. A most subtle form of eristic is the kind of writing labelled sentimental. Yet how are we to detect or measure *sincerity* in a writer – a writer not merely on philosophy but on any subject of rational inquiry? If, as T. E. Hulme says, 'style is a way of subduing the reader', we understand again why there must be an eristic element in all style. But we can be subdued in more than one way. We can be made to surrender our rational faculties altogether, or we can be persuaded to compose them in an act of voluntary assent.

In order to approach nearer to the criterion of sincerity, let us shift our attention from philosophy proper to another subject. First we must make a generalization, if only because limitations of space preclude lengthy examples. No writer, whatever his subject, can be judged solely on excerpts. He has his own particular range. In assessing him, this whole range must be taken into account, together with the level on which he deploys his ideas, and his prevailing tone. To know whether a writer rings true, we must sound him at regular intervals. His personality must show coherence; this is revealed often in the degree to which his argument is systematic.

The science of economics is of comparatively recent origin; it is an abstraction from political science. Consequently, works on economics show a tendency towards one of two extremes: either, like linguistic philosophy, they seek to employ pure symbolic notation, or, reacting against their own abstractness, they become a branch of 'social studies'. The style will vary accordingly. A work such as Marx's *Das Kapital* oscillates between the two poles; but because it is in the classical tradition of Adam Smith and Ricardo, as well as in the Hegelian philosophical tradition, and equally in the tradition of Hebrew prophecy, it is never, except in some of Part II, pure economic theory. Indeed, the assumption that Marxism is an economic theory instead of a social gospel has misled not merely individual men, but whole nations. In Britain, unlike France, theories such as Marxism, as well as those of Pareto and Henry George, have exerted little attraction, at least for most academic economists. The result is a tradition of writing at once graceful, clear, judicious; Alfred Marshall is still read for the possession of these qualities. With wider culture and greater powers of irony, J. M. Keynes continued the tradition of Marshall; but he combined objectivity with considerable social concern. In his work the eristic element is evident, though well under control: thus one of his volumes was aptly called *Essays in Persuasion* (1931).[7] A writer on economics of remarkable literary gifts was his senior, Philip Wicksteed. Wicksteed's *Commonsense of Political Economy* (1910) represents one of the most successful expositions of ideas, or of a single idea, of modern times. The idea is no less 'philosophical' for being an economic concept, that of marginalism. Written in prose of sustained elegance, this great book possesses a clarity to be expected of the translator of Dante, though the style recalls that of Newman. There can be few treatises in which successive *sondages* over 800 pages yield such excellence of matter and manner:

We have seen that a man's economic position depends not only on his powers but on his possessions. These possessions may embody the fresh output of current effort, or they may be accumulations, or they may consist in the control, secured by law, of the prime sources of all material wealth. The differentiation between the taxation of earned and unearned income reminds us that there is a vast revenue that someone is receiving though no one is earning it. Thus it is clear that if no one receives less than his current effort is worth, many receive a great deal more. There seems, then, to be nothing intrinsically monstrous in the idea of looking into this matter. If there are sources from which, apparently, anyone or everyone might receive more than he earns, or is worth to others, no proposal need be condemned simply because it contemplates certain classes receiving more than their output of effort is worth, as certain other classes do at present. Proposals for land nationalization, or for the collective control of the instruments of production, are dictated by the belief that we are in possession of a common patrimony which is not being administered in the common interest. But we should distinguish very clearly in our own minds between saying that a person is 'underpaid for his work', and saying that he has a claim to something more than 'mere payment for his work at its worth'.[8]

(Vol. I, p. 341)

In intellectual works, the temptation of the learned expositor, or the gambit of the charlatan, is the adoption of a tone of unrelieved solemnity. The pedant, the legalist, and often the theologian, are perennial butts of satire; their manner of writing, inflated, lays itself open to parody. The test of sincerity may be not so much prolonged high seriousness or fervour, as the occasional ironic aside, the play of wit. These are means to the preservation of balance and sanity. In all serious writing, a certain elevation of tone is to be expected; flippancy and facetiousness are out of place. But we can be serious without being solemn. The portentousness and aridity of much economic writing, which at one time earned economics the name of the 'dismal science' and Coleridge's epithet 'solemn humbug', may have masked a vagueness about fundamentals, and in the case of those defending the established order a sense of moral uncertainty. Both are characteristic of John Stuart Mill, prior to his mental crisis and before the influence of Harriet Taylor. The muscle-bound prose of the young Mill, modelled on that of his father, contrasts markedly with the fine and flexible medium of the *Essay on Liberty* and the *Autobiography*: a mastery which, save for obvious reasons in the latter work, fell away sadly after the guiding-hand was removed. Today, the revival of economic studies and the liberation of that science from dogmas such as psychological hedonism have been responsible, one may suggest, for an increase in works at once serious and readable. Lord Robbins's well-known essay entitled *The Nature and Significance of Economic Science* (1932) and Mrs Joan Robinson's book *The Economics of Imperfect Competition* (1933), despite their abstract subject-matter, show command of the prose of thought as much by their abundant irony and wit as by their patient analysis of particular doctrines. An example is Mrs Robinson's 'Digression on Rent' (ch. viii), a topic not as a rule productive of liveliness. Such qualities belong to effective dialectic; the sarcasm characteristic of the unbalanced or wayward personality belongs to eristic. Given space, one would have wished to pursue this investigation in the realm of law and related subjects. Sir

Carleton Allen's *Law in the Making* (1927), to take but one example, would be difficult to surpass for sustained lucidity. Indeed, in the work of eminent jurists the prose of thought reaches that temporary equilibrium in which dialectic and eristic enter into partnership.

The course of a man's style can reflect, sometimes with uncanny fidelity, the progress or deterioration of his thought. Whereas the level of writing of such a work as *The Golden Bough* (1890–1912) remains even and steady throughout a succession of volumes, the prose of the last volumes of Arnold Toynbee's *Study of History* (1954) sometimes falls below the level of the earlier part, rallying again in *An Historian's Approach to Religion* (1956), and in the excellent *Reconsiderations* (1961). There is a study to be made of the variations in quality, throughout a long and colourful career, of the prose of Earl Russell. In his middle period, this penetrating thinker seems to have lost his bearings. The result is an excess of eristic writing and some measure of flatness, in contrast to the early superb command of dialectic.

To suggest that a change in a man's outlook exerts direct or immediate influence upon his style would be to venture too far; but apart from the fact that ideas, if coherent at all, are *expressed* ideas, the movement of a man's thought can and does thus reflect itself. There are not two things, the thought and the style; there is either one thing, or a mere string of words. Nor is this to say that the *manner* necessarily changes; the prevailing manner may remain the same, but transformed into mannerism or caricature. By way of illustration, we may take five modern writers, differing widely in outlook but sufficiently long-lived to have demonstrably exchanged one mood for another. The early prose of W. R. Inge possessed a cutting-edge which, towards the end, had become blunted. A writer who admired Inge's prose, if nothing else about him, was Hilaire Belloc. The Belloc of *The Path to Rome*, the early historical studies, and even *The Cruise of the Nona* (1925), especially the philosophical digressions, wrote eloquent and noble English; the later Belloc often makes heavy and painful reading. Although H. G. Wells was not a professional thinker, he was very much a 'man of ideas'; his early novels and essays have an incandescent quality which lifted their style, otherwise undistinguished, to considerable heights. The Wells of *The World of William Clissold* (1927) was a tired and disillusioned idealist: hence the invective, the sarcasm, the querulous loquacity of much of the later work. Bernard Shaw, after persistent practice, evolved a style so fine and swift that even his sectarian political essays, such as that which he wrote and several times revised for *Fabian Essays* (1889), are still worth reading; but the later plays and their prefaces, for all their violence, are often lifeless.[9] That remarkable philosopher R. G. Collingwood wrote trenchantly about the style appropriate to philosophy, and in such early works as *Speculum Mentis* (1924) and *An Essay on Philosophical Method* (1933) he practised what he preached almost to perfection. Some rift or hesitancy in his thought, due not necessarily to increasing ill-health, makes his work from the *Essay on Metaphysics* (1940) onwards both uneven and erratic.

In the work of all these man we find the style mirroring, however subtly, a change in outlook. The ageing Inge had come to distrust the mysticism to which he was early devoted; Belloc lost not his faith but the sense of beatitude; Shaw's early social idealism gave way to a cynical admiration for despotism; Collingwood fell into the historicism against which he had issued repeated warnings. Consistently enough, the five men came to show a preponderance of the eristic outlook over the dialectic; and this is reflected in the inner quality of their prose.

An essay such as the present must not neglect to take into account a form of prose embodying not so much thought as an attitude to thought. This is reflective prose. In this genre many great writers may be included; two obvious examples are Bacon and Sir Thomas Browne. The twentieth century has witnessed the revival of the essay; but if England has no equivalent to Alain, it has produced some distinguished practitioners of this form; the early essays of Middleton Murry and Aldous Huxley may be cited. Our greatest modern essayists are usually men who imagined they were working in a different genre. The prose works of Wyndham Lewis, particularly *The Art of Being Ruled* (1926) and *Time and Western Man* (1927), fall naturally into separate essays, while such pieces as *The Diabolical Principle and The Dithyrambic Spectator* (1931), despite a marked eristic vein, show a vigorous mind wrestling with new ideas and generating an original prose to embody them, so that Eliot could describe Lewis as 'one of the permanent masters of style in the English language'. Another master of the essay form is Havelock Ellis. Some of the *Little Essays in Love and Virtue* (1922), the two volumes of *Impressions and Comments* (1914–23), and above all *The Dance of Life* (1923) reveal the workings of a fastidious mind, though Ellis could fall into rhetoric.[10] As he confessed in his *Autobiography*, he was essentially a dreamer, viewing life (and sex for that matter) in terms of art; and this quality of reverie, like that of Yeats, translated itself into a style of hypnotic charm but often imperfect conceptual realization.[11]

The prose of T. S. Eliot falls naturally into two categories: the reflective and the logical. His studies of individual writers, particularly the Elizabethan poets and Dante, are judicious studies in assessment. To quote Hazlitt, his task is 'to lead the mind into new trains of thought'. But Eliot is likewise a master of logical exposition. Some of the early essays, above all the famous *Tradition and Individual Talent* (1917), or even later works such as *Notes towards the Definition of Culture* (1950) are masterpieces of dialectic. The prose moves forward almost with the movement of thought itself; the result is a succession of illuminations.[12]

The case for a society with a class structure, the affirmation that it is, in some sense, the 'natural' society, is prejudiced if we allow ourselves to be hypnotized by the two contrasted terms *aristocracy* and *democracy*. The whole problem is falsified if we use these terms antithetically. What I have advanced is not a 'defence of aristocracy' – an emphasis upon the importance of one organ of society. Rather it is a plea on behalf of a form of society in which an aristocracy should have a peculiar and essential function, as peculiar and essential as the function of any other part of society. What is important is a structure of society in which there will be, from 'top' to 'bottom', a continuous gradation of cultural levels: it is important to remember that we should not consider the upper levels as possessing *more* culture than the lower, but as representing a more conscious culture and a greater specialization of culture. I incline to believe that no true democracy can maintain itself unless it contains these different levels of culture. The levels of culture may also be seen as levels of power, to the extent that a smaller group at a higher level will have equal power with a larger group at a lower level; for it may be argued that complete equality means universal irresponsibility; and in such a society as I envisage, each individual would inherit greater or less responsibility towards the commonwealth, according to the position in society which he inherited – each class would have somewhat different responsibilities. A democracy in which everybody had an equal responsibility in everything would be oppressive for the conscientious and licentious for the rest.

(*Notes towards the Definition of Culture*: 'The Class and the Elite')

*

A survey of the language of thought of the twentieth century reveals a certain rhythmic and even cyclic development. In this development we may detect, at each stage, a dialectic and an eristic aspect. This suggests that between the dialectic and eristic elements themselves there operates a higher dialectic. Indeed, without such a higher dialectic, language would constantly be moving towards one or the other extreme and thus failing as a means of communication. The idealist philosophers, taking the Hegelian system as their point of departure, found themselves confronted with the New Realism. Failure to establish communications called out the eristic side of their minds. The analytical school, taking its stand upon empiricism, tended to assume another form of eristic, that directed towards the demolition of speculative systems in general.[13] Meanwhile, a more balanced view of philosophy was slowly emerging: Sir Alfred Ayer replaced the eristical prose of his anti-metaphysical manifesto *Language, Truth and Logic* (1935) by the measured urbanity of his *Philosophical Essays* (1954), *The Problem of Knowledge* (1956), and *The Concept of a Person* (1963), where the subject-matter was largely metaphysical. Indeed, there was a remarkable and perhaps significant resemblance between the syle of the later Ayer and that of McTaggart. It was only too clear that analysis, the weapon of every genuine philosopher, had its own metaphysical assumptions, even if it were only that 'reality' could be conceived as divisible into parts.[14] Moreover, analysis was a process which, in able hands, must be pushed to the limit; but *if* it be pushed to the limit, it finds itself grappling with metaphysical problems. Thus, despite certain signs to the contrary, there was brought about something in the nature of metaphysical revival, though not a return to the old idealism.

In order to judge the quality of the language of thought over a period, it is useful by way of summing up to examine the attitude to literature in general, since philosophical writing is a branch of literature. *The Problem of Style*, by John Middleton Murry, written just after the First World War, differed radically from a work such as Sartre's *Qu'est que la littérature?*, published just after the Second, and for which there was no English analogue. To Murry, literature was still an ornament of life; to Sartre, it was an explosive force enlisted in the service of social transformation. The difference was between diversion and *engagement*. The 1930s were a period in which the attitude to 'letters' or language was undergoing subtle change, though the *theory* behind this change was to be elaborated, along with much else, by the post-existentialist generation in France. That is why we have observed some flexibility over our time-scale; for the influential Saussure (a Swiss), with his distinction between *langue*, a super-individual system, and *parole*, the manifestation·of this system in speech, died in 1913, whereas the structuralists became articulate half a century later. Indeed, structuralism, once elaborated, split into sects. It received a Marxist and a Freudian interpretation, was repudiated, and in due course emerged as post-structuralism, thus undergoing the kind of development which had been followed, though with less addiction to abstract argument, by logical positivism. In general, however, structuralism involved a radical re-thinking of the nature of language which had begun in Britain with the work of Russell, Moore, and Wittgenstein, and was continued by J. L. Austin; but it adopted from the first an anti-empiricist stand. Even so, the ideas of Rowland Barthes throw retrospective light on the preoccupation of I. A. Richards and F. R. Leavis – however different their approach – with the *text*, though neither pursued his speculations to the point of believing, with Barthes and Derrida, that the text inhabited a dimension all its own, removed from any world that it might reflect (and incidentally with *Finnegans Wake* as its text of texts). And although Richards was more concerned than Leavis with the mechanism of the expression of thought, even to the point of comparing in *Mencius on the Mind* (1931) traditional oriental with occidental mental processes, he never freed himself from a Benthamite theory of 'fictions' and a Humian utilitarianism, which Leavis, though not a systematic thinker, found increasingly uncongenial.

But what light does all this shed on philosophy itself and its language? Certainly, the analytical philosophers were already distrustful of language, because their search for a medium wholly transparent to logical thought – a window giving directly on the realm of concepts – implied the exclusion of anything 'literary'. The prevailing hostility to idealism, especially of the Hegelian variety, was based on the conviction that the ideas there expounded were the result of a kind of metaphorical conspiracy. Idealism, to the logical analysts, was a form of metaphorical intoxication. But, as we

have argued, no analytical philosopher – and certainly not Wittgenstein, who habitually resorted to metaphor (though not always good
metaphor: 'bumping up against the limits of language', etc.) – succeeded in isolating this pure medium.

It is possible that the pursuit of accuracy lies along a different
path. To quote Murry, 'try to be precise and you are bound to
be metaphorical'.[15] This apparent paradox contains an important
truth. A diet of philosophical reading, especially of a thinker such
as Carnap or some of the young philosophers, leaves one often *affamé*
for a vivid image, a figure which shall bring illumination. But to
be bound to be metaphorical does not mean to be bound by
metaphor. To the thinker, language must be kept in subservience:
which is why, despite the verse of Empedocles, or what we have
of it, or Lucretius, there is only a *prose* of thought. For prose – the
form of expression most difficult to sustain – is an exercise in verbal
restraint in the interests of conceptual clarity. It is intelligence on
the move. In some of George Santayana's work, fine though it is,
the incantatory nature of the style draws attention to itself rather
than to the argument, and seems on occasion to be a substitute for
argument: a book such as *Scepticism and Animal Faith* (1923), re-read
after an interval of years, is found to yield precious little intellectual
satisfaction.

What, then, to revert to our starting-point, is the fundamental
difference between the language of thought and what may be called
literary language? The answer is simple. There is no fundamental
difference. The distinction, launched upon the intellectual scene by
Richards, between emotive language and scientific or referential
language is an unreal one, and has been responsible for two unfortunate results: first, the assumption that literary prose, being ballasted
with metaphor (to adapt Bergson's phrase), is to that extent irreduci-
bly opaque; and secondly, that scientifice or referential prose, by eject-
ing such ballast, can eliminate this opacity. The distinction has a further
consequence, perhaps the most unfortunate of all. In rebellion against
such exclusion from artistry, some scientists, anxious to display literary powers, have gone to great lengths to express themselves in what
they conceive to be a literary manner, in which exercise they have
sometimes outdone the literary folk in 'fine writing'. The criticism, so
far as style is concerned, of such works as D'Arcy Wentworth

Thompson's massive *Growth and Form* (1917) and to some degree
Charles Sherrington's *Man on his Nature* (1932), is that they are too
literary. D'Arcy Thompson even ventured, in his enthusiasm, to
introduce stylistic archaisms.[16] The language of thought is ordinary
language. Ordinary language is already mobilized. If this were not
so, the thinker would find himself unable to argue his case intelligibly,
and his readers would fail to grasp the case he was presenting. The
most successful language of thought has always exhibited what
Collingwood described as a 'disposition to improvise and create, to
treat language as something not fixed and rigid but infinitely flexible
and full of life'.[17]

NOTES

1. cf. Stephen Toulmin, *The Uses of Argument* (Cambridge, 1958): 'It
cannot be custom alone which gives validity and authority to a form of
argument, or the logician would have to wait upon the results of the anthro-
pologist's researches' (5).

2. *On Philosophical Style* (Manchester, 1954), 23.

3. The point is well brought out in the symposium *Metaphysical Beliefs*,
eds Macintyre and Gregor Smith (London, 1957), 5, though a change came
with John Robinson's *Honest to God* (London, 1963).

4. I make no comment here, or elsewhere, on the *validity* of the argument.
The reader who is curious on that point should consult W. D. Ross's *The Right
and the Good* (Oxford, 1930), 88.

5. See *The Bloomsbury Group*, J. K. Johnstone (London, 1954).

6. *Preliminary Studies for the 'Philosophical Investigations': generally known as
the Blue and the Brown Books* (Oxford, 1958), 174.

7. 'It was in a spirit of persuasion that most of these essays were written,
in an attempt to influence opinion' (v).

8. Observe how, in the hands of less objective writers, this passage could
have degenerated into eristic.

9. An exception must be made of the Preface to the World's Classics edition
of *Back to Methuselah*, written in his tenth decade and a most spirited performance.

10. e.g. *The Dance of Life* (London, 1923), ch. III, iv.

11. cp. in the case of Yeats, the prose of *Per Amica Silentia Lunae* (London,
1917).

12. I have argued elsewhere (*T. S. Eliot, A Tribute from Japan*, Kenkyusha,
1967) that 'the discipline of prose' was that which laid the foundation of Eliot's
poetic eminence.

13. e.g. Stuart Hampshire's claim that system-building has been killed 'stone dead' by the 'devastating discoveries of modern linguistic philosophers' (*The Nature of Metaphysics*, edited by D. F. Pears, (London, 1957), 25).

14. This is the assumption behind a book by Sir Peter Strawson, which bears the significant title of *Individuals: an essay in descriptive metaphysics* (London, 1959).

15. *The Problem of Style* (Oxford, 1922), 83.

16. Sir Peter Medawar described *Growth and Form* as 'beyond comparison the finest work of literature in all the annals of science that have been recorded in the English tongue'. He also described it as 'the equal of anything of Pater's or Logan Pearsall Smith's in its complete mastery of the *bel canto* style'. It is all the more significant, therefore, that J. T. Bonner, in his abridged edition of 1961, eliminates much of this 'literary' accretion, presumably in the interests of science.

17. R. G. Collingwood, *An Essay on Philosophical Method* (Oxford, 1933), 'Philosophy as a branch of Literature', 214.

E. M. FORSTER'S GOOD INFLUENCE

G. D. KLINGOPULOS

Anyone familiar with the writings of E. M. Forster for a fair number of years is likely to feel some discontent at his gradual transformation into a 'minor classic', even if his own account of work he has admired for so long might have to admit that a claim to 'major' status, if it is to be advanced at all, cannot be made to apply to more than one or two of the novels. There is even something in the stories themselves which discourages and seems to mock the whole business of careful definition and appraisal. Is he, perhaps, guilty of what his author would regard as a radical fault, a lack of 'humour'?

> Bring out the enjoyment. If 'the classics' are advertised as something dolorous and astringent, no one will sample them. But if the cultured person, like the late Roger Fry, is obviously having a good time, those who come across him will be tempted to share it and to find out how.
>
> (*Two Cheers for Democracy*, 1951, 'Does Culture Matter?')

Surely these are sentiments to which the bosom of every 'cultured person' returns an echo? Or is Forster himself, in this rare instance, slightly lacking in humour in his anxiety about 'having a good time'? Questioned about this in conversation with the present writer, Forster was almost too ready to see another point of view: 'Were I professionally committed to evaluation, my attitude would of course be different.' The concession is so large that it makes agreement more remote. Is the distinction between the 'professional' and the general reader a sound one, and is not the ideal critic the ideal reader? There is, of course, much more than this to Forster's emphasis on the need for 'humour'.

Whatever the fanciful surface of some of his prose, Forster is a consistent moralist and intellectual. He addresses himself primarily and almost exclusively to those who share his assumptions.

> I distrust Great Men ... I believe in aristocracy though – if that is the right word and if a democrat may use it. Not an aristocracy of power based upon

rank and influence, but an aristocracy of the sensitive, the considerate, and the plucky ... They represent the true human tradition, the one permanent victory of our queer race over cruelty and chaos.

(*Two Cheers for Democracy*: 'What I Believe')

The essay 'What I Believe' was the meeting-point for many different sorts of people between 1939 and 1946, and it seemed, with all its frailty and absurdity, exactly right. Anything stronger would have been useless. Some of his other writing became strangely more poignant and meaningful during that period. This indisputable and long-lasting contemporary importance is, inevitably, the most evanescent part of a writer's achievement. It is what the 'minor classic' accounts of Forster have taken less and less into consideration. In a century which has produced a surfeit of Great Men, bullying, brutality, dogmatism, and noise, Forster represented an attractive, though not easily imitable, intellectual shrewdness, delicacy, and responsibility. These qualities are not to be explained in terms of Bloomsbury affiliations, and Forster has told us that he never read Moore's *Principia Ethica*. An idealized Cambridge, arising out of an exceptionally lucky imaginative experience of Cambridge,[1] is certainly one source of his charm. He has offered other clues. Jane Austen, obviously, but not, it appears, Meredith, not consciously at any rate. Hardy, as we should expect, is 'my home'. Later there was India which made a deep fusion with some of his earlier attitudes and preoccupations. And the astringent, timeless impact of the Alexandrian recluse Cavafy. One would have guessed the influence of Butler, but not the order of importance which Forster himself gives him.

Samuel Butler influenced me a great deal. He, Jane Austen, and Marcel Proust are the three authors who helped me most over my writing, and he did more than either of the other two to help me to look at life the way I do.

If the remark implies a slight overestimation of *The Way of All Flesh*, that too is relevant.

The enumeration of influences, however extended, will not add up to an explanation of the impression which Forster gives. Perhaps no literary influences could compare in importance with the world described in *Marianne Thornton* (1956). He is one of the few modern English writers whose work reveals the process of assimilation and growth of a genuine sensibility, by which we mean something different from style, or technique, or learning. It is as rare among poets as among novelists, for determination and a certain amount of verbal skill often suffice for the production of quite reputable verse. It is not manner, though Forster wrote much that is only mannered and Lamb-like. It is a quality of interest, sympathy, and judgement which is no more to be achieved by the activity of the will than the idyllic effect of the best of Hardy's prose and poetry. To acknowledge this genuine, experiencing centre in all Forster's work is as important as making up one's mind about the variable quality of the writing in each of his books. Because of this principle of life and growth, he remained consistently responsive to new people, new books, and new lands, without becoming in the least miscellaneous or indiscriminate. He did not become pompous or, like the scientific progressive H. G. Wells, turn gloomily prophetic in old age.

With all these virtues, Forster might well appear a finely representative 'humanist' and 'liberal', and if he had written only criticism and biography, there would have been no need to go beyond these descriptions which he frequently applied to himself. But Forster is also and primarily a novelist. The special value of novels, when they rise above ordinary brilliance, is that they enable us to dispense with the labels and slogans which are the currency of professional moralists, philosophers, and politicians, so that we may examine human relationships and motives more inwardly and completely in terms of presented experience. Henry James, it may be recalled, considered the value of a novel to depend directly on 'the amount of felt life concerned in producing it', and thus, ultimately, on 'the kind and the degree of the artist's prime sensibility, which is the soil out of which his subject springs'. The value one puts on Forster's 'sensibility' will decide one's attitude to, for example, his early abandonment of the novel, and to the question whether his gifts really fulfilled their promise.

Some of his earliest short stories are related, though in a slighter mode, to Hardy's theme of Wessex and the consequences of complete industrialization, and one, *The Machine Stops*, is 'a reaction to one of the earlier heavens of H. G. Wells'. In his earlier work, Forster was precariously poised between forms of resistance and of escape – a flight to the Mediterranean world, to 'the other side of the hedge' or to the terminus of the celestial omnibus. Among his short stories, *The Story of a Panic* and *The Curate's Friend* are not far removed from R. L. Stevenson's slight fantasies.

> Pan is not dead, but of all the classic hierarchy alone survives in triumph; goat-footed, with a gleeful and an angry look, the type of the shaggy world: and in every wood, if you go with a spirit properly prepared, you shall hear the note of his pipe ... It is no wonder, with so traitorous a scheme of things, if the wise people who created for us the idea of Pan thought that of all fears the fear of him was the most terrible, since it embraces all. And still we preserve the phrase, a panic terror.
>
> (*Virginibus Puerisque*, 1881)

But though Forster defended 'escape', he was never a whole-hearted escapist. 'I cannot shut myself up in a Palace of Art or a Philosophic Tower and ignore the madness and misery of the world.' Nor was he tempted to insist on optimism or fatalism or any doctrinal position which would simplify the stresses of life. His slighter works of fantasy must be regarded as attempts to organize and bring to a focus certain intuitions which at first derive from books, and later from experience and from travel. They attempt to open windows for enclosed and regimented men, and to evoke intuitive or childlike memories, as in dreams, of other levels of existence – 'the magic song of nightingales, and the odour of invisible hay, and stars piercing the fading sky'. Criticism is forestalled by the description of Rickie's stories in *The Longest Journey* (1907), but these fragile reworkings of classical myth have their place in any account of Forster's development.[2]

Rickie's stories are, of course, rather ambiguously treated and the novel of which he is the hero has too much of the arbitrary fanci-fulness of *The Celestial Omnibus* (1911) to provide an entirely adequate context of appraisal. *The Longest Journey*, which is the weakest of the novels, was the author's personal favourite, possibly because it contains an autobiographical element which does not have the same value for the reader. The book is about a theme which recurs in all the novels. How can men and women remain loyal to their generous and best impulses in a world which inevitably imposes mere conformity with its coldness, its cowardice and polite deceit? How can men achieve a good relationship with nature and with other men, and avoid the self-sufficiency which is based on various forms of pride or hubris or hardness of will? These themes are as old as European literature, and, recognizing them, we confer importance even on work which embodies them faintly and elusively. They certainly help to give an impression of continuity and completeness to Forster's work, whatever our views of the individual novels may be.

Like everything of Forster's, *The Longest Journey* is immensely readable, but one cannot avoid the impression that a subject-matter requiring some of Lawrence's powers is, in the end, only very sketchily dealt with. The moral disintegration of Rickie and the fulfilment of Ansell's prophecy that Rickie's marriage would fail are never sharply focused. The novelist, one feels, should have given the marriage more of a chance.

Neither by marriage nor by any other device can men insure themselves a vision: and Rickie's had been granted him three years before, when he had seen his wife and a dead man clasped in each other's arms. She was never to be so real to him again.

Why should Agnes not have become real? The novel does not provide a satisfactory answer, and the business about inherited deformity in Rickie and his child is an evasion, a feeble symbol for over-civilized decadence. Agnes is made unsubtly incapable of realizing that the marriage was a failure. 'She moves as one from whom the inner life has been withdrawn.' Is it much more than a phrase, this 'inner life' which is understood by the philosophizing Ansell and unconsciously represented by Stephen, though only guessed at by Rickie? The novel gives the impression of having been written out of convictions, feelings, and prejudices – about public schools, about townspeople and countrymen and Cambridge – which do not hang together convincingly. The equation between the dead Gerald and the living Stephen as seen by the domineering, disappointed, self-ignorant Agnes, is one of many attempts to 'connect' in Forster which are not quite effective. It is certainly tantalizing. There should have been a deep sense of loss and a tragic song of praise and renewal, but the reader has to guess and invent these for himself because what he is offered is sentimentally vague. Stephen should have had some of the symbolic power of Hardy's Giles Winterborne, but in fact he is not much more substantial than the Pan of the stories. Where the 'pattern and rhythm' which Forster aims at in all his novels, and describes in *Aspects of the Novel* (1927), become conspicuous in set passages of evocative prose, we are reminded not of Hardy but of Meredith:

> The riot of fair images increased. They invaded his being and lit lamps at unsuspected shrines. Their orchestra commenced in that suburban house where he had to stand aside for the maid to carry in the luncheon. Music flowed past him like a river ... In full unison was love born, flame of the flame, flushing the dark river beneath him and the virgin snows above. His wings were infinite, his youth eternal: the sun was a jewel on his finger as he passed it in benediction over the world ...
>
> (*The Longest Journey*, ch. 3)

As an attempt to define the 'reality', 'vision', and 'inner life' this is disappointing. The poetic style, though partly insured against bathos by its own exaggeration, appears self-conscious and uncertain in intention. The more elaborate pages of descriptive or impressionistic writing in the earlier novels, especially when they attempt to display the larger significance of events, usually leave a feeling of strain. Only in *A Passage to India* are the descriptive passages deeply evocative, secure, through their real connection with the novelist's experience, against the incursions of the Comic Spirit or of the little god Pan. The distinction I am making here is not one between 'success' and 'failure'. All the earlier novels remain fresh and individual even after much rereading, and they will probably remain current for a long time to come. But if, despite their deceptive surface lightness, they did not aim at something more than the success of 'light entertainment', they would not require and repay the detailed study which they have received. They have affinities with the novels of Hardy on the one hand, and with those of Lawrence on the other. The affinities are more a matter of differences than of resemblances, yet the differences imply a deeper, though scarcely formulable, connection with Hardy and Lawrence than the conscious indebtedness to Butler or Proust. If Forster had ever written extensively, as he did at times briefly, about his relation to Hardy and Lawrence he might perhaps have stressed, in the case of Hardy, the ironic contrast of his own birthplace in Melcombe Place, Dorset Square, London, and might have established his own connection with Lawrence through his sharp awareness that the admirable Victorian liberal outlook 'has lost the basis of gold sovereigns upon which it originally rose, and now hangs over the abyss'. If we cannot claim for Forster the same intensity of moral exploration that characterizes Lawrence, then we must add that no modern English writer challenges comparison with Lawrence in this respect.

The continuity between the short stories and the novels is felt most strongly in the two Italian novels, both unquestionable successes. In both, Italian landscape and people enable some English middle-class characters to achieve an increase in freedom and self-knowledge, but confirm the prejudices and self-righteousness of others. At the centre of Forster's hostility is genteel Sawston with its 'culture' and 'principles' and its fear of vulgarity that seems almost a negation of life. Forster does not idealize his Italians to make his point. What he sees in them appears objective and real. Harriet Herriton is blind to this reality. Miss Abbott is transformed by it. The expedition from Sawston to recover the dead Englishwoman's child from its unacceptable Italian father is confused by the living significance of the infant.

> She had thought so much about this baby, of its welfare, its soul, its morals, its probable defects. But, like most unmarried people she had only thought of it as a word – just as the healthy man only thinks of the word death, not death itself. The real thing, lying asleep on a dirty rug, disconcerted her. It did not stand for a principle any longer. It was so much flesh and blood, so many inches and ounces of life – a glorious and unquestionable fact, which a man and another woman had given to the world ... And this was the machine on which she and Mrs Herriton and Philip and Harriet had for the last month been exercising their various ideals – had determined that in time it should move this way or that way, should accomplish this and not that. It was to be Low Church, it was to be high-principled, it was to be tactful, gentlemanly, artistic – excellent things all. Yet now that she saw this baby, lying asleep on a dirty rug, she had a great disposition not to dictate one of them, and to exert no more influence than there may be in a kiss or in the vaguest of heartfelt prayers.
>
> (*Where Angels Fear to Tread*, 1905, ch. 7)

When Harriet succeeded in stealing the baby, she 'dandled the bundle laboriously, like some bony prophetess'. The child is accidentally killed. This violence, like the scuffle which hurries Fielding's departure from the Chandrapore club, reminds us sharply that, though the mode is comedy, Forster is very much in earnest about his subject-matter. Later, this discontent with middle-class manners deepened into a recognition of the difficulty of all good relationship, especially without the mediation of a common religious tradition and vocabulary. Forster's clergymen were all facets of Sawston worldliness and self-importance. He never attempted to describe religious vocation from the inside – partly because (and not only for Victorian liberals) the 'inside' of modern religious experience tends to be outside ecclesiastical institutions. Like many other observers, Forster doubted the value of fashionable literary Christianity. But the satire against the Rev. Mr Eager and the Rev. Mr Beebe in *A Room with a View* (1908) would be still more effective if we could be clearer about the rationalist Mr Emerson, with 'the face of a saint who understood'. The fact that the gout-stricken Mr Emerson takes refuge instinctively in the rectory study, its walls lined with black-bound theology, is surely meant to carry meaning, though to Lucy 'it seemed dreadful that the old man should crawl into such a sanctum when he was unhappy, and be dependent on the bounty of a clergy-man'. The stock descriptions – 'agnostic', 'liberal sceptic', 'anti-clericalist' – suggest clear-cut attitudes unlike Forster's. He knows when clarity falsifies, and that it is very often better to tolerate muddle as nearer to the actual conditions of intellectual and moral life. But old Mr Emerson is an unimpressive representative of this sort of attitude. Nor can one be quite happy about the kind of generalization Forster makes on very common problems of adjustment to cultural differences within society. Here is an example from Lucy's defence of the priggish London intellectual Cecil:

> 'You can't expect a really musical person to enjoy comic songs as we do.'
> 'Then why didn't he leave the room? Why sit wriggling and sneering and spoiling everyone's pleasure?'
> 'We mustn't be unjust to people,' faltered Lucy. Something had enfeebled her, and the case for Cecil, which she had mastered so perfectly in London, would not come forth in an effective form. The two civilizations had clashed – Cecil had hinted that they might – and she was dazzled and bewildered, as though the radiance that lies behind all civilization had blinded her eyes. Good taste and bad taste were only catchwords, garments of diverse cut; and music itself dissolved to a whisper through pine-trees, where the song is not distinguishable from the comic song.

The discriminations are not subtle or sharp enough either in these general comments which remind one of Meredith – and of the anxious geniality about critical 'astringency' mentioned in our first paragraph – or in the presentation of Cecil. So that a measure of sentimental vagueness must be tolerated as part of the experience of 'enjoying' the novel.

This is also the case in the more substantial work *Howards End* (1910). Here Forster is again concerned with the interaction of cultural levels, and he returns to the attempt made in *The Longest Journey* to analyse and describe the drift of modern English life as it had been transformed by a century of industrialization and imperial expansion. The novel shows the harmonizing, genial, and intensely patriotic sides of the novelist at odds with his radicalism. The date was 1910 and the subject, as Forster put it, 'a hunt for a home'. It is the equivalent in his work of Hardy's *Return of the Native* and is similarly oversimplified. The hunt is genuine enough, but one may well doubt whether the home was ever found. Nevertheless the novel was in some ways a pioneer work and it helped to modify attitudes and educate manners for half a century. Even *The Times* printed leading articles weightily agreeing that the British Empire was undermined by bad manners. A future Gibbon

will have to discover just what part was played in the decline by the behaviour of Englishmen – not to mention Englishwomen – who lived their lives in the East. How much are the angry young men of Singapore a product of an exclusive transplanted Wimbledon?

(*The Times*, 16 September 1959)

The question can be put so calmly largely because *A Passage to India* (1924) made it possible. This major work is, of course, much more than a comment on colonialism, but it is worth saying that one's impression of the courage needed to write it is no less strong now than it was then. Democracy has its frivolous side, and questions of principle and moral responsibility for unrepresented populations overseas do not decide parliamentary elections. Forster did more to educate large numbers of the electorate ('two cheers for democracy') than any English writer of his time. Because *A Passage to India* has been a best-selling paperback for decades, discussion can dispense with political watchwords and slogans and go straight to the heart of the matter. Written after a silence of fourteen years, the book revealed none of the old Meredithean associations, and the simple pieties of Thomas Hardy were also outgrown. Seen in relation to Forster's work as a whole, it represents as significant a process of development as any in modern literature. In the earlier novels, the correcting of intellectual arrogance in Cecil Vyse by contrast with Mr Emerson, in Rickie by Stephen, or in the Schlegels by Mrs Wilcox, had left a suggestion of falsity or sanctimoniousness. What Forster recoiled from was clear enough, but his alternatives seemed oversimplified. His major novel does not offer alternatives and solutions. India acts as a solvent not only to the churchy serenity of Mrs Moore (who is related to several other characters in earlier novels) but also to the rationalism and self-confidence of Fielding.

And he felt dubious and discontented suddenly, and wondered whether he was really and truly successful as a human being. After forty years' experience, he had learnt to manage his life and make the best of it on advanced European lines, had developed his personality, explored his limitations, controlled his passions – and he had done it all without becoming either pedantic or worldly. A creditable achievement, but as the moment passed, he felt he ought to have been working at something else the whole time, – he didn't know at what, never would know, never could know, and that was why he felt sad.

(*A Passage to India*, ch. 20)

Some readers have seen this novel as essentially pessimistic and 'defeatist', but this seems to be the result of misinterpreting the incidents in the cave. Value must still be affirmed despite the dark rumblings of negation and nullity, and it was the strain of this task which overtaxed Mrs Moore. 'Everything exists, nothing has value.' It was her distinction to have had the experience.

She had come to that state where the horror of the universe and its smallness are both visible at the same time – the horror of the double vision in which so many elderly people are involved ... In the twilight of the double vision, a spiritual muddledom is set up for which no high-sounding words can be found. (ch. 23)

But the experience was also her punishment for having declared earlier, much too complacently, 'I like mysteries, but I rather dislike muddles.' To Adela and Fielding she left a hint of other modes of responsiveness to 'India' than their own. 'Were there worlds beyond which they could not touch, or did all that is possible enter their consciousness? ... Perhaps life is a mystery, not a muddle; they could not tell.'

The Hindu ceremonies with which the novel concludes strike one as the acceptance and sanctification of muddle which appears more tolerable and nearer the truth than more orderly religious systems and patterns of belief. The effect of this conclusion to the elaborate tapestry of the book is positive and far from depressing. And it is naïve to see evidence of a lack of moral vitality in the last words of a novel which, with few reservations, is an impressive structure of carefully pondered experience. 'Love in public affairs does not work', Forster wrote in an essay on Tolerance. He was not the first novelist to distrust 'good intentions'. After the violence and change of the intervening years, the balance of antipathy and sympathy in *A Passage to India* still seems the undistorted response of a mind of rare courage, delicacy, and integrity, and it plays an important part in the total music of this major work.

NOTES

1. It is characteristic of Forster that he should conclude his biography of Goldsworthy Lowes Dickenson (1934) in this way: 'Mephistopheles, who should inhabit a cranny in every biography, puts his head out at this point, and asks me to set all personal feelings aside and state objectively why a memoir of Goldsworthy Lowes Dickenson need be written ... The case for Mephistopheles would appear to be watertight, and a biography of my friend and master uncalled for.'

2. See my essay in *Essays in Criticism*, Vol. VIII, no. 2.

VIRGINIA WOOLF:
THE THEORY AND PRACTICE OF FICTION

FRANK W. BRADBROOK

There are probably no writers whom it is more difficult to discuss with a proper critical disinterestedness than those that one first admired many years ago, as a student. Their influence, however modified by what has been written since, and by one's subsequent reading and experience, remains a deep and permanent one. Moreover, the writers whom one admired in the late thirties have not been outmoded in the sense that H. G. Wells, John Galsworthy, and Arnold Bennett were for Virginia Woolf when she started publishing fiction at the beginning of the First World War. The problem of the relationship between the generations was for her a matter of breaking free from an inadequate technique and a limited vision. Her own achievement may appear now to be a more limited one than it did when her novels were first read, and her lasting contribution to fiction may be reduced to a single novel, *To the Lighthouse*. Yet she had imagination, great sensitiveness, delicacy, wit, and the infinite capacity of genius for taking pains. She, at least, did not curb the spirit, or erect barriers that her followers have had to break down. If one thinks of her limitations, it is only compared with the greatest of her predecessors, Jane Austen and George Eliot, two artists whom she admired and whose work as a whole gives one a sense of achievement and triumph beside which the writings of the twentieth-century novelist, inevitably perhaps, appear, for all the flashes of brilliance, curiously fragmentary and inconclusive.

'That fiction is a lady, and a lady who has somehow got herself into trouble, is a thought that must often have struck her admirers', Virginia Woolf remarks at the beginning of a review of E. M. Forster's *Aspects of the Novel*. There now exist numerous books containing essays on the art of fiction and kindred subjects by Virginia Woolf herself. Here one can see the artist working out her technical problems. The essay 'Modern Fiction' in *The Common Reader* (First

Series) is largely taken up with destructive criticism of the Edwardians:

> ... materialists ... they are concerned not with the spirit but with the body ... they write of unimportant things ... they spend immense skill and immense industry making the trivial and the transitory appear the true and the enduring.

Life escapes H. G. Wells, John Galsworthy, and Arnold Bennett:

> ... look within and life, it seems, is very far from being 'like this'. Examine for a moment an ordinary mind on an ordinary day. The mind receives a myriad impressions – trivial, fantastic, evanescent, or engraved with the sharpness of steel. From all sides they come, an incessant shower of innumerable atoms; and as they fall, as they shape themselves into the life of Monday or Tuesday, the accent falls differently from of old ... Life is not a series of gig lamps symmetrically arranged; life is a luminous halo, a semi-transparent envelope surrounding us from the beginning of consciousness to the end.[1]

This may be inadequate psychology, it may involve a too passive conception of perception,[2] but it describes what life meant for Virginia Woolf, and it made necessary the creation of new techniques and methods. Plot, character, comedy, tragedy, and the concentration on 'love interest', the old conventional themes and categories, were no longer adequate to communicate the stream of the modern consciousness. Virginia Woolf had certain models for what may be called the 'hit-or-miss' style, such as the Elizabethan novelists, particularly Thomas Nashe, odd eccentrics such as Sterne, and, in her own day, James Joyce. These writers, rather than Thackeray, Thomas Hardy, and Joseph Conrad, whom she also esteemed, provided her with something in the nature of a tradition, though she 'felt the lack of a convention, and how serious a matter it is when the tools of one generation are useless for the next' (*The Captain's Death Bed*). Her attitude is primarily that of the innovator, experimenting, conscious of infinite possibilities, and ready to try anything. There is no such thing as 'the proper stuff of fiction': 'everything is the proper stuff of fiction, every feeling, every thought; every quality of brain and spirit is drawn upon; no perception comes amiss' (*The Common Reader*, First Series). Such all-inclusiveness has its dangers, and in trying to record everything, in refusing to select and discriminate between the significance and value of different experiences, the novelist may merely end by reproducing the chaos from which it is the function of intelligence to save us.

Virginia Woolf believed that the novelist must 'expose himself to life' and yet be detached from it. In *Granite and Rainbow*, using a vivid image of Ernest Hemingway, she remarks that 'the true writer stands close up to the bull and lets the horns – call them life, truth, reality, whatever you like – pass him close each time'. Life, as she describes it in *A Writer's Diary*, is (this was written in 1920) 'for us in our generation so tragic – no newspaper placard without its shriek of agony from someone ... Unhappiness is everywhere; just beyond the door; or stupidity, which is worse.' Yet it has its moments of happiness, which would be more frequent if 'it weren't for my feeling that it's a strip of pavement over an abyss' (*A Writer's Diary*). 'The Russian Point of View', of which Virginia Woolf was very much aware – her essay with this title is in *The Common Reader* (First Series) – deepened her sense both of the comedy and tragedy of life, but it was supremely embodied in the novels of Tolstoy, whom she saw as a kind of Sir Thomas Browne creating nineteenth-century Slavonic Hamlets who were perpetually asking themselves the question 'Why live?' Modestly realizing her limitations, it was the less massive genius Chekhov with whom she tended to sympathize. His art had that economy which she also found in the novels of Jane Austen, who was, in this respect, she thought, superior to George Eliot herself (*The Common Reader*, First Series).[3]

Virginia Woolf was very conscious of her place in the tradition of women writers, and her determination to maintain the dignity of her sex could at times even tempt her into the unartistic faults of stridency, exaggeration, and overemphasis. *A Room of One's Own*, which directly deals with the problems of the woman writer, is interesting and occasionally amusing, but there is a sense of strain and even of viciousness in the attack on various types of masculine pomposity and self-importance in *Three Guineas*. A good case and legitimate attitude are spoilt by an unusual crudity of presentation.[4] Writing about women and fiction in 1929, she prophesied that

the greater impersonality of women's lives will encourage the poetic spirit, and it is in poetry that women's fiction is still weakest. It will lead them to be less absorbed in facts and no longer content to record with astonishing acuteness the minute details which fall under their own observation. They will look beyond the personal and political relationships to the wider questions which the poet tries to solve – of our destiny and the meaning of life.

(*Granite and Rainbow*)

This 'poetic spirit', together with the concern with the meaning of destiny and life, had been characteristic of Virginia Woolf's own fiction from the first. 'A method essentially poetic and apparently trifling has been applied to fiction', as E. M. Forster noted (*Two Cheers for Democracy*).

Fiction, for Virginia Woolf, was not a 'criticism of life' in any Arnoldian sense, but rather a re-creation of the complexities of experience. Just as life was a most subtle and complicated succession of experiences, so fiction must be infinitely adaptable and supple in order to catch the 'tones', the light and shade of experience. The art of the novelist was similar to that of the painter, and painting for Virginia Woolf did not mean the Dutch School, who were admired by George Eliot, but Roger Fry and the Post-Impressionists, Van Gogh rather than the Van Eycks, Cézanne, Gauguin, and Matisse. There were various 'phases' of fiction and different types of novelists, equivalent to the different schools of painting, and the task of the modern novelist was to make use of whatever was of value in the past. The truth-tellers, the romantics, the character-mongers and comedians, the psychologists, the satirists and fantastics, and the poets, were like the different paints on the palette. How did one combine their various methods to produce the perfect picture?

Experience is a flux, and the novelist must communicate it. Yet there must be some sort of order in the art by means of which it is presented:

For the most characteristic qualities of the novel – that it registers the slow growth and development of feeling, that it follows many lives and traces their unions and fortunes over a long stretch of time – are the very qualities that are most incompatible with design and order. It is the gift of style, arrangement, construction to put us at a distance from the special life and obliterate its features; while it is the gift of the novel to bring us into close touch with life. The two powers fight if they are brought into combination. The most complete novelist must be the novelist who can balance the two powers so that the one enhances the other.

(*Granite and Rainbow*)

345

Virginia Woolf's values are those of Bloomsbury, the group of writers and artists that included, in addition to Roger Fry, Vanessa and Clive Bell, Duncan Grant, Lytton Strachey, Leonard Woolf, J. M. Keynes, Desmond MacCarthy, and (rather on the fringe) E. M. Forster.[5] The danger of the clique spirit in the modern literary world does not require stressing to anyone who is sufficiently alert and informed to see what goes on, and the Bloomsbury group suffered like any other school of writers from a tendency towards mutual admiration that was merely a form of narcissism. There were also certain blind-spots. Virginia Woolf refers to 'the chants of the worshippers at the shrine of Lawrence', and then, in the following essay, proceeds to chant at the shrine of Roger Fry, who is praised for his honesty and integrity, qualities that he may have owed in part to his Quaker blood. He also went to Cambridge (King's College) and is meant to represent the Cambridge mind at its best. While giving a sympathetic account of *Sons and Lovers*, Virginia Woolf asserts that D. H. Lawrence

is not a member, like Proust, of a settled and civilized society. He is anxious to leave his own class and to enter another. He believes that the middle class possess what he does not possess ... the fact that he, like Paul, was a miner's son, and that he disliked his conditions, gave him a different approach to writing from those who have a settled station and enjoy circumstances which allow them to forget what those circumstances are. (*The Moment*)

The Lawrence of Virginia Woolf's imagination is not interested in literature, the past, or the present except in so far as it affects the future, or in human psychology, and in comparison with Proust again, he is said to have no tradition behind him. He is lacking in style, civilization, and a sense of beauty.[6] When discussing *A Passage to India*, Virgina Woolf can be more detached because she is talking about the writings of someone with whom she is acquainted and can even be ironical about the place that provided the group with its standards – 'it is a relief for a time, to be beyond the influence of Cambridge'. In that 'for a time' there is an unconscious irony.

To pass from Virginia Woolf's theories, ideas, and criticism to the study of her practice as a novelist is to realize how much more conventional she was than she imagined. *The Voyage Out* (1915), her first novel, is quite traditional in form, and the best moments occur when she is being autobiographical. In chapter XIII, Rachel visits the room of Mr Ambrose, her uncle, and one is reminded of the education that Virginia Woolf's father, Leslie Stephen, gave her:

> to read what one liked because one liked it, never to pretend to admire what one did not – that was his only lesson in the art of reading. To write in the fewest possible words, as clearly as possible, exactly what one meant – that was his only lesson in the art of writing. (*The Captain's Death Bed*)

There, is the essential strength of Virginia Woolf, the tradition that was to produce Mr Ramsay of *To the Lighthouse*. She did not mean to be prejudiced against the poor, but her intense intellectual life was accompanied by a vein of snobbery, however much she tried to sympathize. George Eliot, the granddaughter of a carpenter, is described as 'raising herself with groans and struggles from the intolerable boredom of petty provincial society.' She was lacking in charm: 'she had none of these eccentricities and inequalities of temper which give to many artists the endearing simplicity of children' (*The Common Reader*, First Series). George Eliot might well reply that the simplicity of children is not always endearing, and that it is the duty of artists to be adult in their attitudes and ideas. When, in *The Voyage Out*, a character called Hewet says 'I want to write a novel about Silence, the things people don't say. But the difficulty is immense', one feels that Virginia Woolf is merely being clever in a Bloomsbury kind of way.[7] One is reminded of Jane Austen – 'What did she say? – Just what she ought, of course. A lady always does,' describing Emma's response to Mr Knightley's proposal. The world of Virginia Woolf's characters is supposed to be a sophisticated and cosmopolitan one, yet it, too, has its provincial aspects. Evelyn, in *The Voyage Out*, is going to found a club '– a club for doing things ... It was brains that were needed ... of course, they would want a room ... in Bloomsbury preferably'. There, the essential naïvety of Virginia Woolf manifests itself.

Night and Day (1919), like *The Voyage Out*, is a conventional, realistic story, showing many of the characteristics that Virginia Woolf ridiculed in her criticism of the English realistic novelists. Early in the novel, one is introduced to Katherine Hilbery,

> belonging to one of the most distinguished families in England ... when they were not lighthouses firmly based on rock for the guidance of their generation, they were steady, serviceable candles, illuminating the ordinary chambers of life. (*Night and Day*)

She typifies Bloomsbury humanity as well as Bloomsbury snobbery. 'Not to care' is the unforgivable sin. Ralph Denham, whom she eventually marries, is metaphorically united with her towards the end of the novel, and one sees here the beginnings of the later, more subtle use of symbolism and poetic technique:

an odd image came to his mind of a lighthouse besieged by the flying bodies of lost birds, who were dashed senseless, by the gale, against the glass. He had a strange sensation that he was both lighthouse and bird; he was steadfast and brilliant; and at the same time he was whirled with all other things, senseless against the glass.

In Mrs Hilbery's reverie and its conclusion in the statement that 'love is our faith', which is compared by her daughter to the 'breaking of waves solemnly in order upon the vast shore that she gazed upon', there is a foreshadowing of the Mrs Ramsay–Lily Briscoe relationship in *To the Lighthouse*.

Jacob's Room (1922) marks a further development in this poetic method. There are flashes here, too, of that almost vicious, satirical wit, usually aimed at men, and their attempts to think or to keep up the appearance of thinking. Even Cambridge is not lacking in insensitive characters: at George Plumley's luncheon at 'Waverley', on the road to Girton, there were 'on the table serious sixpenny weeklies written by pale men in muddy boots – the weekly creak and screech of brains rinsed in cold water and wrung dry – melancholy papers'. The real culture of Cambridge, however, 'the light of Cambridge', is implicitly opposed to the provincial prudishness of Professor Bulteel of Leeds, who 'had issued an edition of Wycherley without stating that he had left out ... several indecent words and some indecent phrases'. The astringent wit of Virginia Woolf, combined with the quite open snobbery, as in the reference to Soho, 'and so again into the dark, passing a girl here for sale, or there an old woman with only matches to offer', derives from Jane Austen, the Jane Austen of *The Letters*, *Northanger Abbey*, and the ironical observer of the fate with which Jane Fairfax is threatened in *Emma*, though the subject-matter is that of Defoe (cp. the end of the essay on Defoe in *The Common Reader*, First Series). Virginia Woolf also shares with Jane Austen a sense of the importance of the apparent trivialities of life: 'it's not catastrophes, murders, deaths, diseases, that age and kill us; it's the way people look and laugh, and run up the steps of omnibuses' (*Jacob's Room*).

The use of imagery to connect different moments in the novel, and to form patterns apart from character and plot, becomes more confident and consistent in *Mrs Dalloway* (1925). Images, in Virginia Woolf's novels, are even carried over from one book to another. 'Darkness drops like a knife over Greece', in *Jacob's Room*; Mrs Dalloway 'sliced like a knife through everything'; again in *Mrs Dalloway*, Peter Walsh is frequently described as playing with a knife, and it is connected with his habit of 'making one feel, too, frivolous; empty-minded; a mere silly chatterbox'. The image of a knife is also used in *To the Lighthouse*, in connection with Mr Ramsay, to describe the ruthlessness and insensitiveness of the male intellect, as opposed to the feminine imagination of Mrs Ramsay. (There is, perhaps, too, a suggestion here of Time's 'scythe and crooked knife', one of the themes of Shakespeare's sonnets.[8]) The use of the background of the rhythm of the waves when evoking those isolated, significant moments in experience with which Virginia Woolf is so concerned, appears in *Mrs Dalloway*, looking forward to the extended use of this image in *To the Lighthouse* and *The Waves*. A mood of serenity and resignation is usually conveyed by this image (though sometimes the thundering of the waves can suggest terror). The hypnotic rhythms of the falling waves induce the appropriate response in Mrs Dalloway: ' "Fear no more," says the heart, committing its burden to some sea, which sighs collectively for all sorrows, and renews, begins, collects, lets fall'.[9] One cannot help feeling that there is a certain complacency in the novel here, and it appears again in the character of Peter Walsh who, growing old, 'has gained − at last! − the power which adds the supreme flavour to existence − the power of taking hold of experience, of turning it round, slowly in the light'. He, in other words, is another Sir Thomas Browne in modern dress, Hamletizing, as Virginia Woolf imagined the heroes of Tolstoy did, but he makes a comparatively poor showing intellectually. The detachment from life and experience has been too easily won. Clarissa Dalloway is tinged with the same complacency. Living for her parties, she 'could not think, write, even play the piano ... she must be liked; talked oceans of nonsense'. No one liked a party more than Jane Austen's Emma, and she is equally ignorant and undisciplined, but she is only twenty when the novel begins, and has grown up by the end of the story. It is a weakness in Virginia Woolf's novels that her models of mature, feminine wisdom are essentially adolescent – Mrs Ramsay also has an 'untrained mind'. In *Mrs Dalloway*, the macabre Septimus Smith episode is less effective than it would be if Virginia Woolf was more capable of describing the subtleties and complications of normal, mature living.

To the Lighthouse (1927) is generally recognized as Virginia Woolf's masterpiece. The combination of autobiographical material with the poetic method of presentation and the larger structural pattern results in the final reconciliation between life and art. The symbolism of the lighthouse, used spasmodically in *Night and Day*, becomes as natural and inevitably right as the

> ever-fixèd mark,
> That looks on tempests and is never shaken.

There is, of course, a danger in making a comparison between a sonnet of Shakespeare (No. 116) and an image used in a modern novel. Yet, *To the Lighthouse* may with justice be described as 'an expanded metaphor', as Wilson Knight has described a Shakespearian play. Here the individual images have the same organic relationship with the allegory of the general theme that we find in Shakespeare's greatest plays. The themes of *To the Lighthouse* are those of the sonnets – time, beauty, the survival of beauty through the means of art, absence, and death:

> Like as the waves make towards the pebbled shore,
> So do our minutes hasten to their end ...
>
> (No. 60)
>
> How with this rage shall beauty hold a plea,
> Whose action is no stronger than a flower? ...
>
> (No. 65)
>
> From you have I been absent in the spring,
> When proud-pied April, dress'd in all his trim,
> Hath put a spirit of youth in every thing ...
>
> (No. 98)

It is, surely, in Shakespeare rather than (as has been suggested) in Bergson that the source of Virginia Woolf's themes is to be found.[10]

The method is that of poetry not philosophy, and to discuss *To the Lighthouse* and *The Waves* in terms of mystical experience is equally dangerous.[11] The symbolism of the lighthouse is clear, and Virginia Woolf is no more mystical than E. M. Forster in *Howards End*, where the symbolism of the house performs a similar function and music replaces painting as the source of aesthetic experience. Forster has, perhaps, been less successful in his 'poetic' effects, but in the way in which he makes use of Beethoven's Fifth Symphony there is an example of the larger rhythm and theme comparable to Virginia Woolf's image of the waves.

These rhythms and themes transcend plot and character, and appear at significant moments during the novels, when the trivialities and pettinesses of ordinary life are surpassed. During isolated moments of intense experience, when 'the miracle happens', life takes on the intensity of art. The long steady stroke of the lighthouse beam is Mrs Ramsay's stroke, and symbolizes the stability and security which her presence imposes on the flux of life. The flashing of the beam is the equivalent in life to the movements of the painter's brush – Mrs Ramsay and Lily Briscoe are equally artists – and the novel ends with the long steady stroke of the brush that also completes Lily Briscoe's picture in the mind, of the perfect woman whom she loves. Both in the novel and in painting, formality and discipline are imposed on the chaos of experience. To make, Virginia Woolf seems to be saying, something of permanent importance out of one's momentary experiences is the aim of the poet, such as Shakespeare in his sonnets, the novelist, the artist in living, such as Mrs Ramsay, and the painter; and in order to express one's personality, one must lose it by absorbing it in something larger and seeing its place in the artistic pattern of the whole: 'losing personality one lost the fret, the hurry, the stir' and gained the peace which passeth all understanding. Virginia Woolf, for once, used directly religious terminology, but the experience she describes frequently occurs in non-religious poetry.

Opposed to this poetic experience is the rationalism of Mr Ramsay, with the endurance, stoicism, and tyranny that it involves. This is the world of Victorian agnosticism:

We stand on a mountain pass in the midst of whirling snow and blinding mist, through which we get glimpses now and then of paths which may be deceptive. If we stand still we shall be frozen to death. If we take the wrong road we shall be dashed to pieces. We do not certainly know whether there is any right one. What must we do? 'Be strong and of good courage.' Act for the best, hope for the best, and take what comes ... If death ends all, we cannot meet death better.[12]

Such an attitude, of course, can result in self-dramatization which is very far removed from the heroism that it pretends to be. The greatness of Virginia Woolf's portrait of Mr Ramsay is that she finally acknowledges and succeeds in convincing us of his heroism, despite her prejudice against the tyranny of the male intellect, its essential egoism and pettiness. The contrast between Mr and Mrs Ramsay is comparable to that of Jane Austen's Emma and Mr Knightley: the end of Virginia Woolf's greatest novel also vindicates 'the wishes, the hopes, the confidence, the predictions of the small band of true friends' (the conclusion of *Emma*) as Mr Ramsay reaches the end of his journey to the lighthouse, and Lily Briscoe completes the painting inspired by Mrs Ramsay. The world of prose has been united with those of poetry and of art.

Orlando (1928), though it has brilliant passages, has not the unity of *To the Lighthouse* and the indulgence of fantasy is inclined to pall. Genius, Virginia Woolf remarks,

resembles the lighthouse in working, which sends one ray, and then no more for a time; save that genius is much more capricious in its manifestations and may flash six or seven beams in quick succession ... and then lapse into darkness for a year or for ever. To steer by its beams is therefore impossible, and when the dark spell is on them men of genius are, it is said, much like other people.

That, unfortunately, is what appears to have happened to Virginia Woolf herself. *The Waves* (1931) deals with the theme of the progress of time, the days, months, and seasons following each other like the waves and ending, for the individual, with death. There are beautiful passages, such as Bernard's final monologue, with which the novel concludes, but there is not 'an intimate autobiographical sense of life'. *The Years* (1937) contains, near the beginning, a flash of the old satirical wit in the description of the hypocrisy of Colonel Pargiter and the death, after a painful, protracted illness, of his wife. The novel, as a whole, shows signs of tiredness, and is dull and monotonous. It ends with the sun rising on a new day, 'and the sky above the houses wore an air of extraordinary beauty, simplicity and peace'. It is a conventional, not a strenuously achieved ending, like the serenity of the conclusion of *To the Lighthouse*. There is a reference to 'the heart of darkness', the title of Conrad's tale, and it also appears at the end of the posthumously published *Between the Acts* (1941). The heart had gone out of Virginia Woolf's work.

That her genius had burned itself out is confirmed by the six previously unpublished short stories at the end of *A Haunted House* (1944). Her short stories, despite some brilliancies, tend to confirm the sense of a minor talent. Yet if she is not among the very greatest of English novelists, her fiction leaves one with the impression of a delicate and subtle artist in words, who upheld aesthetic and spiritual values in a brutal, materialistic age. Forster reminds one of the permanent significance of her work:

> Order. Justice. Truth. She cared for these abstractions, and tried to express them through symbols ... The epitaph of such an artist cannot be written by the vulgar-minded or by the lugubrious ... She triumphed over what are primly called 'difficulties', and she also triumphed in the positive sense: she brought in the spoils. And sometimes it is as a row of little silver cups that I see her work gleaming. 'These trophies,' the inscription runs, 'were won by the mind from matter, its enemy and its friend.'
>
> (*Two Cheers for Democracy*)

To these eloquent words one may, perhaps, add the comment that Virginia Woolf had not only the sensitiveness, poetry, and imagination of Mrs Ramsay. She retained and exemplified the integrity and heroism of Mr Ramsay and of Leslie Stephen, her father.

The recent publication of Leslie Stephen's *Mausoleum Book*, together with autobiographies and biographies of various members of the Bloomsbury Group, including the memoirs of Leonard Woolf and the letters and diaries of Virginia, has greatly increased one's knowledge of the personal backgrounds and of the relationships between the members of this set of writers. The relevance of all this information to criticism of their creative achievement is debatable. However, the letters and diaries of Virginia Woolf give illumination and insight into the struggles and tensions of artistic creation which are almost unique in their detail and which are intimately related to the fiction, the letters representing something like the equivalent of dialogue and the diary recording that perpetual interior monologue from which the novels were produced. There is a sense in which Virginia Woolf was her own best critic, and as she recalls her efforts, constant fears of failure, and moments of triumph, and explains her intentions and difficulties, an element of moral courage, heroism of character and self-knowledge emerges, which is reflected in the enduring and permanent significance of her fiction, however much it may have been coloured by period influences, and however little it may lend itself to imitation by later novelists and the establishment of a tradition.

NOTES

1. The quotations from the works of Virgina Woolf are taken from the uniform edition, published by the Hogarth Press.

2. See D. S. Savage, *The Withered Branch* (1950), quoted by Arnold Kettle in *An Introduction to the English Novel*, Vol. II, 105.

3. For the influence of Turgenev on Virginia Woolf, see Gilbert Phelps, *The Russian Novel in English Fiction*, 132–7.

4. See the review by Q. D. Leavis in *Scrutiny*, Vol. VII, No. 2 (September 1938).

5. See Frank Swinnerton, *The Georgian Literary Scene* (Everyman's Library), ch. XIII, J. K. Johnstone, *The Bloomsbury Group*, and Quentin Bell, *Bloomsbury*.

6. F. R. Leavis might have found in Virginia Woolf's notes on D. H. Lawrence an interesting footnote to his accounts of the social prejudice and intellectual antagonism shown by J. M. Keynes and his circle and others.

7. Perhaps Virgina Woolf is indebted for the idea to Flaubert: 'what I should like to do is to write a book about nothing, a book with no reference to anything outside itself, which would stand on its own by the inner strength of its style, just as the earth holds itself without support in space, a book which would have hardly any subject, or at any rate one that is barely perceptible, if that were possible'. Letter to Louise Colet (16 January 1852), quoted by Miriam Allott, *Novelists on the Novel*, 242.

8. cp. Nos 95 and 100.

9. The immediate reference here is to the song to Fidele in *Cymbeline*, IV, ii.

10. J. W. Graham in 'A Negative Note on Bergson and Virginia Woolf' (*Essays in Criticism* VI, No. 1, January 1956), argues convincingly that the influence of Bergson on Virginia Woolf was both more general and limited than has frequently been assumed.

11. e.g. Peter and Margaret Havard-Williams: 'Mystical Experience in Virginia Woolf's *The Waves*' (*Essays in Criticism* IV, No. 1, January 1954).

12. Fitzjames Stephen: *Liberty, Equality, Fraternity*, 353 (2nd edn, London, 1874), quoted by William James, *Selected Papers on Philosophy* (Everyman's Library), 124. Virginia Woolf possibly read the passage in William

James's *The Will to Believe* (1897), as well as in its original context in Fitz-james Stephen; she was also, of course, a great admirer of the philosopher's brother, the novelist Henry James, to whom there are some interesting references in *A Writer's Diary*. For the intellectual background of the Stephens, see Q. D. Leavis's article on Leslie Stephen, *Scrutiny*, Vol. VII, No. 4, March 1939, and the study by Noel Annan.

D. H. LAWRENCE AND
WOMEN IN LOVE

W. W. ROBSON

D. H. Lawrence was destined to become what is called a 'controversial' author, because he sought to deal directly and candidly with human sexual relationships. Like Ibsen and Hardy before him, he was accused by self-appointed spokesmen for public morality of trafficking in filth and obscenity; like them he was installed for a time as the object of a cult by people, some of them very remote in sentiment and outlook from what the writer really cared for, who felt that in acclaiming him they were showing their enlightened superiority to the vulgar herd and the journalists who pandered to it. And, like his predecessors, he was in the end to be established as a famous author and canonical literary figure for a younger generation who found it difficult to understand what all the fuss had been about.

Lawrence made a vivid impression on his contemporaries before the controversies began. His first two novels were poor, but with *Sons and Lovers* (1913) and the short stories collected as *The Prussian Officer* (1914) he came to be widely recognized as the most brilliant young writer of his time. His social background, north of the river Trent and working-class, was no disadvantage to him in the era of Edwardian radicalism, and by the beginning of the First World War he seemed on the verge of a splendid literary career. It was *The Rainbow* (1915) that brought the storm and stress – a strange, visionary novel, without precedent in English fiction, it seems to many now the expression of a refined and noble art and a high purpose. Yet it incurred legal proceedings, and the first edition was destroyed with the acquiescence of Lawrence's publishers. From then on there was a cloud over Lawrence's literary reputation. He was thought sinister, immoral, dangerous. Nor did the criticism of his time do much to crystallize and clarify his achievement. The note of stridency in the posthumous critiques of him by his most influential champion,

F. R. Leavis – culminating in *D. H. Lawrence: Novelist* (1955) – is understandable when we consider how many prejudices had accumulated in the years since 1915. Silly books by people who knew Lawrence had made him seem silly too. *Lady Chatterley's Lover* (1928), the most sexually explicit of Lawrence's novels, was banned in its unexpurgated form and circulated clandestinely, again suggesting pornography, until a famous court case of 1960 released it to a huge, curious, expectant public.

Since that time much of the smoke has cleared away, and Lawrence, while remaining popular, has become an academically respectable author, a recognized glory of English literature. Indeed what is now found difficult and problematic in his writings, by younger readers, is not anything aggressively modern and subversive, but a traditionalism, or 'male chauvinism', which for them associates him not with our contemporaries but with the past.

But some of the difficulties of Lawrence's work are of a different order. The problem is often not whether Lawrence's point of view in this or that book is acceptable, but just what it is: what he is 'up to'. This is largely because in Lawrence it is impossible to separate, for long, his work and his life. The work represents the writer's dramatization of his own personal problems and conflicts; while the life seems to take on the shape of a symbolic story or legend.

The outlines of this story are very familiar. The childhood of the son of a Midland miner and a woman of marked character, in a country village transformed by the mining industry, which helped to give us *Sons and Lovers* (1913) and *The Rainbow* (1915), with their insights into the emotional and moral problems arising between husband and wife, and between child and parent, in a working-class environment; the youth and early manhood of a provincial elementary-school teacher, with an early success as a writer which distinguished him as one of the most gifted of his time; the union with a German wife of patrician origin, their later marriage which (all difficulties admitted) was to give so much sustenance to the man and subject-matter to the writer; the conflict with the authorities over *The Rainbow*'s alleged immorality (as later over that of *Lady Chatterley's Lover*); the horrors of the war-time years, the 'nightmare' described in *Kangaroo* (1923), the petty persecution, the suspicion and fear; the Utopian dream of Rananim, with its corollaries partly absurd and partly sad; the years of restless wandering, to all quarters of the earth; the intense, difficult, usually ambivalent personal relationships with men and women, both distinguished and obscure; the temptations to primitivism and Messianism, explored and abandoned; the growing bitterness and depression, illustrated in the satirical quality of so many of Lawrence's later stories, now and then alleviated by flashes of gaiety, sardonic humour, and robust common sense; the long-drawn-out and pathetic struggle with illness, the death in his forty-fifth year – these things have been so much written about that detailed rehearsal of them is unnecessary. But the story will be read over again and probably with more objectivity as the years go by and the personalities and topicalities involved cease to irritate or to divert. Lawrence is a person that future students of English literature and English civilization will have to meet; and it may be said that his 'personality' is the central subject for criticism for the student of his life – not only the Lawrence of anecdote, the brilliant letter-writer, journalist, and travel-book writer, but the wider personality-pattern which informs his creative work. Only one or two facets of Lawrence's 'personality' can be examined here; no comprehensiveness will be attempted, but merely a clearing-away of some of the manifest obstacles to judgement and appreciation.

Many of the works of Lawrence that follow his 'Nottingham' period do present obstacles. Now it should be said at once that where he is most completely a *poet* these seem to disappear; where, for example, he is evoking the life of nature: not merely the 'nature' of nature-poets, but the ancient feeling of the cosmic mystery, the pre-human and inhuman power of the universe, which we may suppose archaic man to have felt, and which Lawrence, with that strong 'archaic' strain in his genius, can make articulate more wonderfully than any other modern writer in English. When this poetry appears in Lawrence – more often in his prose than in his verse – our doubts, objections and questions are silenced. But Lawrence is a novelist and storyteller as well as a poet of the cosmos, and when he deals in human relationships – and he himself described his own subject-matter as 'the relations between men and women' – we are often disturbed and challenged, and sometimes repelled, by what we sense of the point of view of the author. This is not only because Lawrence preaches to the reader, and many of us dislike being preached to anyway, apart from disliking what he preaches. Even when Lawrence is more fully an artist and makes us feel what he wants us to feel, instead of insisting that we ought to feel it, bafflement and irritation often occur. It is at such times that our attention is drawn away from the work to the man behind the work, and we cannot but deviate into thoughts about those well-known sexual obsessions and social unease which critics and biographers have so much dwelt on. So we lose contact with the world of the author's imagination and find ourselves on the plane of ideas and opinions. It is easy then to discover that Lawrence as a moralist is thoroughly incoherent. Any attempt to institutionalize his moral, social, or political teaching would produce chaos – assuming we could imagine what the attempt would be like. Lawrence is too obviously generalizing improperly, and at times erroneously, from his own case. This is especially clear in the matter of sex. There is obviously self-deception, hence insincerity, in a work like *The Plumed Serpent* (1926), with its insistence that a woman must not seek complete physical satisfaction from the act of sex, but must find contentment instead in a reverent 'submission' to male 'authority'.

But this disagreeable side of Lawrence, though it exists, is relevant to the literary student only in so far as it reflects a failure in Lawrence's art. It is true that this failure is frequent and characteristic – perhaps especially in those post-war years when the suffering and defeated mood of the author is more evident, and coincides with, if it is not indeed partly due to, a decline in his creative powers. But we must be careful to distinguish between those works of his which are disturbing in the wrong way – those which deflect us on to the plane of opinions and arguments – and those which are healthily disturbing, which compel us to a valuable reappraisal, and perhaps readjustment, of our familiar assumptions and attitudes. Roughly speaking, we may say that in his successful works Lawrence makes us *see* the complexity of many of the concrete human situations to which moral judgements are undoubtedly relevant, but which do not lend themselves to description and analysis in straightforward moral terms. Thus (whatever we may think of the success of the novel as a whole) his presentation in *Aaron's Rod* (1922) of the deadlock in Aaron's marriage, the impasse into which Aaron's life has got, is so powerful that we are no more inclined than we would be in real life to pronounce readily on the rights and wrongs of Aaron's decision to leave his wife and children. It is not that we are persuaded to excuse Aaron, though as the novel goes on we soon realize that the author is on Aaron's side. It is rather that, owing to Lawrence's art, we are able to see this sort of situation 'in depth' – in a way that we rarely can, either in our own lives or in the lives of others. When it comes to explaining *why* Aaron took the step that he did, Lawrence is perhaps not able to translate his own convictions about the matter into art – not able to dramatize them; the amateur psychologist may indeed feel that this is because Aaron's decision is not consciously enough related, in the book, to his difficulties revealed there in forming a relationship with *any* woman and his curious quasi-homosexual relationship with the writer Rawdon Lilly. But what Lawrence can and does do is to show *how* it happened. We *see* that the Aaron we meet in his pages would, and did, act in this way. Lawrence's imagination has been sufficient to provide the data, the 'facts' of the situation; though when it comes to interpreting them, his imagination – perhaps because of some personal psychological 'block' – seems to function less powerfully.

Even where Lawrence has clearly fallen into special pleading, we can find this fullness in the presentment of the *données* of the situation which gives us room to make up our own minds. And it should be added that Lawrence's didacticism is characteristically apt to turn into self-questioning; just as those works of his (like *Lady Chatterley's Lover*) where a kind of near-allegorical simplicity is clearly intended, turn into something more complex because Lawrence, in 'becoming' the gamekeeper, cannot but bring into the gamekeeper his own un-certainties and self-mistrust. (A simpler example is the short story *The Daughters of the Vicar*, in the character of the miner Durant, who represents instinctive 'life' in the fable, but who turns out to have intense inner difficulties.) It is notable that Laurentian didactic prose is at its best when it reveals, in its oscillatory, fluctuating movement, this recurrent self-questioning.

Lawrence's over-insistence on 'telling' us things – and sometimes telling us things we cannot accept – should not, then, be allowed to obscure from us the very real extent to which he often succeeds in conveying the feel of actual life and actual human problems. A man who spent so much of his life as Lawrence did in preaching to women, or to one woman, may fail (as Lawrence so often does) to pay due regard to the rules which govern valid argument, illustration, and proof; but this does not mean that he is lacking in the essential intelligence required of a novelist to realize the full human reality of the *people* who argue, puzzle, and suffer. Furthermore, the inner stresses and strains which cause incoherence in the abstract thinker may in the novelist and story-teller provide the creative driving-force.

Perhaps it is something in Lawrence's manner of writing, rather than his matter, which has proved a stumbling-block for many readers. If we take up *The Tales of D. H. Lawrence* – the volume which contains a great part of his most unquestionably successful work as an artist – we will soon be struck by an obvious difference in quality between Lawrence's style and most of the educated English fiction we are accustomed to. Probably a superficial impression of lack of 'style' had counted for much in the opinion, once very common, that Lawrence is an uneducated writer. This opinion, stated baldly, is absurd. Nevertheless, the quality in Lawrence's style which prompts it is certainly there. When Lawrence lapses from his highest level he is apt to move towards Marie Corelli or Rider Haggard, not towards Galsworthy. In his good as in his inferior works he has something in common with the great 'lowbrow' best-sellers: the vitality which they have and the 'middlebrow' novelists have not, though the best-sellers are coarse where Lawrence is sensitive and spiritual. He can use a vocabulary perilously like theirs in which to register his sharpest intuitions into modern civilized life, and allow himself confident generalizations about racial, philosophical, and sexual matters which have a tone and ring uneasily reminiscent of the intellectual underworld of 'British Israel', Count Keyserling, or Max Nordau. This is a pity, because it nourishes the various animosities which ordinary vulgar snobbery, prudery, philistinism, or Bloomsbury superciliousness already have towards Lawrence on other grounds.

But it is now becoming common to praise the directness and vitality of Lawrence's style in general. What seems still an open question, even among his admirers, is whether he succeeded in expressing his full powers in self-sufficient works of art. It is well known that Lawrence rejected the traditional canons of structure and method in the novel. He wanted Arnold Bennett (the 'old imitator') to be told that the principles Bennett invoked held good only for novels that were 'copies' of other novels, and he spoke in exasperation about the 'ossiferous skin-and-grief' form which others wanted to impose on him. Some of what Lawrence said on this subject can be dismissed as mere special pleading. A judicious admirer of Lawrence will not cite *Aaron's Rod* or *Kangaroo* as triumphs of originality of form. They are meandering, repetitious, padded-out. Lawrence, especially in his later years, wrote too much and wrote it too quickly. Nor can the artistic objection to a great part of his work be regarded only as a misguided application of the Flaubertian principles which he rejected. Lawrence allows himself liberties, in what purport to be works of fiction – works of imagination – which are incompatible with the practice of any art, not merely the art of Flaubert. He openly abandons the pretence of dramatic objectivity and admits that this or that character is a mere mouthpiece. He addresses the reader directly, to explain, emphasize, or preach. He permits details from his personal life, not fully coherent with the presented fiction, to get into the book. It is unnecessary to elaborate these faults. Much can be urged in mitigation: the circumstances of Lawrence's life as a professional writer, the treatment meted out to the novels on which he *did* work hard, the growing urgency of his feeling (hence the overwrought, violent, didactic tone so frequent in those later books) about the decadence of modern civilized life. But faults are faults. If Lawrence is to be defended as an original artist of the novel, it will not be on the strength of *Aaron's Rod* or *Kangaroo*. Each has the makings of a good novel: but these are lost in a wilderness of preaching, autobiography, and journalism.

Nor will *The Plumed Serpent* or *Lady Chatterley's Lover* serve to substantiate the artistic claim for Lawrence. These he certainly worked hard on, especially the latter. They are different from one another, and their didactic messages differ. But they have this in common, that the writer is concerned with a single-minded intentness to 'put over' those didactic messages. Certainly his own maxim (in *Studies in Classic American Literature*, 1923) 'Never trust the artist. Trust the tale' applies to those two books. The tale can get the better of the artist. The fantasy-revival of the old Mexican paganism in the one, and the insistent sexual outspokenness in the other, do not make up the whole interest of *The Plumed Serpent* and *Lady Chatterley*. The fables themselves, in important points, do not serve the unequivocal purpose they were meant to serve. *The Plumed Serpent* in places can impress and move the reader who is most convinced that Lawrence's aim in this book was tragically mistaken and perverse – as well as being somewhat absurd. *Lady Chatterley's Lover* can inspire a sympathy with Clifford which was probably not intended, but can be genuinely grounded in what the story tells us. But neither book can be 'lived in': that is, neither book creates an imagined domain in which the reader simply finds himself, and finds *for* himself the moral bearings of the world which the artist has imagined; a world which we are not just told about, but which seems to exist in itself and be discovered by us. In these books, as in other stories of Lawrence, the poles of truth and falsity, good and evil, sickness and health are imposed by the direct moral intervention of the author. The books cohere as wholes and make sense (morally speaking) only if looked at from a point of view already predisposed to accept the author's ideas. Too much of what seems to come out of genuine experience has passed through the moralist's filter. The high proportion in these books of merely sketched, diagrammatic characters is significant.

Now it is easy to show – from explicit remarks of Lawrence's in the novels, as well as in his criticism and in letters and so on – that in this didacticism Lawrence was going against his own proclaimed principles. What is harder to make out is just what *positively* those principles come to: just what is the formal character of the works that do come more or less completely out of 'pure passionate experience'. Some may think that *Sons and Lovers* is the text to choose in order to discover this. It is rightly one of the best known and most popular of Lawrence's books. But much that is essential to the study of Lawrence would be missed if we took that novel as fully representative. It is certainly the easiest to understand, being the only one of his first-rate books which is like an ordinary novel. Though much of it takes on a fuller significance when we know the rest of Lawrence's life and work, it is self-sufficient and undoubtedly the novel that a reader ignorant of him should begin with. Furthermore, the life-choices that the hero, Paul, makes in *Sons and Lovers* show their consequences in Lawrence's later work. Some have thought that in Paul's failure to see through his mother's pathetically false values, and in the cruelty, due to his mother's thwarting of his development, shown in his attitude to his father and later in his treatment of Miriam, we discover Lawrence himself taking the wrong turning. But however this may be, Paul's choices are self-explanatory within the book itself. If in some respects it seems to be a confessional work, the power of the literary artist is shown in the objectivity with which the confession is treated. Yet *Sons and Lovers* is the work of a potential rather than an actual genius. Its great superiority over Lawrence's previous novels – *The White Peacock* (1911) and *The Trespasser* (1912) – lies in its freedom from literariness. They are over-written: the directness and naturalness of *Sons and Lovers* mark the great *literary* evolution which is the result of Lawrence's decision (encouraged by 'Miriam') to deal directly with urgent personal matter. But by reason of its very merits it cannot be a triumph of imagination. There is little in the book to make us feel that the author's future strength would lie in the imagining of characters and themes outside his immediate personal situation. In this respect it shows no clear anticipation of the best parts of *The Rainbow*.

It is *The Rainbow*, together with *Women in Love* (1920) and the best of the tales, on which F. R. Leavis, in his study of Lawrence, has chosen to lay the main stress. And whether or not we can go all or most of the way with Leavis in what he says about Lawrence in general, I am sure his selection here is right. And out of this selection *Women in Love* seems a suitable particular choice to illustrate Lawrence's mature art. Lawrence seems to have thought it, together with *The Rainbow*, his greatest work – though in later years his preoccupation with the Chatterley book may have caused him to alter his judgement. Leavis, having given good reasons for treating it (despite the carry-over of names of characters) as a separate work from *The Rainbow*, ranks it above the earlier novel. Whether this is so or not, it seems clear that it is best considered as a separate work (though one initial problem that confronts the reader of *Women in Love*, the uncertainty about the social status of the two girls Ursula and Gudrun whom he meets in the first chapter, is cleared up if we come to the later novel from the earlier). Perhaps it is a pity that Lawrence did not change the names of the characters who are carried over when he separated out the two works from the originally envisaged single novel of *The Sisters*. The Ursula of *Women in Love* is not like the Ursula of *The Rainbow*. To simplify for the moment, Ursula of *The Rainbow*, though quite convincingly dramatized and a girl, lives mainly out of the experience of the young Lawrence himself. The Ursula of *Women in Love* has much more in her of Lawrence's wife Frieda. Any effort by the reader to fuse the two Ursulas in his reading of *Women in Love* would lead to difficulties. It is true that the later part of *The Rainbow* – what bears on the failure of the affair between Ursula and Skrebensky – contains germinally some of the substance of *Women in Love*. But the connection is thematic, rather than narrative. *Women in Love* is thus best treated separately.

There are two reasons for choosing it, rather than its predecessor, for discussion. First, the cyclical, repetitive method of *The Rainbow* is not hard to grasp, once it is seen for what it is. The book contains patches of local obscurity (as often with Lawrence, the love-scenes are obscure), but it has not on the whole been found so radically puzzling as *Women in Love*. But above all *Women in Love* is the more 'modern' of the two, the one in which Lawrence is more concerned with what we recognize as contemporary life. There is something of a pastoral, idealizing, idyllic quality about *The Rainbow* – at any rate, in the earlier part, before the advent of 'modern' life in the story of the childhood and youth of the girl Ursula. That earlier part has a certain epic spaciousness which is unlike anything else in Lawrence. *The Rainbow* compares with *Women in Love*, in this respect, as *War and Peace* does with *Anna Karenina*. Its idyllic quality is beautiful. But that quality is only possible because of the background to the story, the older England which has gone for ever; it is the work of the Lawrence whom Leavis can see as the successor to the George Eliot of *The Mill on the Floss*. *Women in Love*, then, is chosen here as the more complex, difficult, and 'modern' of the two novels of Lawrence's creative prime – not necessarily as the better.

'Difficult', however, is not the right word for the immediate impression *Women in Love* is likely to make on a reader who comes to it unprepared. John Middleton Murry's review in the *Nation and Athenaeum* (13 August 1921) gives an account of the shock and bewilderment such a reader is more likely to feel, and at the same time throws down a critical challenge which those who admire the book have in some way to meet. He calls *Women in Love* 'five hundred pages of passionate vehemence, wave after wave of turgid, exasperated writing'. He speaks of an 'underworld whose inhabitants are known by this alone, that they writhe continually, like the damned, in a frenzy of sexual awareness of one another'. 'Their creator,' says Murry, 'believes that he can distinguish the writhing of one from the writhing of another; he spends pages and pages in describing the contortions of the first, the second, the third, and the fourth. To him they are utterly and profoundly different; to us they are all the same.' The core of Murry's complaint is that he cannot make out what the book is about, 'the experience x', as he calls it, which takes place between Birkin and Ursula. He can see no difference between it and 'the experience y', which takes place between Gerald and Gudrun. 'Yet x leads one pair to undreamed-of happiness, and y conducts the other to murder and suicide.'

What is *Women in Love* about? It is natural (though not, I think, best) to set about answering this question by beginning at the beginning of the novel, with the conversation between the two sisters, Ursula and Gudrun Brangwen. This opening scene impressively illustrates Lawrence's power of suggesting undercurrents of feeling and atmosphere: in this case the suppressed sexual tension and, more dimly in the background, the social unease of the girls – yet all is done dramatically, through the conversation, picking up and fading out in an apparently casual, natural way. Their conversation is about marriage; and there presently follows a description of a wedding at which the two are present, and during which we are introduced to most of the principal characters of the novel. All this is simply but adroitly done, and as the book gets going we are ready to assume that it is to be about marriage, and the varying attitudes of the two girls (who are already contrasted) to men in marriage. We are thus tempted to regard the girls as central characters. And indeed Gudrun's attitude to Gerald Crich in this chapter, the nature of her attraction to him, does point forward to what their relationship is to become. But it soon becomes clear that the organizing principle of the novel is not to be found in the difference between the two girls nor in the theme of marriage. True, we are given to understand at the end that Ursula, the more sympathetic of the two girls, does marry Birkin. But this marriage has no climactic effect. If, then, we begin our analysis of *Women in Love* from what seems the natural starting-point, we soon get into difficulties, such as have made less analytically minded readers in the past give up the book in exasperation.

It seems to me, then, that the structure – and hence the total meaning – of the book is better understood not by beginning at the natural starting-point suggested by the book's title and the first chapter, but by beginning at what might be called the logical starting-point, which is Birkin. This is not to assume that as an actual fact of composition Lawrence himself began here – though it seems significant that in an early draft of *Women in Love* the book did begin with Birkin's meeting with Gerald on holiday on the Continent. All that is claimed is that the effective structure of the book is more clearly revealed by taking Birkin to be the principal centre of interest. It may well turn out – indeed in my view it does – that Birkin does not in the end have quite the kind of central and standard-supplying role in the book which Lawrence may have intended. But he is, after all, virtually a self-portrait of Lawrence, and as such he carries whatever weight of doctrine about the relations of men and women is to be found in the novel. And it will be seen that all the other principal characters and themes of the book are in a sense causally dependent on the conception of Birkin.

Though modelled on the author, Birkin is definitely a character *in* the book and not overshadowing it. He is exasperating and touching, protean, sometimes unpleasant, sometimes likeable, in a credible way. If his peculiarities are Lawrence's own, they are presented by Lawrence quite objectively. It is not even clear that when Birkin and Ursula are in conflict the reader's sympathy is automatically presupposed to be with Birkin. This objectivity is comparatively rare in Lawrence. The passage in chapter XIX, in which the two sisters discuss Birkin, suggests how this effect is obtained:

'Of course,' she [Gudrun] said easily, 'there is a quality of life in Birkin which is quite remarkable. There is an extraordinary rich spring of life in him, really amazing, the way he can give himself to things. But there are so many things in life that he simply doesn't know. Either he is not aware of their existence at all, or he dismisses them as merely negligible – things which are vital to the other person. In a way he is not clever enough, he is too intense in spots.'

'Yes,' cried Ursula, 'too much of a preacher. He is really a priest.'

'Exactly! He can't hear what anybody else has to say – he simply cannot hear. His own voice is too loud.'

'Yes. He cries you down.'

367

'He cries you down,' repeated Gudrun. 'And by mere force of violence. And of course it is hopeless. Nobody is convinced by violence. It makes talking to him impossible – and living with him I should think would be more than impossible.'

'You don't think one could live with him?' asked Ursula.

'I should think it would be too wearing, too exhausting. One would be shouted down every time, and rushed into his way without any choice. He would want to control you entirely. He cannot allow that there is any other mind but his own. And then the real clumsiness of his mind is its lack of self-criticism. No, I think it would be perfectly intolerable.'

Ursula 'assents vaguely' to this, but she 'only half agrees', and presently she feels a 'revulsion from Gudrun'.

She finished life off so thoroughly, she made things so ugly and so final. As a matter of fact, even if it were as Gudrun said, about Birkin, other things were true as well. But Gudrun would draw out two lines under him and cross him out like an account that is settled. There he was, summed up, paid for, settled, done with. And it was such a lie. This finality of Gudrun's, this dispatching of people and things in a sentence, was such a lie.

It is a measure of the success in the presentation of Birkin that we are made both to feel the applicability of what Gudrun says and the understandableness of Ursula's reaction to it. We see him often as Ursula does in chapter XI, where we hear of

... this duality of feeling which he created in her ... his wonderful life-rapidity, the rare quality of an utterly desirable man: and there was at the same time this ridiculous, mean effacement into a Salvator Mundi and a Sunday-school teacher, a prig of the stiffest type.

In this treatment of his self-dramatization Lawrence shows himself one of the great realists of literature. Not that he is always convincing in his treatment of material facts, settings, and milieux: anyone who has read much of Lawrence will know that that is not so. But when he is at his best he can give expression in the most effective way – in the dramatic treatment of character – to the refutation of that 'finality' which Ursula here imputes to Gudrun: the moralist's wish for the ultimate and definitive 'placing' of live human creatures in their life and growth, in relation to some static and preconceived notion of purpose and value. And correspondingly the novelist's positive achievement is the communication of a sense of life as it is lived, not merely in the day-by-day or moment-by-moment fluctuations of perception and emotion, but in the shifts of judgement and attitude which are inevitable in any live human relationship. The result is that we are involved in the experiences described in a fuller way than as mere spectators, because we are made to feel that it is continuous with ours. Sometimes, indeed, the involvement is too great, as in the quarrels between Mr and Mrs Morel in *Sons and Lovers*, or Birkin's obscure battles with Ursula in this novel; the 'frame' of the book is broken and we are drawn into the quarrel as if it were real life, forced to take sides, to want to intervene. This is a serious fault in the art, but it shows the strength of Lawrence's conceptions: a strength which in his best work is surprisingly compatible with the 'distancing' that good art requires. But this compatibility would not be possible without the dual nature of the character Birkin. Lawrence is personally involved with him but – in the best passages anyway – without this interfering with our sense of Birkin as a dramatic character, open to objections which are forcibly put, either by himself or by the tenacious Ursula.

Birkin, then, is a spokesman for Lawrence's changing moods. He is also, just credibly, a school-inspector; this enables Lawrence both to give some trace of plausibility to the restless wandering which seems to characterize his form of life, and to put him in touch with Ursula in her fictional capacity as a school-mistress. But he is above all the opportunity for Lawrence to imagine an experiment in life. Birkin is a man of religious temperament who cannot believe in the God of Christianity, or in any formal religion. He feels a revulsion from the mechanized wilderness of the modern world, the loss of supernatural sanctions, the disappearance of clear significance and purpose in living from every class of society. This revulsion is accompanied by a deep repugnance for the whole social structure of England. Birkin has no clear positive idea of just what he wants changed, and what he wants to put in its place. This no doubt deprives his jeremiads of any definite significance; but it does not invalidate them as expressions of his state of soul. He evinces the same passionate dislike of the bourgeoisie among whom he lives (with Bohemian intervals) as the clever cultivated Gudrun does for the working-class life in which she has grown up and from which she has broken away. The book ends, as Lawrence's stories so often do (*The Fox*, *The Daughters of the Vicar*, and others), with the 'fugue', the flight abroad of the Lawrence-character with the woman he loves, into a social void. But although Birkin can find no general practical cure for the social disease that disgusts him, he seeks for a personal way of salvation for himself. He wants to try to live by a religion of love. This 'love' is not to be interpreted in a romantic or Christian sense. It is to be a relationship between 'fulfilled' individuals, who remain individuals (Birkin shrinks in horror from the idea of any kind of 'merging', loss of individuality in the union of love) but who each achieve through the other some contact with a hitherto unknown, non-human, and trans-human power. One lover is to be the 'door' of the other to this unknown power, the life-source to which Christianity (as Birkin–Lawrence understands it), and still more modern humanitarianism and democracy, have no access.

The Birkin theme is thus mainly concerned with his choice of Ursula as the woman with whom he is to try this 'way of freedom' in love, and to whom he preaches – against her understandable resistance – a curious doctrine of sexual *Apartheid* that goes with it. His failure with another woman, Hermione, which we learn about early in the novel, and the consequent embarrassing, embittered, and prolonged epilogue to their love-affair, represent the wrong kind of relationship between a man and a woman. Birkin has to escape from this. He has also to escape from an inner temptation which he feels very strongly towards a cult of purely sensual, 'mindless' experience evoked in the novel by a West African statuette which is introduced, with effective dramatic symbolism, in the chapter called 'Totem'. Here, of course, we have an instance of Lawrence's famous primitivism. But we note that in the book it is a temptation which Birkin sees as such. That sensual mindlessness, which he calls the 'African way', is a sort of barbaric equivalent to the sentimental Western idea of love which he feels to be decadent: but it too he supposes to be a product of decadence. But Birkin also thinks he must educate Ursula out of the sentimental and romantic love-ideal which she wants to impose on their relationship. He senses behind it that devouring and essentially egocentric maternal possessiveness which readers of Lawrence will not be surprised to learn that he regards as the enemy of human life and growth. It is this would-be 'education' of Ursula which makes up the main positive part of the Birkin theme.

This purpose of Birkin's can be taken as the logical starting-point of the novel. We have it foreshadowed in chapter v, in a conversation between Birkin and his friend Gerald Crich, in which Birkin asks Gerald the characteristically Laurentian question: 'What do you think is the aim and object of your life?' It is a characteristic question, because it demands, and permits, only a certain kind of answer, the kind that is suggested when Birkin says presently: 'I find that one needs some one *really* pure single activity.' It is also characteristic because it seems to be as much a question asked of himself as of Gerald. Gerald finds some difficulty in answering, and finally admits that he has no answer to it, or to the equivalent question: 'Wherein does life centre for you?' 'It doesn't centre at all. It is artificially held *together* by the social mechanism', is what he eventually has to say. Birkin agrees, but presses his view that 'there remains only this perfect union with a woman – sort of ultimate marriage – and there isn't anything else'. Gerald's rejection of this idea of 'ultimate marriage', a rejection which expresses his essential nature, and the psychological consequences of that rejection, underlie the extended story of his relations with *his* chosen woman right down to its disastrous close, his extinction in an inhuman world of snow and ice.

The Gerald theme is thus both complementary and contrasting to the Birkin theme. It is so much easier to work out analytically, after reading the book, that to some readers it seems to be the main 'story' in *Women in Love*. But this is not its place in the intended structure of the work. The two men, Gerald and Birkin, show a kind of contrast which is familiar to all readers of Lawrence. No subject does he write about more, whether well or badly, in his fiction. It is a contrast easier to illustrate than describe: the contrast between what is meant to be represented, in their different ways, by the game-keeper in *Lady Chatterley*, by Count Dionys in *The Ladybird*, or by Alexander Hepburn in *The Captain's Doll*, and on the other hand by Sir Clifford Chatterley, by Rico in *St Mawr*, or by the Bricknells in *Aaron's Rod*. One says 'meant to be represented', because sometimes confusions and contradictions vitiate Lawrence's handling of it. But in its outlines the nature of the contrast is clear: that between the man who has the right kind of human naturalness, showing itself in a play of emotional spontaneity and mobility and a capacity for tenderness – a man whose form of life grows from that 'life-centre' without which Lawrence thought modern living was mere auto-matism; and the man who lets 'will-power', 'personality', and 'ideals',

in the strongly derogatory sense Lawrence gives to such words, interfere with his proper relation to other men and women and the
universe, and who thus lacks the emotional depth and the capacity for
sincere relationships and tenderness which for Lawrence were the
evidence of a connection with some power above and beyond the
individual. In his various novels and tales Lawrence sees people's
superficially different or unconnected characteristics – such as ex-
ecutive or intellectual domineering, sentimentality, aestheticism,
flirtatiousness, smart flippancy – as all symptoms of living at too
shallow a level, excessive 'consciousness' (as Lawrence likes to call
it) drawing its perverse power from thwarted and misdirected
emotional forces. He is apt to weight the scales against such people
by representing them as sexual failures, but it is clear that this is only
the sign or symbol of a more general failure. And Lawrence in his
later years came with an increasing bitterness to see people of Gerald's
Weltanschauung as the real rulers of the modern world.

Now we may argue that Lawrence's sense of proportion, and at
times his sense of reality, desert him in some of his treatments of
this theme. Rico and Sir Clifford Chatterley, for example, are too
slight characters to bear the symbolic weight which their part in the
chosen fable imposes on them. Worse than that, many of them, like
Rico (though unlike Sir Clifford), are badly drawn, unconvincing,
and presented with such obvious animosity as to invalidate their
functioning as art. But one of the notable things about *Women in
Love* is that the treatment of the Gerald theme is wholly convincing;
Gerald as a character does really enact the symbolic role which he
is assigned. He is done from within as almost no other characters
of this kind are done in Lawrence: Lawrence *is* Gerald in important
ways, and this identification is reflected in the strong and deep relation
that there is in the book between Birkin and Gerald, who are close
friends, ambivalent, intermittent, and obscure as the presentment of
their friendship is in chapters like 'Man to Man' and 'Gladiatorial'.
Lawrence is not weighting the scales this time; as a result he realizes
much more fully the potentialities of the Gerald theme.

So thoroughly, indeed, is the Gerald theme worked out that
F. R. Leavis is able to base on it the greater part of his account of
Women in Love. Once the intention behind the creation of Gerald
is grasped his drama is felt to unfold itself convincingly. Gerald's

strength is a mechanical strength, a strength of 'will-power' and 'ideals'. He has not the inner reserves to meet the mounting crisis of his life, and the strain in him is felt like the tighter and tighter winding-up of a mechanical toy which at last flies loose and bounds away to its final destruction. It is worth noting that Gerald's realistic status in the novel, as an efficient colliery owner, does not (whatever Lawrence may have intended) derive its validity from any faithfulness to social history. The judgement on Gerald would still be valid even if there were in fact no general correlation between the qualities needed for success in industry and the particular *malaise* of which he is the victim. The point of making him an industrial tycoon is symbolic: he is a man who makes the machine his god, and it is a god that fails.

Yet Gerald himself is not a machine, but a human being, and by no means an unsympathetic one. Lawrence gives a pretty full account of his previous life and his background – his father, his mother with her significant 'queerness', due to the ruining of her life by her husband's 'idealism', the childhood in which he accidentally killed his brother. When he grows up his knowledge of his father's inefficient paternalism as 'industrial magnate' spurs him on to improve on and supersede his father. He makes himself efficient and ruthless, and though the colliers hate him they respect him as they did not respect his father, because even if he despises them and they know it, they are slaves themselves to the 'values' which he seems so successfully to embody. But his strength is not true strength. He has limitations. The machine fails him already in the 'Water-Party' chapter, where he 'assumed responsibility for the amusements on the water' – lest this 'responsibility' for what happens, the drowning of his sister, should seem too tenuous, the point is driven home by the failure of his attempt at rescue. And ironically this cruel expression of his limitations comes just at the moment when he has been able to achieve one of the rare moments of 'apartness' and peace with the woman he loves. It is not Lawrence's purpose to show that strength and tenderness are incompatible. On the contrary, it is Gerald's inner weakness which is the corollary of his incapacity for true love. The slow disintegration and death of his father brings sickeningly home to him the void in his life which 'will-power' is powerless to fill. He turns in his need to the woman, Gudrun. But it is part of the dialectic of their relationship – their similar incapacity for true love – that this need should call out in Gudrun the mocking, destructive, malicious side of her nature. This has throughout been shown as a possible development in Gudrun, and it is one of the ways in which the two sisters are shown as different types of woman. The dramatic consequences of the conflict between the lovers are worked out in the long chapter called 'Snowed Up'. The final death of Gerald in the snow is only the symbolic expression of the inexorable consequence of his life-defeating idealism. Lawrence often uses the contrast of warmth and cold in a symbolic way: human warmth is a spiritual reviving-power in stories like *The Horse-Dealer's Daughter* or *The Virgin and the Gipsy*. Here the intense cold is the symbol of spiritual death.

Everything in *Women in Love* that bears on this theme is finely organized. And it is noteworthy that, although the drama of Gerald and Gudrun mostly happens on an esoteric plane, most of it is made to happen also on a plane where the ordinary criteria for successful fiction can be employed. In spite of some avant-garde critics, a general credibility of characters and setting is necessary for successful fiction. 'People don't do such things' remains a valid adverse criticism of a novel. Now, once the total structure of *Women in Love* has been understood – and it is this on the whole that has been found difficult – the characters do affect us as belonging to a life we know, and behaving in keeping with it (given a certain amount of poetic licence in the presentation of the social setting).

This keeping in touch with ordinary reality is a remarkable achievement. It broadens the scope of the novel. It enables Lawrence to introduce, quite naturally, characters like Gerald's father and mother – indeed the whole of the Crich family – who are very relevant to the Gerald theme, and yet are given the kind of dramatic presence, natural dialogue, and ordinary credibility which the novel-reader expects. Some of them may be 'odd', but they are odd as people in real life are odd. Lawrence takes similar opportunities in depicting Birkin's relation to Hermione. Much of this is on an esoteric level, half-conscious swirls of emotion, since Hermione is a sort of feminine counterpart of Gerald, in her blend of domineering will-power and inner weakness, just as her need for Birkin, which he knows he cannot meet, is a counterpart of Gerald's need for Gudrun.

Yet Hermione is vividly depicted as a picturesque serio-comic character, and her house-party makes the appropriate occasion for Lawrence
to bring in some satire both on the 'Establishment' of the day and
the sophisticated radical intelligentsia he had encountered in such
quarters (he takes the chance to pay off an old score against Bertrand
Russell). Even the chapters describing artistic Bohemian life, though
their relevance is less obvious, have a function in making the
Bohemian side of Birkin's and Gerald's life more real, and in one
place at least – the night Gerald spends with Halliday's mistress –
their bearing on the Gerald theme is important, as illustrating the
superficiality of Gerald's attitude to sex. And there is no need to
emphasize the functional importance of minor characters like the
artist Loerke, who plays his part in the climax of Gerald's tragedy.
Thus *Women in Love* has a structure which arises naturally from
Lawrence's firm grasp of his dual theme. The filling-up and population of the book seems thereby also to be accomplished with inevitability and naturalness.

Women in Love, then, does seem in part to justify the unusualness
of its formal conception: a novel whose 'plot', if it is to be so called,
does not answer to the usual account of 'character in action'. There
is development, but it is at a deeper level than that of 'personality'.
If the whole book had a convincingness equal to what we find in
the treatment of the Gerald theme, it could be judged an assured
artistic success. But it suffers from a grave central weakness. The
book's strong pattern derives from the contrast between the
destinies of the two couples, and the subsidiary, though important,
masculine relationship between Birkin and Gerald. (We may compare the strong pattern given to *Anna Karenina* by Tolstoy's use of
the three marriages of Anna, Dolly, and Kitty, the 'unhappy,' the
'ordinary', and the 'happy' marriages respectively.) But what is the
significance of this pattern in expressing the intended total meaning
of *Women in Love*? Leavis would have us believe that the Birkin–
Ursula relationship sets up a standard – or at least moves towards
a standard – from which the Gerald–Gudrun experience is a devi-
ation. But do we feel this in reading the novel? Surely what we feel
in reading the novel is that Birkin too is a sick and tortured man,
who does not (except at a few ideal moments which give rise to some
of the worst writing in the book) achieve with Ursula the kind of

fulfilment which he has made his *raison d'être*. Perhaps if Lawrence had conveyed the positive quality of those moments – as distinct from the mere feeling of repose and relief after fighting and tension, which as always he conveys wonderfully – our sense of Birkin's 'normative' standing in the novel would have been induced. But as it is, those ideal moments – as in Chapter XXIII, 'Excurse' – are among the weaknesses of the book. Lawrence expresses the ineffable no better here by his obscure, repetitious, periphrastic style than he does in the notoriously direct passages of *Lady Chatterley's Lover*. And if it is urged that, given the nature of the experience in question, those portentous wordinesses are all he could do, that is enough to prove the enterprise mistaken.

But this is not the most radical question. To understand Birkin fully we must understand the state of mind of the Lawrence who wrote of him. It is true that *Women in Love*, as part of *The Sisters*, was presumably conceived before the horror of the war-years had closed down on Lawrence: conceived during the happy interval between the break with 'Miriam' and the coming of the war. But it is hard not to see in Birkin the Lawrence of 1916, amid the penury and misery of his life in Cornwall, and in his mind always the horror of the war and the nightmare of suspicion and persecution. How else can we explain Birkin's hatred of human life? 'Mankind is a dead tree, covered with fine brilliant galls of people', he says, and there is much in the same strain. But this is a defect in a work of imagination. Birkin's hatred is not clearly accounted for in particular terms. It remains in the book just a *donnée*, an idiosyncrasy, which is so strongly rendered that it seriously limits Birkin's value as a representative of the normal man. No doubt it is unfair to attack *Women in Love* on the ground that Birkin himself is obviously not a normal man. Some imaginative licence must be granted in the presentation of this experiment in love: for the character who thinks of making it to be at all convincing, he would have to be rather unusual. But it is clear that Lawrence intended Birkin to be searching for, and perhaps eventually reaching, conclusions about the relations of men and women in marriage which *could* be held to be valid for normal men.

This suggests a more serious criticism. For we cannot ignore Birkin's own sense of his failure. After all, the last chapter, in which Birkin gazes down at the dead Gerald, is a final taking-up of the issues first proposed between them in the chapter called 'In the Train'. Birkin has come to realize that his ideal of 'ultimate marriage' was not sufficient. It needed completion by the male relationship with Gerald. But this too has failed. What makes Gerald's death tragic – and there is an unmistakable note of tragedy in Birkin's thoughts as he turns away – is not the death itself (Gerald is not a figure of tragic stature) but its effect on Birkin. And the whole effect of the book – though Birkin even at the end will not directly admit this to Ursula – is to show that the kind of love he wanted is illusory. And to say this is not to bring extrinsic standards to bear on a work of imagination. It is what the work itself seems to say: pointing a moral of its own, which is not the author's.

THE CONSISTENCY OF JAMES JOYCE

ARNOLD KETTLE

James Joyce was no flincher. There is a consistency about his life and development as a writer, a coherence and a completeness which has the sort of aesthetic rightness at which he aimed with such single- and multi-mindedness in his work.

From the writing of the first stories of *Dubliners* (1914) to the moment when, the extraordinary work at last complete, its progress rounded off with an unending sentence, he announced the title of *Finnegans Wake* (1939), he seems to have known precisely what he was doing. If there is a false start amidst his oeuvre, a cul-de-sac leading off the Vico road, it is the two volumes of lyric poetry. Looking back at the total achievement these do seem, with their reliance on a less radical use of language, to do him less than justice. If it is as a poet that he is to be remembered it is not by this kind of poetry.

Everywhere else – in *Dubliners, A Portrait of the Artist* (1916), even *Exiles* (1918), as well as *Ulysses* (1922) and *Finnegans Wake* – the organization of words and the final effect of the whole has the stamp and intensity of a supreme effort to achieve a newly creative use of language. *Stephen Hero* (published posthumously, 1944) has not this quality to anything like the same degree, though it has plenty of interest of another sort.

From *Stephen Hero* we get, explicitly, the theory of epiphanies:

... By an epiphany he meant a sudden spiritual manifestation, whether in the vulgarity of speech or of gesture or in a memorable phase of the mind itself. He believed that it was for the man of letters to record these epiphanies with extreme care, seeing that they themselves are the most delicate and evanescent of moments. He told Cranly that the clock of the Ballast Office was capable of an epiphany. Cranly questioned the inscrutable dial of the Ballast Office with his no less inscrutable countenance.

'Yes,' said Stephen. 'I will pass it time after time, allude to it, refer to it, catch a glimpse of it. It is only an item in the catalogue of Dublin's street furniture. Then all at once I see it and I know at once what it is: epiphany.'

'What?'

'Imagine my glimpses at that clock as the gropings of a spiritual eye which seeks to adjust its vision to an exact focus. The moment the focus is reached the object is epiphanised. It is just in this epiphany I find the third, the supreme quality of beauty.'

'Yes?' said Cranly absently.[1]

I do not think Joyce ever again expressed more clearly in analytical terms what he was after. This passage and the whole, more highly-wrought discussion on aesthetics in *A Portrait of the Artist* is worth reading in conjunction with Virgina Woolf's well-known essays on modern fiction and worth considering too in relation to the aims and achievements of contemporary French painting. Joyce is a far bigger figure than Virginia Woolf – his work bristles with an intellectual and moral toughness which hers only achieves at its very best – and it is perhaps the measure of his superiority as a writer that his concern with literary creativity should exercise itself in verbal and intellectual rather than visual or descriptive terms. Even if his emphasis on the word was to be, in the end, destructive, it was also his incomparable strength.

It is right at this point to emphasize also the importance of the theory expounded by Stephen of 'esthetic stasis':

An esthetic image is presented to us either in space or in time. What is audible is presented in time, what is visible is presented in space. But, temporal or spatial, the esthetic image is first luminously apprehended as self-bounded and self-contained upon the immeasurable background of the space and time which is not it. You apprehend it as *one* thing. You see it as one whole. You apprehend its wholeness. That is *integritas* ...

... The radiance of which [Aquinas] speaks is the scholastic *quidditas*, the whatness of a thing. This supreme quality is felt by the artist when the esthetic image is first conceived in his imagination. The mind in that mysterious instant Shelley likened beautifully to a fading coal. The instant wherein that supreme quality of beauty, the clear radiance of the esthetic image, is apprehended luminously by the mind which has been arrested by its wholeness and fascinated by its harmony is the luminous silent stasis of esthetic pleasure, a spiritual state very like to that cardiac condition which the Italian physiologist Luigi Galvani, using a phrase almost as beautiful as Shelley's, called the enchantment of the heart.[2]

Stephen goes on, incidentally, to develop a theory of the depersonalization of the artist which reminds us that T. S. Eliot's was not, in

1917, a lone voice. But what is particularly interesting is, first, the remarkable emotional force which in their context in the *Portrait* these apparently abstract passages have – they are part and parcel of Stephen's own life-adventure – and, secondly, their connection with the famous climax of the book in which Stephen, having uttered his devil's vow of 'non serviam' and rejected utterly the claims of church and state, sets forth upon his life of silence, exile, and cunning to encounter 'the reality of experience and to forge in the smithy of my soul the uncreated conscience of my race'.

The contradiction so powerfully expressed at the conclusion of *A Portrait of the Artist* is embedded deep in the whole of Joyce's life and achievement. He leaves Dublin in 1904, to return to the city endlessly in every page he writes. As Sydney Bolt has put it:

> It was the Irish, rather than the English, whose oppression he fled from. The struggle for Irish independence did not, of course, leave him unmoved. He held decided views on the major issues involved, and even after his departure continued to follow political developments with interest in the nationalist press. But his conception of national enslavement was deeper and subtler than that of the patriots. He believed that the condition of slavery had produced a slavish mentality in Ireland.[3]

It is the writer whose work gives so deep an impression of self-sufficiency who developed a style – if that is the right word – more cosmopolitan than any in modern literature.

Ulysses begins straightforwardly enough. No one has evoked more richly and movingly the awakening hours of a city and its people. These wonderful pages – the Telemachaia – which act as lead-in to the epic of Bloomsday and as a bridge between *A Portrait of the Artist* and Joyce's later work combine also the Chekhovian realism of *Dubliners*, the passionate intellectual argumentation of the *Portrait*, and the techniques of complex leitmotiv and verbal association upon which Joyce was more and more to concentrate. They form therefore a remarkably convenient starting-point for the would-be initiate and one which requires the minimum of outside support. The reader need not know or worry that Stephen is to be Telemachus; he will grasp soon enough what is at this stage of the book far more important, that Stephen is his mother's son and that the mother, though she is one and unique, is also something more impersonal, Irish and

Catholic, and so linked – not just arbitrarily but in the complex inter-relations of life itself – with mother-figures more pervasive; and Stephen, though he is Stephen Dedalus, student and artist, mummer and pedant, is a little boy lost, partaking of the problems and nature of Hamlet and of Jesus, as well as of Parnell and Ulysses' son. Ireland-Island is also all islands, the sea all seas, and the key in Stephen's pocket has not just in the ordinary sense 'dramatic significance', like the pipe in Ibsen's *Ghosts*, but is a symbol of all keys, locking, unlocking ...

Ulysses can be approached from a whole number of directions. One of the best, as Richard Ellmann's fine biography indicates, is through an awareness of Joyce's own life.[4] The Homeric parallels, though too heavy weather can be made of them, are important. 'Homer is my example and his unchristened heart.' No less than Yeats and Pound, Joyce turned to epic and mythology as a release from the tyranny of abstract ideas. *Ulysses*, like *Joseph Andrews*, is a comic epic poem in prose, and the framework is no more arbitrary than that of Fielding or Cervantes. It is an epic with a difference and the difference is conveyed partially in the word comic, which Joyce in his later years would doubtless have found some means of linking verbally with cosmic.

Bloom's journey through a Dublin day is given form by being seen – with all rules broken – from behind Homer. But one should most certainly not conclude that Joyce's interest in his hero is there-fore schematic or second-hand. He does not just exist to prove some-thing, unless it is his creator's art. Frank Budgen, who saw Joyce frequently while *Ulysses* was being written and read passages as they were completed, relates that the author's first question, on getting back a section of the manuscript, almost always bore on the con-vincingness of Bloom as a 'character', not on the effectiveness or subtlety of the presentation or method which appeared to be his first concern in composition. Bloom was to be the first complete all-round character presented by any writer, an advance on Homer's Ulysses. And the extraordinary thing is that, in a sense, the ambition was fulfilled. 'He's a cultured all-round man, Bloom is.' With him, human manysidedness achieves a new level of literary expression. Which is not to say that he makes a more vivid or convincing impression than, say, Falstaff or Mr Boffin or Isabel Archer. What one can confidently say is that one knows more about Bloom than about these others.

Ulysses is at the same time a triumphant piece of 'realism' – a book about convincingly 'real' people in an actual city, presented with a regard for detail that would have made a French naturalist envious – and a microcosmic evocation of certain themes and patterns in human life as such. Thus Leopold Bloom, middle-aged, Jewish, kind, abused, unheroic is at the same time Ulysses the Wanderer, an archetypal Father searching for a Son, an Exile homing (the word is applied to a sailing ship entering Dublin Bay) in a hostile and yet not un-friendly world. In the conversation of medical students in a hospital where a woman is having a baby all human history – or at least chronology – is implied through a series of literary parodies. When Molly Bloom thinks of tomorrow's breakfast as she lies in bed the whole flux and continuity of life is involved.

The difference between the significance of theme and symbol in *Ulysses* and in, say, Dickens's *Bleak House* is worth emphasizing. The fog which shrouds *Bleak House* is often called, for want of a better word, symbolic. That is to say, it has a significance in the novel which is more than a part of the realistic description of London: it is bound up with and illuminates (in the way poetic images do) Dickens's vision of a whole society and the fog of Chancery is moral and mental as well as physical. Yet although this image of fog is so pervasive, so extraordinarily 'significant' in *Bleak House*, there is nothing mystical or metaphysical about Dickens's use of it, no impli-cation that the image is somehow or other touching the bounds of cosmic processes as such. One never feels the need to put a capital letter to the fog. But the father–son theme in *Ulysses*, for instance, like the theme of exile, has, in a subtle but essential sense, a quite different status. Between Bloom and Stephen, who do not meet until the last third of the book, late in the evening of Bloomsday, there is through-out the whole day a tenuous but insistent *rapport*, achieved by a sort of literary counterpoint, which is quite different from the sort of significance Dickens gets through his inter-connected images and subtly complicated plot. You cannot usefully compare the relation-ship of Esther and Lady Deadlock, even though they are in a very important sense searching for one another and are indeed daughter and mother, with the relationship of Bloom and Stephen. Nor does the word 'psychological', in its more workaday sense, help us much in defining this new significance which Joyce expresses. Bloom's need for a son is not to be thought of primarily in terms of an individual 'psychological' need.

Although Bloom's Odyssey is rightly to be seen as an epic of dis-integration, it is at the same time (before *Finnegans Wake*) the most consciously integrated book in history. The disintegration is – to make a division which can only be temporarily and perilously main-tained – in the content of the book, the integration is in the form. 'It is not my fault that the odour of ashpits and old weeds and offal hangs round my stories'[5] Joyce had written of *Dubliners*, sixteen years before the publication of *Ulysses*, and had referred to Dublin as 'the centre of paralysis'. In *Ulysses*, the odour remains: Bloom's first waking act is to collect offal from the butcher's; Stephen (and later Bloom) watches the writhing weeds lift languidly on the Dublin shore as he waits for his ash-plant to float away, the ash-plant (did it grow in an ashpit?) which is to be one of the key symbols in the climactic moments of the scene at Bella Cohen's. And the paralysis remains too, deep in the book. Harry Levin makes the point well:

Streets intersect, shops advertise, homes have party walls and fellow-citizens depend upon the same water supply; but there is no co-operation between human beings. The individual stands motionless, like Odysseus becalmed in the doldrums.[6]

In this crowded Dublin, at least as full of leitmotivs and symbolic phrases as it is of human beings, nothing is achieved but a series of epiphanies.[7] Things and people 'belong' only in the sense that they are there and willy-nilly mingle with one another. It is this that leads ultimately to the arbitrariness of Joyce's verbal associations, for as he goes on he becomes progressively less interested in words as sym-bols for real things and actions and more interested in the word as such. As Alick West pointed out in a very perceptive essay as long ago as 1937:

What Joyce spends most care on is the formal side, watching that a phrase used on one page has the right echoes with phrases used on fifty other pages. But this sovereign importance of the verbal phrase is in contradiction to the life of the book. For it implies that the fabric is stable, and that its surface can be decorated with the most subtle intricacy, like the Book of Kells ...

It assumes something as permanent as the church was for its monks. Yet Stephen and Bloom are both drawn as symbols of humanity in the eternal flux. On the other hand the sense of change in the book is so strong that this static formal declaration is felt to be a mechanism of defence against the change, and only valuable to Joyce as such defence. Joyce seems to play with the two styles of change and stability as he plays with his two chief characters. He plays with the contradictions; he does not resolve them. Where in Milton there is advancing movement, Joyce only shifts from one foot to the other, while he sinks deeper into the sand-flats.[8]

What is good about *Ulysses* is the enormous vitality and human insight, as opposed to mere virtuosity, of many of the parts, the poetic evocation of the city itself, the inter-relationships which Joyce's *leit-motivs* establish and illuminate often with a power as intellectually stimulating as it is sensuously haunting. What is unsatisfying about the book is perhaps best pinpointed by a word that almost everyone writing about Joyce finds himself coming back to: the word 'play'.

It is not an arbitrary word, for it takes one to the heart of Joyce's mystery, and it is a mystery in the old craft sense, with Joyce the artificer. If we call Joyce an aesthete (and I think we should) we must be conscious of just what the word implies for worse and for better. The better side is expressed in the joy and vigour and mastery of play, done beautifully and, more nearly than almost any activity, for its own sake. It would be naïve to imagine that Joyce, the admirer of Ibsen, believed that the activity of the artist ignored morality. When he wrote of forging the uncreated conscience of his race he meant what he said and knew as well as James or Conrad or Hamlet the ramifications of the word conscience. 'I believe that in composing my chapter of moral history in exactly the way I have composed it I have taken the first step towards the spiritual liberation of my country.'[9] But Joyce the liberator worked in his own way, the exile's way, through art, a conception of art not only above but also below and around all other struggles, as many-worded as many-sided, reaching for the kind of ultimate involved in the word he used about Bloom – all-round.

It is not by chance that *Ulysses* ends with Molly Bloom's half-awake reverie. The final chapter pushes to the furthest extent the 'stream of consciousness' method – the attempt to find a verbal equivalent for the inner thought-processes of a character. ('I try to give the unspoken, unacted thoughts of people in the way they occur.'[10])

Joyce's purpose in developing this method is primarily to enrich his objective evocation of a total situation by adding a new dimension, another side to the many-sidedness of complex life. This attempt, though it has often been associated historically with the development of psychology as a science, is no more 'scientific' than any other literary attempt to give the impression of reality. You cannot in the nature of things find a precise verbal equivalent for unformulated thoughts; the interior monologue may give the *impression* of an actual thought-track, but it cannot do more than that.

Joyce knew plenty about contemporary developments in psychiatric research. He knew what it was to be jung and easily freudened.[11] He did not live in Zürich for nothing. But while he *used* the material of modern psychology for his purposes (just as he used among much else a considerable knowledge of anthropology and scholastic philosophy and a life-long passion for vocal music), his aim was not that of the analyst, the scientist. And he was bound to run up against an outstanding difficulty: you cannot isolate the individual's consciousness from what is happening around and to him. Hence, throughout most of *Ulysses*, 'stream of consciousness' is mingled continuously and sometimes uneasily with 'objective' narrative and the description of outside fact.

In the final chapter 'stream of consciousness' finally comes into its own and for the simple reason that Molly Bloom is half-asleep. She is *doing* nothing and can therefore dispense with punctuation. Joyce, in this remarkable chapter, seems to have stumbled – not that one normally thinks of him as stumbling – on one ideal possibility in his constant battle against the fact of time and its implications. By concentrating on the moment of sleep he defeats his enemy; but it is at the cost of presenting consciousness not as an active apprehension of the present (and therefore involving the challenge of action and the possiblity of progress) but passively as a mode of recollection and impulse divorced from actual activity. The only affirmation that Molly Bloom is permitted is in fact the sort of affirmation associated with a principle rather than a person. Her yes, like Anna Livia's, is the yes of the Eternal Feminine, no more an act of volition than the journey of the river to the sea, without which life would stop altogether, a possibility which even Joyce does not seem seriously to contemplate.

Finnegans Wake follows *Ulysses* inevitably. If Bloom is an all-round character, *Finnegans Wake* is an all-round book. I think it is unrealistic not to recognize it as – for better or worse – Joyce's masterpiece and one of the great odd masterpieces of all literature. That it is 'difficult', more difficult than any novel ever written, cannot be denied; but most of the general theoretical rejections of it, because it is hard or queer or private, seem to be beside the point. The commonly expressed view that it is a 'private' book, in the sense of involving a rejection of the artist's obligation to communicate, is simply untrue. Whatever Joyce was up to he was not bogged down in the subjective theory of 'self-expression'. The language of *Finnegans Wake* is not a private language, it is a very extraordinary development of public language, involving a use of the resources of half a dozen different tongues, though fundamentally it is English, with the spoken (or sometimes sung) note of Dublin guiding its cadences. Every sentence, indeed every word, can be logically explained. It is true that for any one person to be in a position to give such an explanation is virtually impossible; and like some other truths this may properly be held to be a pity. It is also true that there is a kind of cosmic pedantry about Joyce's total achievement which is in the end perhaps its most vulnerable quality. I am not arguing that *Finnegans Wake* can be regarded as popular literature or is ever likely to be. I am arguing, however, that the book is not to be dismissed as a mere private eccentricity, a gigantic mistake, least of all the product of a charlatan.

The case for *Finnegans Wake* is that it can stimulate and delight the reader, acting in such a way that (in Shelley's words) 'it awakens and enlarges the mind itself by rendering it the receptacle of a thousand unapprehended combinations of thought', and that these combinations are not just arbitrary and casual but very often intimately connected with the actual experiencing and interpreting of reality.

It is not easy, in a few words, to substantiate this claim and one can only propose to sceptical readers that they should, duly armed, if they wish, with some of the information now quite easily available,[12] take the plunge into one of the more accessible areas of the book – say the opening of the 'Shem the Penman' passage (pp. 169ff.) – assured at least that in this of all books they will not be cheating by starting in the middle. Better still, that they should listen, if they can find means of acquiring it, to the gramophone record in which Joyce himself reads a part of 'Anna Livia Plurabelle'. It should perhaps be mentioned, however, that this particular passage is unusually lyrically 'attractive' and may possibly raise false expectations. Those passages, both in *Ulysses* and *Finnegans Wake*, in which the author indulges – rivers and seas seem to tempt him to it – in somewhat lush and easy rhythms, do not show Joyce at his best.

The core of the method of *Finnegans Wake* is contained in a famous anecdote related by Frank Budgen:

> I enquired about *Ulysses*. Was it progressing?
> 'I have been working hard on it all day,' said Joyce.
> 'Does that mean that you have written a great deal?' I said.
> 'Two sentences,' said Joyce.
> I looked sideways but Joyce was not smiling. I thought of Flaubert.
> 'You have been seeking the *mot juste*?' I said.
> 'No,' said Joyce, 'I have the words already. What I am seeking is the perfect order of words in the sentence. There is an order in every way appropriate. I think I have it.'
> 'What are the words?' I asked.
> 'I believe I told you,' said Joyce, 'that my book is a modern Odyssey. Every episode in it corresponds to an adventure of Ulysses. I am now writing the *Lestrygonians* episode, which corresponds to the adventure of Ulysses with the cannibals. My hero is going to lunch. But there is a seduction motive in the Odyssey, the cannibal king's daughter. Seduction appears in my book as women's silk petticoats hanging in a shop window. The words through which I express the effect of it on my hungry hero are: "Perfume of embraces all him assailed. With hungered flesh obscurely, he mutely craved to adore." You can see for yourself in how many different ways they might be arranged.'[13]

This seems to tell us a great deal about Joyce's use of language, as well as about his method of work in general. By putting 'assailed' at the end of its sentence, the physical impact of the word is allowed, so to speak, to pile up: by putting the object before the verb a suggestion comes through of a possible reversal of object and subject. Just how passive is the character concerned? The position of 'all' in the sentence likewise gives it a maximum effect, referring back to 'embraces' and forward to 'him'. This last would be lost, or weakened, if Joyce had written 'all of him', and at the same time the maleness of 'him' would have been less potent too. Just as the perfume, placed anywhere else in the sentence, would have impregnated it less thoroughly.

What Joyce is up to here is – it can be argued – not anything so very extraordinary. Is he not playing the game all poets play? There is nothing sacred about the order of words. Poets arrange them in the way that will make them work best for their particular purposes, organizing, if they can, their every reverberation, controlling the fall-out of any verbal explosion.

No one – not even Shakespeare – carried the experiment as far as Joyce did; but, in its essence, is the method of *Finnegans Wake* really so different from that of, say, *Paradise Lost* or *The Waste Land*? And cannot one say much the same about the subject-matter? Is it more misleading than any other statement about this extraordinary book to say that it is about the Fall?

One of the new things, of course, is the *extent* to which Joyce builds and manipulates words, including non-English ones: he uses syllables, rhymes, half-rhymes, inventions, anagrams and every kind of associative device. This helps make his rhetoric uniquely and many-sidedly rich. Compare Fielding on the subject of Tom Jones's lowness, social and literary, with Joyce on Shem:

How is that for low, laities and gentlenuns? Why, dog of the Crostiguns, whole continents rang with this kairokorran lowness! Sheols of houris in chems upon divans (revolted stellas vesperine vesamong them) at a bare (O!) mention of the scaly rybald explained: Poisse![14]

The problem, though, about stressing the links between Joyce's uses of language and those of his predecessors is that a doubt arises as to whether, in gathering him as much as possible into the 'mainstream' of modern literature, we may not be underplaying the radicalism of his innovations. There is surely an important sense in which he has to be seen to be out to undermine not simply the clichés and inadequacies of our familiar ways of seeing and describing reality, but also all assumed relationships between language and reality altogether. To attempt to incorporate his 'revolution of the word' into our familiar ways of dealing with a literary text may be to refuse the very challenge his writing offers us.[15]

In *Finnegans Wake*, narrative in the usual sense, which presumes a beginning and an end, is dispensed with. But that is not all. The reader, in trying to get his bearings, is denied any certain 'reality' which he can assume to be somehow *basic* to what the language is evoking. It is impossible to be quite sure that, or whether, *Finnegans Wake* is Earwicker's dream; for the question is, in the light of Joyce's preoccupations, irrelevant. Similarly it is not possible to evaluate the 'success' of particular images. Always in the later Joyce there is hovering in the air the suspicion that words have *in themselves* some mystic significance. Because of his refusal to commit himself to the proposition that dream is in the end less real than reality, he ends up, it sometimes seems, with the implication that nothing is real except words.

Finnegans Wake can only be read and enjoyed in its own terms, i.e. by an acceptance, for the purposes of the book, of the whole Joycean bag of tricks. And because reality is more important, complex and pervasive than theories about it, the great odd book has a way of breaking through many of the objections which commonsense consideration will plausibly erect. That is why, while it is fair enough to point out that *Finnegans Wake* is 'a book written to a theory', with the problems this implies, it would be wrong to regard such a judgement either as a defence (because the theory is true) or as a dismissal (because it isn't).

A reader prepared to approach Joyce's later work with the right kind of openness (a kind that can, as it seems to me, only be defined in terms of its own success in coping with the text) is likely to get from it a new sense of the possibilities of language and of the complexities and contradictions of human life. One who is not an out-and-out Joycean, philosophically and aesthetically, hesitates to make a larger claim than that, for there remains an unreduced element of scepticism. Does Joyce the writer succeed in beginning to restructure the world he has so persistently broken up? Certainly he does things with words that no one previously had done, but is the final predominant effect one of liberation and enrichment or of a stupendous yet ultimately rather arid *tour de force*? Certainly, in the best of Joyce, laughter and tears assert themselves as a humanizing force, counteracting with their sanity the tendencies towards pedantry and isolation. Perhaps it is the very consistency of his total effort, the very completeness of the structure he creates, that has in it something which also makes us question whether he who accepted so boldly all the implications of his exile – poorjoist unctuous to polise nopebobbies – had flinched at nothing except life itself.

PART THREE

NOTES

1. *Stephen Hero* (1944), 188. See also *Introduction*, 13ff., by Theodore Spencer.

2. *A Portrait of the Artist as a Young Man* (Travellers Library, 1930), 241ff. See also the discussion of this point in *James Joyce* by Harry Levin (1944), especially Part I, ch. 3 and Part II, ch. 3.

3. S. Bolt, *A Preface to James Joyce* (1981), 12.

4. Richard Ellmann (*James Joyce*, Oxford, 1959) shows very clearly the direct autobiographical basis of almost all Joyce's literary preoccupations. It is a fruitful emphasis not only because it explains much in the two major books that is otherwise almost incomprehensible, but also because it counteracts the over-metaphysical approach to Joyce which many of his admirers (including Messrs Campbell and Robinson, see n. 12) have encouraged.

5. *Letters*, ed. Stuart Gilbert (London, 1957), 64.

6. *James Joyce* (1944), 96.

7. Ellmann's description of *Ulysses* (*James Joyce*, 370) as 'pacifist' seems to me suggestive and useful but not quite satisfactory. 'The theme of *Ulysses* is simple . . . Casual kindness overcomes unconscionable power' (390). But does it?

8. Alick West, *Crisis and Criticism* (London, 1937), 178.

9. *Letters*, 62–3.

10. Frank Budgen, *James Joyce and the Making of Ulysses* (Oxford, 1934), 94.

11. *Finnegans Wake*, 115.

12. e.g. S. Bolt, *A Preface to James Joyce* (London, 1981); M. H. Begnall and F. Senn (eds), *A Conceptual Guide to Finnegans Wake* (Penn. State, U.S.A., 1974); J. Campbell and H. M. Robinson, *A Skeleton Key to Finnegans Wake* (London, 1947); C. Hart, *Structure and Motif in Finnegans Wake* (London, 1962), *A Concordance to Finnegans Wake* (Appel, N.Y., 1963); M. J. C. Hodgart, *James Joyce: A Student's Guide* (London, 1978); Roland McHugh, *Annotations to Finnegans Wake* (London, 1980); W. Y. Tindall, *A Reader's Guide to Finnegans Wake* (London, 1969).

13. *James Joyce and the Making of Ulysses*, 20.

14. *Finnegans Wake*, 177.

15. This is, at least as I understand it, the underlying argument of Colin McCabe's *James Joyce and the Revolution of the Word* (London, 1978), which brings to bear the theories of structuralist linguistics and post-structuralist psychoanalysis on Joyce's enterprise.

L. H. MYERS AND BLOOMSBURY

G. H. BANTOCK

The work of L. H. Myers presents at least two points of interest. There are the novels in themselves – one of which, at least, is of sufficient merit to warrant inclusion among the best of this century (and the company would not be large); and there is what has happened to the novels – the literary situation which has quietly ignored Myers's work. As might be guessed, the two points are not unconnected; and by defining the attitude to experience that Myers's work entailed and by examining the particular nature of his moral preoccupations, something will already have been done to uncover the motives behind the neglect. Indeed, the use of the word 'moral', necessarily forced upon one in the most preliminary consideration of the novels, may already have provided a clue.

Frederic W. H. Myers, Leo's father, an essayist and poet of minor distinction, was one of the founders of the Society for Psychical Research, in 1882, an undertaking which interested a number of the best minds of late Victorian intellectual society. Thus, Leckhampton House, Cambridge, at which the young Leo was brought up, became a centre of intellectual life attended by many of the distinguished minds of the late Victorian period, Henry Sidgwick, Montagu Butler, Lord Rayleigh, F. W. Maitland, Balfours, Lyttletons, and many others. This was the Cambridge of the Puritan-Whig tradition of common sense and the dry light of reason, as Leslie Stephen described it. Though F. W. H. Myers was subject to a more turgid emotionalism than were many of his friends, his major preoccupation was still primarily rationalistic and moralistic – the attempt to prove, by controlled scientific experimentation, the immortality of the soul.

To the father the common enterprise of psychical research provided an adequate social and intellectual milieu. Given the particular circumstances of the breakdown of dogmatic creeds in the late Victorian era, psychical research was obviously something to engage the united attention of 'serious' minds. This is worth stressing because Leo Myers constantly sought for, and perpetually failed to find, some group which would enable him to achieve at least a tolerable degree of what nowadays is referred to as social integration. As early as at Eton, he reacted strongly against the social tone of his environment. The school provided Myers's first contact with what in his books he called 'the world'; and there is good evidence from friends that he found repugnant the covert insincerities which even this adolescent world demanded. All his life he concerned himself with the Idols of the Market-Place, those which are 'formed by the intercourse and association of men with each other', and the insincerities of behaviour to which men are led by their need to live in society.

Myers was well-to-do and, except for a brief period at the Board of Trade during the First World War, had no regular employment. As a young man, he had a mystical experience in America. Though he had no liking for any orthodox Christian faith, he retained a sense of powers extra-human and transcendental throughout his life. Intellectually he developed late. His first novel, *The Orissers*, took him twelve or thirteen years to write, and was not published until 1922, when he was just over forty. Other novels appeared at regular intervals, until *The Pool of Vishnu* (1940). After that, attempts to write were unsuccessful. An abstract indictment of contemporary society failed, though he attempted at least three versions of it. Just before he died he destroyed an autobiographical study, intended to display the evils of his own social class. He committed suicide in 1944.

As a writer, Myers is much nearer to the practice of, say George Eliot, than to those modern 'experimental' writers whose aim is to convey experience through the 'stream of consciousness'. He is perpetually aware of the implications of the experience he is conveying. Hence what might be termed the 'literary' flavour of his novels; they are consciously shaped, like Victorian novels, and they seek not to convey the 'moment', but events winnowed and sifted. And the sense which guides and selects is the moral sense. He comments adversely on Proust:

When a novelist displays an attitude of aesthetical detachment from the ordinary ethical and philosophical preoccupations of humanity, something in us protests ... Proust, for instance, by treating all sorts of sensibility as equal in importance, and all manifestations of character as standing on the same plane of significance, adds nothing to his achievement, but only draws attention to himself as aiming at the exaltation of a rather petty form of aestheticism.

Thus Myers seeks to be a 'connoisseur' of character, and criticizes the lack of moral and spiritual discrimination which fails to appreciate the 'deep-seated spiritual vulgarity that lies at the heart of our civilization'.

Hence it is the exercise of the moral judgement which actuates the discriminations among his characters. His novels, though they appear at first sight to be remote in subject-matter, are in fact strictly contemporary; and he worked out in them, after the manner of his own Jali, some of his most pressing personal problems, chiefly the problem which he remembered exercising him from his childhood: 'Why do men choose to live?', and the problem of personal relationships. What he investigated through his 'serious' characters was the possibility of a way of life which should at once stand the test of a morally fastidious taste and end his feeling of social and personal isolation. The books, therefore, are peculiarly autobiographical. Fundamentally, as I have suggested, his mind was of a religious tendency; his major work, *The Near and the Far*, is set in India in the sixteenth century, because this not only allows him the detachment from strictly local and contemporary settings that, significantly, he always needed, but permits him to explore a selection of Eastern and Western approaches to the problem of ultimate 'Being'.

In *The Near and the Far*, Ranee Sita is pointing out to the Brahmin, Gokal, the extent to which she disagrees with her husband Amar's outlook:

'I, for my part, shall always affirm what Amar denies. Between us there is a gulf.'
Gokal leaned forward earnestly, 'The gulf lies not between those who affirm and those who deny, but between those who affirm and those who ignore. Listen!' he went on ... 'Fundamentally your mind and Amar's are similar in type; you both raise the same problems and the answers you give are the same in essence, if their substance is not the same. You advocate life's intensification, Amar its extinguishment; but you both recognize imperfection and you both aim at perfection!'

For Myers this distinction between those who affirm and those who ignore – the Fastidious and the Trivial, as he called them – was fundamental. An examination of how these two groups manifest themselves, what characteristics they reveal, and on what terms they exist in society, will take us far in an understanding of Myers's work.

In all his books there is a small group of characters – the Fastidious – who stand over against society as it manifests itself in the life of social classes and institutions. There, standards of conduct are derived, ultimately, not from an apprehension of spiritual forces comprehending something greater than, and apart from, man but from a glorificaion of society's own spirit, a judgement in terms of its own materialistic values. Most people, he considered, live by appearances; by 'appearances' (illusion, Maya) he usually meant those modes of behaviour, those masks, which a man adopts so that he may find himself accepted. Such a man presents to his companions a recognizable 'personality', a 'persona'; all real genuineness vanishes. Of such are the Trivial.

Myers was always strongly convinced of the reality of the 'Evil Will' in human intercourse. This accounts for his unwillingness to allow for compromise in the conflict between the Trivial and the Fastidious. Such a conflict is the subject of his first novel, *The Orissers*, which is concerned with the struggle between the Maynes and the Orissers for the possession of the family seat of the Orissers, Eamor. The Maynes represent in their varying degrees of spiritual obtuseness the worldly and material values of that type of society in which Myers moved. Whatever the faults of the Orissers, they recognize a standard beyond social opinion. In the end John Mayne is defeated; and his defeat springs from the forced recognition of a moral obligation. Contact with Lilian Orisser convinces him of his inadequacy; his handing over of the house, Eamor, is the tacit recognition of a standard beyond public opinion and common law, the sources from which the Maynes of the world are accustomed to draw their instinctive self-justification.

Nevertheless, the position of the Orissers is not really satisfactory – and the problem of the Orissers is ultimately Myers's own problem. They are self-isolated; and they are critical enough of their own position to be aware of the fact that to be cut off from 'life', even in John Mayne's intrepretation of the word, is not to their advantage. Eamor symbolizes an ordered way of life, uncontaminated by the material spirit of the society of the day; to gain it the Orissers are prepared to offend against the conventional moral code, even to commit murder. Yet, even when they are successful, they feel themselves cut off in Eamor's 'dreadful peace'. If the Orissers are the spiritually aware, they are, nevertheless, aware of themselves as the self-conscious members of an effete and dying social order.

Myers's first novel, then, reveals quite starkly – too starkly – the problem; 'too starkly' because the moral distinctions involved (the dichotomy between the Orissers and the Maynes) are too crudely made – we descend too quickly to melodrama. There is more egotism in the make-up of the Orissers than Myers seems aware of. At the same time, it was right that the concern for standards of conduct should not be regarded as illusory, even as those standards are interpreted in the novel; and Myers does sense that the moral isolation of the Orissers is equivocal, and that such isolation represents a desiccation.

The 'Clio' hardly merits serious consideration; Myers wrote it because he wished to produce something in the Aldous Huxley vein. It is in The Root of the Flower (1935), the first three sections of The Near and the Far, that the implications of the Orissers are taken up and explored more fully. The Orisser group – the sensitive and fastidious – reappear in the characters of Rajah Amar, his wife, Sita, and their son Jali, together with Amar's brother-in-law, Hari, and a friend, Gokal. Through the 'education' (using the word in the sense in which Henry Adams employed it) of Jali we explore the effect of society on a young and sensitive mind and the pretentiousness of various social and artistic circles is revealed. The Rajah himself, mature and critically aware of the corruptions of the world, seeks to retire from an active to a contemplative life. But his political responsibilities for his small state and the struggle for the throne which is bound to break out between Akbar's two sons, Salim and Daniyal, after the emperor's death, ensure that the contact between the 'fastidious' group and the rest of society shall be much closer than in The Orissers. The Rajah believes in an absolute division between the political and spiritual life. He imagines that he can readjust his allegiance in accordance with expediency alone, on the principle of 'Render unto Caesar'. He does not realize that the policy and the person are inextricably bound together. For he feels that, despite his personal distaste for Daniyal, he can side with him on purely abstract grounds. It is not until Daniyal by a superficially trivial, but brutal, act of cruelty reveals the corruption of spirit which he represents that the Rajah strikes at the prince with his sword. The action is unavailing, but symbolically Myers has indicated that the evil of the world is a quality of the personality and must be met by opposition and action.

There are various gross manifestations of the trivial materialistic outlook in India in the book. Myers's analysis of the Pleasance of the Arts, a meeting place of contemporary aesthetes, has interest beyond the novel, for here he is satirizing a prominent literary group of his times, Bloomsbury.

Daniyal, the leader of the Pleasance, is the 'poet, the Artist, the enraptured lover of Beauty'. The camp glories in its independence of thought, its freedom from conventions, its emancipation from the Philistine and the Prig. It casts off 'dreary actuality' and basks in the glitter of its own pretentiousness. Here everybody flatters himself that he is somebody; 'in artificiality the spirit finds its own true life'; revolt is the order of the day, revolt against the old, outworn conventions, prejudices, and, above all, 'the bullying, nagging disposition of nature'. A closer acquaintanceship with the members of the Pleasance shows, however, that the camp has its own inverted orthodoxy. Not only is the apparent freedom of the camp entirely illusory, for all its inhabitants are bound by a rigid necessity to share the same vices and applaud the same apparently heterodox opinions, but they also depend basically upon a

solid, shockable world of decorum and common sense. They had to believe that a great ox-like eye was fixed upon them in horror. Without this their lives lost their point.

It is not hard to see why Bloomsbury was distasteful to Myers; for Bloomsbury was aesthetic rather than moralistic, even though its outlook was profoundly influenced by a work on moral philosophy. The last chapter of G. E. Moore's *Principia Ethica*, where his intuitionist moral theory led him to set up personal relations and a sense of beauty as the two supreme goods, formed the starting place for the development of an aesthetic philosophy to which the Bloomsbury intellectuals subscribed with varying degrees of personal emphasis. Clive Bell, in defining what he understood by Civilization, declared that 'Works of art being direct means to aesthetic ecstasy are direct means to good'. The potential value of a work of art lay in the fact that it could 'at any moment become a means to a state of mind of superlative excellence'. The aim of every civilized man was the 'richest and fullest life obtainable, a life which contains the maximum of vivid and exquisite experiences'. Civilized man desired 'complete self-development and complete self-expression'.

What Bloomsbury made of Moore's doctrine, then, was subjectivist and aesthetic, something very different from Myers's transcendentalist position. As Keynes put it in his *Memoir*:

Nothing mattered except states of mind, our own and other people's, of course, but chiefly our own. These states of mind were not associated with action or achievement or with consequences. They consisted in timeless passionate states of contemplation and communion, largely unattached to 'before' and 'after' ...

The effect was to 'escape from the Benthamite tradition' – there was no place for social effort or moral strenuousness of the Victorian type:

... social action as an end in itself and not merely as a lugubrious duty had dropped out of our Ideal, and, not only social action, but the life of action generally, power, politics, success, wealth, ambition ...

The anti-traditional element in all this was strong:

We claimed the right to judge every individual case on its merits, and the wisdom, experience and self-control to do so successfully ... We repudiated entirely customary morals, convention and traditional wisdom.

The self-regarding mind, then, freed itself from locality and background which might have carried a hint of continuity and obligation. This represents a position very different from that to which Amar came, with its underlying acceptance of social responsibility. But what Myers particularly detested was the Bloomsbury 'tone', the element of communal self-congratulation implicit in the self-conscious spirit of social aloofness and 'difference': 'The life of a first-rate English man or woman', urged Clive Bell, 'is one long assertion of his or her personality in the face of unsympathetic or actively hostile environment' (*Civilization*). Roy Harrod, in his book on Keynes, reveals something of the origin and behaviour of the group. It developed from 'The Society' at Cambridge; not all members of Bloomsbury had been members of the Society, but Bloomsbury was, undoubtedly, 'strongly influenced by some who had been members'. Its growth was spontaneous rather than contrived: but frequent meetings and social intercourse induced a reasonably homogeneous outlook. The intimacy of personal relationship manifested itself in a private language; letters and talk between members abounded in esoteric jokes and allusions. It is true that members criticized each other, frequently in a spirit of mockery and raillery, and often displayed considerable differences of opinion; but the criticisms themselves implied a common acceptance of iconoclastic irreverence for all normal taboos and conventions: 'they shared a taste for discussion in pursuit of truth and a contempt for conventional ways of thinking and feeling', admits Clive Bell, while seeking to deny any real homogeneity of outlook (*Old Friends*). Such protestation of liberty of expression and a pervasive scepticism of outlook formed a barrier against an outer world in the grip of superstition and convention. Thus there came to be a Bloomsbury manner – composed of mockery, 'gentle dissection, fun, and ridicule', all 'in the greatest good humour'. There was even a Bloomsbury voice:

> The voice was emphatic but restrained. Certain syllables, or even letters, were rather strongly stressed, but not at all in the manner of a drawl. The presupposition of the cadence was that everything one said mattered. Emphasis had to be applied.
>
> (R. F. Harrod: *The Life of John Maynard Keynes*)

In Bloomsbury, then, it might be said, as Myers so ironically wrote of the Pleasance:

> Here you might come across people of every variety – except one, the commonplace. Dull, conventional people – people who weren't lit by the divine spark, had no chance of gaining admission here. Daniyal had thrown away the shackles of ordinary prejudices and cant.

In this, the reasons why Myers, who had formed many Bloomsbury acquaintances, gradually but effectively dissociated himself from the group become clear. They were both moral and personal.

The Pool of Vishnu, Myers's continuation and conclusion of *The Root and the Flower*, contains the positive answer to the meretricious materialist world of Akbar's India. In the story of Mohan and Damayanti, Myers reveals the positive nature of a married relationship based on complete candour as between absolute equals working through communion with transcendental powers ... 'All communion', says the Guru, the wise man who defines, too overtly for good novel writing, the moral implications of the book, 'is through the Centre. When the relation of man and man is not through the Centre it corrupts and destroys itself.' This notion, of course, was very similar to that expressed in Martin Buber's *I and Thou*. Personal relationships conceived in such terms – a very different matter from Bloomsbury's conception of them – Myers believed to be capable of infinite extension in a manner which would finally overthrow the old, stratified social order, represented here by Rajah Bhoj and his wife and their cult of first-rateness. And in the relationship between Mohan and Damayanti and their peasants a new brotherhood of man is foreshadowed. At their house Jali discerns a correspondence between the outward things and the inner landscape of his mind – the 'near' and the 'far' coalesce. The material requirements of everyday life are spiritualized in true community. Over all is Vishnu – and Vishnu is a preserver.

This last novel contains Myers's dream of spiritual home. Someone suggested, as he stated, that 'I put serenity into the book instead of finding it in my life'. And he accepted this as being 'shrewd, and, in fact, right'. But he went on, in the same letter, to observe that the Guru does not preach a doctrine of serenity nor do any of the other characters find a resolution of their difficulties and conflicts. A life of effort was always necessary because it implied a transcendence of self in relationship to others. It is this that makes the vision of personal relationships mature and convincing. Here, at any rate, faith and community could combine. In the real world Myers thought that they would manifest themselves in communism; during the last years of his life he became violently pro-Russian. Yet he held such beliefs with the vehemence of desperation. In his own life, he never found the community that he sought. 'Many of my old friends and acquaintances move in a world of thought and feeling that is distasteful to me', he wrote. And in the last five years of his life he withdrew from many long-standing friendships.

It is significant that all the characters in his book inhabit imaginary environments, places to which Myers himself had never been. Their problems are real problems as problems of the mind, but the characters themselves are rootless. Myers did not have, say, George Eliot's capacity, despite the intellectual nature of her mature life, for setting characters in an immediate and closely realized English environment; nor did he, like Lawrence, possess the 'spirit of place'. Myers's characters exist rather as self-consciousness than as intimately observed individuals. He was, in any case, never interested in the setting and he would brush aside praise of his descriptive powers with the remark that he was completely uninterested in description.

Yet Myers remains an important writer. For one thing, he had integrity; behind his work there is a kind of moral honesty which refuses to be taken in by the worldly and the meretricious. His analyses of behaviour are often extremely acute; he realized how very important group appreciation is to man and had an unerring eye for the social insincerity which marks a desire to be approved. He has, in fact, a notion of the civilized life, involving honesty and frankness of relationship, a basic genuineness of personality, which saw beyond the normally accepted criteria of such a life – polite conversation and a dabbling acquaintanceship with the arts. He sees the inadequacy of liberal humanism for the sort of being man is; and one remembers certain scenes – Daniyal's stepping on the cat's head is an example – because they challenge the easy optimism of the liberal tradition. He has, that is, a sense of evil. Had he had more 'imagination' in the Coleridgean sense – a quality necessitating a greater vitality, perhaps – he might have been a great writer. Greatness he misses; but he is never trivial. Fundamentally he is serious, concerned, and intelligent; and in a literary world which seems increasingly to find 'amusing' a term of critical approbation, he has not retained favour. The neglect into which he has fallen invokes a comment on our debilitation of standards; there are not so many with such virtues in our times that we can afford to neglect what he had to say.

CRITICISM AND THE READING PUBLIC

ANDOR GOMME

Criticism ... must always profess an end in view, which roughly speaking, appears to be the elucidation of works of art and the correction of taste. The critic's task, therefore, appears to be quite clearly cut out for him; and it ought to be comparatively easy to decide whether he performs it satisfactorily, and in general, what kinds of criticism are useful and what are otiose. But on giving the matter a little attention, we perceive that criticism, far from being a simple and orderly field of beneficent activity, from which impostors can be readily ejected, is no better than a Sunday park of contending and contentious orators, who have not even arrived at the articulation of their differences. Here, one would suppose, was a place for quiet cooperative labour. The critic, one would suppose, if he is to justify his existence, should endeavour to discipline his personal prejudices and cranks – tares to which we are all subject – and compose his differences with as many of his fellows as possible, in the common pursuit of true judgment. When we find that quite the contrary prevails, we begin to suspect that the critic owes his livelihood to the violence and extremity of his opposition to other critics, or else to some trifling oddities of his own with which he contrives to season the opinions which men already hold, and which out of vanity or sloth they prefer to maintain. We are tempted to expel the lot.

This famous passage from one of the most distinguished of T. S. Eliot's essays, on 'The Function of Criticism', was written in 1923. Reviewing the essay himself thirty-three years later, Eliot said that he found it impossible to recall what all the fuss was about. The facts, so far as the early twenties are concerned, are there to discover simply by looking in the files of the literary and semi-literary magazines of the day. But actually Eliot's words would quite accurately describe the situation thirty, even fifty, years later. The most immediately noticeable change is that there has been a certain congealing: a good many differences *have* been composed, though the result has not generally been any advance towards true judgement (and Eliot's later bewilderment may well have been the outcome of composing too many differences with the wrong kind of fellow). If there is now a rather less confusing array of contention and dispute, the element of clique and coterie, with its snobbism, its pushing of personal and arbitrary values, is perhaps even more apparent. It remains true, as Arnold said in *Culture and Anarchy* (1869), that

Each section of the public has its own literary organ, and the mass of the public is without any suspicion that the value of these organs is relative to their being nearer a certain ideal centre of correct information, taste, and intelligence, or farther away from it.

What is not true is that there would be agreement between those counting themselves educated on the direction in which the ideal centre lies. With much talk of the relativity of values, there is often doubt as to whether the ideal centre exists; and for the rest the idea of the elite, implying a dedication to values that are generously and broadly human, has been superseded by that of the gang,[1] with its motivation derived from private or arbitrary sources. The confusion of critical standards has remained as marked as ever it was: it has merely become a little more lumpy.

The period has been one of a great general cultural upheaval, in which mass literacy and the enormous increase in the power and range of mass media have been accompanied by an apparently final decay and disintegration of traditional sanctions of belief and behaviour. Thus the literary tradition comes to have a greater importance than ever, as on it alone now depends the possibility of maintaining a link with the past by which we can draw on the collective experience of the race. We are at a stage in civilization which demands more and more consciousness, when the individual cannot be left to be formed by the environment but must be trained to discriminate and resist.

The 'collective experience' sounds now almost an empty phrase, so fragmentary are the relics of any homogeneous culture that we may have had. Yet this is the kind of culture that the person for whom literary criticism seriously matters must strive towards; the culture in which it will be possible to appeal to the common reader as Johnson did, in which individual judgements will be confirmed and amplified in an experience of civilized living which is more than individual, where personal concerns meet in the creation of the standards by which a civilization lives.

Only on the basis of a common reader who can be appealed to in this way, who is part of a homogeneous culture with 'more-than-individual judgement, better-than-individual taste', can literature flourish and perform its function in the community. The 'literary court of appeal', then, which James looked for[2] is the very reverse of an academic preserve of rules of good writing. The appeal must always be from the general judgement to the particular, but to the particular seen as part of a coherent, educated, and influential reading-public, one capable of responding intelligently and making its response felt, for it is only then that 'standards are "there" for the critic to appeal to: only where there is such a public can he invoke them with any effect'. Standards are 'there' only in a community, a coherent (though not necessarily conscious) body of thought and feeling, because the standards appealed to, common to all men, are not created individually; for living is a more-than-individual process.

The absence of adequate standards of intelligence and taste, together with the inflation of private and temporary ones, is naturally seen at its worst in the dance of the reviews. Already in 1893, Henry James could remark that reviewing is 'a practice that in general has nothing in common with the art of criticism'; and his description of the way in which 'the great business of reviewing' carries on 'in its roaring routine' holds admirably for today:

> Periodical literature is a huge open mouth which has to be fed ... It is like a regular train which starts at an advertised hour, but which is free to start only if every seat be occupied. The seats are many, the train is ponderously long, and hence the manufacture of dummies for the seasons when there are not passengers enough. A stuffed manikin is thrust into the empty seat, where it makes a creditable figure till the end of the journey. It looks sufficiently like a passenger, and you know it is not one only when you perceive that it neither says anything nor gets out. The guard attends to it when the train is shunted, blows the cinders from its wooden face and gives a different crook to its elbow, so that it may serve for another run. In this way, in a well-conducted periodical, the blocks of *remplissage* are the dummies of criticism – the recurrent, regulated breakers in the tide of talk.[3]

Yet reviews are the nearest that most people get to most books and that some people get to any books at all; they have become a substitute literature speeding the decay of critical standards, a way of talking about books which obscures and flattens out their differences in adequacy and interest. And in the fairly short run the result is that literature is demoralized. There is a close connection between the extraordinary thinness of our contemporary literature on the one hand, and on the other the proliferation of nine-day masterpieces, the manufacture of easy reputations based on unsubstantiated promise, and the resulting ambience in which minor but interesting talent is stunted and prevented from developing in the pink haze of admiration without discretion or respect. James's strictures are indeed justified:

> The vulgarity, the crudity, the stupidity which this cherished combination of the offhand review and of our wonderful system of publicity have put into circulation on so vast a scale may be represented ... as an unprecedented invention for darkening counsel. The bewildered spirit may ask itself, without speedy answer, What is the function in the life of man of such a periodicity of platitude and irrelevance? Such a spirit will wonder how the life of man survives it, and, above all, what is much more important, how literature resists it; whether, indeed, literature does resist it and is not speedily going down beneath it. The signs of this catastrophe will not in the case we suppose be found too subtle to be pointed out – the failure of distinction, the failure of style, the failure of knowledge, the failure of thought.

Failure of thought, however, not just among writers but in the nation at large. It isn't merely that literary standards look outwards and reflect – as we make judgements – an attitude to civilization and to day-to-day habits of living; failure to maintain a critical spirit means a decay in the very processes of thought and feeling. The language is kept alive by a living literature and a living commerce with it: the effect of the genuine writers of the time is felt far and wide:

> ... our language goes on changing; our way of life changes, under the pressure of material changes in our environment in all sorts of ways; and unless we have those few men who combine an exceptional sensibility with an exceptional power over words, our own ability, not merely to express, but even to feel any but the crudest emotions, will degenerate.
>
> (Eliot, 'The Social Function of Poetry')

Literature, as Ezra Pound said in one of his manifestos,[4]

has to do with the clarity and vigour of 'any and every' thought and opinion. It has to do with maintaining the very cleanliness of the tools, the health of the very matter of thought itself. Save in the rare and limited instances of invention in the plastic arts, or in mathematics, the individual cannot think and communicate his thought, the governor and legislator cannot act effectively or frame his laws, without words, and the solidity and validity of these words is in the care of the damned and despised *litterati*. When their work goes rotten – by that I do not mean when they express indecorous thoughts – but when their very medium, the very essence of their work, the application of word to thing goes rotten, i.e. becomes slushy and inexact, or excessive or bloated, the whole machinery of social and of individual thought and order goes to pot. This is a lesson of history, and a lesson not yet half learned.

The absence of a responsive and responsible public, and the consequence of not living in 'a current of ideas in the highest degree animating and nourishing to the creative power', will always be felt most tellingly by the artist, who is thereby deprived of the critically healthy and creatively stimulating environment necessary for the making of work which has a value and meaning both in its own time and place, and permanently, acting as 'nutrition of impulse'. Society in Sophocles' and in Shakespeare's time was, says Arnold, 'in the fullest manner permeated by fresh thought, intelligent and alive; and this state of things is the true basis for the creative power's exercise, in this it finds its data, its materials, truly ready for its hand'. And James saw the reverse in his time, commenting that 'to be puerile and untutored' about literature 'is to deprive it of air and light, and the consequence of its keeping bad company is that it loses all heart'. The great artist, the really distinguished individual, will suffer, no doubt, less in his art than others. Yet even he cannot write entirely without an audience; and the want of a reciprocal and health-giving relation between the writer and his public marks – a notable example – much of the late work of James himself, a work clearly and painfully deriving much more from the writer's own intense mental effort than from real commerce with a living environment. On the other hand, coming to too easy terms with an intellectually ingrown and complacent society led Eliot, in his writing after *Four Quartets*, into modishness and triviality.

The worst effect is unquestionably seen in the way in which the age makes use of its minor talent, which will always be the majority of talent and has much to do with keeping society 'fresh, intelligent and alive' or letting it become the reverse. And here the history of poetry and of poetical reputations since the 1920s, a period in which immature talent has again and again been hailed as genius, and caught and held in an atmosphere wholly subversive and hostile to mature development, amply documents the dangers of not living in an animating and nourishing current of ideas. For as F. R. Leavis put it, in discussing this very 'Poetical Renascence':

Favourable reviews and a reputation are no substitute for the conditions represented by the existence of an intelligent public – the give-and-take that is necessary for self-realization, the pressure that, resisted or yielded to, determines direction, the intercourse that is collaboration (such collaboration as produces language, an analogy that, here as so often when art is in question, will repay a good deal of reflecting upon: the individual artist to-day is asked to do far too much for himself and far too much as an individual).

The resistance always required of the writer to his age is now of a deeper and more exhausting kind: he must write, as it were, against the public potentially so willing to do him the wrong kind of honour. The environment, and its vocal representation in the reading public, is the reverse of nourishing.[5]

It is inevitable, therefore, that for anyone seriously concerned for the function of criticism at the present time, the creation and maintenance of a coherent and responsible reading public must be a matter of the greatest urgency. That there has been an extraordinary amount of writing about writing is no indication that the issue is being faced. A notable aspect of the situation has indeed been the display of new literary organs, the enormous number of reviews, 'little magazines', and book sections whose production became one of the major small industries of the century. Almost all of these have seen their function as catering for the local interests of small sections of the public, and presenting them as matters of universal concern. Almost none has been devoted to maintaining or re-creating human values in literature, or human criteria of relevance in judgement. An early (and partial) exception was the *Athenaeum*, which kept up an independent existence as a weekly from 1919 to 1921, before being submerged in the *Nation*. Under the lively if uneven editorship of John Middleton Murry, it was responsible (among much that was infuriatingly silly) for a standard of reviewing which at its best – particularly in the regular work of Murry and Katherine Mansfield – was incomparably better than anything in weekly journalism today.

Even the *Athenaeum*, however, was something of a catering agency. The first real attempt this century to create the nucleus of an influential reading public coherent enough to keep the function of criticism served at all came with *The Calendar of Modern Letters* (1925–7), a first-rate review whose early death was one sign of the difficulty of the undertaking. *The Calendar* in fact saw its purpose as the creation of such a body as had (in its own comparison) been represented by *The Quarterly*, *The Edinburgh*, and *Blackwood's*. Its position was stated bluntly in the first editorial:

In reviewing we shall base our statements on the standards of criticism, since it is only then that one can speak plainly without offence, or give praise with meaning.

That these standards represent – in so far as *The Calendar*'s critics were able to call on them – a mature public attesting to the existence of a 'contemporary sensibility' is evidenced throughout in the continuously high level of response and attention expected from readers,[6] and in the tone of its confident appeal to a judgement embracing far more than the personal reaction of the writer. At its most explicit, *The Calendar*'s relation to its reading public is brought out in Douglas Garman's excellent article on 'Audience', one of the first after Arnold to realize the importance of the audience in the creation of literature and to distinguish between poetry and various types of pseudo-poetry which only exist 'to season the opinions which men already hold, and which out of vanity or sloth they prefer to maintain'.

The strength of *The Calendar* – which in only two years and a half yielded three anthologies of reviews and articles of permanent critical value[7] – is manifested not only in the quality of individual contributions (including the first appearances of Lawrence's 'Art and Morality' and 'Morality and the Novel': Lawrence was a fairly regular reviewer), but in the high level of work maintained by the various writers as a team of reviewers. It comes out at its most characteristically impressive in such a review as Edgell Rickword's of Eliot's *Poems 1909–1925*, an article whose significance lies in an exact appreciation of the importance of Eliot's work – the struggle with technique by which he 'has been able to get closer than any other poet to the physiology of our sensations' – with an insight which can pinpoint the dangerous 'personal' tendencies (the arbitrary or obstinately private collocations) to which Eliot was prone and which lessened the public availability of his poetry. The value of Eliot's contribution is thus all the more surely established and the essay, written in 1925, is an amazing achievement at a time when Eliot was everywhere greeted with bewildered or contemptuous hostility.[8]

The Calendar's weakness – seen from time to time in a rather un-thinking acceptance of the counters of the poetical academy (awe in front of *Prometheus Unbound* or *Samson Agonistes*), in a naïvety of tone (as when Muir complains that Eliot doesn't appreciate Milton and Wordsworth as much as Marvell and Dryden), and in occasional un-certainty of judgement with regard to contemporary writers (an over-estimation of Joyce and even Wyndham Lewis at the expense of Lawrence) – seems to come partly from a refusal to attempt live critical judgements of past literature in terms of present needs and aspirations as well as present viewpoint and availability; and partly in a refusal to go outside literature (in the directions in which litera-ture leads), and thus display and strengthen the foundations of literary judgement. Possibly it is this last that lies behind the cryptic hint thrown out in the 'Valediction forbidding Mourning' in the final issue: 'the present situation requires to be met by a different organiza-tion, which we are not now in a position to form'.

Scrutiny (1932–53), by far the most important and – it will prove – most influential critical review of the century, started not only with the experience of *The Calendar* behind it, but also with the immediate stimulus of Q. D. Leavis's *Fiction and the Reading Public* (1932), a book whose fully documented account of the development of popular reading habits during the hundred years or so in which fiction-reading had become largely responsible for spreading a lazy shod-diness of thought and feeling, represented a new realization of the cultural crisis of mass literacy accompanied by the collapse of a widely held community of taste and judgement. *Scrutiny*'s aim and practice were more widely and firmly grounded than those of *The Calendar*, with a concern not merely for literary values, but that their influence should be felt in a world which hardly holds literature to matter at all: the 'intelligent educated and morally responsible public' which *Scrutiny* sought to nourish was to be one which had, with its experi-ence of a training in sensitive judgement, a real effect in fostering a free play of constructive thought on all the conditions of the human situation:

> *Scrutiny* stands for co-operation in the work of rallying such a public, the problem being to preserve (which is not – need we say? – to fix in a dead arrest) a moral, intellectual and, inclusively, humane tradition, such as is

essential if society is to learn to control its machinery and direct it to intelligent, just and humane ends.

(*Scrutiny*, II, iv. 332)

While first place was always given to the importance of literary culture, as the guardian of collective wisdom, the standards discovered in live contact with the literature of the present and that of the past which is vital for us today were applied in criticism of other issues in the contemporary cultural and social scene, and particularly in the educational movement with which *Scrutiny* was associated from the start.[9] Indeed, the whole project of *Scrutiny* involved necessarily a movement towards the resurrection of standards in education to ensure a training of general non-specialist sensibility adequate to meet the pressures of contemporary life – not only for the sake of individual well-being but to lead to a common realization of human ends, unrelated to which practical and political action is likely to be worse than useless.

The bringing of literature, and of the values inherent in it, to bear on the conditions of everyday practical affairs is something that can only happen through a public educated in this way. *Scrutiny*'s main effort, then, was towards the defining – that is, forming – of a 'contemporary sensibility':

What it should be possible to say of 'the skilled reader of literature' is that he 'will tend, by the nature of his skill', to understand and appreciate contemporary *literature* better than his neighbours. The serious critic's concern with the literature of the past is with its life in the present; it will be informed by the kind of perception that can distinguish intelligently and sensitively the significant new life in contemporary literature.

(XIX, iii. 178)

The function, as an early editorial put it,

is essentially cooperative – involving cooperation and fostering it ... The critic puts his judgements in the clearest and most unevadable form in order to invite response; to forward that exchange without which there can be no hope of centrality. Centrality is the product of reciprocal pressures, and a healthy criticism is the play of these.

(II, iv)

For if standards are only 'there' in an intelligent, educated, morally responsible public, they are only worked out and displayed in collab-

orative exchange between critics. In a later article Dr Leavis expanded
the conception of the process hinted at above:

> A judgement is a real judgement, or it is nothing. It must, that is, be a
> sincere personal judgement; but it aspires to be more than personal. Essentially
> it has the form: 'This is so, is it not?' But the agreement appealed for must
> be real, or it serves no critical purpose and can bring no satisfaction to the
> critic. What his activity of its very nature aims at, in fact, is a collaborative
> exchange or commerce. Without a many-sided real exchange – the collabora-
> tion by which the object, the poem (for example), in which the individual
> minds meet, and at the same time the true judgements concerning it, are
> established – the function of criticism cannot be said to be working.
>
> (XVIII, iii. 227)

Standards derive from centrality (which is 'the product of reciprocal
pressures'), the many-sided exchange working to eliminate the
merely personal element of prejudice and eccentricity, which characterizes to some degree the initial individual response, and to develop
the genuine individual judgement into an understanding of the
significance of the .work in the community of values upon which
the culture is built. And the kind of exchange found throughout
Scrutiny is in fact almost the only example we have of a cooperative
attempt to discover and make palpable values which are essentially
and broadly human and not simply those of a coterie. The initial
agreement of its contributors was on *function*, on the nature of the
discipline undertaken in literary criticism and its relation outside itself
in the influence it can bring to bear in the world at large.[10] They
formed in fact a group of highly intelligent common readers (whose
intelligence was certainly *not* common in the usual sense), who had
trained themselves in the discipline of a central but non-specialist
cultural activity: they were, in short, one centre of the élite upon
whose existence the survival of humane values has come entirely to
depend.

Scrutiny's contribution to the defining of a contemporary sensibility (its firm but sensitive assessing, in the first place, of contemporary writing) depended upon a revaluation of our past literature which
was pursued rigorously and intelligently. As one friendly but impartial critic put it, this work amounted to a whole new conception
of the English literary tradition; and the same writer's judgement
elsewhere may be allowed to stand:

Richards wrote *Practical Criticism* but *Scrutiny* was practical and criticized. Cleanth Brooks wrote notes for a new history of English poetry but in essay after essay *Scrutiny* accumulated a new history *in extenso*. Burke and Ransom extended the boundaries of critical discussion but *Scrutiny* actually occupied the territory and issued new maps.

(Eric Bentley, in *Kenyon Review*, Autumn 1946)

And as F. R. Leavis himself was able to claim, not only have the main *Scrutiny* revaluations become generally current, but all the work of 'affecting radically the prevailing sense of the past' was done in *Scrutiny*.

So impressive was this achievement that it has been implied by the editor of a review with claims towards something of *Scrutiny*'s vigilance that *Scrutiny*'s 'task of revaluation' had been completed, the work done and now safely docketed so that the judgements could be drawn on by those with the more urgent purpose in hand of 'responding' to the contemporary literary scene. The apparent compliment, of course, distorts the place that this radical, critical, and scholarly rewriting of English literary history had in *Scrutiny*'s programme. Revaluation is not something that is done once for all, the judgements being established for all time: it is the discovery of how the literature of the past is alive in the present. As such – and because the present is always changing – no revaluation is ever final, however much permanent conditions may be pointed to: the many differences within *Scrutiny* itself testify to an understanding of this.

Scrutiny lasted for twenty-one years – in itself something remarkable. Its final decline and death came not directly from the hostility and neglect with which it was normally treated in more institutional quarters so much as from the dislocation caused by the war, which dispersed the contributors and destroyed the network of collaboration which had been made. *Scrutiny* outlasted the war by eight years, but 'never again was it possible', as the valedictory editorial says, 'to form anything like an adequate nucleus of steady collaborators'. This way of putting it shows immediately how important to the whole scheme was essential agreement among contributors on the function of the discipline they were engaged in. *Scrutiny* was never a haphazard collection of articles on literary matters. A breadth of interest and concern was implicit in the conception from the start; and the marked narrowing of attention which is so plain in the later issues is a sign that to some degree the world had triumphed, and the literary critic was no longer to be found who could feel that he had anything important to say outside his own 'literary' field. Fewer books were reviewed, and those on a much smaller range of subjects. Moreover articles became longer, more 'exhaustive', and at the same time less stimulating. Where earlier essays (for example, Leavis's on *Othello*) had taken one or two central issues raised by their subject to suggest lines where further inquiry would be profitable, there seemed to be a tendency towards the end to assume that the work had not been properly done unless every possible aspect had been covered, every possible approach explored. Sometimes indeed subject-matter seems to have been embarked on just for the sake of having something new to say. The opening, for example, of D. A. Traversi's essay on *Henry V* [11] must immediately arouse in the reader concerned for relevance a suspicious, defensive attitude: 'There are, among Shakespeare's plays, those which seem to have eluded criticism by their very simplicity'.

The implication (alas, borne out in the sequel) seems to be that Derek Traversi will now set out to remedy not only the shortage of criticism but also the simplicity. Indeed the heavyweight treatment that Shakespeare received at the hands of Traversi and others seems to lead away altogether from an interest in the plays as live literature and to find its significance in the tracing of patterns of imagery almost for its own sake – an activity which is pursued quite intensively enough in universities and academic journals as it is. This kind of treatment is at times only too close in feeling and intention to such an offering (to take an example conveniently to hand) as appeared in *Essays in Criticism*, where a contributor has ploughed through 'the structure of imagery in *Harry Richmond*' – an undertaking which immediately demonstrates the futility of engaging in literary business without a live critical sense: for the right critical deduction would have shown at the start that the subject itself couldn't maintain the interest required of the reader or rightfully demand his spending time and attention on it.

Mention of *Essays in Criticism* (founded 1950) in connection with *Scrutiny*, however, can only be made in order to establish their essential difference, which is the difference, in general, between academic literariness uncontrolled by critical insight, and the benefit of working with a sense of relevance, always in sight of Arnold's 'central, truly human point of view'. And *Scrutiny*'s limitations and shortcomings seem in retrospect a small thing compared with the entire failure of any other journal to maintain anything like a true perception of the function of criticism at the present time.

For the function of criticism to be properly served the media must be created in which individuals can carry on 'the common pursuit of true judgement'. But there must, too, be distinguished critics ready to use the occasion to its best advantage. In this, our age has been peculiarly fortunate; it isn't possible here to do more than point to four critics whose work seems now to have the greatest permanent value as well as being significant in the development of the general cultural state during the last hundred years. Inevitably this is unfair to a number of critics whose work is not considered and yet has much value. Of the four writers whom I glance at here three are among the greatest creative writers this century, and the relation of their main work to their criticism is what gives the latter its largest interest. Among these, Eliot – especially in his early work – had so notable an influence in the spreading abroad of certain literary ideas that his inconsistencies and loosenesses of thought may be historically as significant as his more assured successes.

Of the most recent of the four, F. R. Leavis, it is only necessary to say in introduction that of all the critics in the period under discussion he was the most actively and continuously concerned for the creation of a worthy and stimulating critical environment, as well as providing in his own work a body of criticism of the utmost consistency and distinction. It is impossible to separate a discussion of *Scrutiny* from that of his own contribution to it, for one cannot doubt that the review's incisiveness, centrality, and sense of relevance were the mark more than anything of his genius, and that without this its continuance for even half its actual lifetime would have been out of the question.

'A sense of relevance' not only led Leavis to see in a continuance of Arnold's spirit the critic's true business in the world, to see criticism as essentially practical and theory as subservient and secondary to practice, but also to find in values stemming from a fine sense of the whole breadth of life the standards by which literature must be judged. The truly relevant criteria – the futility, also, of ignoring them – come out admirably in a passage where he is discussing Jane Austen's position at the start of the great tradition of the English novel:

> As a matter of fact, when we examine the formal perfection of *Emma*, we find that it can be appreciated only in terms of the moral preoccupations that characterize the novelist's peculiar interest in life. Those who suppose it to be an 'aesthetic matter', a beauty of 'composition' that is combined, miraculously, with 'truth to life', can give no adequate reason for the view that *Emma* is a great novel, and no intelligent account of its perfection of form. It is in the same way true of the other great English novelists that their interest in their art gives them the opposite of an affinity with Pater and George Moore; it is, brought to an intense focus, an unusually developed interest in life. For, far from having anything of Flaubert's disgust or disdain or boredom, they are all distinguished by a vital capacity for experience, a kind of reverent openness before life, and a marked moral intensity.
>
> (*The Great Tradition*, 1948)

This grasp of criteria is what enabled Leavis to map out and define the significant tradition of the English novel from Jane Austen, through George Eliot, James, and Conrad, to Lawrence – which, as Leavis himself says, 'has become a fact of general acceptance ... with the implication that it has always been so'.

The appropriateness of these criteria in criticism of the novel would now perhaps be generally granted. But, as Leavis has shown in the course of practical analysis and revaluation of English poetry, they carry over into all literature, remain central to our judgement. In the sensitive and penetrating analysis of verse Leavis has certainly no master, but always his concern for 'practical criticism', for close attention to 'the words on the page', is a concern for something which far transcends the limits usually implied by these phrases: the accuracy arises out of a need to establish the relevance of a passage in the work as a whole and, by extension, the place which the work should take up in our cultural consciousness.[12]

Technique, in short, 'can be studied and judged only in terms of the sensibility it expresses'. The need to find and realize our contemporary sensibility should lie behind all discussions of technique, and justifies, in Leavis's case, the attention given to it.[13]

The *locus classicus* for inquiry into the relation between technique and the feelings and attitudes which it expresses has long been a passage from one of the finest of Eliot's essays which has been reprinted as 'Poetry in the Eighteenth Century', in Volume 4 of the *Guide* (*From Dryden to Johnson*):

... after Pope there was no one who thought and felt nearly enough like Pope to be able to use his language quite successfully; but a good many second-rate writers tried to write something like it, unaware of the fact that the change of sensibility demanded a change of idiom. Sensibility alters from generation to generation in everybody, whether we will or no; but expression is only altered by a man of genius. A great many second-rate poets, in fact, are second-rate just for this reason, that they have not the sensitiveness and consciousness to perceive that they feel differently from the preceding generation, and therefore must use words differently.

Eliot's own work as the man of genius who altered expression is intimately bound up with that of the critic who saw that 'every vital development in language is a development of feeling as well'. The technique that has mattered in our day is the outcome of

an intense and highly conscious work of critical intelligence [which] necessarily preceded and accompanied the discovery of the new uses of the words, the means of expressing or creating the new feelings and modes of thought, the new rhythms, the new versification. This is the critical intelligence manifested in those early essays: Eliot's best, his important, criticism has an immediate relation to his technical problems as the poet who at that moment in history, was faced with 'altering expression'.[14]

'Never', Leavis has said, 'had criticism a more decisive influence.' The intimate connection between Eliot's poetry and criticism was what drew attention to the truly classical statements that his early essays contain. In 'The Perfect Critic', which came out first of all in *The Athenaeum* and was reprinted in *The Sacred Wood*, Eliot noted the likelihood that the critic and the creative artist should frequently be the same person. And more recently he rightly said of his own best criticism that it consists of essays on poets and poetic dramatists who had influenced him. The essay on Marvell, for example, is a model of critical conciseness, accuracy, and suggestiveness – evaluating (with a little helpful practical analysis by the way) Marvell's own personal distinction, generalizing to probe the nature of the quality (wit) which he shared with the earlier metaphysicals and with Dryden and Pope, then back again to isolate the precise tone of its appearance in Marvell. No better introduction to a poet could be found; it leaves most of the work to be done by the reader himself, while making clear the lines which can profitably be followed up. And in so doing it makes generalizations which open up new ways of approach to English poetry as a whole. It is hardly too much to say that this essay and its two companions in the pamphlet *Homage to John Dryden* began the whole movement of re-appraisal in which *Scrutiny* later played the most important part.

But the connection between Eliot's decline as a poet (decline, that is, from *Four Quartets* to the subsequent plays in verse) and the frequency with which he came to produce arbitrary and unsubstantiated critical dogmas will not seem a chance one. And just as there are forced and unrealized collocations in *The Waste Land*, as Edgell Rickword pointed out, so even in the early criticism appear ideas and doctrines (among them some that have been widely influential) which are arbitrary, being unrelated to his general critical insights or to the creative successes that seemed to lend them force. The dogma of impersonality, which began its career in 'Tradition and the Individual Talent' (see in *Selected Essays*) is the most notorious of these. In this essay, Eliot, extending the idea of the poet as the supreme representative of consciousness in his time, expels the poet's mind and individuality from having any part in the poetic process. The poet's mind is represented as

a receptacle for seizing and storing up numberless feelings, phrases, images, which remain there until all the particles which can unite to form a new compound are present together.

How this uniting happens we never learn – only that 'floating feelings' come together:

The ode of Keats contains a number of feelings which have nothing particular to do with the nightingale, but which the nightingale, partly perhaps because of its attractive name, and partly because of its reputation, served to bring together.

The mind of the poet is said during this process to be as unaffected as the shred of platinum used as a catalyst (even though somehow it 'digests' and 'transmutes' 'the passions which are its material'). We hear a good deal – here and throughout Eliot's work – of the business of poetry being to express emotions, though whose or what must remain in doubt. In the end the complete divorce postulated between 'the man who suffers and the mind which creates' opens the door for a determination in which the distinguished individual has no part and the poet is a mere mouthpiece of his age, whose business is 'to express the greatest emotional intensity of his time, based on whatever his time happened to think'.

It is difficult to makes short statements about Eliot's criticism because of the radical inconsistency which it so often displays, a habit which moved Yvor Winters to exclaim that 'at any time he can speak with equal firmness and dignity on both sides of almost any question, and with no realization of the difficulties in which he is involved'. But a generalization about his later work would be bound to take note of the increasing (but possibly always deep-seated) conventionality of his judgement, curiously contradicting his very real achievement. His record (inconsistencies and all) with regard to his contemporaries was all along very unhappy; rather less to be foreseen was his acceptance of academic or even Book Society standards and attitudes, maintained without a substantiating relation to the work in hand and upheld, one feels (especially in the proposal of interest in Kipling as a 'great verse-writer'), for reasons other than those of a literary critic.

Eliot's best – his lasting – criticism, then, is 'a by-product of his poetry workshop'. It in a sense codified the 'change of expression' which his poetry had made to correspond with the change of sensibility that he had found. It was the poetry, as Leavis has said, that drew attention to the criticism, and not the other way round; inevitably the poetic achievement, with its so notably new distinction, lent speciousness to much in the criticism that has since seemed hollow or arbitrary.

The same qualifications do not need to be made about the two other great practitioner-critics, in whom none the less a close link between the two sides of their work is always apparent: Henry James and D. H. Lawrence. Both wrote much about the fiction of their own and earlier periods, and related it to the problems, opportunities, and challenges which faced them as novelists; but both also have produced judgements on novelists and novels which achieve classical rank in their accuracy and the keenness of their understanding as well of the particular concerns of their subject as of the general conditions under which the novel can be met, and against which it is to be judged. James's book on Hawthorne, his essays on Flaubert, Maupassant, and Zola, and on Arnold, Lawrence's on Galsworthy, and

Verga, his 'Morality and the Novel', and his *Study of Thomas Hardy*
are classics of criticism which should have far more recognition than
they have received.[15]

The parallels can be interestingly extended. Both did much practical criticism in the way of reviewing: for James and Lawrence at
least, a review was an occasion for delicate and precise judgement;
and the valuations they then directly made have remained astonishingly secure. James's review of *Our Mutual Friend* is in its way a
masterpiece, a model of accurate and refined judgement, excellent in
its tone, in the seriousness with which it treats its subject, in the way
in which, while condemning Dickens's work, it enables one to see
by what high standards it is being, and must be, judged. James's
poise at the age of twenty-two is amazing:

> Insight is perhaps too strong a word [for Dickens]; for we are convinced
> that it is one of the chief conditions of his genius not to see beneath the
> surface of things. If we might hazard a definition of his literary character,
> we should, accordingly, call him the greatest of superficial novelists. We are
> aware that this definition confines him to an inferior rank in the department
> of letters which he adorns; but we accept the consequence of our proposition.
> It were, in our opinion, an offence against humanity to place Mr Dickens
> among the greatest novelists. For, to repeat what we have already intimated,
> he has created nothing but figures. He has added nothing to our under-
> standing of human character.

The assurance with which these generalizations are made and
grounded on accurate and pertinent observations of detail in the novel
is entirely convincing. An even more impressive case is the review,
written nine years later, of Flaubert's *La Tentation de Saint Antoine*,
particularly its magnificent ending in which James fixes permanently
the deficiencies of the society which produced the book in such a
way as to make quite clear the measures against which it is found
wanting:

> His book being, with its great effort and its strangely absent charm, the
> really painful failure it seems to us, it would not have been worth while to
> call attention to it if it were not that it pointed to more things than the
> author's own deficiencies. It seems to us to throw a tolerably vivid light on
> the present condition of the French literary intellect. M. Flaubert and his
> contemporaries have pushed so far the education of the senses and the cul-
> tivation of the grotesque in literature and the arts that it has left them morally
> stranded and helpless. In the perception of the materially curious, in fantastic
> refinement of taste and marked ingenuity of expression, they seem to us now

to have reached the limits of the possible. Behind M. Flaubert stands a whole society of aesthetic *raffinés*, demanding stronger and stronger spices in its intellectual diet. But we doubt whether he or any of his companions can permanently satisfy their public, for the simple reason that the human mind, even in indifferent health, does after all need to be *nourished*, and thrives but scantily on a regimen of pigments and sauces. It needs sooner or later – to prolong the metaphor – to detect a body-flavor, and we shall be very surprised if it ever detects one in 'La Tentation de Saint Antoine'.

This measure James to a great extent found in the American society for whom he was writing (most of the best reviews were for *The Atlantic Monthly* and the American *Nation*), and which evidently provided him with an intelligence and responsiveness of a high order, on which he could continuously count. There is, in his early criticism, a sense of being secure among values which were accepted as the natural basis of a civilized society: for James's poise and self-confidence are more than personal – they are those of a distinguished individual who is none the less closely related to a poised and confident society (though one which he understood well enough to criticize shrewdly – see especially *The Europeans* and *Washington Square* – and which in the end failed to provide him with what, as a novelist, he needed). This feeling of knowing for whom he was writing disappears in some degree from James's later work. The criticism which James wrote at the same time as his last novels has something of the same air of having been written in unread loneliness, so strained and involved is the very process of writing. And the work is correspondingly more cautious, more hesitant even – and more distant from us. Even in the essay on Flaubert, one of his best, which has all James's admirable perceptiveness and understanding, he doesn't push his judgements to their logical conclusions:

Emma Bovary, in spite of the nature of her consciousness and in spite of her reflecting so much that of her creator, is really too small an affair ... Why did Flaubert choose, as special conduits of the life he proposed to depict, such inferior and in the case of Frédéric such abject human specimens? I insist only in respect of the latter, the perfection of *Madame Bovary* scarce leaving one much warrant for wishing anything other. Even here, however, the general scale and size of Emma, who is small even of her sort, should be a warning to hyperbole. If I say that in the matter of Frédéric at all events the answer is inevitably detrimental I mean that it weighs heavily on our author's general credit. He wished in each case to make a picture of experience – middling experience, it is true – and of the world close to him; but if he imagined nothing better for his purpose than such a heroine and such a hero, both such limited reflectors and registers, we are forced to believe it to have been by a defect of his mind. And that sign of weakness remains even if it be objected that the images in question were addressed to his purpose better than others would have been: the purpose itself then shows as inferior.

This is excellent, not only in the directness with which the individual judgements are made, but, again, in their grounding. How fine a sense James has of what it is relevant to bring in, and how delicate a feeling for the life to which Flaubert seems to offer an insult. But James's perception and honesty have undermined the general judgement: 'the perfection of *Madame Bovary*'. The particular and the general judgements don't hang together, and Flaubert's genius, after James's criticism, is not enough to resolve the contradiction. Much the same applies, rather less obviously because the writing is more confused, to the extremely high rank that James gives to Balzac in face of very severe limiting judgements.

Like Lawrence's, James's competence as a reviewer extends over an extraordinarily wide field: his essay on Arnold remains one of the finest broad assessments we have, as well as being itself a model of taste and discretion. But it is for his work on the novel that one returns to him with most profit, and this again links him to Lawrence, in whose work too the importance of the novel is central. For James the novel must 'represent life', its province is 'all life, all feeling, all observation, all vision', the essence of its 'moral energy' is to 'survey the whole field'. And so for Lawrence the novel is 'the one bright book of life', which 'can make the whole man alive tremble. Which is more than poetry, philosophy, science, or any other book-tremulation can do'. In these terms, the novel was of course more than just prose fiction:

The Bible – but *all* the Bible – and Homer, and Shakespeare; these are the supreme old novels. These are all things to all men. Which means that in their wholeness they affect the whole man alive, which is the man himself, beyond any part of him. They set the whole tree trembling with a new access of life, they do not just stimulate growth in one direction.

('Why the Novel Matters')

For Lawrence 'the business of art is to reveal the relation between man and his circumambient universe, at the living moment'. It is the living moment that is all-important: in the novel 'everything is true in its own time, place, circumstance, and untrue outside of its own place, time, circumstance. If you try to nail anything down in the novel, either it kills the novel, or the novel gets up and walks away with the nail. Morality in the novel is the trembling instability of the balance ...' true to the ever-changing relationships between men and between man and the universe, never fixed in one place or one attitude. As the relations change, so the living novel changes, informing and leading 'into new places the flow of our sympathetic consciousness, and [leading] our sympathy away in recoil from things gone dead'.

This clearly is something very different from the poor conventional accounts which even quite distinguished critics give of the business of the novel, and its relation to the life it celebrates or describes. The acuteness and originality of Lawrence's criticism, so much a piece with his actual practice of the novel, are natural products of his deep feeling (a religious feeling, he would have called it) of the need to be fully alive, which means not being 'nailed down', not reacting by convention or out of part of oneself, but with one's whole being, seeing the living moment as it really is in all its changing aspects. And the novel will be true to this only if it presents life whole and openly: so its morality is never a fixed counter, but always draws its validity from the conditions of the time and place. Or when the novelist denies this and forgets the demand of honesty and has an axe to grind, 'when the novelist has his thumb in the pan, the novel becomes an unparalleled perverter of men and women'.

The relevance of these passages to Lawrence's own work is very clear. But the insight they show – the insight of a novelist of supreme moral openness and integrity – acts also as a marvellously sure foundation for his criticism of other novelists, and enables him to go to the heart, for instance, of the fatal weakness which makes Galsworthy so palpably second-rate, while it also accounts for his continuing popularity:

Why do we feel so instinctively that [the Forsytes] are inferiors?
It is because they seem to us to have lost caste as human beings, and to have sunk to the level of the social being, that peculiar creature that takes the place in our civilization of the slave in the old civilizations. The human individual is a queer animal, always changing. But the fatal change to-day is the collapse from the psychology of the free human individual into the

psychology of the social being, just as the fatal change in the past was a collapse from the freeman's psyche to the psyche of the slave. The free moral and the social moral: these are the abiding antitheses.

Lawrence, then, all the time traces the links between the books he writes of and the wider interests that they raise, and which he brings relevantly to bear, generalizing to their presence and significance in the world itself. The relation of the novel to the life it serves is always the criterion. So it is in the brilliant short essays on Verga, where so much is said, so many openings made, Verga himself sensitively placed and the value of his work surely indicated, while the issues that his books bring to the fore are further explored and generalized; and so, on a larger scale, in the *Study of Thomas Hardy*, where the novels provide the natural occasion for some of Lawrence's most daring and impressive statements on the morality of art and the morality of life.

Lawrence's genius as a critic is one with his genius as a novelist; there is in him no division of personality: everything he deals with he approaches as 'whole man alive'. It is this which enabled him to write the finest brief statement on the nature of criticism that we have:

Literary criticism can be no more than a reasoned account of the feeling produced upon the critic by the book he is criticizing. Criticism can never be a science: it is, in the first place, much too personal, and in the second, it is concerned with values that science ignores. The touchstone is emotion, not reason. We judge a work of art by its effect on our sincere and vital emotion, and nothing else. All the critical twiddle-twaddle about style and form, all this pseudo-scientific classifying and analysing of books in an imitation-botanical fashion, is mere impertinence and mostly dull jargon.

A critic must be able to *feel* the impact of a work of art in all its complexity and force. To do so, he must be a man of force and complexity himself, which few critics are . . .

More than this, even an artistically and emotionally educated man must be a man of good faith. He must have the courage to admit what he feels, as well as the flexibility to *know* what he feels. So Sainte-Beuve remains, to me, a great critic. And a man like Macaulay, brilliant as he is, is unsatisfactory, because he is not honest. He is emotionally very alive, but he juggles his feelings. He prefers a fine effect to the sincere statement of the aesthetic and emotional reaction. He is quite intellectually capable of giving us a true account of what he feels. But not morally. A critic must be emotionally alive in every fibre, intellectually capable and skilful in essential logic, and then morally very honest.

(Essay on Galsworthy)

In a short chapter it isn't possible to do more than sketch a few lines of approach. One cannot possibly include all those critics whose work has been influential in one way or another, or even all those to whom one can now return with some prospect of profiting by the journey. For since Eliot wrote the polemic quoted at the start, there have emphatically been 'certain books, certain essays, certain sentences, certain men, who have been "useful" to us'. So much so, indeed, that one can only be appalled at the forces at large in the world which have prevented their making the great impression on contemporary life – or even on the literary scene – which one might expect, and which comparable or lesser critics of earlier periods could certainly count on making. In the early eighteenth century, the thought of the *Spectator* and *Tatler* reviewers *was* the thought of the common reader ('who *were* common, because to live in a homo-geneous culture is to move among signs of limited variety'); the influence of the incisive critical insight of Johnson was great; Cole-ridge's presence was felt very impressively. By the end of the nine-teenth century, the effect of Arnold, of James, of Leslie Stephen, was a very much less substantial affair and had tended to become almost exclusively literary: that it had not been so before the influence of Coleridge on Mill testifies. But the situation by the middle of the twentieth century was very much worse than ever Arnold or James conceived. During the period covered by this book we have had the astonishing good fortune of at least three and a half great critics: it is not too much to say that their influence on the larger issues of contemporary life has been negligible. Yet this influence is something that we do without at our peril.

✳   ✱   ✱

That was 'how it struck a contemporary' in 1960 (the essay has been reprinted with minor corrections and a new footnote 13): a piece of the history of the twentieth century from the point of view of one who saw himself as engaged in its process and who believed him-self to share its overall preconceptions. There has never been such intense critical activity; and now, to the writer looking back after another twenty years of it, the dangers and burdens bulk enormously higher and the benefits shrink away. Indeed, criticism as burden has become almost a definition of much of the student's task: it is only the bravest or the maturest who will risk themselves on a creative work new to them without first consulting a shelf of approved criticism. I don't suggest that any critic worth reading would explicitly subscribe to this view; but the academy does, in the expectations it imposes on its staff of teacher–critics, and they dutifully (or self-protectively) oblige. The critic has become an intermediary, a necessary preparation for meeting the original work. Yet Leavis said that the perfect critic is simply the ideal reader, and more recently (in *The Living Principle*) that 'every intelligent reader of creative literature' is a critic. That may seem disarming – and it is a position which Leavis always maintained. Yet the weapons of criticism have not really been discarded: he maintained equally the necessity of literary criticism in a much more formal sense. Moreover, a critic is etymologically one who separates, judges, brings to trial, and though the meanings have broadened, they have changed in essence remarkably little: to be critical is still, in popular speech, to find fault. And though literary criticism need not be, nor has been in the work of those who seem on reflection to have genuinely enlightened us, fundamentally negative, the great majority of this century's criticism reflects both Johnson in the eighteenth century and Arnold in the nineteenth in assuming as axiomatic the existence of 'a certain ideal centre of correct information, taste, and intelligence', an agreed 'scale of value for judgements'. 'This is so, isn't it?' – with its implication that basic and permanent disagreement is either unthinkable or indicates an invincible impercipience in the unpersuaded. I now feel most unhappy in assenting to what underlies such an approach, in agreeing that there is a 'this' to be 'so' or not. What there are are works of creative art and the personal responses of individuals – which may overlap but need not – and what will bring true benefit is not criticism as it has largely been understood and practised in our times, but the ability, to adapt Lawrence's words, to be 'men in their wholeness wholly attending'.

NOTES

1. 'The gang' – a term used of themselves by prominent members of 'the poetical renascence', who, amongst other things, had the run of Eliot's review, *The Criterion*. Spender's autobiography, *World Within World*, is, from its title onwards, a revealing document of the operation of a metropolitan literary clique. It can hardly be recommended on other grounds.

2. In 'The Lesson of Balzac', reprinted in Edel, *The House of Fiction* (London, 1957) '... the appeal I think of is precisely from the general judgement, and not to it; it is to the particular judgement altogether: by which I mean to that quantity of opinion, very small at all times, but at all times infinitely precious, that is capable of giving some intelligible account of itself.'

3. 'Criticism', included in *The Art of Fiction*, ed. Morris Roberts (New York, 1948). Orwell's essay, 'Politics and the English Language' (reprinted in the Penguin *Selected Essays*), is an interesting extension of this theme.

4. *How to Read*, reprinted in *Literary Essays of Ezra Pound* (London, 1954). This and other of Pound's manifestos have useful propaganda material (especially 'The Teacher's Mission'), though what active criticism they contain is generally perverse. Pound's frequent impercipience and irresponsibility make even the use of his propaganda a dangerous business and liable to misinterpretation. See Leavis, *How to Teach Reading*, reprinted as Appendix II to *Education and the University* (2nd edn, London, 1948).

5. 'If a poet gets a large audience very quickly, that is a rather suspicious circumstance: for it leads us to fear that he is not really doing anything new, that he is only giving people what they are already used to.' (Eliot, 'The Social Function of Poetry'.) Eliot had said in his essay on the Metaphysical Poets (1921) that 'it appears likely that poets in our civilization, as it exists at present, must be *difficult*. Our civilization comprehends great variety and complexity, and this variety and complexity, playing upon a refined sensibility, must produce various and complex results.' An interesting comparison can be made between the reception of Eliot's own (admittedly difficult) poetry and that of more recent 'modern' poets, who have had it far too much their own way. And cf. a review by Edwin Muir in *The Calendar*: 'The writer who does not resist his age, defending himself against all its claims crowding in upon him and overwhelming him, will belong to the literature of fashion. The writer who refuses to realize his age is not likely to belong to literature at all.'

6. Muir's review already cited is a good – and typical – example. The difference between work like this and the reviews that Muir later wrote for *The Observer* is a significant and distressing one: it reflects very largely on what the two journals expect in their readers.

7. *Scrutinies I* and *II*, edited by Edgell Rickword; *Towards Standards of Criticism*, edited by F. R. Leavis.

8. 'The impression we have always had of Mr Eliot's work ... may be analysed into two coincident but not quite simultaneous impressions. The first is the urgency of the personality, which seems sometimes oppressive, and comes near to breaking through the so finely-spun aesthetic fabric; the second is the technique which spins this fabric and to which this slender volume owes its curious ascendancy over the bulky monsters of our time. For it is by his struggle with technique that Mr Eliot has been able to get closer than any other poet to the physiology of our sensations (a poet does not speak merely for himself) to explore and make palpable the more intimate distresses of a generation for which all the romantic escapes had been blocked. And,

though this may seem a heavy burden to lay on the back of technique, we can watch with the deepening of the consciousness, a much finer realization of language . . .' (*Calendar*, II, 278–9).

9. A glance at the contents of a typical issue illustrates the range tackled: for instance, Vol. II, No. 4 contains essays on Burns (John Speirs) and on Swift (Leavis); on the Scientific Best Seller (J. L. Russell); 'What shall we teach?' (Denys Thompson); 'Fleet Street and Pierian Roses' (Q. D. Leavis). The books reviewed included three popular books on art, *Music and the Community*, Baden Powell's autobiography, *Change in the Farm*, and books on anthropology, history, and sociology as well as a number on more strictly literary topics. Nor was this variety ever allowed to become indiscriminate.

The most important product of this educational movement was Leavis's *Education and the University*, a book of great and central significance.

10. cf. 'The Kenyon Review and Scrutiny', *Scrutiny*, XIV. ii. 136: '*Scrutiny* has no orthodoxy and no system to which it expects its contributors to subscribe. But its contributors do, for all the variety represented by their own positions, share a common conception of the kind of discipline of intelligence literary criticism should be, a measure of agreement about the kind of relation literary criticism should bear to "non-literary" matters, and, further, a common conception of the function of a non-specialist intellectual review in contemporary England. They are, in fact, collaborators.'

The work of Yvor Winters, as being that of an impressive intelligence apparently isolated from collaborative exchange, is the most notable case of a fresh and vigorous taste and judgement, which, while aspiring to be much more than individual, have too often remained obstinately personal and idiosyncratic. His work is however of great interest, strikingly original and often penetrating, particularly noteworthy in a scene in which reputations are too easily made and taken for granted.

11. Vol. IX, No. iv. His *Coriolanus* essay (VI. i) is a different matter. I owe to Mr J. M. Newton much of my understanding of these trends in *Scrutiny* and elsewhere.

12. '. . . to insist that literary criticism is, or should be, a specific discipline of intelligence is not to suggest that a serious interest in literature can confine itself to the kind of intensive local analysis associated with "practical criticism" – to the scrutiny of the "words on the page" in their minute relations, their effects of imagery, and so on: a real literary interest is an interest in man, society and civilization, and its boundaries cannot be drawn.' F. R. Leavis, *Scrutiny*, XIII, i, 78.

13. It is now clear that Q. D. Leavis shared deeply not only in the inception but also in the writing of several of F. R. Leavis's earlier books, perhaps most notably *The Great Tradition*, of which it is probably correct to attribute much, including the introductory chapter, to her. The exceptional sharpness of her intelligence, together with her acerbic wit, give a peculiarly astringent and bracing character to her criticism which deserves to be recognized as a fully independent force, sometimes indeed working against what might be taken to be a *Scrutiny* line, though one which may be seen as still exploring the

quasi-sociological concern with literature which marked her first book, *Fiction and the Reading Public* (1932). Mrs Leavis came more prominently to public notice towards the end of her life, appearing as joint author with her husband of *Dickens the Novelist* and *Lectures in America* and also as editor of new texts of several major works of Victorian literature.

14. Leavis, 'T. S. Eliot's Stature as Critic', *Commentary* (New York), Vol. 26, No. 5, November 1958, a valuable essay from the point of view of both its author and its subject. It contains a very fine treatment of the whole doctrine of 'Impersonality'.

15. James's and Lawrence's criticism has never been properly collected, though in Lawrence's case there is a useful volume edited by Anthony Beal, *Selected Literary Criticism* (London, 1955), which contains all the essays mentioned in this chapter as well as much of the *Hardy* and the *Studies in Classic American Literature*. The Galsworthy essay and one or two others are in the Penguin *Selected Essays*; many more appear in *Phoenix* (new edition, London, 1961). James's *Hawthorne* (and Lawrence's *Studies*) is reprinted in Wilson, *The Shock of Recognition* (London, 1956). James's own collections *French Poets and Novelists*, *Partial Portraits*, and *Notes on Novelists* have long been out of print; and the only readily available work now is in Mordell, ed., *Literary Reviews and Essays* (a compendious anthology of James's excellent early reviews) (Grove Press, 1957), Edel, *The House of Fiction* (London, 1957), and M. Shapira, *Selected Literary Criticism of Henry James* (London, 1963).

EZRA POUND'S
HUGH SELWYN MAUBERLEY

GEORGE DEKKER

Critics who acclaim the American poet Ezra Pound as one of the great masters of modern literature usually do so on the basis of the polyglot post-Whitmanian epic of his middle and later years, *The Cantos*. Others feel sure that he is best remembered as the devoted young scholar-poet-publicist who, living in London from 1908 to 1921, earned himself a permanent place in the history of British literature as the friend and advocate of Yeats, Ford, Wyndham Lewis, Eliot and Joyce; as a cranky and yet discerning pioneer in the appreciation of James's fiction and Lawrence's poetry; and above all as the unsparing anatomist of the modern British world of letters in the paired sequences of short poems entitled *Hugh Selwyn Mauberley* (1919–20). Still others urge that Pound's is essentially the negative capability of a translator, arguably the greatest since Dryden, and that his masterpiece is the extraordinary paraphrase from the Latin, *Homage to Sextus Propertius* (1917).

Whatever the final reckoning, it must be owned that his major poems have all proven highly problematic, as elusive in form and meaning as unstable in critical reputation over the years. *Mauberley* is shorter than the others and speaks more directly to the interests of most readers, and yet it too is formidably difficult. Most of its allusions have by now been glozed satisfactorily and present no insuperable obstacles to readers who can cope with Yeats or Eliot.[1] But the ground in *Mauberley* is most treacherous where it appears most firm.

Unlike *Propertius* and *The Cantos*, which are written in free verse and proceed from image to image without regard for the reader's expectations of a narrative or discursive order, *Mauberley* has the seeming advantage of a more traditional format. It is written mainly in rhymed quatrains and has a narrative frame. The 'story' it tells, of the American poet 'E. P.' and his English double 'Mauberley', is clear enough in broad outline and intention. Like such variations on the *doppelgänger* theme as *Heart of Darkness* and James's *The Jolly Corner*, it projects the disasters (in this case artistic sterility) that might have befallen the protagonist had his luck been different (had he not been 'born/ In a half-savage country, out of date'). *Mauberley* is subtitled 'Life and Contacts', and as we discover in the second sequence of poems, Mauberley's personal and artistic life is destroyed by his contacts with the cultural milieu depicted in the first sequence. E. P., on the other hand, like Conrad's Marlow, survives his contacts with the same hostile environment to recount the 'Life' of his wraith. 'Of course, I'm no more Mauberley than Eliot is Prufrock,' Pound explained shortly after the poem was published, and went on to describe it as 'a study in form, an attempt to condense the James novel'.[2] The parallel with Eliot and Prufrock is just and helpful as a gauge of the ironic distance between Pound and Mauberley, but the suggestion that *Mauberley* might be read as a condensed James novel should give us pause.

For there are several abrupt and puzzling shifts of point-of-view in the poem such as Eliot's monologue form proscribes and such as James, of all novelists, would never have allowed himself. This means that at several key moments we are unsure of the identity of the speaker or the value, from Pound's perspective, of what he says. Some of these obscurities, especially in the narrative frame provided by 'E. P. Ode' and the entire second sequence, seem to be due to the author's inexperience in handling point-of-view in an extended narrative. The problems of interpretation thus occasioned are doubtless among the most teasing in modern poetry and must receive further scrutiny in the present essay. But I believe that the enduring interest of *Mauberley* lies much less in the E. P.–Mauberley narrative than in the Contacts sequence, from Poem II through the 'Envoi', and that it should be our first concern.

The Contacts section richly exemplifies the qualities that admirers have always claimed for *Mauberley*. From Eliot to F. R. Leavis to Hugh Kenner, distinguished critics have insisted on its technical virtuosity and cultural centrality. Eliot's is the classic summing-up.[3]

... the poem seems to me, when you have marked the sophistication and great variety of the verse, verse of a man who knows his way about, to be a positive document of sensibility. It is compact of the experience of a certain man in a certain place at a certain time; and it is also a document of an epoch; it is genuine tragedy and comedy; and it is, in the best sense of Arnold's worn phrase, a 'criticism of life'.

The life criticized is not so much English life as that which was experienced, especially by artists, in the capital city of the British Empire during its period of greatest power and affluence. Indeed, Poems II–V have a still wider range and offer a critique of the social and cultural values of the North Atlantic nations during the most expansionist phase of capitalism, roughly since the American Civil War and the Franco-Prussian War. (There are allusions to both wars.) This section of the sequence, which attacks the secularization, mass-production, sexual repressiveness and egalitarianism of modern life, culminates in two bitter poems on the First World War and establishes the larger economic and social context for the London literary scene depicted in the rest of the sequence.

Poem II poses what Pound took to be the central dilemma of the twentieth-century artist and implies a strategy for dealing with it:

> The age demanded an image
> Of its accelerated grimace,
> Something for the modern stage,
> Not, at any rate, an Attic grace;

What is special about the artist–patron relationship envisaged in these lines is suggested first of all by 'demanded', a word that conveys both an imperious tone and, like 'at any rate', an association with commerce. ('Supply and demand', 'pay on demand'.) And the patron that demands its portrait is no individual person but a featureless abstraction, 'The age', representative of mass-consumership and mass-production:

> The 'age demanded' chiefly a mould in plaster,
> Made with no loss of time,
> A prose kinema, not, not assuredly, alabaster
> Or the 'sculpture' of rhyme.

In its second appearance the phrase 'age demanded' means what it did before but also contains the poet's reply: in a sense at once colloquial and commercial the age 'asked for it', i.e. demanded and received the 'mould in plaster' which was its due. This shift of meaning is articulated by a shift of tone and perspective as the speaker takes the offensive, dissociating the art he values from the products and materials which do indeed most truly portray the age.

The slighting references to 'the modern stage' and 'A prose kinema' do not imply hostility to literary realism as such: Pound admired Flaubert, the Goncourts, Ibsen and James for their craftsmanship and/or candour. But he was hostile to the deterministic theory developed by some of their friends and followers (notably Henry Adams) that confused the relationship between art and life by requiring art in its every aspect, including form and mode of presentation, to be a mere reflector of the contemporary scene. What the 'age demands' is the *reductio ad absurdum* of this theory. Pound's own art in these quatrains feigns acquiescence to the demands of the age, but its imperfect rhymes and stuttering rhythms belong to the deeper realism which judges and interprets what it reflects. Moreover, like similar allusions in the mock-heroic poems of Dryden and Pope, such phrases as 'inward gaze' and 'sculpture of rhyme' remind us of ranges of experience and performance which are no less true and perennially relevant for being neglected or denied. At the end of the Contacts sequence stands, italicized in its foreignness, a lyric which recreates the 'sculpture of rhyme' of the English song tradition at its height, and which asserts, against the modern view that time is money and therefore not to be lost, the view that the true measures of time are human life and beauty, which can be 'saved' only by the poet's lavish expenditure of time.

Poem III carries forward the offensive initiated in the third quatrain of II but surveys the same topics from a temporal perspective as long as the previous one was grotesquely short:

> The tea-rose tea-gown, etc.
> Supplants the mousseline of Cos,
> The pianola 'replaces'
> Sappho's barbitos.

Did Pound fully recognize just how distorting such contrasts between the cultural high points of one age and the low points of another must be? So long as the conflict is limited to fabrics and musical instruments, we may not care greatly that the method is reductive and anti-historical. We may even applaud its use against modern 'Puritanism':

Christ follows Dionysius,
Phallic and ambrosial
Made way for macerations;
Caliban casts out Ariel.

The terse line 'Caliban casts out Ariel' calls to mind Ernest Renan, whose parable of the triumph of utilitarian democracy in the play *Caliban, suite de La Tempête* (1878) anticipates Pound's own. Renan's demagogic Caliban also casts out Ariel, spirit of art and magic, and there can be no doubt that Renan would have appreciated the anti-egalitarian invective of the fifth and sixth quatrains of this poem.[4] Now that we are on to politics, and politics too of a kind that might be described (misleadingly, I think) as 'proto-fascist', we may be more concerned to know whether Pound appreciated it also.

The letters and essays he wrote at this time – the time of Prohibition, the Bolshevist take-over in Russia, the Versailles Treaty, censorship of *Ulysses*, etc. – confirm that the sentiments of Poem III were close to Pound's own. They were close as well to those of his friends Yeats, Ford, Eliot and Lewis, and their provenance may be traced either through intermediaries like Lionel Johnson and T. E. Hulme or directly to the great anti-democratic literary intellectual tradition of nineteenth-century France. Equally characteristic of that tradition were Baudelaire's savage coinage 'zoocracy' and Huysmans's Romantic castle of art. Renan belonged to it and so, more importantly for Pound, did Flaubert and Théophile Gautier, literary artists of the first rank who dedicated their lives to uncompromising craftsmanship and truthfulness in the face of bourgeois incomprehension and outrage. Flaubert is described in the opening poem of *Mauberley* as Pound's 'true Penelope', and Gautier's quatrains are the principal model for Pound's. As John Espey has shown, Gautier's influence is nowhere stronger than in Poem III.[5]

Des dieux que l'art toujours révère
Trônaient au ciel marmoréen;
Mais l'Olympe cède au Calvaire,
Jupiter au Nazaréen;

If the voice we hear in Poem III has a decidedly French inflection, it is because Pound believed that French authors of the nineteenth century provided his own generation with a model not only of technical discipline but also of spirited resistance to basically the same

432

kind of social pressures. Therefore any suggestion that Pound does not sympathize with the views expressed in that poem fails to take adequate account of his likely (and, it may be added, thoroughly characteristic) strategy in Englishing earlier foreign writers. Poem III is his 'homage' to his French forebears. All the same, sympathy does not mean total identification with their views.

If he had attributed the poem to a *persona* like Fra Lippo Lippi or Crazy Jane, clearly distinct from himself although apparently claiming his good will and sometimes even his intellectual assent, we should infer Pound's attitudes to the speaker, but no more expect explicit judgements and declarations of principle than we should from Browning or Yeats, or more to the point, the author of *The Ambassadors*. As James gradually refined the omniscient narrator out of existence, his fiction became increasingly 'dramatic'; that is, he had, like a playwright, to indicate his attitudes by means of the indirect commentary of pointed juxtapositions, parallels and contrasts of scene, motive and situation. In his 'attempt to condense the James novel' Pound provides a similar commentary, but one which requires greater powers of inference from the reader. Thus the shift of temporal perspective between Poems II and III — a shift as vertiginous in its way as that between Books One and Two of *Gulliver's Travels* — ought to warn us that the positions taken in III are extreme. They are advanced not as a judicious weighing of all the evidence, but as a vigorous debater's rebuttal of a position which, if accepted, would mean that the highest form of contemporary art is a *March of Time* newsreel. That Pound does not identify himself unreservedly with the rebuttal is made more certain by the relationship between Poems IV and V, on the Great War, and the final quatrain of III:

> O bright Apollo,
> τίν' ἄνδρα, τίν' ἥρωα, τίνα θεὸν,
> What god, man, or hero
> Shall I place a tin wreath upon!

The clear implication of these lines, in which the Greek of Pindar's Second Olympic Ode is rearranged and then immediately translated, is that the age is as lacking in heroes as in Sapphic lyres. But in the poem that follows Pound celebrates heroes compared with whom the Panhellenic games' victors were paltry:

> Daring as never before, wastage as never before.
> Young blood and high blood,
> fair cheeks, and fine bodies;
>
> fortitude as never before ...

Pound is on record as considering Pindar 'the prize wind-bag of all ages',[6] i.e. an inflated and inflationary writer; whereas Poem IV is marked throughout by recognition of the sordid as well as the nobler aspects of motivation and behaviour. It is the cautious and balanced historical assessment which III is not, and all of the internal and external evidence indicates that the identification between author and speaker is as close here as it ever is in *Mauberley*.

In a letter quoted earlier, Pound remarked that 'The meter in *Mauberley* is Gautier and Bion's "Adonis"; or at least those are the two grafts I was trying to flavour it with'. The Bion model imitated with some closeness in Poem IV, and fleetingly elsewhere, is characterized by irregular line lengths, hesitations and the lavish use of syntactical parallelisms and other forms of verbal repetition. Had we not been referred to Bion, we might have guessed a severe pruning and disciplining of the prosodic forms that Whitman adapted from the English Bible. For Whitman was, after all, the great elegist of the first major Machine-Age war as well as the progenitor of much of the sprawling free verse that *Mauberley* was meant to criticize by example:[7]

> I saw battle-corpses, myriads of them,
> And the white skeletons of young men – I saw them;

Pound's lines are stricter and have only a hint of Whitmanian plangency:

> There died a myriad,
> And of the best, among them,
> For an old bitch gone in the teeth,
> For a botched civilization, ...

The tone in Poem V modulates rapidly from elegy to unpurged bitterness – just the opposite of the emotional progression in *When Lilacs Last in the Dooryard Bloom'd*. Pound believed that the First World War had been fought 'for' civilization, but he could not forget that armaments factories and colonial possessions now belonged as much to European civilization as Dante or the Rheims cathedral.

With *Yeux Glauques*, Pound moves in for a close-up of the British world of letters during the previous half-century, exchanging the generalizing force and grandeur of the early poems for a piquant particularity. Indeed, so packed with biographical anecdote are Poems VI and VII that a detailed exegesis would require several pages. However, the two poems – one concerned with the Pre-Raphaelites, the other with the Nineties Poets – are obscure *only* in details, which are usually more important for what they readily suggest to an intelligent reader than for anything which scholarly annotation could explain. Thus it is a fact that Ruskin wrote a lecture entitled *Of Kings' Treasuries*, but the actual lecture appears to have little bearing on the first quatrain of 'Yeux Glauques':

> Gladstone was still respected,
> When John Ruskin produced
> 'Kings' Treasuries'; Swinburne
> And Rossetti still abused.

Fresh from reading *The Education of Henry Adams*, Pound may well have had in mind Gladstone's duplicitous role in British diplomacy during the American Civil War, and he doubtless had his reasons for pillorying Ruskin as well. But what really matters is the obvious contrast between 'official' Victorian culture as represented by Gladstone and Ruskin ('respected', 'produced', 'Kings' Treasuries') and the 'counter-culture' represented by Swinburne and Rossetti. Poems VI and VII are about that counter-culture: its Bohemian charm and squalor; its confusions of art, life and religion; and its few slender masterpieces, especially of painting and translation. The anecdotal particulars which embody these themes are often strictly legendary. That is, they convey impressions often factually inaccurate but memorable and revealing:

> ... how Johnson (Lionel) died
> By falling from a high stool in a pub ...
> But showed no trace of alcohol
> At the autopsy, privately performed –
> Tissue preserved – the pure mind
> Arose toward Newman as the whisky warmed.

A witty combination of ancestral tall tale and literary saint's legend, this apocryphal story does not ask to be accepted as historistic; on the contrary, the 'evidence' of sanctity (no deterioration of the body) is plainly as bogus as the purity of the 'spiritual' uplift is suspect. The story has the 'impressionistic truth' that Ford claimed for his memoir of Conrad.

Ford's example is pertinent in other ways as well. He is usually taken to be the 'stylist' of Poem x, and he is a likely source of the (mis)information on which Pound based the other two portraits – 'Brennbaum' and 'Mr Nixon' – in a brief series dealing with eminent contemporary men of letters. The first of these shows how Pound 'improved' on history:

> The sky-like limpid eyes,
> The circular infant's face,
> The stiffness from spats to collar
> Never relaxing into grace;

The infantile sexual development associated with the infant's face of 'Brennbaum "the Impeccable" ' actually belonged to Lionel Johnson, since what Johnson's autopsy *did* reveal was that he had never matured physically. If Brennbaum is impeccable, Pound implies, it is because he is incapable of sinning. (The epithets 'sky-like' and 'circular', like the subsequent mention of Horeb and Sinai, confirm a very Poundian *double entendre* in 'grace'.) Brennbaum's stiff refinement is juxtaposed with the unbuttoned vulgarity of Mr Nixon:

> In the cream gilded cabin of his steam yacht
> Mr Nixon advised me kindly, to advance with fewer
> Dangers of delay. 'Consider
>   Carefully the reviewer.

'Anal' and 'oral' might be the terms a psychologist would use: we note, as well, the contrasts between choir stall and naval headquarters, static and energetic syntax, upper and middle class. With each of these writers, success is a matter of skilful self-promotion in the appropriate market. The dedicated stylist of Poem x, however, is obliged to retreat, 'Unpaid, uncelebrated', to the country where

> Nature receives him;
> With a placid and uneducated mistress
> He exercises his talents
> And the soil meets his distress.

Clearly, his 'distress' is financial as well as emotional. Whether the 'mistress' is Nature personified, an actual 'earthy' woman, or both, is uncertain, and deliberately so, since the ambiguity makes Pound's point – of first importance in the poems that follow – that it is through sexual union that civilized man is best able to maintain a vital contact with nature.

Pound discovered in the literature of several cultures – Greek, Roman, French – reasons for believing that sexual love and poetic expression were closely and sometimes causally related phenomena. It could be maintained for instance that sexuality, in this case highly refined and sublimated, inspired the rebirth of secular verse and music in the love songs of the Provençal troubadours and their heirs – among the most notable of these being the English lyric poets from Chaucer to Waller. Pound even speculated that poetry was 'phallic' in nature while (his eye on Rabelais, Flaubert and Joyce) prose fiction was 'excremental'.[8] In this light the censorship and sexual repressiveness attacked earlier in *Mauberley* take on a particularly sinister significance: they threaten to cut off the poet from his primary source of inspiration and energy. And of knowledge likewise, since according to the aphorism of Rémy de Gourmont adapted in the first line of Poem XI, women are 'conservatrices des traditions milésiennes'. Gourmont's reference to the ancient and erotic Milesian tales is a tribute to women's capacity to transmit the wisdom (and not solely erotic wisdom) of the race in spite of fads and fashions. Presumably it was this kind of wisdom and renewal that the stylist gained from his 'placid and uneducated mistress' and could not have received from the class-corseted suburban woman of Poem XI or the society dame of Poem XII. The portrait of Lady Valentine is especially damning because the traditions she fails to keep alive are those which have been in the keeping of women of her class since the beloved *domnas* of the troubadours:

> Doubtful, somewhat, of the value
> Of well-gowned approbation
> Of literary effort,
> But never of The Lady Valentine's vocation:

In an ironic reversal of roles the poet rather than the lady is the conservator. His mythopoeic imagination is still able to transform a tawdry or merely well-upholstered object into a thing of beauty:

> 'Daphne with her thighs in bark
> Stretches toward me her leafy hands' –
> Subjectively.

The moment may strike us as Prufrockian. (The quotation is from Gautier but the manner, like Eliot's early manner, is derived from Laforgue.) But this *persona* retains, as Prufrock could not, a sense of personal and vocational worth and dignity in the face of standards he considers false.

Developing his distinction between prose as excremental and poetry as phallic, Pound hypothesized in his essay on James that the former 'arises, perhaps, from an instinct of negation', of the need to analyse 'something one wants to eliminate'. On the other hand, poetry is 'the assertion of a positive, i.e. of desire', and poetic satire is 'only an assertion of this positive inversely, i.e. as of an opposite hatred'.[9] Other words he associates with poetry are 'synthesis' and 'emotional'. Without arguing for their perfect transparency, I believe that the distinctions he ventures in this analysis can help us understand what was involved in his 'attempt to condense the James novel'. Merely to condense it was impossible; he had instead to transform James's leisurely analysis and accumulation of data into something equivalent and yet radically different: poetic satire. *Mauberley* is full of hatred and what often strikes us as over-simple assertions of value. But its syntheses of the disparate particulars of history into luminous paradigms (especially in Poems VI–XII) are memorable and true as only poetry can be, and it everywhere implies the opposite of hatred, the positive ideals of a rich and humane civilization. In the 'Envoi' he at last gives us the 'assertion of a positive, i.e. of desire' in the appropriate form of a lyric modelled upon and echoing a host of medieval and renaissance English love songs. The shift from negative to positive at this moment is in no respect more exhilarating than in the impression of rhythmic release that the 'Envoi' creates, of verse finally given its head by an expert and loving hand.

In outline and intention, I have said, the narrative design of *Mauberley* is fairly clear. E. P. is dismissed in the opening poem as, in various ways, unable to meet the demands of the age; the Contacts section reveals what he was up against. The second sequence, 'Mauberley/1920', is a third-person narrative which recounts the life of

an imaginary British poet who, lacking virility and personal toughness, pursues a course of aesthetic escapism to the point of personal
and artistic extinction. Each sequence concludes with a poem which
appears to be the last bow of E. P. and Mauberley respectively. That
some such pattern of ironic doubling exists cannot be doubted. The
doubts concern the identities of Pound's *dramatis personae* at several
junctures and hence, inevitably, of the specific targets of his irony.

The most notorious crux is the identity of the speaker of the first
poem, *E. P. Ode*. If, as seems likely, the 'biographer' of Mauberley
in the second sequence is E. P., the dismissive voice of *E. P. Ode*
ought for symmetry's sake to be Mauberley's. And sure enough,
Pound told a correspondent some thirty years later that 'Mauberley
buries E. P. in the first poem; gets rid of all his troublesome
energies'.[10] This may be so, but I am one reader who cannot accept
that the insecure aesthete portrayed later is the obtuse and magisterial
critic who concludes:

> Unaffected by 'the march of events',
> He passed from men's memory in *l'an trentiesme*
> *De son eage*; the case presents
> No adjunct to the Muses' diadem.

On the contrary, this speaker appears to confound E. P. with Mauberley, attributing the latter's weaknesses to the American. And the
rest of *Mauberley* appears to be an *éclaircissement* of the muddle deliberately created in *E. P. Ode*. But if this reading is accepted, as I
think it should be, what are we to make of the doubling 'pattern' or
of Pound's later gloss?

A related problem arises in connection with the last poem, 'Medallion'. Here the poet's vision of a woman singing metamorphoses her
into an object – firstly into a plate in a tome on comparative religion
and secondly into something metallic or intractable:

> Honey-red, closing the face-oval,
> A basket-work of braids which seem as if they were
> Spun in King Minos' hall
> From metal, or intractable amber;

Pound's implicit judgement on this reification might seem too
obvious to require further comment. And yet there are passages in his
contemporary prose works which have been construed to endorse
such alchemy. Donald Davie notes passages extolling Joyce's 'metal

finish' and the 'hardness' of Gautier's *Émaux et Camées*. Jo Brantley Berryman, demonstrating that the woman portrayed in both *Medallion* and *Envoi* was the singer Raymonde Collignon, quotes Pound's admiring description of her: 'As long as this *diseuse* was on the stage she was non-human; she was, if you like, a china image . . .'[11] On Dr Berryman's showing, *Medallion* conforms to Pound's aesthetic ideals and is offered as a poem as excellent of its kind as the *Envoi*; and it is Pound's poem, not Mauberley's!

What can be said in favour of Mauberley's authorship? We have seen that *Mauberley* is much preoccupied with confused values and identities, counterfeits and misattributions. And in the *Envoi* – companion poem of *Medallion* and unquestionably a touchstone for *Mauberley* as a whole – Pound is scrupulously careful to distinguish between the attributes of life (transient and particular) and art (permanent and archetypal). In *Medallion* the poet's singleness of vision converts all things – and especially things sexual – into the terms of art. That is Mauberley's way of dealing with life, as it so consummately was of one of his chief fictional forebears, Adam Verver of *The Golden Bowl*. James remarks ironically:

> Nothing perhaps might affect us as queerer, than this application of the same measure of value to such different pieces of property as old Persian carpets, say, and new human acquisitions . . . As it had served him to satisfy himself, so to speak, both about Amerigo and about the Bernardino Luini he had happened to come to knowledge of at the time he was consenting to the announcement of his daughter's betrothal, so it served him at present to satisfy himself about Charlotte Stant and an extraordinary set of oriental tiles . . .[12]

An artist rather than a collector, Mauberley makes his own 'Luini in porcelain', but his priorities and confusions are the same as Verver's. Just as life takes its revenge on Verver (cuckolded by his son-in-law Amerigo), so it does on Mauberley as well. For, like himself in sexual relations, his poem is 'frigid'. That is Pound's word for the poetry of those who tried to be 'poetic' by duplicating the 'hardness' of Gautier's *manner* rather than his 'intentness on the quality of the emotion to be conveyed'.[13] *Medallion* is all manner, all surface – hard and brilliant, to be sure, but lending itself to the evasion rather than the conveyance of emotion.

Dr Berryman's findings do suggest one refinement of this reading.

Pound's description of Collignon specifies that she was 'non-human', a 'china image', as long as she was *on the stage*. The singer in *Medallion* is on stage, i.e. an artist in concert, and this may be the sole occasion when Mauberley's habitual way of viewing women would be the appropriate one. If this 'refinement' strikes the reader as finical and imported from outside the poem, I can reply only that the narrative frame of *Mauberley* constantly drives its interpreters to such shifts. Nobody has been able to give a wholly convincing account of it. Therefore Donald Davie may be right to say that *Mauberley* 'falls to pieces, though the pieces are brilliant, intelligent always, and sometimes moving'.[14] But how large is the largest piece? The more we read the Contacts section, the more aware we become both of coherent linear progression and of parallels and cross-references that make the individual poems within it mutually illuminating parts of a larger whole. Where among modern poems written in English do we find a poem or passage of comparable length that combines so much variety and profound 'criticism of life' with such sustained perfection and power of execution?

NOTES

1. Basic resources for the study of *Mauberley* are John J. Espey, *Ezra Pound's Mauberley: A Study in Composition* (London, 1955) and K. K. Ruthven, *A Guide to Ezra Pound's Personae* (Berkeley and Los Angeles, 1969).

2. *The Letters of Ezra Pound 1907–1941*, ed. D. D. Paige (London, 1950; reprinted 1971), 180.

3. T. S. Eliot, 'Introduction: 1928', *Selected Poems by Ezra Pound* (London, 1928; new edn 1949), 20. This, the most widely circulated selection of Pound's early poems, is the source of my quotations. F. R. Leavis's and Hugh Kenner's discussions appear in *New Bearings in English Poetry* (London, 1932; new edn 1951) and *The Poetry of Ezra Pound* (London, 1951).

4. The best account of Pound's politics is in William Chace, *The Political Identities of Ezra Pound and T. S. Eliot* (Stanford, 1973).

5. Quoted by Espey, 36. Gautier's poem is *Bûchers et Tombeaux*.

6. *Letters*, 87.

7. '. . . two authors . . . decided that the dilutation of *vers libre*, Amygism, Lee Masterism, general floppiness had gone too far and that some counter-current must be set going . . . Results: Poems in Mr Eliot's *second* volume . . . also "H. S. Mauberley".' Quoted from 'Harold Munro' (1932) by Espey, 25.

8. *Pound/Joyce*, ed. Forrest Read (London, 1968), 144, 146–7. The sexual

motifs in Pound's poetry are discussed by Espey and, more fully, by George Dekker, *Sailing After Knowledge* (London, 1963).

9. 'Henry James' (1918), *Instigations of Ezra Pound* (1930, reprinted Freeport, N. Y., 1967), 147–8.

10. Thomas E. Connolly, 'Further Notes on *Mauberley*', *Accent*, XVI (1956), 59.

11. Donald Davie, *Ezra Pound: Poet as Sculptor* (London, 1965), 100. Jo Brantley Berryman, ' "Medallion": Pound's Poem', *Paideuma*, II (Winter 1973), 391–8.

12. *The Golden Bowl*, Vol. I (New York, 1909), 196–7.

13. 'A Study in French Poets', *Instigations*, 6.

14. Davie, *Ezra Pound*, 101.

T. S. ELIOT: POET AND CRITIC

L. G. SALINGAR

Since T. S. Eliot published his first volume in 1917, his poetry has overcome the incomprehension or dislike of critics bound by nineteenth-century literary conventions and won for him an authority such as no other poet in English has enjoyed since Tennyson – an authority seconded by his prestige as a critic, publicist and playwright. Eliot restored the intellectual dignity of English poetry; at a time when few people would take it seriously, he formed a means of expression in poetry for the surface and the depths of a representative modern mind, intensely aware of his surroundings, their place in history, and his intimate reaction to them. And with his sensitive, multi-lingual scholarship he has contributed more than any other modern writer to the framework of ideas within which English poetry, past as well as present, is read and interpreted. A decisive literary achievement; yet one that, by its very power, drives the reader to ask whether it has not been gained at a heavy cost, the cost of ignoring or suppressing a great deal of common feeling and experience. Precisely because of his great influence on modern literature, it is important for us to try to judge Eliot's work clearly and in perspective.

Two impressions stand out from his first volume, *Prufrock and Other Observations* (written 1909–15). One is the impression of a remarkable technique, already flexible and accomplished. The other is that the poet is usually dealing with involved or obscure or painful states of mind. And the special question raised by this poetry of 'observations', written in some sense from the outside, is whether the accomplishment is serving to elucidate the states of mind, or doing something else instead.

The flexible technique springs largely, as Eliot has told us, from his early study of Jacobean stage verse and the free verse of Jules Laforgue[1] (though to these should perhaps be added the influence

443

of Browning and of Henry James). Webster and Laforgue speak together, for example, in lines such as these from the *Portrait of a Lady* (written 1910):

> I feel like one who smiles, and turning shall remark
> Suddenly, his expression in a glass.
> My self-possession gutters; we are really in the dark.

It is a sign of Eliot's originality and insight that he should have turned to these two models in verse and studied them together; and especially that he should have been one of the first English writers to respond to the most significant developments in modern French poetry. For the prevailing influence in these early poems is that of Laforgue, with Baudelaire behind him. From this source, besides his fluid metre, Eliot has adapted his urban settings, with their burden of tedium and nostalgia, and his notation of feelings by means of fugitive and intermingled sense-impressions, diversified with literary allusions or ironic asides:

> You will see me any morning in the park
> Reading the comics and the sporting page ...
>
> I keep my countenance,
> I remain self-possessed
> Except when a street piano, mechanical and tired
> Reiterates some worn-out common song
> With the smell of hyacinths across the garden
> Recalling things that other people have desired.
> Are these ideas right or wrong?

This is very like Laforgue; so, too, is Prufrock's 'No! I am not Prince Hamlet, nor was meant to be'. But whereas Laforgue's verse, with its 'sentimental irony', is concentrated on himself – *pauvre, pâle et piètre individu* [poor, pale and paltry individual] – Eliot's monologues remain 'observations', detached from the imagined speaker and reaching beyond him. The origin of disturbance within his poetry appears to be, not merely the sense that the feelings imagined are inadequate (as with Laforgue), but the more radical intimation that they are somehow unreal. F. R. Leavis has pointed out how Eliot's mature poetry carries the effect of a 'de-realizing of the routine common-sense world' while hinting at the same time at a hidden spiritual reality;[2] and this description brings out the central preoccupation and the central problem of Eliot's work from the outset. Imagining characters whose feelings are insubstantial or puzzling to themselves, the poet moves swiftly – and often too swiftly – from asking what these feelings are worth on the plane of personal living to asking what their status is in relation to the absolute. In the long run the feelings are left even emptier than at first.

The Love Song of J. Alfred Prufrock (finished in 1911, when he was twenty-three) already shows Eliot's distinctive manner and indicates the range of his wit in the quizzical title followed by a sombre epigraph from Dante. His break from Victorian poetry comes out in the opening lines, where colloquial language presents a situation at once distinct and mystifying:

> Let us go then, you and I,
> When the evening is spread out against the sky
> Like a patient etherised upon a table;
> Let us go, through certain half-deserted streets,
> The muttering retreats
> Of restless nights in one-night cheap hotels
> And sawdust restaurants with oyster-shells:
> Streets that follow like a tedious argument
> Of insidious intent
> To lead you to an overwhelming question ...
> Oh, do not ask, 'What is it?'
> Let us go and make our visit.
>
> In the room the women come and go
> Talking of Michelangelo.

The speaker is vague, but the images he uses are distinct, acutely so; and the precise movement of these irregular lines tells us directly how Prufrock feels: they reach forward only to fall back. The two striking lines ending in 'table' and 'question' are left without the support of rhyme, but when Prufrock clinches his words in rhyming couplets he only seems to be losing balance. Similarly, there is a continuous undercurrent of half-audible images from the 'muttering' streets with their 'tedious argument' to the thought of the women talking, where it peters out, for the moment, in irrelevance and anti-climax. Eliot has said that the most interesting verse is that which constantly approaches a fixed pattern without quite settling into it: 'it is this contrast between fixity and flux, this unperceived evasion of monotony, which is the very life of verse' (*Reflections on 'Vers*

Libre', 1917[3]). This is an apt and fundamental comment on his own practice.

And contrast between fixity and flux applies to much more than the versification of these lines. Prufrock's surroundings consist of hard, gritty objects; his thoughts are fluctuating and evasive. He is witty, nervous, self-important, and illogical. With a side-glance at romantic sunsets, he merges the evening into his own state of trepidation. The 'retreats' he notices are neither calm nor silent. He reads 'an overwhelming question' into the layout of the city blocks. What that question is – a proposal of marriage? the question of human dignity? – is not put into words; but the way it emerges expresses the condition of seeing a problem and shrinking away from it.

Beyond Prufrock's vacillation, moreover, there are hints of something permanent which he can dimly perceive but cannot grasp. The sky and the table are more enduring than the presence of any single evening or any single patient; and by a striking and characteristic compression of meanings, 'etherised' suggests 'going under' and 'spiritualized' at the same time. Oyster-shells and Michelangelo recall high values, however empty of content at present; conversely, 'restless nights in one-night cheap hotels' and again the image of the women talking suggest a coming-and-going of many lives across fixed points of loneliness or boredom. Prufrock's irony is made to reflect a general human predicament besides being directed against himself. But if Eliot's attitude here is already more complex than that of Laforgue, it is hardly as yet more mature: Prufrock's fear of ordinary living is measured by his own standards.

Eliot's *Prufrock* volume belongs to Boston and Paris. His next group of poems was written in London about the end of the war. Here (acting on Ezra Pound's advice) he turns from free verse to the strict rhyming quatrains of Gautier. With the new form of verse goes a sharper satiric edge, but also a more startling conjunction of images and ideas, as if Eliot were compensating for more fixity in one direction by more elasticity in another. In his disconcerting wit we seem to feel the pulse of the generation for whom (as he wrote soon after) 'the dissolution of value had in itself a positive value'.[4] These poems are dry, fantastic, astringent. But they leave the poet's essential attitude to life still unresolved.

Sweeney Among the Nightingales (1918) illustrates the method of the rhyming poems. The narrative is kept obscure but it appears that in a tavern somewhere in South America a number of shady characters are plotting against Apeneck Sweeney. Possibly he escapes. But at the end, as if in a film, the images of the present scene are transposed into others emerging from a remote and tragic past:

> The host with someone indistinct
> Converses at the door apart,
> The nightingales are singing near
> The Convent of the Sacred Heart,
>
> And sang within the bloody wood
> When Agamemnon cried aloud,
> And let their liquid siftings fall
> To stain the stiff dishonoured shroud.

Agamemnon and Sweeney, and music, blood and droppings, are coupled together; religion and poetry (the Convent and the nightingales) have always been witnesses of the same squalid agony. And yet what these lines emphasize most is not the horror of the spectacle but its monotony, with an overriding sense of the neatness of the versification. Technique here is not a means of clarifying the tangle of human experience but of withdrawing from it towards an artificial objectivity.

Although this passage is not one of Eliot's best, it reveals the purpose behind his finest poetry. His central purpose can be described as a search for detachment, or impersonality (as Eliot calls it in his programmatic essay of 1917 on *Tradition and the Individual Talent*). Detachment is the counterpoise to his deep sense of unreality, or equivocal reality, in personal emotions. The people he creates in his early work embody detachment in the negative sense that they have no satisfying hold on life. They have no personal roots or affections and cannot trust their own impulses. They are acutely conscious of some spiritual absolute, but only in the form of a privation, as 'the Shadow' that falls 'Between the emotion And the response' in *The Hollow Men* (1925). Or they feel they are exiles in the midst of life, somewhat like Orestes, because of their contact with a dreadful but unidentifiable guilt – as with the heroes of *Sweeney Agonistes* (1924–6) and *The Family Reunion* (1939). Eliot speaks of a poet's desire to escape from the burden of private emotion; and he comes to recognize that the name of impersonality may cover a variety of attitudes to life, from self-discipline to indifference or revulsion. His ideal of impersonality is ambiguous. But at its clearest, it stands for an intense effort to pass through a baffling, oppressive sense of unreality, to free himself of it by converting it into a mode of detached contemplation.

In the same essay, Eliot insists on a poet's obligation to transcend his private self by loyalty to the tradition of European literature as a whole – for which he needs 'the historical sense'. The historical sense is not antiquarian; for Eliot, it means a constant attention to changes in literary styles and values, but also to continuity and permanence; a sense of fixity together with flux; and further, 'a sense of the timeless as well as of the temporal and of the timeless and of the temporal together'. In his reaching out from America to the tradition of Europe, Eliot resembles Henry James.[5] But he goes far beyond James; and, especially in his sense of the relativity of values, he speaks for the general mind of his own age, imbued with the historical and evolutionary thought of the nineteenth century and at the same time perplexed by the problem of discontinuity in culture and belief. From Eliot's sense of history and his search for a metaphysical reality beyond the self comes a series of meditations in his poetry on the idea of Time – time as an aspect of individual lives or the succession of generations, time in relation to the discredited idea of progress, time in relation to eternity. In Eliot's poetry, the idea of Time has the same kind of prominence as the idea of Nature in the poetry of the romantics. It is latent there from the beginning (for instance, in Prufrock's references to Michelangelo and Hamlet or in the coupling of Agamemnon with Sweeney). It comes to the forefront in *Gerontion* (1919), the most important poem in his second volume. And thereafter meditation on time remains an essential aspect of his poetry, from *The Waste Land* to *Four Quartets*, where it supplies both a subject and a method.

Gerontion is important in other respects as well. Gerontion ('the little old man') is apparently a former seaman or business man at the end of his tether, 'an old man driven by the Trades To a sleepy corner'. He is blind; he lives in 'a decayed house' which is not his own; as he considers his possible future and the memories left by his travels he realizes with anguish that he has no genuine life behind him, no achievements, 'no ghosts', no faith, no passions. In *Prufrock*, Eliot had made the speaker confuse his sensations with his thoughts; in *Gerontion*, he makes the effort of thinking itself almost a physical sensation, a straining to grasp at elusiveness and illusion:

> After such knowledge, what forgiveness? Think now
> History has many cunning passages, contrived corridors
> And issues, deceives with whispering ambitions,
> Guides us by vanities. Think now
> She gives when our attention is distracted
> And what she gives, gives with such supple confusions
> That the giving famishes the craving. Gives too late
> What's not believed in, or if still believed,
> In memory only, reconsidered passion. Gives too soon
> Into weak hands, what's thought can be dispensed with
> Till the refusal propagates a fear. Think
> Neither fear nor courage saves us. Unnatural vices
> Are fathered by our heroism. Virtues
> Are forced upon us by our impudent crimes.
> These tears are shaken from the wrath-bearing tree.

This passage, with its quick interplay between sound, metaphor and idea, shows Eliot triumphantly applying his study of the Jacobean dramatists. And it shows what he means in his own practice by 'metaphysical' quality or texture in verse, the quality he describes as 'a direct sensuous apprehension of thought, or a recreation of thought into feeling'. His dramatizing tendency works together with his tendency to seize ideas at their point of contact with sensations.

Yet the poem as a whole is unbalanced precisely where it is most obviously dramatic. The concentration in Gerontion's mind, the urgent rhetorical 'Think now', gives way to an impulse to hypnotize himself with his own despair; the 'corridors' lead him to a private nightmare (like the streets in *Prufrock*), a maze where he loses his identity. He merges himself with the whole of mankind, with the failures imposed by history or else – the argument shifts – resulting from original sin. But there is no clear relation between the private and the universal phases of Gerontion's despair, for the personal memories he has just recalled (the immediate objects of his guilty 'knowledge') are no more, in themselves, than provocative but trivial fragments; in the phrase Eliot himself applies to *Hamlet*, they do not constitute an 'objective correlative' to Gerontion's feelings about history.[6] Nevertheless, his despair is presented as something more weighty than a personal outburst. The intimate and the rhetorical elements in the poem are brought together by force.

Eliot might have left a different impression if he had been willing to treat Gerontion as a character with particular qualities and a particular story. But he is evidently reluctant to shape a narrative, with its chain of proximate causes and effects. He dismisses these as predetermined by or in History –

> while the world moves
> In appetency, on its metalled ways
> Of time past and time future.
> (*Burnt Norton*, 124; 1935)

And when he praises *Ulysses* for giving 'a significance to the immense panorama of futility and anarchy which is contemporary history', the point of his admiration is that Joyce uses analogies drawn from myths 'instead of narrative method'.[7] Eliot's indifference to narrative in his own work is another aspect of his search for impersonality.

In his critical essays, especially the early ones, Eliot is deeply (and rightly) concerned with his practical interests as a poet. He is brilliant and illuminating when he declares his own taste or when he deals with versification and certain aspects of poetic language. But he becomes evasive and inconsistent when he touches on poetic composition as a whole or on a poet's attitude to life, although he regularly assumes an incisive and even dogmatic tone. Hence his critical pronouncements form a tricky instrument to use for the understanding of his own poetry and still more for that of other poets.[8]

Although he once proclaimed himself a classicist, his view of poetry derives from the nineteenth century, not from the seventeenth or the eighteenth; it comes from Flaubert and Baudelaire and their French successors and from the more direct influence of Irving Babbitt and Santayana at Harvard and Ezra Pound and T. E. Hulme in London. The Flaubertian strain in his doctrine of impersonality comes out where he argues (as in his essay on tradition) that a poet's mind should remain 'inert' and 'neutral' towards his subject-matter, keeping a gulf between 'the man who suffers and the mind which creates'; or again, where he tries to equate literature with science (comparing the method of *Ulysses*, for example, to 'a scientific discovery'). The influence of Baudelaire and his successors is powerful both in the moral colouring of Eliot's poetry and in his views on poetic symbolism, on the use of mythological or literary parallels and allusions, on the music in poetry, and on sensibility.

The poetic world of Baudelaire contains 'forests of symbols'. His images blend the resonance of differing sense-impressions; they signify a hidden unity between matter and spirit, or else disclose an ironic contrast-in-resemblance between the actual and the ideal. And Mallarmé claims that a poet can evoke the ultimate mystery of things in and through the non-conceptual properties of words, especially their music. Eliot takes the same direction. He admires in Baudelaire the power of bringing 'imagery of the sordid life of a great metropolis' to a pitch of 'the *first intensity* – presenting it as it is, and yet making it represent something more than itself'; and in Dante he emphasizes the physical immediacy of the allegory – 'Dante's is a *visual* imagination ... in the sense that he lived in an age in which men still saw visions.'[9] The important factor here is rather sensory apprehension than the visual as such, for elsewhere Eliot claims, rather like Mallarmé, that a poet's 'auditory imagination' can pass through the conventions of language accumulated by history to return to 'the most primitive', 'penetrating far below the conscious levels ... seeking the beginning and the end'. Similarly, he holds that the true function of the poetry in poetic drama is to 'touch the border of those feelings which only music can express' – thus preparing the audience for a religious insight transcending the spectacle of human action.[10] Here Eliot differs from Mallarmé and the cult of pure poetry, in that he considers poetry an auxiliary to religion and not a substitute for it. As to poetry in its own sphere, however, he sketches out a similar view: the poet apprehends what is below or above the plane of practical consciousness through a heightened activity of his senses, which includes his response to language. And this perception, crystallized in language, is as much independent of the writer's everyday personality as the vision of a mystic or the discovery of a scientist. What Eliot leaves unclear in his statements is the part he assigns to the poet's intelligence.

At first sight, it appears that he values the intellect and the senses together – the 'recreation of thought into feeling'. But he repeatedly implies that the senses are both vital and trustworthy for a poet, whereas the intellect is irrelevant. In one place he writes that 'the keenest ideas' have 'the quality of a sense-perception'; elsewhere, that poets like Donne and Mallarmé pursue philosophical speculation simply in order to 'develop their power of sensibility' – without believing in their ideas or even thinking consecutively.[11] In his essay on *Shakespeare and the Stoicism of Seneca* (1927) he maintains that 'the poet who "thinks" is merely the poet who can express the emotional equivalent of thought' – which looks plausible. 'But' (Eliot goes on) 'he is not necessarily interested in the thought itself' – which is almost nonsense. However, 'in truth neither Shakespeare nor Dante did any real thinking'; although Dante relied on a superior philosophy, the philosophy of St Thomas, 'that was just his luck'; and the so-called thinking of both poets is simply 'the thought current at their time, the material enforced upon each to use as the vehicle of his feeling'. Now, it is one thing to say that a poet is not a systematic philosopher; quite another to suggest that he merely drifts on the stream of his age. It is difficult to see how Eliot supposes Dante leaned on St Thomas, or Shakespeare leaned on Seneca to the neglect of St Thomas (who, after all, was pretty much as accessible to him as to Eliot); or how Dante or Donne or Shakespeare could have represented their feelings coherently at all. But his theory maintains that during the process of composition a poet's mind is inert or neutral towards his experience (including his reading and his emotions alike), while the real work of creation is done by his sensibility; as, for example, in a now famous passage in his essay on *The Metaphysical Poets* (1921):

> Tennyson and Browning are poets, and they think; but they do not feel their thought as immediately as the odour of a rose. A thought to Donne was an experience; it modified his sensibility. When a poet's mind is perfectly equipped for its work, it is constantly amalgamating disparate experience; the ordinary man's experience is chaotic, irregular, fragmentary. The latter falls in love, or reads Spinoza, and these two experiences have nothing to do with each other, or with the noise of the typewriter or the smell of cooking; in the mind of the poet these experiences are always forming new wholes ... The poets of the seventeenth century, the successors of the dramatists of the sixteenth, possessed a mechanism of sensibility which could devour any kind of experience.

When Eliot wrote these words, it required a highly creative taste to bring home the difference between Browning and Donne; but his general statement is another matter. What is valuable or suggestive in it comes, directly or indirectly, from previous critics – the concept of the poet's amalgamating power from Coleridge, the concept of multiple sensibility from Baudelaire and Rémy de Gourmont.[12] What Eliot has contributed is the stark alternative between order and chaos and the notion that a poet achieves order through some privileged internal 'mechanism'. Instead of fastening upon the real strength of such a poet as Donne – his power of sensitive concentration – Eliot reduces the writing of poetry to a sort of conjuring trick. Apparently he does so because of his dislike of romantic opinions; on one occasion, he says he prefers to think of poetry as 'a superior amusement'. But it surely comes nearer to our understanding of good poetry (and nearer to the classical tradition as well) to say, with Wordsworth, that it is 'the spontaneous overflow of powerful feelings' in a man 'who, being possessed of more than usual organic sensibility, had also thought long and deeply'; or even, with Arnold, that it is 'a criticism of life'.

The essential vision for a poet, Eliot has also said, is a vision of 'the boredom, and the horror, and the glory' (*The Use of Poetry*, ch. vi, 1933). His own poetry is defective as a criticism of life because he is too deeply occupied with horror and boredom. He shares very little of Baudelaire's moral passion or the human sympathy of Gerard Manley Hopkins. But his greatness as a poet lies in his striving to grasp a metaphysical reality – to maintain a detachment resembling that of the mystics against the pressure of his own scepticism. There is no parallel in English to the poetry of sustained and strenuous contemplation in *Four Quartets*. Eliot there does not define his metaphysical reality or describe a contemplative experience, so much as recreate the experience dramatically, in a new form of monologue which embodies a logical conclusion to his previous work. Here, more completely than anywhere else in his writing, the resolution of tensions, the experience of achieving detachment, takes place within the poetry itself.

His dramatic impulse, inadequate to the action of a play, finds a natural outlet in the poetic monologue, focused on the awareness of shifting and irreconcilable values within a single perception or state of mind. Through all his poetry there runs the same constructive principle of dramatized meditation, of searching for fixity in and through the flux of time. As Eliot himself suggests, this is the principle behind his masterly handling of verse, which is more sensitive to fine shades of feeling in irregular forms hinting at a pattern than it is, as a rule, in regular stanzas with rhyme. And this is the principle behind his treatment of images – behind his 'sensuous apprehension of thought' and 'recreation of thought into feeling'. In his 'de-realizing of the routine common-sense world' (to revert to Leavis's defining phrase), Eliot breaks down habits of sentiment, moral or literary, breaks down the comforting sensation that mind and feelings are resting on something solid, and exposes himself to a profoundly dismaying experience of disintegration. His development has been a progress from treating experiences of such a nature with indecisive irony or contained horror to the hard-won composure of *Four Quartets*.

Prufrock shrinks away from definite consciousness, Gerontion is quivering with it. *The Waste Land* (1922) is an amazing anthology of indeterminate states of mind and being, of 'memory and desire' resisting present awareness, of vivid perception passing over into hallucination, of phrases, situations, personalities blended and superimposed across the boundaries of time and place. Reluctance and bewilderment, as between sleep and waking, are given, for example, in the very rhythm of the first lines, with their dragging participial endings suggesting life and immobility together:

> April is the cruellest month, breeding
> Lilacs out of the dead land, mixing
> Memory and desire, stirring
> Dull roots with spring rain.

This in-between state, neither spring nor winter, neither dull nor alert, but straining between the two, provides the model of everything that follows. Sometimes it rises to fever-pitch, as in these lines (352–8), where the absence of punctuation contributes to the sense of lurching hopelessly forward:

> If there were the sound of water only
> Not the cicada
> And dry grass singing
> But sound of water over a rock

> Where the hermit-thrush sings in the pine trees
> Drip drop drip drop drop drop drop
> But there is no water.

Or else the sense of hovering between consciousness and unconsciousness is made part of a complex synthetic image, as in the lines (215ff.) introducing the scene of the typist's seduction (or rather, mechanical surrender):

> At the violet hour, when the eyes and back
> Turn upward from the desk, when the human engine waits
> Like a taxi throbbing waiting,
> I Tiresias, though blind, throbbing between two lives ...

The light, the moment of city routine, the feel of the engine, all work together – and against each other; and Tiresias, who, 'though blind', is to 'see' the seduction, belongs to the same mode of being. He is both male and female, time-bound and timeless, a withered demi-god, a prophet hypnotized by an eternal machine.

In *The Waste Land* Eliot has applied the 'mythical method' he admires in *Ulysses* with brilliant but finally incoherent results.[13] All the fragmentary passages seem to belong to one voice, recalling memories, meditating, crossing spoken and unspoken thoughts; but the one voice pertains to a multiple personality beyond time and place. He is Tiresias (who resembles Gerontion) and, as such, suffers with the women he observes; he is the knight from the Grail legend; he moves through London ('Unreal City') and Baudelaire's Paris and a phantasmal post-war Middle Europe; he is Ferdinand from *The Tempest* and a Phoenician sailor anticipating his own shipwreck (and hence, conceivably, Dante's Ulysses as well). But the moral sequence or development is lost in this tangle of myths. Early in the poem, for instance, there is a striking and poignant moment (35ff.):

> 'You gave me hyacinths first a year ago;
> 'They called me the hyacinth girl.'
> – Yet when we came back, late, from the Hyacinth garden,
> Your arms full, and your hair wet, I could not
> Speak, and my eyes failed, I was neither
> Living nor dead, and I knew nothing.
> Looking into the heart of light, the silence.

The moment of ecstasy has been ambiguous, and the memory of it now is followed by passages of hallucination, boredom, or disgust;

but nothing is gained for the understanding of this crucial phase in the poem by accumulating parallels and multiplying costumes and dates. Eliot relies on allusion and analogy to do more work than they can. At another important passage (307ff.) he explains in a footnote that he is echoing both St Augustine and Buddha –

> To Carthage then I came
>
> Burning burning burning burning
> O Lord Thou pluckest me out
> O Lord Thou pluckest
>
> burning

– but the words are quite insufficient for the constructive effect intended, while at the the same time 'burning' seems excessively violent to describe the emotions of the people in the Waste Land. Instead of reducing these emotions to order, the 'mythical method' reflects their confusion.

The Hollow Men (1925) forms a sardonic elegy on the unreal beings in the previous poems; Ash-Wednesday (1927–30) marks a decisive 'turning' to religious faith. Nevertheless, the Four Quartets can still be described as a return to early themes and symbols, a return to the garden glimpsed in The Waste Land and to 'the heart of light, the silence'.[14] The central problem, both personal and universal, is still the unreality of time, the unreality of human life so governed by time that the present dissolves into memories of the past and desires for the future; and each of the Quartets follows a pattern fore-shadowed in the earlier work. Each introduces the central problem by means of a meditation aroused by a particular season and place – the vanished rose garden in Burnt Norton (1935), the country lane in East Coker (1940), the Mississippi and the New England coast in The Dry Salvages (1941), the chapel with its Civil War associations visited during war-time in Little Gidding (1942). The second section re-states the opening themes, first lyrically and then in more abstract terms; the third describes a revulsion or withdrawal from the world, a kind of negative ecstasy; the fourth, a short lyric, forms a prayer; and the last section suggests a resolution, in 'hints and guesses', supported by reference to the satisfaction of creating a work of art or responding to it. As in the earlier poems Eliot dwells on indeterminate states of mind, dissolving common-sense reality: for instance, the introduction of *Burnt Norton*, delicately hovering between actuality, memory, and speculation; or the powerful opening of *The Dry Salvages*, where the throb of the lines evoking the river calls up the menace 'of what men choose to forget' and yet blends with cheerful memories of boyhood; or the 'midwinter spring' at Little Gidding, where 'the soul's sap quivers'. But there is a surer control in such passages than before, and a firmer progression of thought through the *Quartets* as a group. *Burnt Norton* presents the themes in a general, abstract form (the half-historical, half-imaginary garden representing both childhood and the Garden of Eden). The middle poems deal more concretely with history and the lesson of experience; the mood here comes closer to despair. And *Little Gidding* carries the despair to a climax, changing the general pattern to this effect by bringing forward to its second section the main passage dealing with literature (the meeting with the ghost) and also making it the strongest passage of negative emotion; but on the other hand *Little Gidding* gathers together the positive symbols and affirmations of the whole sequence. In detail and organization, *Four Quartets* is a superb achievement, the masterpiece of modern English poetry.

One sign of Eliot's mastery is his having perfected a new form of verse, resembling Langland's measure and challenging, without being distracting to, a modern ear. It might be called a poised measure, distinct alike from *vers libre* and irregular blank verse. It consists of lines of varying length, commonly with four strong beats, pausing midway as if for deliberation; it upholds that most precarious of poetic flights, calm abstract statement:

> Time present and time past
> Are both perhaps present in time future,
> And time future contained in time past.
> If all time is eternally present
> All time is unredeemable.
>
> *(Burnt Norton, 1)*

The same cadence is heard again at the end of this *Quartet*, but on this occasion with echoes and repetitions seeming to check (or 'contain') the flight of time:

> Words move, music moves
> Only in time; but that which is only living
> Can only die. Words, after speech, reach
> Into the silence. Only by the form, the pattern,
> Can words or music reach
> The stillness, as a Chinese jar still
> Moves perpetually in its stillness.

And the same cadence is heard throughout the passages in a longer line:

> There are three conditions which often look alike
> Yet differ completely, flourish in the same hedgerow:
> Attachment to self and to things and to persons, detachment
> From self and from things and from persons; and, growing
>   between them, indifference
> Which resembles the others as death resembles life,
> Being between two lives – unflowering, between
> The live and the dead nettle . . .
>
> <div align="right">(<i>Little Gidding</i>, III)</div>

This has the deliberateness of prose, but the effect of poetry – even (in its subdued manner) of dramatic monologue; the verse movement underscores the act of the mind in distinguishing 'between' neighbouring concepts. Eliot has found the exact rhythm and tone of voice for his purpose.

And this tone and rhythm hold at the opposite pole of his 'detachment', where he is contemplating emptiness or disintegration:

> I said to my soul, be still, and let the dark come upon you
> Which shall be the darkness of God. As, in a theatre,
> The lights are extinguished, for the scene to be changed
> With a hollow rumble of wings, with a movement of darkness on
>   darkness,
> And we know that the hills and the trees, the distant panorama
> And the bold imposing façade are all being rolled away –
> Or as, when an underground train, in the tube, stops too long
>   between stations
> And the conversation rises and slowly fades into silence
> And you see behind every face the mental emptiness deepen
> Leaving only the growing terror of nothing to think about;
> Or when, under ether, the mind is conscious but conscious of
>   nothing –
> I said to my soul, be still . . .
>
> <div align="right">(<i>East Coker</i>, III)</div>

Here the 'going under' is more distinctly and more steadily conveyed than in the earlier poems; it is placed in a clearer framework of experience. So, too, the moving 'Death by Water' from *The Waste Land* is surpassed in the corresponding passage, the sestina in *The Dry Salvages* (II):

> Where is the end of them, the fishermen sailing
> Into the wind's tail, where the fog cowers?
> We cannot think of a time that is oceanless
> Or of an ocean not littered with wastage
> Or of a future that is not liable
> Like the past, to have no destination.
>
> We have to think of them as forever bailing,
> Setting and hauling, while the North East lowers
> Over shallow banks unchanging and erosionless
> Or drawing their money, drying sails at dockage;
> Not as making a trip that will be unpayable
> For a haul that will not bear examination.

Eliot's verbal invention comes out here in 'oceanless' and 'unpayable', with its compound of opposites – the solemn ('beyond profit or loss') and the sardonic ('priceless'). And his ever-present sense of the futility of human effort is now more compassionate and more objective than before.

The description of the aftermath of an air-raid that introduces the Dantesque episode of the ghost in *Little Gidding* (II) is one of the most sustained passages of tragic intensity in English verse; if nothing else, it is an unforgettable record of war. With extraordinary intimacy, Eliot catches the nervous tension of such a moment, merging together the frightful throbbing of the machines and the ebbing sensations of relief, breathlessness, bewilderment:

> In the uncertain hour before the morning
>   Near the ending of interminable night
>   At the recurrent end of the unending
> After the dark dove with the flickering tongue
>   Had passed below the horizon of his homing
>   While the dead leaves still rattled on like tin
> Over the asphalt where no other sound was
>   Between three districts whence the smoke arose
>   I met one walking, loitering and hurried
> As if blown towards me like the metal leaves
>   Before the urban dawn wind unresisting.

By a daring paradox, the enemy bomber ('the dark dove') suggests the Holy Ghost, and the 'uncertain hour' becomes an 'intersection time' between London and Purgatory. But the paradox emerges from an experience directly met and unflinchingly received. Eliot has not only turned sensation into thought, he has made sensation universal.

In a sense, then, Eliot becomes more impersonal in *Four Quartets* by speaking in the first person. Nevertheless, he still leaves the reader to balance his creative achievement against his scepticism. There are, for example, the relatively mechanical passages of satire on the ordinary mind in *East Coker* (101–11) and *The Dry Salvages* (184–98); and there is the prevailing sense of effort wasted – after which it comes as poor encouragement to be urged to 'fare forward' or to be told that the apprehension of timelessness is 'an occupation for the saint'. The consolatory message from the dead in *Little Gidding* (III) appears to come to no more than that they *are* dead. And this follows the utterance of futility and exasperation on the part of the ghost, who recalls the despair of Gerontion, but with more force and more authority, since Eliot makes him represent the whole European literary tradition. Against such feelings, there is the effect of Eliot's superb command of language and his determination to find a pattern in human experience. The poems rest on a statement of faith. But it is difficult to feel sure how far the total pattern they communicate is due to the mastery of horror and boredom, and how far it is simply an aesthetic ideal.

We owe an immense debt to Eliot for extending the range of English poetry. But it is a chilling reflection on the poet and on his age that so distinguished a writer should have spent so much of his energy in negation.

NOTES

1. See T. S. Eliot's Introduction to *Selected Poems* of Ezra Pound (London, 1928), and 'From Poe to Valéry' (1948: repr. in *Literary Opinion in America*, ed. M. D. Zabel, New York, 1951). For details of French influence on Eliot, see E. J. H. Greene, *T. S. Eliot et la France* (Paris, 1951) and Grover Smith, *T. S. Eliot's Poetry and Plays: a Study in Sources and Meaning* (2nd edn, Chicago, 1974); cp. Arthur Symons, *The Symbolist Movement in Literature* (London, 1899); Edmund Wilson, in *Axel's Castle* (New York, 1931); and P. Mansell Jones, *The Background of Modern French Poetry* (Cambridge, 1951) and *Baudelaire* (Cambridge, 1952).

2. F. R. Leavis, *Education and the University* (London, 1943), 96.

3. Eliot, *Selected Prose*, ed. F. Kermode, 31–6.

4. *The New Criterion* IV (1926), 752–3; cp. Eliot in *A Garland for John Donne*, ed. T. Spencer (Cambridge, Mass., 1931), 8.

5. cp. Van Wyck Brooks, *New England: Indian Summer, 1865–1915* (London, 1940).

6. See Eliot's essay on *Hamlet* (*Selected Essays*), of the same year as *Gerontion*; cp. Leavis, 'T. S. Eliot as Critic' (*Commentary* XXVI, 1958; repr. in *'Anna Karenina' and other essays*, London, 1967).

7. Eliot's review of *Ulysses* is repr. from *The Dial* (1923) in *Selected Prose*, 175–8.

8. On Eliot's criticism, see Leavis, 'T. S. Eliot as Critic', and in *The Common Pursuit* (London, 1952) and *English Literature in Our Time and the University* (London, 1969); also Yvor Winters, *The Anatomy of Nonsense* (Norfolk, Conn., 1943: repr. in L. Unger, ed., *T. S. Eliot: a Selected Critique*, New York, 1948); D. Newton–de Molina, ed., *The Literary Criticism of T. S. Eliot* (London, 1977).

9. *Selected Essays* (1932 edn), 229, 374. cp. Mario Praz, 'T. S. Eliot and Dante', repr. in *The Flaming Heart* (New York, 1958); also A. C. Charity (on Eliot and Dante) and Nicola Ward (on Eliot and Baudelaire), in A. D. Moody, ed., *'The Waste Land' in Different Voices* (London, 1974).

10. *The Use of Poetry*, pp. 118–19; *On Poetry*, pp. 30, 86–7; see Matthiessen, 89–90, and Ronald Peacock, *The Art of Drama* (London, 1957) ch. IX.

11. Eliot, in *The Athenaeum* (1919), 362, and *La Nouvelle Revue Française* (1926: quoted, René Taupin, *L'Influence du symbolisme français sur la poésie américaine, 1910–20* (Paris, 1929), 224–5); cp. *Selected Essays* (1932 edn), 96, 134ff.

12. See F. W. Bateson and Eric Thompson in *Essays in Criticism* I–II (1951–2).

13. See the original drafts of *The Waste Land*, ed. Valerie Eliot (London, 1971; discussed in A. D. Moody, *Thomas Stearns Eliot, Poet* (Cambridge, 1979; enlarged, 1980, 310ff.); cp. Grover Smith (n. 1, above). For critical studies of *The Waste Land*, see Leavis (in *New Bearings*); the collections of essays ed. Unger, Moody and Rajan (nn. 8, 9, 14), and Part IV. Moody, *T. S. Eliot, Poet*, 79ff., gives a subtle and searching reading of 'the poem as an organic whole'.

14. On *Four Quartets*, see Harding and Leavis (*Education*, 87ff.; also in Bergonzi, ed., *'Four Quartets': a Casebook* (London, 1969)). Preston, *'Four Quartets' Rehearsed* (London, 1949), Unger, 374ff., Philip Wheelwright, (in *T. S. Eliot: a Study of his Writings by Several Hands*, ed. B. Rajan, London, 1947), and Smith give studies of the imagery. For general studies of the poems and for studies of their successive drafts, see Dame Helen Gardner, *The Art of T. S. Eliot* (London, 1949) and *The Composition of 'Four Quartets'* (London, 1978), and Moody, *T. S. Eliot, Poet* (1980 edn), 185ff., 327ff.

THE POETRY OF W. H. AUDEN

R. G. COX

One could expect fairly general assent to the statement that of poets still writing during the Second World War Auden ranks next in importance to Eliot. When, however, we ask just how near is 'next' and what is the precise nature of the importance, opinions at once diverge. He has no universally accepted masterpieces, nothing as central as *The Waste Land* or *The Tower*, and there is little agreement either about the relative success of his poems or the best way to describe their nature. Auden, we hear, is the Picasso of verse; Auden is mainly a poet of general ideas; Auden is primarily a satirist; Auden's poetry is fundamentally romantic; Auden is most successful in light verse. Some of this is due to the variety of stages that his thought and feeling passed through and to the immediate sensitivity with which he registered the changing moods and opinions of his time. For many of his contemporaries there was a sense of being directly and personally implicated in his poetry. Such topical urgency may lend a spurious liveliness to work which later appears dated and ephemeral, and it would seem that Auden's younger readers today show some tendency to be bored by the social and political concerns of the 1930s and to question their permanent interest as poetic themes. With the problem of sifting out the mere journalism from Auden's work go fundamental questions of pre-suppositions and belief – psychological, moral, political, and religious. At a more technical level there is a constant experimenting with new forms and manners. And perhaps most essentially confusing to the critic is the presence throughout of a peculiarly deep-seated inequality and unevenness, cutting across all the changes in thought, subject-matter, and general attitude.[1] Having regard to the variety of stages through which Auden's work passed, it seems best to take a broadly chronological view of his development.

Auden's first volume, published in 1930 when he was twenty-three, made an immediate impact. Here was unquestionably a new talent, the voice of an individual sensibility alive in its own time and capable of vigorous expression. Everywhere there were striking and memorable phrases: 'gradual ruin spreading like a stain', 'spring's green Preliminary shiver', 'Events not actual In time's unlenient will', 'brave sent home Hermetically sealed with shame'. Imagery of un-usual force was often matched with expressive and moving rhythms:

> O watcher in the dark, you wake
> Our dream of waking, we feel
> Your finger on the flesh that has been skinned . . .
>
> The song, the varied action of the blood
> Would drown the warning from the iron wood
> Would cancel the inertia of the buried:
>
> Travelling by daylight on from house to house
> The longest way to the intrinsic peace,
> With love's fidelity and with love's weakness.

The originality was of course tempered by a normal proportion of the derivative: it is easy to find echoes here of Eliot, Edward Thomas, Wilfred Owen, Emily Dickinson, Robert Graves, Laura Riding, and perhaps the Pound of *Mauberley*:

> Issued all the orders expedient
> In this kind of case:
> Most, as was expected, were obedient,
> Though there were murmurs, of course;

as well as of Skelton, Old English poetry, and the sagas. Less healthy signs were an excessive dependence on purely personal associations and a frequent use of private jokes and allusions. The difficulty of some of these poems seems far beyond what is demanded by the depth or complexity of the thought to be expressed. Some of it is a trick of over-elliptical grammar and syntax: some of it can be cleared up by reading the psychoanalytical writings in which Auden was so deeply interested at this time, but there remains much that looks merely irresponsible. Christopher Isherwood recorded has Auden's early habit of constructing poems out of good lines salvaged from poems that his friends had condemned, 'entirely regardless of gram-mar or sense.'[2] We need not take this too literally, but the suggested attitude is revealing. However, this was, after all, a first volume and it still seems reasonable that its positive originality and its promise should have received the main stress. If the feeling for words and imagery could be controlled by a fuller and profounder organization of experience there was every reason to expect a great deal.

Meanwhile the themes and atmosphere were new and exciting, however much the genuine feeling might seem mixed with adolescent elements. The sense of a doomed civilization, the references to disease and the death-wish symbolized as a mysterious Enemy, the imagery of guerrilla warfare, ruined industry, railheads, and frontiers, had not yet become the stock-in-trade of all up-to-date verse as they were to a few years later – a point that modern readers may easily forget. And in *Paid on Both Sides*, the 'charade' which so curiously mingles the heroic and modern worlds, the sagas, and the spy-story, Auden seems to penetrate at times to a level of something like universal human tragedy. The most successful of the *Poems* are perhaps XI, the typical landscape with symbolic overtones subsequently called *The Watershed*; II, the archetypal quest poem now entitled *The Wanderer*; III, the address of the Life Force to modern man later given the whimsical caption 'Venus Will Now Say a Few Words'; and XVI, the long personal meditation on the element of dissolution in modern culture, which, in spite of some awkward passages of elliptical grammar not unfairly described by John Bayley as 'pidgin English', has an unusual accent of personal sincerity and maturity in its better parts. The opening paragraph arrests the attention with a powerful contrast:

> It was Easter as I walked in the public gardens
> Hearing the frogs exhaling from the pond,
> Watching traffic of magnificent cloud
> Moving without anxiety on open sky –
> Season when lovers and writers find
> An altering speech for altering things,
> An emphasis on new names, on the arm
> A fresh hand with fresh power.
> But thinking so I came at once
> Where solitary man sat weeping on a bench,
> Hanging his head down, with his mouth distorted
> Helpless and ugly as an embryo chicken.

and the rest of the poem develops the relation between death and growth with, for the most part, a sense of complexity, a refusal of easy simplification often lacking in later work.[3] The characteristic unevenness of these early poems appears most strikingly in the concluding sonnet (*Petition* in the collected volume). It has the arresting phrases – 'a sovereign touch Curing the intolerable neural itch'; the psychological insight and moral urgency – 'Prohibit sharply the rehearsed response'; the private allusions – 'the liar's quinsy'; the throw-away bathos of 'country houses at the end of drives'; and the queer Kipling–Wells uplift of 'look shining at New styles of architecture, a change of heart'. No wonder Edwin Muir remarked that it was hard to tell whether the person addressed was 'the Head of the universe or of the school'.[4]

This inequality is accentuated in *The Orators* (1932), that curious experiment, largely in prose, which Auden subsequently thought a good idea imperfectly executed. Here a great part is played by the theories of Groddeck and Homer Lane, especially that of the psychological origin of disease. Once more inertia, ossification, fear, and death in the individual consciousness and in society generally are symbolized as the Enemy, and there is a constant atmosphere of military campaigns, conspiracy, and intrigue, that is continually slipping back into the world of scouting, O. T. C. field-days, and the schoolboy thriller. It is as if the author never quite made up his mind whether he was really concerned with more than amusing his friends. The brilliance appears chiefly in the more intelligibly satirical prose sketches, 'Address for a Prize Day' and 'Letter to a Wound': the verse marks no advance on *Poems* and sometimes drops to the level of popular lampoon (*Beethameer*) or undergraduate parody, as when the stanza of *The Wreck of the Deutschland* is ingeniously used to celebrate a Rugger victory.

In the more political phase which followed, Auden often exploited popular light verse, partly in an attempt to reach a wider public, and much of this is associated with writing for the stage. An extreme instance is *The Dance of Death* (1933): with more direct Marxist propaganda and more sheer doggerel than any other work, it is the only one from which later collections salvaged nothing. The three later plays in collaboration with Isherwood had a more varied scope, and although they all contain passages looking like attempts to beat Noel Coward on his own ground, they also include quite ambitious serious verse, for which Auden is generally assumed to be responsible. The best of this is choric, and it often picks up that technique of the cinematic survey interspersed by vivid close-ups of typical detail that had already been developed in *Poems* (the use in Poem xxix of the view of the hawk or 'helmeted airman' has been discussed by a number of critics):[5]

> The Summer holds: upon its glittering lake
> Lie Europe and the islands; many rivers
> Wrinkling its surface like a ploughman's palm ...
> We would show you at first an English village ...
> A parish bounded by the wreckers' cliff: or meadows where
>   browse the Shorthorn and the map-like Frisian
> As at Trent Junction where the Soar comes gliding out of green
>   Leicestershire to swell the ampler current.

Sometimes this choric verse lapses into preaching on Marxist and psychoanalytical texts, either solemnly and directly or through satire whose force tends to be blunted by a facile knowingness. As in *The Orators*, almost anything may be a symptom:

> Beware of those with no obvious vices; of the chaste, the non-
>   smoker and drinker, the vegetarian
> Beware of those who show no inclination towards making money:
>   there are even less innocent forms of power ...

When in *The Ascent of F6* (1936) verse is used for serious dialogue it tends to be rather heavy, and Ransom's climactic soliloquy is an extraordinary piece of imitation Shakespeare: not surprisingly it can hardly stand up to the invited comparison.

The problem of the popular song manner as used by a serious poet is that too often his nature is subdued to what it works in. The banal rhythms and language simply cannot carry effectively the more sophisticated meanings and deeper intentions. Where in Auden's revue lyrics and doggerel ballads these are attempted, the result is too often a peculiarly distasteful air of smartness. The section of 'Lighter poems' in *Another Time* (1940) provides instances: why in volume after volume should Auden have gone on reprinting *Victor* and *Miss Gee*? He always championed light verse – even editing an Oxford Book of it in 1938 – as a proper use of talent and an anti-dote to Victorian over-solemnity about poetry, but it often betrayed him into a peculiar uncertainty of tone and recourse to irony of the self-protective kind.[6] *The Witnesses*, an early poem which survives in the short version used in *The Dog Beneath the Skin* (1935), seems to me typically unsure how serious it intends to be. An allied uncertainty affects some of the political satire: the once popular *A Communist to Others* (reprinted without title in *Look, Stranger!* (1936) but dropped from later collections) is typical in its hesitation between virulent intensity and facetious exuberance.

Auden's more serious poetic output of the thirties is to be found in the two volumes *Look, Stranger!* (entitled in the U.S.A. *On this Island*) and *Another Time*, with the verse sections of *Journey to a War* (1939). As compared with the first poems these show less taut bareness of language, less elliptical compression, and less awkwardness; but at the same time something has been lost in pressure and urgency of feeling. The technique has more surface competence, and this can give at its best a greater ease and fluency, but it sometimes emerges as a smooth slickness which provides a ready mask for irresponsibility or the absence of a deeper organization. That often-quoted song 'Our hunting fathers', for example, owes rather too much to sheer rhetorical vigour and assurance (borrowed, perhaps, partly from Yeats). It appears to combine subtle complexity with epigrammatic logic in a way that analysis cannot quite substantiate:[7]

> Our hunting fathers told the story
>   Of the sadness of the creatures,
> Pitied the limits and the lack
>   Set in their finished features;
> Saw in the lion's intolerant look
>   Behind the quarry's dying glare,
> Love raging for the personal glory
>   That reason's gift would add,
> The liberal appetite and power,
>   The rightness of a god.
>
> Who nurtured in that fine tradition
>   Predicted the result,
> Guessed love by nature suited to
>   The intricate ways of guilt?
> That human ligaments could so
> His southern gestures modify,
> And make it his mature ambition
>   To think no thought but ours,
> To hunger, work illegally
>   And be anonymous?

The general meaning is fairly clear: 'Love' must of course be taken as something like instinctive energy, or the Life Force: it has vague over-tones from psychoanalytical theory and constitutes the main positive value explicitly recognized in Auden's earlier work. The 'result' in the second stanza is presumably the result of the tradition, not the result of love's achievement of reason's gift, but why then insist on the modification of love's southern gestures by 'human ligaments'? The important contrast would seem to be that between the 'fathers' and the present generations, and surely 'love' must have been embodied in 'human ligaments' in both? One may find answers to these questions individually, but the fact is there are, throughout, various loose ends of possible meaning not completely organized. If we rule them out the poem becomes a simpler statement of Marxist or Freudian doctrine than it appears at first: if not, it must be seen as a less unified whole.

Technical facility, indeed, comes to seem Auden's chief danger henceforward. Poem after poem contains brilliant or powerful lines but is less successful as a whole because he has not been able to resist the irrelevant elaboration, the chasing of too many hares at once, the smart epigram, or the multiplication of self-conscious ironies. Too many possibilities present themselves as he writes, and he accepts them without adequate discrimination. Some of his methods lend themselves particularly to these dangers. The illustration, for example, of a general state or mood by a series of revealing details or particular instances can sometimes become a mere catalogue. The acknowledged inequality of *Spain* arises chiefly from the list of activities typical of the present and future, where almost any item, one feels, might have something else substituted for it, yet at its best the poem focuses sharply on the immediate crisis:

> On that arid square, that fragment nipped off from hot
> Africa, soldered so crudely to inventive Europe,
>   On that tableland scored by rivers,
> Our fever's menacing shapes are precise and alive.

Other technical mannerisms which sometimes get out of hand are the surprising simile and epithet. The first, which is often an effective source of expressive vitality:

468

> such a longing as will make his thought
> Alive like patterns a murmuration of starlings
> Rising in joy over wolds unwittingly weave

sometimes degenerates into a kind of compulsive nervous tic: 'And
lie apart like epochs from each other', 'Encased in talent like a uniform', 'Anxiety receives them like a grand hotel', 'added meaning
like a comma'. The second is that peculiar feature of Auden's style
which often concentrates all the more striking part of his meaning
into the adjectives, or into the tension between an adjective and the
noun it qualifies. Edwin Muir, reviewing *Another Time*,[8] objected
that Auden used the adjective to express a controversial attitude
to things rather than the qualities of things, but Richard Hoggart[8]
has reasonably argued that this adjectival comment may function as a
play of wit and irony bringing experiences into new relationships
– as perhaps in 'the habit-forming pain', 'eternal and unremarkable
gestures Like ploughing or soldiers' songs', 'Death's coercive
rumour', 'the low recessive houses of the poor'. It must be admitted,
however, that often the adjective adds nothing or merely injects a
perfunctory sophistication: 'the necessary lovers touch', 'the striped
and vigorous tiger', 'the luscious lateral blossoming of woe', 'the
flower's soundless hunger'.

With an increasing tendency in the later thirties to general intellectual comment, there went a remarkable fondness for personifying
abstract qualities. Some lines in *A Summer Night 1933* evoking

> evenings when
> Fear gave his watch no look:
> The lion griefs loped from the shade
> And on our knees their muzzles laid
> And Death put down his book

show the gain in concreteness achieved by this incarnation in vivid
gestures, but also the temptation to excessive ingenuity and the difficulty of control, since Death's movement might in itself be equally
well taken as ominous. *August for the People* provides a list of
personified ills (emulating Shakespeare's Sonnet 66) which ranges
from 'Courage to his leaking ship appointed' through the over-smart
'Greed showing shamelessly her naked money' to the flat bathos of
'Freedom by power shockingly maltreated'. Later poems up to *New
Year Letter* (1941) tend to make personification an automatic habit:[10]

> Violence successful like a new disease
> And Wrong a charmer everywhere invited . . .
>
> And when Truth met him and put out her hand
> He clung in panic to his tall belief . . .

To an easy mastery of free verse there is increasingly added in the later thirties a fluent use of regular forms. Sometimes this contributes to a new lyrical quality, as in the title poem of *Look, Stranger!* or some of the love songs – 'May with its light behaving', 'Fish in the unruffled lakes', 'Lay your sleeping head', 'Underneath the leaves of life'. Sometimes it is recognizably another poet's music that is reproduced, and difficult problems arise as to how far the pastiche is deliberate and how far it can be justified in the total effect – the use of Housman and Blake, for example, in 'Now the leaves are falling fast' or of Blake in the elegy on Yeats:

> Intellectual disgrace
> Stares from every human face,
> And the seas of pity lie
> Locked and frozen in each eye.

Monroe K. Spears[11] has defended this device as a deliberate use of a *persona*, but it seems doubtful whether it can always be accepted so easily. Yeats himself is laid under contribution in a number of poems, not perhaps always consciously, but Auden generally contrived to make the characteristic trimeter his own and to marry the Yeatsian rhetoric to a new moral content:

> What mad Nijinsky wrote
> About Diaghilev
> Is true of the normal heart;
> For the error bred in the bone
> Of each woman and each man
> Craves what it cannot have,
> Not universal love
> But to be loved alone.

This comes from *September 1st, 1939*, a poem in which world events precipitate a more than usually mature blending of Auden's psychological and political concerns. Here the self-consciousness falls away and the feeling is conveyed with sufficient conviction to avoid the opposite fault of propagandist solemnity. The poems of this period which have worn best are those showing a somewhat similar balance: in the best of the lyrical group mentioned above (say, 'Underneath the leaves of life') the emotion controls the technique and the eye is less on the audience: elsewhere in a number of poems dealing with personal experiences certain urgent needs of self-analysis and understanding seem to have had the same effect, as in *Through the Looking Glass, Two Worlds*, and, in part, *Birthday Poem*. One characteristic vein which generally results in a more convincing tone and feeling is that of general meditation linking the mood of a place with comment on the general drift of the world: *Perhaps, The Malverns, Dover 1937, Oxford*, and the *Commentary* concluding *In Time of War*: with these may be mentioned one or two reflections in a loose discursive manner such as *Musée des Beaux Arts*. Space does not permit the full quotation that would be desirable here, but I hope the reader will be able to follow up these references.

Two groups not yet mentioned deserve a brief note. The first is a series of critical essays or epigrams, sometimes obituary, but including past writers back to Voltaire and Pascal. At their worst these run to glib reach-me-down psychoanalysis (on Housman, Arnold, Edward Lear); at their best they provide distinguished reflective verse as in most of the elegy on Freud. The second group consists of the poems, mostly sonnets, written under the influence of Rilke. D. J. Enright, who has discussed this influence in some detail,[12] thinks that it 'encouraged Auden's gift for the brief dramatic situation', and notes that Auden applies Rilke's symbols and techniques to his own anti-aesthetic ends and emphatically human concerns. Even here he remains the generalizing moralist:

> We envy streams and houses that are sure
> But we are articled to error; we
> Were never nude and calm like a great door,
>
> And never will be perfect like the fountains;
> We live in freedom by necessity,
> A mountain people dwelling among mountains.

These lines from the last sonnet *In Time of War* call to mind a technical device present in Auden from the first but strongly confirmed by Rilke's influence – the use of geography and landscape to symbolize spiritual and mental states:

> Lost in my wake the archipelago
> Islands of self through which I sailed all day . . .

> To settle in this village of the heart . . .

This, too, is a device that can be overworked:

> Our money sang like streams on the aloof peaks
> Of our thinking . . .

> He hugged his sorrow like a plot of land . . .

but in a wider development it leads on to one of the more successful aspects of Auden's later work.

The second Rilkean sonnet sequence, *The Quest*, was published in the same volume as *New Year Letter* (called in the U.S.A. *The Double Man*) which is the first of the group of longer poems constituting Auden's chief work of the 1940s. The years of his emigration to America and the beginning of the Second World War saw a considerable change in his intellectual outlook, principally towards a much more serious and more explicit concern with religion. The influence of Marx and Freud gives way to that of Kierkegaard and modern Protestant theologians, and there is an increasing employment of orthodox Christian doctrines. *New Year Letter* records in octosyllabic couplets, with a remarkable proliferation of notes, references and appended after-thoughts, part of the intellectual debate accompanying this change. The critic who called it 'a kind of Hundred Points of Good Husbandry for contemporary intellectuals'[13] presumably had his eye on the verse style as well as the matter and it must be admitted that much of the poem is near doggerel in its loose prosaic informality. Critics have not usually tried to defend it as a whole; they have been content to discuss the new developments of thought in the abstract, especially the new recognition that 'Art is not life, and cannot be A midwife to society', to note the instances of frank self-criticism:

> Time and again have slubbered through
> With slip and slapdash what I do,
> Adopted what I would disown,
> The preacher's loose immodest tone . . .

and to point to the occasional passages of greater life and sensitiveness such as the last lines of the concluding affirmation of faith or the description of man and his development in terms of remembered Northumbrian landscape.

The next volume, *For the Time Being* (English edition 1945), contained also *The Sea and the Mirror*, a 'commentary' on *The Tempest* in the form of verse monologues by the chief characters, all except Caliban who has a mannered prose which starts as a close imitation of later Henry James. The main theme of this work seems to be the relation between art and life, and its treatment brings in a wide range of religious and philosophical problems and perceptions, but the result is hardly a complete artistic success. The symbolic possibilities tend to become too wide for adequate control, and the attempts at profounder analysis to be dissipated in surface brilliance, so that we are left with a number of effective fragments that look rather more impressive out of their context. The title piece of the volume is described as a 'Christmas Oratorio': it has a Narrator, Chorus, and allegorical characters, as well as the persons of the Nativity story. Two sections, the meditation of Simeon and the speech of Herod, are in prose, the first a complex theological statement and the second a kind of Shavian soliloquy. The verse seems in general to rehearse the whole gamut of Auden's previous manners. We find a particularly unfortunate instance of the personification trick – 'tortured Horror roaring for a bride' – and at times there is a general effect of self-parody:

> Our plans have all gone awry
> The rains will arrive too late,
> Our resourceful general
> Fell down dead as he drank ...

Elsewhere there occur some jarring transitions of tone: it is difficult to see what is gained by the Gilbertian element in the song of the Wise Men or the excessively exuberant nastiness of the Voices of the Desert. Among the more impressive parts are the Annunciation song and Mary's lullaby in the Manger scene, but on the whole the apparent intellectual and doctrinal intention is far from being adequately realized.

The Age of Anxiety, the 'Baroque Eclogue' of 1948, is again experimental both in substance and style. Through the minds of four characters meeting by chance in a New York bar in wartime Auden attempts to create a general modern consciousness – rootless, isolated, insecure, obscurely dominated by fear, guilt, and the awareness of failure. The verse throughout is highly artificial, an adaptation of old alliterative forms, handled as usual with great virtuosity, but seldom appearing inevitable or unselfconscious, and often showing signs of strain in the choice of words to maintain the sound-pattern ('our dream-wishes Vert and volant, unvetoed our song'). As always there are striking phrases ('the light collaborates with a land of ease') and the occasional memorable expression of a profounder insight:

> We would rather be ruined than changed,
> We would rather die in our dread
> Than climb the cross of the moment
> And let our illusions die

But the general unsatisfactoriness remains: as G. S. Fraser remarked, in this poem 'the theme of our awkward malaise was all too faithfully mirrored in the elaborate maladroit handling'.[14]

Auden's work of the 1950s is found in the two partly over-lapping volumes *Nones* (1951) and *The Shield of Achilles* (1955). These give a later rendering of most of the moods and qualities of his earlier work. The technical ingenuity continues in a number of experiments with assonance and internal rhyme and in the appearance of a new long line, rather loose and informal, mostly used for discursive reflection and lending itself rather too readily to diffuseness. It is even found linked with the manner of an essay or broadcast talk, so that a poem will begin 'I know a retired dentist who only paints mountains'. The example comes from the sequence of *Bucolics*, meditations on *Winds*, *Mountains*, and so on which are sometimes witty but sometimes sink to the merely whimsical. More than one poem tails off into an uneasy flippancy like the last line of *Lakes*: 'Just reeling off their names is ever so comfy'. More effective use of land-scape and 'the spirit of place' is found in the Horatian *tour de force Ischia*, or *Air Port* with its expression of modern rootlessness, or in what is perhaps the best-known poem of this group, *In Praise of Limestone*. This uses a favourite geographical symbol to convey insights into psychology, history, and man's place in the scheme of things:

> Not to be left behind, not, please! to resemble
> The beasts who repeat themselves, or a thing like water
> Or stone whose conduct can be predicted, these
> Are our Common Prayer ...

and the limestone landscape becomes finally a symbolic aid to imagining 'a faultless love Or the life to come'.

Auden was still fond of the generalizing aerial view of civilization, as in the *Ode to Gaea* or *Memorial to the City* with its vision seen by the 'eyes of the crow and the eye of the camera'. Unfortunately the crow has to be 'on the crematorium chimney' and the sketches of historical epochs in terms of the ideal city of each have the facile quality of some of the earlier biographical epigrams. Similarly the old difficulty of pastiche appears once more: in *The Proof*, for instance, the bemused reader, catching some echoes and suspecting more, wonders what a parody of Tennyson imitating Shakespeare ('When stinking Chaos lifts the latch') has to do with Pamina and Tamino. Something of a new quality appears in the title poem of *The Shield of Achilles*, where Thetis, looking over Hephaestos's shoulder with traditional expectations as he engraves the shield, is confronted with a vision of modern inhumanity stated with considerable directness and force:

> The mass and majesty of this world, all
> > That carries weight and always weighs the same
> Lay in the hands of others; they were small
> > And could not hope for help and no help came ...

This poem is unusual in presenting tragedy without comment: in these volumes an orthodox Christian view is usually in the background if not explicit. The most ambitious attempt at poetry directly on Christian themes is the sequence *Horae Canonicae*, where the seven traditional Church offices provide the framework for a Good Friday meditation on the modern world and the human situation generally. Inevitably there are echoes of Eliot, suggesting comparisons which tend to be damaging:

> This mutilated flesh, our victim,
> > Explains too nakedly, too well,
> The spell of the asparagus garden,
> > The aim of our chalk-pit game; stamps,
> Birds' eggs are not the same, behind the wonder
> > Of tow-paths and sunken lanes,
> Behind the rapture on the spiral stair,
> > We shall always now be aware
> Of the deed into which they lead ...

Here the restless internal rhyming, too, is typical of the general over-conscious experimenting. It is only occasionally that we feel this to be properly controlled by the profounder thoughts and concerns that the poet is clearly trying to express, and the tone is frequently as uncertain as ever: in the culminating stanza of *Compline*, for example, we find:

> ... *libera*
> *Me*, libera C (dear C)
> And all poor s-o-b's who never
> Do anything properly, spare
> Us in the youngest day when all are
> Shaken awake ...

No more than any other of the longer works can the *Horae Canonicae* sequence be said to succeed as a whole.

The three volumes of the 1960s did not make any outstandingly new departures. *Homage to Clio* (1960) contains, notably in the title-poem and *Good-bye to the Mezzogiorno*, some wittily allusive meditations in the loose colloquial manner which became Auden's most characteristic later vein; but there is also much laboured whimsy, and the volume is eked out with mere trivia. The chief technical experimenting now runs to syllabic verse in the style of Marianne Moore, and this continues in *About the House* (1966), half of which is a sequence of reflections suggested by different aspects of the poet's country cottage in Austria, and half a miscellaneous collection whose variety follows lines predictable from the time of *Nones*. *Whitsunday in Kirchstetten*, with which Auden bows himself out of this volume, is the familiar kind of musing, epigrammatic, serious and whimsical by turns, on politics, religion, and the human situation. *City Without Walls* (1969) is a miscellany on lines very similar to the second part of *About the House*.

The problem of unevenness, that arose at every stage in Auden's career, is not resolved even in his later work. It has come to seem a fundamental quality of his talent, almost a necessary condition of his creative activity. He can always be relied on to be more interesting, lively, provocative, wide-ranging, psychologically penetrating, technically skilful, and ingenious than most of his contemporaries. He has given us a small number of successful poems and a great many incidental and fragmentary brilliances. But he never

gathered up and concentrated all his powers in a major achievement, and never quite fulfilled the promise of the first volumes. This
is not merely the obstinate prejudice of those who, in the special
Auden number of *New Verse* fifty years ago, were taken to task for
refusing to recognize that a poet's development might be twisted and
obscure and that 'a wet day in April is not the end of summer'. It
is often Auden's most sympathetic interpreters today whom we find
doubting, even after the fullest possible survey of his poetic range
and quality, whether he can be claimed as a major artist.[15] He
remains a peculiarly representative figure whose work and career raise
the important question: what is it in the present relation of the poet,
his critics, and his public which apparently makes it more difficult
than at any earlier time for genuine talent to grow to its full
stature?

NOTES

1. A further grave complication is Auden's habit of making numerous
textual alterations and revisions at different reprintings. The whole question
has been investigated in detail by Joseph Warren Beach in *The Making of the
Auden Canon*. References to titles added to earlier poems at a later date are
taken from the volume of *Collected Shorter Poems, 1930–44* (1950).

2. In a contribution to the *New Verse* special Auden number (November
1937).

3. An interesting analysis of this poem appeared in an article on 'Marxism
and English Poetry' by D. A. Traversi, *Arena* I, 199 (1937).

4. In *The Present Age from 1914*, 121.

5. e.g. John Bayley in *The Romantic Survival*, A. Alvarez in *The Shaping
Spirit*.

6. The point was discussed in a number of reviews of Auden's early work
by F. R. Leavis (*Scrutiny*, III, 76; V, 323; IX, 200, and see also 'This Poetical
Renascence' in *For Continuity*).

7. Richard Hoggart, in his *Auden, an Introductory Essay*, gives a helpful
commentary on the poem but does not, I think, quite solve the problem.

8. In *Purpose* XII, 149 (1940). The same number contains an essay by Auden
on Thomas Hardy, whom he claims as his 'poetical father'.

9. *Auden, an Introductory Essay*, 90–92. I am indebted to the whole chapter
on Auden's technique, which raises many interesting points.

10. See the review by R. O. C. Winkler, *Scrutiny*, X, 206.

11. In an article 'Late Auden: the satirist as lunatic clergyman', *Sewanee
Review*, Winter, 1951.

12. See the essay 'Reluctant Admiration' in *The Apothecary's Shop*.

13. L. C. Knights in an essay on Bacon (*Explorations*, 110).

14. See 'Auden's Later Manner', in *Vision and Rhetoric*.

15. e.g. Richard Hoggart in his British Council pamphlet (1957): 'We cannot claim that Auden is now a major artist or seems likely to become one'. For a more favourable opinion generally of Auden's achievement, see Monroe K. Spears: *The Poetry of W. H. Auden: The Disenchanted Island* (1963). This book also gives useful and comprehensive factual information about the whole of the poet's work, including his opera libretti and his critical and miscellaneous prose.

NOVELISTS OF SOCIETY:
EVELYN WAUGH, GRAHAM GREENE, C. P. SNOW

GRAHAM MARTIN

In any discussion of minor writers, you really want to say two things: why you think they are minor, and then, given the limitation, what their achievement amounts to. But in a short essay about prolific novelists like Waugh, Greene, and Snow – together they have written over fifty novels – it is impossible to deal fairly with both points. It seems better, then, to concentrate on the second, and hope that a suggestive definition will serve to enforce the undiscussed general assessment. With these writers, this is the more worthwhile, because since each speaks from a distinct social situation, their juxtaposition underlines major changes in the structure of English society between the late 1920s and the present day. Moreover, since at least one of the ways in which novelists matter arises from their ability to interpret their social preoccupations more or less penetratingly, a basis already exists for the view that they *are* limited. None of these novelists, that is, seems completely in control of his material; or at least, of the kind of issues which his presentation of the material raises. Greene's awareness is certainly more acute and more arresting than that of either Waugh or Snow, and he is, correspondingly, a more considerable figure. Snow, of course, has the special interest of a contemporary whose retrospective view of the period could never be inferred from any acquaintance with Waugh or Greene. Waugh, on the other hand, with the exception of *The Sword of Honour* trilogy, offers mainly a period interest. He is essentially a pre-war novelist, and the post-war interest in him is a kind of hang-over, a nostalgic reaction, socially, but not critically, interesting. Greene spans the gap between Waugh and Snow. His deeper penetration releases him from the strictures of both 'pre-war' and 'post-war'. This judgement coincides with the strikingly different social settings favoured by each novelist: Waugh's upper-middle class, Greene's middle-middle, and Snow's professional and working or lower-middle class. Simply in that shift, the process

479

of social change is plain enough. Snow, of course, is not the only witness to the results of the process – one needs *Anglo-Saxon Attitudes* and *Lucky Jim* as well – but he does effectively qualify the complacent Forward-With-The-People version of it, without obliging us to accept Waugh's helpless disgust. (See the opening pages of *Brideshead Revisited*.) As Edward Hyams remarks, 'People forget that the Managers began their revolution in the second year of the war'.[1]

Evelyn Waugh

Evelyn Waugh's first novel, *Decline and Fall*, appeared in 1928, his last, *Unconditional Surrender*, in 1961. In all, he wrote fifteen novels, a collection of short stories (1936), some travel books, a study of Rossetti (1928), biographies of Edmund Campion (1935) and Ronald Knox (1959). The novels fall into two well-defined groups: up to and including *Put Out More Flags* (1942); and from *Brideshead Revisited* (1945) onwards. The second group is less homogeneous than the first. There are satires in the earlier manner of which *The Loved One* (1948) is the best known; some shorter pieces which include the quasi-autobiographical *The Ordeal of Gilbert Pinfold* (1957); and those in which the author's Roman Catholic faith prominently figures, *Brideshead*, a historical novel, *Helena* (1950); and the trilogy of *Men at Arms* (1952), *Officers and Gentlemen* (1955), and *Unconditional Surrender* (1961), collectively entitled *The Sword of Honour*, about the war. For reasons which will appear, it is possible to discuss Waugh as a pre-war novelist.

Waugh objected to the common description of his early work as social satire on the ground that this is impossible in a society which provides the satirist with no acceptable norms of behaviour, attitude, and belief.[2] The analysis is arguable, though, in view of the negative emphasis of the novels themselves, it is worth bearing in mind. But in the first instance, 'satire' is hard to do without. The kind of observation – 'Mrs Ape watched them benignly, then, squaring her shoulders and looking (except that she had really no beard to speak of) every inch a sailor, strode resolutely to the first-class bar' – the recourse of parody – 'you will find that my school is built upon an ideal – an ideal of service and fellowship. Many of the boys come from the very best families' – the stretches of dead-pan quotation from real speech, the sequence of fantastic and grotesque events, run in the end to an impression reasonably described in the Penguin editions as 'pungent satire upon the coteries of Mayfair'. It seems pointless to wonder whether this is *really* satire because it lacks moral indignation – it doesn't – or farce, or comedy of manners, or a peculiar amalgam of all three. These terms have no precise modern application. With the exception of *A Handful of Dust* (1934), 'social satire' provides at least a starting point for discussion of Waugh's novels from *Decline and Fall* to *Put Out More Flags*.

As a narrator, Waugh is usually neutral, concealing his attitude behind a front of impersonal reporting. Sometimes, however, he is more open, and the result is interesting.

> Various courageous Europeans, in the seventies of the last century, came to Ishmaelia, or near it, furnished with suitable equipment of cuckoo clocks, phonographs, opera hats, draft-treaties and flags of the nations which they had been obliged to leave. They came as missionaries, ambassadors, tradesmen, prospectors, natural scientists. None returned. They were eaten, every one of them; some raw, others stewed and seasoned – according to local usage and the calendar (for the better sort of Ishmaelites have been Christian for many centuries and will not publicly eat human flesh, uncooked, in Lent, without special and costly dispensation from their bishop). Punitive expeditions suffered more harm than they inflicted, and in the nineties humane counsels prevailed. The European powers independently decided that they did not want that profitless piece of territory; that the one thing less desirable than seeing a neighbour established there was the trouble of taking it themselves. Accordingly, by general consent, it was ruled off the maps and its immunity guaranteed. As there was no form of government common to the peoples thus segregated, nor tie of language, history, habit, or belief, they were called a Republic.
>
> (*Scoop*, pp. 74–5)*

This attack on the benefits of 'civilization' typifies the spirit of much of *Scoop* (1938), of *Black Mischief* (1932), and of many incidental gibes at 'humanism' elsewhere; yet in neither of the novels can we point to any alternative position in whose terms the attack can be understood. Moreover, in the details of passage itself, the novelist deliberately withdraws, at the actual moment of utterance, the only morality to which the paragraph might successfully have appealed (see the sentence in brackets, above). If the passage accepts anything, it is only the honest Ishmaelites who ate the European colonists raw.

* Page references to the Penguin editions in this and subsequent cases.

Scoop and *Black Mischief* move into a slightly different world from that represented by Lady Metroland and the coteries of Mayfair, though the two are not unconnected, of course. But in doing this, they only extended to new material a manner and an attitude already characteristic.

> It was called a Savage party, that is to say that Johnnie Hoop had written on the invitation that they were to come dressed as savages. Numbers of them had done so; Johnnie himself in a mask and black gloves represented the Maharanee of Pukkapore, somewhat to the annoyance of the Maharajah, who happened to drop in. The real aristocracy, the younger members of the two or three great brewing families which rule London, had done nothing about it. They had come on from a dance and stood in a little group by themselves, aloof, amused but not amusing. Pit-a-pat went the heart of Miss Mouse. How she longed to tear down her dazzling frock to her hips and dance like a Bacchante before them all. One day she would surprise them all, thought Miss Mouse.
>
> (*Vile Bodies*, p. 53)

The *nouveau riche* Miss Mouse is at one point the object of the satire – she is a social climber into *this* society – and at another, the focus of a satirical comment upon it. She innocently longs for the real barbarism of which the Mayfair party provides a bored, decadent imitation. Waugh does not exactly accept her (comparative) sincerity – as he accepts the honesty of the more frank of the Ishmaelian cannibals – but, by implying this alternative, and at the same time mocking its foolishness, he complicates the simpler attack of the rest of the paragraph. This is more of a piece with the manner dominating most of the novel.

> There was a famous actor making jokes (but it was not so much what he said as the way he said it that made the people laugh who did laugh). 'I've come to the party as a wild widower,' he said. They were that kind of joke – but, of course, he made a droll face when he said it.
>
> Miss Runcible had changed into Hawaiian costume and was the life and soul of the evening.
>
> She had heard someone say something about an Independent Labour Party, and was furious that she had not been asked.
>
> (*Vile Bodies*)

The cumulative effect of this is actually to dissipate the greater satirical energy of the passage about Miss Mouse. (The same is true of *Scoop*.) But that passage still does represent something important about the whole novel, because the series of accidents which make up 'the story' is no more successful in establishing a secure point of view than this, or any other, seeming confession of one. The satirical bias, which we begin by assuming is simply hidden from view by the parodic report, turns out to have no definable status. When Waugh appears to offer one, it is only a trick. He lures the reader into a judgement – in the context of neutral narration we are eager to accept one – and then leaves him there, the target of a hostility more supple and more deep-seated than he had guessed. In both a local and a general view, this is more important than the dissection of Mayfair high life. It commits Waugh to his so-called (but the word is misleading) dramatic presentation. The world is disliked, but it is not understood; the report on it must therefore communicate a generalized unselective distaste. To angle the view (as, for example, Angus Wilson does) would be to expose a particular animus, and so a criterion of judgement. But there is no criterion. And, as a consequence, the neutral manner is not simply a satirist's tactic, but the statement of what we have to call, for lack of another term, an attitude.

If this is largely true of all Waugh's satires, it applies more exactly to the two earliest: *Decline and Fall* (1928) and *Vile Bodies* (1930). *Black Mischief* (1932) and *Scoop* (1938) offer (in part at least) a contrast between types of social and political folly and a *relative* normality. *Put Out More Flags* (1942) opposes the job-hunting of the phoney war to the patriotic realities of personal sacrifice (though the presentation of Basil Seal and the 'comic' victimization of Ambrose Silk are deeply ambiguous). It is, then, the earlier pair that best represent the 'pure' Waugh statement. In each, the novelist organizes the social report around the story of young man's adventures in Society. Each is, formally speaking, the hero, presented on the whole more sympathetically than his milieu. But neither is allowed to focus upon that milieu anything like a criticism. In *Decline*, Paul Pennyfeather is very explicitly *not* allowed to do so (see pp. 187–8). In *Vile Bodies*, Adam Fenwick-Symes is, like his predecessor, the passive victim of his group, but in a subtler way. He belongs to the coterie, but even though he suffers from the trivializing folly of its attitudes, he still accepts them. The action details his unsuccessful attempts to get rich so that he can marry Nina. With her, he shares a feeling towards which we are expected to be sympathetic. Yet neither this feeling (nor even the old Edwardian order represented by Anchorage House) is set up in opposition to the demonstrated meaninglessness of their social life. Adam fails to get rich, Nina marries someone who is, and Adam ingeniously cuckolds her husband by pretending to be that husband on a Christmas visit to Nina's home. War interrupts this idyll, and the novel concludes ('Happy Ending') with Adam reading a letter from Nina in the midst of 'the biggest battlefield in the history of the world'.

As a sort of reason for all this misery, Waugh offers in the mysterious person of Father Rothschild, S.J. this comment on the Bright Young Things: 'But these people have got hold of another end of the stick, and for all we know it may be the right one. They say, "If a thing's not worth doing well, it's not worth doing at all." It makes everything very difficult for them' (p. 132). And an exchange between Adam and Nina at a crisis in their fortunes appears to make the 'difficulty' more general:

'Adam, darling, what's the matter?'
'I don't know ... Nina, do you ever feel that things simply can't go on much longer?'
'What d' you mean by things ... us or everything?'
'Everything.'

(p. 192)

It would, of course, be impressive to describe this as an intimation of class-decadence, but the view is so restricted, the analysis so slight, and the treatment so external, that 'class' is not a possible term. It is never more than a question of Society.

We have to conclude, I think, that in these two novels the writer is reporting a situation which, strictly, he cannot interpret. His feeling towards its particular meaninglessness is one of half-fascinated, half-indulgent horror. He makes gestures of protest, but does not follow them through. On the other hand, his is far from a ruthlessly amoral exploration. The neutral assurance again and again exposes sudden crystallizations of hatred and disgust; and the story moves easily towards the grotesque and the nightmarish. But one thing distinguishes the two earlier satires: a quality of nihilistic acceptance which refuses to escape into the general securities – the country-house, patriotism, 'culture' – hinted at (though never wholly accepted) in the later ones. This makes for a peculiar tension which, already slackening in *Scoop* and *Put Out More Flags*, disappeared altogether from the post-war writing (except in *The Loved One*). Waugh later allowed himself to take up attitudes for which in the early period he had nothing but distaste.

Waugh's only novel of the decade, not merely satirical, is *A Handful of Dust* (1934). It is not possible to discuss it in detail, but since it is sometimes referred to as a minor classic, one comment is necessary. We seem to be reading about a typical relationship of upper-middle-class society in the thirties. Yet when we explore for the real substance of the marriage and its breakdown, try to realize the motives and sympathies of wife, lover, and husband, as the seriousness of their situation appears to invite us, we run up against a blank silence. The neutral presentation seems designed to baffle and confuse the development of those very responses it begins by invoking. Our sympathies are engaged, but never exactly. We are manipulated into accepting as 'real' characterizations and substantial moral involvements people and a story that are scarcely there at all. Except in a kind of brilliant faking, Waugh never goes beyond the external accuracy of observation which served him in the satires. We are left, as a result, with an extreme statement of personal disillusion, but masked as an impersonal analysis and an objective account.

Waugh then represents the pre-war period in a peculiar way. His novels do not provide insights into the special aspect of his time that he knows, but they recognize its symptoms. (Compare *Vile Bodies* with Greene's *A Gun For Sale*.) The situation he speaks about is a fragmentary social experience scarcely related at all to the encompassing society and culture to which it belonged. Auden and Huxley, writing from a comparable condition, generalize and interpret in a way that sometimes disguises and even falsifies. Waugh avoids this. He seems admirably careful to submit to the discipline of a faithful report. But the report itself is really serving the rigidities of fixed emotion ('those vile bodies'); a state of affairs which can obstruct 'meaning' quite as effectively as an over-zealous pursuit of it. In this respect, the later 'Roman Catholic' novels show a development. Ryder's dislike of 'the age of Hooper' (*Brideshead Revisited*, p. 332) is presented as one element in a general truth, that all human life is 'vanity', and devotion to the True Faith the only virtue. Token gestures, perhaps, given the story as a whole, but *The Sword of*

Honour attempts to realize them in detail. Crouchback's hatred of the modern age is rooted in a romantic illusion as damaging as any other signs of the times (see *Unconditional Surrender*, p. 232), while his father's Christian virtues are seen as nothing in the sight of God (p. 65). Yet rejection is the final emphasis. Crouchback effectively retires from the world, leaving it to sinister figures like Ludovic, or to the merely careerist Kilbannock or Box-Bender. Of Gilbert Pinfold we are told that 'he wished no-one ill, but he looked at the world *sub specie aeternitatis* and he found it flat as a map' (*The Ordeal of Gilbert Pinfold*, p. 14). It is a judgement which Waugh's post-war fiction repeatedly under-writes.

Graham Greene

Graham Greene's writing career, more or less contemporaneous with Waugh's until the latter's death in 1966, now extends over half a century. His first novel, *The Man Within*, was published in 1929, and his most recent at the time of writing, *Dr Fischer of Geneva*, appeared in 1980. To date, he is the author of twenty-one novels; or excluding the first three, which he had described as *juvenilia*, and starting with *Stamboul Train* (1932), of eighteen main titles. Full novels alternate with 'entertainments' (Greene's name for his less serious works) more or less evenly over the whole period. There is an early volume of poems (1925). There are collections of short stories, travel books, plays, and essays both critical and biographical, the latter collected in *Ways of Escape* (1980).

Unlike Waugh, Greene has always been a highly topical writer. The depression, international capitalist monopolies, war-scare, survivors from torpedoed ships, diamond-smuggling by neutrals, spy-scare, the Cold-War, anti-Americanism – this list of headlines comes only from *England Made Me* (1935), *The Heart of the Matter* (1948), and *The Quiet American* (1955); and even if Greene's topicality extended only to the sensations of the national dailies, it would still be worth stressing. This is one of the ways in which Greene has been popular, without being any the less serious. But the sense for news penetrates more deeply than this. Greene is also very sensitive to climates of opinion, and in his novels these emerge, not through spokesmen for (quaintly) period-views, but through their mood, their general feeling about the topical events made use of by the plots. In *A Gun For Sale* (1936), for example, the fear of war is neither simply a device for the story, nor an emotion certain people experience: it emerges also from the way the scene of the action is presented, from the buildings, the streets, the anonymous crowds who fill them. Its presence 'in the air' of the novel is underlined in a contrast with *Vile Bodies*, whose conclusion adopts the same topical fact of war-scare, without any of Greene's compelling social actuality. Waugh's 'biggest battlefield in the history of the world' belongs to a nightmare appropriate enough to his novel, but remote from the thing itself. Again, *The Ministry of Fear* (1943), *The Heart of the Matter* (1948), and *The End of the Affair* (1951) all recognize the presence of the war, less as something to be fought, or stopped, or worried about, than as a social fact to be lived with, and put up with, like some chronic but not fatal disease. Simply as social history, 'topicality' at this level is not to be despised. And the question it immediately raises, i.e. how does it relate to Greene's serious themes? is central to Greene's importance.

Kenneth Allott, in his discussion of the way Greene establishes in each novel his characteristic attitudes and interpolations, has stressed the dominant role of his metaphorical prose.[3] Now this (through scene-setting and the detailed response of key-characters to the scene) is also the source of the topical mood, so that between Greene's peculiar sensibility and his topical sense, there must be a very close connection; and a connection, moreover, which rules out two common views of Greene's social observation. Neither the view which confines the *value* of this to the novels of the thirties (where it is certainly more obvious), nor the view which commends it as a superior kind of social-documentary padding really accounts for the character of Greene's prose. This implies that Greene's 'social consciousness' is both more extensive and more important than that, and at the same time calls for very careful definition. For if the topicality is always more than a record, if, then, it does verge on explicit social comment, it is never easy to decide what this comment amounts to. The fact is that none of Greene's novels from any period ever succeeds in challenging, much less in revising the rough social images of the different periods which we already possess. As far as its social insight goes, each novel remains an isolated statement. There is

no sense in which, collectively, 'the world of Greene's novels' outlines the significant experience of an epoch. With Greene or without
him, we still experience the different decades of his career as
still-to-be-interpreted sequences of roughly known facts and partial
insights. Greene's topicality, therefore, remains ambiguous, however
pervasive, however deep-seated. On the one hand, whatever social
insight it portends seems locked within the parochial details of the
thirties, the forties, the fifties, etc. On the other hand, the fact of its
persistence points to an equally persistent social condition which
Greene's sensibility is particularly able to express. The only way to
identify this condition, and at the same time to account for its literal
obscurity, is to consider the actual art which is its vehicle.

In *Brighton Rock* (1938), the first of Greene's Catholic novels, the
corrupt lawyer, Mr Drewitt, to whom Pinkie applies for advice about
his marriage, fittingly quotes Mephistopheles. 'Why, this is Hell,' he
says, 'nor are we out of it', and the remark applies, of course, to the
career of the damned Pinkie. But it also indicates a feature of the
novel less explicit than its theology. The presentation of Brighton,
full as it is of convincing period detail, can be called 'realistic', but
'hell' is also a very fair description. Apart from Ida – and the novel's
argument sets her apart – Pinkie's individual response to the scene is
completely endorsed throughout the novel, even when the viewer is
Hale. The novel's 'realism', that is, cooperates with Pinkie's state of
mind by the language it uses and the currents of feeling this sets
going, through, in a word, its mood. This mood has been compared
with the relevant sections of *The Waste Land*, and the comparison
underlines not only a common emphasis on seediness, sterility, and
despair, but a common method of establishing it. Like Eliot, Greene
works through metaphor to convey a particular range of feeling
which ratifies, almost proves, an unstated general view of life. (E.g.
'Jug, jug to *dirty ears*' – the last two words overpower the whole
implication of what has gone before, and somehow exclude protest or
dissent.) Yet unlike the poem's, the novel's mood emerges not within
a formal poetic organization (with all the reservations that that brings
into play), but underwritten by the apparently unquestionable
guarantees of 'realism'. This is not to imply that in *Brighton Rock*
Greene is 'a poet' trying to be 'a novelist' and failing. *Brighton Rock*
is a successful novel, and this part of its structure contributes to that

success. Greene's earliest work, *Stamboul Train* for example, is over-metaphorical, but as he develops, Greene turns not to the 'symbolist' inventions of Lawrence, but to the analytical procedures of James and Conrad: distanced characterization, significant description, multiple point-of-view narrative, 'credible' plots. The ambiguous 'realism' is, in a sense, Greene's particular addition to these methods. In *Brighton Rock* the effect of this is to objectify Pinkie's moral condition. Brighton/Hell exists both in its own right, and as a vehicle for Pinkie's character, a projection of his sterile guilt. This balance works both ways, so that the personal guilt and the particular character define themselves in 'real' social environments. Neither environment nor moral condition predominates; neither is the cause of the other; and as a result, both together, Pinkie *and* Brighton, combine in the novel to suggest an absolute human condition, of no particular social or historical identity. The modified 'realism' helps both to make topical *and* to generalize Pinkie's total estrangement from the meaning of his life. Greene, of course, goes on to interpret this condition theologically. But novels can be more socially conscious than novelists, and this is the case here and with a number of Greene's novels; Pinkie's condition is socially meaningful, not because he is the victim of a particular kind of social outrage which Greene, blinkered by his religion, refuses to name. It is his failure to belong to his own experience that matters. Loss of meaning, loss of control, loss of contact, not simply with others, but, except in crude glimmerings, with one's own actual experience – there is no need to elaborate the reasons for this having been felt more generally, more acutely, and more persistently in our society between 1930 and 1945. What Greene diagnoses as an absolute human condition – 'why, this is hell, nor are we out of it' – existed as an experienced social fact. And as a result, Greene's sense for topical mood was able to connect, and connect significantly, with his own themes. The same reason may account in his more recent work for the falling-off in relevance of this kind.

What, of course, makes it hard to identify the social consciousness of Greene's novels is either the exclusion in the early ones of any explicit comment, or, in the later ones, the insistence of the theology. More and more, this works to convert the novels into parables with just sufficient contemporary detail to make them apply. That does not mean that *ipso facto* the Catholic novels fail; or that their theses can, either for agreement or dismissal, be disengaged from the situations they interpret. But it does make possible two critical questions: does the official interpretation evade or confuse the meaning of the novel's situation? or if it does not, *as an argument*, how seriously is it being offered? The first applies to *The Heart of the Matter*, discussed below, but since *The Power and The Glory* (1940) is also a candidate for Greene's most characteristic novel, it is worth applying the second question there. Clearly, its thesis is appropriate enough to the situation, but in at least one instance it seems disingenuously offered. The 'radical' policeman is completely routed in his arguments with the 'reactionary' priest, but only for two reasons which have little to do with the real content of the argument. The policeman's position is a parody of what it is supposed to be, and the priest's arguments get their real force from the priest's experience. That experience, especially in the prison scene, is so much finer, so much more vivid than the hollow interchanges of the subsequent argument, that it seems to justify the novelist's glaring partiality for the priest's view of the case. In a slightly different way, the same holds for some of the earlier novels of the thirties. Admittedly there is no thesis there, but the richness of scene and characterization accumulates an effect powerful enough to underline the novelist's refusal to be explicit about it.* *It's A Battlefield* (1934) and *England Made Me* (1935), certainly studies in the moral absolutes of betrayal, guilt, and loneliness, are also novels about identifiable social and political conditions. But these conditions are never identified in the novels, and this withholding portends the cruder juggling of the issues in *The Power and The Glory*. The final stage in this process seems to be *The End of the Affair*, where an over-articulate thesis dominates characters and setting so completely that 'social-documentary padding' does seem the correct description for the presence of the blitz, and wartime London. From this point of view, then, *The Heart of the Matter* is Greene's most successful novel because it best coordinates argument and example; better even than *Brighton Rock*, where the plan is more unevenly realized, perhaps because it is only an 'entertainment'. Thus, the West African colony is familiar enough in being English, because a colony; but strange, because for the same reason it is not England.

---

* But perhaps the climate of literary opinion in the thirties accounts for this reticence.

The scene is better able to provide Scobie's tragedy with its objective guarantee; yet the details of this successfully inhibit any irrelevantly 'social' interpretation of his state of mind. (Put Scobie in London, and his troubles either dissolve, or generalize themselves into recognizable social tensions. Compare the Assistant Commissioner in *It's A Battlefield*.)

Scobie's experience hovers in a kind of no-place between the condition of personal nightmare, subdued only because he feels he has chosen it; and that of a general waste land in which, though they do not know it so thoroughly as Scobie, all human beings share.

> Why, he wondered, swerving to avoid a dead pye-dog, do I love this place so much? Is it because here human nature hasn't had time to diguise itself? Nobody here could ever talk about a heaven on earth. Heaven remained rigidly in its proper place on the other side of death, and on this side flourished the injustices, the cruelties, the meanness that elsewhere people so cleverly hushed up. Here you could love human beings nearly as God loved them, knowing the worst: you didn't love a pose, a pretty dress, a sentiment artfully assumed.

(pp. 33–4)*

Evidently, 'here' is crucial to the argument, and it supports it both by being offered as 'real', and at the same time as being the projection of the attitudes and assumptions on which the argument really depends. The point of the 'dead pye-dog', not the only one to be picked out in this way, is to mobilize the support of earlier examples of such projections, and such arguments. This early description of the police-station, for example:

> In the dark narrow passage behind, in the charge-room and the cells, Scobie could always detect the odour of human meanness and injustice – it was the smell of a zoo, of sawdust, excrement, ammonia, and lack of liberty. The place was scrubbed daily, but you could never eliminate the smell. Prisoners and policemen carried it in their clothing like cigarette smoke.

(p. 6)

Or the description of Scobie's wife Louise:

> He saw the fist open and close, the damp inefficient powder lying like snow in the ridges of the knuckles ... He lifted the moist hand and kissed the palm: he was bound by the pathos of her unattractiveness.

(p. 23)

---

* Page references to the 1951 Uniform Edition by William Heinemann.

Even Wilson's seemingly casual perceptions are laid under contribution:

> A vulture flapped and shifted on the iron roof and Wilson looked at Scobie. He looked without interest in obedience to a stranger's direction, and it seemed to him that no particular interest attached to the squat grey-haired man walking alone up Bond Street. He couldn't tell that this was one of those occasions a man never forgets: a small cicatrice had been made on the memory, a wound that would ache whenever certain things combined – the taste of gin at midday, the smell of flowers under a balcony, the clang of corrugated iron, an ugly bird flopping from perch to perch.
>
> (p. 4)

In each case, a combination of physical accidents generates a mood and a point of view whose main consciousness is Scobie. Thus, because the prison's 'lack of liberty' is, by metaphor, an actual smell, it emerges not as a particular social condition with particular causes, but as an irreducible fact of life. The argument of the first quotation grows, therefore, from a context which makes it seem the only possible one. It is in this way that Scobie's personal morality is projected on to an environment from which, at the same time, it seems inevitably to grow. In most extreme cases, the result is nightmare. Here is Scobie's act of self-damnation:

> Father Rank came down the steps from the altar bearing God. The saliva had dried in Scobie's mouth: it was as though his veins had dried. He couldn't look up: he saw only the priest's skirts like the skirt of the mediaeval war-horse bearing down upon him: the flapping of feet: the charge of God. If only the archers would let fly from ambush ... But with open mouth (the time had come) he made one last attempt at prayer, 'O God, I offer up my damnation to you. Take it. Use it for them', and was aware of the pale papery taste of his eternal sentence on the tongue.
>
> (p. 272)

As well as being a poetic statement of mood and attitude, *The Heart of the Matter* narrates the history of certain human relationships. Scobie's isolation, his sense of being moral in relation to a world which is immoral, and yet immoral in relation to the morality of God, has to be proved there as well. And since he is, in a sense, an Everyman, the voice of the moral man's complaint against the nature of life itself, his story must protect him from over-specific charges against his character as an individual man. Here Greene runs into difficulties: the story purports to be an unbiased record, concealing nothing significant to the moral situation. Yet there is more than one point at which the record seems to have been too carefully arranged. In an account of actual relationships, selective 'realism' is only a possible method if the basis of the selection (as in satire) is fully confessed. Yet Greene's method, his generalizing intention, necessarily conceals this basis. Thus, Scobie's mistrust of Ali, his only real friend, leads to the latter's brutal death. The narration makes this seem an inevitable tragedy arising from Scobie's quixotic surrender to Helen Roth's demands upon him – Scobie's 'responsibility' perhaps, but not his fault. But in fact, either this catastrophe *does* reveal a moral fault in Scobie which particularizes his condition; or, if not, then it is imposed on to his likely behaviour to 'prove' how brutally meaningless life really is. The novel very skilfully refuses to choose: the first would affect Scobie's general significance; the second the inevitability which the 'realism' of behaviour attempts to convey. So, the incident counts against him only in the way that Scobie allows it to count. We are forced to accept his vague self-contempt. There is no other standard to go by. In the same way, Scobie's relationship with his wife seems less than fully declared. What he calls his 'pity' for her can be more simply described as lack of love. In fact, Louise actually says this, but the effect is merely to prevent us saying it, because the structure of the novel carefully allows her no moral rights. Scobie's is the only effective view. In both relationships, then, Greene covertly indulges his hero's faults, and in the case of the two women, his 'pity' for them is allowed to attract the same kind of admiration (despite the results of his bungling) as his feeling for the survivors of the torpedoed ships, or of the dying child. The attitudes within such terms as 'pity' and 'responsibility' are, in fact, more complex than the author lets us think. Scobie is both more and less admirable than the formal view of him which the novel offers. This view, which the contrivance of the plot works for with great skill, explains Scobie's suicide by the nature of life itself, rather than by the nature of Scobie's life. But many different causes cooperate in Scobie's damnation: the significantly obscure failure of his marriage, the place he works in, the heat, the war, money, his job, and so forth. This makes it 'realistic' of course, but it proves nothing absolute about the human condition. It is one thing to detail a particular story, and invite sympathy for it – 'Here was a man who ..., etc.' It is quite another to manipulate the presentation so that the story proves a hidden argument. The argument may be right or wrong – that is not the point – but to insinuate it into Scobie's story by way of plot-contrivance (however subtly and skilfully) is to invite at least the charge of limited seriousness. Put beside the more candid intensities of local feeling and particular vision (e.g. the last of the above quotations, Scobie's reaction to the dying child, or to the dawn-sea) the argument of the plot seems rather shabby.

The point is impossible to discuss fairly in short space, but because it emerges so intimately from Greene's method as a novelist, it has to be mentioned. Greene's art attempts to reconcile the narrow strength of a very specialized vision – Kenneth Allott has described Greene's world as 'an underworld' – with an easily accessible novel structure whose purpose is to generalize the vision. At the level of what I have called 'mood', the reconciliation succeeds, but beyond that it begins to involve serious evasions and ambiguities. And this is certainly one of the ways in which Greene is a minor novelist. A 'major' treatment of his underworld would involve either a different quality in the supporting argument or a fuller commitment to the special vision – in either case, a very different kind of novel. On the other hand, the ambiguities evidently spring from the writer's belief that the condition he diagnoses *is* absolute, and demands an expression of itself which says so. And though Greene's subsequent writing is occasionally more genial, and often more comic, though it is a comedy that is never far from macabre, these inner convictions continue to dominate. Of Wilson we are told that he 'felt the loyalty we all feel to unhappiness – the sense that that is where we really belong' (*The Heart of the Matter*, p. 213). Greene's later novels remain equally loyal to that personal vision.

C. P. Snow

C. P. Snow's reputation rests upon the sequence of eleven novels, published 1940–70, whose title is that of the first-member, *Strangers and Brothers* (1940).[4] (*The Search*, which first appeared in 1934 and was reprinted in 1958, does not belong to this sequence.) In the preface to *The Conscience of the Rich* (1958), Snow describes the series as having two aims: to give 'some insights into society' by relating the stories of several individuals over a period of time, roughly 1920 to 1968; and to follow the moral growth of Lewis Eliot, the narrator of these stories, as he experiences the struggle for power, both private and public, within his own life and in that of his friends. Each novel can be separately read, but they are all closely linked, not only by their common themes, but by the persons, incidents, and places used in the narration. Eliot's presence is of course the main link, and even where, as in *The Masters* (1951), his part in the story is marginal, he is still more than a narrative convenience. Eliot is not exactly a Jamesian 'consciousness', but the experience related is very certainly his, whether its ostensible interest is social history as in *The New Men* (1954), or personal biography as in *A Time of Hope* (1949). He is the only character in the whole sequence with whom we feel any degree of intimacy.

The scheme is ambitious, and though for a reason which I will suggest it is not really successful, it makes Snow interesting as no other contemporary writer is. Quite apart from the social history it recounts, Eliot's own career – provincial clerk, rising barrister, Cambridge don, industrial legal consultant, upper civil servant – is a significant one. (It is, in fact, A Career.) The road from the working or lower-middle class to Whitehall is never likely to be very busy; but the spirit in which successful travellers journey, the kind of experience the journey brings, the kinds of observation it encourages – and discourages – these have a general relevance (to other kinds of contemporary social travelling) which it is difficult to overrate. More especially, perhaps only Eliot's career could make available the classic pattern of English society and at the same time display so clearly its altered significance. 'Society' (in the Waugh sense) is no longer the place where the ambitious man, having arrived at the summit, begins to enjoy his reward. Society has become 'contacts', something to be made use of on the way to the top. The goal to be achieved (in Eliot's case to be renounced) is not social elevation, but effective power; and the criteria of judgement not finally manners or culture, though these help, but ability, weightiness, acumen, and, above all, an instinct for backing the winning side.

As an observer, Snow is accurate and painstaking rather than sensitive (cp. Greene). He has little success in conveying any mood or atmosphere which does not fall within the reflective sensibility of

Lewis Eliot, so that between us and the portrayal there is a certain remoteness. But the accuracy is convincing.

[After the war] we had to recognize that English society had become more rigid, not less, since our youth. Its forms were crystallizing under our eyes into an elaborate and codified Byzantinism, decent enough, tolerable to live in, but not blown through by the winds of scepticism or individual protest or sense of outrage which were our native air. And those forms were not only too cut-and-dried for us: they would have seemed altogether too rigid for nineteenth-century Englishmen. The evidence was all about us, even at that wedding-party: quite little things had, under our eyes, got fixed, and, except for catastrophes, fixed for good.

(*Homecomings*, 1956, p. 283)

He was propounding the normal Foreign Office view that, since the amount of material was not large, it was the sensible thing to distribute it in small portions, so that no one should be quite left out; we should thus lay up credit in days to come. The extreme alternative view was to see nothing but the immediate benefit to the war, get a purely military judgment, and throw all this material there without any side-glances. There was a whole spectrum of shades between the two, but on the whole Eggar tended to be isolated in that company and had to work very hard for small returns. It was so that day. But he was surprisingly effective in committee; he was not particularly clever, but he spoke with clarity, enthusiasm, pertinacity and above all weight. Even among sophisticated men, weight counted immeasurably more than subtlety or finesse.

(*The Light and The Dark*, 1947, pp. 333–4)

There was a chance, how good I could not guess, that the [atomic] pile would still work quickly; it meant giving Luke even more money, even more men.

'If you're not prepared for that,' I said, hearing my voice sound remote, 'I should be against any compromise. You've either got to show some faith now – or give the whole thing up in this country.'

'Double or quits,' said Rose, 'if I haven't misunderstood you, my dear chap?'

I nodded my head.

'And again, if I haven't misunderstood you, you'd have a shade of preference, but not a very decided shade, for doubling?'

I nodded my head once more.

Rose considered, assembling the threads of the problem, the scientific forecasts, the struggles on his committees, the Ministerial views.

'This is rather an awkward one,' he said. He stood up and gave his polite youthful bow.

'Well,' he said, 'I'm most indebted to you and I'm sorry to have taken so much of your valuable time. I must think this out, but I'm extremely grateful for your suggestions.'

(*The New Men*, 1954, pp. 123–4)

This social documentation is only one aspect of these three novels. Into each account of public events Snow interweaves a personal story; and this structure roughly corresponds on the one hand to the social insights, and on the other to the struggle for power. But the private histories are the least successful parts of these novels. Snow's powers of characterization, limited chiefly to speech-style, and very often amounting to little more than a few typical phrases per character, are scarcely adequate to the demands of his scheme. The novels are very thin in their physical and emotional life. Thus, Eliot's difficult relationship with his first wife as told in *Homecomings* (1956), or equally difficult friendship with Roy Calvert (*The Light and the Dark*, 1947) are present in the novels only through Eliot's personal account of his own feelings. His responses are 'there', but not the objects which are supposed to account for them. This failure in realization is important enough in itself, but it extends farther, to the narration of the public events as well. The various incidents, considered apart from the local use that Eliot makes of them, resolve into mere aggregate of social-documentary detail. Eliot is therefore the only explicit source of each novel's judgements, so that a contradiction between his essential attitudes and the ostensible scheme of the novels cannot be compensated elsewhere. The success of the scheme stands or falls by Eliot's ability to unify and interpret its material. In two ways it seems to me that he fails to do this, so that the necessary connection between his history and the social insights he mobilizes is never forged.

The first dissonance between Eliot and 'the material' concerns the theme of power. On this issue, Eliot is principally an interested observer, who rarely passes judgements, except in the special cases of his own renunciations (see *A Time of Hope*, *Homecomings*, *Last Things*). Ostensibly, the illustrative incidents are left to speak for themselves, and on a number of occasions it is possible to discern the submerged workings of an attitude which, since it is not Eliot's, can only be the novelist's. This attitude can be described as a quickened feeling for the actual process of decision-taking, as distinct, that is, from the content

497

or the meaning of the decision. In, for example, *The Light and The Dark*, Snow recounts the arguments for and against the decision to launch regular night-bombing against the Germans. Bomber Command's view is that it will boost civilian morale in such a way that the great expense in men and materials will be worthwhile. Eliot and, more importantly, his friend Francis Getliffe think the expense too great. Getliffe is an influential man because of his war-work on radar, and he throws himself into the business of pressuring and lobbying the appropriate committees. However, the decision goes against him, and because he continues the fight to the very last moment, he hopelessly identifies himself with a losing cause. As a result, he is relegated to unimportant work. Now, in the meanwhile, Eliot's friend Roy Calvert, who already knows about the heavy losses from conversations with Eliot, decides to become a bomber pilot. His personal life (whose tensions the novel is mainly concerned with tracing) has reached the point at which he no longer cares whether he lives or dies. Bomber Command provides him with an honourable solution; and so, in due course, he becomes one of the 'losses who might have fought longer' and his friend Eliot is left alone with his memories and grief. This, very briefly, is the point at which the public decision, whose mechanics we know in some detail, interlocks with the private history. But in doing so, its *public* significance disappears, to be replaced by its *private* effect on three individual lives. Calvert dies *privately*, not as a patriot; Eliot mourns him as a friend, not as a type of the heavy losses; Getliffe is demoted; and as everybody knows, the bombing went on. This implies (and I say 'implies' because it is a case of what is not said, rather than what is) that the only kind of individual participation in public life is at the level, not of responsibility, but of power. Eliot's neutrality (unawareness?) at this point offers no other solution. Choice, control, understanding: these ideas are confined to the private histories, which are lived out in a public context determined on quite different principles. In their private lives, some people stoically accept the fact that they are victims of uncontrollable forces. In public, however, other people make decisions which direct these forces one way or another to the more or less severe detriment of many private lives. But the two kinds of decision remain separate, and their meeting in Eliot's narration of his experience only underlines their hiatus. Eliot's attitudes belong to the sphere of private life; the public history remains significantly uninterpreted.

The second dissonance can be more briefly mentioned. Eliot's deepest response to the complexities of personal friendship is that of Arnold: 'Yes! in the sea of life enisled ... We mortal millions live *alone*'. And since Snow is unable to provide Eliot with a context which speaks up for the opposite feeling (i.e. that we mortal millions live socially if we live at all), Eliot's morality dominates the novels, becomes in fact the felt morality of the novelist, and this considerably magnifies the importance of his failure to complement Eliot by means of the realization of other and different characters. It is this failure that makes Snow's ambition to show realistic 'insights into society' virtu-ally impossible to achieve – except, that is, in the external manner of the above quotations. Necessarily, the novelist of 'social insights' whose presentation of social experience is so remote and so static as Snow's defeats his own hope. In the last analysis, the sequence seems less to be about society than about Lewis Eliot's personal journey through various sections of the English class-structure.

However, where the sequence has a limited success is in its accumu-lated sense of Eliot's long life, whose intensities of loss and achieve-ment, despair and recovery, especially in the later novels, sustain the reader's otherwise flagging interest in the 'social' narrative. In contrast with the general thinness of characterization, Eliot's reflections about his friends, acquaintances and family, his steady and not unsubtle wrestling with the complexities of human behaviour, command respect. As a very different novelist wrote, 'on balance life is suffering, and only the very young or the very foolish imagine otherwise.'[5] Despite his genial accommodations with the material benefits of satisfied ambition, Eliot would not have disagreed.

NOTES

1. *Taking It Easy* (1958), 5.
2. F. J. Stopp, *Evelyn Waugh: Portrait of an Artist* (1958), cited 194–5.
3. K. Allott and M. Farris, *The Art of Graham Greene* (1951).
4. *Strangers and Brothers* has since been retitled *George Passant*.
5. George Orwell, *Selected Essays* (Penguin, 1957), 115.

THE ANATOMY OF MASS
COMMUNICATIONS IN BRITAIN

RICHARD HOGGART

This chapter is not about 'serious' or 'good' literature; nor is it about literature alone. It is about that extraordinary and complicated range of recreational activities put out by the media of mass communication, activities which reflect and affect aspects of British 'culture' in this century. Somewhere outside them stands the work of the novelists, poets and dramatists discussed elsewhere in this volume; so do older forms of popular urban entertainment such as working-men's club concerts, brass bands, chapel choirs, comic postcards and *Peg's Paper*; so do officially established cultural organizations and arrangements, such as the Arts Council and that part of the rates which local authorities spend on the arts. But here, in the centre for the moment, are the popular newspapers and weekly magazines (from the 'sexy' to the 'women at home' kind of magazine); comedy radio-shows (a particularly rich seam, especially during the last war); the gossip columnists; Hollywood films of all kinds and the *sui generis* Ealing films; domestic radio serials and advertisements of all sorts. After television began to come into full flower, roughly from the late 1950s, examples multiplied: television is by nature a main creator of instant, disposable popular folk-lore.

In general, examples here will be drawn from mass media up to the last war. In referring to broadcasting I will emphasize the pre-television and pre-competitive days. However, where it seems helpful to use foresight born out of hindsight – and where it would be formalistic to do otherwise – the period will be stretched.

How the creations of mass media relate to literature, and to the 'high culture' of which literature is a part, is not immediately clear. But there are relationships, direct and important, relationships which anyone interested in literature and in society will do well to think about more than is generally done. Discussion about mass communications has been persistent, confused, and heated in this century; but it is not essentially new. It is a development in contemporary terms of a larger debate, with a long history. A major historian and critic of this larger debate, Raymond Williams, began his examination with Edmund Burke and moved – to name only some major figures – through Coleridge, Newman, Lawrence, and T. S. Eliot. This list spans more than one hundred and fifty years, and in Britain alone. If we look more widely, to European and American writers, we can span a roughly similar period by moving, say, from Alexis De Tocqueville to Ortega y Gasset and well beyond.

The larger debate is about culture and society, that is about the quality of life which democracies offer and encourage. Culture here, then, has to do with the quality of the imaginative and intellectual life these societies express, most obviously though not only through the place they give to the creative arts and to intellectual inquiry. The debate is also, inevitably, about the relation of culture to class, to wealth, to work, and to educational provision. What place, if any, do traditional forms of 'high culture' (those arts and inquiries largely produced and sustained, formerly, by members of the middle and upper classes) have in a universally literate and fairly prosperous democracy? What future, if any, have the elements of a differently phrased and local working-class culture? Is a good, widely diffused, popular or demotic culture possible in such democracies? What kinds of persuasion, by government or by non-statutory bodies, are legitimate and desirable?

Such a debate is not expressed only in writing. In nineteenth-century Britain the sustained and devoted efforts by some members of the privileged classes to disseminate the benefits of education and culture to those less fortunately placed is part of the same movement (as in the development of extra-mural teaching by the universities, which was begun by Cambridge). Similarly, many of those resourceful nineteenth-century reformers who were themselves from the working classes believed that they had a cultural as well as a political and economic mission. To take another example from adult education: the universities did not there plough a virgin field; many grass-roots organizations for the cultural improvement of working people existed before the universities entered.

This is a very simple outline of a complex background, meant to indicate chiefly that the discussion of mass communications is part of a larger and longer inquiry. But there are sound reasons why the inquiry should be especially active in this century and should have the particular emphasis I go on to describe. The twentieth century is the first century of the truly *mass* media of communication, and this gives a special force to questions of the kind enumerated above. Is high culture bound to be peripheral to the driving and overriding forces of mass communications? Are all older types of culture likely to be submerged in new substitute forms, in 'kitsch'? What is the relation of the creative arts and of disinterested intellectual activity to these new means of communication?

First, however, what are the mass media and how did they arise? No definition can be precise, but a workable definition can be reached. The chief forms of mass communication, as the phrase is normally used, are sound and television broadcasting, the press (with certain exceptions), the cinema, and some types of advertising. In general, and this is their distinction, all these activities are addressed regularly to audiences which are very large and relatively undifferentiated by class, income, background or locality (thus, most books are not in this sense mass media). All these activities are products of the twentieth century. Before then, broadcasting and the cinema did not exist, and the press and advertising existed only in a small way.

Several social and technological factors combined to produce these modern forms of communication. Two are usually given overriding importance and must be mentioned first, although the illumination they give of the more subtle aspects of the problem – those to do with direction and quality – is in fact not great. These two factors are technological advance and universal literacy. Obviously the two interact and some mass media (especially popular publications) have particularly developed from the interaction; on the other hand cinema and broadcasting need hardly attend on literacy. The most striking primary cause for the appearance of contemporary mass communications, then, was technical knowledge and its application. The last decades of the nineteenth century, in particular, saw an enormously accelerated development in all parts of this field.

In Britain, it is true and important, these advances roughly coincided with the appearance of a new reading public. Towards the end of the nineteenth century the Registrar-General was able to announce that Britain – no other nation had preceded her – was substantially literate. The total population was growing, and has continued to grow. There is plenty of evidence, especially in the biographies of the first press-lords, that some energetic men appreciated the commercial opportunities presented by this large, new, literate, but not intellectually critical audience.

Three further qualifications have to be made, however, so that universal literacy is not given too much weight in the general development of mass communications. First, it would be wrong to infer that before the late nineteenth century only a tiny minority in Britain could read. Mid-twentieth-century research has shown that by the middle of the nineteenth century a substantial proportion were able to read, even among the working classes. Second, there was a considerable amount of cheap publication for working people by, for example, 1840; these productions divided roughly into two types, the 'improving' and the sensational. Third, if too simple a relationship is assumed between statutory education for the body of the people and the rise of certain types of mass communication, then one more easily assumes that these productions are addressed chiefly to working people, that working people, almost alone, are affected by them. This was never substantially true and has steadily lost most of its relevance.

Two other factors lie behind the rise of mass communications and tell more about their nature and quality. The first is the development, in both democracies and totalitarian states, of centralized social planning. In almost all societies, and especially in those which are becoming increasingly industrialized, a kind of national self-consciousness is greater today than ever before. This does not necessarily mean that what is commonly called a 'nationalist spirit' is more powerful, but that these societies need more and more to speak to their citizens as a body, to persuade them in certain directions. This is the public or governmental pressure behind mass communications and can be seen in a great number of forms: in authoritarian countries as a support to state ideologies (Mussolini's Italy, Hitler's Germany, Soviet Russia, Communist China); in democratic countries chiefly in time of war or 'cold war'; but increasingly in the day-to-day peacetime life of any technologically advanced state. It would be difficult to decide the relative importance of various factors when comparing the *speed* with which the means of mass-communication have been adopted in different countries. In the democracies we tend to overestimate the effect of commercial forces. We should give more importance to larger social forces, to public and governmental pressures.

Still, there are immense commercial pressures in the democracies. In spite of the damage of two major wars and the increases in population, the twentieth century has seen a considerable increase in the real wealth of most Western countries. In Britain a large body of people (though not from all parts of society) who previously spent almost the whole of their income in providing, and often barely providing, for necessities have, since the mid-1950s, had money to spend on goods which are not essential – though they may be pleasant to have. Marginal spending by teenagers, in particular, has encouraged, and been encouraged by, substantial businesses; by contrast, pensioners and others past working age have not so much benefited from this prosperity (compare the attention paid by the mass media to youth with that to the aged). This general improvement may or may not accompany a levelling of incomes within a society. The crucial element is the over-all rise in real wealth which has ensured that a large number of people who were previously below the level at which they attracted serious and concerted attention from the makers of non-essential consumer goods are now above that level. These are what market-research specialists call 'new markets', especially for tastes previously enjoyed chiefly by middle- and upper-class groups, or 'potential markets' where a more novel taste or invented 'need' has to be encouraged.

In the Soviet Union and China the mass media are substantially arms of government, with positive and comparatively single-minded functions. In different democracies their use differs according to the structure and underlying assumptions of each society. We can say roughly that in America the main emphasis is on the commercial use of the means of mass communication – they tend to be aids to selling, or profit-making organizations in their own right. In Britain, which is both a stratified society with a responsible and still fairly powerful 'establishment' and yet a commercial 'open' democracy, the use of mass communications reflects this piebald character. The British like to use direct governmental controls as little as possible, but their strong tradition of public service and public responsibility causes them (where it is not possible or relevant to support existing voluntary agencies) to establish semi-autonomous chartered bodies under regular, but not day-by-day, government surveillance. The Universities Grants Committee and the Arts Council (its progenitor was the wartime C.E.M.A. – Council for the Encouragement of Music and the Arts) are typical of such bodies. This tradition helped to ensure that, once broadcasting had begun to show its powers in the mid-1920s, a new chartered body was created – the British Broadcasting Corporation – charged with the responsibility for public service broadcasting.

The history of the B.B.C. in this period and some way beyond has been very fully written by Asa Briggs.[1] By the outbreak of the Second World War, the B.B.C. had become an extremely competent and a proud organization; its pre-eminent rights had never been seriously challenged. It was not simply 'the main instrument of broadcasting' in Britain, as it more and more came to be described after the appearance of a competing system: it was the only instrument. Hence its very special and particular character. On the one hand it was unmistakably the voice of – and an instrument for sustaining the idea of – not so much the 'establishment' as an assumed established consensus. What other broadcasting system agonized so much over the responsibilities of the broadcasters to propriety in all its aspects, to the idea of an acceptable 'standard' form of speech, to established and unestablished religion, to the Monarchy, the Empire and later the Commonwealth, to its own artistic duties, to the relations between the national and the regional? It was an amazingly sustained seminar, and so serious that it sometimes verged on the comical. What other broadcasting system would produce a flurry of argumentative memoranda on the duty of the system to do right by poetry? The B.B.C. in its upper echelons was in the pre-war years staffed largely from Oxford and Cambridge. Hence their conviction, which they no doubt shared with other readers of *The Times*, that the annual university boat race was a 'national' event. This odd conviction persists: the Boat Race is now televized.

On the other hand, the B.B.C. was not and is not an arm of government. It is funded if not directly by, at least in relation to the size of, the licence fee rather than by Exchequer grant; and that strangely Platonic formula strengthens its sense of independence. This independence has expressed itself powerfully at crucial moments, as we shall see. It also helped ensure that the B.B.C., more than any other broadcasting system, pondered endlessly and with great catholicity on the nature of its audiences, their tastes and – more important – the potentialities of their range of interests. To do this is not necessarily to be a blind 'do-gooder' ('giving people what they ought to have') but may rather be a sign of respect for the individuals who make up broadcasting's huge audiences (as distinct from the implicit contempt in aiming only to 'give people what they want'). So the B.B.C. was a far more complex organization than the received view allows. It had pronounced weaknesses and cultural limitations; it had also great virtues and considerable achievements. It was often stuffy but had important moral strengths. This process was orchestrated not by but through the presence of Sir John (later Lord) Reith. His personal role is often given too much weight. He was certainly a very powerful factor, but we would do well to see him, during his decade in charge of the B.B.C. (1927–38), as less a conscious cause than a remarkable symptom of qualities in British pre-war society very much wider and larger than any one personality, qualities which he did not himself greatly understand.

So the B.B.C. entered the last war in good heart and came out of it having firmly established two important positions. It had become in some sense 'a part of the war effort'. But such a phrase can cover a wide range of behaviour. By the end of the war the B.B.C.'s reputation internationally had never stood higher. It had given the news day by day so nearly objectively that even enemy nations trusted it. It had also, in response to the wartime need both to increase the sense of community and to provide relief from grimness, discovered that whatever its class or regional differences 'the nation' did have a common 'funnybone', that people did laugh at the same things – surrealist knockabout situations, mad inventiveness in language, the interplay of ranges of eccentric characters.

The B.B.C. has never since had such an easy time. But the clouds were gathering. By an odd irony the mid-1950s saw two important moments in the B.B.C.'s life, one a reinforcement of its proven strengths, the other its greatest continuing problem for the future. In the autumn of 1958 it met the most direct challenge it had ever had.

The Prime Minister, Sir Anthony Eden, ill and beset with the complicated mess that was his Suez intervention, argued that, since the country was at war, the B.B.C. should become an arm of government and forgo the effort at objective reporting. The B.B.C. replied that since Parliament was divided on the Suez issue we could not be said to be 'at war' as a nation, and refused to comply. There was a morning when it looked as though the Governors might be overridden and have to resign. Then Eden pulled back from the brink.

The same period saw the arrival of commercial television, financed by advertisement revenue. The Independent Television Authority was established, to oversee that network, in 1954. With it came the biggest opposition yet offered to the B.B.C.'s role, standing, definition of its objects, sense of its audiences and of itself. These redefinitions inevitably led to a heightening of both weaknesses and strengths and to the emergence of new strengths and new weaknesses. That process is not completed; in some ways it never can be.

The advocates of British commercial broadcasting always point out that its programmes are not sponsored by the advertisers as they are in the United States. This is true, but the similarities between American television and independent British television are considerable. And the general tendencies of both are markedly different from those of the B.B.C. It would be more accurate to call the British second channel commercial television rather than independent television. In media so centralized and which reach instantaneously so large an audience there can be no full independence: one chooses to try to fulfil, as objectively as possible, one's public-service responsibilities; or one is pulled by the pervasive general requirements of those who pay for the advertisements. These two channels, each competing for the attention of the British people, and each representing one main form of dependence, are the most striking evidence for the two themes of this essay: the intrinsic power and importance of the organs of mass communication; and the curiously mixed relationships of Great Britain with these organs – relationships decided partly by history and tradition, and partly by newly emerging commercial and cultural pressures.

In Great Britain, particularly during the last half-century, the four factors already discussed – technological advances, universal literacy, increased public self-consciousness, and increased consumption of goods – have encouraged two striking changes in almost all forms of public communication. To some extent these changes, towards centralization and concentration, *must* develop as the means of communication become means of mass communication; in Britain they have developed very quickly.

Centralization denotes the tendency for local or regional sources of communication to give way to one metropolitan source. The metropolitan area itself progressively subdivides into segments, each providing nationally most of the popular material within a given branch (e.g. pre-war Denmark Street and its environs for popular songs). There are a number of reasons why this process should have moved particularly quickly in Britain. The country is highly industrialized, densely populated, small in area, and has good communications. Practically everyone can be reached instantaneously by broadcasting, or within a few hours by a national newspaper. The United States has roughly four times the population of Britain but thirty times the land area. Holland and Belgium have most of the characteristics listed above, but the relative smallness of their populations makes it less likely that really massive organizations can be founded in the field of communications. Nor has Britain any strong regional centres of cultural and intellectual activity. Edinburgh and Manchester can make some claim, but a comparison with, say, Naples or Milan shows how limited the claim is.

Centralization in communications reflects a similar pattern in commerce and industry, just as concentration reflects larger economic movements. If centralization makes for the production of almost all material of one kind from one source, concentration makes for a reduction in variety within each kind. In industry, the production of cars is an obvious instance. Several kinds of car are available (family saloon, sports car, limousine, estate car) but the number of different makes and so of models within each kind is small. The large markets thus ensured bring obvious advantages: lower price, relative stability of employment, concentration of resources for research. Occasionally, some of these advantages can be usefully taken in the *distribution* of good intellectual and imaginative works as in the issue of good books in paperback which used to be called 'the paperback revolution' (though it is now a rather faded revolt). But that is chiefly a matter of 'marketing' an existing product of good quality (and for every publication of this sort the same machines produce several which are purely commercial fabrications). The real problems which concentration in cultural matters poses lie here: that concentration does not simply distribute existing material but to a large extent decides the form and nature of all new material, reduces variety in approach and attitudes, seeks manners which will gain a mass audience most of the time. Cars are not really very important; if by centralizing and concentrating their production we get workable models cheaply we may well be satisfied. But cheapness, speed, modernity, smartness are all profoundly irrelevant to intellectual and imaginative affairs and, worse, are often bought at the cost of what *is* relevant to them. The intense difficulties of serious publishing in the last ten or twenty years – especially of new fiction, poetry and critical writing, and the falling out of print of minor classics, even in paperback – are only a few indications of the force of this argument.

Broadcasting is the product of a highly technological period and has been since its birth both centralized and concentrated. The cinema, since it is almost entirely a profit-making industry, has been centralized and concentrated almost since its beginnings, and our pleasure when something even mildly exploratory is attempted in a film sufficiently suggests what a loss this has meant. For films too the last war was a watershed. In the 1930s they were the supreme form of international mass entertainment. During the long-drawn-out years of the war that position was protected and strengthened. They, too, like the B.B.C. had a falsely secure decade thereafter. But as television arose so their power waned. They would survive but in greatly changed forms and no longer as the dominant popular visual medium.

Nevertheless, in Britain changes in the press and in periodical publication during the last fifty years show most clearly the trend towards centralization and concentration, since these types of production originally had a great variety of outlets and attitudes. The number of provincial papers still published might seem to suggest that here at least centralization and concentration have not gone far. Certainly the evening provincial papers sometimes have a more independent life than those published in the morning. But a close reading of most provincial papers reveals that centralization and concentration are here too. Ostensibly a paper may belong to a provincial town and the editor may live in its suburbs. But in most important respects these papers are often no more than provincial outlets, printing offices, for large London concerns, and, though they include a moderate amount of local news and views (rather after the manner of the local insets in a parish magazine), the major comment and editorials, the background articles, the judgements on all topics other than those of a purely local interest, are likely to be issued from London each day and so be syndicated in papers under the same central control all over Britain.

Concentration is particularly striking in the national press. During the 1920s Britain still had eight or nine popular daily newspapers of roughly equal effect. In the 1930s there were ruthless price wars which accelerated the process of concentration. Rationing of newsprint during the war meant that even ailing papers could survive, artificially protected. After that the fights began again, for massive circulations and the increased advertising that brings. Quite soon, only two or three newspapers were fighting for the main spoils, and so the process has continued. To achieve concentration on a few outlets you must also concentrate your themes. But to pursue that argument would take us into the 1960s and 70s which have seen not only further concentration in the popular press but an increasing polarization between popular and 'posh' newspapers. The 'posh' or 'quality' or 'serious' newspapers have increased their readerships but still reach a minority of the population. The populars, in two or three huge blocks, have more and more narrowed and trivialized their areas of interest.

It is simply not sufficient to say, as some do, that the mass media are only means of communication, channels for the large-scale distribution of material whose character is not affected by the manner in which it is distributed. Yet there is some truth in the claim, and it underlines the undoubted advantages mass communications can bring. Broadcasting, and especially television, can, as we are so frequently told, suggest a range of worthwhile interests and pleasures far wider than most of us would otherwise have known. It can give millions the chance to hear at the same time a really informed discussion on some matter of public interest; it can occasionally give an unusually close sense of the characters of impressive individuals who would otherwise be no more than names to us; it can present from month to month plays, well acted and produced, which most of us would have passed a life-time without hearing or seeing. In all this broadcasting is acting as a transmitter, a very valuable multiple transmitter.

Some other forms of mass communication also seem to be acting as 'straight' transmitters, in less obvious or simple ways. They appear to have taken over from scattered and varied oral agencies the work of sustaining an elementary folklore. In this shadowy but powerful symbolic world some of the strip-cartoons now work alongside and are probably beginning to replace a dark network of urban stories and myths. This harsh but meaningful sub-world has not been much examined either by writers on mass communications or by students of literature or – we may be glad, since they might make use of it – by the advertising copywriters.

Most of the work of the mass media is done in a more self-conscious light. And the fact that this work is produced for a mass audience radically affects its character. The position of the media forces certain qualities upon it; and these are usually weakenings of the qualities of those established arts on which mass communications must feed.

Mass communications are led, first, to avoid clear psychological and social definition. Sharp definition is possible in 'high' art, and concrete definition of a certain kind is possible in 'low' art, since each depends on a limiting of the audience. The first audience is nowa-days largely self-selected, without overriding reference to social or geographical factors. This is, for want of a better term, the 'high-brow' audience composed of people who, during the times that they are being 'highbrows', are not in a disabling sense also clerks in Sheffield, mechanics in Manchester, or stockbrokers in Croydon – though these may be their everyday occupations and could in different ways reinforce their reading. Yet they are, whilst forming this audience, in a certain sense disinterested. A clerk can read *Anna Karenina* with essentially the same kind of attention as a stockbroker or a mechanic, though the life of upper-class Russian civil servants in the nineteenth century has little social similarity with any of theirs. The second audience is limited by class or geography or both. It can allow a kind of definition within a specific way of life because this way of life is local or socially accepted. This is the audience of, say, both the popular and the posh women's magazines.

The mass media can only occasionally accept either of these types of audience. The first is too small to be of much use; the second is a *series* of audiences, of roughly the same type though divided by habit and custom. Essentially the job of the mass media is to weld this second series of audiences into one very much larger group. There is an immediate loss. Compare only the texture of working-class life in Lawrence's *Sons and Lovers*, or even the particularity and denseness of working-class life assumed in an old-fashioned working-class women's magazine, with the life embodied and assumed in one of the mid-twentieth century classless women's magazines, or that in the posters and pamphlets issued by the main political parties in Britain.

The overwhelming use of the 'realist' or photographic method in mass art underlines this situation. The mass media, especially in a commercial society, dare not genuinely disturb or call into question the status quo. Basically their function is to reinforce the given life of the time, to help their new or emerging mass audience accept the 'reality' that is offered them. Everything has to be shown as 'interesting' and yet as equally interesting, since to do otherwise would be to inspire distinctions and so create minorities. By this means most of existence is presented as a succession of entertaining items, each as significant as the next: a television 'magazine' programme or a weekly illustrated magazine will successively give the same sort of treatment – the visual, the novel, the interesting – to a film actress, a nuclear physicist, a teenage singing star, a great 'man of letters'; similar treatment will be given to close-up photographs of a personal tragedy or a new technique for building roads. Order and significance give way to sheer spectacle, the endlessly fragmented curiousness of brute experience.

Although they are exceptionally aware of their huge audience as a huge audience, the mass media dare not have a real closeness to the individuals who compose that audience. they can rarely be so precise and particular as to inspire any one of that audience to say, 'There, but for the grace of God . . .' or, 'This attitude I cannot accept . . .' They retreat from the immediate dramatic presentations of art to the sterilized world of the 'documentary', where the close detail of individual existence is reduced, by being generalized, to the status of 'problems which concern us all', problems which are examined in a 'neutral', a 'fair-minded' and 'objective' way. This is the foundation of that standardization, that stereotyping, of character which marks almost all works produced expressly for the mass media.

We are told that the mass media are the greatest organs for enlightenment that the world has yet seen, that in Britain, for instance, several million people see each issue of a television current affairs programme. We have already agreed that the claim has some foundation. Yet it is not extensive. It is true that never in human history were so many people so often and so much exposed to so many intimations about societies, forms of life, and attitudes other than those which obtain in their own local societies. This kind of exposure may well be a point of departure for acquiring certain important intellectual and imaginative qualities: width of judgement, a sense of the variety of possible attitudes. Yet in itself such an exposure does not bring intellectual or imaginative development. It is no more than the masses of stone which lie around in a quarry and which may, conceivably, go to the making of a cathedral. But the mass media cannot build the cathedral, and their way of showing the stones does not always prompt others to build. For the stones are presented within a self-contained and self-sufficient world in which, it is implied, simply to look at them, to observe – fleetingly – individually interesting points of difference between them, is sufficient in itself.

Life is indeed full of problems on which we have to make decisions, or at least try to, as citizens or as private individuals. But neither the real difficulty of these decisions nor their true and disturbing challenge to each individual can always be communicated through the mass media. The disinclination to suggest real choice, individual decision, which is to be found in the mass media is not simply the product of a commercial desire to keep the customers happy. It is within the grain of *mass* communications. The 'establishments', however well-intentioned they may be and whatever their form (the State, the Church, some voluntary agencies, political parties), have a vested interest in ensuring that the public boat is not violently rocked, and will so affect those who work within the mass media that they will be led insensibly towards forms of production which, though they go through the motions of dispute and inquiry, do not break through the skin to where such inquiries might really hurt. They will tend to move, when exposing problems, well within the accepted cliché-assumptions of democratic society and will tend neither radically to question those clichés nor to make a disturbing application of them to features of contemporary life; they will stress the 'stimulation' the programmes give, but this soon becomes an agitation of problems for the sake of the appeal of that agitation in itself; they will therefore, again, assist a form of acceptance of the status quo. There are exceptions to this tendency, but not enough to break the soft mould.

In Britain a habitual uneasiness about intellectual and, even more, artistic debate reinforces this process. On issues which require some prior thinking about general principles the mass media tend to shy away quickly into stereotyped generalities and personalization. In radio 'magazine' programmes, to take an outstanding example of the style, any item which involves, let us say, academic matters or the life of art and artists brings out a deep uneasiness. Surely an audience out there assumes only that all professors are absent-minded and all artists wild and bohemian? So 'nudge, nudge' goes the commentator into the conventionalities he has himself fathered on the audience out there. The relief when he returns to more manageable, more 'Fleet Street-style' issues – politics, the unions, odd animals, crime – is almost palpable.

The results of all this can be seen in a hundred radio and television programmes as plainly as in the normal treatment of public issues in the popular press. Different levels of background in the readers or viewers may be assumed, but what usually takes place is a substitute for the process of arriving at judgement. Programmes such as this – they occur under both broadcasting authorities – are important less for the 'stimulation' they offer than for the fact that that stimulation (repeated at regular intervals) may become a substitute for and so a hindrance to judgements carefully arrived at and tested in the mind and on the pulses. Mass communications, then, do not ignore intellectual matters; they tend to castrate them, to allow them to sit on one side of the fireplace, sleek and useless, family playthings.

Similarly, mass communications do not ignore imaginative art. They must feed upon it, since it is the source of much of their material and approaches; but they must also seek to *exploit* it. They tend to cut the nerve which gives it life – that questioning, with all the imaginative and intellectual resources an artist can muster, of the texture and meaning of his experience; but they find the body both interesting and useful. Towards art, therefore, the mass media are the purest aesthetes; they want its forms and styles but not its possible meanings and significance. Since they are *mass* communications they have both a pressing awareness of their audience and a pressing uncertainty about that audience. There is a sense in which we may say that a serious artist ignores his audience (assuming that they will share his interest in exploring the subject); or in which we may say that a popular artist with a defined audience simply assumes that audience because his work is embedded in, and expresses, attitudes which are never called into question. But the worker in the mass media is not primarily trying to explore anything or express anything: he is trying to capture and hold an audience. Manner is more important than matter. The fact that very often there is not one writer on a specific programme but a 'team', each member contributing his tactical items, underlines how far is this process from the serious artist's single strategy towards his recalcitrant material.

If an artist will co-operate with the mass media on their terms (to their credit some artists go on working with the media for the sake of such success as they can gain in their own imaginative terms), he may have exceptional rewards. For in the age of mass communications art becomes one of the most elusive and therefore most sought-after forms of 'marginal differentiation'. Culture becomes a commodity. And just as the dilemmas of experience are reduced to a series of equally interesting but equally non-significant snapshots, or to the status of documentary 'problems', so the products of art become an eclectic shiny museum of styles, each of them divorced from its roots in a man or men suffering and rejoicing in certain times and places. You may buy by subscription and renew, as often as you renew the flowers in your sitting room, examples of Aztec art or African art or Post-Impressionist painting or Cubist painting or the latest book (probably about the horrors of mass-society) which a panel of well-publicized authorities have selected for you. And all has the same effect as the last instalment of the television magazine. You have sipped and looked and tasted; but nothing has happened. Culture has become a thing for display not for exploration; a presentation not a challenge. It has become a thing to be consumed, like the latest cocktail biscuit.

The above point needs to be stressed because it is altogether too easy to think that the mass media affect only 'them'; that the 'masses' are some large body of people in an outer uncultured darkness. There are probably no masses at all – only operators in the mass media trying to form masses and all of us from time to time allowing them. But these 'masses' cannot be identified with one social class or even with our usual picture of the lowbrows and the middlebrows (against the highbrows). Not everyone who reads the book pages of the 'quality' papers is automatically free from mass persuasions, even in his cultural interests.

For, as we have persistently noted, one primary need of mass communications is to reach as wide an audience as possible. Class divides. Where the mass media are commercially influenced this need is all the stronger. To sell their centralized and concentrated goods they must seek a centralized and concentrated audience. In this, therefore, the mass media are both reflecting and encouraging much wider social changes. Centralized production, changes in the nature of work (partly through more effective automatic processes), the higher general level of incomes, greater social mobility, educational changes – all these are helping to alter the local and class lines of British life. In part those lines are also related to divisions in types of cultural activity. British society may well be forming new stratifications, by brains, education, and occupation rather than by birth and money. But such a society will need, if it is not to be irritated by constant inner dissent, a sort of common meeting ground of acceptable attitudes. In democracies this assent has to be brought about by a winning persuasion. In commercially powerful and densely populated democracies the acceptable attitudes can include a wide range of seemingly varying attitudes. There is room there for the *Daily Star* as much as for *Vogue*, for the *Miss United Kingdom Competitions* as much as for the highbrow Book Clubs. But the variety is only apparent; the texture of the experience they offer is not significantly different at any point in the spectrum. You have then arrived at a sort of cultural classlessness.

Here, again, the Second World War can be seen as a watershed. Those who spent several years as servicemen in that war know they entered a hierarchic, unaware, closed society, whose style was typified by the confidence of the rapidly promoted ex-Territorial Army officers. They left more often than not as servicemen ready for change far beyond anything envisaged by Churchill. The vote for Attlee was unmistakably a vote for a more open and democratic Britain. Looking back from near the end of the century, one sees that that spirit was dissipated above all in the prosperous 1960s and was not regained in the disordered 1970s. We await the book which will trace the role of the mass media in all these changes. This role will not be a slight or merely reactive one.

The need to reach a large and (whilst they are listening) classless audience ensures that the mass media can take little for granted. What sort of furniture, reactions, assertions may be used here? How far dare one go on this line without running the risk of alienating some group? It follows that mass communications tend to flatter, since they will take the more plainly winning attitude before the one which may disconcert. Much more important, they have little opportunity for exploring a living relationship towards their material. Some existing attitudes they may use, after a fashion; others they must freshly introduce, with great care. This explains the strange and limited narcissism of the mass media towards attitudes which have been traditionally acceptable to large numbers of people, especially towards attitudes which can be made to assist in creating the most suitable atmosphere in the productions of the mass media themselves. They will accept certain well-established working-class attitudes such as tolerance, lack of meanness, generosity, quirkiness, and extend them into a friendly public buyers' and sellers' world in which – like stuck flowers – they look the same but may soon wither, for want of the soil (of difficulty and tension) in which they had first been nurtured. Programmes such as 'This Is Your Life' and 'That's Life' are typical instances of this kind of process; so is the whole tone of much popular journalism, especially that in the gossip columns and in the editorial responses within the correspondence columns.

This kind of extension can only go so far and soon risks foundering on the reefs of excessive generality (over-extending the stereotype) or excessive particularity (alienating part of the audience).

Therefore, in a society marked with the fine complicated lines of class distinction, mass communications have to move towards a world which is not too specifically recognizable by any one group or class but is acceptable by all. They have to invent a world which most of us, in the times that we are consumers, are happy to inhabit. This is the origin of the glossy advertising copywriters' world, a world with a fixed grin which most of us at some times could imagine inhabiting, but which is artificial, 'dreamed-up'. Such is the sophistication of mass communications (they are rarely naïve) that there are also built into this world allowances for idiosyncrasy, for the odd 'highbrow', and even for the 'bloody-minded' individual. But all will have in the process been effectively neutered. Mass communications naturally tend towards a bland, a nice, a harmless but bodiless range of attitudes. For more and more of the time more and more of us become consumers of more and more things – from material goods to human relations.

Here we come to the overriding danger of mass communications, unless they are constantly criticized and checked against individual judgement. We are not primarily concerned with whether 'highbrow' books will be read in a society dominated by mass communications (as we have seen, they will still be read, in a certain way); we have to ask what will be the quality of the life expressed through all the arts and at all levels in such a society. It may be that literature will have relatively a much smaller place in the society which is now emerging than most people who read this chapter have assumed and hoped.

The intricate social pattern which produced, among much else, 'high culture' as that is normally recognized is being changed. At the same time great numbers of people are in some respects freer than before. In a changed society the best qualities which inform 'high culture' may have to find other ways of expressing themselves; so will the best qualities in the old local and oral life of people who were not in a position to make much contribution to 'high culture'. At the moment the one seems likely to be bypassed and the other eroded by the impact of massively generalized communications. There is a considerable fund of common imaginative strength in all parts of society. The poorest prefabricated art may draw on good impulses. If a thinner consumers' culture is not to spread overall much more care will have to be taken in seeking relevant connections, genuine links between things which show the strengths (some features of day-to-day life, some work in the arts today, some social organizations, some forms of recreation). It is not possible to define in advance the nature of a good demotic culture. Unless one believes that such a culture is not possible one has to try to keep open all lines which may allow for good development as well as to oppose those which are likely to lead to a dead smartness. At present most people with literary interests keep open less effectively than they oppose.

Looked at from the perspective of the late 1980s, this chapter's story seems to belong to a distant era. The idea of the public service in broadcasting has been weakened on all fronts and seems unlikely to survive into the 1990s except as a pale simulacrum.

NOTE

1. A. Briggs, *The History of Broadcasting in the United Kingdom* (Oxford, 1961–79).

PART IV

APPENDIX

VOLUME 7

COMPILED BY JOHN LYON AND ANNE VARTY

List of Abbreviations

ed.	edited
edn	edition
enl.	enlarged
comp.	compiled
pub.	published
repr.	reprinted
rev.	revised
trans.	translated
vol. (s)	volume(s)
b.	born
d.	died
c.	circa
?	probably

The lists which follow are intended as a guide to literature written in the British Isles, and concentrate on the first half of the twentieth century. Such other writers as Henry James and Ezra Pound, both important for British literature of this period, are also included. Readers are also invited to refer to the bibliographies in Volumes 6 and 8 of the Guide where much that is of direct relevance to this period will be found.

FOR FURTHER READING
AND REFERENCE

The Social and Intellectual Setting

I. HISTORIES: GENERAL AND POLITICAL

Beloff, M. *Wars and Welfare: Britain 1914–1945*, 1984
  Britain's Liberal Empire, 1897–1921, 1988
  Dreams of Commonwealth, 1921–42, 1989
Blake, R. *The Conservative Party from Peel to Thatcher*, 1985
Brand, C. F. *The British Labour Party: A Short History*, 1974
Briggs, A. (ed.) *They Saw It Happen*, 1960
Bullock, A. and Shock, M. (eds.) *The Liberal Tradition from Fox to Keynes*, 1956
Butler, D. *The Electoral System in Britain, 1918–1951*, 1953 (second edn, 1963)
Churchill, W. S. *The World Crisis, 1911–1914*, 5 vols., 1923–31
  The Second World War, 6 vols., 1948–54
Cole, G. D. H. *A History of the Labour Party from 1914*, 1948
Cook, C. *A Short History of the Liberal Party, 1900–1976*, 1976
Cross, C. *The Fall of the British Empire, 1918–1968*, 1968
Ensor, R. C. K. *England 1870–1914* (Oxford History of England Vol. XIV) 1936
Foot, M. R. D. *British Foreign Policy since 1898*, 1956
Halévy, E. *The Rule of Democracy, 1905–1914*, 1952 (first published 1934)
Halsey, A. H. *Trends in British Society since 1900*, 1972
Kellas, J. G. *Modern Scotland: The Nation since 1870*, 1968
Lloyd, T. O. *Empire to Welfare State: English History, 1906–1976*, 1979
Lyons, F. S. L. *Ireland since the Famine*, 1971, rev. 1973
Marriott, J. A. R. *Modern England: 1885–1945*, 4th edn, 1960
Marwick, A. *Britain in Our Century: Images and Controversies*, 1984
Medlicott, W. M. *Contemporary England, 1914–1964; with epilogue, 1964–74*, 1976
Morgan, K. O. *Rebirth of a Nation: Wales, 1880–1980*, 1981
Mowat, C. L. *Britain between the Wars, 1918–1940*, 1955
Pelling, H. *The Origins of the Labour Party, 1880–1990*, 2nd edn, 1965
Porter, B. *The Lion's Share: A Short History of British Imperialism, 1850–1983*, 1984

Sampson, A. *The Changing Anatomy of Britain*, 1982

Shannon, R. *The Crisis of Imperialism, 1865–1915*, 1974, rev. 1976

Smellie, K. B. *A Hundred Years of English Government*, 1937, rev. 1950

Steiner, Z. *Britain and the Origins of the First World War*, 1977

Taylor, A. J. P. *English History, 1914–1945* (Oxford History of England, Vol. XV) 1965

Thomas, H. *The Spanish Civil War*, 3rd edn, 1977

Thomson, D. *England in the Twentieth Century, 1914–1963*, 1965, rev. 1981

White, R. J. (ed.) *The Conservative Tradition*, 1950, 2nd edn, 1964

Winter, J. *Socialism and the Challenge of War: Ideas and Politics in Britain, 1912–1918*, 1974

    The Great War and the British People, 1985

    The Experience of World War I, 1988

II. HISTORIES: SOCIAL AND ECONOMIC

Aldcroft, D. H. *The Inter-war Economy, 1919–1939*, 1970

Ashworth, W. *An Economic History of England, 1870–1939*, 1960

Bedarida, F. *A Social History of England, 1851–1975*, 1979

Britain, I. *Fabianism and Culture: A Study of British Socialism and the Arts, c. 1884–1918*, 1982

Burnett, J. *Plenty and Want: A Social History of Diet, 1815 to the Present Day*, 1966, rev. 1979

Fraser, D. *The Evolution of the British Welfare State: A History of Social Policy since the Industrial Revolution*, 1973, 2nd edn, 1984

Glynn, S. and Oxburrow, J. *Interwar Britain: A Social and Economic History*, 1976

Graves, R. and Hodge, A. *The Long Week-end: A Social History of Great Britain, 1918–1939*, 1940

Lambert, A. *Unquiet Souls: The Indian Summer of the British Aristocracy, 1880–1918*, 1984

Lewis, J. *Women in England 1870–1950: Sexual Divisions and Social Change*, 1984

Lovell, J. C. and Roberts, B. C. *A Short History of the TUC*, 1968

Marwick, A. J. B. *The Deluge: British Society and the First World War*, 1965

Mitchell, D. J. *Women on the Warpath: The Story of the Women of the First World War*, 1966

Montgomery, J. *The Twenties: An Informal Social History*, 1957

Nowell-Smith, S. (ed.) *Edwardian England, 1901–1914*, 1964

Pankhurst, E. S. *The Suffragette Movement: An Intimate Account of Persons and Ideals*, 1931

Peden, G. *British Economic and Social Policy*, 1985

Pelling, H. *History of British Trade Unionism*, 4th edn, 1987

Pollard, S. *The Development of the British Economy, 1914–1980*, 3rd edn, 1983

Read, D. *Edwardian England*, 1972

Robbins, L. *The Great Depression*, 1934

Royle, E. *Modern Britain: A Social History 1750–1985*, 1987

Stevenson, J. *British Society, 1914–1945*, 1984

Symons, J. *The General Strike: A Historical Portrait*, 1957

Thompson, F. M. L. (ed.) *The Cambridge Social History of Britain, 1750–1950*, 3 vols., 1990

Webb, S. and Webb, B. *The History of Trade Unionism*, 1950 (first published 1894)

Williams, F. *Magnificent Journey: The Rise of the Trade Unions*, 1954

Winter, J. (ed.) *The Working Class in Modern British History*, 1983

III. PHILOSOPHY AND HISTORY OF IDEAS, RELIGION, EDUCATION

Ayer, A. J. *Language, Truth and Logic*, 1936, rev. 1946

Broad, C. D. *Five Types of Ethical Theory*, 1930

Butterfield, H. *The Whig Interpretation of History*, 1931

Collingwood, R. G. *Religion and Philosophy*, 1916
    The Principles of Art, 1938
    The Idea of History, 1946

Copleston, F. *A History of Philosophy*, Vol. 8, 1966

Cox, C. B. and Dyson, A. E. (eds.) *The Twentieth-Century Mind: History, Ideas and Literature in Britain*, 3 vols., 1972

Frazer, J. G. *The Golden Bough*, 3rd edn, 12 vols., 1907–15

Keynes, J. M. *The Economic Consequences of the Peace*, 1919
    The General Theory of Employment, Interest and Money, 1936

Mace, C. A. (ed.) *British Philosophy in the Mid-Century*, 1957

Moore, G. E. *Principia Ethica*, 1903
    The Philosophy of G. E. Moore, ed. P. A. Schlipp, 1939

Passmore, J. A. *A Hundred Years of Philosophy*, 2nd edn, 1968

Pears, D. *Bertrand Russell and the British Tradition in Philosophy*, 1967

Russell, B. *Problems of Philosophy*, 1912
    An Outline of Philosophy, 1927
    A History of Western Philosophy, 1945

Ryle, G. *The Concept of Mind*, 1949

Tawney, R. H. *The Acquisitive Society*, 1921

Urmson, J. O. *Philosophical Analysis: Its Development between the Two World Wars*, 1956

Warnock, G. J. *English Philosophy since 1900*, 1958

Warnock, M. *Ethics since 1900*, 1960

Whitehead, A. N. and Russell, B. *Principia Mathematica*, 3 vols., 1910–13

Williams, B. and Montefiore, A. (eds.) *British Analytic Philosophy*, 1966

Wittgenstein, L. *Tractatus Logico-Philosophicus*, 1922
    Philosophical Investigations, ed. G. Anscombe, 1953
    The Blue and Brown Books, 1958

Cowling, M. *Religion and Public Doctrine in Modern England*, 2 vols., 1980–85

Davies, H. *Worship and Theology in England, V: The Ecumenical Century, 1900–1965,* 1965

Eliot, T. S. *The Idea of a Christian Society,* 1939

Garbett, C. F. *In An Age of Revolution,* 1952

Lewis, C. S. *The Screwtape Letters,* 1942

Lloyd, R. *The Church of England, 1900–1965,* 1966

Norman, E. R. *Church and Society in England, 1770–1970,* 1976

Spinks, G. S. et al. *Religion in Britain since 1900,* 1952

Armytage, W. G. H. *Civic Universities,* 1955

Bagley, J. J. and Bagley, A. J. *The State and Education in England and Wales, 1833–1968,* 1969

Board of Education Consultative Committee, *The Teaching of English in England,* 1921; *The Education of Adolescents,* 1927; *Primary Education,* 1930; *Education in Grammar and Technical High Schools,* 1938

Curtis, S. J. *Education in Britain since 1900,* 1952

Dent, H. C. *1870–1970: Century of Growth in English Education,* 1970

English Association series of pamphlets, including: Chambers, R. W. *The Teaching of English in the Universities of England,* 1922; McKerrow, R. B. *Note on the Teaching of English Language and Literature,* 1921

Isaacs, S. *Intellectual Growth in Young Children,* 1930
    Social Development in Young Children, 1933

Leavis, F. R. *Education and the University,* 1943, rev. 1948

Lowndes, G. A. N. *The Silent Social Revolution: An Account of the Expansion of Public Education in England and Wales, 1895–1935,* 1937

Palmer, D. J. *The Rise of English Studies,* 1965

Potter, S. *The Muse in Chains: A Study in Education,* 1937

Russell, B. *Education and the Social Order,* 1932
    On Education, 1926

Sampson, G. *English for the English,* 1921, rev. 1952 and 1970

Stocks, M. *The Workers' Educational Association: The First Fifty Years,* 1953

Tillyard, E. M. W. *The Muse Unchained,* 1958

Whitehead, A. N. *The Aims of Education,* 1929

IV. SCIENCE AND TECHNOLOGY

Dingle, H. (ed.) *A Century of Science, 1851–1951,* 1951

Dunsheath, P. (ed.) *A Century of Technology, 1851–1951,* 1951

Harre, H. R. (ed.) *Scientific Thought, 1900–1960: A Selective Survey,* 1969

Kuhn, T. S. *The Structure of Scientific Revolutions,* 1962

Mason, S. F. *A History of the Sciences: Main Currents of Scientific Thought,* 1953

Rose, H. and Rose S. *Science and Society,* 1969

Whitehead, A. N. *Science and the Modern World,* 1926

Williams, T. I. *A Short History of Twentieth Century Technology c. 1910–1950,* 1982

FOR FURTHER READING AND REFERENCE

V. MUSIC, ART AND ARCHITECTURE, THE MEDIA AND PUBLISHING

Ford, B. *The Cambridge Guide to the Arts in Britain, 8. The Edwardian Age*, 1989
Cooper, M. (ed.) *The Modern Age, 1890–1960 (The New Oxford History of Music Vol. X)*, 1974
Howes, F. *The English Musical Renaissance*, 1966
MacKerness, E. D. *A Social History of Music*, 1964
Pirie, P. J. *The English Musical Renaissance*, 1979
Scholes, P. A. *The Mirror of Music 1844–1944*, 2 vols., 1947
Trend, M. *The Music Makers*, 1985
Walker, E. *A History of Music in England*, rev. by J. A. Westrup, 1952
Young, P. M. *A History of British Music*, 1967

Farr, D. *English Art, 1870–1940 (Oxford History of Art, Vol. XI)*, 1978
Harrison, C. *English Art and Modernism, 1900–1939*, 1981
Hitchcock, H. R. *Architecture: Nineteenth and Twentieth Centuries*, 1977
Richards, J. M. *An Introduction to Modern Architecture*, 1940
Rothenstein, J. *British Art Since 1900: An Anthology*, 1962
Service, A. *Edwardian Architecture and its Origins*, 1975
Shone, R. *The Century of Change: British Painting Since 1900*, 1977
Spalding, P. *British Art Since 1900*, 1987

Angell, N. *The Press and the Organization of Society*, 1922, rev. 1933
Ayerst, D. *The Manchester Guardian: Biography of a Newspaper*, 1971
Betts, E. *The Film Business: A History of British Cinema, 1896–1972*, 1973
Black, P. *The Biggest Aspidistra in the World: Fifty Years of the BBC*, 1972
Briggs, A. *Mass Entertainment: The Origins of a Modern Industry*, 1960
    The History of Broadcasting in the United Kingdom, 4 vols., 1961–79
    The BBC: The First Fifty Years, 1985
Durgnat, R. *British Movies from Austerity to Affluence*, 1970
Hamilton, H. (ed.) *Majority, 1931–1952: An Anthology of 21 Years of Publishing*, 1952
The History of 'The Times', 5 vols., 1935–84
Hodges, S. *Gollancz: The Story of a Publishing House, 1928–78*, 1978
Leavis, Q. D. *Fiction and the Reading Public*, 1932
Lee, A. J. *The Origins of the Popular Press in England, 1855–1914*, 1976
Lewis, J. *The Left Book Club*, 1970
Martin, B. Kingsley, *The Press the Public Wants*, 1947
Morpurgo, J. E. *Allen Lane, King Penguin: A Biography*, 1979
Pegg, M. *Broadcasting and Society, 1918–39*, 1983
Richards, J. *Best of British: Cinema and Society, 1930–1970*, 1983
    The Age of the Dream Palace: Cinema and Society in Britain, 1930–1939, 1984
Rotha, P. *The Film Till Now*, 1930, rev. 1949

Scannell, P., and Cardiff, D. *A Social History of British Broadcasting 1922–1939,* 1991
Ullswater Committee on Broadcasting, *Report,* 1935
Woods, O., and Bishop, J. *The Story of The Times,* 1984

The Literature

VI. BIBLIOGRAPHIES

Daiches, D. (ed.) *The Penguin Companion to Literature, 1: Britain and the Commonwealth,* 1971
The English Association: *The Year's Work in English Studies,* 1919–
Jones, B. (comp.) *A Bibliography of Anglo-Welsh Literature, 1900–1965,* 1970
Mikhail, E. H. *A Bibliography of Modern Irish Drama, 1899–1970,* 1972
     English Drama, 1900–1950: A Guide to Information Sources, 1977
Modern Humanities Research Association: *Annual Bibliography of English Language and Literature,* 1921–
Modern Language Association of America: *Annual Bibliography* (English section), 1886–
Reilly, C. W. *English Poetry of the First World War: A Bibliography,* 1978
Temple, R. S. (comp.) *Twentieth Century British Literature: A Reference Guide,* 1968
Vinson, J. (ed.) *Twentieth-Century Western Writers,* 1982
Ward, A. C. *Longman Companion to Twentieth Century Literature,* 1970, rev. 1975
Watson, G. (ed.) *The New Cambridge Bibliography of English Literature,* Vol. 3, 1800–1900, 1969
Willison, I. R. (ed.) *The New Cambridge Bibliography of English Literature,* Vol. 4, 1900–1950, 1972
Wilson, N. (ed.) *Scottish Writing and Writers,* 1977

VII. GENERAL STUDIES

Aldritt, K. *Modernism in the Second World War,* 1989
Bell, M. *1900–1930: The Context of English Literature,* 1980
Bell, Q. *Bloomsbury,* 1968
Bergonzi, B. *Heroes' Twilight: A Study of the Literature of the Great War* 1965, rev. 1980
     (ed.) *The Twentieth Century* (Penguin History of Literature in the English Language, Vol. 7), 1970
     The Turn of a Century, 1973
     Reading the Thirties, 1978
Bigsby, C. W. E. *Dada and Surrealism,* 1972
Blamires, H. *Twentieth-Century English Literature,* 1982, rev. 1986
Bradbury, M. *The Social Context of Modern English Literature,* 1971
Carpenter, H. *The Brideshead Generation,* 1989

Clark, J. et al. (eds.) *Culture and Crisis in Britain in the Thirties*, 1979

Coombes, J. *Writing from the Left*, 1989

Craig, C. (ed.) *The History of Scottish Literataure, Vol. 4: The Twentieth Century*, 1987

Craig, D. and Egan, M. *Extreme Situations: Literature and Crisis from the Great War to the Atom Bomb*, 1979

Cunningham, V. *British Writers of the Thirties*, 1988

Donoghue, D. *The Ordinary Universe: Soundings in Modern Literature*, 1968

Ellman, R. (ed.) *Edwardians and Late Victorians*, 1960

    (ed. with C. Fiedelson) *The Modern Tradition: Backgrounds of Modern Literature*, 1965

    Eminent Domain: Yeats Among Wilde, Joyce, Pound, Eliot and Auden, 1967

    Four Dubliners, 1987

Enright, D. J. *The Apothecary's Shop: Essays in Literature*, 1957

Faulkner, P. *Modernism*, 1977

    A Modernist Reader: Modernism in England, 1910–1930, 1986

Fussell, P. *The Great War and Modern Memory*, 1975

    Abroad: British Literary Travelling Between the Wars, 1980

Glen, D. *The Individual and the Twentieth-Century Scottish Literary Tradition*, 1971

Green, M. *Children of the Sun: A Narrative of 'Decadence' in England after 1918*, 1976, rev. 1977

Hamilton, I. *The Little Magazines: A Study of Six Editors*, 1976

Harmer, J. B. *Victory in Limbo: Imagism, 1908–17*, 1975

Hillis Miller, J. *Poets of Reality: Six Twentieth-Century Writers*, 1966

Hoggart, R. *The Uses of Literacy*, 1957

Hough, G. *Image and Experience*, 1960

Hynes, S. *The Edwardian Turn of Mind*, 1968

    The Auden Generation: Literature and Politics in England in the 1930s, 1976

Jarrell, R. *Kipling, Auden & Co.: Essays and Reviews, 1935–1964*, 1981

Johnstone, J. K. *The Bloomsbury Group*, 1954

Kenner, H. *A Sinking Island: The Modern English Writers*, 1988

Kermode, F. *Continuities*, 1968; *Modern Essays*, 1971; *History and Value*, 1988

Lester, J. A. *Journey Through Despair: Transformations in British Literary Culture, 1880–1914*, 1968

Light, A. *Forever England: Femininity, Literature and Conservatism Between the Wars*, 1991

Lucas, J. (ed.) *The 1930s: A Challenge to Orthodoxy*, 1978

Materer, T. *Vortex: Pound, Eliot and Lewis*, 1979

Matthews, J. H. *The Imagery of Surrealism*, 1977

Morris, J. A. *Writers and Politics in Modern Britain, 1880–1950*, 1977

Muir, E. *Transition: Essays on Contemporary Literature*, 1926

O'Brien, C. C. *Writers and Politics*, 1965

Pritchard, W. H. *Seeing Through Everything: English Writers, 1918–1940*, 1977

Robson, W. W. *Critical Essays,* 1966; *Modern English Literature,* 1970
Rosenbaum, S. P. (ed.) *The Bloomsbury Group,* 1975
Rutherford, A. *The Literature of War: Five Studies in Heroic Virtue,* 1978, rev. 1989
Simpson, L. *Three on the Tower: The Lives and Works of Ezra Pound, T. S. Eliot and W. C. Williams,* 1975
Spacks, P. A. M. *The Female Imagination,* 1976
Starkie, E. *From Gautier to Eliot: The Influence of France on English Literature, 1851–1939,* 1960
Steiner, G. *Language and Silence,* 1967
Stewart, J. I. M. *Eight Modern Writers,* 1963
Symons, J. *The Thirties: A Dream Revolved,* 1960
    Makers of the New: The Revolution in Literature, 1912–1939, 1987
Ward, A. C. *Twentieth-Century Literature, 1901–1960,* (first pub. 1928), 1964
Wees, W. C. *Vorticism and the English Avant-garde,* 1972
Williams, R. *Culture and Society 1780–1950,* 1958
    The Long Revolution, 1961
Wilson, E. *Axel's Castle: A Study of the Imaginative Literatue of 1870 to 1930,* 1931

VIII. POETRY

Allen, D. C. (ed.) *Four Poets on Poetry,* 1959
Alvarez, A. *The Shaping Spirit,* 1958
Baker, W. E. *Syntax in English Poetry, 1870–1930,* 1967
Banerjee, A. *Spirit Above Wars: A Study of the English Poetry of the Two World Wars,* 1976
Bayley, J. *The Romantic Survival,* 1957
Brown, T. and Grene, N. (eds.) *Tradition and Influence in Anglo-Irish Poetry,* 1988
Carter, R. (ed.) *Thirties Poets: 'The Auden Group' – A Casebook,* 1984
Davie, D. *Thomas Hardy and British Poetry,* 1973
    The Poet in the Imaginary Museum, 1979
Draper, R. P. *Lyric Tragedy,* 1985
Duncan, J. E. *The Revival of Metaphysical Poetry,* 1959
Dyson, A. E. *Yeats, Eliot and R. S. Thomas: Riding the Echo,* 1981
    (ed.) *Poetry Criticism and Practice: Developments Since the Symbolists,* 1986
Ford, H. D. *A Poet's War* (Spanish Civil War), 1965
Fraser, G. S. *Essays on Twentieth Century Poetry,* 1977
Gregson, J. M. *Poetry of the First World War,* 1976
Hamburger, M. *The Truth of Poetry: Tensions in Modern Poetry from Baudelaire to the 1960s,* 1969
Hibberd, D. (ed.) *Poetry of the First World War: A Casebook,* 1981
Hoffman, D. G. *Barbarous Knowledge: Myth in the Poetry of Yeats, Graves and Muir,* 1967
Holbrook, D. *Lost Bearings in English Poetry,* 1977

Johnston, J. H. *English Poetry of the First World War*, 1964

Kahn, N. *Women's Poetry of the First World War*, 1988

Kermode, F. *Romantic Image*, 1967

Langbaum, R. *The Poetry of Experience*, 1963

Leavis, F. R. *New Bearings in English Poetry*, 1932

Longley, E. *Poetry in the Wars*, 1986

Lucas, J. *Modern English Poetry: From Hardy to Hughes*, 1986

McDiarmid, L. *Yeats, Eliot and Auden Between the Wars*, 1984

Mackinnon, L. *Eliot, Auden, Lowell: Aspects of the Baudelairean Inheritance*, 1983

Martin, G. and Furbank, P. N. (eds.) *Twentieth-Century Poetry: Critical Essays and Documents*, 1975

Maxwell, D. E. S. *Poets of the Thirties*, 1969

Millard, K. *Edwardian Poetry*, 1991

Parfitt, G. *English Poetry of the First World War: Contexts and Themes*, 1990

Riding, L. and Graves, R. *A Survey of Modernist Poetry*, 1927

Robinson, A. *Poetry, Painting and Ideas, 1885–1914*, 1985

Rogers, T. (ed.) *Georgian Poetry, 1911–1922: The Critical Heritage*, 1977

Rosenthal, M. L. *The Modern Poets: A Critical Introduction*, 1960
    Sailing into the Unknown: Yeats, Pound and Eliot, 1978

Scannel, V. *Not Without Glory: Poets of the Second World War*, 1976

Shires, L. M. *British Poetry of the Second World War*, 1985

Silkin, J. *Out of Battle: The Poetry of the Great War*, 1972

Sisson, C. H. *English Poetry, 1900–1950; An Assessment*, 1971

Smith, S. *Inviolable Voice: History and Twentieth-Century Poetry*, 1982

Stead, C. K. *The New Poetic: Yeats to Eliot*, 1964
    Pound, Yeats, Eliot and the Modernist Movement, 1986

Tolley, A. T. *The Poetry of the Thirties*, 1975

Trotter, D. *The Making of the Reader: Language and Subjectivity in Modern American, English and Irish Poetry*, 1984

Van Wyk Smith, M. *Drummer Hodge: The Poetry of the Anglo-Boer War, 1899–1902*, 1978

IX. PROSE

Allen, W. *Tradition and Dream*, 1964
    The Short Story in English, 1981

Anderson, L. R. *Bennett, Wells and Conrad: Narrative in Transition*, 1988

Batchelor, J. *The Edwardian Novelists*, 1982

Bayley, J. *The Short Story: Henry James to Elizabeth Bowen*, 1988

Bewley, M. *The Complex Fate*, 1952
    The Eccentric Design, 1959

Caveliero, G. *The Rural Tradition in the English Novel, 1900–1939*, 1977

Davie, D. (ed.) *Russian Literature and Modern English Fiction*, 1965

Dusinberre, J. *Alice to the Lighthouse: Children's Books and Radical Experiments in Art*, 1987

Edel, L. *The Psychological Novel, 1900–1950*, 1955

Ford, F. M. *The English Novel*, 1929

Forster, E. M. *Aspects of the Novel*, 1927
    The Development of English Prose between 1918 and 1939, 1945

Friedman, A. *The Turn of the Novel*, 1966

Gorra, M. *The English Novel at Mid-Century*, 1990

Graham, K. *Indirections of the Novel: James, Conrad and Forster*, 1988

Green, M. *The English Novel in the Twentieth Century: The Doom of Empire*, 1984

Greicus, M. S. *Prose Writers of World War I*, 1973

Hanson, C. A. *Short Stories and Short Fictions, 1880–1980*, 1984
    (ed.) *Re-reading the Short Story*, 1989

Hardy, B. *The Appropriate Form*, 1964

Hazell, S. (ed.) *The English Novel: Developments in Criticism since Henry James – A Casebook*, 1978

Hillis Miller, J. *Fiction and Repetition*, 1982

Hunter, J. *Edwardian Fiction*, 1982

Johnstone, R. *The Will to Believe: Novelists of the Nineteen-Thirties*, 1982

Kaplan, S. J. *Feminine Consciousness in the Modern British Novel*, 1975

Kermode, F. *Essays on Fiction 1971–82*, 1983

Kiely, R. *Beyond Egotism: The Fiction of James Joyce, Virginia Woolf and D. H. Lawrence*, 1980

Klein, H. (ed.) *The First World War in Fiction: A Collection of Critical Essays*, 1976

Leavis, Q. D. *Fiction and the Reading Public*, 1932

Liddell, R. *A Treatise on the Novel*, 1947

Lodge, D. *The Language of Fiction*, 1966
    The Modes of Modern Writing, 1977
    After Bakhtin, 1990

Lubbock, P. *The Craft of Fiction*, 1921

Mack, M. and Gregor, I. (eds.) *Imagined Worlds: Essays on Some English Novels and Novelists*, 1968

Mahood, M. *The Colonial Encounter: A Reading of Six Novels*, 1977

Meyers, J. *Fiction and the Colonial Experience*, 1972

Muir, E. *The Structure of the Novel*, 1928

O'Connor, F. *The Mirror in the Roadway*, 1956; *The Lonely Voice*, 1963

O'Faolain, S. *The Vanishing Hero: Studies in Novelists of the Twenties*, 1956

Page, N. *Speech in the English Novel*, 1973

Parrinder, P. *Science Fiction: A Critical Guide*, 1979

Russell, J. *Style in Modern British Fiction*, 1978

Sandison, A. *The Wheel of Empire: The Imperial Idea in Some Late Nineteenth-Century and Early Twentieth-Century Fiction*, 1967

Schorer, M. (ed.) *Modern British Fiction: Essay in Criticism*, 1961

Schwarz, D. R. *The Humanistic Heritage: Critical Theories of the English Novel from James to Hillis Miller*, 1986
    The Transformation of the English Novel, 1890–1930, 1989

Shaw, V. *The Short Story*, 1983

Showalter, E. *A Literature of Their Own: British Women Novelists from Brontë to Lessing*, 1977

Stubbs, P. *Women and Fiction: Feminism and the Novel, 1880–1920*, 1981

Trodd, A. *A Reader's Guide to Edwardian Literature*, 1991

Van Ghent, D. *The English Novel: Form and Function*, 1953

Walcutt, C. C. *Man's Changing Masks: Characterization in Fiction*, 1966

West, P. *The Wine of Absurdity*, 1966

Williams, R. *The English Novel from Dickens to Lawrence*, 1970

X. DRAMA AND THE THEATRE

Agate, J. *The Contemporary Theatre*, 1925
    A Short View of the English Stage, 1900–1926, 1926

Archer, W. *The Old Drama and the New*, 1923

Beerbohm, M. *Around Theatres: Reviews, 1898–1910*, 1924, rev. 1953

Bentley, E. R. *The Playwright as Thinker: A Study of Drama in Modern Times*, 1946
    The Modern Theatre, 1948

Bogard, T. and Oliver, W. I. (eds.) *Modern Drama: Essays in Criticism*, 1965

Booth, M. R. *Victorian Spectacular Theatre, 1850–1910*, 1981

Browne, M. *Verse in Modern English Theatre*, 1963

Cole, T. and Chinoy, H. K. (eds.) *Directors on Directing: A Source Book for the Modern Theatre*, 1964 (rev. of 1953 edn)

Craig, G. *On the Art of the Theatre*, 1911

Donoghue, D. *The Third Voice: Modern British and American Verse Drama*, 1959

Gascoigne, B. *Twentieth Century Drama*, 1962

Hinchliffe, A. P. (ed.) *Drama Criticism: Developments Since Ibsen – A Casebook*, 1979

Hogan, R. and Kilroy, J. *The Modern Irish Drama*, 1975–8

Kennedy, A. *Six Dramatists in Search of a Language*, 1975

Kennedy, D. *Granville Barker and The Dream of Theatre*, 1985

Leeming, G. *Poetic Drama*, 1989

Lumley, F. *Trends in Twentieth-Century Drama*, 1956

McDonald, J. *The New Drama, 1900–1914*, 1986

Mikhail, E. H. (ed.) *The Abbey Theatre: Interviews and Recollections*, 1988
    The Revels History of Drama in English, Vol. VII, 1880 to the Present Day, 1978

Samuel, R., MacColl, E. and Cosgrove, S. *Theatres of the Left 1880–1935*, 1985

Shaw, G. B. *Shaw on Theatre* ed. E. J. West, 1958

Sidnell, M. *Dances of Death: The Group Theatre of London in the Thirties*, 1984

Taylor, J. R. *The Rise and Fall of the Well-made Play*, 1968

Trewin, J. *The Theatre since 1900*, 1951

The Edwardian Theatre, 1976
Weales, G. *Religion in Modern English Drama,* 1961
Williams, R. *Modern Tragedy,* 1966
 Drama in Performance, 1954, rev. 1968
 Drama from Ibsen to Brecht, 1968 (enlarged edn of *Drama from Ibsen to Eliot,* 1952)
Worth, K. J. *Revolutions in Modern Drama,* 1973
 The Irish Drama of Europe from Yeats to Beckett, 1978

XI. CRITICS AND PERIODICALS

Bodkin, M. *Archetypal Patterns in Poetry,* 1934
Bradley, A. C. *Shakespearean Tragedy,* 1904
 Oxford Lectures on Poetry, 1909
Grierson, H. J. C. (ed.) *The Poems of John Donne,* 2 vols., 1912
Hulme, T. E. *Speculations,* 1924
Knight, G. Wilson, *The Wheels of Fire,* 1930
Knights, L. C. *Drama and Society in the Age of Jonson,* 1937
 Explorations, 1946
Lewis, C. S. *The Allegory of Love,* 1936
Lodge, D. (ed.) *20th Century Criticism: A Reader,* 1972
Murry, J. Middleton *The Problem of Style,* 1922
Richards, I. A. *The Meaning of Meaning* (with C. K. Ogden), 1923
 Principles of Literary Criticism, 1924
 Science and Poetry, 1926
 Practical Criticism, 1929
Tillyard, E. M. W. *The Elizabethan World Picture,* 1943

The Adelphi, 1923–27, and *The New Adelphi,* 1927–30, ed. J. Middleton Murry
The English Review, 1908–37, ed. F. M. Heuffer *et al.*
Horizon, 1940–50, ed. C. Connolly
The Mask, 1908–29, ed. E. G. Craig
The New Age, ed. A. R. Orage, 1907–34
The Times Literary Supplement, 1902–
New Verse, 1933–9, ed. G. Grigson, (–1937)
New Writing, 1936–8, ed. J. Lehmann

See also AUTHOR entries for C. Caudwell, T. S. Eliot, W. Empson, F. M. Ford, E. M. Forster, H. James, D. H. Lawrence, F. R. Leavis, E. Muir, E. Rickword, E. Pound, G. Bernard Shaw, V. Woolf and W. B. Yeats for other major periodicals and criticism.

AUTHORS AND WORKS

Collections and Anthologies

Blythe, R. (ed.) *Components of the Scene: Stories, Poems and Essays of the Second World War*, 1966

Kermode, F. and Hollander, J. (eds.) *Modern British Literature* (*The Oxford Anthology of English Literature*), 1973

McEwan (ed.), *The Twentieth Century* (*1900–Present*) (*Macmillan Anthology of English Literature*), 1989

Allott, K. (ed.) *The Penguin Book of Contemporary Verse*, 1950, rev. 1962

Brophy, J. and Partridge, E. (eds.) *The Long Trail: What The British Soldier Said and Sang in the Great War of 1914–18*, 1965

Cecil, D. and Tate, A. (eds.) *Modern Verse in English, 1900–1950*, 1958

Cunningham, V. (ed.) *The Penguin Book of Spanish Civil War Verse*, 1980

Freer, A. and Andrew, J. (eds.) *Cambridge Book of English Verse, 1900–1939*, 1970

Gardner, B. (ed.) *Up the Line to Death: The War Poets, 1914–18*, 1964
   (ed.) *The Terrible Rain: The War Poets, 1939–1945*, 1966

Germain, E. B. (ed.) *English and American Surrealist Poetry*, 1978

Hamilton, I. (ed.) *The Poetry of War, 1939–45*, 1965

Heath-Stubbs, J. and Wright, D. (eds.) *The Faber Book of Twentieth Century Verse*, 1953, rev. 1965 and 1967

Hibberd, D. and Onions, J. (eds.) *Poetry of the Great War: An Anthology*, 1986

Holloway, J. (ed.) *Poems of the Mid-Century*, 1957

Hussey, M. (ed.) *Poetry of the First World War*, 1967

Jones, P. (ed.) *Imagist Poetry*, 1972

Jones, R. G. (ed.) *Poetry of Wales, 1930–1970* (in Welsh and English), 1974

Larkin, P. (ed.) *Oxford Book of Twentieth-Century Verse*, 1973

Lindsay, M. (ed.) *Modern Scottish Poetry: An Anthology of the Scottish Renaissance 1920–45*, 1946, rev. 1966

MacBeth, G. (ed.) *Poetry 1900 to 1975*, (first published 1967), 1979

Mahon, D. (ed.) *Modern Irish Poetry*, 1972

Marcus, D. (ed.) *Irish Poets, 1927–74*, 1975

Parsons, I. M. (ed.) *Men Who Marched Away* (World War I), 1965

The Poet Speaks (10 gramophone records of eighty poets reading their own verse), Argo PLP 1081/90

Reeves, J. (ed.) *Georgian Poetry*, 1962

Rodway, A. E. (ed.) *Poetry of the 1930s*, 1967

Silkin, J. (ed.) *The Penguin Book of First World War Poetry*, 1979

Skelton, R. (ed.) *Poetry of the Thirties*, 1964
     (ed.) *Poetry of the Forties*, 1968

Williams, J. S. and Stephens, M. (eds.) *The Lilting House: Anglo-Welsh Poetry, 1917–1967*, 1969

Yeats, W. B. (ed.) *The Oxford Book of Modern Verse, 1892–1935*, 1936

Young, D. (ed.) *Scottish Verse, 1851–1951*, 1952

Davin, D. (ed.) *Short Stories from the Second World War*, 1982

Hadfield, J. (ed.) *Modern Short Stories*, 1939

Jones, G. (ed.) *Welsh Short Stories*, 1956

Marcus, D. (ed.) *Best Irish Short Stories*, 1976

O'Connor, F. (ed.) *Modern Irish Short Stories*, 1957

Armstrong, W. A. (ed.) *Classic Irish Drama*, 1964

Browne, E. M. (ed.) *Four Modern Verse Plays*, 1957

Authors

AUDEN, WYSTAN HUGH (1907–73): Poet, playwright, critic and collaborator in writing plays and libretti; b. York; educated at Gresham's School, Holt and Christ Church, Oxford; privately printed *Poems*, 1928; spent year in Berlin, 1928–29; *Poems*, 1930; schoolmaster, 1930–35; *The Orators*, 1932; *Look Stranger!*, 1936; collaborated with Christopher Isherwood in writing three plays, *The Dog Beneath the Skin*, 1935; *The Ascent of F6*, 1936, and *On the Frontier*, 1938; *Letters from Iceland* (with Louis MacNeice), 1937; in 1937 volunteered as an ambulance driver for the Republicans in the Spanish Civil War but in fact worked as a journalist there; 'Spain', 1937; in 1938 travelled with Isherwood to China, and together they produced *Journey to a War*, 1939; settled in United States, 1939; *Another Time*, 1940; *New Year Letter*, 1941; *For the Time Being*, 1945; *The Age of Anxiety*, 1948; *Nones*, 1952; collaborated with Chester Kallman in writing libretto for Stravinsky's *The Rake's Progress*, 1951; in 1956 elected Professor of Poetry, Oxford; died in Vienna.

(For further details of writings after 1945 see Volume 8 of the *Guide*.)

Life by H. Carpenter, 1981; C. Osborne, 1980

Collected Shorter Poems 1927–57, 1966

Collected Longer Poems, 1968

Collected Poems ed. E. Mendelson, 1976

The English Auden: Poems, Essays and Dramatic Writings, 1927–37 ed. E. Mendelson, 1977

See:

J. W. Beach, *The Making of the Auden Canon*, 1957

J. G. Blair, *The Poetic Art of W. H. Auden*, 1965

E. Callan, *Auden: A Carnival of Intellect*, 1983
R. Carter (ed.), *Thirties Poets: 'The Auden Group' – A Casebook*, 1984
V. Cunningham in *British Writers of the Thirties*, 1988
B. Everett, *Auden*, 1964
J. Fuller, *A Reader's Guide to W. H. Auden*, 1970
J. Haffenden (ed.), *W. H. Auden: The Critical Heritage*, 1983
S. Hynes in *The Auden Generation*, 1976
R. Jarrell in *The Third Book of Criticism*, 1969
    in *Kipling, Auden and Co.*, 1981
L. McDiarmid in *Saving Civilization: Yeats, Eliot and Auden Between the Wars*, 1984
E. Mendelson, *Early Auden*, 1981
S. Smith, *W. H. Auden*, 1985
M. K. Spears, *The Poetry of W. H. Auden: The Disenchanted Island*, 1963
    (ed.), *Auden: A Collection of Critical Essays*, 1964
S. Spender (ed.), *W. H. Auden: A Tribute*, 1975
R. Williams in *Drama from Ibsen to Brecht*, 1968–9 revision of 1952 edition

BELLOC, JOSEPH HILAIRE PIERRE RENÉ (1870–1953): Essayist, historian, poet and novelist; b. Saint Cloud, near Paris, the son of a French barrister and his English wife, moved to London, 1872, and to Sussex, 1878; educated at Cardinal Newman's Oratory School, Birmingham, and Balliol College, Oxford; *Verses and Sonnets*, and *The Bad Child's Book of Beasts*, both 1896; *The Path to Rome*, 1902; British naturalization, 1902; literary editor of the *Morning Post*, 1906–10; Liberal MP for Salford, 1906–10; founded journal, *Eye Witness*, 1911; *The Servile State*, 1912; *A History of England*, 1925–31; *The Crisis of Our Civilization*, 1937.

Other writings include:
(novels) *Emmanuel Burden, Merchant*, 1904; *Mr Clutterbuck's Election*, 1908;
    Pongo and the Bull, 1910; *The Green Overcoat*, 1912
(autobiography) *The Cruise of the 'Nona'*, 1925
(biography) *Danton*, 1899; *Robespierre*, 1901; *Milton*, 1935

Life by R. W. Speaight, 1957; A. N. Wilson, 1984
Collected Verse, 1958
Letters ed. R. W. Speaight, 1958
See:
R. Haynes, *Hilaire Belloc*, 1953, rev. 1958
J. P. McCarthy, *Hilaire Belloc*, 1978

BENNETT, ENOCH ARNOLD (1867–1931): Novelist and journalist; b. Hanley, Staffs.; educated at Burslem Endowed School and the Middle School, Newcastle under Lyme; in 1888 became clerk in London solicitors' firm; became assistant editor, 1893, and editor, 1896, of *Woman* magazine, resigning in 1900; first novel, *A Man from the North*, 1898; *Anna of the Five Towns*, 1902; lived in France, 1902–10; *The Old Wives' Tale*, 1908;

'Clayhanger' trilogy – *Clayhanger*, 1910, *Hilda Lessways*, 1911, *These Twain*, 1916; collaborated with Edward Knoblock on play, *Milestones*, 1912; *Riceyman Steps*, 1923; *Imperial Palace*, 1930.

Stories include: *Tales of the Five Towns*, 1905; *The Grim Smile of the Five Towns*, 1907.

Life by M. Drabble, 1974
Journals ed. N. Flower, 3 vols., 1932–3
Letters ed. J. Hepburn, 4 vols., 1966–86
Sketches for Autobiography ed. J. Hepburn, 1979
See:
J. Hepburn, *The Art of Arnold Bennett*, 1963
    (ed.), *Arnold Bennett: The Critical Heritage*, 1981
J. Lucas, *Arnold Bennett: A Study of His Fiction*, 1974

BLUNDEN, EDMUND CHARLES (1896–1974): Poet and critic; b. London; educated at Christ's Hospital and Queen's College, Oxford; *Poems*, 1914; commissioned 1915; fought in France and Belgium; awarded MC, 1916; *The Waggoner*, 1920; *The Shepherd*, winner of the Hawthornden prize, 1922; between 1924–7 Professor of English Literature at Tokyo Imperial University; prose memoir, *Undertones of War*, 1925; *English Poems*, 1925; *Retreat*, 1928; *Near and Far*, 1929; *Poems 1914–30*, 1930; Fellow of Merton College, Oxford, 1931–43; *Charles Lamb and his Contemporaries*, 1933; *Choice or Chance*, 1934; *Thomas Hardy*, 1942; joined staff of *Times Literary Supplement*, 1943; CBE, 1951; Professor of English, Hong Kong, 1953–64; *Poems of Many Years*, 1957; Professor of Poetry, Oxford, 1966–8.

Life by B. Webb, 1990
Selected Poems ed. R. Marsack, 1982
See:
B. Bergonzi in *Heroes' Twilight*, 1965, rev. 1980
D. Graham in *The Truth of War: Owen, Blunden, Rosenberg*, 1984
A. Hardie, *Edmund Blunden*, 1958, rev. 1971
M. Thorpe, *The Poetry of Edmund Blunden*, 1971

BOURNE, 'GEORGE BOURNE': See STURT, GEORGE (1863–1927)

BOWEN, ELIZABETH DOROTHEA COLE (1899–1973): Novelist and short-story writer; b. Dublin; educated at Harpenden Hall School, Herts., and Downe School, Kent; first book, *Encounters* (short stories), 1923; first novel, *The Hotel*, 1927; worked as ARP warden during Second World War; CBE, 1948.

Other writings include:
(novels) *The Last September*, 1929; *The House in Paris*, 1935; *The Death of the Heart*, 1938; *The Heat of the Day*, 1949
(short stories) *Joining Charles*, 1929; *Look at All Those Roses*, 1941; *The Demon Lover*, 1945; *Collected Stories*, 1980

Life by P. Craig, 1986; V. Glendinning, 1977
See:
J. Bayley in *The Short Story: Henry James to Elizabeth Bowen*, 1988
P. Lassner, *Elizabeth Bowen*, 1990

BROOKE, RUPERT CHAWNER (1887–1915): Poet, b. Rugby; educated at Rugby School and King's College, Cambridge where he became a member of the 'Apostles'; *Poems*, 1911; Fellow of King's, 1912; between 1913–14 visited United States, the islands of the Pacific and New Zealand; commissioned 1914; on the way to the Dardanelles, died of septicaemia and buried at Scyros; *1914 and Other Poems*, 1915.

Life by C. Hassall, 1964
Collected Poems (with a Memoir by E. Marsh), 1918, rev. 1928, 1942 and 1989
Poetical Works ed. G. Keynes, 1946
Letters from America, 1916
Letters ed. G. Keynes, 1968
Letters to Noel Oliver, ed. P. Harris, 1991
The Prose of Rupert Brooke ed. C. Hassall, 1968
(criticism) *John Webster and Elizabethan Drama*, 1916
See:
P. Delany, *The Neo-Pagans: Friendship and Love in the Rupert Brooke Circle*, 1987

CARY, ARTHUR JOYCE LUNEL (1887–1957): Novelist; b. Londonderry; educated at Clifton College; studied art in Edinburgh, 1907–9; graduated in law from Trinity College, Oxford, 1912; served with the British Red Cross in the Balkan Wars (1912–13); joined the Nigerian political service in 1913; returned from West Africa to live in Oxford, 1920; first novel, *Aissa Saved*, 1932; *Mister Johnson*, 1939; *Charlie is My Darling*, 1940.
(For further details of writings after 1945 see Volume 8 of the *Guide*.)

Other works include:
(novels) *An American Visitor*, 1933; *The African Witch*, 1936; *A House of Children*, 1941; a trilogy – *Herself Surprised*, 1941, *To Be a Pilgrim*, 1942, and *The Horse's Mouth*, 1944; a second trilogy – *Prisoners of Grace*, 1952, *Except the Lord*, 1953, and *Not Honour More*, 1955
(short stories) *Spring Song*, 1960
(political treatises) *The Case for African Freedom*, 1941; *Britain and West Africa*, 1946
Selected Essays ed. A. G. Bishop, 1974

Life by A. G. Bishop, 1988; M. Foster, 1968
See:
C. Cook, *Joyce Cary: Liberal Principles*, 1981
M. J. C. Echeruo, *Joyce Cary and the Novel of Africa*, 1973
    Joyce Cary and the Dimensions of Order, 1979

M. Mahood, *Joyce Cary's Africa,* 1964
R. W. Noble, *Joyce Cary,* 1973
A. Wright, *Joyce Cary: A Preface to his Novels,* 1958

CAUDWELL, CHRISTOPHER – pseudonym of Christopher St John Sprigg – (1907–37): Poet and critic; b. London; educated at Ealing Priory School; journalist and writer on aviation; developed interest in Marxism and politics, 1934; novel, *This My Hand,* 1936; machine-gun instructor for the Republicans in Spanish Civil War; killed in action in Spain; criticism, *Illusion and Reality,* 1937; *Poems,* 1939.

Other works include:
Studies in a Dying Culture, 1938; *Further Studies in a Dying Culture,* 1949; *Romance And Realism,* 1970; *Scenes And Actions: Unpublished Manuscripts* ed. J. Duparc and D. Margolies, 1986
Collected Poems ed. A. Young, 1986
See:
D. Margolies, *The Function of Literature: A Study of Caudwell's Aesthetics,* 1969
D. Margolies and L. Peach (eds.), *Caudwell: Marxism and Culture,* 1989
C. Pawling, *Caudwell: Towards a Dialectical Theory of History,* 1989

CHESTERTON, GILBERT KEITH (1874–1936): Essayist, critic, novelist and poet; b. London; educated at St Paul's School, and the Slade School of Art; worked as a journalist; first published books were verse – *Greybeards at Play* and *The Wild Knight,* both 1900; first novel, *The Napoleon of Notting Hill,* 1908; *Orthodoxy,* 1908, *The Innocence of Father Brown* (stories), 1911; in 1916, became editor of *New Witness,* later revived as *G. K.'s Weekly,* 1925; became Roman Catholic, 1922.

Other works include:
(stories) The 'Father Brown' stories: collected editions, 1929 and 1947; *Collected Poems,* 1927, rev. 1933
(criticism) *Robert Browning,* 1903; *Charles Dickens,* 1906; *R. L. Stevenson,* 1927 *Autobiography,* 1936

Life by M. Coren, 1989; A. S. Dale, 1982; M. Finch, 1986; M. Ward, 1943
See:
I. Boyd, *The Novels of G. K. Chesterton,* 1975
J. Sullivan (ed.), *G. K. Chesterton: A Centenary Appraisal,* 1974

COMPTON-BURNETT, IVY (1884–1969): Novelist; b. Pinner, Middlesex; educated at Addiscombe College, Hove and Royal Holloway College, London; first novel, *Dolores,* 1911, a work which she later disowned; *Pastors and Masters,* 1925; *Brothers and Sisters,* 1929; *Daughters and Sons,* 1937; *Parents and Children,* 1941; *Manservant and Maidservant,* 1947; created Dame, 1967.
   (For further details of writings after 1945 see Volume 8 of the *Guide.*)

Life by E. Sprigge, 1973; H. Spurling, *Ivy When Young,* 1974

See:
C. Burkhart (ed.), *The Art of I. Compton-Burnett,* 1972
K. J. Gentile, *Ivy Compton-Burnett,* 1991
R. Liddell, *The Novels of Ivy Compton-Burnett,* 1955

CONRAD, JOSEPH – Józef Teodor Konrad Korzeniowski – (1857–1924): Novelist and short-story writer; b. Berdyczów in partitioned Poland, son of a Polish nationalist; brought up by an uncle, Tadeusz Bobrowski; travelled to Marseilles to become a seaman, 1874; suicide attempt, 1878; entered British Merchant Navy, 1878, travelled widely as a seaman; became a British subject and gained a master's certificate, 1886; Congo journey, 1890; first novel, *Almayer's Folly,* 1895; left sea to write; *The Nigger of the 'Narcissus',* 1897; *Heart of Darkness,* 1899; *Lord Jim,* 1900; *Nostromo,* 1904; *The Secret Agent,* 1907; suffered nervous breakdown, 1910; *Under Western Eyes,* 1911; *Victory,* 1915; *The Shadow-Line,* 1917.

Other works include:
(novels) *An Outcast of the Islands,* 1896; *Chance,* 1913; *The Arrow of Gold,* 1919, *The Rover,* 1923; *Suspense,* 1925; and, with Ford Madox Ford, *The Inheritors,* 1901, *Romance,* 1903, and *The Nature of a Crime,* 1924
(stories) *Tales of Unrest,* 1898; *Youth,* 1902; *Typhoon,* 1903; *A Set of Six,* 1908; *'Twixt Land and Sea,* 1912; *Within the Tides,* 1915; *Tales of Hearsay,* 1925
(essays) *Notes on Life and Letters,* 1921; *Last Essays,* 1926; *Selected Literary Criticism* ed. A. Ingram, 1986
(autobiographical writings) *The Mirror of the Sea,* 1906; *A Personal Record,* 1912

Life by J. Baines, 1959; F. R. Karl, 1979; Z. Najder, 1980; C. Watts, 1989
Collected Works, 22 vols., 1946–55
Cambridge Edition, 1990–
Collected Letters ed. F. R. Karl and L. Davies, 1983–
Letters to R. B. Cunninghame Graham ed. C. T. Watts, 1969
See:
R. Ambrosini, *Conrad's Fiction as Critical Discourse,* 1991
J. Berthoud, *Joseph Conrad: The Major Phase,* 1978
J. Batchelor, *Lord Jim,* 1988
C. B. Cox (ed.), *'Heart of Darkness', 'Nostromo' and 'Under Western Eyes': A Casebook,* 1981
A. Fleishman, *Conrad's Politics: Community and Anarchy in the Fiction of Joseph Conrad,* 1967
J. D. Gordan, *Joseph Conrad: The Making of a Novelist,* 1941
A. J. Guerard, *Conrad the Novelist,* 1958
R. Hampson, *Joseph Conrad: Betrayal and Identity,* 1992
J. Hawthorn, *Joseph Conrad: Language and Fictional Self-Consciousness,* 1979
  Joseph Conrad: Narrative Technique and Ideological Commitment, 1992
B. Johnson, *Conrad's Models of Mind,* 1971

O. Knowles, *A Conrad Chronology*, 1989

F. R. Leavis in *The Great Tradition*, 1948

J. Lothe, *Conrad's Narrative Method*, 1989

M. Mudrick (ed.), *Conrad: A Collection of Critical Essays*, 1966

Z. Najder (ed.), *Conrad Under Familial Eyes*, 1983

E. Said, *Joseph Conrad and the Fiction of Autobiography*, 1966
    in *Beginnings: Intention and Method*, 1975

N. Sherry, *Conrad's Eastern World*, 1966
    Conrad's Western World, 1971
    (ed.), *Conrad: The Critical Heritage*, 1973
    (ed.), *Joseph Conrad: A Commemoration*, 1976

D. Thorburn, *Conrad's Romanticism*, 1974

D. E. Vulcan, *Conrad and the Modern Temper*, 1992

I. Watt, *Conrad in the Nineteenth Century*, 1980

C. Watts *Conrad's 'Heart of Darkness'*: 1977
    A Preface to Conrad, 1982

A. White, *Joseph Conrad and the Adventure Tradition*, 1993

M. Wollaeger, *Joseph Conrad and the Fiction of Scepticism*, 1990

DE LA MARE, WALTER (1873–1956): Poet and writer of children's books; b. Charlton, Kent; educated at St Paul's Cathedral Choristers' School; worked for Anglo-American Oil Company, 1890–1908; first publication, *Songs of Childhood*, 1902; *Henry Brocken* (prose), 1904; *Poems*, 1906; *The Return* (prose), 1910; *The Listeners* (verse), 1912; *Poems for Children*, 1930; awarded Order of Merit, 1953.

Life by T. Whistler, 1993
Collected Stories for Children, 1947
Collected Poems, 1969
See:
F. R. Leavis in *New Bearings in English Poetry*, 1932, rev. 1950

DOUGLAS, KEITH CASTELLAIN (1920–44): Poet; b. Tunbridge Wells; educated at Christ's Hospital and Merton College, Oxford; joined army, 1940; served in the Middle East; *Selected Poems*, 1943; killed in action; *Alamein to Zem Zem* (war experiences), 1946.

Life by D. Graham, 1974
Collected Poems ed. J. Waller, G. S. Fraser and J. C. Hall, 1951, rev. 1966
Selected Poems ed. T. Hughes, 1964
Complete Poems ed. D. Graham, 1978
A Prose Miscellany ed. D. Graham, 1985
See:
W. Scammell, *Keith Douglas: A Study*, 1988

ELIOT, THOMAS STEARNS (1888–1965): Poet, playwright, essayist and critic; b. St Louis, Missouri; educated at Smith Academy, St Louis, Milton

Academy, Mass., Harvard, the Sorbonne and Merton College, Oxford; graduate work on the philosopher, F. H. Bradley; met Ezra Pound, 1914; worked as a schoolmaster and, between 1917 and 1925, for Lloyd's Bank, London; *Prufrock and Other Observations*, 1917; *Poems*, 1919; *The Sacred Wood* (criticism), 1920; *The Waste Land*, 1922; editor of *The Criterion*, 1922–39; joined board of directors of Faber and Gwyer (later Faber and Faber); joined Church of England and became British subject, 1927; *Ash-Wednesday*, 1930; poetic drama, *Murder in the Cathedral*, 1935; *Four Quartets*, 1943, collecting together *Burnt Norton*, 1936, *East Coker*, 1940, *The Dry Salvages*, 1941, and *Little Gidding*, 1942; awarded Order of Merit and Nobel Prize, 1948.

(For further details of writings after 1945 see Volume 8 of the *Guide*.)

Other writings include:

(poetry) *Ara Vos Prec*, 1920; *Collected Poems 1909–1935*, 1936; *Old Possum's Book of Practical Cats*, 1939; *The Cultivation of Christmas Trees*, 1954; *Poems Written in Early Youth* ed. J. Hayward, 1967; *The Waste Land: A Facsimile and Transcript of the Original Drafts* ed. V. Eliot, 1971

(verse drama) *Sweeney Agonistes*, 1932; *The Rock*, 1934; *The Cocktail Party*, 1950; *The Confidential Clerk*, 1954; *The Elder Statesman*, 1959

(criticism and essays); *For Lancelot Andrewes*, 1928; *The Use of Poetry and the Use of Criticism*, 1933; *Selected Essays 1917–32*, 1932, enlarged 1951; *After Strange Gods*, 1934; *The Idea of a Christian Society*, 1939; *Notes Towards the Definition of Culture*, 1948; *On Poetry and Poets*, 1957

Life by P. Ackroyd, 1980; L. Gordon *Eliot's Early Years*, 1977, and *Eliot's New Life*, 1988
Complete Poems and Plays, 1969
Selected Prose ed. F. Kermode, 1975
Letters ed. V. Eliot, 1988–
See:
B. Bergonzi, *T. S. Eliot*, 1972
    (ed.), *T. S. Eliot, 'Four Quartets': A Casebook*, 1969
M. E. Browne, *The Making of T. S. Eliot's Plays*, 1969
R. Bush, *T. S. Eliot: A Study in Character and Style*, 1984
A. Calder, *T. S. Eliot*, 1987
G. Clarke (ed.), *T. S. Eliot: Critical Assessments*, 4 vols., 1990
C. B. Cox and A. P. Hincliffe (eds.), *T. S. Eliot, 'The Waste Land': A Casebook*, 1968
M. Ellmann, *The Poetics of Impersonality: The Question of the Subject in T. S. Eliot and Ezra Pound*, 1987
H. Gardner, *The Art of T. S. Eliot*, 1949
    The Composition of 'Four Quartets', 1983
N. K. Gish, *The Waste Land: A Poem of Memory and Desire*, 1988
M. Grant (ed.), *T. S. Eliot: The Critical Heritage*, 2 vols., 1982
P. Gray, *T. S. Eliot's Intellectual and Poetic Development 1909–1922*, 1982
H. Kenner, *The Invisible Poet*, 1960
    (ed.), *T. S. Eliot: A Collection of Critical Essays*, 1962

F. R. Leavis in *New Bearings in English Literature*, 1932, rev. 1950
    in *Lectures in America*, 1969
    in *English Literature in our Time and the University*, 1969
    in *The Living Principle*, 1975
B. Lee, *Theory and Personality: The Significance of T. S. Eliot's Criticism*, 1979
A. W. Litz (ed.), *Eliot in his Time*, 1973
L. McDiarmid in *Saving Civilisation: Yeats, Eliot and Auden Between the Wars*, 1984
C. G. Martin (ed.), *Eliot in Perspective: A Symposium*, 1970
F. O. Matthiessen, *The Achievement of T. S. Eliot*, 1935, rev. 1947 and 1958
A. D. Moody, *Thomas Stearns Eliot: Poet*, 1979
C. Ricks, *T. S. Eliot and Prejudice*, 1988
M. Schofield, *T. S. Eliot: The Poems*, 1988
E. Sigg, *The American T. S. Eliot*, 1989
K. Smidt, *Poetry and Belief in the Work of T. S. Eliot*, 1961
G. C. Smith, *T. S. Eliot's Poems and Plays*, 1956, rev. 1974
B. C. Southam, *The Student's Guide to the Selected Poems of T. S. Eliot*, 1968
    (ed), *T. S. Eliot, 'Prufrock', 'Gerontion', 'Ash-Wednesday' and other Shorter Poems: A Casebook*, 1978
S. Spender, *T. S. Eliot*, 1975
C. K. Stead in *The New Poetic: Yeats to Eliot*, 1964
    in *Pound, Yeats, Eliot and the Modernist Movement*, 1986
A. Tate (ed.), *T. S. Eliot: The Man and his Work*, 1967

EMPSON, WILLIAM (1906–84): Poet and critic; b. Howden, Yorks; educated at Winchester College and Magdalene College, Cambridge; taught in Japanese and Chinese universities in the 1930s; *Seven Types of Ambiguity* (criticism), 1930; *Poems*, 1935; *The Gathering Storm* (poems), 1940; worked for the BBC in London, 1941–6; Professor of English Literature, Sheffield University, 1953–71; knighted, 1979.

(For further details of writings after 1945 see Volume 8 of the *Guide*.)

Other works include:
Collected Poems, 1955
(criticism) *Some Versions of the Pastoral*, 1935; *The Structure of Complex Words*, 1951; *Milton's God*, 1961; *Using Biography* (ed. D. Pirie), 1984; *Essays on Shakespeare* (ed. J. Haffenden), 1986; *Argufying: Essays on Literature and Culture*, 1988
See:
P. H. Fry, *William Empson: Prophet Against Sacrifice*, 1991
P. Gardner and A. Gardner, *The God Approached: A Commentary on the Poems of William Empson*, 1978
R. Gill (ed.), *William Empson: The Man and his Work*, 1974
N. Mapp and C. Morris (eds.), *William Empson: The Critical Achievement*, 1993
C. Norris, *William Empson and the Philosophy of Literary Criticism*, 1978

FORD, FORD MADOX – Jospeh Leopold Ford Hermann Madox Hueffer –
(1873–1939): Novelist and critic; b. Merton, Surrey; educated at University
College School, London; first publication, *The Brown Owl*, a fairy story,
1891; collaborated with Conrad in writing *The Inheritors*, 1901, *Romance*,
1903, and *The Nature of a Crime*, 1924; founded the *English Review*,
1908; commissioned in the Welch Regiment, 1915–19; *The Good Soldier*,
1915; moved to France, 1922; founded the *Transatlantic Review*, 1924; the
Tietjens tetralogy – *Some Do Not*, 1924, *No More Parades*, 1925, *A Man
Could Stand Up*, 1926, and *Last Post*, 1928 (collected as *Parade's End*,
1950); last seventeen years of his life spent between France and the USA.

Other works include:
Collected Poems, 1913, 1936
(novels) *The Benefactor*, 1905; the Fifth Queen Trilogy – *The Fifth Queen*,
   1906; *Privy Seal*, 1907; and *The Fifth Queen Crowned*, 1908; *An English
   Girl*, 1907; *Mr Apollo*, 1908, *A Call*, 1910; *The Rash Act*, 1933
(criticism and reminiscences); *Ancient Lights*, 1911; *Henry James*, 1914; *Joseph
   Conrad: A Personal Remembrance*, 1924; *The English Novel*, 1929; *Return to
   Yesterday*, 1931; *It Was the Nightingale*, 1933; *Provence*, 1935; *Portraits from
   Life*, 1937; *The March of Literature*, 1938; *The Critical Writings of Ford
   Madox Ford* ed. F. MacShane, 1964
(correspondence) *Letters* ed. R. M. Ludwig, 1965; *Pound – Ford: The Story
   of a Literary Friendship* ed. B. Lindberg-Seyersted, 1982

Life by D. Goldring, 1948; A. Judd, 1990; F. MacShane, 1965; A. Mizener, 1971
The Bodley Head Ford Madox Ford, 5 vols., 1962–71
The Ford Madox Ford Reader ed. S. J. Stang, 1986
See:
Agenda, Special Ford Double Issue, 1989/90
R. A. Cassell, *Ford Madox Ford: Modern Judgements*, 1972
W. A. Davenport and R. Hampson (eds.), *Ford Madox Ford: A Reappraisal*,
   1994
R. Green, *Ford Madox Ford: Prose and Politics*, 1981
F. MacShane (ed.), *Ford Madox Ford: The Critical Heritage*, 1972
T. C. Moser, *The Life in the Fiction of Ford Madox Ford*, 1980
A. B. Snitow, *Ford Madox Ford and the Voice of Uncertainty*, 1984
S. J. Stang (ed.), *The Presence of Ford Madox Ford*, 1977
P. L. Wiley, *Novelist of Three Worlds: Ford Madox Ford*, 1962

FORSTER, EDWARD MORGAN (1879–1970): Novelist, short-story writer
and critic; b. London; educated at Tonbridge School and King's College,
Cambridge; lived for a time in Italy; first novel, *Where Angels Fear to Tread*,
1905; *The Longest Journey*, 1907; *A Room with a View*, 1908; *Howard's End*,
1910; worked with the Red Cross in Alexandria during the First World
War; *A Passage to India*, 1924; Clark lectures at Cambridge published as
Aspects of the Novel, 1927; elected Honorary Fellow of King's College, 1946;
Maurice published posthumously in 1971.

Other writings include:

(short stories) *The Celestial Omnibus*, 1911; *The Eternal Moment*, 1928; *The Life to Come*, 1972; *Arctic Summer*, 1980

(criticism and essays) *Abinger Harvest*, 1936; *Two Cheers for Democracy*, 1951; *The Hill of Devi*, 1953

Commonplace Book ed. P. Gardner, 1985

Life by N. Beauman, 1993; P. N. Furbank, 2 vols., 1977–8

The Abinger Edition, 1972–

Selected Letters ed. M. Lago and P. N. Furbank, 2 vols., 1983–5

See:

M. Bradbury (ed.), *E. M. Forster: A Collection of Critical Essays*, 1966

G. K. Das, *E. M. Forster's India*, 1977

G. K. Das and J. Beer (eds.), *E. M. Forster, A Human Exploration: Centenary Essays*, 1978

P. Gardner, *E. M. Forster: The Critical Heritage*, 1973

J. S. Herz and R. K. Martin (eds.), *E. M. Forster: Centenary Revaluations*, 1982

J. S. Martin, *E. M. Forster: The Endless Journey*, 1976

O. Stallybrass (ed.), *Aspects of Forster*, 1969

W. Stone, *The Cave and the Mountain: A Study of Forster*, 1966

L. Trilling, *E. M. Forster: A Study*, 1943

GALSWORTHY, JOHN (1867–1933): Novelist and playwright; b. Kingston Hill, Surrey; educated at Harrow School and New College, Oxford; called to the Bar, 1890; travelled in the Far East where, in 1893, he met Joseph Conrad; first publication, under the pseudonym of John Sinjohn, *From the Four Winds* (stories), 1897; first play, *The Silver Box*, produced 1906; *The Man of Property* (first part of the 'Forsyte Saga'), 1906; awarded Order of Merit, 1929; Nobel Prize for Literature, 1932.

Novels include: Three 'Forsyte' trilogies:

1 *The Forsyte Saga: The Man of Property*, 1906; *In Chancery*, 1920; and *To Let*, 1921; collected, 1922, with the addition of two connecting narratives, *The Indian Summer of a Forsyte* and *Awakening*, 1920

2 *A Modern Comedy: The White Monkey*, 1924; *The Silver Spoon*, 1926; and *Swan Song*, 1928; collected in 1929

3 *End of the Chapter: Maid in Waiting*, 1931; *Flowering Wilderness*, 1932; and *Over the River*, 1933; collected in 1934

Plays include: *Strife*, 1909; *Justice*, 1910; *The Eldest Son*, 1912; *The Skin Game*, 1920; and *Loyalties*, 1934

Life by H. V. Marrot (*Life and Letters*), 1935; C. Dupré, 1976

Collected Works, 30 vols., 1923–35

Collected Plays, 1929

Collected Poems ed. A. Galsworthy, 1934

Letters from Galsworthy 1900–1932 ed. E. Garnett, 1934

See:
J. Conrad in *Last Essays*, 1926
J. Gindin, *John Galsworthy's Life and Art*, 1987
D. H. Lawrence in *Phoenix*, 1936

GERHARDI[E], WILLIAM ALEXANDER (1895–1977): Novelist and critic; b. St Petersburg, Russia, the son of a British industrialist; educated in St Petersburg; served with the Royal Scots Greys and on the staff of the British Embassy in Petrograd during the First World War; OBE, 1920; graduated in Russian from Worcester College, Oxford, 1922; first novel, *Futility*, 1922; *The Polyglots*, 1925; short stories, *Pretty Creatures*, 1927; *Pending Heaven*, 1930; autobiography, *Memoirs of a Polyglot*, 1931; *Resurrection*, 1934; *Of Mortal Love*, 1936; worked for BBC during the Second World War; last thirty-seven years spent in increasing obscurity, leading a hermit-like existence in West London.

Life by D. Davies, 1990
Collected Uniform Edition, 1947
Collected Edition, 10 vols., 1970–74

GRAVES, ROBERT RANKE (1895–1985): Poet and novelist; b. London; educated at Charterhouse; enlisted with the Royal Welch Fusiliers, 1914; wounded and shell-shocked; *Over the Brazier* (poems), 1916; awarded B.Litt from Oxford, 1925; Professor of English at Cairo, 1926; subsequently lived mainly in Majorca; autobiography, *Goodbye to All That*, 1929; *I, Claudius* and *Claudius the God*, 1934; *Collected Poems*, 1938; *Poems 1938–1945*, 1946; *The White Goddess*, 1948; *The Greek Myths*, 1955; Professor of Poetry at Oxford, 1961.

Critical writings include:
A Survey of Modernist Poetry (with Laura Riding), 1927; *The Common Asphodel*, 1949; *The Crowning Privilege*, 1955; *Oxford Addresses on Poetry*, 1962

Life by M. Seymour-Smith, 1982; R. P. Graves, vol. 1, 1986, vol. 2, 1990
Collected Poems, 1975
Selected Poems ed. P. O'Prey, 1987
In Broken Images: Selected Letters, 1914–1946 ed. P. O'Prey, 1982
Between Moon and Moon: Selected letters, 1946–1972 ed. P. O'Prey, 1984
See:
D. N. G. Carter, *Robert Graves: The Lasting Poetic Achievement*, 1989
D. Day, *Swifter than Reason: The Poetry and Criticism of Robert Graves*, 1963
M. Kirkham, *The Poetry of Graves*, 1969

GREEN, HENRY (pseudonym of Henry Vincent Yorke) (1905–1973): Novelist; b. Tewkesbury; educated at Eton College and Magdalen College, Oxford; first novel, *Blindness*, 1926; worked in London for family business.

Works include:

(novels) *Living*, 1929; *Party Going*, 1939; *Caught*, 1943; *Loving*, 1945; *Back*, 1946; *Concluding*, 1948; *Nothing*, 1950; *Doting*, 1952

(autobiography) *Pack My Bag*, 1940

Surviving: The Uncollected Writings of Henry Green, ed. M. Yorke, 1992

See:

O. Holmesland, *A Critical Introduction to Henry Green's Novels*, 1986

R. Mengham, *The Idiom of the Times: The Writings of Henry Green*, 1982

GREENE, GRAHAM (1904–1991): Novelist, short-story writer and dramatist; educated at Berkhamsted School and Balliol College, Oxford; first publication, *Babbling April* (verse) 1925; on the staff of *The Times*, 1926–30; first novel, *The Man Within*, 1929; worked for the Foreign Office during the Second World War; first play, *The Living Room*, 1953; OM, 1986.

(For further details of writings after 1945 see Volume 8 of the *Guide*.)

Other works include:

(novels) *Stamboul Train*, 1932; *It's a Battlefield*, 1934; *A Gun for Sale*, 1936; *Brighton Rock*, 1938; *The Confidential Agent*, 1939; *The Power and the Glory*, 1940; *The Ministry of Fear*, 1943; *The Heart of the Matter*, 1948

(plays) *The Potting Shed*, 1957; *The Complaisant Lover*, 1959

(short stories) *The Basement Room*, 1935; *May We Borrow Your Husband?*, 1967

(travel writing) *Journey Without Maps*, 1936

(autobiography) *A Sort of Life*, 1971; *Ways Of Escape*, 1980

Collected Essays, 1969

Life by N. Sherry, Vol. 1, 1989, Vol. 2, 1994

See:

K. Allott and M. Farris, *The Art of Graham Greene*, 1957

M. Couto, *Graham Greene: On the Frontier*, 1988

S. Hynes (ed.), *Graham Greene: A Collection of Critical Essays*, 1973

J. Meyers (ed.), *Graham Greene: A Revaluation – New Essays*, 1989

P. O'Prey, *A Reader's Guide to Graham Greene*, 1988

R. Sharrock, *Saints, Sinners and Comedians: The Novels of Graham Greene*, 1984

GREGORY, ISABELLA AUGUSTA (Lady Gregory) (1852–1932): Playwright; b. Roxborough, County Galway; met W. B. Yeats, 1898 and worked with him to establish the Irish National Theatre; a director of the Abbey Theatre, opened 1904; first play, *Spreading the News*, 1906

Plays include:

The Unicorn from the Stars (with Yeats), 1908; *The Full Moon*, 1911; *Three Wonder Plays*, 1922; *Selected Plays* ed. E. Coxhead, 1962

(other writings) *Our Irish Theatre: A Chapter of Autobiography*, 1913; *Journals 1916–30* ed. L. Robinson, 1946; *Journal Vol. 1 1916–1925* ed. D. J. Murphy, 1978; *Seventy Years* (autobiography) ed. G. Smythe, 1973

Life by E. Coxhead, 1961, rev. 1966
See:
E. H. Mikhail (ed.), *Lady Gregory: Interviews and Recollections,* 1977

GRIEVE, CHRISTOPHER MURRAY – See HUGH MACDIARMID (1892–1978).

GURNEY, IVOR (1890–1937): Poet and composer; b. Gloucester; educated at the King's School, Gloucester and the Royal College of Music; served in France, 1915–17; gassed; first poems, *Severn and Somme,* 1917; *War's Embers,* 1919; after the war, suffered mental illness and unemployment, culminating in a complete breakdown, 1922; last fifteen years of life spent in an asylum.

Life by M. Hurd, 1978
Collected Poems ed. P. J. Kavanagh, 1982
Selected Poems ed. P. J. Kavanagh, 1990
Severn and Somme; and War's Embers ed. R. K. R. Thornton, 1987
War Letters: A Selection ed. R. K. R. Thornton, 1982

HARDY, THOMAS (1840–1928): The list below is a guide to Hardy's poetry discussed in this volume. For a full bibliography, see the Appendix in Volume 6 of the *Guide.*

Complete Poetical Works ed. S. Hynes, 3 vols., 1982–5
Complete Poems ed. J. Gibson, 1976
A Variorum Edition of the Complete Poems ed. J. Gibson, 1979
The Notebooks of Thomas Hardy ed. F. Hardy, 1955
Personal Writings ed. H. Orel, 1976
Personal Notebooks ed. R. H. Taylor, 1978
Literary Notebooks ed. L. A. Björk, 2 vols., 1974
Letters ed. C. J. Weber, 1954
Collected Letters ed. R. L. Purdy and M. Millgate, 1978–(6 vols. to date)
See:
J. Bayley, *An Essay on Hardy,* 1978
R. G. Cox (ed.) *Thomas Hardy: The Critical Heritage,* 1970
D. Davie, *Thomas Hardy and British Poetry,* 1973
J. Gibson and T. Johnston (eds.), *Thomas Hardy: Poems – A Casebook,* 1979
S. Hynes, *The Pattern of Hardy's Poetry,* 1961
T. Paulin, *Thomas Hardy: The Poetry of Perception,* 1975
F. B. Pinion, *A Commentary on the Poems of Thomas Hardy,* 1976
J. Richardson, *Thomas Hardy: The Poetry of Necessity,* 1977
D. Taylor, *Thomas Hardy's Poetry, 1860–1928,* 1981, rev. 1989
J. P. Ward, *Thomas Hardy's Poetry,* 1993

HOUSMAN, ALFRED EDWARD (1859–1936): See Appendix to Volume 6 of the *Guide.*

HUXLEY, ALDOUS LEONARD (1894–1963): Novelist and essayist; b. Godalming; educated at Eton College and Balliol College, Oxford; first novel, *Crome Yellow*, 1921; moved to the United States, 1937.

Works include:

(novels) *Antic Hay*, 1923; *Those Barren Leaves*, 1925; *Point Counter Point*, 1928; *Brave New World*, 1932; *Eyeless in Gaza*, 1936; *After Many a Summer*, 1939; *Island*, 1962

(stories) *Limbo*, 1920; *Mortal Coils*, 1922; *Brief Candles*, 1930; *Collected Short Stories*, 1969

(essays) *On the Margin*, 1923; *Jesting Pilate*, 1926; *Vulgarity in Literature*, 1930; *Themes and Variations*, 1950; *The Doors of Perception*, 1954; *Heaven and Hell*, 1956; *Brave New World Revisited*, 1958; *Literature and Science*, 1963; *Moksha: Writings on Psychedelics and the Visionary Experience, 1931– 1963* ed. M. Horowitz and C. Palmer, 1980

Letters ed. G. Smith, 1969

Life by S. Bedford, 2 vols., 1973–4, repr. in 1 vol., 1993; L. Huxley, 1969
See:
P. Bowering, *Aldous Huxley: A Study of the Major Novels*, 1968
C. S. Ferns, *Aldous Huxley: Novelist*, 1980
J. Huxley (ed.), *Aldous Huxley, 1894–1963: A Memorial Volume*, 1966
K. M. May, *Aldous Huxley*, 1972
D. Watt (ed.), *Aldous Huxley: The Critical Heritage*, 1975

ISHERWOOD, CHRISTOPHER WILLIAM BRADSHAW (1904–1986): Novelist and dramatist; b. Disley, Cheshire; educated at Repton School and Corpus Christi College, Cambridge; first novel, *All The Conspirators*, 1928; taught English in Berlin 1930–33, then worked in England as a journalist; emigrated to USA, 1939; American citizen, 1946.

Works include:

(novels) *Mr Norris Changes Trains*, 1935; *Goodbye to Berlin*, 1939; *Prater Violet*, 1945; *The World in the Evening*, 1954; *Down There on a Visit*, 1962; *A Meeting by the River*, 1967

(story) *Sally Bowles*, 1937

(plays) (all with W. H. Auden) *The Dog Beneath the Skin*, 1935; *The Ascent of F6*, 1936; *On the Frontier*, 1938

(travel writing) (with W. H. Auden) *Journey to a War*, 1939

(autobiography) *Lions and Shadows*, 1938; *Christopher and His Kind*, 1977; *My Guru and His Disciple*, 1980

Life by B. Finney, 1979; J. Fryer, 1993
See:
S. Wade, *Christopher Isherwood*, 1991

JAMES, HENRY (1843–1916): Novelist, short-story writer and critic; b. New York, second son of Henry James, philosopher, and younger brother of William James, the pragmatist; irregular education in Europe and United States; entered Harvard Law School, 1862; began publishing articles and reviews, 1864; revisited Europe, 1869; spent a year, 1875–6, in Paris where he met Turgenev, Flaubert and Zola; *Roderick Hudson*, 1875; settled in London, 1876; *The Europeans* and *Daisy Miller*, 1878; *Washington Square*, 1880; *The Portrait of a Lady*, 1881; *The Bostonians* and *The Princess Casamassima*, 1886; between 1890–95 tried, with little success, to write for the theatre and abandoned the attempt after the failure of *Guy Domville*, 1894; *What Maisie Knew*, 1897; moved to Lamb House, in Rye, Sussex, in 1898; *The Awkward Age*, 1899; *The Wings of the Dove*, 1902; *The Ambassadors*, 1903; *The Golden Bowl*, 1904; between 1905–10 revisited the United States, and edited New York Edition of his works; became British subject, 1915; awarded Order of Merit, 1916; died in London leaving two novels and a third volume of autobiography all unfinished.

Other works include:

(novels) *The American*, 1877; *Watch and Ward*, 1878; *The Reverberator*, 1888; *The Tragic Muse*, 1890; *The Spoils of Poynton*, 1897; *The Sacred Fount*, 1901; *The Ivory Tower*, 1917; *The Sense of the Past*, 1917

(stories) *The Aspern Papers*, 1888; *The Real Thing*, 1892; *In The Cage*, 1898

(criticism) *Hawthorne*, 1879; *Partial Portraits*, 1888; *Notes on Novelists*, 1914; *The Art of the Novel* (Prefaces) ed. R. P. Blackmur, 1934; *The Scenic Art* ed. A. Wade, 1948; *The House of Fiction* ed. L. Edel, 1957; *Literary Reviews and Essays* ed. A. Mordell, 1957; *The Art of Criticism* ed. W. Veeder and S. M. Griffin, 1986

(autobiographical writings) *The American Scene*, 1907; *A Small Boy and Others*, 1913; *Notes of a Son and Brother*, 1914; *The Middle Years*, 1917

Life by L. Edel, 5 vols., 1953–72; and F. O. Matthiessen (ed.) *The James Family: A Group Biography*, 1947
The New York Edition, 24 vols., 1907–9
Complete Tales ed. L. Edel, 12 vols., 1962–4
Tales ed. M. Aziz, 1973– (3 vols. to date)
Complete Plays ed. L. Edel, 1949
Complete Notebooks ed. L. Edel and L. H. Powers, 1987
Literary Criticism, 2 vols., 1984
Letters ed. P. Lubbock, 2 vols., 1920
Letters (selected) ed. L. Edel, 4 vols., 1974–84
Henry James and Edith Wharton: Letters, 1900–1915 ed. L. H. Powers, 1989
See:
Q. Anderson, *The American Henry James*, 1958
A. Berland, *Culture and Conduct in the Novels of Henry James*, 1981
M. Bewley, *The Complex Fate*, 1952
    The Eccentric Design, 1959
R. Chase in *The American Novel and its Traditions*, 1957
S. Chatman, *The Later Style of Henry James*, 1972

F. C. Crews, *The Tragedy of Manners: Moral Drama in the Later Novels of Henry James*, 1957

F. W. Dupee (ed.), *The Question of Henry James*, 1947
Henry James, 1951

R. Gard (ed.), *Henry James: The Critical Heritage*, 1968

D. Gervais, *Flaubert and Henry James: A Study in Contrasts*, 1978

J. Goode (ed.), *The Air of Reality: New Essays on Henry James*, 1972

K. Graham, *Henry James: The Drama of Fulfilment*, 1975

W. Isle, *Experiments in Form: Henry James's Novels 1896–1901*, 1968

D. W. Jefferson, *Henry James and the Modern Reader*, 1964

V. Jones, *James the Critic*, 1985

D. Krook, *The Ordeal of Consciousness in Henry James*, 1962

F. R. Leavis in *The Great Tradition*, 1948

B. Lee, *The Novels of Henry James: a Study of Culture and Consciousness*, 1978

F. O. Matthiessen, *Henry James: The Major Phase*, 1944

R. Poirier in *A World Elsewhere: The Place of Style in American Literature*, 1966

E. Pound in *Literary Essays*, 1954

P. Rahv in *Image and Idea*, 1957

S. Sears, *The Negative Imagination: Form and Perspective in the Novels of Henry James*, 1968

T. Tanner (ed.), *Henry James: Modern Judgements*, 1968
Henry James, 3 vols., 1979–81

J. A. Ward, *The Search for Form: Studies in the Structures of James's Fiction*, 1967

JOYCE, JAMES AUGUSTINE ALOYSIUS (1882–1941): Novelist, poet and playwright; b. Dublin; educated at Belvedere College and University College, Dublin; left Ireland, 1902, living chiefly in Paris and Trieste; first publication, *Chamber Music* (poems) (ed. W. Y. Tindall, 1954), 1907; *Dubliners*, 1914; 1914–18 spent in Zürich; *Portrait of the Artist as a Young Man*, 1916; *Exiles* (play) 1918; 1920–39 lived in Paris; *Ulysses*, 1922; *Pomes Penyeach*, 1927; *Collected Poems*, 1936; *Finnegans Wake*, 1939 (published in extracts as 'Work in Progress', 1928–37); from 1940 lived in Zürich where he died.

Life by R. Ellmann, 1959, rev. 1982
Stephen Hero: Part of the First Draft of 'A Portrait of the Artist as a Young Man' ed. T. Spencer, 1944, rev. 1963
Ulysses: The Corrected Text ed. H. Gabler *et al.*, 1986
Ulysses: A Facsimile of the Manuscript ed. C. Driver, 3 vols., 1975
The Critical Writings of James Joyce ed. E. Mason and R. Ellmann, 1959
Letters Vol. 1 ed. S. Gilbert, 1957, rev. 1966; Vols. 2 and 3 ed. R. Ellmann, 1966
See:
D. Attridge, ed., *The Cambridge Companion to James Joyce*, 1990
S. Beckett *et al.*, *Our Exagmination Round His Factification For Incamination of 'Work in Progress'*, 1929

M. Beja (ed.), *James Joyce: 'Dubliners' and 'A Portrait of the Artist as a Young Man' – A Casebook*, 1973

H. Blamires, *The Bloomsday Book: A Guide through Joyce's Ulysses*, 1966, rev. 1988

S. Bolt, *A Preface to James Joyce*, 1981 2nd edn 1992

F. Budgen, *James Joyce and the Making of Ulysses*, 1972

A. Burgess, *Here Comes Everybody*, 1965

R. H. Deming (ed.), *James Joyce: The Critical Heritage*, 2 vols., 1970

R. Ellmann, *Ulysses on the Liffey*, 1972
    The Consciousness of Joyce, 1977

D. Gifford and R. J. Seidman, *Ulysses Annotated*, 2nd edn 1988

A. Glasheen, *A Third Census of Finnegans Wake: An Index of the Characters and their Roles*, 1956, rev. 1977

S. L. Goldberg, *The Classical Temper: A Study of James Joyce's Ulysses*, 1961

J. Gross, *James Joyce*, 1970

H. Kenner, *Dublin's Joyce*, 1955; *Joyce's Voices*, 1978; *Ulysses*, 1980

R. B. Kershner, *Joyce, Bakhtin and Popular Literature*, 1989

R. McHugh, *Annotations to Finnegan's Wake*, 1980
    The Finnegans Wake Experience, 1981

P. Parrinder, *James Joyce*, 1984

C. H. Peake, *James Joyce: The Citizen and the Artist*, 1977

W. Thornton, *Allusions in Ulysses*, 1968

W. Y. Tindall, *A Reader's Guide to James Joyce*, 1959

K. Wales, *The Language of James Joyce*, 1992

KIPLING, RUDYARD (1865–1936): See the Appendix in Volume 6 of the *Guide*.

LAWRENCE, DAVID HERBERT (1885–1930): Novelist, poet, dramatist and essayist; b. Eastwood, near Nottingham; educated at Nottingham High School and University College, Nottingham; worked as a teacher in Croydon until the publication of his first novel, *The White Peacock*, 1911; *Sons and Lovers*, 1913; lived in Italy, returning to England for the duration of the First World War; *The Rainbow*, 1915; after the war, travelled widely in Italy, Australia and New Mexico; *Women in Love*, 1920; *The Plumed Serpent*, 1926; *Lady Chatterley's Lover*, 1928; died of tuberculosis in Vence, near Nice.

Other writings include:
(novels) *The Trespasser*, 1912; *The Lost Girl*, 1920; *Aaron's Rod*, 1922; *Kangaroo*, 1923; *Mr Noon* ed. L. Vasey, 1984
(stories and novella) *The Prussian Officer*, 1914; *England, My England*, 1922; *The Ladybird*, 1923; *St Mawr*, 1925; *The Woman Who Rode Away*, 1928; *The Virgin and the Gypsy*, 1930; *Love Among the Haystacks*, 1930; *The Man Who Died*, 1931
(plays) *The Widowing of Mrs Holroyd*, 1914; *Touch and Go*, 1920; *David*,

1926; *A Collier's Friday Night,* 1934

(poems) *Amores,* 1916; *Look! We Have Come Through,* 1917; *New Poems,* 1918; *Birds, Beasts and Flowers,* 1923; *Collected Poems,* 2 vols., 1928; *Pansies,* 1929; *Nettles,* 1930; *Last Poems,* 1932

(travel writing) *Twilight in Italy,* 1916; *Sea and Sardinia,* 1921; *Mornings in Mexico,* 1927; *Etruscan Places,* 1932

(essays and criticism) *Movements in European History,* 1921; *Psychoanalysis and the Unconscious,* 1921; *Fantasia of the Unconscious,* 1922; *Studies in Classic American Literature,* 1923; *Reflections on the Death of a Porcupine,* 1925; *Apocalypse,* 1931

Life by E. Delavenay, 1972; H. T. Moore, 1954, rev. 1974; E. Nehls (A Composite Biography) 3 vols., 1957–9; K. Sagar, 1980 and 1985; J. Worthen, 1989

The Cambridge Edition of the Complete Works, 1979–

Complete Short Stories 3 vols., 1955

Complete Poems ed. V. de Sola Pinto and W. Roberts, 2 vols., 1964

Complete Plays, 1965

Phoenix ed. E. D. McDonald, 1936

Phoenix II ed. W. Roberts and H. T. Moore, 1968

Letters ed. A. Huxley, 1932

Collected Letters ed. H. T. Moore, 2 vols., 1962

Letters (Cambridge Edition) ed. J. Boulton et al., 1979–

See:

M. Black in *The Literature of Fidelity,* 1975
    D. H. Lawrence: The Early Fiction, 1986

K. Brown (ed.), *Rethinking Lawrence,* 1990

C. Clarke, *D. H. Lawrence and English Romanticism,* 1969
    (ed.), *D. H. Lawrence: 'The Rainbow' and 'Women in Love'* – *A Casebook,* 1979

H. Coombes (ed.), *D. H. Lawrence: A Critical Anthology,* 1973

P. Delany, *D. H. Lawrence's Nightmare,* 1979

R. P. Draper (ed.), *D. H. Lawrence: The Critical Heritage,* 1970

D. Ellis and H. Mills, *D. H. Lawrence's Non-Fiction,* 1988

G. H. Ford, *Double Measure: A Study of the Novels and Stories of D. H. Lawrence,* 1965

S. M. Gilbert, *Acts of Attention: The Poems of D. H. Lawrence,* 1972

A. H. Gomme (ed.), *D. H. Lawrence,* 1978

E. Goodheart, *The Utopian Vision of D. H. Lawrence,* 1963

C. Heywood (ed.), *D. H. Lawrence: New Studies,* 1987

G. Holderness, *D. H. Lawrence: History, Ideology and Fiction,* 1982

D. H. Holbrook, *Where D. H. Lawrence was Wrong About Women,* 1992

G. M. Hyde, *D. H. Lawrence,* 1990

M. Kalnins (ed.), *D. H. Lawrence: Centenary Essays,* 1986

F. Kermode, *D. H. Lawrence,* 1973

M. Kinkead-Weekes, 'The Exploratory Imagination of D. H. Lawrence' in

Imagined Worlds ed. M. Mack and I. Gregor, 1968
F. R. Leavis, *D. H. Lawrence: Novelist*, 1955
    Thought, Words and Creativity, 1976
J. C. F. Littlewood, *D. H. Lawrence I: 1885–1914*, 1976
M. J. Lockwood, *A Study of the Poems of D. H. Lawrence*, 1987
J. Meyers (ed.), *D. H. Lawrence and Tradition*, 1985
S. J. Miko, *Toward 'Women in Love'*, 1971
K. Sagar, *D. H. Lawrence: A Calendar of his Works*, 1979
    D. H. Lawrence: Life into Art, 1985
G. Salgado and G. K. Das (eds.), *The Spirit of D. H. Lawrence: Centenary Essays*, 1988
S. Sklar, *The Plays of D. H. Lawrence*, 1975
A. Smith (ed.), *Lawrence and Women*, 1978
J. Worthen, *D. H. Lawrence and the Idea of the Novel*, 1979

LEAVIS, FRANK RAYMOND (1895–1978): Critic; b. Cambridge; educated at the Perse School and Emmanuel College, Cambridge; stretcher-bearer on Western Front between 1914 and 1918; married Queenie Dorothy Roth, 1929; *Mass Civilization and Minority Culture*, 1930; *New Bearings in English Poetry*, 1932, rev. 1950; Director of Studies in English, Downing College, Cambridge, 1932; editor of *Scrutiny* (1932–53), to which he was the main contributor; made CH, 1978.

(For further details of writings after 1945 see Volume 8 of the *Guide*.)

Other critical works include:
For Continuity, 1933; *Culture and Environment* (with D. Thompson) 1933; *Revaluation*, 1936; *Education and the University*, 1943; *The Great Tradition*, 1948; *The Common Pursuit*, 1952; *D. H. Lawrence: Novelist*, 1955; *Dickens the Novelist* (with Q. D. Leavis) 1970; *The Living Principle*, 1975

Life by R. Hayman, 1976
See:
M. Bell, *F. R. Leavis*, 1988
R. P. Bilan, *The Literary Criticism of F. R. Leavis*, 1979
E. Greenwood, *F. R. Leavis*, 1978
F. Mulhern, *The Moment of 'Scrutiny'*, 1979
A. Samson, *F. R. Leavis*, 1992
W. Walsh, *F. R. Leavis*, 1978

LEHMANN, ROSAMOND NINA (1901–1990): Novelist; b. Bourne End, Buckinghamshire; educated at Girton College, Cambridge; first novel, *Dusty Answer*, 1927.

Works include:
(novels) *A Note in Music*, 1930; *Invitation to the Waltz*, 1932; *The Weather in the Streets*, 1936; *The Ballad and the Source*, 1944; *The Echoing Grove*, 1953; *A Sea-grape Tree*, 1976

(stories) *The Gipsy's Baby and Other Stories*, 1946
(play) *No More Music*, 1939
(other) *The Swan in the Evening: Fragments of an Inner Life*, 1967
See:
J. Simons, *Rosamund Lehmann*, 1992

LEWIS, CECIL DAY (1904–72): Poet and, under the pseudonym of Nicholas Blake, detective novelist; b. Ballintubbert, Ireland; educated at Sherborne School and Wadham College, Oxford; first publication, *Beechen Vigil*, 1925; schoolteacher 1927–35; *From Feathers to Iron*, 1931; manifesto, *A Hope for Poetry*, 1934; moved to Devon, 1938; worked for the Ministry of Information during Second World War; *Word Over All*, 1943; *Poems 1943–1947*, 1948; Oxford Professor of Poetry, 1951–6; Poet Laureate, 1968.

Life by S. Day-Lewis, 1980
Poems ed. I. Parsons, 1977

LEWIS, PERCY WYNDHAM (1882–1957): Novelist and painter; b. on a yacht off Nova Scotia; educated at Rugby School and the Slade School of Art; edited *Blast*, the Vorticist review, 1914–15; served as a gunner and later as an official war artist in the First World War; first novel, *Tarr*, 1918; edited *Tyro*, 1921–2 and *Enemy*, 1927–9; spent Second World War in United States and Canada; returned to England, 1945; art critic of *The Listener*, 1946

Writings include:
(novels) *The Childermass*, Section 1, 1928; *The Apes of God*, 1930; *Snooty Baronet*, 1932; *The Revenge for Love*, 1937; *Self-Condemned*, 1954; *The Human Age*: Book 2 *Monstre Gai* and Book 3 *Malign Fiesta*, 1955; Book 1, a revision of *The Childermass*, 1956
(essays and criticism) *The Caliph's Design*, 1919; *The Art of Being Ruled*, 1926; *The Lion and the Fox: A Study of the Hero in the Plays of Shakespeare*, 1927; *Time and Fiction*, 1930; *Hitler*, 1931; *Men Without Art*, 1934; *Left Wings over Europe*, 1936; *Blasting and Bombardiering* (autobiographical essays), 1937; *The Jews, are they Human?*, 1939; *The Hitler Cult*, 1939; *The Writer and the Absolute*, 1952; *The Demon of Progress of the Arts*, 1954

Life by J. Meyers, 1980
Collected Poems and Plays ed. A. Munton, 1979
The Essential Wyndham Lewis ed. J. Symons, 1989
Wyndham Lewis on Art: 1913–1956 ed. W. Michel and C. J. Fox, 1969
Enemy Salvoes: Selected Literary Criticism ed. C. J. Fox, 1975
Letters ed. W. K. Rose, 1963
Pound/Lewis: The Letters ed. T. Materer, 1985
See:
D. Ayers, *Wyndham Lewis and Western Man*, 1992
D. G. Bridson, *The Filibuster: Political Ideas of Wyndham Lewis*, 1972

R. T. Chapman, *Wyndham Lewis: Fictions and Satires,* 1973
F. Jameson, *Fables of Aggression,* 1979
H. Kenner, *Wyndham Lewis,* 1954
T. Materer, *Wyndham Lewis the Novelist,* 1976
   Vortex: Pound, Eliot and Lewis, 1979
J. Meyers (ed.), *Wyndham Lewis: A Revaluation,* 1980
W. Pritchard, *Wyndham Lewis,* 1968
D. Schenker, *Wyndham Lewis: Religion and Modernism,* 1992

MACDIARMID, HUGH – Christopher Murray Grieve – (1892–1978): Poet
and prose writer; b. Langholm, Dumfriesshire; educated at Langholm
Academy; pupil-teacher in Edinburgh; worked as a journalist; army, 1915–
19; first collection of poems, *Annals of the Five Senses,* 1923; first verse in
Scots, *Sangschaw,* 1925 and *Penny Wheep,* 1926; *A Drunk Man Looks at the
Thistle,* 1926; founder member of Scottish Nationalist Party, 1928; expelled,
1933; *First Hymn to Lenin,* 1931; *Second Hymn to Lenin,* 1932; joined
Communist Party, 1934; expelled, 1948; rejoined in 1957 after the Russian
invasion of Hungary; *In Memoriam James Joyce,* 1955.
   (For further details of writings after 1945 see Volume 8 of the *Guide.*)

Life by A. Bold, 1988; G. Wright, 1977
Complete Poems 1920–1976 ed. M. Grieve and W. R. Aitken, 1978
Letters ed. A. Bold, 1984
Selected Essays ed. D. Glen, 1969
(autobiography) *Lucky Poet,* 1943; *The Company I've Kept,* 1966
See:
A. Bold, *Hugh MacDiarmid: The Terrible Crystal,* 1983
G. E. Davie, *The Crisis of the Democratic Intellect,* 1986
N. K. Gish, *Hugh MacDiarmid: The Man and his Work,* 1984
D. Glen (ed.), *Hugh MacDiarmid: A Critical Survey,* 1972
W. N. Herbert, *To Circumjack MacDiarmid,* 1992
R. Watson, *Hugh MacDiarmid,* 1985

MACNEICE, LOUIS (1907–63): Poet; b. Belfast; educated at Marlborough
College and Merton College, Oxford; first poems, *Blind Fireworks,* 1929;
lectureship in Classics, Birmingham University, 1930–36; lectureship in
Greek, Bedford College, London, 1936–40; translation of Aeschylus' *Aga-
memnon,* 1936; visited Iceland with W. H. Auden and together they wrote
Letters from Iceland, 1937; joined BBC, 1941; CBE, 1958.

Works include:
(poems) *Poems,* 1935; *The Earth Compels,* 1938; *Autumn Journal,* 1939; *The
   Last Ditch,* 1940; *Collected Poems 1925–48,* 1949
(radio plays) *Christopher Columbus,* 1944; *The Dark Tower,* 1947; *The Mad
   Islands* and *The Administrator,* 1964
(criticism) *Modern Poetry,* 1938; *The Poetry of W. B. Yeats,* 1941; *Varieties of
   Parable,* 1965

(travel writing) *I Crossed the Minch,* 1938
(autobiography) *The Strings are False* (unfinished), 1965

Collected Poems ed. E. R. Dodds, 1966
Selected Literary Criticism ed. A. Heuser, 1987
See:
T. Brown, *MacNeice: Sceptical Vision,* 1975
B. Coulton, *Louis MacNeice in the BBC,* 1980
E. Longley, *Louis MacNeice: A Study,* 1988
P. McDonald, *Louis MacNeice: The Poet in his Contexts,* 1991
W. T. McKinnon, *Apollo's Blended Dream: A Study of the Poetry of Louis MacNeice,* 1971
R. Marsack, *The Cave of Making: The Poetry of Louis MacNeice,* 1982

MANSFIELD, KATHERINE – Katherine Mansfield Beauchamp – (1888–1923): Short-story writer; b. Wellington, New Zealand; educated at Wellington Girls' High School and Queen's College, London; first collection of stories, *In A German Pension,* 1911; 1911, met John Middleton Murry, whom she married in 1918; *Bliss,* 1920; died of tuberculosis.

Other stories include: *The Garden Party,* 1922; *The Dove's Nest,* 1923; *Something Childish,* 1924

Life by A. Alpers, 1953 and 1980; G. Boddy, 1988; J. Meyers, 1978; C. Tomalin, 1987
Collected Stories, 1945
Stories ed. A. Alpers, 1984
Undiscovered Country: The New Zealand Stories ed. I. A. Gordon, 1974
Poems ed. V. O'Sullivan, 1988
Journal ed. J. M. Murry, 1927, rev. 1954
Collected Letters ed. V. O'Sullivan and M. Scott, 1984–
The Letters and Journals: A Selection ed. C. K. Stead, 1977
Critical Writings ed. C. Hanson, 1987
See:
K. Fullbrook, *Katherine Mansfield,* 1986
C. A. Hankin, *Katherine Mansfield and Her Confessional Stories,* 1983
C. Hanson and A. Gurr, *Katherine Mansfield,* 1981
S. J. Kaplan, *Mansfield and the Origins of Modernist Fiction,* 1991

MASEFIELD, JOHN EDWARD (1878–1967): Poet; b. Ledbury, Herefordshire; educated at the King's School, Warwick and the training ship, HMS *Conway*; sailed round Cape Horn as a merchant seaman and subsequently lived in New York until his return to England in 1897; worked as a journalist; *Salt Water Ballads,* 1902; *Ballads,* 1903 and 1910; *The Everlasting Mercy,* 1911; *Dauber,* 1913; during the First World War served with the Red Cross in France and on a hospital ship; *Reynard the Fox,* 1919; *Collected Poems,* 1923, 1932 and 1938; Poet Laureate, 1930; Order of Merit, 1935.

Other works include:
(plays) *The Tragedy of Nan*, 1909; *The Coming of Christ*, 1928; *Easter*, 1930
(novels) *Lost Endeavour*, 1910; *Sard Harker*, 1924; *Odtaa*, 1926; *The Bird of Dawning*, 1933
(autobiography) *So Long to Learn*, 1952

Life by C. Babington Smith, 1978
Collected Works, 5 vols., 1935–7
Complete Poems, 1953
Selected Poems ed. D. E. Stanford, 1984
Letters to Florence Lamont ed. C. Lamont and L. Lamont, 1979
Letters to Reyna ed. W. Buchan, 1983
Letters from the Front 1915–17 ed. P. Vansittart, 1984

MAUGHAM, WILLIAM SOMERSET (1874–1965): Novelist, short-story writer and playwright; b. Paris; educated at King's School, Canterbury, Heidelberg University and St Thomas's Hospital, London; first novel, *Liza of Lambeth*, 1897; first play, *A Man of Honour*, 1903; worked under cover for Intelligence in Geneva during First World War; *Of Human Bondage* (novel), 1915; lived permanently in the South of France since 1928; made CH, 1954.

Novels include:
The Moon and Sixpence, 1919; *The Painted Veil*, 1925; *Cakes and Ale*, 1930; *The Razor's Edge*, 1944

Life by R. Maugham, 1966; T. Morgan, 1980
Complete Short Stories, 3 vols., 1951
See:
A. Curtis and J. Whitehead (eds.), *W. Somerset Maugham: The Critical Heritage*, 1987

MUIR, EDWIN (1887–1959): Poet, critic and (with Willa Muir) translator; b. Orkney; educated at Kirkwall Burgh School; family moved to Glasgow, 1901; worked as a clerk; first publication, *We Moderns*, 1918; moved to London, 1919, where he worked for the *New Age*; travelled widely in Europe, 1921–4; earned his living as a critic and translator; worked for the British Council, 1942–50, and as Warden of Newbattle Abbey, 1950–55; CBE, 1953.

Works include:
(poetry) *First Poems*, 1925; *Chorus of the Newly Dead*, 1926; *Variations on a Time Theme*, 1934; *Journeys and Places*, 1937; *The Narrow Place*, 1943; *The Voyage*, 1946; *The Labyrinth*, 1949; *Prometheus*, 1954; *One Foot in Eden*, 1956; *Collected Poems, 1921–1958* ed. W. Muir and J. C. Hall, 1960
(essays and criticism) *Latitudes*, 1924; *Transition: Essays on Contemporary Literature*, 1926; *The Structure of the Novel*, 1928; *Scott and Scotland: The Predicament of the Scottish Writer*, 1936; *The Present Age from 1914*, 1939;

Essays on Literature and Society, 1949, rev. 1965; *Uncollected Scottish Criticism*
ed. A. Noble, 1982; *The Truth of the Imagination* ed. P. H. Butter, 1988
(translations with Willa Muir) a number of contemporary German writers
including the following by Kafka: *The Castle*, 1930; *The Trial*, 1937;
America, 1938
(autobiography) *The Story and the Fable*, 1940; rev. as *An Autobiography*, 1954
(letters) *Selected Letters* ed. P. H. Butter, 1974

Life by P. H. Butter, 1966; W. Muir (*Belonging*), 1968
See:
R. Knight, *Edwin Muir: An Introduction to His Work*, 1980
G. Marshall, *In a Distant Isle: The Orkney Background of Edwin Muir*, 1987
C. Wiseman, *Beyond the Labyrinth: A Study of Edwin Muir's Poetry*, 1978

MYERS, LEOPOLD HAMILTON (1881–1944): Novelist; b. Cambridge; educated at Eton College and Trinity College, Cambridge; first publication,
Arvat (verse drama), 1908; worked for the Board of Trade, 1914–18; first
novel, *The Orissers*, 1922; visited Ceylon, 1925; committed suicide.

Novels include:
The 'Clio', 1925; *The Near and the Far*, 1929, with its sequel *Prince Jali*,
1931, and *Rajah Amar* appeared as *The Root and the Flower*, 1935; *Strange
Glory*, 1936; *The Pool of Vishnu*, 1940, republished with *The Root and the
Flower* as *The Near and the Far*, 1943
See:
G. H. Bantock, *L. H. Myers: A Critical Study*, 1956

O'BRIEN, FLANN (also Myles na Gopaleen – both pseudonyms of Brian
O'Nolan) (1911–66): Novelist; short-story writer and journalist; b. Strabane,
Tyrone; educated at Blackrock College and University College, Dublin;
worked for the Irish Civil Service.

Works include:
(novels) *At Swim-Two-Birds*, 1939; *The Third Policeman* (completed 1940),
1967; *An Béal Bocht*, 1941 (translated as *The Poor Mouth*), 1973; *The Hard
Life*, 1961; *The Dalkey Archive*, 1964
(plays) *Faustus Kelly*, 1943
(stories) *Stories and Plays*, 1973; *The Various Lives of Keats and Chapman* and
The Brother ed. B. Kiely, 1976
See:
A. Clissman, *Flann O'Brien: A Critical Introduction to His Writing*, 1975
A. Cronin, *No Laughing Matter*, 1989

O'CASEY, SEAN (1880–1964): Playwright; illness prevented formal education; worked as a labourer; first publication, *The Grand Oul' Dame Britannia*
(ballad), 1916; first play, *The Shadow of a Gunman*, performed 1923; *Juno
and the Paycock*, performed 1924; *The Plough and the Stars*, 1926; moved to
England, 1926.

Writings include:

(plays) *The Silver Tassie*, 1928; *Within the Gates*, 1933; *Five Irish Plays*, 1935; *The Star Turns Red*, 1940; *Purple Dust*, 1940; *Red Roses for Me*, 1942; *The Drums of Father Ned*, 1960

(autobiography) *I Knock at the Door*, 1939; *Pictures in the Hallway*, 1942; *Drums Under the Window*, 1945; *Inishfallen, Fare Thee Well*, 1949; *Rose and Crown*, 1952; *Sunset and Evening Star*, 1954

(selections) *Feathers from the Green Crow, 1905–25* ed. R. Hogan, 1962; *Blasts and Benedictions* ed. R. Ayling, 1967

Life by H. Hunt, 1980; D. Krause, 1960, rev. 1975; E. O'Casey, 1971
Complete Plays, 5 vols., 1984
Seven Plays ed. R. Ayling, 1985
Letters ed. D. Krause, 1975– (2 vols. to date)
See:
W. A. Armstrong, *Sean O'Casey*, 1967
R. Ayling (ed.), *Sean O'Casey: Modern Judgements*, 1969
    O'Casey: The Dublin Trilogy – A Casebook, 1985
R. Hogan and R. Burnham, *The Years of O'Casey 1921–1926*, 1992
T. Kilroy (ed.), *Sean O'Casey: A Collection of Critical Essays*, 1975
D. Krause and R. G. Lowery (eds.), *Sean O'Casey: Centenary Essays*, 1980
R. G. Lowery (ed.), *O'Casey Annual*, 1, 1982, 2, 1983, 3, 4, 1985
R. G. Rollins, *Sean O'Casey's Drama: Verisimilitude and Vision*, 1979
J. Simmons, *Sean O'Casey*, 1983
B. L. Smith, *O'Casey's Satiric Vision*, 1978

O'CONNOR, FRANK (pseudonym of Michael Francis O'Donovan) (1903–66): Short-story writer, critic and translator of Irish poetry; b. Cork; educated at the Christian Brothers School, Cork; worked as a librarian; first publication, *Guests of the Nation*, 1931.

Works include:

(stories) *Crab Apple Jelly*, 1944; *The Common Chord*, 1947; *Domestic Relations*, 1957; *My Oedipus Complex*, 1963; *Collection Two*, 1964; *Collection Three*, 1969

(biography) *The Big Fellow: A Life of Michael Collins*, 1937

(autobiography) *An Only Child*, 1961; *My Father's Son*, 1968

(criticism) *The Lonely Voice*, 1963

See:
M. Sheehy (ed.), *Michael/Frank: Studies on Frank O'Connor*, 1969
M. Wohlgelernter, *Frank O'Connor: An Introduction*, 1977

O'FAOLÁIN, SÉAN (1900–1991): Novelist, short-story writer, and biographer; b. Cork; educated at University College, Cork and Harvard University; worked as a lecturer; first publication, *Midsummer Madness* (stories), 1932; Director of the Arts Council of Ireland, 1957–9.

Works include:

(novels) *A Nest of Simple Folk*, 1933; *Bird Alone*, 1936; *Come Back to Erin*, 1940

(stories) *A Purse of Coppers*, 1937; *Teresa and Other Stories*, 1947; *I Remember! I Remember!*, 1961; *The Heat of the Day*, 1966; *Collected Stories*, 3 vols., 1980–82

(criticism) *The Short Story*, 1948; *The Vanishing Hero*, 1956

(biography) *The Life of Eamon de Valera*, 1933; *Constance Markievicz*, 1934

See:

M. Harmon, *Sean O'Faolain: A Critical Introduction*, 1966

O'FLAHERTY, LIAM (1896–1984): Novelist and short-story writer; b. Aran; educated at Rockwell College, Cashel, Blackrock College and University College, Dublin; served in the First World War; travelled widely and settled in England, 1922; first publication, *Thy Neighbour's Wife*, 1923.

Works include:

(novels) *The Black Soul*, 1924; *Skerrett*, 1932; *The Martyr*, 1933; *Famine*, 1937; *Land*, 1946

(stories) *Spring Sowing*, 1923; *Civil War*, 1925; *The Tent*, 1926; *The Mountain Tavern*, 1929; *Stories*, 1956; *The Pedlar's Revenge* selected by A. A. Kelly, 1976

(autobiography) *Shame the Devil*, 1934

See:

A. A. Kelly, *Liam O'Flaherty, The Storyteller*, 1976

P. F. Sheeran, *The Novels of Liam O'Flaherty*, 1976

ORWELL, GEORGE – Eric Arthur Blair – (1903–50): Novelist, journalist and critic; b. Motihari, Bengal; educated at Eton College; served with the Imperial Police in Burma, 1921–6; *Down and Out in Paris and London*, 1933; *Animal Farm*, 1945; *Nineteen Eighty-four*, 1949; died of consumption.

Other writings include:

(novels) *Burmese Days*, 1934; *A Clergyman's Daughter*, 1935; *Keep the Aspidistra Flying*, 1936; *The Road to Wigan Pier*, 1937; *Homage to Catalonia*, 1938

(essays) *Inside the Whale*, 1940; *Shooting an Elephant*, 1950; *England, Your England*, 1953; *Collected Essays* ed. S. Orwell and I. Angus, 4 vols., 1968

Life by B. Crick, 1980; M. Sheldon, 1991

See:

J. Meyers (ed.), *George Orwell: The Critical Heritage*, 1975

C. Norris (ed.), *Inside the Myth: George Orwell, Views from the Left*, 1984

R. Williams, *Orwell*, 1971

 George Orwell: A Collection of Critical Essays, 1974

D. Wykes, *A Preface to Orwell*, 1987

OWEN, WILFRED EDWARD SALTER (1893–1918): Poet; b. Oswestry; educated at the Birkenhead Institute, Shrewsbury Technical School and University College, Reading; taught English in France 1913–15; served with the

Artists' Rifles during First World War; suffered shell-shock and was sent to Craiglockhart War Hospital, near Edinburgh; there met Siegfried Sassoon and was encouraged by him to write; returned to the Front in France, September, 1918; awarded MC; killed seven days before the Armistice; *Poems* ed. S. Sassoon, 1920.

Life by H. Owen, 3 vols., 1963–5; K. Simcox, 1987; J. Stallworthy, 1974
Collected Poems ed. C. Day Lewis, 1963
Complete Poems and Fragments ed. J. Stallworthy, 2 vols., 1983
Selected Poetry and Prose ed. J. Breen, 1988
Collected Letters ed. H. Owen and J. Bell, 1967
See:
B. Bergonzi in *Heroes' Twilight*, 1965, rev. 1980
D. Graham, *The Truth of War: Owen, Blunden, Rosenberg*, 1984
D. Hibberd, *Owen the Poet*, 1986
D. S. R. Welland, *Wilfred Owen: A Critical Study*, 1960, rev. 1978

POUND, EZRA LOOMIS (1885–1972): Poet, translator and critic; b. Hailey, Idaho; educated at Hamilton College and the University of Pennsylvania; travelled in Europe, 1907; lived in London 1908–20, and subsequently in Paris and Rapallo; *A Lume Spento*, 1908; *Personae*, 1909; *Ripostes*, 1912; *Quia Pauper Amavi* (including *Homage to Sextus Propertius*), 1919; Cantos published at intervals throughout his life, beginning in 1919; *Hugh Selwyn Mauberley*, 1920; *Poems 1918–21*, 1921; in 1945, taken back to the United States to stand trial for pro-Fascist broadcasts made from Italy during Second World War, but declared unfit to plead and confined in a Washington asylum until 1958; returned to Italy after release; died in Venice.

Essays and critical writings include:
The Spirit of Romance, 1910; *Gaudier-Brzeska*, 1916; *Antheil and the Treatise on Harmony*, 1924; *How to Read*, 1931; *ABC of Reading*, 1934; *Make it New*, 1934; *Jefferson and/or Mussolini*, 1935; *Guide to Kulchur*, 1938

Life by H. Carpenter, 1988; M. de Rachewiltz (memoir *Discretions*), 1971; N. Stock, 1970
Selected Poems ed. T. S. Eliot, 1971
Collected Shorter Poems, 1968
Collected Early Poems ed. M. J. King, 1976
Cantos, revised, collected edition, 1975
The Translations of Ezra Pound, 1953
Confucius, 1969
The Literary Essays of Ezra Pound ed. T. S. Eliot, 1954
Selected Prose 1909–1965 ed. W. Cookson, 1973
Ezra Pound and Music: The Complete Criticism ed. R. M. Schafer, 1977
Ezra Pound and the Visual Arts ed. H. Zinnes, 1980
Letters:
Letters 1907–1941 ed. D. D. Paige, 1950

Pound/Joyce ed. F. Read, 1967

Pound/Ford ed. B. Lindberg-Seyersted, 1982

Pound/Lewis ed. T. Materer, 1985

Ezra Pound and Dorothy Shakespear: Their Letters 1909–1914 ed. O. Pound and A. Walton Litz, 1985

Pound/Zukofsky ed. B. Ahearn, 1987

Pound/The Little Review (letters to Margaret Anderson) ed. T. L. Scott and M. J. Friedman, 1988

See:

M. Alexander, *The Poetic Achievement of Ezra Pound*, 1979

G. Bornstein (ed.), *Ezra Pound Among the Poets*, 1985

P. Brooker, *A Student's Guide to the Selected Poems of Ezra Pound*, 1979

W. Cookson, *A Guide to the Cantos of Ezra Pound*, 1985

D. Davie, *Ezra Pound: Poet as Sculptor*, 1965
    Pound, 1975

M. Ellmann, *The Poetics of Impersonality: The Question of the Subject in T. S. Eliot and Ezra Pound*, 1987

W. S. Flory, *The American Ezra Pound*, 1989

P. N. Furbank, *Pound*, 1985

A. Gibson (ed.) *Pound in Multiple Perspective*, 1993

E. Hesse (ed.), *New Approaches to Ezra Pound*, 1969

E. Homberger (ed.), *Ezra Pound: The Critical Heritage*, 1972

G. Kearns, *Ezra Pound, the Cantos*, 1989

H. Kenner, *The Pound Era*, 1972

P. Makin, *Pound's Cantos*, 1985

M. Perloff, *The Dance of the Intellect: Studies in the Poetry of the Pound Tradition*, 1985

M. L. Rosenthal in *Sailing into the Unknown: Yeats, Pound and Eliot*, 1978

C. K. Stead, *Pound, Yeats, Eliot and the Modernist Movement*, 1986

J. P. Sullivan, *Ezra Pound and Sextus Propertius: A Study in Creative Translation*, 1964
    (ed.), *Ezra Pound: A Critical Anthology*, 1970

H. Witemeyer, *The Poetry of Ezra Pound: Forms and Renewal, 1908–1920*, 1969

THE POWYS BROTHERS:

JOHN COWPER (1872–1963): Novelist; b. Shirley, Derbyshire; educated at Sherborne School and Corpus Christi College, Cambridge; *Odes* (poems), 1896; first novel, *Wood and Stone*, 1915; *Wolf Solent*, 1929; *A Glastonbury Romance*, 1932; *Autobiography*, 1934.

THEODORE FRANCIS (1875–1953): Novelist; b. Shirley; educated at Dorchester Grammar School and Aldeburgh; farmed in Suffolk, 1896–1901, then moved to Dorset; *The Soliloquy of a Hermit*, 1916; *Mr Tasker's Gods*, 1925; *Mr Weston's Good Wine*, 1927

LLEWELYN (1884–1939): Essayist; b. Dorchester; educated at Sherborne School and Corpus Christi College, Cambridge; *Confessions of Two Brothers*, with John Cowper, 1916; *Ebony and Ivory*, 1923; *Black Laughter*, 1925; *Earth Memories*, 1934; *Love and Death*, 1939.
See:
J. A. Brebner, *The Demon Within: A Study of John Cowper Powys's Novels*, 1973
C. A. Coates, *John Cowper Powys in Search of a Landscape*, 1982
H. Coombes, *T. F. Powys*, 1960
R. P. Graves, *The Powys Brothers*, 1983
K. Hopkins, *The Powys Brothers*, 1967
B. Humphrey (ed.), *Recollections of the Powys Brothers*, 1980
    J. C. Powys's Wolf Solent: Critical Studies, 1990
L. Marlow, *Welsh Ambassadors*, 1936, rev. K. Hopkins, 1971

PRIESTLEY, JOHN BOYNTON (1894–1984): Novelist, dramatist, critic and essayist; b. Bradford; educated at Belle Vue High School; worked as a junior clerk; entered the army, 1914; after the war studied at Trinity Hall, Cambridge; first publication, *The Chapman of Rhymes* (verse), 1918; first novel, *Adam in Moonshine*, 1927; novels include *The Good Companions*, 1929 (dramatized, 1931) and *Angel Pavement*, 1930.

Other works include:
(plays) *Dangerous Corner*, 1932; *Time and the Conways*, 1937; *When We Are Married*, 1938; *An Inspector Calls*, 1947
(essays and criticism) *The English Comic Characters*, 1925; *The English Novel*, 1927; *The English*, 1973
(autobiography) *Margin Released*, 1962; *Instead of the Trees*, 1977

RHYS, JEAN – Ella Gwendolen Rees Williams – (1890–1979): Novelist and short-story writer; b. Roseau, Dominica; educated at the island's convent school, the Perse School, Cambridge, and at Tree's School of Dramatic Art (later RADA); worked as actress until marriage in 1919, when she moved to Paris; in 1923 befriended and encouraged to write by Ford Madox Ford; first publication, a volume of sketches, *The Left Bank*, 1927; first novel, *Postures*, 1928 (retitled *Quartet*, 1969); in the 1950s lived in obscurity and was thought dead until she answered a BBC advertisement seeking information about her in 1957; *Wide Sargasso Sea*, 1966.
    (For further details of writings after 1945 see Volume 8 of the *Guide*.)

Other works include:
(novels) *After Leaving Mr Mackenzie*, 1931; *Voyage in the Dark*, 1934; *Good Morning, Midnight*, 1939
(stories) *Tigers are Better Looking*, 1968; *Sleep It Off, Lady*, 1976
(autobiography) *Smile Please* (unfinished), 1979
Letters 1931–1966 ed. F. Wyndham and D. Melly, 1984

Life by C. Angier, 1985

See:
C. A. Howells, *Jean Rhys*, 1991
T. F. Staley, *Jean Rhys: A Critical Study*, 1979

RICHARDSON, DOROTHY MILLER (1872–1957): Novelist; b. Abingdon, Berks; first publication, *The Quakers Past and Present*; first novel, *Pointed Roofs*, 1915, the first of her works published collectively as *Pilgrimage*. Other novels in *Pilgrimage* include: *Backwater*, 1916; *The Tunnel*, 1919; *Deadlock*, 1921; *The Trap*, 1925; *Dawn's Left Hand*, 1931; *Dimple Hill*, 1938.

Life by G. G. Fromm, 1977
Pilgrimage Collected Edition, 1938, rev. and ed. W. Allen, 4 vols., 1967
Journey to Paradise (short stories and autobiographical sketches) ed. T. Tate, 1981
See:
J. Radford, *Dorothy Richardson*, 1991

RICKWORD, EDGELL (1898–1982): Poet and critic; educated at Colchester Grammar School; joined the Artists Rifles, 1916; awarded M C; four terms at Pembroke College, Oxford; first poems, *Behind the Eyes*, 1921; editor of *The Calendar of Modern Letters* 1925–7; edited *Scrutinies by Various Writers*, 1928, second volume, 1931; *Twittingpan and Some Others* (poems), 1931; *Collected Poems*, 1947

Between the Eyes: Selected Poems and Translations, 1976
Essays and Opinions, 1921–1931 ed. A. Young, 1974
Literature and Society: Essays and Opinions (II), 1931–1978 ed. A. Young, 1978
See:
C. Hobday, *Edgell Rickword: A Poet at War*, 1989

ROSENBERG, ISAAC (1890–1918): Poet; b. Bristol; educated at elementary schools in London; apprenticed to an engraver; Slade School of Art, 1911–14; *Night and Day*, 1912; visited South Africa, 1914–15; enlisted 1915; killed in action.

Life by J. Cohen, 1975; J. Liddiard, 1975
Collected Works ed. I. Parsons, 1979 (revision of the edition by G. Bottomley and D. Harding, 1937)
Collected Poems ed. G. Bottomley and D. Harding, 1949
See:
B. Bergonzi in *Heroes' Twilight*, 1965, rev. 1980
D. Graham, *The Truth of War: Owen, Blunden, Rosenberg*, 1983
D. W. Harding in *Experience into Words*, 1963

SASSOON, SIEGFRIED LORRAINE (1886–1967): Poet and prose writer; b. Kent; educated at Marlborough College and Clare College, Cambridge; first publication, *Poems*, 1906; commissioned in the Royal Welch Fusiliers, 1915; awarded M C; wounded 1917; literary editor of the *Daily Herald*, 1919; CBE, 1951.

Works include:

(poems) *The Old Huntsman*, 1917; *Counter-Attack*, 1918; *The War Poems*, 1919; *The Heart's Journey*, 1928; *Collected Poems 1908–56*, 1961

(novels) *Memoirs of a Fox-Hunting Man*, 1928; *Memoirs of an Infantry Officer*, 1930; *Sherston's Progress*, 1936 (these three published as *The Complete Memoirs of George Sherston*, 1937)

(autobiography) *The Weald of Youth*, 1942; *Siegfried's Journey 1916–1920*, 1945 *Diaries 1920–1922* ed. R. Hart-Davies, 1981; *Diaries 1923–25* ed. R. Hart-Davies, 1985

See:

B. Bergonzi in *Heroes' Twilight*, 1965, rev. 1980

M. Thorpe, *Sassoon: A Critical Study*, 1966

SHAW, GEORGE BERNARD (1856–1950): Playwright, essayist and critic; b. Dublin; educated at Wesley Connexional School; junior clerk, 1871–6; moved to London, 1876; joined Fabian Society, 1884; first novel, *Cashel Byron's Profession*, 1886; *The Quintessence of Ibsenism*, 1891, rev. 1913; first play, *Widowers' Houses*, performed 1892; dramatic critic of the *Saturday Review*, 1895–8; Borough Councillor for St Pancras, 1897–1903; helped found the *New Statesman*, 1913; Nobel Prize for Literature, 1925; *Sixteen Self-Sketches* (autobiography), 1949.

Plays include:

Plays Pleasant and Unpleasant, 1898 (Pleasant: *Arms and the Man, Candida, The Man of Destiny, You Never Can Tell*; Unpleasant: *Widowers' Houses, The Philanderer, Mrs Warren's Profession*); *Three Plays for Puritans*, 1901 (*The Devil's Disciple, Caesar and Cleopatra, Captain Brassbound's Conversion*); *Man and Superman*, 1903; *Major Barbara*, 1907; *The Doctor's Dilemma*, 1911; *Pygmalion*, 1913; *Androcles and the Lion*, 1916; *Heartbreak House*, 1919; *Back to Methuselah*, 1921; *St Joan*, 1924; *The Apple Cart*, 1930; *In Good King Charles's Golden Days*, 1939

Life by St J. Ervine, 1956; F. Harris, 1931; M. Holroyd, 4 vols., 1988–92; H. Pearson, 1942, rev. 1961; S. Winsten, 1956

Collected Plays with Their Prefaces, 7 vols., 1970–74

Bernard Shaw's Ready-Reckoner: A Guide to his Ideas ed. N. H. Leigh Taylor, 1966

Selected Non-Dramatic Writings ed. D. H. Laurence, 1965

Bernard Shaw's Non Dramatic Literary Criticism ed. S. Weintraub, 1972

Shaw's Music: The Complete Musical Criticism ed. D. H. Laurence, 3 vols., 1981

Shaw on Language ed. A. Tauber, 1963

The Matter with Ireland ed. D. H. Laurence and D. H. Greene, 1962

Shaw on Shakespeare ed. E. Wilson, 1961

Shaw on Theatre ed. E. J. West, 1958

Platform and Pulpit ed. D. H. Laurence, 1961

Major Critical Essays ed. M. Holroyd, 1986

Collected Letters ed. D. H. Laurence, 4 vols., 1965–88

See:

T. F. Evans (ed.), *G. B. Shaw: The Critical Heritage*, 1976
A. Ganz, *George Bernard Shaw*, 1983
A. M. Gibbs (ed.), *The Art and Mind of Shaw*, 1983
D. J. Gordon, *Bernard Shaw and the Comic Sublime*, 1990
N. Grene, *Bernard Shaw: A Critical View*, 1984
K. M. May, *Ibsen and Shaw*, 1985
M. M. Morgan, *The Shavian Playground*, 1972
R. F. Whitman, *Shaw and the Play of Ideas*, 1977

SITWELL, EDITH LOUISA (1887–1964): Poet; b. Scarborough, elder sister of Osbert and Sacheverell; educated privately; *The Mother*, 1915; *Façade*, a collaboration with the composer, William Walton, given first public performance, 1923; created Dame, 1954; became Roman Catholic, 1955; *Taken Care Of* (autobiography), 1965.

Life by V. Glendinning, 1981
Collected Poems, 1957
Selected Poems ed. J. Lehmann, 1965
Selected Letters ed. J. Lehmann and D. Parker, 1970
See:
J. Pearson, *Façades: Edith, Osbert and Sacheverell Sitwell*, 1978

SMITH, 'STEVIE' – FLORENCE MARGARET – (1902–71): Poet and novelist; b. Hull; educated at Palmers Green High School and North London Collegiate School for Girls; in 1918, her aunt became the most important figure in her life; worked for a publishing house; *Novel on Yellow Paper*, 1936; first book of poems, *A Good Time Was Had by All*, 1937; further novels – *Over the Frontier*, 1938 and *The Holiday*, 1949; poems, *Not Waving but Drowning*, 1957; awarded The Gold Medal for Poetry, 1969.

Life by J. Barbera and W. McBrien, 1985; F. Spalding, 1988
Collected Poems, 1975
Me Again: Uncollected Writings ed. J. Barbera and W. McBrien, 1981
See:
S. Sternlicht (ed.), *In Search of Stevie Smith*, 1991

SNOW, CHARLES PERCY (1905–79): Novelist; b. Leicester; educated at Alderman Newton's Grammar School and University College, Leicester; scientific research at Cambridge; Fellow of Christ's College, Cambridge, 1930; first novel, *Death Under Sail*, 1932; *Strangers and Brothers* (first novel giving its title to a series of eleven volumes) 1940; CBE, 1943; knighted, 1957; life peerage, 1964.

(For further details of writings after 1945 see Volume 8 of the *Guide*.)

Other works include:
(novels) *The Search*, 1934; *The Masters*, 1951; *The Corridors of Power*, 1964

(non-fiction) *The Two Cultures and the Scientific Revolution*, 1959; *Science and Government*, 1961; *Postscript*, 1962

Life by P. Snow, 1982
See:
F. R. Leavis, *Two Cultures? The Significance of C. P. Snow*, 1962
D. Shusterman, *C. P. Snow*, 1975

SPENDER, STEPHEN (1909–95): Poet and critic; b. London; educated at University College School and University College, Oxford where he met Auden, Day Lewis and MacNeice; first publication, *Nine Experiments*, 1928; travelled with Isherwood; *Vienna*, 1934; *The Still Centre*, 1939; *Ruins and Visions*, 1942; Professor of English, University College, London, 1970–77; knighted 1983; *The Temple* (novel), 1988.

Criticism includes: *The Destructive Element*, 1935; *The Creative Element*, 1953; *The Struggle of the Modern*, 1963

Collected Poems 1930–1985, 1985
Journals 1939–1983, 1985
Letters to Christopher: Stephen Spender's Letters to Christopher Isherwood 1929–1939, 1980

STURT, GEORGE – 'George Bourne' – (1863–1927): Writer on the countryside; b. Farnham, Surrey; educated at Farnham Grammar School; worked as a teacher, 1878–85; then entered family business, a firm of wheelwrights; first publication, *A Year's Exile*, 1898.

Works include:
The Ascending Effort, 1910; *Change in the Village*, 1912; *The Wheelwright's Shop*, 1923; *A Small Boy in the Sixties*, 1927; *The Journals of George Sturt* selected and ed. E. D. Mackerness, 2 vols., 1967

SYNGE, JOHN MILLINGTON (1871–1909): Playwright; b. Dublin; educated by a tutor and at Trinity College, Dublin; travelled in Europe; met W. B. Yeats in Paris, 1899; first play, *The Shadow of a Glen*, performed 1903; director of the Abbey Theatre from 1904.

Plays include: *Riders to the Sea*, 1905; *The Well of the Saints*, 1905; *The Playboy of the Western World*, 1907; *The Tinker's Wedding*, 1907; *Deirdre of the Sorrows*, 1910

Life by M. Bourgeois, 1913; D. H. Greene and E. M. Stephens, 1959
Collected Works, 4 vols., ed. R. Skelton *et al.*, 1962–8
Complete Plays ed. T. R. Henn, 1981
Collected Letters ed. A. Saddlemyer, 2 vols., 1983–4
See:
R. Ayling (ed.), *J. M. Synge: Four Plays*, 1992
E. Benson, *J. M. Synge*, 1982

N. Grene, *Synge: A Critical Study of the Plays*, 1975
M. Harmon, *J. M. Synge: Centenary Papers 1971*, 1972
D. Kiberd, *Synge and the Irish Language*, 1979
E. H. Mikhail (ed.), *J. M. Synge: Interviews and Recollections*, 1977

THOMAS, PHILIP EDWARD (1878–1917): Poet, critic and essayist; b. London; educated at St Paul's School and Lincoln College, Oxford; *The Woodland Life*, 1897; earned his living by reviewing, and by critical essays and studies of country life; *The Heart of England*, 1906; *Richard Jeffries* and *The South Country*, both 1909; in 1914 began writing poetry under the pseudonym of Edward Eastaway; enlisted, 1915; killed in action at Arras; *Poems*, 1917; *Last Poems*, 1918.

Life by W. Cooke, 1970; R. P. Eckert, 1937; J. Moore, 1939; R. G. Thomas, 1985
Collected Poems ed. R. G. Thomas, 1978
'Poems' and 'Last Poems' ed. E. Longley, 1973
Prose selected by R. Gant, 1948
Edward Thomas on the Countryside ed. R. Gant, 1977
A Language Not to Be Betrayed: Selected Prose ed. E. Longley, 1981
Letters from Edward Thomas to George Bottomley ed. R. G. Thomas, 1968
Letters to Jesse Berridge ed. A. Berridge, 1983
See:
J. Barker (ed.), *The Art of Edward Thomas*, 1987
M. Kirkham, *The Imagination of Edward Thomas*, 1986
F. R. Leavis in *New Bearings in English Poetry*, 1932, rev. 1950
E. Longley in *Poetry in The Wars*, 1986
A. Motion, *The Poetry of Edward Thomas*, 1980
H. Thomas, *As It Was*, 1926, and *World Without End*, 1931, (both republished together, 1956 and 1972)

WAUGH, EVELYN ARTHUR (1903–66): Novelist; b. London; educated at Lancing College and Hertford College, Oxford; schoolmaster 1924–7; *Decline and Fall*, 1928; *Vile Bodies*, 1930; became Roman Catholic, 1930; *A Handful of Dust*, 1934; *Scoop*, 1938; served with Marines and Commandos in Second World War; *Put Out More Flags*, 1942; *Brideshead Revisited*, 1945; first volume of autobiography, *A Little Learning*, 1964.

(For further details of writings after 1945 see Volume 8 of the *Guide*.)

Life by M. Stannard, 2 vols. 1986, 1992; C. Sykes, 1975
Diaries ed. M. Davie, 1976
Letters ed. M. Amory, 1980
Essays, Articles and Reviews, ed. D. Gallagher, 1983
See:
M. Bradbury, *Evelyn Waugh*, 1964
R. F. Garnett, *From Grimes to Brideshead*, 1990

J. McDonnell, *Waugh on Women,* 1986
  Evelyn Waugh, 1988
M. Stannard (ed.), *Evelyn Waugh: The Critical Heritage,* 1984

WELLS, HERBERT GEORGE (1866–1946): Novelist, short-story writer and essayist; b. Bromley, Kent; haphazard education; worked for a chemist and a draper, and as a student teacher; won scholarship to the Normal School of Science (later Imperial College); gained B.Sc. as external student, 1890; *The Time Machine,* 1895; joined Fabian Society, 1903; break with Fabians, 1906; much engaged with sociological issues, conceiving of himself as a world teacher; life dogged by recurrent ill health.

Works include:
(novels) *The Invisible Man,* 1897; *The War of the Worlds,* 1898; *Love and Mr Lewisham,* 1900; *Kipps,* 1905; *Tono-Bungay,* 1909; *The History of Mr Polly,* 1910; *The New Machiavelli,* 1911; *Marriage,* 1912; *Mr Britling Sees It Through,* 1916; *The Shape of Things to Come,* 1933
(short stories) *The Stolen Bacillus,* 1895; *Tales of Space and Time,* 1899; *The Short Stories,* 1927
(non-fiction) *Mankind in the Making,* 1903; *A Modern Utopia,* 1905; *A Short History of the World,* 1922; *Experiment in Autobiography,* 1934

Life by N. and J. MacKenzie, 1973; D. C. Smith, 1986; A. West, 1984
The Atlantic Edition of the Works, 24 vols., 1924–8
Letters: *Henry James and H. G. Wells* ed. L. Edel and G. N. Ray, 1958
  Arnold Bennett and H. G. Wells ed. H. Wilson, 1960
  G. Gissing and H. G. Wells ed. R. A. Gettmann, 1961
H. G. Wells's Literary Criticism ed. P. Parrinder and R. M. Philmus, 1980
See:
J. Batchelor, *H. G. Wells,* 1985
B. Bergonzi, (ed.), *H. G. Wells: A Collection of Critical Essays,* 1976
J. R. Hammond (ed.), *H. G. Wells: Interviews and Recollections,* 1980
  H. G. Wells and the Modern Novel, 1988
  H. G. Wells and the Short Story, 1992
P. Parrinder (ed.), *H. G. Wells: The Critical Heritage,* 1972

WOOLF, VIRGINIA (1882–1941): Novelist and critic; b. London, second daughter of Leslie Stephen; educated by her father at home; after father's death (1904), set up home in Bloomsbury with her brother and sister, inaugurating the famous 'Bloomsbury Circle' of writers which included E. M. Forster, J. M. Keynes, Lytton Strachey and Roger Fry; married Leonard Woolf, 1912; first novel, *The Voyage Out,* 1915; *Night and Day,* 1919; *Jacob's Room,* 1922; *Mrs Dalloway,* 1925; *To the Lighthouse,* 1927; *Orlando,* 1928; *The Waves,* 1931; *The Years,* 1937; *Between the Acts,* 1941; much dogged throughout her life by depression and nervous disorders; committed suicide.

Other writings include:

(short stories) *Monday or Tuesday*, 1921; *A Haunted House*, 1943

(biography) *Flush*, 1933; *Roger Fry*, 1940

(essays and criticism) *Mr Bennett and Mrs Brown*, 1924; *The Common Reader*, First series, 1925, Second series, 1932; *A Room of One's Own*, 1929; *Three Guineas*, 1938

Life by Q. Bell, 2 vols., 1972; L. Gordon, 1984; P. Rose, 1978

Letters ed. N. Nicholson and J. Trautmann, 6 vols., 1975–80

Virginia Woolf and Lytton Strachey: Letters ed. L. Woolf and J. Strachey, 1956

A Writer's Diary ed. L. Woolf, 1953

Diary ed. A. O. Bell and A. McNeillie, 5 vols., 1977–84

Essays ed. A. McNeillie, 2 vols., 1986

Complete Shorter Fiction ed. S. Dick, 1985

See:

T. E. Apter, *Virginia Woolf: A Study of Her Novels*, 1979

E. Auerbach in *Mimesis*, 1953

J. Batchelor, *Virginia Woolf*, 1991

N. T. Bazin, *Virginia Woolf and the Androgynous Vision*, 1973

G. Beer in *Essays in Narrative from Woolf to Sidney*, 1989

M. Beja (ed.), *'To the Lighthouse': A Casebook*, 1970

E. Bishop, *A Virginia Woolf Chronology*, 1988

R. Bowlby, *Virginia Woolf*, 1988

A. Fleishman, *Virginia Woolf: A Critical Reading*, 1975

R. Freedman (ed.), *Virginia Woolf: Revaluation and Continuity*, 1980

H. Lee, *The Novels of Virginia Woolf*, 1977

R. Majumdar and A. McLaurin (eds.), *Virginia Woolf: The Critical Heritage*, 1975

A. McLaurin, *Virginia Woolf: The Echoes Enslaved*, 1973

J. Marcus (ed.), *New Feminist Essays on Virginia Woolf*, 1981
   Virginia Woolf and Bloomsbury: A Centenary Celebration, 1987

A. D. Moody, *Virginia Woolf*, 1963

J. Naremore, *The World Without a Self: Virginia Woolf and the Novel*, 1973

R. Poole, *The Unknown Virginia Woolf*, 1978

C. Sprague (ed.), *Virginia Woolf: A Collection of Critical Essays*, 1971

E. Warner (ed.), *Virginia Woolf: A Centenary Perspective*, 1984

L. Woolf in his autobiography, Volume III, *Beginning Again, 1911–1918*, 1964, and Volume IV, *Downhill All the Way, 1918–1939*, 1967

YEATS, WILLIAM BUTLER (1865–1939): Poet and dramatist; b. Dublin; educated at the Godolphin School, Hammersmith and Dublin Grammar School; studied art; first publication, *Mosada: A Dramatic Poem*, 1886; *The Wanderings of Oisin*, 1889; influential figure in the Celtic Renaissance; first play, *The Countess Kathleen*, 1892; involved with Lady Gregory in the founding of the Irish National Theatre Society, of which Yeats was president, and in the Abbey Theatre, opened 1904; member of the Irish

Senate, 1922–8; Nobel Prize for Literature, 1923; died at Roquebrune, France.

Works include:

(poems) *The Wind among the Reeds*, 1899; *The Green Helmet*, 1910; *Responsibilities*, 1914; *The Wild Swans at Coole*, 1917; *Michael Robartes and the Dancer*, 1920; *The Cat and the Moon*, 1924; *The Tower*, 1928; *The Winding Stair*, 1929; *Words for Music, Perhaps*, 1932; *Last Poems*, 1939

(plays) *The Land of Heart's Desire*, 1894; *Cathleen ni Houlihan*, 1902; *The Hour-Glass*, 1903; *The King's Threshold, On Baile's Strand*, 1904; *Deirdre*, 1907; *The Unicorn from the Stars* (with Lady Gregory), 1908; *Four Plays for Dancers*, 1921; *The Player Queen*, 1922; *The Herne's Egg*, 1938.

(essays and criticism) *Ideas of Good and Evil*, 1903; *Discoveries*, 1907; *Synge and the Ireland of his Time*, 1911; *The Cutting of an Agate*, 1912; *Per Amica Silentia Lunae*, 1918; *A Vision*, 1925, rev. 1937; *A Packet for Ezra Pound*, 1929; *Modern Poetry*, 1936; *Essays, 1931 to 1936*, 1937; *Mythologies*, 1959; *Essays and Introductions*, 1961; *Explorations*, 1962; *Uncollected Prose*, 2 vols., ed. J. P. Frayne and C. Johnston, 1970–75; *Prefaces and Introductions* ed. W. H. O'Donnell, 1988; *Uncollected Prose*, 2 vols., ed. J. P. Frayne and C. Johnson, 1990; *Letters to the New Island* ed. G. Bournstein and H. Witemeyer, 1989

(autobiography) *Autobiographies* (a collection of previously published writings), 1955; *Memoirs: autobiography, first draft journal* ed. D. Donoghue, 1972

(letters) *Collected Letters*, Vol. 1, 1865–95, ed. J. Kelly, 1986; *W. B. Yeats and T. S. Moore: Their Correspondence* ed. U. Bridge, 1953; *Letters to Katharine Tynan* ed. R. McHugh, 1953; *Letters* ed. A. Wade, 1954; *Letters on Poetry to Dorothy Wellesley*, 1940; *The Gonne–Yeats Letters, 1893–1938*, ed. A. MacBride and A. N. Jeffares, 1992

Life by R. Ellmann, 1948; J. Hone, 1942, rev. 1989; A. N. Jeffares, 1988

Collected Edition of the Works, 1984–

Collected Poems, 1950

The Poems: A New Edition ed. R. J. Finneran, 1984

Variorum Edition of the Poems ed. P. Allt and R. K. Alspach, 1957

Selected Poems ed. T. Webb, 1991

Collected Plays, 1952

Variorum Edition of the Plays ed. R. K. Alspach, 1966

The Secret Rose, Stories by W. B. Yeats, a Variorum Edition ed. W. Gould, P. L. Marcus and M. J. Sidnell, 2nd edn 1992

See:

H. Bloom, *Yeats*, 1970

C. Bradford, *Yeats at Work*, 1965

E. Cullingford, *Yeats, Ireland and Fascism*, 1981
    (ed.), *Yeats: Poems, 1919–1935 – A Casebook*, 1984

D. Donoghue, *Yeats*, 1971

A. E. Dyson in *Yeats, Eliot and R. S. Thomas: Riding the Echo*, 1981

R. Ellmann, *The Identity of Yeats*, 1954

I. Fletcher, *Yeats and His Contemporaries*, 1987

W. Gould (ed.), *Yeats Annual* nos. 3–8, 10 (1993 to date)

J. Hall and M. Steinmann (eds.), *The Permanence of Yeats*, 1961

T. R. Henn, *The Lonely Tower: A Study in the Poetry of W. B. Yeats*, 1950, rev. 1965

G. Hough, *The Mystery Religion of W. B. Yeats*, 1984

A. N. Jeffares (ed.), *W. B. Yeats: The Critical Heritage*, 1977
    A New Commentary on the Poems of W. B. Yeats, 1984

A. N. Jeffares and K. G. W. Cross (eds.), *In Excited Reverie: A Centenary Tribute to William Butler Yeats*, 1965

A. N. Jeffares and A. S. Knowland, *A Commentary on the Collected Plays of W. B. Yeats*, 1975

F. Kermode, *Romantic Image*, 1957

L. McDiarmid in *Saving Civilization: Yeats, Eliot and Auden Between the Wars*, 1984

L. MacNeice, *The Poetry of Yeats*, 1941, ed. R. Ellmann, 1967

T. Parkinson, *W. B. Yeats, Self-Critic*, 1971

W. H. Pritchard (ed.), *W. B. Yeats: A Critical Anthology*, 1972

M. L. Rosenthal in *Sailing into the Unknown: Yeats, Pound and Eliot*, 1978

J. Stallworthy, *Between the Lines: Yeats' Poetry in the Making*, 1963
    (ed.), *W. B. Yeats: Last Poems – A Casebook*, 1968

P. S. Stanfield, *Yeats and Politics in the 1930s*, 1988

C. K. Stead in *Pound, Yeats, Eliot and the Modernist Movement*, 1986

R. Taylor, *A Reader's Guide to the Plays of W. B. Yeats*, 1984

D. Toomey (ed.), *Yeats and Women: Yeats Annual no. 9*, 1992

J. Unterecker, *A Reader's Guide to W. B. Yeats*, 1959
    (ed), *Yeats: A Collection of Critical Essays*, 1963

P. Ure, *Yeats the Playwright*, 1963

F. A. C. Wilson, *Yeats and Tradition*, 1958

ACKNOWLEDGEMENTS

For permission to reprint copyright matter, the following acknowledgements are made: for extracts from the *Collected Poems* of W. H. Auden to Faber & Faber and to Random House in USA.; for extracts from poems by Walter de la Mare to his literary trustees and the Society of Authors as their representative; for extracts from T. S. Eliot's *Collected Poems, Four Quartets* and *Notes towards the Definition of Culture* to Faber & Faber and to Harcourt, Brace & World, New York; for part of a poem by William Empson ('Villanelle') to Chatto & Windus and to Harcourt, Brace & World, New York; for extracts from *The Longest Journey, Where Angels Fear to Tread, A Room with a View*, and *A Passage to India*, by E. M. Forster to Edward Arnold, and to Alfred A. Knopf, Inc. and Harcourt, Brace & World, New York; for extracts from poetry by Ezra Pound to the Estate of the author; for extract from *The Concept of Mind* by Gilbert Ryle to the author and Hutchinson & Co., for poems by Siegfried Sassoon ('Dreamers', 'The General', 'Suicide in the Trenches', '*They*', 'On Passing the Menin Gate, 1927', 'An Unveiling', 'Disabled') to the Estate of the author; for part of a poem by Dylan Thomas to J. M. Dent & Sons and to New Directions in USA; for poems by Edward Thomas ('A Tale', 'March', 'The Glory') to Mrs Thomas and Faber & Faber; for extracts from the Uniform Edition of the Works of Virginia Woolf and from her critical writings to the Hogarth Press and to Harcourt, Brace & World, New York; and for extracts from poems by W. B. Yeats to Macmillan & Co., and to the Macmillan Co. in USA.

NOTES ON CONTRIBUTORS

G. H. BANTOCK Emeritus Professor of Education, University of Leicester. Author of *Freedom and Authority in Education* (1952), *L. H. Myers* (1956), *Education, Culture and the Emotions* (1967) and *Studies in the History of Educational Theory* (vol. 1, 1980; vol, 2, 1984).

T. R. BARNES. Formerly Head of English, Bishop Wordsworth's School, Salisbury. He is the author of *English Verse: Sound and Movement from Wyatt to Yeats* (1967) and *Poetry Appreciation* (1976). He contributed to *Scrutiny* and *The Use of English*.

F. W. BRADBROOK (d. 1983) Was Senior Lecturer in English, University College of North Wales, Bangor. Author of *Jane Austen: Emma* (1961) and *Jane Austen and her Predecessors* (1966); editor (with James Kingsley) of *Jane Austen: Pride and Prejudice* (1970).

DOUGLAS BROWN (d. 1964) Was Senior Lecturer in English Literature at the University of Reading, and had just been appointed Professor of English at York. Author of *Thomas Hardy* (1954); editor of *Selected Poems of George Herbert* (1960), Conrad's *Nigger of the Narcissus* (1960) and *Three Tales from Conrad* (1960).

R. C. CHURCHILL (d. 1986) Was author and journalist. His books include *Disagreements* (1950), *The English Sunday* (1954), *The Frontiers of Fiction* (1970) and *The Revised Concise History of English Literature* (1970).

H. COOMBES (d. 1980) Lectured extra-murally for Bristol University in Gloucestershire. His published works include *Literature and Criticism* (1953), *Edward Thomas* (1956), *T. F. Powys* (1960); he edited the Penguin Critical Anthology on D. H. Lawrence (1973).

R. G. COX (d. 1981) Was Reader in English Literature, University of Manchester; author of articles and reviews in *Scrutiny*, *The Times Literary Supplement*, *The Sewanee Review* and other periodicals; editor of *Thomas Hardy: The Critical Heritage* (1970).

PART FOUR

GEORGE DEKKER Professor of English, Stanford University. Author of *Sailing after Knowledge: The Cantos of Ezra Pound* (1963), *James Fenimore Cooper the Novelist* (1967), *Coleridge and the Literature of Sensibility* (1978) and *The American Historical Romance* (1987).

D. J. ENRIGHT Writer, formerly university teacher. Publications include *Shakespeare and the Students* (1970), *The Alluring Problem: An Essay on Irony* (1986), and *Collected Poems, 1987*; editor of *A Choice of Milton's Verse* (1975), *Rasselas* (1976), *The Oxford Book of Contemporary Verse 1945–1980* (1980) and *The Oxford Book of Death* (1983).

GRATTAN FREYER Founder-director of the Irish Humanities Centre in Dublin, providing courses in Irish Studies for overseas students. Works include *A Prose and Verse Anthology of Modern Writing* (1979), *W. B. Yeats and the Antidemocratic Tradition* (1981) and articles in various periodicals from *Scrutiny* onwards.

HENRY GIFFORD Emeritus Professor of English and Comparative Literature, University of Bristol. His books include *The Novel in Russia* (1964), *Comparative Literature* (1969), *Pasternak: A Critical Study* (1977), and the text of the Clark Lectures for 1985, *Poetry in a Divided World* (1986).

NANCY K. GISH Professor of English at the University of Southern Maine. Author of *Time in the Poetry of T. S. Eliot* (1981), *The Waste Land: A Poem of Memory and Desire* (1988), *Hugh MacDiarmid: The Man and His Work* (1984) and editor, *Hugh MacDiarmid: The Man and Poet* (1992).

ANDOR GOMME Held a personal chair in English Literature and Architectural History at the University of Keele. Author of *Attitudes to Criticism* (1966), *Dickens* (1971); editor of *Coriolanus* (1968), *Jacobean Tragedies* (1969–75) and *The Roaring Girl* (1976). Has also written (in collaboration) books on the architecture of Glasgow and Bristol.

RICHARD HOGGART Author of *Auden* (1951), *The Uses of Literacy* (1957), *Speaking to Each Other* (1970), *Only Connect* (1972), *An Idea and its Servants* (1978), *An English Temper* (1982). *A Local Habitation* (1988), *A Sort of Clowning* (1990), *An Imagined Life* (1992) and *Townscape with Figures* (1994).

JOHN HOLLOWAY Emeritus Professor of Modern English, Cambridge; publications in or largely in the Victorian field include *The Proud Knowledge* (1977), *Narrative and Structure* (1979) and *The Slumber of Apollo* (1983); numerous critical articles and tapes; editions of *Little Dorrit* (1962) and *Silas Marner* (1967, enlarged 1977), and *The Oxford Book of Local Verses* (1987). Also *Civitatula* (1994), a long poem about Cambridge.

ARNOLD KETTLE (d. 1987) Was Professor of Literature, The Open University. Author of *An Introduction to the English Novel* (1951); editor of *Shakespeare in a Changing World* (1964) and *The Nineteenth-Century World* (revised 1981).

G. D. KLINGOPULOS Formerly Senior Lecturer in English, University College, Cardiff. Contributor to *Scrutiny*.

GRAHAM MARTIN Formerly Professor of Literature at the Open University. Publications include OU Courses on Dickens, George Eliot, D. H. Lawrence. Editor of *Eliot in Perspective* (1970); co-editor of *Twentieth-Century Poetry: Essays and Documents* (1975) and *Industrialization and Culture, 1832–1914* (1971) and the *Everyman Book of Romantic Verse*. Is currently editing the *Faber Book of 20th Century Criticism*.

W. W. ROBSON Emeritus Professor of English Literature, University of Edinburgh. Author of *Critical Essays* (1966) and *Modern English Literature* (4th impr. 1979). Recent publications include *The Definition of Literature* (1982) and *Prologue to English Literature* (1986).

LEO SALINGAR Fellow of Trinity College and formerly Lecturer in English, Cambridge University; author of *Shakespeare and the Traditions of Comedy* (1974) and *Dramatic Form in Shakespeare and the Jacobeans* (1986).

DENYS THOMPSON (d. 1988) Formerly Head of Yeovil Grammar School. He assisted F. R. Leavis with *Culture and Environment* (1933) and was one of the early editors of *Scrutiny*. Also the first editor of *The Use of English*. Author of innumerable books linked to the teaching of English – most recently *The Uses of Poetry* (1978) and *Change and Tradition in Rural England* (1980).

E. W. F. TOMLIN (d. 1988) Served with the British Council and was Representative and Cultural Counsellor in Ankara, Tokyo and Paris. Also held professorships at the universities of Nice and Southern California. Author of a number of books on philosophical and literary subjects, including *Living and Knowing* (1955), *Simone Weil* (1954) and *Philosophers of East and West* (1986).

ANNE VARTY is a Lecturer in English and Drama at Royal Holloway, University of London. She has published work on Walter Pater and is currently writing a book on Oscar Wilde.

INDEX

READ MORE IN PENGUIN

In every corner of the world, on every subject under the sun, Penguin represents quality and variety – the very best in publishing today.

For complete information about books available from Penguin – including Puffins, Penguin Classics and Arkana – and how to order them, write to us at the appropriate address below. Please note that for copyright reasons the selection of books varies from country to country.

In the United Kingdom: Please write to *Dept. EP, Penguin Books Ltd, Bath Road, Harmondsworth, West Drayton, Middlesex UB7 0DA*

In the United States: Please write to *Consumer Sales, Penguin Putnam Inc., P.O. Box 12289 Dept. B, Newark, New Jersey 07101-5289*. VISA and MasterCard holders call 1-800-788-6262 to order Penguin titles

In Canada: Please write to *Penguin Books Canada Ltd, 10 Alcorn Avenue, Suite 300, Toronto, Ontario M4V 3B2*

In Australia: Please write to *Penguin Books Australia Ltd, P.O. Box 257, Ringwood, Victoria 3134*

In New Zealand: Please write to *Penguin Books (NZ) Ltd, Private Bag 102902, North Shore Mail Centre, Auckland 10*

In India: Please write to *Penguin Books India Pvt Ltd, 11 Community Centre, Panchsheel Park, New Delhi 110017*

In the Netherlands: Please write to *Penguin Books Netherlands bv, Postbus 3507, NL-1001 AH Amsterdam*

In Germany: Please write to *Penguin Books Deutschland GmbH, Metzlerstrasse 26, 60594 Frankfurt am Main*

In Spain: Please write to *Penguin Books S. A., Bravo Murillo 19, 1° B, 28015 Madrid*

In Italy: Please write to *Penguin Italia s.r.l., Via Benedetto Croce 2, 20094 Corsico, Milano*

In France: Please write to *Penguin France, Le Carré Wilson, 62 rue Benjamin Baillaud, 31500 Toulouse*

In Japan: Please write to *Penguin Books Japan Ltd, Kaneko Building, 2-3-25 Koraku, Bunkyo-Ku, Tokyo 112*

In South Africa: Please write to *Penguin Books South Africa (Pty) Ltd, Private Bag X14, Parkview, 2122 Johannesburg*

READ MORE IN PENGUIN

LITERARY CRITICISM

The Practice of Writing David Lodge

This lively collection examines the work of authors ranging from the two Amises to Nabokov and Pinter; the links between private lives and published works; and the different techniques required in novels, stage plays and screenplays. 'These essays, so easy in manner, so well-built and informative, offer a fine blend of creative writing and criticism' *Sunday Times*

A Lover's Discourse Roland Barthes

'May be the most detailed, painstaking anatomy of desire we are ever likely to see or need again ... The book is an ecstatic celebration of love and language ... readers interested in either or both ... will enjoy savouring its rich and dark delights' *Washington Post*

The New Pelican Guide to English Literature Edited by Boris Ford

The indispensable critical guide to English and American literature in nine volumes, erudite yet accessible. From the ages of Chaucer and Shakespeare, via Georgian satirists and Victorian social critics, to the leading writers of the twentieth century, all literary life is here.

The Structure of Complex Words William Empson

'Twentieth-century England's greatest critic after T. S. Eliot, but whereas Eliot was the high priest, Empson was the *enfant terrible* ... *The Structure of Complex Words* is one of the linguistic masterpieces of the epoch, finding in the feel and tone of our speech whole sedimented social histories' *Guardian*

Vamps and Tramps Camille Paglia

'Paglia is a genuinely unconventional thinker ... Taken as a whole, the book gives an exceptionally interesting perspective on the last thirty years of intellectual life in America, and is, in its wacky way, a celebration of passion and the pursuit of truth' *Sunday Telegraph*

READ MORE IN PENGUIN

The New Pelican Guide to English Literature

Edited by Boris Ford

'The best and most lively general survey of English literature available to schools, students and general readers' – *The Times Educational Supplement*

Authoritative, stimulating and accessible, the original seven-volume *Pelican Guide to English Literature* has earned itself a distinguished reputation. Now enlarged to ten volumes and a readers' guide, this popular series has been wholly revised and updated.

What this work sets out to offer is a guide to the history and traditions of English literature, a contour-map of the literary scene. Each volume includes these standard features:

(i) An account of the social context of literature in each period.

(ii) A general survey of the literature itself.

(iii) A series of critical essays on individual writers and their works – each written by an authority in their field.

(iv) Full appendices including short author biographies, listings of standard editions of authors' works, critical commentaries and titles for further study and reference.

The *Guide* consists of the following volumes:

1. Medieval Literature:
   Part One: Chaucer and the Alliterative Tradition
   Part Two: The European Inheritance
2. The Age of Shakespeare
3. From Donne to Marvell
4. From Dryden to Johnson
5. From Blake to Byron
6. From Dickens to Hardy
7. From James to Eliot
8. From Orwell to Naipaul
9. American Literature
   A Guide for Readers